Computers and Exceptional Individuals

Computers and Exceptional Individuals

Second Edition

Edited by
Jimmy D. Lindsey
Southern University

8700 Shoal Creek Boulevard
Austin, Texas 78758

Library of Congress Cataloging-in-Publication Data

Computers and exceptional individuals / [edited by] Jimmy D. Lindsey.
— 2nd ed.
        p.   cm.
    Includes bibliographical references and index.
    ISBN 0–89079–547–9
    1. Handicapped children—Education—United States—Data
processing.   2. Special education—United States—Data processing.
3. Computer-assisted instruction—United States.   I. Lindsey, Jimmy D.
LC4024.C64   1992
371.9′043—dc20   91–48182
                                                                         CIP

pro·ed
8700 Shoal Creek Boulevard
Austin, Texas 78758

1 2 3 4 5 6 7 8 9 10   97 96 95 94 93 92

I dedicate the second edition of *Computers and Exceptional Individuals* to my family (Renee, Christiaan, Jonathan, and Camille) and to the chapter and appendix authors and their families.

Contents

Preface

The purpose of the second edition of this text is to again provide a practical discussion of current computer technology with individuals with disabilities or those that are gifted and talented. It delineates specific and generic computer concepts presently being used (or to be used in the near future) with and by exceptional individuals. Computer and special education jargons have been minimized. Practicality is stressed in the suggested activities and resources included in the chapters and appendixes.

Intended for a varied audience, this text can be used by undergraduate and graduate students taking an introductory or method course on computers and exceptional individuals. It can also be used by regular and special educators, other professionals (e.g., speech-language clinicians, physical and occupational therapists, and psychologists among others), and paraprofessionals in in-service activities designed to advance competencies in computer technology and special education. Computer theorists and manufacturers can significantly increase their insight into computer concepts

related to exceptionality by reading this text. Finally, individuals with disabilities, gifts, or talents interested in learning about specific hardware and software can develop a foundation for this knowledge by reading this book.

The second edition of *Computers and Exceptional Individuals* has three sections, composed of 14 chapters. Section One, "Foundation," uses five chapters to introduce general and specific computer concepts related to exceptional individuals. Chapter 1 defines exceptional individuals and discusses current knowledge of and opinions of the use of computers with and by exceptional individuals in the home, school, and community. Chapters 2 and 3 outline specific and generic hardware and software concepts. Chapter 4 outlines principles and procedures relative to evaluating and developing software. Chapter 5 focuses on the use of interactive videodisc systems in special education. Section Two, "Categorical Applications," has five chapters. Chapters 6 through 10 define five exceptional populations, provide a brief review of the computer literature related to this topic, and delineate general and specific computer applications. Section Three, "Administrative and Instructional Applications," uses four chapters to outline principles and procedures relative to implementing and evaluating administrative and teaching technological applications with exceptional individuals. Chapter 11 presents concepts to consider when starting or expanding computer systems. Chapters 12 and 13 delineate specific and generic procedures for data base management and teaching applications in special education. Chapter 14 discusses how to evaluate technology concepts and summarizes the text. Finally, six appendixes (computer terms, history, languages, professional competencies, software, programming, and a software evaluation form) and two indexes (name and subject) are available to promote reading economy, enhance research purposes, and extend the practical resource information.

I believe the second edition of this text to be a needed addition to the growing number of works on computers and exceptional persons because it takes a very practical approach to computer technology and provides activities and resources to reinforce or extend the reader's knowledge. The authors and I have done everything we can to ensure that the content (e.g., hardware nomenclature and attributes, software descriptions and additions) is current. However, computer technology is advancing so rapidly that what you will read, as Carl Steinhoff and Teresa Lyons state in Chapter 2, is only a portent of what is to come. Computer hardware is evolving; software is being revised. The rapid progress of computer technology, as Ronald Kelly notes in Chapter 9, is reported in newspapers and periodicals weekly. This reporting can only serve to advance computer concepts for individuals with disabilities, gifts, and talents. It goes without saying that the reader of this text should use current publications to supplement the information we have given.

Jimmy D. Lindsey

Acknowledgments

I am especially indebted to a number of people for helping me develop this text. I want to thank Drs. Donald Hammill and Jim Patton, PRO-ED publisher and executive editor respectively, for making this second edition a reality and for providing insightful suggestions for revisions. I want to thank my colleagues at Southern University for their confidence and support and for directly and indirectly helping me find the time to complete this book. I am indebted to the authors, who did everything I asked of them to ensure that their chapters and appendixes reflect the current state of the art. An editor could not have worked with a more willing and competent group of writers. Thank you for the valuable time you devoted to writing your chapters and appendixes. I am also indebted to a number of Southern University graduate students for their clerical, proofreading, and library research support. These individuals are Natee Banderjakul, Rodney Woods, Carolyn Woods, Victor Kirk, and Jerri Smith.

I want to thank those persons who, in addition to the authors, provided the photographs used throughout this book. These individuals include Jesse Kempter and Pat Davis (IBM), Nancy Guittard and Rosa Radicchi (Apple), R. Gayle Persac (Education and Technology Resources), Linda L. Repp (Prentke Romich Company), Laurence H. Weiss (ZYGO Industries), Pat Kallio (MECC), Marcia B. Dugan (National Technical Institute for the Deaf/Rochester Institute of Technology), Ray Jagger (Northeast Missouri State University), Paul C. Arcell (Kay Elemetrics Corporation), Robin T. Berard (New Iberia, LA), David M. Aultz (Bear, DE), and Ed Washington (Lafayette, LA). I want to also thank my colleagues (especially Cora Blanks and Henry Teller), selected graduate students and their children, family members (especially Jonathan and Camille Lindsey and Brett and Ellion Berard), and friends (especially Ed Washington) for giving me permission to take their pictures for inclusion in this book.

I must express my sincere appreciation to selected individuals at PRO-ED for their efforts. I want to thank Rebecca Fletcher for her editorial assistance. I also thank Alan Grimes (production manager), Lori Kopp, and Chris Anne Worsham for their production activities. Sincere and special thanks are also expressed to my copyeditor, Letitia Blalock, for her thorough and accurate editing of this second edition.

Finally, I would like to again recognize a number of individuals who made the first edition of this book a reality or contributed to its success: Drs. Greg H. Frith, Earl H. Cheek, A. C. Blanks, Timothy H. Little, Gary E. Rushakoff, Tom Lough, and Mrs. Carole Lick. Greg and Earl were instrumental in the developmental and contractual processes, and A. C. Blanks was my chairperson and constant support during the writing and production stages. Tim, Gary, Tom, and Carole were chapter authors. Sadly, I must express recognition in memoriam to Drs. Blanks and Rushakoff.

Foundation

SECTION

This section introduces the concept of computers and exceptional individuals, the hardware and software domains, software evaluation and development, and interactive videodisc technology.

Computers can be found in all segments of society. *(Photograph by Jimmy D. Lindsey)*

Computers and Exceptional Individuals

CHAPTER

Alonzo E. Hannaford
Western Michigan University ■

Societies measure their greatness in many ways. One measure of society is how it uses its technology. For decades, those concerned about exceptional individuals have sought ways to use emerging technologies to help handicapped and gifted people achieve their potential. For many exceptionally able persons in the United States (Johnson, 1991) and in Europe (Botlik, 1992), in the Pacific Rim (Huh, 1992), and in the former Soviet Union (Kiselev, 1992), computer technology has offered a way to improve the quality of life for children, youths, and adults in the home, school, or community. Many Americans have also explored how computer technology might aid disabled citizens.

Because of the relative unavailability, high cost, large size, and complexity of computers, widespread use of the technology with exceptional persons was slow in coming. The introduction of the smaller, less expensive, and less complex microcomputer or personal computer was met with enthusiasm. It was thought that computers would dramatically improve the lives of many exceptional individuals, and that

there would be a great rush to use this technology to do that. After almost 20 years of trial and error, some of this enthusiasm has waned. While computers can extend, expand, and amplify our work, they cannot generate new and innovative solutions to problems faced by exceptional persons. Such solutions require human thoughtfulness and knowledge about human needs.

What makes computer technology attractive to advocates for exceptional persons? Why is it that both the popular and professional literatures are replete with articles related to computer technology and its potential for this population? Why are tens of millions of dollars being spent to explore possible uses for computers with exceptional individuals? It is because computers can carry out instructions more quickly and accurately than humans. But we must remember that it is the human mind that develops the use and functions of the computer.

We are now entering a phase of informed decision making in which our awareness of the computer's capabilities and limitations is

---

TABLE 1.1
Using computers successfully with handicapped and gifted/talented individuals

---

1. While computer capabilities are continually expanding, there are still technological as well as practical limits to what computers can do.

2. We must know the needs of handicapped and gifted individuals who will use computers.

3. We must be able to instruct computers to do what we want them to do. Before a programmer can turn an idea into a set of meaningful instructions to the computer, there must be a very careful analysis and specification of what is to be done, by whom, when, under what conditions, and with what effect.

4. The technology must be integrated into instructional, managerial, and adaptive systems that are themselves effective.

5. We must adapt the technology to fit the needs of the individual rather than forcing the individual to adapt to the technology.

---

being teamed with our knowledge of the needs of exceptional persons to make appropriate and efficient use of computer technology. We are implementing evaluation procedures to show how the computer can accomplish specific tasks (see Chapter 14). Special educators and others working directly and indirectly with exceptional persons now need to learn when, where, and how computers can best be used to help this population. Table 1.1 delineates the five elements that must be present to effectively use computers with individuals who have disabilities, gifts, or talents.

This chapter will define what is meant by exceptional people, their characteristics, and the ways computers can help compensate for their deficits and augment their strengths. This chapter will also overview topics addressed in later chapters. What is currently known about the use of computers with exceptional individuals and the use of computers in various educational settings will be discussed. The use of computers in the home and ways that this technology can improve the quality of life for exceptional persons will be shown.

COMPUTERS AND EXCEPTIONAL INDIVIDUALS

Exceptional persons are those who, due to their mental, emotional, learning, social, physical, sensory, or communication abilities, require assistance in school to reach their full potential as happy, self-supporting, contributing adults. This text groups these individuals into five categories: mildly handicapped, speech or language disordered, severely or physically handicapped, sensory impaired, and gifted/talented.

Mildly Handicapped

Individuals with mild handicaps have disabilities in learning, perception, cognition, or socialization, or have difficulty in appropriately handling their emotions to such an extent that they may require special education (e.g., resource room instruction) or related services (e.g., counseling) in schools or in society. Included in this group are those who have been identified as mildly mentally retarded, learning disabled, and behavior disordered. For mildly handicapped individuals, the computer helps in the educational process (e.g., learning to read), at work (e.g., cataloging items), and at home (e.g., communicating with relatives). In school, students with mild handicaps can profit from computer programs designed to teach or reteach basic and content skills. Computers have been successfully used

Computer use is increasing and user age is decreasing. *(Photograph by Jimmy D. Lindsey)*

to help these students achieve in such areas as reading (Harper & Ewing, 1986; Rosegrant, 1985), spelling (Hall, McLaughlin, & Bialozor, 1989; Kinney, Stevens, & Schuster, 1988; Varhagen & Gerber, 1984), personal adjustment (Cress, 1986; Ryba & Chapman, 1983), socialization (Larson & Roberts, 1986), and study skills (Day, Golden, & Sweitzer, 1989). Computers have also been specifically used with students with behavior disorders (Manion, 1986). Chapter 6 discusses in depth the use of computers with individuals with mild disabilities.

Speech and Language Disordered

Computers are being used in educational and clinical settings to address a wide range of communication problems (Hanley, 1987; Johnson, 1987; Kinzer, 1987; Rushakoff & Bull, 1987; Story & Sbordone, 1988). Problems that may require special services include articulation disorders (e.g., saying "wabbit" for "rabbit"), voice problems (e.g., extreme hoarseness), dysfluency (e.g., stuttering), and disorders preventing communication and understanding (e.g., problems in using syntax or sentences). Further, children and adults are finding computer devices that produce speech helpful (Mason, Tanaka, & Lian, 1987). An assessment of computer technology with persons who have various disorders of communication has been presented by Houle (1988, 1989). Chapter 7 delineates general and specific uses of the computer for individuals with speech and language disorders.

Severely and Physically Handicapped

Individuals with severe and physical handicaps are two very different exceptional populations. The severely mentally handicapped are those with very limited cognitive ability. Not able to care for themselves, use abstract concepts, or learn basic academic skills, they may also be nonambulatory, unintelligible, and have other handicapping conditions. Individuals with physical handicaps, on the other hand, have difficulty engaging in appropriate motor activity (e.g., gross or fine motor skills) due to

neurologic, bone, joint, or muscle disorders (e.g., cerebral palsy, spina bifida, muscular dystrophy, osteogenesis imperfecta, or the absence of limbs). Persons with physical handicaps may be able to move with or without prostheses or may be totally nonambulatory. Their intellectual abilities range from gifted/talented to severely mentally handicapped, and they may also be handicapped in other ways.

Computer applications with individuals who have severe and physical handicaps are as diverse as the characteristics of the two populations. Individuals with severe mental handicaps usually cannot use most computers. However, people working with them do use computers to manage the environment, increase comfort levels, and provide stimulation. Computer applications with the physically handicapped can be very similar to traditional functions or specifically related to their disabilities. Students and adults with physical handicaps use the computer for educational purposes (e.g., drill and practice, programming), at home (e.g., leisure games, budgeting), and in the community (e.g., at work, at the bank). However, through adaptive devices (e.g., computer speech synthesizers), persons with physical handicaps can use the computer to compensate for the absence of an ability (e.g., the ability to talk), to help them move (e.g., computerized wheelchair), or to take care of themselves (e.g., accessing information services).

Computer technology is now helping previously nonambulatory individuals to walk and achieve a degree of independent mobility unthought of only a few years ago. For example, the advancements in computer-controlled muscular stimulation at Wright State University in Ohio have been the focus of television specials and have been widely reported in the popular literature. This use of computers certainly is one of the most exciting for this exceptional population. Chapter 8 provides general and specific applications for individuals with severe and physical handicaps.

Sensory Impaired

Individuals with sensory impairments are those who have difficulty with vision or hearing and require special education or related services. Since we learn about the world through our senses, the absence, loss, or reduction of sensory function is obviously significant. Besides requiring special methods of instruction, visual and auditory impairments slow down the process of education or adapting to society.

Computers are having a positive impact on the visually and hearing-impaired populations. Computer-generated speech or speech synthesis (i.e., turning text into speech) means visually impaired persons can hear information rather than having to try to read it, resulting in quicker information acquisition. The computer is also being used to produce easily read, enlarged print and electronic paper braille.

Hearing-impaired persons who have difficulty acquiring basic academic skills, understanding higher-level concepts, and communicating may have difficulty learning and adapting in and out of the schools. The pupil who cannot hear has difficulty acquiring both spoken and written language. Since the computer is largely a visual medium, it is possible for hearing-impaired persons to gain a great deal of information from it. Computers can also be used to generate speech and to permit use of telecommunication devices attached to telephone lines. Wilson (1989) has studied the development of cognition in hearing-impaired and severely language-disabled/learning-disabled students at the University of Minnesota. This research has centered on the use of the computer to teach mathematical problem-solving to these students.

Chapter 9 describes computer applications with the sensory impaired. Many of the computer uses discussed with communication disorders (Chapter 7) also apply to the hearing impaired.

Gifted/Talented

The gifted/talented are those who have very high levels of ability in understanding, problem solving, thinking, or creative ability. The computer is a tailor-made technology for gifted/talented persons. Many gifted/talented individuals are interested in computers and how to program them. They are adept at developing computer algorithms (i.e., the sequence of instructions to the computer) and are able to use the computer as a tool to help solve problems they encounter in other areas. And many talented individuals are using the computer to create musical compositions or pictures. In science and mathematics, computers are used directly in the education of gifted students and have become nearly indispensable for effective learning. Gifted children, youths, and adults are also routinely using computers with modern capabilities (discussed in Chapter 2) to access data bases and information services (e.g., CompuServe, discussed later in this chapter) to pursue their special interests. Chapter 10 specifically addresses computers and gifted/talented individuals.

CURRRENT KNOWLEDGE AND OPINION

A considerable body of literature exists regarding computers and exceptional persons. However, if it is to be meaningfully read and understood and pertinent concepts gleaned, it is imperative that the reviewer use an organized perspective based on specific categories. A very selective review of the existing literature found in popular and professional publications using three categories (synthesis/opinion, reports, and research) follows. Additional literature specific to each exceptionality and special computer concepts will be presented in subsequent chapters.

Synthesis/Opinion Literature

Synthesis/opinion literature, the largest category of literature published to date, consists of authors' syntheses of information and their opinions regarding the use of computers with exceptional persons. While such literature may be based on empirical information, what is reported is generally personal interpretation and synthesis. This body of literature provides general information about almost any topic, what is believed about it, and what is hoped for it.

Journals and magazines have devoted special issues to the use of computers with exceptional individuals. Many of the articles that have appeared in such issues can be categorized as synthesis or opinion. Journals in which an issue contained only articles related to special education technology applications include *Exceptional Children* (vol. 49, no. 2, 1982), *Exceptional Education Quarterly* (vol. 4, no. 4, 1984), *Journal of Special Education Technology* (vol. 5, no. 4, 1982), *Computing Teacher* (vol. 10, no. 6, 1982), *Educational Computer* (vol. 4, no. 1, 1984), *Byte* (vol. 7, no. 9, 1984), *Focus on Exceptional Children* (vol. 18, no. 9, 1986), *Technological Horizons in Education* (vol. 13, no. 6, 1986), *Computers in the Schools* (vol. 3, no. 3/4, 1987), and *Learning Disabilities Focus* (vol. 5, no. 1, 1989). The publication of these and other journal issues increased awareness about the possibilities of using computers with exceptional persons. Such literature also stimulated a great deal of discussion and served as impetus for research activities.

Synthesis/opinion literature addresses both general and specific uses of computers with handicapped and gifted/talented individuals. A portion of this literature consists of books written by such noted writers as Behrmann, 1988; Cain and Taber, 1987; Church and Bender, 1989; Johnson, 1987; Male, 1988; and Russell, Corwin, Mokros, and Kapisovsky, 1989. Additionally, articles from professional journals have also addressed the general uses of computers with exceptional persons (see Blaschke, 1985, 1986; Keefe & Chandler, 1989; Woodward, Carnine, & Collins, 1988; Yates, 1987) as well as specific technology applications with the mildly handicapped (Deming & Valeri-Gold, 1987; Farrell & Kaczka, 1988; Lehrer, Harckham, Archer, & Pruzek, 1986; Maddux, 1987), speech and language disordered (Houle, 1988), severely and physically handicapped (Becker & Schur, 1986), sensory handicapped (Hill & Bradfield, 1987; Mason, Tanaka, & Lian, 1987; Wilson, 1989), gifted/talented (Hersberger & Wheatley, 1989; Jones, 1990), and autistic learners (Hedbring, 1985).

Conference proceedings also represent a source of synthesis/opinion literature as well as more empirically based literature. A variety of specific conferences have been held to ad-dress computer and technology-related concepts for exceptional individuals, and the proceedings of many of these conferences are available. For example, conference proceedings that can be reviewed to get synthesis/opinion information include the annual International Conferences of the Association for the Advancement of Rehabilitation Technology (RESNA) of 1983, 1984, 1985, 1986, and 1988 and the Computer Technology and Persons with Disabilities Conference held in Northridge, California, in 1985. The Technology and Media (TAM) Division of the Council for Exceptional Children also holds an annual conference specifically devoted to technology and the exceptional learner, as does Closing the Gap.

As would be expected, the past decade and a half has resulted in significant changes in the general orientation of synthesis/opinion publications. The initial literature was overwhelmingly optimistic, assuming that computers were going to have a nearly instant and dramatic impact on the education and lives of exceptional persons. As people began to understand the technology better (its capabilities and limitations), readers began to be cautioned not to have blind faith that the computer was an instant solution (see Budhoff & Hutten, 1982; Hannaford, 1983). More recently the emphasis has shifted to informed consumerism. Literature now appears (Becker, 1987, 1989; Hanley, 1987; Hasselbring & Goin, 1988; Howell, 1988; Leles & Culliver, 1986; Lieber & Semmel, 1985) that includes the message "Now that we have the technology and know its potential strengths and limitations, let's work to find out how we can best put it to appropriate use."

Reports

A number of reports have been published of results from funded projects on the use of computers with exceptional persons. Some of these reports are case studies or testimonials of existing uses of computers. In such reports, school districts or public agencies provide information regarding what they attempted with computers, the results of their efforts, problems encountered, and recommendations or suggestions for future use (Cress, 1986; Gray, Hammerbacher, & Simon, 1989). While most of such reports are quite optimistic, this does not mean that uniform success with computers is assured but rather that those producing such reports (and/or those publishing them) are more inclined to report successes than failures. Too frequently, reports do not contain objective data or empirical evidence to support stated findings or conclusions; uncritical acceptance of such reports can lead to false assumptions regarding the use of computers with exceptional individuals.

Research

Research studies investigating the use of computers with handicapped or gifted individuals have also been published. A few years ago very little systematic research had been done in this area. Fortunately the picture is changing and there is an ever-increasing body of research related to the use of computers with exceptional populations. Unfortunately, this category still comprises but a small fraction of available literature on the topic. Some of this research is descriptive of current conditions, reports status or user survey results, or outlines empirical findings. Descriptive research, status surveys, and empirical research results should be included in any literature review to enable the reader to gain an understanding of what is known based on empirical data

Computers promote exceptional individuals' independence. *(Photograph courtesy of IBM Corporation)*

about computer applications with exceptional individuals.

Surveys

The literature now contains a variety of survey results reporting how computers are used in both general education and special education environments. One of the earliest surveys was that conducted by the Cosmos Corporation (see Hanley, 1983a, 1983b). Twelve geographically diverse school districts provided a variety of information regarding the collaborative efforts between regular and special education; the decision-making process involving computers; administrative and instructional uses; the type of computer preparation needed by special education teachers; and the skills, responsibilities, and opportunities surrounding the use of computers in educational settings. As a follow-up to the 1983 survey, Hanley (1987) developed case studies of 27 programs including those serving handicapped learners. The study validated most of the early findings, especially those related to the promotion or inhibition of the use of computers by schools. There was improvement found in the number of administrators using the technology, the expanded role of special education administrators in making technology-related decisions, greater availability of in-service training and technical assistance in the schools, and greater diversity in instructional uses of computers. The most common form of instructional application remained drill-and-practice, and there was still a problem with availability and accessibility. Hanley concluded that while progress has been made, it will take years to incorporate new technologies systematically into the educational programs of handicapped learners.

The findings of a survey of special education teachers conducted by Lance (1984) revealed that 80% of the teachers felt microcomputers to be essential or of moderate educational value to handicapped learners. The teachers felt the value was in the instructional aspects rather than in management or assessment. There was, however, a discrepancy between the teachers' perceived need and the amount of use. Unavailability of hardware and software and the need for additional in-service preparation in the use of technology were seen as the reasons for this discrepancy.

Cosden, Gerber, Goldman, Semmel, and Semmel (1986) surveyed the access and use of microcomputer-based technology by mildly handicapped learners in 300 Southern California elementary schools. They found that two-thirds of the schools allowed learning-handicapped students access to the technology but only half of the schools provided actual computer instruction to this group. It was further found that the number of computers available was related to the amount of access to the technology by the learning handicapped. It appears from this survey that in schools where computers are present there still is a way to go to make certain disabled students have adequate access to and use of this technology.

National surveys of the use of computers in the general educational environment have also been undertaken. The most important of these have been reported by Becker (1985, 1987, 1990). The latest of these is the second national survey of more than 10,000 school personnel in over 2,300 elementary and secondary schools. It was reported by Becker (1986) that in a typical school almost half of the elementary and middle school students and nearly one-third of the high school students used computers in their education. Only about 25% of the teachers were found to be regular users of computers with their students. A wide range of locations for computers within the schools was found, ranging from laboratories to halls. The greatest uses were found to be in mathematics, language arts, computer literacy, programming, and business education. Compared with the first national survey in 1983, it was found that students have greater access to computers because there are greater numbers of computers available in the schools.

These and other surveys continue to provide a baseline for comparing future developments. The results also suggest that computers are being used in much the same way in special education as in regular education with the exception of their use as adaptations by certain populations.

While the surveys published present extensive information on how computers are being used, they do not provide much infor-

mation as to their effectiveness. Such knowledge can only be gained through systematic evaluations and through more experimental research.

Experimental Studies

There is an increasing number of experimental research studies appearing in the literature that focuses on various aspects of using computers with exceptional populations. A perusal of the literature surrounding computer technology and handicapped learners reveals studies investigating the effect of the technology on attitudes (Watkins, 1989), games (Axelrod, McGregor, Sherman, & Hamlet, 1987; Bahr & Rieth, 1989), synthesized speech (Hannaford, Icabone, & Barbus, 1990; Helsel-Dewert & Van Der Meiracker, 1987), mathematics (Robinson, DePascale, & Roberts, 1989), problem solving (Lieber & Semmel, 1987; Woodward, Carnine, & Collins, 1988; Zimmerman, 1988), reading (Fiedorowicz & Trites, 1987; Harper & Ewing, 1986; Keene & Davey, 1987; Torgesen, Waters, Cohen, & Torgesen, 1988), social studies (Horton, Boone, & Lovitt, 1990), spelling (English, 1985; Kinney, Stevens, & Schuster, 1988), word processing (Jacobi, 1986), adaptive devices (Battenberg & Merbler, 1989; Elf, 1988), writing (MacArthur & Graham, 1987), and other areas.

Studies have been conducted with ages from infants to adults and in quite diverse educational settings. It is interesting to note that in recent years the vast majority of the research reported has been conducted with students with learning disabilities. This parallels the dramatic increase in the number of students in this category in recent years, which makes them far more accessible as a population to be studied. No attempt will be made here to provide a comprehensive review of the research in the field. Rather, a few studies that are representative of the diversity present in the research literature will be presented. That will be followed by a synthesis of computer-related research literature in the form of meta-analyses of research in the area.

The effect of the use of computer technology on the attitudes of learners was the focus of an investigation by Watkins (1989).

One group of elementary-level students with learning disabilities received computerized drill-and-practice in spelling and mathematics. A second group of the same type of students did not receive computerized math and spelling instruction. After a year, the attitudes of students in the two groups toward academic learning in general and specifically toward the subjects of math and spelling were determined. Elementary-level students with learning disabilities who had received computerized instruction not only had more positive attitudes toward the two subjects in which they received computerized instruction than did the students who did not receive computerized instruction, but also more positive attitudes toward academic subjects in general than the noncomputerized group.

Rieth, Bahr, Okolo, Polsgrove, and Eckert (1988) studied the impact that the presence of microcomputers had on the ecology of secondary-level special education classrooms. Through the use of direct classroom observation in 26 classes, they found that although there was ready access to computers in the classes, only about 60% of the teachers made use of them. They further found that the microcomputers were used only about one-fourth of the time. The authors identified the low level of use to be due to lack of appropriate software, problems in scheduling use of the computers, and lack of training for teachers. The investigation also found that teachers who made use of microcomputers spent less time directly instructing students and did not integrate their instruction with the instruction provided by the computer.

Delivery of spelling instruction to fourth- and fifth-grade students with learning disabilities was the topic of an investigation by MacArthur, Haynes, Malouf, Harris, and Owings (1990). This research compared computer-assisted instruction and paper-and-pencil instruction in the delivery of independent spelling practice. The content was the same for both groups and the activities were similar but differed in the way they were delivered. Factors like the teacher, the teacher's role, time of day, amount of time spent, presence of peers and teachers in the classroom were controlled. After a 4-week period of time, the group of students who received computer-assisted instruction scored significantly better in spelling achievement and in time on-task, which was positively correlated with achievement.

Woodward, Carnine, and Gersten (1988) investigated the effectiveness of combining effective teaching techniques and computer-based instruction with secondary-level students with learning disabilities. The students studied a unit in health in which computer-assisted instruction was combined with teaching methods based on effective teaching research (teacher-guided practice and high rate of teacher-student interaction). The total group was presented 40 minutes of structured instruction for 12 days. Half of the students then went to a computer laboratory and engaged in guided and independent computer simulation activities while the other half remained in their classroom with a teacher who helped them review and apply previously learned information. The computer simulation group scored significantly higher on a posttest of facts and concepts that was administered immediately after the training. They also performed significantly better after 2 weeks on a separate test of application of the learned information. The results suggest that well-developed and well-applied computer-assisted instruction combined with good instruction can be a powerful educational tool.

The impact of computer-supported writing instruction on the quality of writing of students with learning disabilities was investigated by Morocco, Dalton, and Tivnan (1989). Pencil-and-paper and computer-supported writing instructional programs were evaluated on the quality of writing and attitudes of normally achieving and learning-disabled fourth-grade students. Modest support was found for the computer-supported writing intervention. It was concluded that the computer, when used in conjunction with an instructional approach based on extensive composition, revision, and individualized help, contributed to gains in the quality of writing. The students who had access to computer-supported writing expressed more enjoyment of writing at the end of the year than they did at the beginning.

McDermott and Hessemer (1987) investigated the effects of three different presentation formats on the learning disabled and normal achieving children's mathematical achievement and motivation. The drill-and-practice methods used were: (a) computer-assisted instruction with a reward game, (b) computer-assisted instruction without a reward game, and (c) pencil and paper. Students were identified as achievers and underachievers. Each of the groups was then randomly assigned to one of the three treatments. Both computer-assisted instruction groups were found to spend more time on the tasks than the pencil and paper group. The students receiving computer-assisted instruction without a reward game completed more problems correctly than the other computer-assisted instruction group. When achievement was measured by pre-and posttest performance there were no significant differences among the three groups.

In 1985, the Council for Exceptional Children sponsored an invitational research symposium on special education technology. Contained in the proceedings of that symposium are 42 summaries of technology-based research. Kulik reported in his review of meta-analysis of the studies that in virtually all studies the criterion measure used was student learning. Most computer-based educational programs have been shown to have a positive effect on learning. Students generally learn more in classes where computers are used: they remember longer, learn in less time, like their classes, and develop more positive attitudes. Kulik pointed out, however, that the effects are not positive in every case.

Rieth reviewed and presented research conducted at the secondary school level to study the impact of microcomputers on student behavior, teacher behavior, and the content of the curriculum. He reported that the highest use was in the area of mathematics, with the computer generally used in conjunction with other pencil-and-paper activities. Use of the computer was found to free up teacher time, but this free time was used for supervision of activities rather than for additional instruction. Students were found to generally function in isolation and to receive very little feedback. Another study has demonstrated that when students receive feedback there is an increase in academic performance.

It was found that teachers were unable to provide feedback to students using the computers and to other students as well.

In reporting on the first year of a 4-year study, Semmel indicated that the study had found that schools go through a natural evolution with respect to the allocation of computer-based hardware. This process begins informally with interest and evolves as technology enters the schools. Eventually this evolves into competition for resources and results in pressure to centralize resources into a laboratory arrangement. Teachers reported that computers are used to deliver group instruction as opposed to individual instruction. Computers were found to be used to supplement or reinforce rather than to supplant or replace instruction. Students were found to be active users of the technology but the rate of teacher contact and monitoring remained low.

Malouf indicated that there is a tendency to look for simple answers to complex questions in research on technology. He suggested research is more likely to provide complex answers to simple questions than vice versa. Also, a number of hypotheses have been advanced to account for the equivocal findings reported when traditional paper-and-pencil procedures and computer-based instruction were compared. It has been suggested that "instruction over an extended period of time is necessary in order to effectively evaluate the effectiveness of computer mediated treatment conditions" (Swanson & Trahan, 1992, p. 84). Future researchers conducting experimental studies to investigate the advantages and disadvantages of traditional and computer-based instructional procedures should give careful thought to length of time of the intervention and treatment conditions.

What the Literature Tells Us

Synthesis/opinion articles, reports, and research articles lead to the following conclusions:

1. Within the synthesis/opinion literature, there still is a note of cautious optimism about the use of computers with exceptional populations. While many potential applications

have been identified and many have been put into use, there are still realities and problems associated with the appropriate use of this technology. The question seems to be how the application *should* be used rather than how it *can* be used.

2. Much of what is presented as being known about the use of computers with exceptional persons is actually what is believed, felt, or hoped. While there is an increasing amount of research and evaluation support associated with various uses of the technology, there is still relatively little empirical support for many statements found in the popular literature.

3. Most reports indicate that the use of computers with exceptional students has been successful to some extent. This must be tempered with the realization that the very nature of such reports and case studies is such that there is a tendency to omit reports of negative attempts.

4. There continues to be an increase in the use of computers with various groups of exceptional individuals. Most of the recent research literature, however, has addressed the learning-disabled population.

5. Generally, the same research findings noted for nonexceptional populations are found with exceptional populations. Table 1.2 outlines some of the findings that appear to be applicable to both exceptional and nonexceptional children and youths.

COMPUTERS IN THE SCHOOL

Computers are directly and indirectly having an impact on the delivery of special education and related services to exceptional children, youths, and adults in a variety of educational and clinical settings. The primary ways computer technology is being used with handicapped and gifted individuals include its use as a compensatory tool (e.g., to compensate for visual impairment by providing speech output for important information on the computer screen or monitor), use in instructional

---

TABLE 1.2
Parallel findings of computer research studies with nonexceptional and exceptional children and youths

- When computers are used, students tend to learn the material in less time.
- The use of computers seems to result in increased attention, motivation, and time on-task.
- The general effects of computer instruction are similar regardless of the type of software used. This does not imply that the quality of individual software is not a factor, but rather that one category of software has not consistently been found to be superior to others.
- Exceptional as well as nonexceptional learners tend to view the computer in the instructional setting quite positively.
- Drill-and-practice is the most frequent type of program used. This type of program is most useful with lower-ability students but has been found to be effective overall.
- Higher-ability students appear to benefit the most from the use of computers in terms of the amount and diversity of learning attained. This would appear consistent with the learning charcteristics of this group.
- Using computers appears to more easily provide education to students who have typically been difficult to reach and teach.
- Computers are helpful in reviewing previously learned material. This may be a very significant factor in mainstreaming settings.
- The most effective use of computers is when they are used to supplement other instruction.
- Use of computers leads to better social interaction when students work jointly than when they work in isolation or when they work in traditional ways with traditional instruction.
- Computers do not stifle creativity nor do they dehumanize education.
- The benefits of computers are not inherent. The environment in which they are used and the way in which they are used are the determining factors.
- Teachers remain excited about the technology but do not spend much time actually using computers in the instructional process. Computers continue to be used in ways that are isolated from the instructional mainstream.

management (e.g., to write, file, and revise individual education plans [IEPs]), and use in instructional delivery (e.g., to individualize instruction for each student).

Compensatory Tool

The power of the computer to augment, accelerate, and enhance functioning in certain areas has proved to be a boon to exceptional students. Devices such as the Adaptive Firmware Card (described in Chapters 7 and 8) and Access to Adaptive Devices for Microcomputers (COMPUTE, 1988) allow individuals with physical handicaps to operate computers with a single key or switch rather than through a regular keyboard. Voice command systems such as IntroVoice (Voice Connection, 17835 Skypark Circle, Suite C, Irvine, CA 92714) and Shadow Vet (Scott Instruments, 1111 Willow Springs Drive, Denton, TX 76201) enable persons to enter information or commands into a computer verbally. Pneumatic switches (sip and puff switches) and the electromyographic switch (sometimes called the brow-wrinkle switch) are other such compensatory devices.

The flexibility of the computer also enables it to control other devices, resulting in numerous applications of this technology in helping exceptional individuals with disabilities compensate for the loss or absence of body parts or functions. Deaf students can more readily communicate with hearing students or other deaf persons in classrooms over long distances using computer-controlled telecommunications devices (e.g., modems discussed in Chapter 2 and FAX machines). Computer-generated enlarged print, braille translations, and synthesized speech can assist the visually impaired to communicate. Inexpensive speech synthesizers, such as Echo Plus (described in Chapter 7), Type-'N-Talk, or The PC Voice, are great communication advancements for students with expressive language problems.

Students with mild handicaps are also being helped to compensate for their problems through the use of computers. Individuals with mental retardation, learning disabilities, behavior disorders, and/or difficulty with hand-writing can use the computer as a word processor to compose, edit, and print language. Likewise, mildly handicapped students with severe grammar and spelling problems can use computerized grammar and spelling programs such as Sensible Grammar and Mega-Works the Spelling Checker & Mail-Merge program to produce work that is not only acceptable but also of a quality of which they can be proud.

There is little doubt that educational uses of computers as compensatory tools will continue to increase. While the cost of some of these devices and accompanying software is high, the cost of not having them is even greater to those students whose education literally depends upon them.

Instructional Management

More demands have been made of teachers because of the increased diversity in the types and levels of functioning of exceptional students found in schools; the increase in the number of students to be served; local, state, and federal requirements for data collection; mandated educational planning; the increased regular class placement of handicapped learners; and accountability. Faced with increasing noninstructional responsibilities, regular and special educators have had a very difficult choice to make. They could reduce the amount of time and effort devoted to instruction, they could work harder and longer, or they could work more efficiently. With the availability of computers, teachers and other professionals began to see that they could make use of this technology to increase their efficiency and productivity (e.g., individual letters could be sent to all parents by changing only the inside address and the salutation). As an instructional management tool, the computer is being used in special education settings including managing IEPs, assessing students' abilities, writing reports, generating educational prescriptions, keeping and analyzing records, and preparing instructional materials (e.g., using graphics programs to prepare instructional materials and using work sheet generators).

Instructional Delivery

Exceptional students may need extraordinary educational and related services requiring consequence, programmatic, curricular, and consequential instructional modifications if they are to achieve their educational potential. The ways in which computers can be used in the delivery of instruction to exceptional students include individualizing instruction, motivating exceptional learners, and producing interactive learning activities.

Individualizing Instruction

Instruction that adapts to the unique needs and capabilities of the individual results in superior learning. Good software programs are self-pacing (students progress at their own rate); offer flexible branching (when a correct response is made the program continues in the instructional sequence, but if a mistake is made the program lets the user do the task again or attempts to help identify the reason for the error and presents remediation); provide feedback, reinforcement, and reward (the student's response is immediately checked and feedback is provided along with appropriate reinforcement or reward); and are multisensory in presentation (the user's visual, auditory, tactile, and kinesthetic modalities are used). Software possessing these attributes is covered in more depth in subsequent chapters and in Appendix E.

Motivating Learners

Students with disabilities, gifts, and talents who are active in the learning process learn more readily than those who are passive recipients of instruction or who actively resist learning. Experience and research show that exceptional students respond to computers in an educational setting with enthusiasm and become motivated. Computers help motivate exceptional students because they are nonjudgmental, less threatening, and provide educational experiences at the students' present levels of functioning. As one adolescent with emotional disturbance indicated when asked why he liked working with the computer: "Because

it don't yell at me when I get it wrong!" The self-pacing quality of most of the software programs/packages now produced is also a strong motivating factor, as is the fact that many more programs are being produced that have incorporated good instructional design principles that include motivation.

Producing Interactive Learning

Classroom or clinical instruction that requires a high level of active learner involvement is more effective than instruction that relegates the learner to a passive role. With proper programming (e.g., the computer generates questions and the student is directed to input yes or no for each question), good interactive computer software can elicit a high rate of responses and attentive involvement from exceptional learners.

There are advantages to using computers and good software to increase individualized instruction, to help motivate exceptional students, and to provide handicapped and gifted/talented students with a highly interactive learning environment. All of these are important considerations when investigating the computer as an educational tool for exceptional learners. The computer continues to be primarily used as an instructional tool to supplement more traditional instruction in areas such as mathematics, science, and language arts. Widespread and diverse instructional uses of computers with students is still relatively rare, though these uses have dramatically increased in recent years. Hopefully, as we learn more about how this technology can and should be used and team it with other technologies such as interactive videodiscs (see Chapter 5), there will be a gradual expansion of the uses to which it will be put. General and more specific uses of computer hardware and software with exceptional learners are discussed in Chapters 6 through 10.

COMPUTERS IN THE HOME

There can be no question that the advent of the relatively inexpensive Apple, Commodore,

Computers have many uses in the home. *(Photograph courtesy of Apple Computers, Inc.)*

TRS-80, and Atari personal computers in the 1970s was the most important factor leading to the introduction of computers in the schools and for making computer ownership in the home a reality for exceptional persons. The four primary uses of computers by handicapped and gifted/talented individuals in the home environment are recreation and leisure, home management, education, and mobility/communication/independence.

Recreation and Leisure

For many exceptional persons, the computer offers an attractive option in recreation and leisure time use. Although playing popular computer games comes immediately to mind (e.g., video games, chess, flight simulations), computers and related technologies are also being used in hobbies (e.g., inventory of collections and genealogy) and for creative expression (e.g., composing music, artistic expression,

writing) to provide exceptional individuals with recreation, a sense of accomplishment, and feelings of personal worth. These computer activities can also be shared with others (e.g., using a modem). Individuals with disabilities, gifts, and talents are also accessing the major computer information bulletin boards, information services, and data bases (see Table 1.3). For a reasonable fee, access to these services allows persons to communicate (e.g., electronic mail and forums), to have fun (e.g., to play TV-style game shows and soon to participate in interactive television), to shop, to plan travel (e.g., flight and hotel reservations), to access vast amounts of stored information (e.g., encyclopedias and a wide range of data bases), to keep healthy (e.g., access to medical information), to keep abreast of the latest news, weather, and sports (e.g., access wire services, electronic newspapers, sports services), and to review their investments through accessing stock market information. Exceptional individuals can also access information services that are specific to special education such as SpecialNet.

Home Management

Exceptional persons are also finding the computer to be a valuable tool for conducting day-to-day home management. Computer technology (e.g., digital thermostats, satellite dishes) permits handicapped individuals to control environmental factors, select television programs, and do hundreds of other home tasks (e.g., turning any light on or off) with the touch of a button or the utterance of a sound. Also speech synthesizers and modems permit them to communicate in and out of the home, to give directions, and to order needed items or services. Word processing and data base capabilities (discussed in Chapters 3 and 12) have meant new freedom for exceptional persons to process, store, and manipulate any verbal or numerical information they need (e.g., names and addresses, telephone numbers, recipes). The use of electronic spreadsheet software also permits exceptional individuals to engage in simple as well as complex mathematical and financial activities.

Education

Currently there is increasing interest on the part of educators, exceptional individuals, and parents to find new ways in which computers can be used to facilitate the educational process at home. Compatible computers are often available at school and at home so that schoolwork and homework can be done at either location. Parents as well as exceptional persons themselves have sought out, with or without the assistance of educators, computer hardware and educational software that might prove beneficial in acquiring new skills and knowledge. Many exceptional persons have profited educationally from the availability of computers in their homes. They have found this technology not only educationally exciting but also helpful in other kinds of learning (e.g., accessing CompuServe or some other on-line service, for business or pleasure).

Mobility/Communication

Computers in the home are making definite inroads as tools to help persons with handicaps compensate for their disabilities in mobility and communication. For those whose disabilities effectively isolate them from the rest of society, computers, while not providing access to a normal life, have helped significantly (e.g., computerized wheelchairs).

Individuals with handicaps who are confined to their homes have previously had few ways to communicate other than telephone and face-to-face communication with those who come to their home. Today a variety of "tele-information" services are available by which anyone with a touchtone telephone has access to a wide range of information services. Often the same disability that resulted in lack of mobility also greatly hindered options like writing or typing. Today handicapped persons can use computer hardware and word processing programs by inputting information with devices other than the keyboard (e.g., speech recognition units, single switch devices, and scanning devices).

Another major area where computer technology is having a significant impact on the home life of exceptional persons is home control. While the age of the "smart house" is not yet here on a large scale, it is coming. Devices already exist that permit a wide range of home control through voice or remote control input. It is now possible to control a wide range of household functions from a telephone anywhere in the nation. Homes are being built that feature computer control of lighting, security, phone answering, temperature, and automatic phone alarms. For many individuals with handicaps, these features are not a novelty but the difference between their being a part of society or being apart from society.

Telecommunication systems (e.g., computers and modems) that permit exceptional individuals to shop, bank, and pay bills without leaving their homes have obvious advantages to those confined to their homes. In the future the power of computers may be teamed with space satellite technology and robotics to improve the quality of life of many severely handicapped individuals. The type, quantity,

TABLE 1.3
A sampler of information services and data bases exceptional individuals can access

There are over 30 telecommunications services available to the educator. A sampling of those that may be accessed by exceptional individuals includes:

CompuServe
P.O. Box 20212
Columbus, OH 43220
1-800/848-8199

This is the largest information service and provides the most comprehensive array of services to the user. Among the services provided are access to electronic mail (e-mail), computerized shopping, data bases, conferencing, and other consumer services. There are many additional services that are available at additional cost, such as access to the Grolier Electronic Encyclopedia and access to news clipping services.

There is a start-up fee and hourly connect charges.

GEnie
General Electric Information Services
401 N. Washington St.
Rockville, MD 20850
1-800/638-9636

This is a general information service that contains e-mail, forums, weather reports, Grolier Electronic Encyclopedia, etc. It also has a very usable news service with key word searching and an automatic clipping service at no extra charge.

There is a start-up fee and a flat fee for non-prime-time usage. An hourly rate is charged for prime-time use.

Prodigy
Prodigy Services Company
445 Hamilton Ave.
White Plains, NY 10615
1-800/776-3449

This relatively inexpensive information service is designed to provide access to electronic mail, access to various forums, a variety of games, news features, etc. Advertisements are displayed along with the output screens.

There is a flat monthly fee for unlimited access.

America Online, Promenade, PC-Link, Q-Link
Quantum Computer Services
8619 Westwood Center Drive
Vienna, VA 22182
1-800/227-6364 (America Online)
1-800/545-6572 (all other services)

This is a group of four separate services that target specific hardware users: America Online for Apple and MacIntosh users, Promenade primarily for IBM PS/1 users, PC-Link serving the MS-DOS environment, and Q-Link for Commodore users. These services are primarily designed to serve the home user. All four offer standard services such as e-mail, games, and electronic encyclopedia access.

ED-LINE, SpecialNet, NYS NewsLine, and CNN Newsroom
GTE Education Services
8505 Freeport Parkway, Suite 600
Irving, TX 75063
1-800/634-5644

These four subservices are part of a larger global information service serving the educational community. Subscription to one provides access to all of them minus the e-mail capabilities. Each of the areas focuses on a specific area within education. SpecialNet is the service specifically targeting the special education profession. In addition to e-mail, SpecialNet has a wide range of bulletin boards containing specialized information and access to a wide range of data bases. ED-LINE, the general service for educators, provides a wide range of federal and state educational news and access to grant information in addition to e-mail. NYS NewsLine enables exchanges of news among subscribers to permit students and schools to produce daily or weekly newsletters. CNN Newsroom is intended to complement the news presented by the Cable News Network. This service provides downloadable news-related activities for use by students.

There is a monthly fee plus hourly connect charges.

For a more comprehensive listing of data bases of hardware, software, and publications relevant to the use of computers in special education refer to:

DLM Teaching Resources. (1988). *Apple computer resources in special education and rehabilitation*. Allen, TX: DLM Teaching Resources.

and quality of other devices that can be used to normalize the lives of many handicapped individuals will continue to increase.

COMPUTERS IN SOCIETY

Our society is rapidly ascending the crest of what Toffler (1980) referred to as the "Third Wave." We are becoming a society dominated by information rather than one being dominated by industrialization. Computers are nearly everywhere (in supermarkets at checkout counters and even on shopping carts) and assist us in doing many things (they now call us on the telephone and offer to sell us products or solicit donations). Such uses will increase in the future. There is no doubt they will continue to help us move about (e.g., computer care systems and car phones) and take advantage of community activities (e.g., talking at courthouse meetings via telecommunications).

Possibly the most significant aspect of computers in our society is that they are becoming increasingly invisible or transparent to those who use them. While they are becoming more prevalent in our lives, they are also becoming less and less noticeable as computers. From digital watches and clocks to devices that brew our coffee and control our automobiles, the technology of microcomputers surrounds us. Our world is rapidly changing. We have already significantly changed the ways in which we bank and make phone calls. Changes include the increased use of debit cards instead of credit cards. Such cards (e.g., the Washington, DC Subway Fare Card) are bought for a certain amount, and the amount for purchases (e.g., the cost of riding from one DC subway station to another) is automatically deducted from the value of the card. When its value reaches zero, it is discarded or additional money is added. Computer controlled robots independently deliver mail and packages in some businesses. And companies are beginning to issue optical cards that contain hundreds of pages of information such as medical records, X-rays, and so on. The day may soon come when we will be able to carry an actual library of information with us that can be accessed from nearly anywhere.

Advanced telecommunication is changing the workplace. Many exceptional persons can work out of their homes as a result of computers. Already in some work areas computers provide explicit instructions for certain tasks. In the future the necessity for traditional literacy as we know it (reading, writing, and arithmetic) may be increasingly replaced by the necessity for computer literacy. Traditional institutions, jobs, and employees are being changed dramatically as computers change society.

Computers in our society will have an impact on exceptional persons—where and how they learn, live, work, and acquire information. Technology has the potential for improving the quality of life for exceptional persons, but there is nothing inherent in technology to make this happen—the benefits are dependent on how technology is used. Computer technology may prove essential to the exceptional person in the society of tomorrow. If, however, exceptional individuals are not adequately prepared for the new and emerging technologies, the potential of such technologies will most certainly be wasted.

ADDITIONAL COMPUTER ISSUES

A. J. Lotka in 1969 (see Broudy, 1985) coined the term *exosomatics*. Exosomatics "refers to transporting a function from within the human organism to an external machine. Locomotion is a common example, but so is mental arithmetic, mechanical hearts, and, as many hope, artificial intelligence" (p. 8). The concept behind this term is particularly applicable to current and emerging technologies and ways in which computers are and will be used with exceptional persons.

Additional uses of computers with exceptional persons are often related to other technologies that, when teamed with computers, will have an impact on the lives of exceptional individuals. The real power of computers lies in their ability to access and control other technologies. The lives of exceptional persons will continue to be changed because of computers and their associated technologies.

New Computers

Today's computers are made of silicon and use electricity and magnetism to manipulate and store information. Optical computers, however, are being developed that use laser technology and lenses, and in them light replaces traditional silicon/electricity operations. Superfast computers that use chemicals rather than electric impulses to transmit and store information are also being considered. The most startling, yet potentially significant, advance for exceptional individuals is the possible development of biological computers—computers comprised of living matter that can be implanted and will grow. Biologic computers could be implanted in the brain and provide persons with handicaps direct links to other computers or people. Sidestepping the ethical and moral issues, such technology could serve as intellectual prostheses to augment intelligence, provide much faster information processing and thought, and enable the processing of vast quantities of information.

Robotics

Robots are now being used to fabricate automobiles as well as computers, and, in Japanese department stores, they are unloading merchandise, serving food, and helping shoppers. Robots are able to function because computers direct and monitor their movements. As the sophistication of robots increases, so will their ability to provide assistance to exceptional individuals. Indeed, attempts have been made to develop robots to help the severely physically handicapped negotiate their environments and engage in everyday functions (e.g., eating). Experimentation is now occurring in the use of robots as assistive devices, such as robotic arms attached to wheelchairs. The potential of this technology for the handicapped includes robots with very sophisticated manipulators and three-dimensional vision that enable very precise depth perception

Exceptional persons must be prepared to use computers in society.
(Photograph courtesy of Education and Technology Resources)

to locate and grasp and manipulate very complex objects, such as those found within a living environment. Also, robots that are able to understand and respond to natural language commands through the use of computers will be helpful to persons with disabilities unable to move. Robots that move on their own and have a sense of touch could perform delicate tasks for the handicapped (e.g., cooking, reading the newspaper, playing games). The prototypes of the lovable *Star Wars* R2D2 and C3PO robots are getting closer and closer.

Artificial Intelligence

Though we sometimes act and speak as though computers are intelligent and have the ability to think, they do not yet do so. While computers have not yet reached that level of sophistication, a great deal of work is taking place in the field of artificial intelligence. Expert systems combine the collected knowledge of experts with the information storage and retrieval capabilities of the computer to allow the information to be used according to a set of "rules" designed to make use of the information in making decisions.

Hofmeister and Ferrara (1986) reported on a research project that investigated the feasibility of using expert systems in special education. Their conclusion was that it is possible to develop such systems, which could provide assistance in numerous areas related to special education.

There has also been rapid advancement in computer systems that understand natural language. Due to research in artificial intelligence, exceptional persons may reap both direct and indirect benefits. Computer artificial intelligence is opening vast new areas of study for gifted/talented persons. The breakthroughs such persons make will be those from which other exceptionalities will benefit. This new technology may develop small computers to serve as "cognitive prostheses" to handicapped persons whose memory, conceptual abilities, or problem-solving capabilities are limited or lost. Computers with artificial intelligence may simulate learning disabilities, mental retardation, and autism so that these conditions can be systematically investigated in ways never before possible and, perhaps, eventually be prevented, eliminated, or circumvented.

Artificial intelligence could also be used to assist the hearing impaired with language development and language usage. Artificially intelligent software that produces speech specifically tailored to the hearing-impaired person's speech reception and residual hearing frequencies would be a dramatic advancement. And a videodisc with sign language attached to an artificially intelligent computer program to interpret verbal input from others would expand the world for the hearing-impaired population.

Mobility and Positioning

Computers are increasingly being used with other technologies to improve the quality of life of those with mobility and physical problems (see Chapter 8). Wheelchair systems with on-board computers are being developed that automatically monitor and adjust speed and avoid obstacles while moving according to a set of preprogrammed instructions. Other systems exist in which the computer monitors the user's position and automatically adjusts posture to accommodate the specific needs of the individual or to enhance physical comfort. It is likely that these and more impressive developments will become more readily available in the near future.

Improved Prostheses

We have begun to see the tip of the iceberg in terms of what computer technology means to the development of vastly improved prosthetic devices. As computers become even smaller and more powerful, we will see other significant advances. The work being done with artificial vision and hearing will continue until both become a reality. Though they may never rival normal vision or hearing, the developments will be significant enough to mean a vastly improved life for many exceptional persons. Work continues on the development of even more sophisticated myoelectric prostheses (electromechanical devices activated and controlled by nerve impulses), a wedding of computer and robotic technologies to give the user more normal range and control of motion, including increased computer control, a rudimentary sense of touch, more precise control of movement, and greater flexibility of use. While such prostheses may never replace the actual body part, they will improve the quality of life for many handicapped persons.

Very sophisticated mechanical devices are on the near horizon that will be totally controlled from a remote location using voice input or using controls that are within the capabilities of many physically disabled persons. The forerunners of such devices are already being used in some industries to handle hazardous radioactive or corrosive materials. Some physically disabled persons may "go to work" without ever leaving home through the use of such devices.

New Computer Inputs

Already information can be entered into computers using voice recognition devices and microswitches controlled by single muscles.

Such voice recognition units enable persons to input a wide range of information using their voices. Persons with disabilities are able to write by simply talking into a voice-activated word processing system. One game manufacturer is already marketing a device that allows computer input through the electrical impulses of the skin. Worn as a headband, the input device detects minute changes in the electrical responses on the skin, and a computer translates these into game control actions. The military, too, has experimented with similar control devices. There are direct and immediate implications of such devices for exceptional persons.

Information Storage and Retrieval

As the information age continues, we can expect to have better information storage and retrieval systems. We already have extremely rapid access to vast banks of information through online information services (see Table 1.3). Kurshan (1990), in her discussion of educational telecommunications in the 1990s, identified a variety of features that are found on such systems:

- Electronic mail
- Bulletin boards
- Conferences
- Real-time conferencing
- Access to a variety of databases
- Curriculum-based projects
- Online tutoring
- Access to experts
- Access to higher education networks & services
- Access to international students, teachers & classrooms
- Online help through moderators
- Training online and through written materials
- Emphasis on graphics and videotext
- Gateways to other networks

- Ability to access projects for limited use
- Local databases
- Menu driven (p. 31)

Compact disks and videodiscs will provide us with even more ready access at work, home, and school. As computers become smaller and able to store even more information, the contents of books or even libraries may be stored on devices the size of a credit card or small calculator. The user will need only to insert the card into a reader to see or hear the contents. Already one major health insurance company is doing just that—each client's card contains entire medical histories including X rays, test results, medications, and other pertinent data. The information is stored, accessed, and updated using laser and computer technologies. Such developments will definitely have an impact on the lives of exceptional and nonexceptional persons. Also, advances in portable communication devices will occur. Today, there is a portable version of the Kurzweil Reader (see Chapter 9) that enables nearly any form of printed material to be read aloud to the user in virtually any location.

Future technologies and their impact on exceptional persons will be stranger than we can imagine. Attempting to look into the future is like peering into a foggy night—the further one attempts to see, the more indistinct the view becomes. However, it is certain that computer developments and their associated technologies will have quite dramatic impacts on the lives of exceptional persons.

REFERENCES

Axelrod, S., McGregor, G., Sherman, J., & Hamlet, C. (1987). Effects of videotapes as reinforcers for computerized addition performance. *Journal of Special Education Technology, 9*(1), 1–8.

Bahr, C. M., & Rieth, H. J. (1989). The effects of instructional computer games and drill and practice software on learning disabled students' mathematics achievement. *Computers in the Schools, 6*(3/4), 87–101.

Battenberg, J. K., & Merbler, J. B. (1989). Touch screen versus keyboard: A comparison of task performance of young children. *Journal of Special Education Technology, 10*(1), 24–28.

Becker, H. J. (1985, July). *The second national survey of instructional uses of school computers.* Paper presented at the World Conference on Computers in Education, Norfolk, VA. (ERIC Document Reproduction Service No. ED 274 307)

Becker, H. J. (1986). *Instructional uses of school computers. Reports from the 1985 national survey.* (Issue No. 3). Baltimore, MD: Johns Hopkins University, Center for Social Organization of Schools. (ERIC Document Reproduction Service No. ED 274 301)

Becker, H. J. (1987, April). *The impact of computer use of children's learning: What research has shown and what it has not.* Paper presented at the annual meeting of the American Educational Research Association, Washington, DC. (ERIC Document Reproduction Service No. ED 287 458)

Becker, H. J. (1989). The effects of computer use on children's learning: Limitations of past research and a working model for new research. *Peabody Journal of Education, 64*(1), 81–110.

Becker, H. J. (1990). Curriculum and instruction in middle-grade schools. *Phi Delta Kappan, 71*(6), 450–457.

Becker, H., & Schur, S. (1986). The advantages of using microcomputer-based assessment with moderately and severely handicapped individuals. *Journal of Special Education Technology, 8*(2), 53–57.

Becker, H. J., & Sterling, C. W. (1987). Equity in school computer use: National data and neglected considerations. *Journal of Educational Computing Research, 3*(3), 289–311.

Behrmann, M. (Ed.). (1988). *Integrating computers into the curriculum: A handbook for special educators.* Austin, TX: PRO-ED.

Blaschke, C. L. (1985). Technology trends in special education. *Technological Horizons in Education, 12*(6), 73–77.

Blaschke, C. L. (1986). Technology for special education: A national strategy. *Technological Horizons in Education, 13*(6), 77–82.

Botlik, O. (1992). Proposing a new paradigm for public education in Czechoslovakia. *T.H.E. Journal, 19*(6), 59–61.

Broudy, H. S. (1985, March). *Past and future in education.* Paper presented at the annual meeting of the Association for Supervision and Curriculum Development, Chicago, IL. (ERIC Document Reproduction Service No. ED 253 969)

Budhoff, M., & Hutten, L. R. (1982). Microcomputers in special education: Promises and pitfalls. *Exceptional Children, 49,* 123–128.

Cain, E. J., Jr., & Taber, F. M. (1987). *Educating disabled people for the 21st century.* Austin, TX: PRO-ED.

Church, G., & Bender, M. (1989). *Teaching with computers: A curriculum for special educators.* Austin, TX: PRO-ED.

COMPUTE. (1988). *Adaptive devices module.* Wayne, MI: Wayne County Intermediate School District.

Cosden, M. A., Gerber, M., Goldman, S. R., Semmel, D. S., & Semmel, M. I. (1986). Survey of microcomputer access and use by mildly handicapped students in southern California. *Journal of Special Education Technology, 7*(4), 5–13.

Cress, C. J. (1986). *Disabled access to technological advances (DATA).* (Final report). Madison, WI: Access to Independence; Madison, WI: Computers to Help People; Madison: Wisconsin Division of Vocational Rehabilitation; Madison: Wisconsin University, Trace Center. (ERIC Document Reproduction Service No. ED 310 598)

Day, V. P., Golden, R. H., & Sweitzer, H. F. (1989). Using microcomputers for instruction and reinforcement of study skills. *Academic Therapy, 24*(4), 461–470.

Deming, M. P., & Valeri-Gold, M. (1987, March). *Computers and the handicapped: A primer.* Paper presented at the 38th annual meeting of the Conference on College Composition and Communication, Atlanta, GA. (ERIC Document Reproduction Service No. ED 295 408)

Elf, B. (1988). Use of the touch sensitive screen with children who have special education needs. *British Journal of Special Education, 15*(3), 116–118.

English, J. P. (1985). Microcomputer-administered spelling tests: Effects on learning handicapped and normally achieving students. *Journal of Reading, Writing, and Learning Disabilities International, 1*(2), 165–176.

Farrell, M. L., & Kaczka, A. (1988). Integrating the computer into resource room instruction. *Computers in the Schools, 5*(1/2), 213–223

Fiedorowicz, C.A.M., & Trites, R. L. (1987). *An evaluation of the effectiveness of computer-assisted components reading subskills training.* (ERIC Document Reproduction Service No. ED 286 163)

Gray, J. B., Hammerbacher, G., & Simon, K. (1989). Teacher use of word processing in rural special education. In *Education and the changing rural community: Anticipating the 21st century.* Proceedings of the 1989 ACE/NRSSC Symposium. (ERIC Document Reproduction Service No. ED 315 242)

Hall, E. R., McLaughlin, T. F., & Bialozor, R. C. (1989). The effects of computer-assisted drill and practice on spelling performance with mildly handicapped students. *Reading Improvement, 26*(1), 43–49.

Hanley, C. (1988, October). *400 systems later: Outcomes of the Pennsylvania Project.* Paper presented at the biennial conference of the Society for Augmentative and Alternative Communication, Anaheim, CA. (ERIC Document Reproduction Service No. ED 304 852)

Hanley, T. V. (1983a). *Microcomputers in special education: Organizational issues. Microcomputers in the schools—implementation in special education. Information product number one.* Washington, DC: COSMOS Corporation. (ERIC Document Reproduction Service No. ED 238 221)

Hanley, T. V. (1983b). *Microcomputer software in special education: Selection and management. Report to RRC's Microcomputer in the schools—implementation in special education. Information product number two.* Washington, DC: COSMOS Corp. (ERIC Document Reproduction Service No. ED 242 121)

Hanley, T. V. (1987). *Case study findings on the implementation of microcomputers in special education.* (ERIC Document Reproduction Service No. ED 304 858)

Hannaford, A. E. (1983). Microcomputers in special education: Some new opportunities, some old problems. *Computing Teacher, 10*(2), 11–17.

Hannaford, A. E., Icabone, D. G., & Barbus, S. (1990). Using a microcomputer and speech synthesizer with learning disabled adolescents. *Educational Technology, 30*(1), 45–48.

Harper, J., & Ewing, N. (1986). A comparison of the effectiveness of microcomputer and workbook instruction on reading performance of high incidence handicapped children. *Educational Technology, 26*(5), 40–45.

Hasselbring, T. S., & Goin, L. I. (1988). Use of computers. In G. A. Robinson (Ed.), *Best practices in mental disabilities* (chap. 10). (ERIC Document Reproduction Service No. ED 304 838)

Hedbring, C. (1985). Computers and autistic learners: An evolving technology. *Australian Journal of Human Communication Disorders, 13*(2), 169–194.

Helsel-Dewert, M., & Van Der Meiracker, M. (1987). The intelligibility of synthetic speech to learning handicapped children. *Journal of Special Education Technology, 9*(1), 38–44.

Hersberger, J., & Wheatley, G. (1989). Computers and gifted students: An effective mathematics program. *Gifted Child Quarterly, 33*(3), 106–109.

Hill, E. W., & Bradfield, A. L. (1987). Electronic travel aids for blind persons. *Journal of Special Education Technology, 8*(3), 31–42.

Hofmeister, A. M., & Ferrara, J. M. (1986). *Artificial intelligence applications in special education: How feasible?* (Final report). (ERIC Document Reproduction Service No. ED 284 402)

Horton, S. V., Boone, R. A., & Lovitt, T. C. (1990). Teaching social studies to learning disabled high school students: Effects of a hypertext study guide. *British Journal of Educational Technology, 21*(2), 118–131.

Houle, G. R. (1988). Computer usage by speech-language pathologists in public schools. *Language, Speech, and Hearing Services in Schools, 19*(4), 423–427.

Houle, G. R. (1989). Teachers of communicatively-impaired students: To use or not to use computer technology. *Educational Technology, 29*(6), 43–45.

Howell, R. (1988, January). *The ethics of technological intervention with disabled learners.* Paper presented at the annual meeting of the Association for Educational Communications and Technology, New Orleans, LA. (ERIC Document Reproduction Service No. ED 295 624)

Huh, U. (1992). Computers in education in the Republic of Korea. *T.H.E. Journal, 19*(6), 72–76.

Jacobi, C. (1986). Word processing for special needs students: Is there really a gain? *Educational Technology, 26*(4), 36–39.

Johnson, D. L. (1987). *Computers in the special education classroom.* New York: Haworth Press.

Johnson, D. L. (1987). *Express yourself: Communication disabilities need not be handicaps.* (ERIC Document Reproduction Service No. ED 303 012)

Johnson, L. B. (1991). Computing with a pen. *PC Today, 5*(10), 8–10.

Jones, G. (1990). *Personal computers help gifted students work smart.* Reston, VA: Council for Exceptional Children; Reston, VA: ERIC Clearinghouse on Handicapped and Gifted Children. (ERIC Document Reproduction Service No. ED 321 488)

Keefe, C. H., & Chandler, A. C. (1989). LD students and word processors: Questions and answers. *Learning Disabilities Focus, 5*(1), 78–83.

Keene, S. & Davey, B. (1987). Effects of computer-presented text on LD adolescents' reading behaviors. *Learning Disability Quarterly, 10,* 283–290.

Kinney, P. G., Stevens, K. B., & Schuster, J. W. (1988). The effects of CAI and time delay: A systematic program for teaching spelling. *Journal of Special Education Technology, 9*(2), 61–72.

Kinzer, G. (1987, April). *Augmentative communication with computer assistance.* Paper presented at the 65th annual convention of the Council for Exceptional Children, Chicago, IL. (ERIC Document Reproduction Service No. ED 288 291)

Kiselev, B. G. (1992). The Soviet Union's large-scale program to computerize education. *T.H.E. Journal, 19*(6), 66–67.

Kurshan, B. (1990). Educational telecommunications connections for the classroom—part 1. *The Computing Teacher, 17*(6), 30–35.

Lance, W. D. (1984). *Use of microcomputers in special education: A survey of special education teachers in the Saddleback Valley Unified School District.* (ERIC Document Reproduction Service No. ED 253 028)

Larson, B. L., & Roberts, B. B. (1986). The computer as a catalyst for mutual support and empowerment among learning disabled students. *Journal of Learning Disabilities, 19*(1), 52–55.

Lehrer, R., Harckham, L. D., Archer, P., & Pruzek, R. M. (1986). Microcomputer-based instruction in special education. *Journal of Educational Computing Research, 2*(3), 337–355.

Leles, S., & Culliver, C. C. (1986, November). *The effects of a computer-assisted instruction program on peer acceptance, teacher acceptance, and self-concept of mildly handicapped students.* Paper presented at the 15th annual meeting of the Mid-South Educational Research Association, Memphis, TN. (ERIC Document Reproduction Service No. ED 293 238)

Lieber, J., & Semmel, M. I. (1985). Effectiveness of computer application to instruction with mildly handicapped learners: A review. *Remedial and Special Education* [RASE], *6*(5), 5–12.

Lieber, J., & Semmel, M. I. (1987). The relationship between group size and performance on a microcomputer problem-solving task for learning handicapped and nonhandicapped students. *Journal of Educational Computing Research, 3*(2), 171–187.

MacArthur, C. A., & Graham, S. (1987). Learning disabled students' composing under three methods of text production: Handwriting, word processing, and diction. *Journal of Special Education, 21*(3), 22–42.

MacArthur, C. A., Haynes, J. A., Malouf, D. B., Harris, K., & Owings, M. (1990). Computer assisted instruction with learning disabled students: Achievement, engagement, and other factors that influence achievement. *Journal of Educational Computing Research, 6*(3), 311–328.

Maddux, C. D. (1987). Issues and concerns in special education microcomputing. *Computers in the Schools, 3*(3/4), 1–19.

Male, M. (1988). *Special magic: Computers, classroom strategies, and exceptional students.* Mountain View, CA: Mayfield Publishing Co.

Manion, M. H. (1986). Computers and behavior disordered students: A rationale and review of the literature. *Educational Technology, 26*(7), 20–24.

Mason, S. D., Tanaka, N. K., & Lian, M. J. (1987). Computer-assisted speech synthesis for severely disabled nonverbal individuals. *Computers in the Schools, 3*(3/4), 131–140.

McDermott, P. A., & Hessemer, J. (1987). *The comparative effects of computer-assisted instruction of motivation and achievement of learning disabled and nonlearning disabled students.* Washington, DC: Department of Education. (ERIC Document Reproduction Service No. ED 309 611)

Morocco, C. C., Dalton, B., & Tivnan, T. (1989). *The impact of computer-supported writing instruction on the writing quality of learning-disabled students.* (Final report). Washington, DC: Special Education Programs (ED/OSERS), Division of Educational Services. (ERIC Document Reproduction Service No. ED 319 181)

Rieth, H., Bahr, C., Okolo, C., Polsgrove, L., & Eckert, R. (1988). An analysis of the impact of microcomputers on the secondary special education classroom ecology. *Journal of Educational Computing Research, 4*(4), 425–441.

Robinson, S. L., DePascale, C., & Roberts, F. C. (1989). Computer-delivered feedback in group-based instruction: Effects for learning disabled students in mathematics. *Learning Disabilities Focus, 5*(1), 28–35.

Rosegrant, T. (1985). Using the microcomputer as a tool for learning to read and write. *Journal of Learning Disabilities, 18*(2), 113–115.

Rushakoff, G. E., & Bull, G. L. (1987). Microcomputers in communication disorders. *Computers in the Schools, 3*(3/4), 141–157.

Russell, S. J., Corwin, R., Mokros, C. R., & Kapisovsky, P. M. (1989). *Beyond drill and practice: Expanding the computer mainstream.* Reston, VA: Council for Exceptional Children.

Ryba, K. A., & Chapman, J. W. (1983). Toward improving learning strategies and personal adjustment training with computers. *Computing Teacher, 11*(1), 48–53.

Story, T. B., & Sbordone, R. J. (1988). The use of microcomputers in the treatment of cognitive-communicative impairments. *Journal of Head Trauma Rehabilitation, 3*(2), 45–54.

Swanson, S. L., & Trahan, M. F. (1992). Learning disabled readers' comprehension of computer mediated text: The influence of working memory, metacognition, and attribution. *Learning Disabilities Research & Practice, 7*(2), 74–86.

Toffler, A. (1980). *The third wave.* New York: William Morrow.

Torgesen, J. K., Waters, M. D., Cohen, A. L., & Torgesen, J. L. (1988). Improving sight-word recognition skills in LD children: An evaluation of three computer program variations. *Learning Disability Quarterly, 11*(2), 125–132.

Varhagen, S., & Gerber, M. M. (1984). Use of microcomputers for spelling assessment: Reasons to be cautious. *Learning Disability Quarterly, 7*(3), 266–270.

Watkins, M. W. (1989). Computerized drill-and-practice and academic attitudes of learning disabled students. *Journal of Special Education Technology, 9*(3), 1989.

Wilson, L. (1989). Application of technology to cognitive development. In D. S. Martin (Ed.), *International Symposium on Cognition, Education, and Deafness. Working Papers: Vol. 2. (2nd, Washington, DC, July 5–8, 1989).* (ERIC Document Reproduction Service No. ED 313 850)

Woodward, J., Carnine, D., & Collins, M. (1988). Closing the performance gap: CAI and secondary education for the mildly handicapped. *Journal of Educational Computing Research, 4*(3), 265–286.

Woodward, J., Carnine, D., & Gersten, R. (1988). Teaching problem solving through computer simulation. *American Educational Research Journal, 25*, 72–86.

Yates, J. R. (1987). Current and emerging forces impacting special education. In *The Future of Special Education: Proceedings of the Council for Exceptional Children Symposium.* (Lake Geneva, Wisconsin, May 1986). (ERIC Document Reproduction Service No. ED 279 139)

Zimmerman, S. O. (1988). Problem-solving tasks on the microcomputer: A look at the performance of students with learning disabilities. *Journal of Learning Disabilities, 21*(10), 637–641.

Suggested Activities

Paper and Pencil

Locate in a popular magazine or newspaper an article on a computer advancement that might have an impact on exceptional individuals. Summarize this development and indicate the exceptionality or exceptionalities that might be affected. Describe the way exceptional learners might be affected by this advancement and speculate on any negative aspects.

Observation

Visit a special education classroom or a classroom in which there are exceptional students. List the specific activities students engaged in where a computer could be effectively used. Also list any problems these students might have using a computer.

Practicum

Find a computer and input the BASIC program listed in Appendix F. Use the embedded REM statements to try to change the program to obtain different but usable results.

Resources

Organizations

Center for Special Education Technology. This is a federally funded project housed at the Council for Exceptional Children. It monitors new and emerging technologies appropriate for use in special education as well as a data base of such technologies. Write to the Center for Special Education Technology, Council for Exceptional Children, 1920 Association Drive, Reston, VA 22091–1589.

Technology and Media Division (TAM). This division of the Council for Exceptional Children has approximately 1,400 members and was formed in 1984 in response to the expansion of technology and media use with exceptional learners. It represents one of the nation's primary organizations specifically addressing the needs of special educators interested in the use of technology with exceptional persons. Write to the Technology and Media Division, Council for Exceptional Children, 1920 Association Drive, Reston, VA 22091–1589.

International Society for Technology in Education. This organization is for professionals and others concerned with computer applications in education. Through its publications it attempts to keep members abreast of current and innovative uses of computers in learning. Write to the International Society for Technology in Education, University of Oregon, 1787 Agate Street, Eugene, OR 97403–9905.

Journals

Journal of Special Education Technology. This is a publication of the Technology and Media Division (TAM) of the Council for Exceptional Children. This publication provides a vehicle for dissemination of information, research, and innovative practices regarding the application of educational technology with exceptional populations. Write to the Journal of Special Education Technology, Peabody College, Box 328, Vanderbilt University, Nashville, TN 37203.

The Computing Teacher. This is one of the journals of the International Society for Technology in Education. It is written for persons with an interest in the educational uses of computers. The emphasis of the journal is on educational and teaching applications and on the impact of the computer on the educational process. Write to the International Society for Technology in Education, University of Oregon, 1787 Agate Street, Eugene, OR 97403–9905.

T.H.E. Journal. This is a journal to which everyone interested in computers should subscribe. It contains excellent reviews and descriptions of computer hardware and software in addition to articles related to the innovative use of technology in education. Write to Information Synergy, 2626 South Pullman, Santa Ana, CA 92705.

The Hardware Domain

Carl R. Steinhoff
Teresa S. Lyons
University of Nevada, Las Vegas ■

Chapter 1 provided a brief overview of the definitions and characteristics of individuals with disabilities, gifts, and talents and described general computer applications with these exceptional children, youths, and adults in the schools, at home, and in the community. This chapter will address how computers actually function, with an emphasis on the practical use of computers with and by persons with special needs.

As defined in Appendix A, hardware is "the physical equipment that makes up a computer system." A generic approach, supplemented by discussions of specific equipment presently available, will be used to delineate and describe pertinent computer components and peripherals. Because of the exponential rate of development of both hardware and software technology, the content and illustrations in this chapter and in the appendixes (see Appendixes B, C, and E) should be viewed as but a portent of things to come. For example, the Wright brothers could not have foreseen the development of the jet airplane within such a short time span. Yet the pace of innova-

tion in computer technology far outstrips the growth of technology in the field of aviation.

The computer is simply a device that multiplies our capacity to perform certain kinds of tasks. Much in the same way that machinery enhanced the productivity of farmers and factory workers during the Industrial Revolution, the computer now enables individuals to engage in a variety of activities at a level of effectiveness previously thought unattainable (see Birkhead [1986] for an excellent discussion and description of computer hardware for educational purposes).

THE COMPUTER

The concept of the computer is not new: the Chinese invented the abacus about 4000 B.C. In the early 19th century the first computerlike device was devised by Charles Babbage, assisted by Ada, the Countess of Lovelace and daughter of Lord Byron. Babbage invented a machine he called an analytical engine that was designed to calculate tables of mathematical functions. In 1889 Herman Hollerith invented a method of storing data that included a type of punched card as well as equipment for processing the information stored. It was first used by the U.S. Census Bureau in 1890.

During the 1930s and 1940s, computing machinery progressed from electromechanical to electronic devices. ENIAC (Electronic Numerical Integrator And Calculator), the world's first all-electronic computer, was completed in 1946. The device had about 19,000 tubes, weighed 60,000 pounds, and could perform 300 calculations per second. However, the real breakthrough in computer design came in 1946 when John von Neumann operationalized his concept of the stored program. Previously, programs (i.e., the sequence of operations of the machine) were determined by the manual setting of plugs or switches or were directed by punched cards or punched paper tape. All modern computers use von Neumann's basic idea of storing a program within the computer's own memory.

Continuing evolution and revolution in the field of electronics have led to the development of the microprocessor—an entire computer circuit printed on an area no larger than a fingernail. This so-called fifth generation technology allows computer processing at speeds of well over a million instructions per second! These amazing chips also provide the means to use sophisticated input/output devices driven by complicated programs with large memory requirements. Over the years, the trend in computer hardware has been toward increased miniaturization, increased capability, and decreasing cost. Appendix B

A basic computer hardware system has numerous components. *(Photograph courtesy of Apple Computers, Inc.)*

has an in-depth discussion of the development of computer principles and theories. Also, Ruggles (1983) has published a very interesting history of the computer prophets and their work that students might find interesting.

THE COMPUTER SYSTEM

A computer system is an interrelated set of components working together as a unit (Spencer, 1985). In its simplest form, a computer system consists of these components:

1. An input device that enables the user to input data to the computer

2. A processing unit that includes the central processing unit (CPU)

3. Disk drives for storage and access of data

4. Main memory

5. Output devices such as a cathode ray tube (CRT) and various printing and/or plotting devices that produce hard copy of processed input

A diagram of a fully configured system is shown in Figure 2.1.

Modern computer systems vary in their speed, size, and complexity. The central processing unit (CPU) of a microcomputer is called a microprocessor, and the latest CPU designs employ RISC (Reduced Instruction Set Code) technology and can process over 27 million instructions per second (IBM's new 6000 system). The computing power of these stand-alone or desktop units exceeds that of the mainframe computer of a decade ago.

Computers with more powerful CPUs, complex peripherals, and the ability to provide for many time-sharing users are called minicomputers. Although in recent years the distinction between microcomputers and minicomputers has become blurred, in general the more powerful CPU of the minicomputer allows a larger number of users to perform a variety of complicated tasks simultaneously.

Recent advances in miniaturization have led to the development of desktop versions of

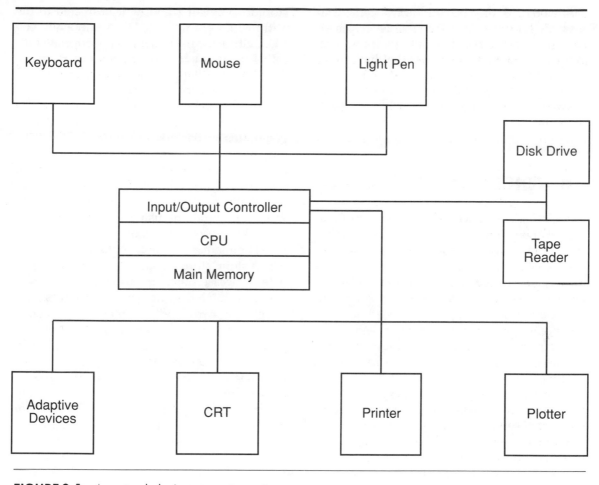

FIGURE 2.1   An extended microcomputer system

popular minicomputer systems. IBM's System/36 and Digital Equipment Corporation's VAX minicomputers are examples of systems now being packaged in desktop units the size of microcomputers but with basically the same computing power as their larger but older cousins.

Larger, faster, and with greater storage capacity than minicomputers, the most complex computer systems are called mainframes. These machines are characterized by great processing speed, enormous memory, many complicated input/output devices, and the capability for a very large number of simultaneous users supported by a number of linked CPUs that control the system. Mainframe computers also support a host of communica-

tions networks that allow users from distant locations to do their computing.

Finally, recent advances in electronic miniaturization have revolutionized the hardware domain and led to the development of innovative and powerful portable computers. For example, laptop and notebook computers—measuring $8\frac{1}{2}$ by 11 inches, weighing 6 to 13 pounds, and possessing the capabilities of state-of-the-art desktop computers—are being used in increasing numbers in the home, school, and community. Also, palm-size computers—measuring 4 by 8 inches when folded, weighing 1 pound, and using standard AA batteries—are being used by nonexceptional and exceptional individuals who find laptop and notebook computers impractical or troublesome

(Johnson, 1991b). The latest advancement in portable hardware has been the development of pen-based personal computers (pen PCs). Pen PCs are tabletlike devices that have built-in handwriting recognition and application software (e.g., spreadsheets) and use an electronic pen as the input device (Glitman, 1992; Johnson, 1991a).

THE CENTRAL PROCESSING UNIT

The CPU is the device that controls the operation of the computer. It has the ability to receive data, decode it, and execute the instructions contained within that data. A CPU acts through a set of specific functions designed into its circuitry. These native functions are enabled through a set of commands known as an operating system, frequently called a disk operating system, or DOS, because they are stored on floppy disks in many microsystems. So, for example, the DOS command SAVE would instruct the CPU to turn on a disk drive, read a file stored in memory, transport the data to that drive, save it, and provide it with a user-selected name. The CPU contains an arithmetic section that enables it to perform calculations and a logic/decision-making section that allows it to perform Boolean functions (i.e., to determine if data is equal to, unequal to, greater than, or less than a reference datum). A diagram of the device in a microcomputer that performs the functions of a CPU, a microprocessor, appears in Figure 2.2.

The input/output controller, the electronic link between the microprocessor and the external environment, makes it possible for data provided by various input devices to be read, stored in memory, and hence directed to the arithmetic logic unit (ALU). Additionally, the I/O controller directs data to appropriate output devices, such as disk drives or printers. The I/O controller provides timing and control for the microprocessor system.

Intel's 80386 is an example of the powerful microprocessor that now powers the current generation of desktop computers. The 80386 has the ability to address over 4 gigabytes (4 billion bytes) of RAM memory and a virtual memory address capability of 64 terabytes (64 trillion bytes). A comparison of popular hardware configurations using current microprocessors is presented in Table 2.1.

The memory section of the microprocessor system stores both programs and raw data. Processed data are also stored in memory in its altered form. Microcomputers generally use two kinds of memory systems. Working or primary memory is generally described as random access memory (RAM). RAM is individually addressable, which means each character or byte of information has its own address and can be located directly. Think of a bank of mailboxes in a post office and you will have a fair idea of what RAM is. Each box has its own address and can be accessed without disturbing any other box. In the case of RAM, each location contains a single piece of information. RAM is volatile, which means that data can be stored only as long as electrical power is applied to the memory circuit; if power is not maintained, the data stored in RAM are lost.

Read-only memory (ROM) permanently stores program data. Information needed over and over again, such as an operating system or an application program (word processing, for example) can be permanently stored in ROM in the latest microcomputers; ROM memory cannot be erased or overwritten. An example of a microcomputer that has made extensive use of these devices is the Tandy 2810, which has its operating system and several applications programs included in ROM. Some ROM chips can be individually programmed, and they are called programmable read-only memory (PROM). A form of ROM that can be used many times is called erasable programmable read-only memory (EPROM).

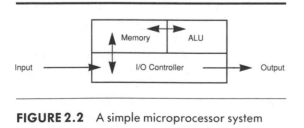

FIGURE 2.2 A simple microprocessor system

TABLE 2.1
Popular hardware configurations of current microprocessors

Macintosh		IBM/Clones	
Classic	68000 chip 2/40 MB 8 MHz	IBM—PS/1	80286 chip 1/30 MB 10 MHz
LC	68020 chip 2/40 MB 16 MHz	AST Research— Bravo/386SX	80386sx chip 2/45 MB 16 MHz
IIsi	68030 chip 5/80 MB 20 MHz	Compaq—Deskpro 386s/20	80386sx chip 4/120 MB 20 MHz
IIci	68030 chip 4/80 MB 25 MHz	IBM—PS/2 Model 70	80386 chip 12/60 MB 25 MHz
IIfx	68030 chip 8/80 MB 40 MHz	Compaq—Deskpro 386/33	80386 chip 2/84 MB 33 MHz

INPUT/OUTPUT DEVICES

I/O devices are the components of the computer system that allow a user to command and control the processing of data. Input devices provide the means for the CPU or microprocessor to read data for processing, while output devices provide the end product, or outcome of processing in a form specified by the user. These devices are controlled by the I/O controller described previously, which in turn is under the control of the operating system, which in turn is under the control of an application program loaded in memory. While some devices function as either input or output mechanisms, some can function in both roles. Spencer (1984) and Shelly and Cashman (1990) have provided excellent discussions of the technical aspects and utility of these devices.

Keyboards

The device most frequently used to enter data is the keyboard, while the device most frequently used to display information is the cathode ray tube (CRT). If a child were to push the A key on the keyboard, the encoder chip within the keyboard circuit would transmit the BCD (binary coded decimal) representation of that letter in ASCII (American Standard Code for Information Interchange), or 01000001, to the CPU where it is stored. The output section of the CPU would "instruct" the CRT to display a pattern of dots on the CRT that the child would recognize as the letter which was typed. The letter would be placed next to the cursor, a visible symbol that indicates where on the screen characters are to be displayed. In its simplest form, a keyboard is a typewriterlike device containing a set of keys for letters, numbers, and special characters. Some keyboards contain a 10-key numeric pad for fast data entry. Additionally, some keyboards contain function keys that can be programmed for special use when used with the appropriate software.

Light Pens

Light pens are input devices used with specialized software to draw images in color di-

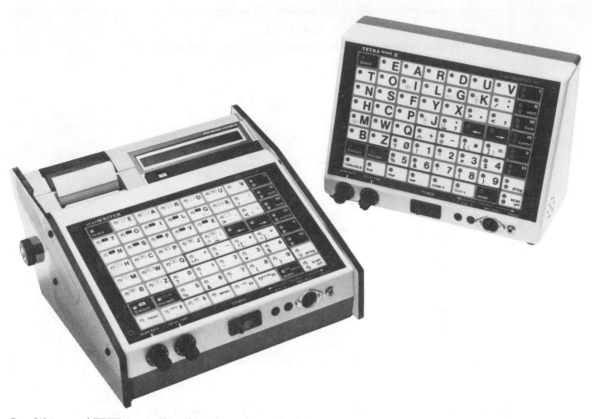

ScanWriter and TETRAscan II keyboard emulators facilitate input. *(Photograph courtesy of ZYGO Industries, Inc.)*

rectly on the display screen of the CRT. They can also be used by educators and exceptional individuals who have problems using the keyboard to run programs by pointing the light at objects or instructions on the CRT. For example, pointing the light at a picture of a trash basket will clear the screen and create a new file.

Graphics Tablets

These touch-sensitive controllers allow a user to select shapes or specialized images from a palette using a styluslike device, thus eliminating the need for the tedious and painstaking programming of shapes. The Koala Pad (Koala Technologies, 206 Junction Avenue, San Jose, CA 95131) is a very popular graphic device that has been used with and by exceptional individuals to call up and run software programs. Graphics tablets, like light pens, eliminate the need for using the keyboard to input data.

Optical Character Readers

Optical character readers (OCRs) are input devices that can read hand-printed or type-written characters directly into the memory of a computer. A video camera at the end of the OCR translates letters into electrical impulses that are then converted to an ASCII text file. This data can then be edited by most standard word processing programs. The utility of using OCRs to input text is excellent for physically handicapped individuals or exceptional persons with limited keyboard skills. Curran and Curnow (1983) have an easy-to-read discussion of OCR technology.

The Mouse

The mouse, invented by Xerox and popularized by Apple, has revolutionized the control and manipulation of text and graphics. The device is a ball held against a set of sensors that convert relative motion into signals that control the screen position. There are now devices that seem to be the reverse of a mouse. For example, the Macintosh portable has a ball built into the keyboard. Ball-type devices are also available that plug in like the mouse (serial or bus) but lie in one spot and are moved with the fingers. Some people who have used the ball devices say that they are more sensitive than the mouse. Mouse devices that are directed by foot as well as by hand are currently available.

The Cathode Ray Tube (CRT, Screen)

The most common output device is the CRT. The CRT is a televisionlike device that can display upper- and lowercase letters and complex graphic displays, as well as special characters. Screen types include monochrome, color, plasma, and liquid crystal displays (LCD). Plasma and LCD are sometimes called flat panel display screens and are most often used as output devices for notebook-size computers because of their small size. While early screens displayed white characters on a black background, today's screen displays feature green or amber characters or even full color. Modern systems use a memory (bit) mapped display that allows each pixel or dot on the CRT to have its own address in the computer's memory.

The most advanced systems feature touch input, inverse video, flexible sizing of characters, boldfacing, scrolling, split screen images, paging, and the graphical user interface (GUI). The latest GUIs go beyond bit-mapped images to PostScript for image generation (the NeXT uses PostScript while the new Macintosh II using Macintosh Operating System version 7.0 is reputed to employ PostScript for image generation). Several new display technologies feature virtual image where the action moves from display to display in a multiple screen setup.

The Printer

Another common output device is the printer. The most frequently used printers, dot matrix printers, use a series of wires that, when pressed against a ribbon, cause small dots to be printed on a sheet of paper or acetate. The pattern of dots forms the desired letter or character. Operating under the control of appropriate software commands (a printer driver) embedded within an applications program, a dot matrix printer reproduces dots in the same fashion as the CRT. Initially thought to be good only for drafts, the modern dot matrix printer using up to 24 wires in its print head now provides low-cost, high-speed, high-quality output. Additional types of printers include the following:

1. *Impact printers.* An example of this kind of printer is the daisy wheel printer. A printing element spins until the selected character lines up with a hammer. The hammer drives the element against an inked ribbon, thus imprinting a high-quality or letter-quality character on the paper.

2. *Ink jet printers.* Ink jet printers spray ink onto a page, producing a dense, high-quality image. Ink jet printers can also produce high-quality color graphics on acetate to create overhead transparencies.

3. *Laser printers.* Laser printers are the latest innovation in microcomputer printer technology (Kehoe, 1992). Laser light is used to create high-quality images that now rival those produced by conventional printing technologies.

4. *Plotters.* Plotters use pens of different colors to create high-quality graphics output. Plotters are generally used in the production of business graphics.

Under certain circumstances, a printer may be used as an input device. Using a specially designed piece of hardware, the Thunderscan, the Apple ImageWriter II printer can copy any image scanned by this device and place it in the memory of the computer where, using specialized software, it can then be customized and copied into other documents.

Disk Drives

Computers need to access data as well as store it. Data may be in the form of a program needed to drive the computer, or it may be in the form of information, such as in a small data base needed by an application program already resident in memory. Processed data likewise need to be stored accurately and in a manner that facilitates rapid retrieval. The input/output device that performs this function is called the disk drive.

Disk drives made for personal computers are generally of two types. The most common uses a 5¼- or 3½-inch "microfloppy" diskette that has a storage capacity of between 100,000 characters and 3,000,000 characters per diskette. Greater storage capacity is achieved by the use of a Winchester or hard disk system. Hard disks are sealed units that operate at a higher speed than do floppy drives and have a storage capacity of 5-million to 2½-billion characters of storage. In addition to their vastly increased storage capacity, hard disks access data at speeds that are significantly higher than those of floppies, speeds making them popular for users who need speed and large storage capacity. A number of different kinds of hard disk drives have been developed. The more recent designs feature removable disk cartridges and "streaming tape" devices whose purpose is to provide an inexpensive method of coping with and storing large files for archival purposes.

Optical Disk

The most recently devised storage systems feature the use of optical disks similar in nature to those produced for the home video market. The optical disk system is comprised of a storage medium (optical disk) written to by a beam of intense laser light. The information is stored in digital form and may be read by a computer. Early models of this system did not allow data to be changed or erased; however, recent advances in this technology now allow the user to rewrite the disk at least once. There are now three clearly different technologies: CD-ROM, WORM (Write Once, Read Many), and magneti-optical (the NeXT "floptical," which allows continuous reads, erases, and writes). The advantage of optical disk storage is its fantastic storage capacity—all the pages of a standard encyclopedia can be stored on a single compact disk.

The compact disk holds more than 500 million characters of information. These devices make it possible to store libraries of data and may radically change the way information is presently delivered in many types of educational settings. Certainly the potential this device holds for individuals with special needs is exciting. It should be noted that this is an emerging technology, and any device presently available represents the merest glimpse of things to come.

Modem

Another useful I/O device, the modem, translates digital information (i.e., ASCII data) into electrical waveforms that can be transmitted over telephone lines or broadcast over the air, and changes this analog data back into its original digital format at a remote receiving site. Modems transmit data at specific baud rates (bits per second); thus a 2400 baud modem (the current choice of most users for personal modem-based communications) allows communication at approximately 240 characters per second. Recent advances in modem technology have resulted in the development of modems for personal computers that transmit and receive at 9600 bauds.

Speech Recognition and Synthesis

Perhaps the most fascinating development in I/O device technology has been in the area of speech recognition. Spoken words are actually used to direct the operation of the computer. It works like this:

1. First, the spoken words are translated into digital components that are stored by the computer.

2. Next, using the appropriate software, these patterns of digitized speech are linked to particular program or operating system commands.

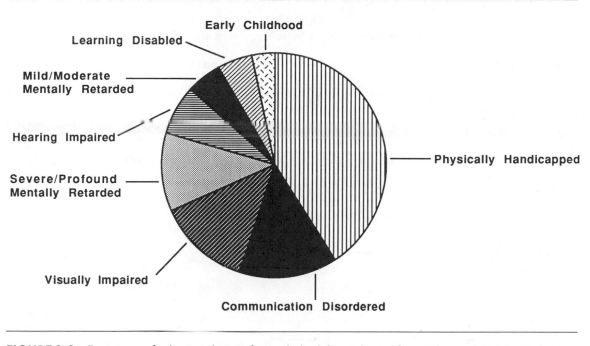

Early Childhood

Learning Disabled

Mild/Moderate Mentally Retarded

Hearing Impaired

Severe/Profound Mentally Retarded

Visually Impaired

Physically Handicapped

Communication Disordered

FIGURE 2.3 Frequency of adaptive devices for each disability. Adapted from "The marketplace: Report on technology in special education" by J. Behrman and E. Lamb, 1988, *The Marketplace, 1,*(2), p. 1. Copyright 1988 by The Center for Special Education Technology. Reprinted by permission.

3. Finally, a system vocabulary is developed (up to several hundred words) that allows the user to command and control the computer and its peripheral devices.

The computer can also be used to transform words stored in memory into sound patterns that resemble human speech. The device that accomplishes this is called a speech synthesizer. This device works in the following manner:

1. A program reads words stored in memory and translates combinations of letters into phonemes, which are then combined into sound.

2. Sophisticated software is used to make these sounds mirror human speech.

3. Application software lets each letter be sounded out individually or in combination with other letters to make words.

Chapters 7 and 8 provide additional information concerning speech recognition and synthesis as they relate to exceptional individuals.

For the special education population, the growing availability of adaptive computer technology provides the opportunity for a quantum improvement in their quality of life. Adaptive devices are commonly grouped into three major categories: assistive devices, input devices, and output devices. As defined by the Center for Special Education Technology, assistive devices permit the user to complete a specific task by modifying or bypassing the conventional method with an alternative method. Input devices provide modified or alternative methods of data entry into a computer or other microprocessor-based device. Output devices provide modified or alternative methods for receiving information from a computer or other microprocessor-based device. Figure 2.3 illustrates the distribution of adaptive devices available to different special education populations by handicapping condition.

Currently, assistive devices far outnumber adaptive input and output devices available to special education populations. Table 2.2 shows the number of devices available by

TABLE 2.2
Frequency of devices by subtype and disability

Subtype of Device	A	C	D	E	H	L	M	P	S	V	Total
Handicapping Condition											
ASSISTIVE DEVICES											
Mobility				1				9		4	14
Communication	2	95	1	2	31	7	7	77	24	14	260
Environment control		7		4	2		3	96	21	1	134
Book handling								7	1		8
Pointing aid	6	7		4		6	7	43	9	10	92
Calculation aid		2			2	3		2		7	16
Vision aid			3		1	9	1			27	41
Basic living	1	11	3	6	40	6	9	44	8	17	145
COMPUTER INPUT											
Input adaptor	2	3		5			2	22	2	1	37
Switches	1	20		2		6		137	39		205
Keyboard emulator		6	3					11	1	1	22
Modified keyboard	1	5		4		1	4	28	5	6	54
Mouse/touchpad/ joystick emulator				1		4	3	19	2		29
Voice recognition		8			1		1	27	2	8	47
Optical character reader										1	1
Infrared receiver				1		1	1	5	1		9
Digitizer		10									10
COMPUTER OUTPUT											
Braille display			2		2					23	27
Large print					1	3				11	15
Synthesized speech	28		1		5		10	6	36		86
Telecommunications		6			15			3		4	28
Security systems								2			2
Infrared transmitter				1		1	1	5	1		9

Key to Handicapping Condition

A = all disabilities
C = communication/speech
D = deaf-blind
E = early childhood
H = hearing impaired
L = learning disabled
M = mild/moderate mentally retarded
P = physically impaired
S = severe/profound mentally retarded
V = visually impaired

Note. From "The marketplace: Report on technology in special education" by J. Behrman and E. Lamb, 1988, *The Marketplace, 1*,(2), p. 2. Copyright 1988 by The Center for Special Education Technology. Reprinted by permission.

subtype and disability; the information is from a survey conducted by the Center for Special Education Technology. The group with the most assistive and input devices is the physically impaired population. The group with the most output devices is the visually impaired population.

Assistive devices include:

1. Environmental control systems that transmit computer information over distance without wires. These devices permit persons with physical disabilities (the physically challenged) to control lamps, appliances, telephones, door openers, and call systems.

2. Voice output communication aids (VOCA) that enable people who cannot speak clearly to communicate by inputting messages into a computer that then converts the messages into synthesized speech.

Adaptive input devices include:

1. Adaptive computer cards that provide access to almost any software application through a variety of input devices. The card also may slow down any interactive program, enabling slow-responding children to participate.

2. Keyboard software that permits the user to modify the standard keyboard for easier access.

3. Keyboard emulators that bypass the keyboard to send information to the computer via a mouse, joystick, headmaster, or scanning device.

4. Voice input devices that permit the user to issue verbal commands or a series of commands to the computer rather than manually inputting the commands.

Adaptive output devices include:

1. Computerized readers such as the Kurzweil Reader that translate the printed word through an optical recognition unit into a synthesized voice. The Kurzweil is capable of translating printed material into six languages for the blind or visually impaired.

This computer system has a keyboard emulator. *(Photograph courtesy of ZYGO Industries, Inc.)*

2. Telecommunications devices for the deaf (TDDs), which permit the hearing-impaired person to communicate over the telephone. A TDD consists of three components: a typewriterlike keyboard, a telephone modem, and a readout display that shows the messages.

3. Computerized embosser printers that produce hard braille copies for the visually impaired.

The devices described represent the beginning of an exciting period of growth in the field. As our understanding of the human body increases and computer technology advances, the marriage between the human body and sophisticated computerlike devices will evolve (e.g., bionic limbs, artificial eyes).

COMPUTER NETWORKING

When one combines elements of two or more computer systems (such as personal computers, minicomputers, or mainframe computers), communications devices, and specialized storage and output devices, the resultant system is called a network. There are basically three types of networks:

1. The star network generally consists of a host CPU (generally a minicomputer) to which several terminals or personal computers are connected (see Figure 2.4).

2. A ring network consists of three or more computers arranged in a circular configuration (see Figure 2.5). Ring networks are useful in situations where it is necessary for each unit in an organization to do its own data processing yet desirable for these departments to update each other's files through direct computer-to-computer communication.

3. The bus network consists of two or more computers and/or peripherals that share a common line of communication (see Figure 2.6). Bus networks are most commonly used in local area networks (LANs).

Star networks are generally used in schools to provide a low-cost, time-sharing environment. In such a system, students use dedicated terminals to access computer-assisted-instruc-

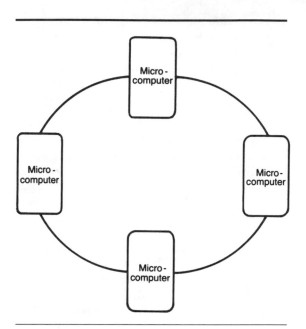

FIGURE 2.5   A ring network

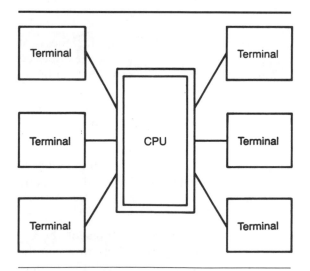

FIGURE 2.4   A star network

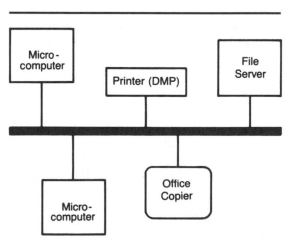

FIGURE 2.6   A modern bus network

tion (CAI) modules or to learn computer programming. The advantages of these systems include the ability to share files, programs, secondary storage, and complex peripherals such as high-speed printers and plotters. A number of school systems have computerized school libraries, thus providing the means to conduct automated bibliographic searches.

The linking of minicomputers and mainframe computers in ring networks has been of great benefit to school administrators who now have the power of distributed data processing. This kind of networking provides more computing power than could be provided by a single unit. Systems of this kind are used for the processing and storage of student records, data base management, and electronic mail. Some state education departments have developed extensive systems for sending to and receiving from local educational units important information electronically. The actual processing of data occurs in steps at each distribution level, making the power of the system greater than that of any single computer.

Microcomputers can be linked together to share expensive peripherals such as plotters, printers, and modems. The bus network or communications system that makes this possible is the local area network (LAN). An example of a modern LAN is the Ethernet system, which allows microcomputers to communicate directly with each other and with peripherals, mainframes, other LANs, and "intelligent" office equipment. Xerox no longer owns Ethernet. Ethernet is only a hardware/transport technology, as are token bus, token ring, and PCnet. As a matter of fact, Novell Netware, a popular LAN software, is available for each of the above transport technologies.

There are a number of companies (e.g., Apple, IBM, and 3M) currently producing LANs for microcomputers. The Corvus system (Corvus Corporation, 2100 Corvus Drive, San Jose, CA 95124) is a popular network with special educators.

Computer networks provide the means to share information electronically. Using a personal computer and a modem, a user can communicate with agencies that provide information about the latest technology and career opportunities through an electronic bulletin

Notebook computers can have speech synthesis capabilities. *(Photograph courtesy of ZYGO Industries, Inc.)*

board. The electronic bulletin board also provides the means for people with disabilities to communicate among themselves and with others.

CONSUMER HARDWARE INFORMATION

The growth of microcomputer applications for individuals with special needs has been spectacular, and the end is nowhere in sight. Those responsible for the selection and purchase of these devices need to choose wisely and to expend scarce funds only after all alternatives have been carefully weighed. The following steps should be considered in the selection and purchase of computer equipment:

1. *Define need.* Try to assess what your mission is and what computer resources are actually needed to accomplish it. What do you intend to do with the equipment you purchase? Since people tend to support what they create, involve a broad spectrum of parents, students (whenever possible), and professionals in the needs-assessment process.

2. *Assess performance.* After specifying the features of the system you require, secure demonstration units from competing vendors, and test each system thoroughly before committing your school district to an

expensive purchase. Determine the availability of specialized software and consider system expansion. Can the system grow with your needs? Choose carefully; you and your students may have to live with your choice for some time to come.

3. *Provide maintenance.* The more complicated the device, the more apt it will be to experience a malfunction. Your school system must have the in-house capability of making timely repairs. The increased emphasis on interoperability and connectivity to accomplish educational goals, coupled with more sophisticated systems and more reliance on software solutions, means that dramatic new strains are placed on support systems, particularly in-house support systems. If your school system does not have the resources to support its hardware, the vendor you choose must be able to assure timely repairs. Additionally, the vendor should be available (and able) to answer questions regarding the operation of the equipment purchased. The selection of a vendor is at least as important as the selection of the equipment itself. Remember, the most advanced device is useless if it cannot be supported in the field. You should also be keenly aware of the fact that software support requires considerably more education and training than does hardware support.

4. *Provide feedback.* Because of the rapid developments taking place in this field, educators are in the unique position of being able to effect change. Make every effort to provide vendors with assessments of how their equipment performs and what changes you deem desirable. They will listen.

Maximizing the effective performance of computer systems involves taking into account who will be using the equipment and the circumstances under which it will be operated. The following suggestions in the design, selection, and evaluation of hardware systems may be helpful:

1. *Purchase quality.* Since students are hard on equipment, it pays to buy industrial/commercial-grade equipment. While it might be politically expedient to purchase more units of a lower-quality brand, the long-term cost of expensive maintenance (not to mention downtime) will negate the initial allure of a low purchase price. Quality is cheaper in the long run.

2. *Try before you buy.* Purchase plug-compatible equipment. Because of the special needs of your clientele, many unique configurations of equipment will be engineered by imaginative educators. Care should be taken to ensure that specialized keyboards, CRTs, CPUs, and voice units adhere to the same I/O standards. What will work with an Apple or IBM may not work with a look-alike clone. Try before you buy.

3. *Prepare the user.* Take steps to provide a receptive professional environment for the introduction of these new devices. Since new technology often requires realignments and adjustments in professional role relationships, the intelligent consumer will create an administrative climate that supports innovation and change.

4. *Get a second opinion.* Get objective opinions from outside experts when evaluating the purchase of complicated and expensive systems. While the local staff usually has the experience and expertise to make a reasoned decision, there is merit in seeking the advice of a disinterested third party.

5. *Check out the manufacturer.* Make every attempt to purchase equipment from manufacturers who have the financial resources to support the equipment they sell. A number of school districts throughout the United States made unwise short-term decisions and now possess inventories of equipment that must be cannibalized for maintenance.

Intelligent consumers are an asset to any school district or agency fortunate enough to have them on their staff. The ability to delineate hardware strengths and weaknesses, design and conduct hardware needs assessment, and purchase and maintain essential equipment are important professional skills that modern educators must possess.

Hardware consumer issues relating to special education and/or exceptional individuals are discussed throughout the remaining chapters.

SUMMARY

This chapter has provided an overview of the concepts necessary to appreciate and understand how a computer functions and to describe frequently used devices. Some practical suggestions were presented to aid the educator in the selection of computer systems. Since the computer hardware field is constantly changing, studying the latest journals, attending the appropriate conferences, and reading the news every day is important. Regular and special educators, other professionals, and exceptional individuals who are willing to master the general concepts of computer technology will be able to communicate their operational needs to hardware designers. The synergy developed from such a partnership will lead to a dazzling array of devices that will magnify the human potential of handicapped and gifted/talented children, youths, and adults.

REFERENCES

Birkhead, E. (1986). Micros for education: New machines offer expanding capabilities. *T.H.E. Journal, 13*(7), 14–17, 105–109.

Curran, S., & Curnow, R. (1983). *Overcoming computer literacy.* Denver, CO: Love Publishing Co.

Glitman, R. (1992). Pen PCs: Mission-critical note takers that return to basics. *PC World, 10*(1), 89–90.

Kehoe, D. M. (1992). A laser on every desk. *PC World, 10*(4), 118–133.

Johnson, L. B. (1991a). Computing with a pen. *PC Today, 5*(10), 8–10.

Johnson, L. B. (1991b). Taking the computer industry by the hand: Options in hand held computing. *PC Today, 5*(9), 8–13.

Ruggles, M. (1983). *An Apple for the teacher.* Denver, CO: Love Publishing Co.

Shelly, G., & Cashman, T. J. (1990). *Computer fundamentals for an information age.* Brea, CA: Anaheim.

Spencer, D. D. (1984). *An introduction to computers.* Columbus, OH: Charles E. Merrill.

Spencer, D. D. (1985). *Computers and information-processing.* Columbus, OH: Charles E. Merrill.

Suggested Activities

Paper and Pencil

Write to the manufacturers of computer-assisted devices and ask to be placed on their mailing lists. Use the information they send you and the descriptions in this text to create your own file of adaptive devices.

Observation

Visit a special education classroom that uses computers and computer-assisted devices. Interview the teacher and (if possible) the students concerning the utility and effectiveness of these devices. Prepare a brief oral report of your findings.

Practicum

Visit a school that has different hardware systems and compatible adaptive devices. Have someone temporarily disable you (e.g., bind your arms, blindfold you, place a gag over your mouth, etc.) and learn to use some of these devices.

Resources

Organizations

ABLEDATA
National Rehabilitation Information Center
4407 Eighth Street NE
Catholic University
Washington, DC 20017

Association for Special Education Technology (ASET)
P.O. Box 152
Allen, TX 75002–0152

Apple Special Education Division
Apple Computer
20525 S. 36M
Cupertino, CA 95014

IBM/Special Needs Exchange
c/o LINC Resources
P.O. Box 434
Pawtucket, RI 02862

IBM National Support Center for Persons
with Disabilities
P.O. Box 2150
Atlanta, GA 30055

Information Center for Special Education
Media and Materials
c/o LINC Resources
4820 Indianola Avenue
Columbus, OH 43214

Information Center for Special Education
Technology
1290 Association Drive
Reston, VA 22091–1589

Journals

Bulletin of Science & Technology for the Handicapped. This quarterly newsletter describes recent computer advances for handicapped persons. Write to American Association for the Advancement of Science, 1776 Massachusetts Avenue, Washington, DC 20036.

Catalyst. This bimonthly newsletter covers a variety of special education computer topics such as software, hardware, and pertinent regulations. Write to Western Center for Microcomputers in Special Education, Suite 275, 1259 El Camino Real, Menlo Park, CA 94025.

Closing the Gap. This compact bimonthly newspaper provides information about microcomputer programs and devices that help handicapped individuals close the gap between themselves and the rest of society. The organization that publishes it, also named Closing the Gap, has a data base of in-depth information on software producers, products, practices, and procedures; a comprehensive text on practices and procedures is also available. One issue of the newsletter is a directory covering producers, products, practices, and procedures related to technology and the disabled. Write to Closing the Gap, P.O. Box 68, Henderson, MN 56044.

Books

Behrman, M. M. (Ed.). (1984). *Handbook of microcomputers in special education.* Austin, TX: PRO-ED.

Behrman, M. M. (1988). *Integrating computers into the curriculum: A handbook for special education.* Austin, TX: PRO-ED.

Budoff, M., Thorman, J., & Gras, A. (1984). *Microcomputers in special education.* Cambridge, MA: Brookline Books.

Burke, B. (1985). *Guide to adaptive devices, software, and services.* (Preliminary draft). Wilmington, DE: IBM.

Fashner, J. H. (Ed.). (1984). *Improving instruction with microcomputers.* Phoenix, AZ: Onyx Press.

Hagen, D. (1984). *Microcomputer resource book for special education.* Reston, VA: Reston Publishing Co.

Lindsey, J. D. (1987). *Computers and exceptional individuals.* Columbus, OH: Merrill.

Roston, A., & Sewell, D. (1984). *Microtechnology in special education.* Baltimore, MD: Johns Hopkins University Press.

Ruggles, M. (1983). *An Apple for the teacher.* Denver, CO: Love Publishing Co.

Shelly, G. B., & Cashman, T. J. (1990). *Computer fundamentals for an information age.* Brea, CA: Anaheim.

Spencer, D. D. (1984). *An introduction to computers.* Columbus, OH: Charles E. Merrill.

Spencer, D. D. (1985). *Computers and information-processing.* Columbus. OH: Charles E. Merrill.

Hardware

Apple Computer
20525 Mariani Avenue
Cupertino, CA 95014

Apricot
47173 Benicia Street
Fremont, CA 94538

Acer America
401 Charcot Avenue
San Jose, CA 95131

AST Research
16215 Alton Parkway
P.O. Box 19658
Irvine, CA 92713

Atari
c/o IB Computers
92244 Beaverton-Hillsdale Highway
Beaverton, OR 97005

AT&T Information Systems
1776 On the Green 3-A13
Morristown, NJ 07960

Austin Computer Systems
10300 Metric Blvd.
Austin, TX 78758

Commodore Electronics
1200 Wilson Drive
West Chester, PA 19380

CompuAdd
12303 Technology Blvd.
Austin, TX 78727

Dell Computer
9505 Arboretum Blvd.
Austin, TX 78759

Digital Equipment
1476 Main Street
Maynard, MA 01754

Epson America
20770 Madrona Avenue
Torrance, CA 90503

Gateway 2000
610 Gateway Drive
North Sioux City, SD 57049

Hewlett Packard
19310 Pruneridge Avenue
Cupertino, CA 95014

IBM Corporation
One Orchard Road
Armonk, NY 10504

Insight Computers
1912 West 4th Street
Tempe, AZ 85281

Leading Technology
4685 South Ash Avenue
Suite H-5
Tempe, AZ 85282

NCR
1700 South Patterson Blvd.
Dayton, OH 45479

NEC Technologies
1414 Massachusetts Avenue
Boxborough, MA 01719

Northgate Computer Systems
7075 Flying Cloud Drive
Eden Prairie, MN 55344

Samsung Information Systems America
3655 North 1st Street
San Jose, CA 95134

Tandon
c/o JB Technologies
5105 Maureen Lane
Moorpark, CA 93021

Tandy/Radio Shack
1800 One Tandy Square
Fort Worth, TX 76102

Televideo Systems
P.O. Box 6602
San Jose, CA 95150

Texas Instruments
P.O. Box 202230
Austin, TX 78720

Toshiba America Information Systems
9740 Irvine Blvd.
P.O. Box 19724
Irvine, CA 972713

Wang Laboratories
One Industrial Avenue
Lowell, MA 01851

Xerox
Xerox Square Box 24
Rochester, NY 14644

Zenith Data Systems
1000 Milwaukee Avenue
Glenview, IL 60025

Zeos International
530 5th Avenue NW
St. Paul, MN 55112

Adaptive Devices

Don Johnson Developmental Equipment
900 Winnetka Terrace
Lake Zurich, IL 60047

Adaptive Communications Systems
P.O. Box 12440
Pittsburgh, PA 15231

Creative Switch Industries
P.O. Box 5256
Des Moines, IA 50306

Innocomp
33195 Wagon Wheel Drive
Solon, OH 44139

Laureate Learning Systems
110 East Spring Street
Winnooski, VT 05404

Prentke Romich
1022 Heyl Road
Wooster, OH 44691

Zygo Industries
P.O. Box 1008
Portland, OR 97207–1008

The Software Domain

CHAPTER

James H. Wiebe
California State University, Los Angeles ■

If hardware consists of the physical components of the computer—the plastic, metal, wire, and silicon parts and peripherals discussed in Chapter 2—then what is software? The term *software* may conjure up images of the bath section of a department store or the less durable products used with computers, such as paper or floppy diskettes. Software is a set of instructions (programs) written in BASIC, Pascal, machine language, or some other code (see Appendix C) that a computer can understand and execute and is sold in a package. A software package typically consists of a box containing a set of 5¼- or 3½-inch program diskettes, a reference manual, and often a tutorial manual and/or diskette.

SOFTWARE

Software is soft because it is nonpermanent. Programs on disk or tape may be deleted or changed either by accident or on purpose. Software is also considered soft because it is

stored in RAM, the nonpermanent portion of a computer's memory. A set of instructions placed in the computer's RAM memory may

Software availability and libraries are increasing.
(Photograph by James H. Wiebe)

45

be deleted simply by turning the computer off, by loading another program into memory, or by using a computer command to clear memory.

A computer without software is like an artist's empty canvas. The artist can turn the blank canvas into anything from a line drawing to a colorful abstract or an impressionistic landscape. Likewise, software can turn the computer into an accounting tool, a machine for teaching French, or an arcade game. Software allows a computer to recognize and act upon spoken commands, monitor brain signals to activate artificial limbs, or read text from a book and print the braille equivalent. The possibilities are endless.

A Historical Perspective

Software programs stored on diskettes are a relatively new addition to computer technology. When the first computer was invented (see Appendix B), instructions were given by changing the wiring on what looked like a telephone operator's switchboard. Later, instructions were given to computers by cards with holes punched in them. The holes in the cards represented a language the computer could understand—binary code. Programming a computer in binary code was an extremely difficult and tedious task. Eventually, someone realized that programming could be made simpler by developing an intermediate language between English (or German, French, etc.) and the computer's machine language (i.e, the language built into a computer by the manufacturer). The first types of software were programs that translated between a high-level (Englishlike) language and machine language (programming language).

Early computers had to be specifically programmed by the user for such tasks. The applications programs of today, such as word processing, statistical packages, and spreadsheets, had not yet been invented. A person who wanted a software program to keep track of company sales or inventory wrote a COBOL program (Common Business Oriented Language) to accomplish the task. In the 1950s and 1960s, companies like IBM produced and sold applications programs for their comput-

ers so the users would not have to write their own programs. In the late 1950s and early 1960s, third-party software developers, like Computer Science Corporation, began to create programs for computers sold by other companies, and a new industry was born (Software, 1985).

Now there are tens of thousands of programs and software packages available for almost every imaginable use. These programs range from essential, nonglamorous tools like operating systems (see below) to general purpose tools, like word processors, to highly specific programs such as educational games or programs that allow professionals to generate individual education plans (IEPs). The publishers of these programs range from Fortune 500 companies like Microsoft Corporation and IBM to large educational software corporations, like Sunburst, to professionals who produce and sell a single product out of their home.

SYSTEM SOFTWARE

Before microcomputers came upon the scene (15 or more years ago), a person who wanted to run a computer program or analyze a set of data wrote out lines of code on paper, took them to a keypunch machine and prepared cards, and then carried the cards to the person who operated the computer. The operator stacked the cards into a card reader and punched a series of buttons on the control monitor that caused the cards to be fed into the card reader. The holes on the cards were translated into electrical impulses that the computer could understand, and the computer program was executed.

Operating Systems

Now computers come complete with software that serves the function of the computer operator (the operating system). Operating systems (see Table 3.1), a series of housekeeping programs provided by the computer manufacturer, allow the computer to function. Depending on the computer, the operating sys-

TABLE 3.1
Major computers and their operating systems

Name	Computers	Comments
PC DOS MS DOS	IBM PC, Compaq, Tandy, and many others	Thousands of business and general application programs have been written for PC-DOS or MS-DOS machines. Hundreds of educational programs are now available.
PRO DOS	Apple II +, IIe, IIc	Apple II's operating system. Hundreds of educational programs use this operating system.
MAC OS	Macintosh	Operates the Macintosh computer. Many powerful applications programs, but very few educational programs.
OS-2	IBM	IBM's new operating system, which takes advantage of the power and speed of the newest lines of computers.

tem will load and run programs, save programs, activate a printer, copy disks, rename programs, and perform many more functions. For example, when you point to an icon representing a program and click with a mouse or type its name and press RETURN to start a program (depending on the type and configuration of the computer you have), it is the operating system that recognizes this command, retrieves the program from disk, and gets it going.

In the early days of personal computers (1977–1982), each manufacturer developed its own operating system. The problem with this was that programs written for an Apple computer would not run on a Commodore, Radio Shack, or Atari and vice versa. Control Program for Microcomputers (CP/M) (computer controlled management) was the first successful operating system developed to be used on a variety of computers. When IBM entered the market with the IBM PC, however, other computer makers started using IBM's operating system. As a result, the IBM operating system, PC-DOS (called MS-DOS on other systems) has become the industry standard for the majority of computers sold. Between 80% and 90% of all software sold runs on this operating system.

Operating systems are a major factor in determining whether or not a given piece of software will run on a given computer. Even when computers are somewhat different inter-

nally, like Tandy and IBM computers, they will be able to run the same software if and when they share a common operating system. Operating systems are not the only factor determining whether programs from one system will run on another system: the internal design of the computer also determines whether software designed for one computer will run on another. For example, Macintosh software will not run on the Apple II because these two machines are totally different internally.

Besides the two operating systems already mentioned, there are several other operating systems for computers that might be of interest to small groups of special and regular educators or exceptional individuals themselves, including those developed for Atari, Amiga, and the Radio Shack color computers. Some educational software has been developed for each machine.

Windows and Other DOS Add-ons

Many people, especially beginning computer users, find it difficult to use PC-DOS or MS-DOS on IBM-type computers because they have to remember a set of obscure commands for doing things like preparing new diskettes for use or copying files from one disk to another. For example, to copy a set of files from drive *a* to drive *c*, you might enter the following command:

copy *a:*.* c:*\wp50\group5

Most people find it easier to accomplish such tasks by making selections from a menu or manipulating icons (intuitive pictures that represent objects or actions on the computer) with a mouse.

Fortunately, a new category of software has been designed that makes PC-DOS/MS-DOS easier to use and provides features and utilities—such as disk optimization or printing a map of the organization of disk space—not provided by PC-DOS/MS-DOS add-ons.

The most important of these products is Microsoft Windows. Microsoft Windows provides a user interface similar to that of the Macintosh: it has pull-down windows, scroll bars, icons, and mouse compatibility. Rather than typing commands, the user points, clicks, drags, or makes menu selections with the mouse to do housekeeping tasks like copying a set of files from one disk to another. Microsoft Windows also provides a set of easy-to-use desktop utilities, including a daily calendar with alarm, calculator, notepad, communications program, address file, and drawing program. The newer version of Windows stays resident in the computer's memory and may be called up while in other applications, without having to exit them. For example, if you were working on a report using WordPerfect and wanted to do a quick computation using Windows' calculator, you could pop into Windows, do the computation, and return to WordPerfect without losing your document. Or, if you had set the calendar in Windows to remind you of an important appointment, it would ring and/or flash a message across the screen as you were working. A final benefit is that programs such as word processors and spreadsheets designed to work with Windows have a similar set of commands and techniques for accomplishing tasks, as on the Macintosh. Thus the learning curve is significantly reduced, since the strategies learned with one application will be similar on another.

There are other DOS enhancements that work on other computers and with other operating systems. PC Tools and Norton Utilities (IBM and Apple II) have a range of utilities for managing the computer's hard disk drive.

Programming Languages

The language computers understand is binary code. If you wanted to say hello to a computer directly in its language, your program would look something like Figure 3.1. Besides the tedium and difficulty of communicating with computers in ones and zeros, each major class of computer has its own unique machine language. A program written for an Apple computer in its machine language will not work on a Commodore because they have different types of machine languages. Higher-level programming languages were developed in part to solve this problem. FORTRAN, for example, is virtually the same on all machines. The computer user simply uses a specific interpreter or compiler to translate FORTRAN into the machine language a particular computer understands.

Higher-level programming languages were also designed to allow a human to give instructions to computers in commands that more closely resemble human language. They consist of statements like PRINT, REPEAT, and CALL. Typically, the instructions for translating these high-level, Englishlike commands into machine language are contained on disk and are loaded into the computer just like any other program. Thus, programming languages like LOGO Plus, Quick BASIC, or Turbo C are sold as packages by software vendors, similarly to other software packages.

There are all kinds of programming languages, each with its own particular strengths,

```
00111110    01001000
00110010    00011110    00111110
00111110    01000101
00110010    00011111    00111110
00111110    01001100
00110010    00100000    00111110
00111110    01001100
00110010    00100001    00111110
00111110    01001111
00110010    00100010    00111110
```

FIGURE 3.1 Machine language (TRS-80, M3) routine to print "hello"

uses, and group of proponents. Among the most widely used programming languages are COBOL (used mostly to create business programs), FORTRAN (used by engineers), Pascal (used to solve mathematical and scientific problems), TURBO C (used to solve scientific problems and for developing other software packages), LOGO (a language designed for children), and BASIC (the language included free or at a minimal cost with most microcomputer systems). Of the programming languages mentioned, LOGO, Pascal, and BASIC are the most commonly used in the classroom. LOGO is most often used with elementary school children as a powerful tool for exploring mathematics and other subjects. BASIC is often taught to middle school and high school students and is used by professionals to create their own specific computer applications. Pascal is often taught to high school and college students in formal computer science courses.

Despite the existence of higher-level languages, many programs are still written in machine language. Machine language programs are much faster than programs written in BASIC or LOGO because they make efficient use of a computer's capabilities. They also require much less disk and memory space than LOGO and BASIC programs. Video games, for example, are written in machine language because they require speedy interaction between an input device (e.g., a joystick), an output device (e.g., the monitor), and the computer. A video game written in BASIC or LOGO would be very slow and dull. Most applications packages are written in machine language because they would be too slow and would not fit into memory if written in a high-level language.

APPLICATIONS SOFTWARE

The largest segment of the software market at present is made up of programs designed to organize or manage functions at work, in the home, or at school. These software programs turn computers into smart typewriters, calculators, filing systems, or communication devices and are rapidly changing the way we do

business. They are also making an impact on the way students are taught, particularly handicapped and gifted learners; the way subject matter is presented; and the way classrooms are managed. The six categories of applications software that can be used by educators and exceptional individuals include word processors, desktop publishers, spreadsheets, data base managers, communications programs, and graphics.

Word Processors

Word processing software turns a computer into a smart typewriter, allowing educators and exceptional persons to enter text, format it, and make editorial or format changes. You may cut and paste, moving parts of text from one paragraph to another location, or search for and replace sequences of letters or words. Most important, text you produce can be saved on disk and recalled at any time to make additions or changes.

The possibilities for using word processors in education with or by exceptional individuals are endless. Professionals may use them to correspond, plan lessons, develop examinations, generate IEPs, or produce student work sheets. Combined with data base managers, spreadsheets, and/or graphics programs, word processing software can also be used to prepare evaluation reports that include data about class projects and students' achievements. Exceptional students and adults can gather data and write up the results of a scientific experiment or write a short story with a word processor. Students tend to be more enthusiastic about rewriting and editing their work when using word processors for writing assignments than when they write using pencil and paper (Daiute, 1985).

There are many word processing packages available for every type of computer, ranging from inexpensive programs with few features to powerful programs with many features (Coolidge, 1992). Standard features most users expect in a modern word processor include the ability to insert or overwrite text, move text around within the document, insert footers and headers, number pages, find and replace words or other sequences of characters, underline, center, change margins, and change spacing in the text. For a detailed discussion of the features of a particular word processor, consult the documentation or advertising brochures for the package and the reviews that appear in computer journals when the package is first released.

The list of word processors and their features is far too long and complex to discuss here. Among the more important word processors for business use and serious writers, however, are WordPerfect (IBM and compatibles, Macintosh, and Apple II) and Microsoft Word (IBM and compatibles and Macintosh). For general classroom and home use, the most important word processors are the word-processing subprograms of AppleWorks (Apple II) and Microsoft Works (IBM and compatibles and Macintosh). It should be noted that Apple-Works and Microsoft Works also contain spreadsheets, data base managers, and communications components, while AppleWorks GS has a communications component. The version of AppleWorks that works on the Apple IIe computer (AppleWorks 3.0) does not have a communications subprogram.

A number of word processors are available for exceptional children and youths. The most widely used, Bank Street Writer and HomeWord Plus, are very easy to learn to use and are quite appropriate for writing activities at the elementary and secondary levels or with exceptional adults who might have difficulty using a more complex word processing program. Snoopy Writer is another relatively sim-

ple word processing program that educators may want to teach exceptional pupils how to use. Degnan and Hummel (1985) have published an excellent article on using word processing programs with exceptional students.

Other Writing Programs

Many other programs are available to make writing easier. For example, many word processing packages include spelling checkers. It is also possible to purchase spelling checkers to use with specific word processing programs that do not have their own. For example, Bank Street Speller is designed to compare words in files created with Bank Street Writer against those in its dictionary, while Time Out Quick Spell (Beagle Brothers) for AppleWorks can be used to check the spelling in AppleWorks documents.

More complex writing aids, such as Grammatik and Sensible Grammar work with documents created with a variety of word processors and check the document for errors in grammar, style, usage, and punctuation. Grammatik runs on IBM-type computers and Sensible Grammar works on either Apple II or IBM computers.

Desktop Publishers

Desktop publishing programs are specialized word processors that allow the user to design newsletters, posters, fliers, or similar documents. Typically, they allow the user to create page layouts, to print text in columns, to use a variety of text styles and sizes, to create pictures or other graphics such as boxes to highlight sections of text, and to import graphics created with other programs. Two of the more popular desktop publishing packages are Publish-It (Apple II, IBM and compatibles, and Macintosh) and PageMaker (IBM and compatibles and Macintosh). Furthermore, many modern word processors, especially those that run on Macintosh computers or on IBMs using Windows 3.0, have most features of the better desktop publishers. Microsoft Works and Word (IBM and compatibles and Macintosh) and

Software directions on the screen enhance user-friendliness. *(Photograph courtesy of Apple Computers, Inc.)*

AppleWorks GS (Apple II) are examples of word processors that have desktop publishing features.

Professionals and students will find desktop publishers to be among the most useful of software packages. These products can be used to print documents in bold text for the visually impaired, to create motivating and eye-catching text and graphics for enhancing work sheets, to enliven creative professional-looking reports, and so on.

Electronic Spreadsheets

Spreadsheet programs, originally developed to computerize accountants' planning sheets, have extended far beyond their original use and have become standard fare for computer software developers. A spreadsheet consists of an empty work area of rows and columns. Into this work area, the user may place labels (e.g., months of the year or students' names), numerical data (e.g., students' test scores), or formulas (e.g., @SUM [A1 + B1 + C1]). For example, if you were using a spreadsheet to keep track of student grades, column 1 could contain student names, column 2 ID numbers, and columns 3 to 15 their scores on various assignments and tests. Column 16 could contain a formula for calculating the final grade for each student. Most spreadsheet programs are capable of holding more than 100 rows and 250 columns of information.

Figure 3.2 is a printout of a spreadsheet screen of student grades created with Apple-Works. The shaded rectangular area on the spreadsheet shows the portion that can be seen at one time on the computer's screen. To move the "window" (the computer screen) to other parts of the spreadsheet, the arrow keys or the mouse is used.

One of the major reasons why spreadsheets are so popular is that they allow "what if" speculations. For example, if a school's enrollment drops by 78 exceptional pupils next year, special education staff salaries increase 5%, and utility costs increase 3%, what will the operating budget for the year be? On the other hand, what if utility costs for instructional settings increase only 1%? Spreadsheets are designed to make this type of speculation very simple indeed. If Juanita King's score for quiz 1 in the spreadsheet in Figure 3.2 were changed to 45, the computer would automatically compute and print her average as soon as the score was entered.

Spreadsheet programs may be used to keep track of student grades, pupil cash accounts, or school budgets. They may be used by handicapped and gifted/talented students in scientific and mathematical problem solving. And, when combined with word processing programs, they may be used to print results of computations in documents and reports. For example, if you are running a federal project, you could use your spreadsheet program to keep track of the budget, then incorporate that information into the yearly reports, assuming you have a word processor and spreadsheet that are compatible. Exceptional adults could use spreadsheets to monitor income and expenses and to generate budgets.

Some of the more important spreadsheet packages are Quatro Pro and Lotus 1-2-3 (IBM and compatibles), AppleWorks (Apple), Microsoft Works (IBM and Compatibles and Macintosh), and Excel (Macintosh). All of these, with the exception of AppleWorks, will draw bar, line, or circle graphs using the data in a spreadsheet. This feature can greatly enhance grant proposals or reports on projects involving special individuals.

Data Base Managers

This type of program is designed as a computerized filing cabinet. Data base or file programs allow you to keep records on individuals and inventories of materials, and to recall and manipulate stored data in a variety of different ways.

A data base record or template, equivalent to a file folder in a standard file system, can be designed by the user to fit the application (e.g., for 16 students in a class, 16 records must be created, one for each student). Once the data have been entered and stored using this template, the user can select and print out information on all students living in a certain zip code area, all those with a certain handicap, and those with a certain handicap who

Name	ID #	Chap. 1	Chap. 2a	Chap. 2b	Quiz 1	Chap. 3	Read. 1	Chap. 4	Exp. 1	Writ. 1	Quiz 2	Writ. 2	Chap. 5	Final	Average
Adams, Sean	38-2458	10	10	10	50	8	5	10	10	20	49	15	9	90	.925
Amesqua, Manuel	38-0034	9	10	10	44	8	4	9	10	18	45	18	9	96	.903125
Bavaqua, Brett	36-1056	6	8	10	48	9	5	9	10	18	47	19	9	88	.89375
Bietzo, Ronald	35-9645		2	6	31	8	5	9	10	20	30	16	9	78	.7
Boudreaux, Sally	39-2022	9	10	6	40	10	5	10	10	20	45	17	9	90	.890625
Danielson, Maria	40-5776	7	8	10	37	7	4	10	10	17	35	19	10	76	.78125
Donnaly, Peter	33-9272	6	6	10	39	9	5	8	10	15	44	19	10	88	.84375
Fellini, Stephanie	33-7566	10	7	6	40	5	5	10	10	20	35	20	9	77	.79375
Holly, James	38-8828	10	10	10	49	9	5	9	10	15	48	17	7	97	.925
Huang, Sieu	36-4566	9	8	6	47	6	5	7	10	13	48	18	8	100	.8875
Hyon, Petrie	35-5710	9	9	10	48	10	5	10	10	20	50	19	10	99	.865625
Jenson, Judy	41-0023	5	7	8	28	7	4	4	10	17	35	18	7	66	.675
King, Juanita	38-4723	3	8		22			5		13	20	16		55	.44375
Kyper, Pauline	35-5666	10	10	10	50	10	5	9	10	20	46	20	9	92	.940625
Lundy, Valerie	36-5672	10	10	10	48	9	5	10	10	18	49	19	10	97	.953125
Norse, Henry	40-3485	9	9	10	45	7		5		10	44	14	5	85	.759375
O'Leary, Noreen	38-4888	6	7	8	34	5	4	9	10	20	39	18	8	77	.765625
Pelucia, Robert	37-3303	7	8	8	41	9	5	10	10	20	45	19	10	82	.85625
Roberts, Howard	35-5555				5		3	6	10	10	33	10	10	69	.4875
Sanchez, Victor	39-9923	8	9	10	40	8	5	10	10	20	42	17	8	88	.859375
Tosta, Robert	38-0088	5	9	8	44	10	5	10	10	18	48	20	10	98	.921875
Vivaldi, Maxine	36-5505	7	10	9	36	7	3	8	10	19	40	20	8	89	.83125
White, Wilber	35-8113	8	10	10	42	10	5	9	10	17	46	18	6	83	.85625

FIGURE 3.2 An example of a computer spreadsheet screen

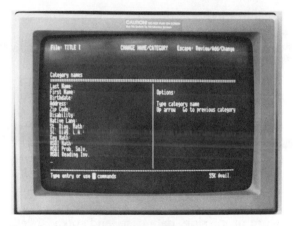

Data base programs permit the user to organize, manipulate, and store information.
(Photograph by James H. Wiebe)

scored below a certain test score. File programs can also arrange information in alphabetical or numerical order for any categories of information contained. Some file programs will even do arithmetical computations, such as finding the average reading score of all pupils who are visually impaired and in the sixth grade or totaling incomes from several sources for exceptional adults.

As with the spreadsheet programs, integrated packages include data base managers together with word processors. For example, addresses in a data base could be used with a word processing program to print mailing addresses on letters. Some of the major data base managers can be used with and by exceptional individuals.

Chapter 12 provides an in-depth discussion of the use of data base managers for administrative purposes, such as keeping track of data about exceptional individuals. These programs may also be used by exceptional individuals themselves to access and manipulate information. At one level, students may manipulate data bases created by others. For example, Sunburst Communications publishes a number of data bases designed for use in the classroom with Bank Street Filer, including Whales Database, North America Database, and Minerals Database. At another level, the professional may design and enter a data base template (the format of a data base), then have the students gather data, enter them into the

data base, and then investigate the data base. Finally, students may design their own data base, gather the appropriate data, and then enter and manipulate the data.

Communications Software

These are programs designed to help computers communicate with each other (Petrosky, 1986). In Chapter 2, modems, which allow computers to communicate over telephone lines, were discussed. Modems by themselves cannot transmit data across the wires. They require software to take the data, program, or file from the computer's memory, disk, or keyboard and set up communications with another computer. Communications software permits handicapped and gifted/talented individuals to communicate with people at different locations through keyboards, computer screens, modems, and telephone lines. It also allows word-processing files or data base records to be transmitted from one location to another. For example, if you had a federal project in Tempe, Arizona, with remote sites on several Indian reservations in northern Arizona, your remote site directors could transmit their reports to you over telephone lines, and you could save them on diskette and compile them later into a larger report.

The great variety of communications software ranges from the least sophisticated (programs that turn the computer into a "dumb" terminal whose keyboard and screen act only as input and output devices for the other computer) to the most sophisticated (programs that allow the user to send files back and forth, to print text from another computer, and to send and receive electronic mail). There are a variety of public domain and commercial programs available for each type of computer. In addition, the integrated packages AppleWorks GS, Microsoft Works, and FrameWork among others include communications subprograms. Check with a local software store to see which package is appropriate for your system.

Graphics

Drawing realistic pictures on a computer screen using BASIC or any other computer language is not easy, especially if they are to be animated. The simplest picture may involve several hundred programming lines. A number of software packages make graphics much easier to produce. These packages often make use of some kind of drawing device, such as a graphics tablet or a mouse. To create pictures, a stylus or mouse is moved across a surface, and these motions are recorded on the computer screen. These packages may allow the individual to choose the type of shade to be drawn, as well as its color, size, and location. Squares, rectangles, circles, and other shapes can be created with a couple of clicks of the mouse button. Some graphics packages also allow defined shapes to be animated. The best computer-assisted instruction (CAI) programs make extensive use of graphics and animation. For example, a program designed to teach about the human digestive system would be incomplete without pictures of the system. Even better would be animated pictures showing food moving down the esophagus and into the stomach and through the rest of the body.

AppleWorks GS and Microsoft Works contain graphics subprograms. DazzleDraw (Apple II), MacPaint (Macintosh), and PC Paintbrush and Corel Draw (IBM and compatibles) are popular graphics packages.

Integrated Software Packages

There are a number of superprograms available for microcomputers that combine many or all of the above applications categories. These integrated packages may contain programs for word processing, data bases, spreadsheets, graphics, and communications. Although it might be possible to do the tasks a superprogram can do with separate programs, integrated programs have the advantage of compatibility. Data created in one application can be easily used in another. This is not likely to be true of stand-alone programs like WordStar and VisiCalc, especially those produced by different publishers. Integrated packages can be used with and by exceptional individuals for business, home, or school purposes to create a file with one type of application and

use it in another. AppleWorks' word processor allows the professional to write a letter to students' parents, while with AppleWorks' data base program the professional can keep information about the class. Because it is an integrated package, only the AppleWorks program needs to be put in the computer to accomplish both functions. It will also merge the letter and information about the class. AppleWorks and Microsoft Works, the integrated software packages that are the most popular with professionals, can be used by many exceptional individuals. AppleWorks has three programs (word processing, data base, and spreadsheet) while AppleWorks GS also includes graphics and communications components. Microsoft Works (IBM and compatibles and Macintosh) has word processing, data base manager, spreadsheets, and communications subprograms. The Macintosh version will also create graphics.

Authoring Systems

An authoring system is a specialized type of program that allows a person to create CAI without writing computer programs (Fitzgerald, Bauder, & Werner, 1992). Instead of writing a sequence of commands to the computer, the software author is confronted with a series of menus and questions presenting available options. One option might be whether an author wishes to enter text or graphics on the screen. Other options might be whether to allow a learner to input an answer from the keyboard, the number of attempts to answer correctly that will be allowed, whether to tell the correct answer, and whether to give specific hints. When all the information has been entered, the system writes the program to produce the desired results. Hyper Studio (Apple II) and Authorware (IBM and compatibles and Macintosh) are excellent authoring systems.

Authoring systems are easier to use than programming languages. No knowledge of BASIC or any other programming language is needed to use them. However, they are not very flexible because they limit the author to a small number of options. According to Alessi and Trollip (1985), "Programs developed on an authoring system look very much alike" (p. 33).

HyperCard and Multimedia Tools

In 1988, Apple developed a new type of computer tool called HyperCard. This tool is essentially an enhanced data base manager that stores information on "cards" (records) in "stacks" (data bases). In addition to storing text and numbers like traditional data base managers, however, it can be used to store graphics and sound. For example, a card could contain a picture of an American robin and text describing its habitat and diet. In addition, the card could be set up so that if you used the mouse to point to and click on the bird's beak, the computer would play its song.

Besides being a powerful data base manager, HyperCard may be used as an authoring tool. It is easier to create certain types of computer-based instruction with HyperCard and similar products than with many authoring systems. Cards may contain text, sound, and pictures designed to teach or practice various concepts. The cards may be linked together in various ways. For example, a lesson prepared for exceptional individuals could branch to various locations in a stack depending on their responses to questions. HyperCard may also be used to control a videodisc player or other media. Numerous HyperCard stacks have been produced for classroom use. For example, Data Disk International produces HyperCard stacks entitled *Presidents, World Data,* and *State Data.* Hyperglot produces HyperCard stacks that teach Spanish, French, and other languages. While HyperCard was the first tool of its type, many similar products have followed. Linkway and ToolBook are similar products for IBM-type computers. Tutor-Tech is a HyperCard-like product for Apple II computers.

EDUCATIONAL SOFTWARE

The applications software discussed above is not designed for any specific setting and may be used in business, home applications, or in educational settings. However, there is a cate-

Multimedia computer presentations incorporate two or more types of media including text, audio, and graphics.
(Photograph courtesy of Apple Computers, Inc.)

gory of software that is used more in schools than anywhere else—educational or instructional software. The following section will introduce educational software and describe its use. Subsequent chapters will describe specific examples of software that can be used with particular exceptional individuals.

Historical Perspective

Before the advent of the personal computer, a number of attempts were made to use the computer as an instructional tool. The PLATO project, started at the University of Illinois in 1959 under support of the National Science Foundation, was to develop computer programs to teach many traditional school subjects. The project has achieved many of its goals and has built up a large library of courses widely used in colleges, high schools, business, and the military. It has not, however, supplanted regular classroom instruction to any degree, and thus has not been nearly as successful as the developers hoped. The PLATO project is now the property of Control Data Corporation. Many of the original PLATO programs have been converted to microcomputer format. Many new programs have been developed as well.

During the first days of PLATO and other similar projects, a number of pioneers predicted a major revolution in education. According to Suppes (1966), "One can predict that in a few more years millions of school children will have access to . . . the personal services of a tutor as well-informed and responsive as Aristotle (computer-assisted instruction [CAI])" (p. 207). Despite predictions like these, little true individualization via computers has crept into our schools in either regular and special education. In fact, with very few exceptions, learning is still delivered by teachers and textbooks. Computers, television, and other media account for only a small fraction of school instruction.

The reason it has taken so long for computers and related technology to contribute to our children's education has to do with the allocation of resources. Before microcomputers, schools—especially elementary schools—had little access to computers, and when they did, the computers were used for administrative rather than instruction purposes. Furthermore, schools had little money to spend for software. Software developers, rather than developing top-quality, inexpensive products for schools, put their efforts into business-oriented products.

During the past few years, there has been a dramatic change. Although a typical professional today is lucky to have a computer in the classroom or to have limited, shared access in a computer laboratory, the installed base of microcomputers has increased to more than 2.5 million microcomputers (Bruder & Chaffin, 1989) and is increasing dramatically each year. There is also a move toward more powerful computing systems such as Macintosh and 80286 and 80386 IBM-type computers. Major companies such as IBM, Microsoft, CBS, and Reader's Digest have become involved in publishing educational software. The result is a new generation of well-designed software products for schools.

Software Categories

There are literally thousands of software packages and programs designed for educational use. They range from free software that may be copied and used at will (see the Public Domain Software and Freeware section below) to published packages costing thousands of dollars. They are available for all types of computing hardware and operating systems. And they are designed to accomplish a wide variety of educational goals from providing a few minutes of exciting practice on multiplication facts to programs that help students write poetry.

There are several major categories of educational software: tutorial, simulation, demonstration/information, drill-and-practice, games, student utilities, tests, and teacher utilities. Even though many software packages do not fit neatly into a single category, it is useful to be acquainted with these categories so that a particular package may be matched with the professional's educational objectives. For example, it would be inappropriate to expect a package to provide initial instruction on the meaning of addition and subtraction of whole numbers if it was designed instead to provide *practice* on addition and subtraction skills (with the assumption that appropriate meanings and computational strategies had already been introduced by the professional).

Tutorial

Tutorial programs present information to the exceptional learner, usually by setting up a dialogue with the student. For example, a program on volcanoes might print a few sentences of text and one or more graphic illustrations on the screen to give information to the learner, then ask one or more questions and, based on the input, go to new material, repeat the previous information, or branch to another part of the program (e.g., less difficult material). Tour of the Macintosh, for example, teaches users how to use the mouse to accomplish basic operations on the Macintosh computer.

A tutorial depends heavily on the ability of the instructional designer to develop an appropriate and effective level of interaction between the learner and the program. Tutorials must be more than electronic page turners and should anticipate the types of errors users will make. If an exceptional student does not understand the concept, a tutorial should provide feedback that leads to improved understanding. This can occur only if the software developer is able to foresee the more common types of mistakes the student will make. The ability to catch these kinds of mistakes and provide appropriate feedback is called instructional error trapping.

Simulation

Simulation programs give the exceptional individual some aspect of a real-life experience. For example, a program written for a high school family life course might simulate household budgeting for new families. One of the most popular simulation programs is Flight Simulator II, which gives the user experience in many aspects of flying a plane without any risk. Another is Sim City, which allows the user to manage a new city or one of seven well-known cities around the world.

A subcategory of simulations is the adventure game. In some ways, these programs are similar to arcade-type games—the player must overcome various obstacles in order to achieve an objective. However, while arcade games are designed merely to entertain, adventure games are designed to teach. One of the best-known adventure games is Oregon Trail. In this program, students relive the experience of crossing the western United States in a covered wagon. If they make the right decisions, they will eventually reach their destination. And, in the process of playing the game, they learn about life in frontier America. Another popular set of adventure games is the Carmen Sandiego series (e.g., Where in the World is Carmen Sandiego? and Where in the U.S.A. is Carmen Sandiego?). In these games, students play the part of a detective and gather clues in the attempt to solve crimes. In order to play the game, students must apply map skills, use reference skills to discover geographical locations and other facts, and record data in a miniature data base.

Demonstration/Information

This type of program is designed to present information to a user. Typically, demonstration programs are designed to be used as part of a lesson presented through a different format or medium and do not make use of interactive instruction.

Demonstration programs can be used the way a film or filmstrip would be used. For example, a high school chemistry class might make use of a program that shows, through graphics, what happens when certain dangerous chemicals are mixed together. The program could be interactive to the extent of asking which chemicals and quantities to mix, but would not query users about the demonstration. Its purpose would be to enhance a lecture or discussion about chemicals.

Informational programs are designed to be a resource, similar to a reference book, dictionary, or encyclopedia. Many of the best informational programs are in the area of social studies. PC Globe, PC USA, and World Geo-Graph are on-line atlases with outstanding maps of various sorts (topographical, demographic, etc.), data bases of information about countries or states, and the ability to create bar charts comparing the countries or states.

Drill-and-Practice

Drill-and-practice programs are the primary software used by professionals working with exceptional individuals (Baby, 1992). In this type of program, no new material is presented. Instead, the user practices on material already presented by responding to questions or other appropriate stimuli about facts, ideas, or relationships. The program will then tell the user whether the response is right or wrong, perhaps giving a hint and another try, then going to the next question.

Drill-and-practice programs vary greatly in sophistication, ranging from the unimaginative electronic ditto sheet to elaborate and exciting video games. A low-end example is a program that simply places math exercises (e.g., "$5.00 – $1.12 = ?") on the screen to which the student responds by typing the answers. At the upper end are programs that embed the problems in arcade-type games or simulations. For example, in Alien Addition students must match the answer on the laser cannon with an addition problem on an invading alien spaceship in order to blast the spaceship. Math Blasters is also an exciting arcade-type program. In Green Globs, students get points by entering algebraic equations to hit green globs appearing on a graph. In most cases, the more sophisticated the equation, the more points scored (e.g., the equation for a circle located in the proper place may hit more green globs than the equation for a straight line).

Games/Problem Solving

Games have long been a part of regular and special education—many teachers have found ways to meet instructional objectives with board games, bingo-type games, and athletic games. The computer has added a new dimension to game playing. Before the computer, games required two or more people. With the computer, it is now possible for an individual to play a game against the computer. Since most children find games to be extremely motivating, computerized educational games may be used to motivate even the most reluctant learner to learn new concepts, practice previously learned skills, or take tests. Word Man is a multilevel (e.g., 1 to 4 increasing in difficulty) and multispeed (e.g., 1 to 9 decreasing user reaction time) game that involves matching homonyms, synonyms, and antonyms. Tetris is a spatial game that involves moving or rotating shapes descending on the screen to fill rows on the screen. Although there is no specific educational objective involved in games like Tetris, one might argue that it develops spatial skills (which in turn are correlated with mathematical achievement).

Some educational games do not really form a separate category of educational software but provide drill-and-practice, instruction, a simulated experience, or a combination of these. Other games have no instructional goal but are intended solely for entertainment. However, some of these games also have educational merit because they teach problem solving and logical thinking, develop motor skills, and/or develop spatial visualization capabilities.

Student Utilities

Another group of educational software programs does not fit into any of the above cate-
gories. These programs help students accomplish some task in the classroom. An example is Kidwriter, designed to encourage and help children write. In this program, children first compose a picture on the screen by choosing from a group of predefined shapes (e.g., a dog) and placing them in desired locations on the screen. Next they use a mini-word processor to write a story about the picture. Note that it does not *teach* children to write—no instruction of any sort is included with the program, and no feedback is given about the text created through the program. Another example is CompuPoem 9, which helps the children write poetry.

Tests

Computerized testing offers some hope of relief from the drudgery of test taking in our schools, especially for handicapped and low-achieving students. By nature, standardized, normed pencil-and-paper tests are time-consuming and require that students face numerous questions, many of which they cannot answer. The computer promises to reduce test-taking time and anxiety considerably by quickly determining the student's level of achievement and presenting questions only at that level. Other exciting possibilities offered by computerized testing are embedding tests in game formats and collecting much more meaningful and accurate information about students.

Computer software programs will also assist regular and special educators in generating, administering, scoring, and assessing tests. For example, QuickTests allow educators with Apple computers to develop objective as well as essay tests in the major subject areas. Quest-Make is available for Apple and IBM computers and can develop test administration and scoring programs. Report Writer: WISC-R can be used to provide a four- to five-page report interpreting the student's demographic information and WISC-R test among other data. Chapter 12 delineates and describes numerous tests that can be used with exceptional individuals.

Teacher Utilities

Somewhere between general applications programs and software that teaches or helps students accomplish some task are programs specifically designed to help teachers manage their classrooms. A number of companies, for example, produce grade-book programs. Others produce programs for writing IEPs, keeping track of educational objectives, and generating examinations and worksheets. Radio Shack and several other companies sell programs that generate mathematics worksheets. The Minnesota Educational Computing Consortium (MECC) has developed several programs to produce a variety of educational puzzles and worksheets. Chapter 12 also provides specific details about pertinent teacher utility programs.

CD-ROM Software

The capabilities of CD-ROM drives were discussed in Chapter 2. At present, the most important educational software available on CD-ROM involves large amounts of data. For example, Grolier and Britannica have put entire sets of encyclopedias on a single disk (Mageau, 1990). Those writing grant proposals or looking for published articles about research findings or specific teaching techniques will find the ERIC CD-ROM resource to be very valuable. The ERIC disk contains the same information that is available to academic libraries via DIALOG. With an appropriate CD-ROM drive and the ERIC disc, professionals may customize their own literature searches and print article titles or abstracts on their own printers.

Videodisc Software

Videodisc software comes in two formats. One format is constant linear velocity (CLV), which is capable of holding two hours of motion video. The other format is constant angular velocity (CAV), which is capable of holding 54,000 still frames, one hour of motion video, or a combination of still and motion video. Both formats produce high-resolution pictures and high-quality stereo sound. While many popular motion pictures and educational films (e.g., episodes of the Nova series) have been recorded in the CLV format, it is the CAV format that has outstanding potential in education.

Videodiscs recorded in the CAV format may be used in a variety of ways in the classroom. One way to use them is in the stand-alone mode. The professional or students may use a hand-held controller to view frames or video sequences on educational videodiscs. For example, students may take a guided tour through the National Gallery of Art or view individual paintings (or details from the paintings) on the National Gallery of Art videodisc.

At another level, a computer may be used to control the videodisc player. HyperCard (Macintosh), Linkway (IBM and compatibles), and Tutor-Tech Hypermedia Toolkit (Apple II) are software packages that may be used to control laserdisc players. These packages may be programmed to show specific still frames, play video sequences, or print text on the video screen. It is also possible to purchase premade HyperCard stacks or other programs that control specific videodiscs. For example, National Gallery of Art Laserguide is a HyperCard stack that may be used to select works on the disc according to the artist, the artist's nationality, the period of the painting, its style, its medium, etc. In the future, we will see more packages providing instruction by combining the interactive capabilities of the computer and the outstanding graphics and sound capabilities of videodisc (Sales, 1989).

OBTAINING SOFTWARE

General purpose and educational software packages are available from a variety of sources. Stores that sell computers systems often sell software too, but typically at retail prices. Software discount houses often sell software at substantially reduced prices. Certain companies, such as Microsoft Corporation, sell software directly to professionals at even greater discounts.

Certain types of educational software are readily available at retail computer hardware and software stores. Examples are Math Blasters, Where in the U.S.A. is Carmen Sandiego?, and Print Shop. Other educational software titles, such as the problem-solving software from Sunburst Corporation, are not typically sold in most software stores. Most major metropolitan areas, however, have professional supply or educational software stores that have a large range of software titles. Another option is mail order companies that specialize in educational software, for example, Scholastic Corporation (P.O. Box 7502, Jefferson City, MO 65102) and Learning Services (P.O. Box 10636, Eugene, OR 97440-2636). Certain, more obscure titles will only be available by dealing directly with the publisher.

Public Domain Software and Freeware

Sometimes software programs developed by individuals or businesses for fun or for specific purposes are not copyrighted or the copyright has expired. This software usually becomes available to the general public and is called public domain software or freeware. These programs include games, educational applications, business routines, and useful utilities. Computer hobbyists have long used and appreciated public domain programs. It is only recently, however, that the business world has considered the use of public domain software ethical and used these programs to increase their profit margin ("Random Access," 1985).

Public domain software and freeware are not always free unless you have a friend who has copies of these programs and gives them to you. Computer user groups have begun to develop libraries of public domain software and freeware and offer their libraries to members for a nominal charge.

Software Needs Assessment

The process of software evaluation focuses on the value of a particular piece of software. Needs assessment, on the other hand, examines a given educational setting to determine what materials can result in maximum learning. The result of needs assessment will usually be a category of software that can form the foundation for a more detailed search for ap-

propriate packages. Needs assessment is often done on a district or programwide basis in order to standardize hardware and software purchases. An added benefit is that you may be able to get multiple-copy discounts on the software you purchase.

Even if you have your own budget and equipment, the process of software selection is never done in a vacuum. There is often a need to coordinate your software usage with that of other classrooms, schools, projects, or sites (See Chapter 11). If you plan to use your computer to write reports about your project, for example, and there are other projects in the school that do similar types of tasks, it would be wise to consider the software they are using. That way, if your computer or software fails, you will have a backup. Nothing is more frustrating than to have a file containing text or data that you cannot use until your computer is repaired or until you get a replacement copy of your software from the publisher. In general, it is often best to make some kind of district or project decision about software purchases based on needs assessments.

SUMMARY

The real computer revolution is taking place in the area of software as people think up new tasks for computers to do and better ways to accomplish them. The most exciting revolution is in software that can help children learn and overcome handicaps. The rest of this book covers more specific aspects of computer hardware and software uses with exceptional individuals.

REFERENCES

Alessi, S. M., & Trollip, S. R. (1985). *Computer-based instruction: Methods and development.* Englewood Cliffs, NJ: Prentice-Hall.

Baby, J. (1992). Curriculum applications in special education computing. *Journal of Computer-based Instruction, 19*(1), 1–5.

Bruder, I., & Chaffin, E. (1989). The K-12 software industry: Where's it going? *Electronic Learning, 8*(7), 26–31.

Coolidge, G. (1992). Importing graphics into Word-Perfect 5.1. *PC Novice, 3*(3), 50–53.

Dauite, C. (1985). *Writing and computers.* Reading, MA: Addison Wesley.

Degnan, S. C., & Hummel, J. W. (1985). Word processing for special students: Worth the effort. *T.H.E. Journal, 12*(6), 80–82.

Fitzgerald, G. E., Bauder, D. K., & Werner, J. G. (1992). Authoring CAI lessons: Teachers as developers. *Teaching Exceptional Children, 24*(2), 15–20.

Mageau, T. (1990). Software's new frontier: Laserdisc technology. *Electronic Learning, 9*(6), 22–28.

Random access. (1985). *Compaq,* Fall/Winter, 46–47.

Sales, G. C. (1989). Videodisc technology: Function and formats. *Computing Teacher, 16*(5), 34–35, 56.

Software. (1985). Alexandria, VA: Time-Life Books.

Stumbling into the computer age. (1984, August). *Forbes, 134,* 35–40.

Suppes, D. (1966). The use of computers in education. *Scientific American, 215*(3), 202.

Suggested Activities

Paper and Pencil

Find a recent journal article reviewing a tutorial, simulation, or drill-and-practice software package in your interest area (e.g., math, science, social studies). What are the hardware requirements for this piece of software? What are the instructional objectives of the program? What features of the program set it apart from other programs in the same area? Would you consider purchasing it for your classroom? Why or why not?

Observation

Interview three or four people who use computers for word processing on a regular basis. Which word processor do they use? What are the strengths and weaknesses of the word processor they are using? What are the advantages and disadvantages of using a word processing system over a typewriter?

Practicum

Find a piece of instructional software covering an area that you normally teach (or will teach) in your classroom. Have one of your students use the program while you observe. What was the student's reaction to the program? What is the instructional objective of the program, and how useful was the program in achieving that objective? Compare the approach and success of the program in meeting its goal with your own classroom approach to meeting the same goal. What advantages/disadvantages does the software have compared to your regular classroom instruction?

Resources

Organizations

See Chapter 6.

Journals

Electronic Learning. This journal is published eight times a year and provides general and specific information about software, computer literacy, instructional applications, and broad issues about computers in education. Write to Scholastic Inc., 730 Broadway, New York City, NY 10003.

The Computing Teacher. This journal addresses elementary and secondary computer issues for beginners and experienced computer users. It is published nine times a year. Write to the International Council for Computers in Education, 135 Education, University of Oregon, Eugene, OR 97403.

Hardware/Software

Alien Addition
DLM
One DLM Place, Box 4000
Allen, TX 75002

Amiga Computer
Commodore Systems
1200 Wison Drive
West Chester, PA 19380

Apple Computer IIe, IIc, GS
Apple Computers
20525 Mariana Avenue
Cupertino, CA 95014

AppleWorks, AppleWorks GS
Claris
5201 Patrick Henry Drive
P.O. Box 58168
Santa Clara, CA 95052

Atari Computer
c/o IB Computers
9244 S. W. Beaverton-Hillsdale Highway
Beaverton, OR 97005

Authorware
8500 Normandal Lake Blvd.
9th Floor
Minneapolis, MN 55437

Bank Street Speller
Brøderbund
17 Paul Drive
San Rafael, CA 94903

Bank Street Writer
Brøderbund
17 Paul Drive
San Rafael, CA 93903

CD-ROM Drive
(Contact local dealer)

CompuPoem
Graduate School of Education
University of California
Santa Barbara, CA 93106

Corel Draw
Corel Systems
1600 Carling Avenue
Ottawa, Ontario
KiZ 8R7

Dazzle Draw
Brøderbund
17 Paul Drive
San Rafael, CA 94093

dBase
Ashton Tate
20101 Hamilton Avenue
Torrance, CA 90509

Excel
Microsoft
One Microsoft Way
Redmond, WA 98052

Flight Simulator
SubLogic
713 Edgebrook Drive
Champaign, IL 61820

Framework
Ashton-Tate
20101 Hamilton Avenue
Torrance, CA 90509

Grammatik
Reference Software
330 Townsend Street
San Francisco, CA 94107

Green Globs
CONDUIT
University of Iowa
Iowa City, IA 52242

HomeWord Plus
Sierra On-Line
P.O. Box 485
Coursegold, CA 93614

HyperCard
Apple Computers
20525 Mariani Avenue
Cupertino, CA 95014

HyperStudio
Roger Wagner Publishing
1050 Pioneer Way
El Cajon, CA 92020

IBM Computer
IBM
One Orchard Road
Armonk, NY 10504

Kidwriter
Spinnaker Software
215 West First Street
Cambridge, MA 02142

Linkway
IBM Corporate
(Contact local dealer)

Lotus 1-2-3
Lotus Development
55 Cambridge Pkwy.
Cambridge, MA 02142

Math Blaster
Davidson & Associates
3135 Kashiwa Street
Torrance, CA 90505

Microsoft Word, Works, and Windows
Microsoft
One Microsoft Way
Redmond, CA 98052

National Gallery of Art Laserguide
Videodisc Publishing
381 Park Avenue South
Suite 1601
New York, NY 10016

Oregon Trail
MECC
6160 Summit Drive North
Minneapolis, MN 55430

PageMaker
Aldus
411 First Avenue South
Seattle, WA 98104

PC Globe
PC USA
PC Globe
4700 South McClintock
Tempe, AZ 85282

PC Paintbrush
Z-Soft
450 Franklin Road
Suite 100
Marietta, GA 30067

PLATO
Control Data
3601 West 77th Street
Bloomington, MN 55435

Presidents
World Data
State Data
(Data Disk International)
Available through Learning Services
P.O. Box 10363
Eugene, OR 97440

Print Shop
Brøderbund
P.O. Box 12947
San Rafael, CA 94913-2947

Publish-It!
Timeworks
625 Academy Drive
Northbrook, IL 60062

Quattro Pro
Borland International
1800 Green Hills Road
Scotts Valley, CA 94025

QuestMake
Slosson Publishers
P.O. Box 280
Past Aurora, NY 14052

QuickTests
Seven Hills Software
2310 Oxford Road
Tallahassee, FL 32304

Report Writer: WISC-R
Psychological Assessment
P.O. Box 98
Odessa, FL 33556

Sensible Grammar
Sensible Software
210 South Woodward
Suite 229
Birmingham, MI 48011

Sensible Speller
Sensible Software
210 South Woodward
Suite 229
Birmingham, MI 48011

Sim City
Brøderbund
P.O. Box 12947
San Rafael, CA 94913-2947

Snoopy Writer
Random House
201 East 50th Street
New York City, NY 10022

Tandy Computer
Tandy/Radio Shack
1400 One Tandy Square
Fort Worth, TX 76102

Tetris
Spectrum HoloByte
2061 Challenger Drive
Alameda, CA 94501

TimeOut QuickSpell
Beagle Bros.
6215 Ferris Square
Suite 100
San Diego, CA 92121

ToolBook
Asymetrix
110 110th Ave. Northeast
Suite 717
Bellevue, WA 98004

Tour of the Macintosh
Apple
20525 Mariani Avenue
Cupertino, CA 95014

Tutor-Tech Hypermedia Toolkit
Techware
P.O. Box 151085
Altamonte Springs, FL 32715

Word Torture
Grammar Exercises (HyperGlot)
Learning Services
P.O. Box 10636
Eugene, OR 97440

World GeoGraph
MECC
6160 Summit Drive North
Minneapolis, MN 55430

Word Man
DLM
One DLM Place Box 4000
Allen, TX 75002

WordPerfect
WordPerfect
1555 North Technology Way
Orem, UT 84057

Wordstar
MicroPro
33 San Pablo Avenue
San Rafael, CA 94903

Software Evaluation and Development

CHAPTER

Florence M. Taber-Brown
Indiana Computer Training Project
South Bend, Indiana ■

Regular and special education professionals often delude themselves into thinking that they write curricula. In reality, educational material producers in general, working with and without professional educators, establish the scope and sequence of instruction in their development of products. This reality is also true of software publications. When educators integrate software into the curriculum, purchases are often based on producer catalog descriptions only, descriptions designed primarily to sell as well as to describe the programs. On the other hand, information gained from a review of the literature or from individuals associated with software evaluation centers suggests that it is very important to evaluate prior to purchase. This importance has been reinforced in numerous conferences around the United States and Canada. Although evaluation is stressed by educators (e.g., Gardner, Taber-Brown, & Wissick, 1992), marketing reports indicate that teachers tend to buy software primarily through catalog advertising. Direct mail catalog houses account for most of the software orders. Many

educators do read reviews or otherwise informally evaluate software before purchase, and a growing number of professionals (see Palin, 1992) are taking an interest in selecting software that meets their needs. An interest in more organized and/or formal evaluations of software would make the purchase of educationally effective software less left to chance.

If there is not appropriate evaluation of software, professionals must depend on the integrity of producers whose primary goal is financial rather than educational. On the other hand, many software producers are interested in developing educationally effective software by using a team approach involving educational specialists, content specialists, and programming technicians. Even if all producers develop proven educationally sound software and include the expense of comprehensive validation studies, professionals must evaluate possible software purchases to determine (a) if the software is appropriate to specific students' needs as stated in the individual education plan (IEP) or individual transition plan (ITP); (b) if the software fits into the core curriculum strands; and (c) if the software complements the approaches and teaching styles of the educator.

Although software is becoming more responsive to good pedagogical theories and practice, professionals still need to know how to evaluate software for their exceptional students. When that software is not available, professionals should consider using authoring systems, programs that permit professionals to add content and make instructional changes. This procedure can be especially important for special educators and clinicians who work with low-incidence populations (e.g., severely handicapped) because software is often unavailable or not validated. Although it traditionally has not been profitable for producers to develop software that caters to a small subgroup of the exceptional population, a number of companies are now developing programs to meet this need.

This chapter is designed to provide the educator of exceptional individuals (a) with information that will be of assistance in evaluating computer-assisted instructional software, to determine if it will meet the needs of the student as well as the needs of the educator; (b) with knowledge to assist in evaluating adaptive devices; and (c) with a system by which the professional can design appropriate software when none is available and with a philosophy that encourages the use of this evaluative information in the selection of emerging technologies (Holden, Holcomb, & Wedman, 1992).

Professionals should personally evaluate software if possible.
(Photograph courtesy of Education and Technology Resources)

SOFTWARE EVALUATION

Evaluation and validation must be of primary concern to the educator of exceptional persons if selection and use of software and any adaptive device is to be effective. Too often software has been used only as a reinforcer for completing assignments (as in the case of drill-and-practice materials) and not to teach concepts or thought processing. Software is all too often being used without an evaluation of the appropriateness of the information it presents and whether it addresses the content in the most educationally effective way. Special care must be taken to assure that the reading and interest levels are matched to those of the student, especially for those handicapped and gifted/talented students who have difficulty using traditional approaches. The software presentation must also be matched to the teaching style of the professional to be employed effectively; this is especially true for lower cognitive functioning individuals. For the gifted/talented, as with all students, care must be taken to stimulate the learner and to employ methods that cause the individual to employ higher cognitive thinking processes (see Chapter 10).

External Evaluation of Software

Regular and special educators cannot evaluate all software personally. Their school systems need to undertake some type of external means of evaluation. Evaluation centers are the major response to this problem. Local education agencies (LEAs), state education agencies (SEAs), regional centers (both within states and across states), and national centers (often university based or connected with periodicals such as *The Computing Teacher*) often have evaluation centers. (The names and addresses of many of these major centers are presented in Table 4.1. Figure 4.1 portrays the steps that the EPIE Institute uses to evaluate software for inclusion in its directory.) More recently, with the passage of Public Law 99–457 and the Technology-related Assistance Act for Individuals with Disabilities of 1989, centers and agencies have

TABLE 4.1
Evaluation and information on special education software sources

Apple Foundation
20525 Mariani Avenue
Cupertino, CA 95014

Center for Special Education Technology
Information Exchange
The Council for Exceptional Children
1920 Association Drive
Reston, VA 22091

Educational Software Exchange Library (EDSEL)
c/o Stanford Avenue School
2833 Illinois Avenue
Southgate, CA 90281

EPIE Institute
Teachers' College
Columbia University
525 W. 120th Street
New York, NY 10027

International Council for Computers in Education
University of Oregon
Eugene, OR 97403

LINC Resources
4820 Indianola Avenue
Columbus, OH 43214

Microcomputer Information Coordination
139 C.R.U., K.U.M.C.
39th and Rainbow
Kansas City, KS 66103

MicroSIFT Project
Northwest Regional Educational Laboratory
710 S. W. 2nd Avenue
Portland, OR 97204

National Education Association
Educational Computer Service
4720 Montgomery Lane
Bethesda, MD 20814

Software Reports
10996 Torreyana Road
P.O. Box 85007
San Diego, CA 92138

Special Education Software Review
3807 N. Northwood
Peoria, IL 61614

been funded within the United States to assist with this function. However, professionals should not assume that programs suggested by these centers and agencies are the only appropriate programs available, because no center or agency can evaluate the multitude of software programs available. Often only those producers large enough to afford the cost of providing free programs to a multiple number of agencies do so for evaluation purposes. Therefore, approved lists of programs tend to not include a number of good programs. Also, many approved state and regional lists of software are based on evaluative processes that represent mere token evaluations and only occasionally represent thorough and well-developed evaluation plans. On occasion, when programs are sent to evaluation agencies, they automatically appear on the approved list, even though they have not been evaluated at all. In other instances, thorough evaluations are completed by a highly trained team that seeks input from the audience(s) for which the software has been designed, the students. Due to the apparent lack of an evaluation standard, professionals need to adopt logical and efficient guidelines for reviewing software evaluations already published. One process is conducting a metaevaluation of available software evaluations to determine the validity of those evaluations. The school system could very easily support and expedite this process by having central office personnel collect and catalog published software evaluations according to their specific areas of content, functioning levels, and grade levels.

In order to conduct an effective metaevaluation, the professional should consider a number of questions addressing various aspects of the evaluation:

1. What are the evaluators' credentials?

2. Was the evaluation based on team effort?

3. Was the intended audience considered in the evaluation?

4. Did the intended audience evaluate the program?

5. How extensive was the evaluation?

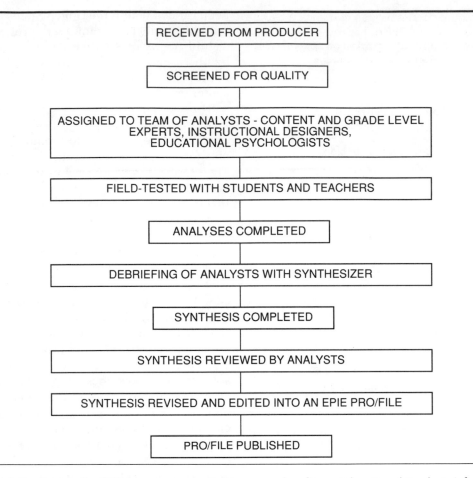

RECEIVED FROM PRODUCER

SCREENED FOR QUALITY

ASSIGNED TO TEAM OF ANALYSTS - CONTENT AND GRADE LEVEL EXPERTS, INSTRUCTIONAL DESIGNERS, EDUCATIONAL PSYCHOLOGISTS

FIELD-TESTED WITH STUDENTS AND TEACHERS

ANALYSES COMPLETED

DEBRIEFING OF ANALYSTS WITH SYNTHESIZER

SYNTHESIS COMPLETED

SYNTHESIS REVIEWED BY ANALYSTS

SYNTHESIS REVISED AND EDITED INTO AN EPIE PRO/FILE

PRO/FILE PUBLISHED

FIGURE 4.1   Steps in the EPIE courseware evaluation procedure [From Educational Products Information Exchange (EPIE), 103-3 W. Montauk Highway, Hampton Bay, NY 11946. Used with permission.]

The evaluators must have pedagogical practice and experience teaching students for whom the program was developed (e.g., of the same age and functioning levels). For example, if an evaluator is an educator and has extensive experience teaching high school algebra, this person may not necessarily be qualified to evaluate the effectiveness of a social studies program written for elementary gifted/talented students, nor is this person necessarily qualified to evaluate mathematical programs written for secondary learning-disabled students. On the other hand, this person may be well qualified to evaluate other mathematics programs written for regular education secondary-level students.

Software, then, must be evaluated by individuals who have had teaching experiences with the subject matter and the audience for which the software is intended. Judgments on software designed for mildly handicapped elementary students should not be made from the point of view of secondary regular education. Such a situation might occur if a secondary school level mathematics teacher evaluated a program designed to teach mathematical concepts to secondary students in a special education program, and the evaluation report indicated the mathematical concepts presented were too basic or simple. Comments such as this may be predicated upon the evaluator's teaching experiences and not on the intended audience for the program. An evaluator not only has to be qualified as a class- or therapy room professional, but must also have had experiences in understanding the dynamics of computing technologies. Further, a team effort evaluation eliminates the bias that occurs when judgment is made by only one person.

An audience similar to the one for which the program was designed should be used when evaluating the program. Programs considered to be exceptionally stimulating and informative by adults, regardless of their characteristics, may receive the opposite reaction from the intended group of students. Field studies conducted by a software developer who writes software primarily for secondary students with learning problems show that some programs considered to be highly educationally effective by an adult can be boring to a student. On the other hand, it is important to realize that software designed for one population may also be appropriate for other populations, as demonstrated by one program developed by MCE/Lawrence Production (Galesburg, MI). Although this program had been designed to develop logic and reasoning in secondary learning disabled and educable mentally retarded students, it was found during the field testing to be equally effective with upper elementary nonexceptional students. The key to the appropriateness of a specific program for a particular audience should be based on the specific objectives of the program plus the interest and reading/presentation levels as validated by each intended specific audience.

The extensiveness of the evaluation is extremely important to the educator's metaevaluation and concerns the entire process employed by the evaluation agency, including all other metaevaluation questions. The evaluative process should permit a sufficient amount of time to follow the steps necessary to make valid and reliable judgments. In the initial stages, software should go through a screening process. If the probability of the software's being an effective instructional program has been ascertained, qualified educators should then thoroughly evaluate the software based on accepted educational principles and the dynamics of the computer. This is a time-consuming process, since every frame and frame sequence must be evaluated based on, for example, all possible responses on input frames.

Software programs as well as printed materials should be evaluated. *(Photograph by Jimmy D. Lindsey)*

Input frames are those components of the program that require the user to respond by selecting from a variety of possibilities or from individualized input. Users may type in yes or no, multiple choices, or variable free input; evaluators should assess what happens after each possible response is entered. As indicated earlier, once the program has been evaluated on specified criteria by qualified evaluators, the program should be used with members of the intended audience to determine if the specified goals and objectives can be reached by their interacting with the program.

Often the professional cannot locate an evaluation report for a particular piece of software. When this occurs, the educator should seriously consider using the LEA's internally developed criteria to evaluate the needed software. Regular and special educators should work with central office personnel to decide their own specific criteria for evaluating software and then use these criteria to develop their particular evaluation form. Although there is some disagreement in special education circles concerning the developing of LEA software evaluation forms (e.g., because forms are already available in the literature), there are a number of reasons for school systems to take the time to develop such forms. If local professionals are involved in the implementation of the software evaluation procedures, they will be more likely to use those procedures. They will also be more knowledgeable about software evaluation principles and the form itself. Software evaluation generated by regular and special educators can be stored in a data base program or on hard copy. The method selected for storing evaluation results should be based on easy access by professionals to the information. At the local level, the evaluator's name, position or role, and how to contact should be included, since colleagues may need further information on the program to determine if it will meet their needs. One form that was developed using educator involvement, locally developed criteria, and directions explaining each of the criteria is the Commack Public School Evaluation Form (no date). There are, of course, many models from which to choose criteria perceived as pertinent for a particular LEA. These models are available from evaluation centers (see Table 4.1), state departmental projects, software companies, and LEAs. Appendix G presents a form developed by SECTOR, a federally funded project.

Internal Evaluation

An appropriate internal evaluation model should be comprehensive and cover instructional information, educational adequacy, technical adequacy, and related technical information. Each of these areas should be based on the intended audience and the intended use of the program.

Instructional Information

Instructional information should include all factors external to the program that deal with implementing the program. The professional should determine if the courseware fits into the curriculum, is appropriate for teaching using the computer, and matches the teacher's style of instruction and the students' needs. The software selected must also consider the students' learning styles. The purpose of the instructional unit should also be determined. The potential types of instruction include drill-and-practice, concept/skill instruction or tutorial, and problem solving/logic development and simulations, which are especially important for learning to make appropriate decisions

in social situations. Another essential factor is the instructional approach, which might include direct presentation of material followed by questions, experiential learning such as simulations, and discovery learning as found in role playing. Since the complexity of the design of the program is different for each type and approach, many of the evaluation factors may be different. A further factor to be considered is the effectiveness of the program with the intended audience. Field test information should either accompany the program or be available upon request. If this information is not available, the effectiveness of the program may be suspect.

Other factors to be evaluated under the area of instructional information should be included in the documentation. At a minimum, documentation should present the pertinent information necessary to operate the program effectively, such as control features (e.g., [Control] T), which may be used to allow certain changes to be made within the program or to run the program. The instructional overview must provide general information about the program as well as information about the goals and behavioral objectives of the program, which can be matched with those in the exceptional student's IEP. If the software itself does not provide information regarding the student's progress in the program, preferably on a printout, the documentation should provide an evaluation plan for assessing the student's progress toward meeting the objectives. Other vital information included in the documentation should be the prerequisite skills, concepts, and vocabulary necessary for the student to be successful with the program, including reading and interest levels. This information is necessary for the professional not only to determine if the program will be used but, if selected, what modifications may be necessary in how the program is presented. The professional will also want to preteach the prerequisite concepts prior to program use. Courseware that involves concept instruction and branching may include more than one reading/conceptual level, thus expanding the use of the program to include multiple audiences. The professional should not assume the levels listed are correct but

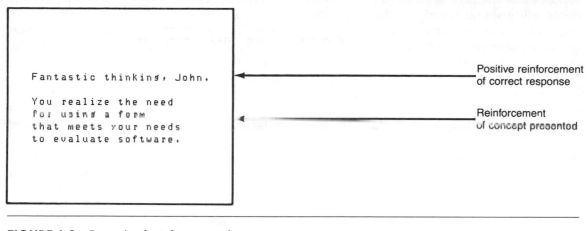

FIGURE 4.2 Example of reinforcement frame

should personally evaluate these levels. Levels are especially important if the student will be using the program with little or no supervision. The professional must consider whether the program is to be run independently of the teacher by the individual, or in small groups.

A final consideration under instructional information is whether the software is adaptable for students with special needs (Project ACCESS, no date). Evaluate whether the teacher can modify the content or alter the sequence of the program, and whether options are provided for printing and turning the sound off. Another important factor is whether the pace can be controlled by the students (Project ACCESS, no date).

Educational Adequacy

Another important evaluation area is educational adequacy, or issues involved with the instruction or program presentation. Included in this category are all the educational principles, some of which involve proceeding from simple to complex, progressing from concrete to abstract, and chaining to develop skills/concepts. When skills/concepts are being introduced, the task analysis must be appropriate for the intended audience and examples should be provided. Transference of learning should be programmed into the presentation, as should evaluation of comprehension. This appropriateness should include a sufficient number of questions or exercises to determine if the concept has been learned, questions of appropriate content to determine competency, and question types from the appropriate level of cognitive functioning based on Bloom's taxonomy (see Chapter 10).

The method in which the program responds to student input should be carefully considered based on reinforcement principles and branching capabilities. Not only should correct responses be reinforced but so should the concepts. Figure 4.2 presents a frame that not only praises the student for an appropriate response but also reinforces the concept. Reinforcing the response and the concept is important because on many input frames students can obtain the correct answer by chance alone.

When student responses are incorrect, the program should either branch for reteaching or allow the student another opportunity to self-correct the response. If the program branches, the task analysis should be broken down into smaller steps and the conceptual and/or reading level may be lower. Students should not merely repeat the program sequence. If the concept/skill was not learned the first time, it will not be learned with subsequent identical presentations. Further, wrong responses should not be punished or, as is sometimes the case, reinforced. Obviously in programs where responses that are incorrect are reinforced, students will respond incorrectly to obtain the exciting replies, thus reinforcing the incorrect answers/responses. In other programs, students are punished for incorrect responses ("Wrong answer, you dummy!"). This type of negative reinforcement may even be accentuated with a loud noise that can be heard by all students in the classroom. Fortunately the program that provided the example used here is no longer on the market.

Software must consider responses that indicate students do not comprehend what is expected of them. On these frames, error messages are required that instruct the student about input expectations. "Type Yes or No," is one type of error message. Although these error messages are necessary, their use can be minimized if the student can access directions whenever necessary (e.g., by using the escape key or F1). Besides being available, directions within programs should be evaluated for clarity.

For software to be motivating, it should provide variable types of input, allow for interaction between the student and the computer program, and branch within the program based on student choice/input. Software must be motivating and based on learning principles, rather than force feeding with regurgitation of information. In fact, research indicates that the more control students have over what they learn and when, the more likely they are to retain that with which they have been involved.

With students who have emotional impairments, typing in free inputs can be a double-edged sword. Software should allow students to interact with the program by allowing them the freedom to type in words and phrases, but the teacher should be aware of reaction by the class and/or the student should profanity be entered, especially if that program "talks."

Besides the variable input capabilities of the computer, programs must be personal, interacting with the student by using his or her name. The psychological value of the student's name entered into the program is obvious.

Too many professionals believe that the more graphics and animation in a program, the better the program. This is simply not true. Graphics or animation must enhance the skill/concept being taught, not detract from it. For students who function at low cognitive levels, the material must be concrete and therefore more graphics should be employed. The needs of the audience must be considered in order to determine the necessity of graphics. These features should always be of high quality with high resolution and represent what is to be taught in a way that is most educationally effective for the student.

Other factors include the use of capabilities inherent in the computer, such as blinks, flashes, and scrolling. Consider the individual who will be using the program. For instance, flashing can cause seizures. For that matter, the constant changes that occur on the screen can also have this effect on some students.

Technical Adequacy and Related Technical Information

Technical adequacy and related technical information is the third major issue to consider in software evaluation. The format of the frame (what is seen on the screen at one time) is extremely important, especially for lower-level functioning individuals. The frame should be uncluttered, phrases should be broken appropriately, and sentences should be of appropriate length for the audience. Single spacing of lines should be avoided because of the difficulty in reading lines placed too closely together. The presentation or format should be variable to increase the program's ability to get and hold the student's attention.

When student inputs are recorded, the assessment of these should be based on the concept and not on typing and/or spelling ability. Furthermore, the software program must take into consideration any probable inputs (e.g., all synonyms for the correct response must be accepted as correct).

The professional must be assured that the program will run to completion, regardless of the inputs of the student. This may sound like an obvious factor to consider, but too often it is overlooked. In one instance, a number of the software products found in a media center would not run to completion. Because most of the programs had been purchased from 3 to 6 months prior to this evaluation, these particular programs were not under warranty and could not be returned. The professional will therefore want to make numerous errors while testing the program to determine if the program will bomb or quit prior to the ending frame. This thorough testing should be done immediately after receiving the program. The educator will also want to check the warranty policy, since policies vary from company to company.

Another issue to consider, one that the educator often assumes is correct, is frame sequence. The frame sequence must make sense. It takes only a small typing error on the part of the programmer for the program to proceed to a wrong frame; although this error is usually caught by the producer, correct sequencing should be verified.

Additional factors to consider include (a) the company's policy for disk replacements, (b) the hardware for which the software is compatible and the general configurations necessary for that software to run (e.g., operating systems and memory), and (c) the peripherals that will operate in conjunction with that software.

Furthermore, as different technologies emerge—such as CD-ROM, interactive video, etc. that are already on the market—basically the same principles of evaluation apply. When selecting programs that are driven using computer technologies, the following should be considered:

1. Can this technology enhance the learning of the student?

2. Can this technology expand the ease with which the professional teaches the skill/concept?

3. Does this medium enhance the reality of the skill/concept presented?

4. Does this medium increase the involvement of the student?

5. Does this medium permit instruction to allow and encourage the student to employ higher-level thinking skills (according to Bloom's taxonomy)?

6. Is the use of this medium cost- and time-effective, based on the first five considerations?

Adaptive Devices Evaluation

Adaptive devices, those electronic devices that operate in conjunction with computers and that adapt or change the input or output possibilities of computers, are a major factor in software evaluation, especially their use with the more severely impaired and physically challenged audiences. For these exceptional persons, the specifics of the individual disability and the functioning of the particular devices are important to consider when determining which evaluation factors are essential. These adaptive devices, when appropriately selected and used, can provide significant freedoms for individuals by assisting them in controlling their environment, in communicating, in achieving mobility, and in learning. To ensure the correct match of the user to the appropriate adaptive device(s), pertinent evaluation procedures should be instituted. Further, it becomes obvious that determination of appropriate adaptive devices for an exceptional individual requires team analysis by those who are most familiar with the individual's needs in a number of situations and environments. This team should consist of parents or caregivers, teachers, speech-language clinicians, occupational and physical therapists, exceptional individuals, and rehabilitation specialists where and when available. All team members should have had previous preservice or in-service training on adaptive technology and experience working or otherwise interacting with exceptional individuals. For individuals with disabilities at the secondary level, the addition of a representative from Vocational Rehabilitation is highly recommended. It is also recommended that exceptional individuals be allowed to use an adaptive device for a period of time on a trial basis to evaluate its effectiveness.

Evaluation of the Individual

In evaluating an individual who will be using an adaptive device, consider the person's capacity to perform functions necessary to operate the technology, that is, whether the device is based on physical or cognitive factors. With those who are physically challenged, the more severe the impairment, the greater the necessity to break down the evaluation of this factor into specific categories (see Chapter 7).

The Microcomputer Applications Programme at the Ontario Crippled Children's Centre in Toronto breaks the physically handicapped individual's assessment into two parts. The first determines what is termed "three possible MSIPs [movement, site, interface, and position]." The second part is designed to monitor the handicapped individual's performance using the MSIPs to determine the most appropriate adaptive device or control system. The MSIPs assessment includes (a) background information on the individual, including communication, mobility, and muscle control; (b) bodily movements, including muscle tone, reflexes, and the most efficient movements "the client can [employ to] initiate control, and return to the resting position"; (c) bodily parts where the adaptive device can most effectively interface with the individual's body; (d) the most effective interface with the body considering the factors of "sensitivity, feedback (tactile, proprioceptive, and auditory), contact surface area, reliability, ease of set-up, cost, and durability"; and (e) the position of the interface based on the above-mentioned factors (Shein, Eng, Eng, & Lee, 1985).

Additional considerations are also necessary in the evaluation of the individual. First, before any determination of an adaptive device can be made, appropriate positioning must be determined. This involves the assistance from a rehabilitation specialist. Second, when selecting these devices, it is important to be aware that more than one device may be necessary. Multiple devices may be needed for control of more than one function, for different environments, and for different purposes such as learning, therapy, environmental control, working, and leisure time. It is important to select a device for therapy that requires a specific amount of energy to assist with therapy, taking into consideration the theory of optimal discrepancy between frustration and

the level of functioning that is so easy it requires little effort. In using adaptives for other purposes—learning, working, leisure time—the minimal amount of energy should go into controlling the device so that the individual's energy can go into cognition. Third, consideration must be given to appropriate adaptive input devices as well as appropriate output devices. For example, an individual with a visual impairment and cerebral palsy may need a particular switch for input purposes and a speech synthesizer for output purposes.

Evaluation of Adaptive Devices

Besides evaluating the individual to determine abilities and adaptive needs, adaptive devices themselves need to be evaluated to determine if they perform as they should. These devices may not always function as expected. Further, although some problems may be due to manufacturing errors, shipment problems, or miscommunication between the producer and the end user, malfunctions may also be caused by unforeseen circumstances connected with the handicap. In one instance, a breathing apparatus interfered with an individual's training of her voice for control on a voice recognition system, and electronic modifications had to be made on the adaptive device. In order to determine the effectiveness of any adaptive device, a thorough evaluation must cover documentation, operation, and service.

Documentation. The documentation should be user friendly. Too often documentation is written by engineers in technical jargon that is

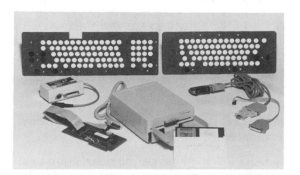

Evaluation of adaptive devices is important to ensure proper fit.
(Photograph courtesy of Prentke Romich Company)

difficult to understand. A user friendly manual is important. Documentation should include (a) how to install the device and what other firmware is necessary for the installation and operation of the device; (b) an overview of how the device operates and a step-by-step guide on how to program and use the device; (c) the field study on how it has been used, including any problems encountered and how these problems were resolved; (d) how to adapt the device to work in conjunction with other devices and with what other devices it is compatible; and (e) any other information necessary for successful operation.

Operation. The evaluation of the operation of an adaptive device includes checking the documentation or manual to determine the device's validity with specific populations and then actually using that device to determine if there are any problems. This is especially important with severely handicapped populations where the functioning capabilities of the individual must be matched to the methods of access of the adaptive device and a determination made of exactly what the device will do for that individual. With less severely handicapped populations, checking on the validity is important but will not require as much specificity in the precise matching of the function of the individual with the function of the device. For example, using voice recognition with a preschool individual who has limited keyboard skills but excellent voice consistency will require less specificity in the evaluation than if this device were to be used with a cerebral palsied individual who has questionable voice consistency and/or difficulty maintaining the mouth close enough to the microphone. Determine also whether the device can be used independently, whether it's portable, and whether a backup is available should the device fail.

The step-by-step guide for using the device must be checked for accuracy and should be easy to follow. When software accompanies devices, it should include comprehensible menus that augment or duplicate the guide found in the documentation. When following the directions on using the accompanying software, the user should be backed up by a program that includes an error-catching system. Then when the user does something wrong, which is inevitable, the device will not cease to function but will provide error statements that assist the user in progressing from that point in the software's program.

Service. The service area of evaluation of adaptive devices is also important. A service contract is essential because difficulties often occur with installation or with operation of the device based on the general functioning of the device or on individual circumstances involving the person who is to use the device. The importance of having a service contract cannot be overemphasized, not only for initial unforeseen problems and general complexities in operating the device, but because of unanticipated problems that can occur. The availability of training and access to a hotline should be built into the contract. Many difficulties that might occur can be avoided with appropriate training, especially with adaptive devices that are complex and/or are going to be employed by the severely handicapped.

Other Factors. Obtain a list of persons who have used or are using a device in order to communicate with them prior to purchase regarding uses and problems they have faced and after purchase to discuss situations as they occur.

Additional information on how this adaptive device has been coordinated with other devices is often necessary. Voice recognition is frequently necessary in conjunction with voice output or with an adaptive firmware card. Control of the environment may need to be coordinated with braille input and output. A list of these combinations must be as extensive as the list of individually determined needs for each handicapped individual. This information may not be available from major producers (see Table 4.2) but may be available from organizations such as LINC Resources (Information Center for Special Education Media and Materials, 4820 Indianola Avenue, Columbus, OH 43214, 1-614-885-5599) or ITTRU (1135 Gun Club Road, Sarasota, FL 34232, 1-813-378-5752). Also see Table 4.3 for some of

---

TABLE 4.2
Adaptive device specialists:
A few suggestions only

AbleNet
1081 10th Avenue SE
Minneapolis, MN 55914

Computability
4000 Grand River Avenue
Novi, MI 48050

Don Johnson Developmental Equipment
P.O. Box 639
1000 Rand Road
Wauconda, IL 60084

Prentke-Romich
1022 Heyl Road
Wooster, OH 44691

TASH (Technical Aids & Systems for the
  Handicapped)
70 Gibson Drive, Unit 12
Markham, Ontario, Canada L3R-4C2

ZYGO Industries
P.O. Box 1008
Portland, OR 97207-1008

---

the many technology access centers across the United States and Canada.

The package price should include all the cables, boards, and software necessary for the installation and operation of the device. Any items not included should be clearly specified.

One example of a comprehensive analysis/evaluation system for adaptive devices that integrates these evaluation factors is described by Lahm and McGregor (1984). This system, HUMAN-SD, covers the phases of requirements analysis, functions analysis, task analysis, interface analysis, and field evaluation. The requirements analysis phase analyzes "the client's goals" and obtains "a general sense of his or her abilities" (p. 225). The functions analysis phase further analyzes the system goals "to determine both the human and machine functions that are required to achieve the goals" (p. 231). Each function is further broken into its component parts in the task analysis phase. Following this phase and dur-

ing the interface analysis phase, "controls and displays are carefully considered in terms of their size, spacing, and placement on a panel or piece of equipment" (p. 235). During the final phase, field evaluation, all functions are performed, evaluated, and modified in the environments in which they will be used.

The technology must be adapted to the exceptional individual's needs and not the other way around. The individual's needs and physical capabilities must be evaluated and that information should be used to select the appropriate adaptive device. Not thoroughly evaluating both the individual and device "is like playing leapfrog with a unicorn—if you are shortsighted, you can be impaled on the horns of a dilemma" (Cain, 1985).

Some systems are designed to evaluate assistive devices for specific audiences, for example, the one reported by Hooper and Hasselbring (1985) on augmentative communication aids for nonreading severely physically handicapped children. This system evaluates assistive devices in the following areas:

TABLE 4.3
Adaptive devices research and development

Center for Special Education Technology
  Information Exchange
Council for Exceptional Children
1920 Association Drive
Reston, VA 22091

LINC Resources
4820 Indianola Avenue
Columbus, OH 43214

PIAM
601 West Maple Street
Lansing, MI 48906

TASH: The Association for Persons with Severe
  Handicaps
7010 Roosevelt Way, NE
Seattle, WA 98115

TRACE Research and Development Center
University of Wisconsin
Waisman Center, Room S-151
1500 Highland Avenue
Madison, WI 53706

---

1. *Indication system.* Is there direct selection of choice for communication by pointing, is the technique based on scanning with one selection at a time presented, or is an encoding technique employed where selection is based on a predefined pattern/ code? This area would also include the type of switch or method of inputting information and the adaptability of the device to changing the method of inputting based on changing needs of the handicapped individual.

2. *Symbols.* Are the symbols predetermined or programmable, and can the language content, format, and symbols be changed?

3. *Number of symbols.* How many sites for symbols are there, and what changes can be made?

4. *Size of sites.* What is the appropriate symbol site size (depending "on the range of motion, visual acuity, and attention span of the particular individual" [p. 43])?

5. *Feedback.* What type of feedback is available and what is its quality?

6. *Speed.* What is the rate of communication for the device and is it modifiable?

7. *Speech.* Is there speech output, what is its quality, and is it easily programmable?

8. *Hard copy printout.* Is there a printout, and what is its quality?

9. *Interfaces.* What, if any, other assistive devices does this communication device interface with?

10. *Correctability.* Can individuals correct their mistakes?

11. *Portability.* Is it portable, lightweight, and battery operated?

12. *Socially pleasing appearance.* How unobtrusive and socially acceptable is it?

13. *Warranty/service.* What warranty and service are available? (pp. 43–48)

TEACHER-DEVELOPED SOFTWARE

The more the professional is involved with evaluation, especially of software, the more the professional learns about the capabilities of the computer and learns that software, especially for low-incidence populations, is either limited or nonexistent. The available software may not have been developed at the appropriate interest level, may involve too much reading, may not have the appropriate number of steps in the task analysis (too few for the gifted and too many for the mildly handicapped), may not address the appropriate level of functioning based on Bloom's taxonomy, may not have appropriate control of stimuli, may not have sufficient interactive qualities, or may not have other of the necessary factors required to meet the needs of individuals within specific areas of exceptionality. However, since software can be invaluable to the functioning and education of many exceptional individuals, professionals need to be able to design software that meets the needs of individuals within identified audiences. That is not necessarily to say that educators should program software—especially if it is an extensive program that can involve hundreds or even thousands of hours. However, the professional can design programs for particular individuals and then give the programs to a programmer to complete or use an authoring system such as Tutor-Tech Hypermedia Toolkit (MECC, Inc.). Designing and programming with authoring systems is an important skill for professionals and exceptional individuals.

Software Design

In order to design educationally effective software, the professional needs a background in pedagogy, computer capabilities, and content. Besides the learning theory discussed under program evaluation, specific individual learner characteristics must be considered:

1. Is the individual an introvert or extrovert?

2. What is the learner's major learning modality?

3. Is there a need to block a specific modality for input or output?

4. What adaptive device, if any, is necessary to meet the individual's specific needs?

5. What is the individual's cognitive functioning level?

6. What is the individual's reading level?

7. What is the individual's interest level (considering chronological age)?

8. What is the individual's optimal discrepancy for learning?

9. What prerequisite skills are necessary?

Other questions involving learning theory include the following:

1. How can I best use assessment before instructional segments (within the program, external to the program, and using which techniques)?

2. How can I best evaluate progress (within the program and external to the program)?

3. How can I make this program motivating?

4. How can I apply appropriate reinforcement principles?

5. How can I make this program personal and interactive based on learner characteristics?

Besides learning theory, the professional will need to have sufficient background in the use of the computer for instruction to determine the purpose of the program, including drill-and-practice, tutorial or concept instruction, simulation, and/or problem solving (see Chapter 3). The professional will want to be able to determine if the program is to provide original instruction or is for enhancement of instruction, as well as to determine if the approach is direct, where information is presented followed by questions that determine comprehension, or is discovery learning. Most of the program design should be determined by the professional's individual instructional approaches, because these approaches will be the ones employed when using other materials and approaches for teaching.

Additional experiences necessary for the development of effective educational software are obtained through evaluation of already developed software, either commercial or public domain. The more professionals use and evaluate software, the more proficient they become in the skills necessary to design software that meets the needs of specific exceptional students. Elements that are considered in evaluation and in designing software include but are not limited to the following:

1. Subject matter must be appropriate for the computer.

2. Software must be interesting and motivating.

3. Software must be nonthreatening.

4. Feedback/reinforcement must be immediate and appropriate.

5. Software must include active involvement and be interactive.

6. Software must be personal (e.g., "Hello, Tom").

7. The lower the functioning level of the individual, the greater the importance of eliminating extraneous text, graphics, and blinks.

8. The higher the functioning level of the individual, the more choices of direction and control of the program should be in the hands of the student.

9. The format of the screen should reflect the functioning and needs of the individual (e.g., content that is centered, lines double-spaced or triple-spaced, appropriate print size and type, appropriate amount of text on the screen, and appropriate placement of words and phrases).

10. Responses by student should be appropriately handled (e.g., right responses, wrong responses, and inappropriate responses).

11. Error catching must be available for any input or output lengths by the student.

12. Management systems should be added where possible.

These elements are designed to integrate the factors used in evaluation with elements used in design and to assist the professional in understanding the importance of experience with

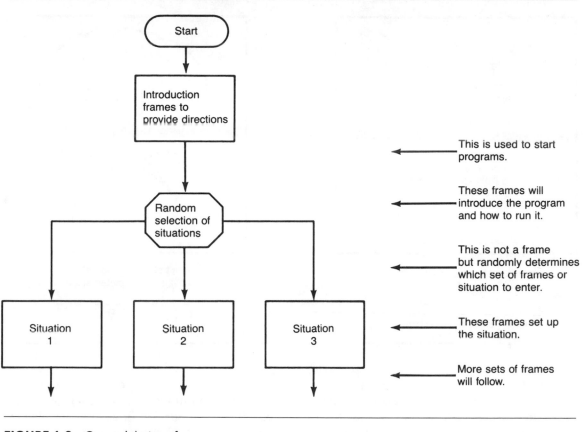

FIGURE 4.3   General design of program

evaluation prior to attempting to design software. The reader should refer to the section in this chapter on software evaluation for further information.

The third area of background information involves content. The professional must know the content to be covered in the software and must obtain assistance from content specialists in the community, from colleges and universities, and from information found in data bases or other sources.

After the professional has acquired the background necessary to develop effective software, a programmer should be contacted (assuming the professional is not going to carry out this aspect of program development). Often a person to do the programming can be a student within the educational system, one hired by the system, or a volunteer programmer from the community. The professional will be creating the design and the script, while the actual programming is done by a programmer.

The programmer's input, from the inception of the project when the goals and objectives are established through the development of the design and script, is essential because of the advice the programmer can give relating to the capabilities of the computer and to the professional's plan for the program design. After discussing implemention ideas with the programmer, a general design for the program is developed such as the one presented in Figure 4.3.

Along with the general or initial design, the professional develops a standard outline for the program in which the professional uses Roman numerals to develop the major objectives of the program and capital letters to designate specific frames. Arabic numerals are

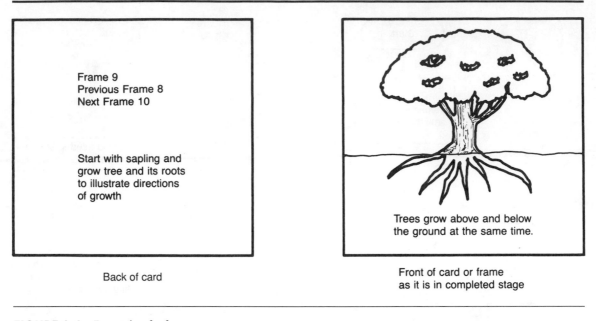

Frame 9
Previous Frame 8
Next Frame 10

Start with sapling and
grow tree and its roots
to illustrate directions
of growth

Trees grow above and below
the ground at the same time.

Back of card

Front of card or frame
as it is in completed stage

FIGURE 4.4   Example of a frame

then used to describe what is to happen to each frame and any other necessary information, such as which frame or frames follow based on the input from the student or what animation is to occur. A major caution to the professional at this point is to limit the content covered in one program. Programs tend to grow after the initial design state if the developer/professional is not careful. Prior to leaving this early developmental state of the program, the programmer is again consulted to ensure that the content can be programmed and to obtain further ideas based on computer capabilities.

Following the initial design stage, the educator develops the specific design of the program. As frames (what is seen on the screen at one time) are created, an educational flowchart is developed to show the frame sequencing. The flowchart may be developed on unlined paper or on other plain paper that can be obtained in rolls, and frames are placed on the flowchart in the appropriate order. The frames can be developed on 4-by-6-inch cards or on graph paper, blocking out the spaces that are available on the screen at one time. Spaces may be perceived as squares on the

screen or as the number of spaces across the screen by the number of lines from top to bottom. Since the number of spaces available on the screen at one time is specific to the particular computer (e.g., Apple, IBM), it is important for the professional to investigate the computer for which the program is being designed. The cards or graph paper used to indicate each frame include text that will be on the screen, graphics, animation of figures, and/or anything else that will be included during the running of that frame. Besides what is seen on the frame, directions need to be written for the programmer on the back of the card or on the side of the graph paper describing any embellishments or actions that will occur during the operation of that frame. Figure 4.4 is an example of a frame that also provides instructions to the programmer. Note that the frame is numbered and that the preceding and following frames are also given, as well as specific information to the programmer. The type and complexity of the flowchart that is developed will depend on the type of program developed. Figure 4.5 presents examples of partial flowcharts.

When the script or set of frames and the flowchart are complete, the programmer will

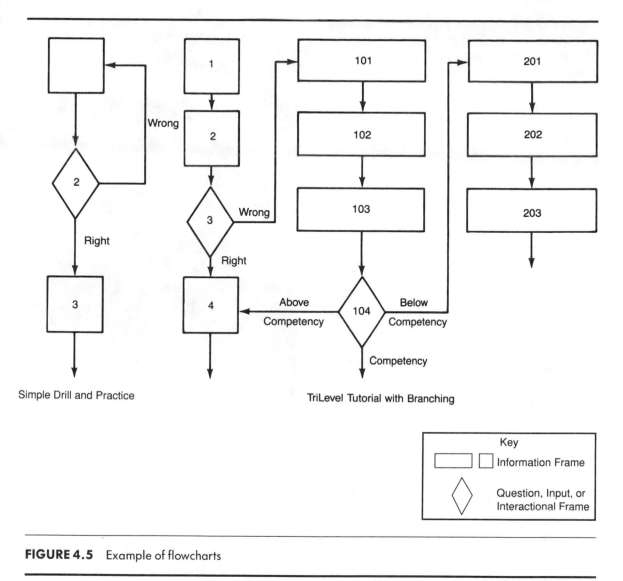

FIGURE 4.5 Example of flowcharts

thoroughly examine them, provide any further suggestions, and return them to the professional. At this point, the professional may wish to share the program (frames and flowchart) with other professionals and with the audience or students for whom the program is being developed for any suggestions that would add to the educational effectiveness and interest value of the program. This is followed by what could be called a program modification stage, in which any changes in the program are made. Following these changes, the frames and flowchart, still in nonprogrammed form, are returned to the programmer for programming.

After the programmer has completed the programming, it is returned to the professional for final, minor editing. It is wise at this point for the educator to validate the program with the proposed audience and allow other educators to interact with the program. If minor changes are to be made, the program can be returned to the programmer. The importance of making only minor changes at this point cannot be stressed too greatly, since only minimal programming changes can be made because of the complexity involved in making the changes and the unforeseen effects that can occur within a program based on any line change.

After the program is virtually completed, the educator should develop documentation incorporating the areas covered earlier in the documentation discussion. Not only will the documentation be of assistance to the professional who developed the program but also to other professionals with whom the program may be shared. Sharing is probably desirable because of the time involved in developing programs, especially those that are more complex than drill-and-practice.

Developing programs that are designed for management requires all the same stages (e.g., investigation, initial or general design, specific design, modification, and final editing), but instead of developing instructional objectives the professional should list all the outcomes expected from the program. In general, it is important to consider in designing management software such factors as (a) the number and types of inputs; (b) the amount of space for each input; (c) the amount of space/memory for the total number of inputs; (d) the type of sorts or how inputs should be accessed in order to obtain the desired combination of outputs for reporting (e.g., disability categories based on chronological ages); (e) user friendliness, including easy-to-operate menus; (f) a method for automatic saving of input information; and (g) the form of the outputs (e.g., hard copy formats, screen formats).

When developing programs for other media, such as interactive videodisc, it is important to apply basic technology principles (e.g., keeping in mind the specific characteristics of the media). See Chapter 5 for further information on interactive videodisc.

RELATED ISSUES

Most of the issues surrounding software involve the purchase of educationally effective programs and packages. All too often, professionals make purchases without appropriate evaluation. They don't always know how to

Professionals and students can work together to evaluate and develop software.
(Photograph by Jimmy D. Lindsey)

evaluate software and lack interest in doing evaluations. As would be expected, the lack of software evaluation by professionals can lead to the purchase of software that does not meet the needs of either the student or the professional. This problem is also augmented by the hesitancy of some producers to allow professionals to preview programs prior to purchase. This hesitancy is often eliminated when the professional sends in a request to preview on a purchase order indicating, "Preview with intent to purchase, if acceptable." It is a good idea for professionals to call the company if they have questions about the appropriateness of particular programs.

A related issue involves the illegal copying of software. In the early 1980s it was estimated by the software industry that up to 80% of software used in and out of the classroom had been illegally copied by professionals. This led to a mistrust on the part of the producer regarding preview of programs, a mistrust that is still a concern in the software industry today. Besides the mistrust created by illegal software copying, pirating also affected the price of software, because producers had to cover the cost of developing and producing software as well as place high-priced protection systems in their programs. Although much of this mistrust has been eliminated and cooperative relationships have been developed between producers and professionals, some illegal copying continues to take place.

Another issue surrounds the field testing of software. Often producers do not extensively field-test their software because the marketing window, or amount of time the software will be profitable on the market, is extremely short. This limited marketing window is due to the rapid changes that occur in what is considered to be state-of-the-art software. Developments in the software industry are occurring so rapidly that if producers are not careful, their software will be out of date before it gets on the market. On the other hand, producers have worked hard with professionals, including special educators, for both developmental and evaluative input. There is still much need, however, for the professional to find a way to evaluate software prior to purchase, since the latest developments in technology may not have been sufficiently validated regarding educational effectiveness.

Other issues involve the need to adapt technology to the learner and not the learner to technology. In the education field, even if the educator purchases technology and software and then desires to make changes based on the needs of the student, these changes are often not possible because of the complexity of the software program and needed technology. Therefore, professionals and producers need to continue communicating to learn about the types of modifications that are necessary to meet the specific needs of the individual and for professionals to understand the types of modification that are possible. This is especially important in the area of exceptional individuals who do not by definition have some of the characteristics when the specific materials and technological devices have been designed for the general population.

There is also a need to develop a peripheral or adaptive input device that is common to all major computers, such as one that involves infrared rays. Then handicapped individuals in particular could have access to different technologies involving computers in a number of environments.

The final but correlative issue mentioned here deals with compatibility: adaptive devices and software should be able to operate effectively on multiple machines. This would involve further standardization within the hardware industry. Presently emulators can be purchased that allow different machines to communicate. However, because of political and economic reasons, full standardization is not the norm.

SUMMARY

This chapter has discussed the major reasons for software and adaptive device evaluation and has provided the professional with a plan for evaluating both as well as a general philosophy for evaluating emerging technologies. The three areas covered that are necessary for effective software evaluation are instructional information, educational adequacy, and technical adequacy. Pertinent evaluation areas to assure effective and nonfrustrating use of adaptive devices include evaluating exceptional individuals (from a developmental and physical functioning standpoint) regarding their needs and relating this information to specific adaptive devices that must be evaluated in the areas of documentation, operation, and service.

Often, even with specific evaluation techniques, the software necessary to meet the particular needs of students, especially those from low-incidence exceptionalities, is limited, and the professional needs to find ways to get that software created. Regular and special education professionals can create the needed software by programming their own software, using authoring systems or more complex programming languages, or can have someone else with programming proficiency do it for them. Regardless of whether professionals program the software or have the software completed by a programmer, they must be able to design effective software and communicate that information to the person who is going to do the programming. For effective designing of software, the professional must have a background in pedagogy, experiences involving the capabilities of the computer, and information on the content to be covered. Effective designing of emerging technologies basically involves the same three knowledge areas.

A number of issues related to evaluation and program development must be addressed by producers and educators working cooperatively to develop educationally effective software and to create appropriate adaptive devices for members of the various exceptionalities.

REFERENCES

Cain, E. J. (1985, March). Potential of advanced technologies: Benefits and barriers. Keynote address at the TAM Computers for the Handicapped Conference, Johns Hopkins University, Baltimore, MD.

Commack Public Schools Evaluation Form. (no date). Commack Public Schools, Hubbs Administrative Center, Clay Pitts Road, East Northport, NY 11731.

Gardner, J. E., Taber-Brown, F. M., & Wissick, C. A. (1992). Selecting age-appropriate software for adolescents and adults with developmental disabilities. *Teaching Exceptional Children, 24*(3), 60–63.

Holden, M. C., Holcomb, C. M., & Wedman, J. F. (1992). Designing hypercard stacks for cooperative learning. *Computing Teacher, 19*(5), 20–22.

Hooper, E. H., & Hasselbring, T. S. (1985). Electronic augmentative communication aides for the nonreading student: Selection criteria. *Journal of Special Education Technology, 7*(2), 39–49.

Lahm, E. A., & McGregor, G. (1984). Hardware selection and evaluation. In M. M. Behrmann (Ed.), *Handbook of microcomputers in special education* (pp. 209–242). Austin, TX: PRO-ED.

Palin, L. (1992). Examining the emperor's new clothes: The use of existing video in multimedia packages. *Computing Teacher, 19*(6), 5–7.

Project ACCESS. (no date). Pontiac, MI: Oakland Schools.

Shein, F., Eng, M., Eng, P., & Lee, K. (1985, April). Assessing severely disabled persons for single-input control of the microcomputer. Presentation at the Personal Computers for the Handicapped Conference, University of Alberta, Edmonton AL, Canada.

Suggested Activities

Paper and Pencil

Review the literature and find a form to evaluate software and one to evaluate adaptive devices. Compare the items on these forms with respect to what was recommended for such forms in this chapter. What areas were not included in either of the forms that would be important in the evaluation process? How does this form compare with the SECTOR form in Appendix G?

Observation

Visit a special education setting that has computer capabilities. Ask the teacher to select one or two software programs used and to list the advantages and disadvantages of the software related to its classroom use. Also talk to students who use the programs and determine their perception of the software's attributes. How did the teacher's and students' opinions differ?

Practicum

Find a computer and run the software program reviewed by the teacher and students in the observation. Were their reviews accurate compared to what you found? Why or why not? What did they not report about the software that they should have put in their reviews and why? Consider using the SECTOR form in Appendix G to complete the practicum.

Resources

Organizations

Apple Computers
Office of Special Education and Rehabilitation
20525 Mariani Avenue
Cupertino, CA 95014

Center for Special Education Technology
Council for Exceptional Children
1920 Association Drive
Reston, VA 22091-1589

IBM
National Support Center for Persons with
Disabilities
Box 2130
Atlanta, GA 30301-2150

Books

Gergan, M., & Hagen, D. (1985). *Computer technology for the handicapped: Proceedings from the 1984 Closing the Gap Conference.* Henderson, MN: Closing the Gap.

Adaptive microcomputer equipment and materials. Write to HCCCP, 7938 Chestnut, Kansas City, MO 64132.

SOFTSEL Product Encyclopedia. Inglewood, CA: SOFTSEL Products. This paperback book has over 3,000 descriptions of computer books, hardware, and software. Write to SOFTSEL, P.O. Box 546, North Oak Avenue, Inglewood, CA 90312.

Interactive Videodisc and Exceptional Individuals

Alan Hofmeister
Ron Thorkildsen
Utah State University ■

Appreciating the instructional potential of videodisc technology requires knowledge about the characteristics of the laser videodisc and about possible instructional formats. This chapter introduces laser videodisc technology and provides a brief description of instructional application levels.

A standard laser videodisc looks like a shiny, white, metallic, LP record. The disc stores the same type of information as videotape, but any of the 54,000 individual, high-quality frames on one side of the disc can be accessed in 1 or 2 seconds. Further, there is no loss of image quality when moving from motion to still-frame presentation. In the laser reflective format, the player directs a low-power laser beam onto the disc surface, where it strikes either a tiny pit or the more reflective surface between the billions of pits etched in the surface. (The pits are protected by thick, clear plastic; only the laser light contacts the disc, resulting in a very robust storage medium and player system.) The laser light is then reflected off the surface to a sensor, which detects the variations in reflected light intensity. These variations are then transformed into a signal fed to a television receiver.

INTERACTIVE INSTRUCTIONAL FORMATS

A widely adopted classification system for individual formats was proposed by the Nebraska Videodisc Design and Production Group

Interactive videodisc player and videodisc can be used for learning. *(Photograph by Ron Thorkildsen)*

in 1979 (Daynes, 1984). This classification system is based on the control methods of different systems. The initial classification scheme included Levels 0 through III, but a Level IV has been added:

Level 0

Systems at this level consist of a linear player. Such systems are primarily designed for home entertainment, have limited interactive functions, and provide many of the same instructional applications as videotape players and movie projectors.

Level I

Level I systems include quick frame access, still frame, and fast visual-scanning functions; two user-selectable audio channels; and chapter and picture stops. Table 5.1 provides a brief description of the capabilities of a Level I system. These functions should be reviewed to fully understand the utility of this level.

Level II

The Level II systems add the intelligence of an internal computer to the Level I functions. A computer program to control the various functions can be placed in an audio track on a videodisc. Complex combinations of functions can then be conducted automatically or triggered by input through the player's control panel. Recording student responses is difficult at this level because of the limited amount of memory available in the internal computer.

Level III

Systems at this level consist of a videodisc player linked to a computer. This type of system allows the simultaneous display of both computer- and videodisc-generated material. At Level III, the read, write, and storage functions of the computer are added.

TABLE 5.1
Capabilities of the Level 1 videodisc system

Quick Frame Access
There are 54,000 individually addressable frames on each side of a videodisc. A frame can be selected and found using the player's remote control panel. When less than 500 frames apart, search time is imperceptible. If the frames are thousands of frames apart, most players will make the change within a maximum of 3 seconds. This facility allows a teacher to branch quickly to any frame on the disc. Using the remote control unit, the teacher can control the videodisc player from any location in the classroom.

Selectable Audio Channels
Although the entertainment industry typically uses two audio channels for high quality stereo, the educator can remotely select either or both channels. This is often done when different audio tracks are used for the same visual display, for example, viewing the same display in two different languages or presenting a display while posing a problem and then replaying, giving the solution on the second audio track.

Chapter Stops
Branching may be done by frame or chapter. To access a frame, a five-digit frame address or a two-digit chapter address is entered. Approximately 70 encoded chapter stops can be placed on one side of a disc. Chapter stop increases the speed and practicality of branching.

Picture Stop
A picture stop is a point or frame at which the player will automatically stop. For example, if students are to work a problem in their workbooks after a demonstration, a picture stop will cause the player to stop automatically, displaying the problem on the screen. The teacher can then signal the player to advance once the students have completed the assignment. This very practical function allows the teacher more time to monitor pupils rather than be distracted by the operation of the player.

Level IV

A Level IV system is distinguished from a Level III system by the additional power of the computer software. If some type of artificial intelligence software is used, it is usually classified as Level IV, although there is considerable disagreement about the functions and components of a Level IV system.

Educational Implications of the Different Levels

Of the different levels, Levels I and III appear at present to have the most instructional value. Level III has received the most attention in industrial and military training efforts. A Level III emphasis implies that the educational institution stresses the individual learning station as a major instructional delivery system and that resources are available to support the installation and maintenance of individual learning stations. Some public school districts have both the interest and resources to support the extensive use of Level III learning stations. However, a large number of school districts are heavily committed to group instruction, with the teacher or therapist as the primary instructional agent and technological aids used in a range of support roles.

Many people in educational technology assume that the individual learning station is the most powerful delivery system and that acceptance of anything less occurs because of lack of resources. The widespread acceptance of this assumption suggests there is a wealth of research to support the clear, comparative advantage of the individual learning station over other instructional delivery systems. Such is not the case. In their comprehensive review of research literature on individualized systems of instruction in secondary schools, Bangert, Kulik, and Kulik (1983) reported that group-paced systems "appeared to produce stronger effects" than self-paced systems. These findings do not suggest that computer-assisted instruction (CAI) and other types of self-paced systems are not effective. Indeed, the findings support the efficacy of CAI. The point is that other instructional delivery systems that monitor the individual's progress, including group-paced systems and systems such as peer tutoring, have been shown to be just as effective as some self-paced systems. Therefore we

should not view the technologically based individual learning station as the ultimate delivery system for classrooms or clinical settings (Pitsch & Murphy, 1992).

The Level I videodisc system adds both a massive storage capacity and fast random-access facility to the combined instructional functions of videotape players and film and slide projectors. For this reason, this versatile instructional medium needs little promotion because it offers the educational potential of any one of the media that videodisc technology can emulate. Of the different instructional presentation functions possible with different media and media combinations, the combination of a Level I videodisc system and individual student workbooks results in one of the most flexible and comprehensive instructional delivery systems (Walker & Butler, 1984). In a typical Level I system, the teacher or therapist can spend a large amount of time moving around the classroom to check individual workbook activities, guide discussion, and control the videodisc player with the aid of a remote control panel. Classroom management and attention to exceptional individuals is enhanced when the professional is not confined to the front of the class or therapy room.

As interest in videodisc technology has grown (cf., Billings & Cobb, 1992), there has been increased concern about the cost effectiveness of different levels for different learner populations and curriculum areas. There is little research data directly related to a comparison of levels and exceptional populations, so caution must be exercised. Given that (a) many exceptional learners are in need of social skills development and (b) there is little evidence to suggest that the physical segregation and individualization of the electronic work station are substantially more effective than less costly group-paced alternatives, the unquestioned promotion of the individual electronic work station is inappropriate.

VIDEODISC APPLICATIONS

The videodisc became commercially available in 1978, and like most new technologies it received both accolades and skepticism from the educational community. Yet while few have questioned the potential of interactive videodisc instruction in health, defense, and industrial training, the potential of videodisc-based instruction in the schools has been questioned. Concerns include the resistance of public educators to technology, hardware costs, and lack of quality courseware to support the investment. Regular and special educators' eagerness to embrace computer technology demonstrates their current ability and willingness to invest in technology on a large scale. Despite this interest, the nature of the public school is such that wide-scale adoption of videodisc technology may not occur until videodisc-based instructional products are specifically designed to meet the needs, restrictions, and strengths of public school instruction.

Potentially the videodisc can meet many of the instructional needs of exceptional persons (Woodward & Gerstern, 1992). For example, a major obstacle to providing individualized instruction for exceptional students is their lack of independent work skills. The need for individual attention increases with the severity of the handicap. The problem is further compounded with students who have limited or no reading skills. Traditional CAI and individualized self-administered assessment instruments and instructional materials require age-appropriate reading skills. This factor prevents a majority of the students with disabilities from profiting from these procedures; spoken instruction is necessary for their interaction. A videodisc player, with its rapid random-access audio capabilities, makes interactive, individualized spoken instruction possible for the exceptional learner (see Table 5.1).

The following sections describe a variety of videodisc technology applications with exceptional individuals. Applications include assessment, academics, social skills, personnel preparation, and artificial intelligence.

Assessment

A complex activity associated with the design of instructional programs for exceptional learners is the diagnostic-prescriptive process. In order to prepare instructional programs that meet the needs of individuals with wide-ranging abilities, assessment activities must be carried out that require processing hundreds of specific objectives. In order to determine the value of using interactive videodisc technology to support assessment activities, a math assessment videodisc was developed and field-tested (Hofmeister, 1984a).

The math assessment videodisc was both a Level II and Level III application, and printed reports were available from both systems. In the Level II system, a printer was connected to the videodisc player. In the Level III system, the disc was used with a touch screen attached to the color monitor.

The disc tested 335 specific math skills in areas of numeration, whole numbers, fractions, decimals, measurement, and geometry. In most testing situations, an item is scored as correct or incorrect, but with the additional processing power of the computer and the videodisc player, the students' wrong answers were also analyzed and reports outlining their computational errors were generated. Twenty-three common computational errors could be identified. With the aid of the second audio track on the math disc, the student could be assessed in either English or Spanish.

Developing and field-testing the math disc involved four major stages. Stage 1 involved content selection and validation. Several commonly used criterion-referenced instruments were analyzed to ensure that items were in agreement with widely used curricula. Research literature on student errors was reviewed to ensure that the more common computational errors were included in the wrong answers provided for each multiple choice item. In the second stage, graphic-print materials were developed and used to simulate test items. Information from associated field testing was used to revise these items.

The third stage involved simulating the videodisc presentation by using videotape. This videotape was then field-tested with 61 individuals at three separate sites. The final stage involved preparation of the videodisc and its field test, concurrent with highly regarded pencil-and-paper instruments. Not only was the videodisc able to do much more than the traditional assessment instruments, but a comparison of performance in common areas indicated that videodisc-based assessment results were valid and reliable. Correlations between videodisc assessment and traditional valid instruments were consistently above .80.

In concluding his review of the math assessment disc, Eastmond (1984) noted that this procedure provides a reliable way of assessing students' abilities by negating the confounding factors of reading prerequisites and primary language bias. Furthermore, tests can be used throughout the instructional process (e.g., assessing gains and losses, pre- and posttest levels, etc.), and the disc's extensive reporting and analysis features free professionals to devote more time to instruction and at the same time generate data that can be used to make teaching more effective.

Academic Programs

The Interactive Videodisc for Special Education Technology (IVSET) Project, begun in 1979 at Utah State University (Thorkildsen, 1982), launched one of the first efforts to use the videodisc with exceptional learners. The technology was very new, and little was known about videodisc production or computer-controlled videodisc players. Developing a hardware system was a major goal of the IVSET Project. Producing an interface to control the videodisc player with a computer was the first challenge. An interface board was designed and developed and was one of the first devices of this type ever developed. The first interface was developed for the IMSAI 8080 computer, and a second board was developed for the Apple II. The IVSET system used a Pioneer 7820-I videodisc player, a Carroll Manufacturing Light Interrupt Touch Panel, and a dot matrix printer. The touch panel eliminated the more complex responding involved in using the computer keyboard.

Students interacted with the system by viewing material on the television screen and then responding to spoken questions or instructions by touching the appropriate image of an object on the screen. The area of the

Interactive videodisc system with touch screen capabilities makes it easy for a student to respond. *(Photograph by Ron Thorkildsen)*

screen touched by a student was detected by the touch panel, and this location was transmitted to the computer. The program in the computer contained the correct location for each segment of instruction. The student's response was compared to the correct location to determine if the response was correct.

In addition to presenting instruction, the IVSET software maintained data on student progress. These data included starting and ending question numbers, the number and percent of correct and incorrect items, the number of times the student did not respond to a question, the number of questions and the length of the session, and the number of times the program signaled for teacher assistance. This information was available from the screen or printer in either graphic or written form and pinpointed areas where the student needed help.

Six programs were developed for use with the microcomputer-controlled videodisc (MCVD) system during the first project, including (a) Matching Sizes, Shapes, and Colors, (b) Time Telling, (c) Identification of Coins, (d) Functional Words, (e) Sight Reading, and (f) Directional Prepositions. These programs were field-tested during the course of the project to obtain information necessary for the continued development and refinement of the system. The following individuals and academic areas were involved in field testing:

1. Elderly persons with moderate mental retardation at the Brigham City Day Care Center—matching

2. Children (4–13 years) with severe to moderate mental retardation at the Center for

Persons with Disabilities—matching and prepositions

3. Individuals with severe to moderate mental retardation of all ages at the Utah State Training School—identification of coins and functional words

4. Children (7–10 years) with learning disabilities and mild mental retardation in a public school resource room—time telling and beginning reading

These populations were used to determine if students learned from the system and if a student could work independently with the system. A major goal required that operation of the system be as independent of the teacher as possible.

In general, the system was least effective with residentially based exceptional children (4–13 years) who needed a great deal of teacher intervention. It was most effective with mainstreamed students with disabilities and students with mild mental retardation. Also the field tests demonstrated the need for continued investigation of instructional videodiscs that take into account varied criteria for judging the acceptability of the videodisc system. What was not effective for one population of students was highly effective for another. A productive direction for the future development of educational videodisc applications may be the determination of effective matches between technology, instructional objectives, and specific learner populations. Clearly all of these aspects must be considered in developing criteria for evaluating successful videodisc instruction.

Reading Programs

Beginning sight reading is a particularly good application for videodisc technology. Students can be prompted with audio to match words with pictures and action sequences.

Prinz and Nelson (1984) developed and tested a beginning reading program for children with hearing impairments. The program teaches nouns, adjectives, and action verbs. The verbs are presented as action sequences,

using computer-generated animation. Based on preliminary research, the authors concluded that the program was effective.

The authors of this program developed and field-tested a videodisc program similar to the above CAI program (Prinz & Nelson, 1985). The same instructional sequences were used, but the computer-generated animations were replaced with videodisc motion sequences. This added a great deal of realism to the program. For example, the CAI program may teach the word *run* by showing an animated dog running toward a house. The videodisc version will show a real dog running toward a real house. A large inventory of realistic action sequences can be placed on the videodisc at a cost much less than that required for creating computer graphics.

Another beginning reading program was developed by the staff at the California School for the Deaf in Riverside, California (Brawley & Peterson, 1983). Between 1980 and 1983, two videodisc sides, an authoring system, and an interfacing card that permits computer-generated text overlays were produced. The reading program was designed for students with hearing impairments. Students were branched through activities that required them to acknowledge captions appearing on the screen, sequence events, recognize grammatical correctness, recognize syntactical correctness, respond to questions, and to categorize, spell, capitalize, punctuate, and construct questions and other sentences. A light pen was used for most student interactions; however, the keyboard was used for spelling tests. Data were collected to establish a baseline that could be used for comparative purposes in subsequent field testing.

Thorkildsen and Friedman (1986) developed and field-tested a beginning sight-reading program. This videodisc-based program was designed specifically to determine differences in the types and intensity of remediation built into the sequence. The effects of different remediation strategies on students' incorrect responses are a major concern when developing technology-based classroom and therapy interventions. Students' needs must be anticipated, and responses to those needs must be built into the program. Information

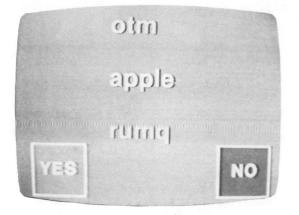

A screen from an interactive videodisc gives immediate feedback. *(Photograph by Ron Thorkildsen)*

regarding the efficacy of different remediation strategies is scarce, at best, for providing guidelines to design instructional videodisc programs. Therefore two versions of the Beginning Sight Reading Program (*BSR-1* and *BSR-2*) were designed to assess two different remedial approaches.

BSR-1 presents a relatively extensive remediation sequence, while BSR-2 presents minimal remediation. For both programs, the first incorrect response produces the same negative feedback: "No, that is not right, try again." The question is then repeated. On the second incorrect response, BSR-1 branches to a remediation segment that consists of a simpler discrimination than the one presented in the original question; BSR-2 simply branches and repeats the previously presented instruction. On the third incorrect response, BSR-1 presents an even simpler version of the original question and adds a prompt to increase the likelihood that a correct response will be elicited; BSR-2 presents the correct answer. On the fourth incorrect response, both programs signal the teacher. In both programs, a correct response results in short praise and transfers to the next instructional unit.

The field test was conducted in two resource rooms with 32 kindergarten and first-grade students who were classified as learning disabled or slow learners. The students were randomly assigned to either BSR-1 or BSR-2 programs. The results of the field test indicated there was no significant difference be-

tween the programs on academic achievement; however, the students in the high remediation program (BSR-1) completed the task of learning seven new words and associated phrases 10% faster than those in the BSR-2 program. The difference in the mean scores of the two groups of students resulted in an effect size of .55, which indicates total mean time on the system for the BSR-1 group was approximately one-half of a standard deviation below the BSR-2 group. The differences in total time on the system mean that the high remediation group (BSR-1) finished 10% lower than the BSR-2 group. A 10% increase in time with just seven words extrapolates to a substantial time savings over a complete reading program. Test scores for both groups doubled between the pre- and posttests. Given the weaknesses of gain scores and the fact that this was an exploratory study with a relatively small sample, these findings are not conclusive, but they suggest that the videodisc programs efficiently taught these resource room students to read seven new words and to read them in the context of sentences.

Time Telling

Time Telling, a program developed by the IVSET Project staff, is another example of a Level III application. The hardware system described earlier managed the instructional interactions. The computer directed the videodisc to present an instructional segment on the screen. One segment presented was "This is the little hand; now you touch the little hand." Instructional segments ended with a command, question, or test sequence, and the student responded by touching one of the answer choices presented on the screen. If the student touched the correct picture (for example, that of the little hand), the computer directed the videodisc to play the next instructional segment. If the answer was incorrect (or the test was not passed), the computer directed the videodisc to branch to a remediation segment or, if the same answer was incorrect several times, the system signaled the teacher with a beeping sound.

Project Rationale

It was not the purpose of the project to compare the instructional effectiveness of teachers and machines. Such an approach would narrowly suggest an either-or situation and would obscure the potential of using both sources to increase productive learning time in the classroom. An alternative approach is to place less emphasis on the competition between teachers and technology and stress their match among known characteristics (e.g., effective instruction, source of instruction, content, and learners' needs). Thus the goal of the project was to structure technological intervention to enhance or minimize the characteristics of effective instruction needed for specific content and learner populations. Project staff hypothesized that an effective match could be made between the system and those instructional objectives best taught in skill hierarchies with intensive interactive instruction and extensive drill and practice for rapid mastery.

Curriculum Content

The Time Telling program was adapted from a paper and pencil package produced by Utah State University's Center for Persons with Disabilities, Outreach and Development Division (Hofmeister, Atkinson, & Hofmeister, 1975). The program consisted of 11 instructional objectives designed to teach children how to tell time to the nearest 5-minute interval. The only prerequisite skills for this program were the ability to recognize the written numbers 0–60 and the ability to count to 60 by ones and fives. The Time Telling program was relatively long and highly interactive. It used two audio tracks and one side of a 29-minute videodisc. To answer every question correctly on the first trial, the student had to make over 700 responses.

The 11 instructional objectives represented a task-analyzed sequence of subskills needed for telling time, including (a) number placement on a clock face, (b) discrimination between the hour hand and the minute hand, (c) identification of values for the minute and hour hands separately, (d) identification of values for the minute and hour hands together, and (e) the ability to read digital format. Stu-

Beginning reading skills can be taught using an interactive videodisc program. *(Photograph by Ron Thorkildsen)*

dents received immediate feedback for correct or incorrect responses after each response. For several consecutive correct responses, a short, cartoonlike reinforcer segment was presented (e.g., frogs leaping and crowds of people applauding). The remediation sequences for incorrect responses consisted of correction procedures and branching back to previous instruction. The program included a criterion-referenced test after each of the 11 instructional segments (e.g., number placement on a clock's face). The system advanced the student through the program only if a criterion level of at least 80% on the segment test was met.

Field Test Procedure

The field test of the Time Telling program was conducted in a resource room in Logan, Utah, from April 1 through May 15, 1982 (Hofmeister & Friedman, 1984). After 1 hour of training, the resource room teacher was responsible for implementation and maintenance of the system throughout the field test. The computer stored all of the student progress data, while project staff members collected observational data.

The four subjects who participated in the field test were 7- to 9-year-old first and second graders; three were classified as learning disabled and one as educably mentally retarded. The average WISC-R score for these students was 82. According to the resource room teacher, these students were able to count to 60 by ones and fives and recognize written numbers but could not tell time. This was verified by administering a pretest in which all students in the resource room were individually asked to count to 60 by ones and fives, identify written numbers 0–60, and identify the time on 20 traditional and digital clocks. Pretest results confirmed that the four students identified by the teacher were the only students in the classroom who met the prerequisite number skills but could not tell time.

The four subjects worked on the system with earphones in a back corner of the resource room to make the system as unobtrusive as possible and to facilitate focusing their attention on the task. They each worked for approximately 15 minutes each day.

Field Test Results

The average completion time was 4 weeks. The consistency of data across the replications was high. All four students could tell time at the end of the program, as measured by the posttests. All posttests were identical in structure but showed different times on the clocks.

Posttest number 1 was administered by the interactive system as part of the Time Telling program. Posttest number 2 was administered to measure the extent to which the subjects could transfer their time-telling skills from videodisc simulations to real clocks in the classroom. Posttest number 3, a retention test, was administered 8 days after posttest number 2. Only three students were available for the retention tests.

On all posttests, the children met or exceeded the criterion of 80% mastery. Based on these test results, it was concluded that the Time Telling program successfully taught four elementary children with mild handicaps to tell time with ease and accuracy. Observational data indicated this goal was met with essentially no instructional teacher intervention. The teacher merely signaled the student to the machines and began the system at the appropriate instructional segment.

Conclusion

The subjects in this study provided a challenging test of the interactive system. The students differed in age, grade level, and handicapping classification. All of them had demonstrated significant learning difficulties, yet they all learned to tell time fluently within 6 weeks and without teacher intervention. The subject matter—telling time—provided a challenging test of the system as well. Telling time can be a difficult skill to master for any child, and interference from past learning often increases the complexity of the task (Hofmeister, 1976). For example, a child being taught to tell time by the "2:45" method, after having been partly taught the "15 till 3:00" method, will often find the learning process confusing. With the typical course of instruction, children usually master time telling over 2 or 3 years of segmented instruction. Alternatively, this program provided intensive instruction, which led to rapid mastery. This approach decreased the probability of interference from past learning. The system also accommodated a wide spread of entry levels, that is, students were able to enter the program at the appropriate skill or objective level.

Based on this study, it appears that interactive instruction and the Time Telling program resulted in a highly successful match among the characteristics of effective instruction, content, and instructional delivery source. The extent to which a regular or special educator could have delivered this instruction and improved the outcomes is not of particular interest here. Most important is the potential to match the capabilities of a technology to specific subject matter and learners' instructional needs, to capitalize on the simultaneous use of teachers and technology, and to increase educationally productive time for handicapped and gifted/talented students in individualized classrooms.

Additional Time Telling Field Tests

The Time Telling videodisc was revised and reedited to allow use in both Level I and Level III applications (Thorkildsen & Findlay, 1991). The revised program was field-tested as a Level I program in three second-grade classrooms. One classroom served as a control group and did not receive the program. The classroom teachers controlled the program through the use of a remote control unit. The classrooms contained no students classified for special education. Because of school policy, students would not have been classified for special education services until the beginning of the following year. The teachers did indicate, however, that there were a number of low-functioning students in each of the classrooms. In order to determine if the program differentially affected low-achieving students, achievement scores were collected and the students were classified as low, medium, or high achieving. Analysis showed statistically and educationally significant differences between the videodisc groups and the control group, but there was no significant interaction between the achievement groups. The low group learned at essentially the same rate as the medium- and high-achieving groups.

Thorkildsen and Reid (1989) also field-tested the revised videodisc program as a Level III application. Students worked individually and responded to the system through the use of a touch panel. Fifty-nine exceptional students and 71 regular education students participated in the field test. Both groups made substantially significant progress in learning to tell time.

Teaching Mathematics

The Mastering Fractions program, produced by Systems Impact, is a Level I videodisc program consisting of 35 lessons. This program is designed for group instruction, with videodisc audio and video instructional segments presented on a color TV in front of the class. Presentations are controlled by the teacher with a hand-held remote-control keypad. The teacher circulates among the students to check their work and provides individual assistance. The program begins with general instructions for students from the videodisc. These instructions, presented both orally and visually, describe how lessons will proceed and what is expected of students. Students watch the screen and listen for explanations, directions, and questions. When a question is asked, the students respond orally. When the program instructs them to work problems in their work-

book or on lined paper, they are told that the teacher will check their written work and help them correct any errors. Graphic prompts are provided for both teachers and students throughout the programs.

A new skill or concept is introduced only when most of the class has mastered the current one. Every skill, once mastered, is reviewed in every other lesson thereafter. Conceptual understanding and problem-solving strategies as well as computational skills are stressed throughout the program. The program presents numerous examples of each concept and capitalizes upon the capabilities of the videodisc to emphasize critical aspects of each concept. For example, important words and numbers change colors, flash on and off, move, or are shown in various pictorial representations that are synchronized with the audio explanation.

Field Test 1

In the fall of 1987, the Mastering Fractions program was installed in seven classrooms in northern Utah (Thorkildsen, 1989). These seven classrooms served as the treatment group, and five additional classes served as a control group. Control group teachers continued with their regular math program but did not teach fractions. Control group teachers were given the opportunity to use the program following the treatment group teachers. Students in each of the 12 classrooms were classified as high achievers, low achievers, or at-risk. High and low achievement was based on scores on a standardized math test. At-risk students were in the low achievement group and were also receiving special education or Chapter 1 services.

The at-risk students normally received math instruction in pullout programs—resource or Chapter 1. During the time the Mastering Fractions program was in use, the at-risk students remained in the regular classroom. The special education teacher was not involved in the regular classroom instruction but provided additional help for the at-risk students using the videodisc program.

Figure 5.1 shows pre- and posttest mean scores for each group (treatment and control)

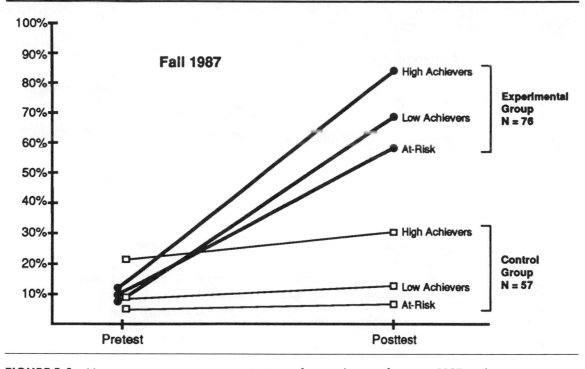

FIGURE 5.1   Mean percentage score on a criterion-referenced test on fractions, 1987 study

and for high-achievement, low-achievement, and at-risk students within each group. Test scores are from a criterion-referenced test in fractions. Posttesting occurred approximately 9 weeks after the pretest.

In 1988, a replication was conducted in 17 classrooms in Cody, Wyoming; Ogden, Utah; and Las Cruces, New Mexico (Lowry & Thorkildsen, 1990). Cody was selected because it is remote and rural; Ogden and Las Cruces were selected because they have a high percentage of minority students (43% Hispanic). Figure 5.2 shows the pre- and posttest mean scores for the 1988 study.

As can be seen from the data in both figures, students from the three achievement classifications increased at approximately the same rate. As could be expected, the control group students showed no increase between the pre- and posttests.

The at-risk students did exceptionally well, considering fractions is a very difficult area and considering the special education teacher was only minimally involved. Thorkildsen and

Lowry (1990) hypothesized that the at-risk students would do even better if the special education teacher teamed with the regular teacher while the videodisc program is being used. Also, they hypothesized that using peer tutors in heterogeneous, cooperative, learning groups would greatly enhance the videodisc instruction.

Teaching Sign Language

Let Your Fingers Do the Talking is a Level II videodisc program developed at the Alberta Vocational Center (Katz, 1984). The videodisc program teaches communication skills to persons who will be working with students with hearing impairments. The disc contains an introduction to the manual alphabet used by the deaf, and includes hand positions, finger spelling, numbers, groups of words, and word signs combined into phrases.

Three Level II computer programs located on the videodisc guide the student through

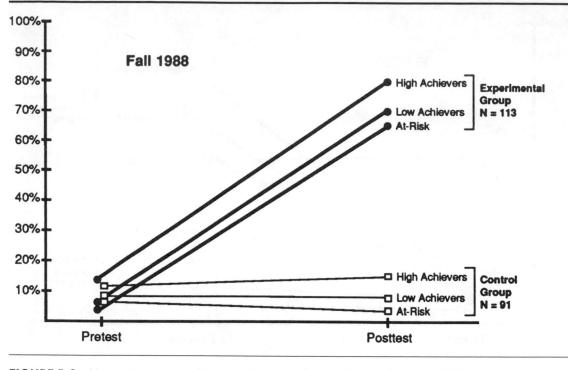

FIGURE 5.2 Mean percentage score on a criterion-referenced test on fractions, 1988 study

the instructional sequences and administer tests at the end of each sequence. Optionally, the student can discontinue control by the internal computer and branch to various places on the videodisc, using the hand-control unit. Material can be reviewed or tests taken at will by the student.

Students in a preliminary field test improved both their receptive and expressive sign language skills, and their attitude toward the system was very positive. They reported that examples on the videodisc were far superior to examples contained in sign language manuals.

The videodisc is fairly complete in its content, which makes it an exceptionally good source of instructional materials for developers who want to create their own Level 3 systems to teach sign language.

Social Skills

Presenting realistic examples and models is a major problem in developing social skills train-

ing programs. A verbal description of a complex social behavior is difficult to write and usually not very compelling; however, actual social situations can be depicted using a videodisc. Screens can be quickly selected and displayed based on the exceptional student's response, presenting the social consequence of the student's decision. The following describes two videodisc applications that have used this decision/consequence strategy to teach various types of social skills.

Social Problem Solving

Think It Through (Nugent & Stone, 1981) is a Level III videodisc-based program developed by staff of the Media Development Project for the Hearing Impaired (MDPHI). This program helps individuals with hearing impairments develop independent thinking skills. Students are presented with problematic situations by the videodisc, and must define the problem and choose a solution. For example, one situation involves a young deaf girl who takes a bus alone for the first time to visit a friend. The girl pays little attention to her mother's directions and gets off the bus at the wrong stop. At this point, the student viewing the situation defines the problem and chooses a solution. The consequence of the student's choice is displayed and evaluated.

A TRS-80 computer is used to control a Pioneer 7820-1 videodisc player. An interface is used to allow computer-generated print to be overlaid on the videodisc image. Questions and comments are presented through the overlaid print. The program prompts student involvement and positive responses to problematic situations. Nugent and Stone's field-testing data indicated that students reacted positively to the instruction and found it fun. Examination of the students' responses reveals that the learners used decision-making strategies. Generalizations to other problem-solving situations were not reported.

Cooperative Interaction

The Interactive Videodisc Social Skills (IVSS) program (Thorkildsen, Fodor-Davis, & Morgan, 1989) combined both videodisc material and written material and taught cooperative interaction skills to fourth-, fifth-, and sixth-grade children with behavioral disorders.

The IVSS program teaches children appropriate phrasing, intonation, and body language in social interactions such as getting involved and being positive. The videodisc presents (a) examples of appropriate and inappropriate social behaviors; (b) models to imitate in role-playing activities; and (c) decision and consequence sequences that depict the social consequences resulting from students' solutions to social problems. A daily lesson guide for the teacher accompanies each videodisc presentation. The program also includes a behavior management system that is used during and after the videodisc and role-playing phase.

A study conducted in a northern Utah school district in 1984 investigated the effectiveness of the IVSS program with main-streamed mildly handicapped children. Six elementary school resource rooms, each containing five mildly handicapped students,

were randomly assigned either to participate in the program (experimental group) or to continue their regular resource room programs (control group). Based on sociometric testing, the students were classified as neglected, accepted, or rejected. Data on the students' social behaviors, acceptance by nonhandicapped peers, self-esteem, and treatment implementation were collected over a 4-month period.

Students who used the IVSS program (experimental group) scored significantly higher on a posttraining measure of peer acceptance than did control group students. The experimental and control group students did not differ on the postmeasure of self-esteem. Experimental group students, irrespective of their classification, were rated significantly higher than control group students on a post-checklist of social skills covered in the program. This checklist was completed by each student's resource room teacher.

From this study, it was concluded that the experimental group students learned the social skills taught by the program. Also, the mildly handicapped students' positive behaviors increased and peer acceptance by their nonexceptional classmates significantly improved.

Personnel Preparation

With increased use of microprocessors and videodiscs in special education classrooms, educators are obliged to be technology literate. Many of the problems now being faced in the effective implementation of communications and computer technology are not due to hardware but to the attitudes and lack of knowledge of participating personnel. Many elementary school children, raised with personal computers at home and in the classroom, are considerably more knowledgeable and have less fear of computer and communication technologies than many practicing teacher educators. The new regular or special education professional faces a world of exploding technologies and must be prepared to interact with and understand their strengths and limitations. Clearly responsibility lies with the teacher education community to ensure that the beginning professional is literate in these areas. What better way to teach technological literacy than through the use of that technology.

Literacy Programs

Videodisc-based computer literacy products are beginning to appear on the market. A computer literacy course completely contained on a videodisc is available from JAM Corporation (300 Main Street, East Rochester, NY 14445) or Digital Controls (5555 Oakbrook Parkway, Suite 200, Norcross, GA 30073). The great advantage of this program is that it can be used individually or by a group. Videodisc players are not readily available for rent, but teachers can conveniently complete a computer literacy course in their own homes when they are provided a videodisc system.

Teacher-training Programs

Videodisc-based teacher-training programs are currently being developed and tested at Utah State University. For example, the IVSS program described earlier contains a teacher-training component (Thorkildsen, 1984). This component is contained primarily on the videodisc but is also included in the teacher-training and reference manuals.

The teacher-training manual is used interactively with the videodisc. The videodisc presents demonstrations and examples of correct use of the social skills training program and gives reading assignments in the manual. The manual also contains explanations of teaching procedures, definitions of terms and rules, suggestions for feedback procedures and reinforcers, and self-check quizzes at the end of each training section. The teacher reference manual contains alphabetically ordered items of information about the entire program and is used during the teacher-training phase and other phases of the IVSS program.

In a field test involving three teachers, training required approximately 3 hours for each teacher. The videodisc system was delivered to the teachers' homes, where they worked individually with the system and manuals. This training did not require assistance from the project staff.

Most social skills training programs require extensive teacher training. One program reviewed required 30 hours of classroom training. Comparatively, the IVSS program required only 3 hours. The developers attribute this efficiency to use of the videodisc and interaction of the videodisc with printed materials.

Another Level III program, developed by Rule, Salzberg, and Schulze (1989) at Utah State University, teaches preservice special educators the interaction skills necessary to provide varied effective instruction, including tutorial instruction, small-group instruction, and individualized instruction. The project focuses on interactive-teaching skills fundamental to instruction that cannot be learned exclusively by didactic classroom instruction or in the field (i.e., in a practicum or in student teaching) due to practical and ethical limitations. It is suggested that thorough training of these skill repertoires across varying instructional formats will improve the general quality of instruction for handicapped persons and enhance the opportunity of special education teachers to assume a leadership role with their colleagues. This may well become an imperative with master teacher and team teaching approaches now rapidly evolving in public school systems.

Research Applications

The interface of videodisc and computer technology opens up new avenues for research in teacher education programs. The ability of videodisc programs to repeat instructional settings reliably and consistently, as well as their ability to record students' responses in considerable detail, provides opportunities in research not previously available from researchers with limited resources. The teacher educator will need to be aware of the increased possibilities in this area and be prepared to incorporate such research opportunities into the thesis and dissertation projects of their students.

There can be little doubt that with microprocessor-videodisc combinations, the teacher educator is facing a new generation of technology. Although considerable research must be conducted to determine the most appropriate applications in special education, there are indications that such applications will be extensive. Should the indicators prove valid, we must be prepared to make changes in curriculum and instructional methodology to ensure that special educators are literate in this new technology.

DIGITAL VIDEO FORMATS AND SPECIAL EDUCATION

Digital audio in the form of optical compact audio discs is now the accepted format in the music-recording industry. Digital video is also very promising but more challenging for developers. Presently, however, digital video is entering the commercial market at relatively low prices.

Merging Television and Computer Technologies

Television and personal computer technologies developed independently in terms of market functions and techniques for storing and displaying information. Television developed around broadcasting and related applications and is primarily an analog technology. An analog approach was the least expensive way of achieving the fidelity of video and audio for a market that could easily accommodate modest amounts of "noise" or errors in the transmission of information.

Personal computer technology evolved from the digital world of mainframe computers, emphasizing error-free storage and transmission of numerical data. According to Luther (1989), video technology and personal computer technology are "heading for the altar." The requirement for this marriage is a common information storage technology; therefore digital storage, because of its superior versatility, has been selected over analog.

Digital Video

Uncompressed digital signals require a great deal of storage (as much as 24 megabytes per second of quality motion video). Consequently, compression and decompression methods are necessary for practical computer applications. In the process of preparing computers to store and retrieve video and audio information, a range of video compression and decompression techniques have been developed. The ability to process digital video signals with an off-the-shelf computer allows the addition of text and graphics of any size and color to any location on the television screen.

Video compression-decompression technology has value in other areas that may eventually exceed its importance in integrating television and computer technologies. If we learn to compress and decompress a television signal in real time with hardware costing hundreds rather than thousands of dollars, then we will have the ability to move broadcast video to the telephone network.

The message is clear: Both storage and delivery methods of television delivery are changing dramatically, and analog approaches are being deemphasized as television, personal computer, and telecommunications merge.

There is nothing futuristic or ambiguous about this trend. The practical union of television and personal computers has been achieved in such technologies as CDI (compact disc interactive) and DVI (digital video interactive). With DVI, personal computers can now store 72 minutes of full-screen, full-motion, quality video and audio on a single 5-inch, CD-ROM disc. This video and audio can be decompressed in real time, integrated with computer text and graphics, and displayed interlaced on the computer color monitor. DVI technology is being jointly developed and marketed by IBM, Intel, and Microsoft.

Digital Video and Special Education

Regarding persons with hearing impairments who are heavily dependent on closed-captioned video, there are both threats and promises in these trends away from the analog-based systems presently used with captioned video. The development of low-cost, multimedia technologies promises educational opportunities for all persons with hearing impairments (Luetke-Stahlman, 1988; Beykirch et al., 1989; Thorkildsen, 1985). For instance, the merging of video and computer technologies provides not only full-motion video but easily accessible audio (Luther, 1989). However, while special educators who deal with nonreaders look forward with some excitement to low-cost computers that talk, persons with hearing impairments may find only another barrier to participation in society. Boatner (1981) documented the consternation generated in the deaf community by the sudden demise of silent films in the late 1920s. He noted, "The advent of sound films in 1927 suddenly deprived the deaf of one of their chief sources of information and entertainment" (p. 520). Given (a) the marketing power of companies such as IBM, Intel, and Microsoft and (b) their clearly demonstrated focus on the promotion of technologies such as DVI in the education and training markets, it is imperative that we monitor these developing mainstream technologies and be alert to every opportunity for making adaptions to meet the needs of persons with hearing impairments (Boothroyd, 1990). An opportunity not to be ignored is the use of DVI to produce low-cost, customized captioning to accommodate individual differences.

Effective instructional use of captioning must be sensitive to even modest individual differences in reading levels and vision. Thorn and Thorn (1989) reported, "If a person has even a small amount of visual loss (20/25), the caption letters become too small for maximum reading performance" (p. 36). Johnson and Whitehead (1989), in an extensive review of the research literature, concluded:

> Because hearing impaired persons are at a higher risk for visual and ocular anomalies which are potentially debilitating, and the anomalies may be subtle and not easily detected, it is essential that programs be initiated which assess and provide a continuity of vision related services for these persons from infancy through adulthood. (p. 241)

Braverman (1981) noted that individual differences in reading ability are "the most potent variable" in determining the effective use of captioning. Given that most captioning tries for a verbatim transcript, unadapted captions may add to the frustration of the user with limited reading skills.

Captioning with DVI will be a relatively simple process because the video and computer signals are merged. Letters and numbers of any size can easily be typed over the video image in any location on the image.

Customized captioning is promising but represents only one opportunity for special educators. The ease of merging audio with computer and video signals opens a multitude of instructional opportunities for nonreaders. With technologies like DVI, instructional developers have an instructional delivery medium that is extremely nonconstraining. Developers can direct their full attention to instructional design with little concern about the limitations of a delivery medium.

ARTIFICIAL INTELLIGENCE AND VIDEODISC TECHNOLOGIES

We have seen the integration of CAI and videodisc technology. As artificial intelligence (AI) applications in special education become more extensive, we will see the integration of artificial intelligence and videodisc technologies.

The Expert System

Expert systems technology is a field within artificial intelligence concerned with the use of the computer to capture and disseminate human expertise. Expert systems have been effective in medicine, geology, chemistry, engineering, and business. Recently, educators have begun to show an interest in expert systems.

An expert system typically engages the user in a dialogue. This dialogue in many ways parallels the conversation a person might have with a consultant who has expertise in a specific area. The system interrogates the user (i.e., asks questions) to pinpoint the problem and to secure the necessary information the expert system needs to suggest a solution. The expert system employs facts supplied by the user and rule-based procedures to solve the problem (Stefik et al., 1983).

Generally the procedures used by expert systems have been developed after examination of examples of problem solving. These examples, generated by one expert or a group of experts, are studied to identify the underlying rules experts use in problem solving or to verify these rules. These underlying rules form the problem-solving processes used by the expert system. It is not unusual for an expert system to use several hundred rules.

Potential Applications in Special Education

Hayes-Roth, Waterman, and Lenat (1983) have documented the generic categories of knowledge engineering. Their listing places an emphasis on prediction, interpretation, diagnosis, remediation, planning, monitoring, and instructional tasks. A review of this listing indicates that a potential exists to match knowledge engineering approaches with problem areas in special education. The categories of diagnosis, planning, and instruction are highly related to important special education activities.

In special education, potential problems might include (a) the development of an instructional prescription based on assessment information, (b) the classification of a child into one of the special education categories (e.g., learning disabled) based on assessment information, and (c) the selection of an appropriate behavior management strategy based on classroom observational data. Most situations where consultant help has value represent potential areas for the development of expert systems in special education.

Expert systems used for direct instruction are sometimes called intelligent computer-assisted instruction (ICAI) or intelligent tutoring systems (ITSs).

The Benefits of Expert Systems

Expert systems product development efforts can have at least three beneficial effects on the field of special education. First, an expert system teamed with a powerful small computer can make low-cost computer consultant services available to classroom teachers. A second benefit is the training value of the intelligent knowledge base generated by the development of the expert system. This knowledge base is a model of reality and can be used in the training of human experts. This training value can reduce the threats presented to special education students by beginning instructors and diagnosticians.

Hofmeister (1984b) developed an expert system, Class.LD, to provide a second opinion regarding the accuracy of the classification "learning disabled." To use the system, the user brings the psychological and educational data used by the assessment team to the computer and responds to a series of questions posed by the computer. The system, which operates on a high-powered personal computer, is under study for its value as a consultant and as a clinical training resource, which graduate students can use to test their diagnostic and classification skills. The system uses Utah and federal regulations related to Public Law 94–142 in its problem-solving processes. The expert knowledge base was built on the opinions of several nationally recognized authorities in learning disabilities.

A third benefit of AI product development is more subtle but just as important. In order to develop an expert system, knowledge engineers must organize and analyze the existing knowledge within a subject area. Expert systems development could, in this way, accelerate the clarification and expansion of knowledge in special education and have research implications of considerable value. At least two well-validated AI programs, Debuggy (Brown & Burton, 1978) and the Computer Guided Diagnosis of Learning Disabilities Prototype (Colburn, 1982; Colburn & McLeod, 1983) have significant implications for special education.

In Debuggy, the knowledge generation aspect is significant. The developers of Debuggy added considerable knowledge about student errors in arithmetic. With Debuggy, the user is trained to identify error patterns in students' attempts at arithmetic problems.

Colburn (1982) developed a prototype expert system that provides the user with a diagnostic report that can be used in the development of a remedial program. The performance of this prototype program suggested that using an expert system for special education diagnosis was clearly feasible. After comparing computer-guided diagnoses with those of humans on 22 files, Colburn and McLeod (1983) noted:

> In general, the results of the evaluation were encouraging; the expert system's diagnoses were accurate. Furthermore, because of the system's speed at analyzing error patterns, its diagnostic reports included more information than those of the human diagnosticians. This was particularly noticeable with regards to the analysis of phonics skills. (p. 37)

Videodisc and Expert Systems

Linking expert systems and videodisc technology presents a variety of possibilities. For example, student response data (e.g., number of correct answers) from an instructional interactive videodisc program could be analyzed with the help of expert systems procedures to determine the most appropriate instructional sequence; an expert system program could select an appropriate behavior management strategy for behavior-disordered students, which would then be exemplified by a supporting videodisc sequence; and when an expert system consultation recommended a solution, the videodisc could provide a specific description and demonstration of the selected solution.

SUMMARY

Special educators have been among the first to assess the feasibility of adapting interactive videodisc technology to meet the needs of exceptional individuals. They have conducted successful demonstrations in a wide range of areas, including language arts, math, and social skills. This technology has also proven effective in personnel preparation, assessment, and prescription.

As regular and special educators and other professionals respond to the need for quality instruction in varied educational settings, they will require vehicles capable of consistently delivering quality instruction in individual, small-group, and large-group settings. Interactive videodisc technology provides a promising vehicle. As special educators explore the application of new technologies to instructional problems, interactive videodisc technology is beginning to emerge as a promising tool for a range of problems. There can be little doubt that a technology that emulates a wide range of instructional media and complements and enhances the functions of computers must be given serious consideration by special educators.

The instructional potential of interactive videodisc technology seems limitless. There is, however, a great and continuing need for research to improve that technology. At this stage of development there is little need to compare videodisc technology to traditional methods of instruction; our energies should be spent on the refinement of procedures, not on the conduct of comparisons that are not justified in terms of available classroom resources. Such comparisons may also condemn a developing procedure to obscurity as a result of premature comparison.

REFERENCES

Bangert, L., Kulik, J. A., & Kulik, C. C. (1983). Individualized systems of instruction in secondary schools. *Review of Educational Research, 53*(2), 143–158.

Beykirch, H. L., Holcomb, T. A., & Harrington, J. F. (1989, March). Isolated sign vocabulary acquisition by hearing adults: CAI vs. videotaped presentation. *American Annals of the Deaf,* pp. 31–34.

Billings, D. M., & Cobb, K. (1992). Effects of learning style preferences, attitude, and GPA on learner achievement using computer-assisted interactive videodisc instruction. *Journal of Computer-Based Instruction, 19*(1), 12–16.

Boatner, E. B. (1981, August). Captioned films for the deaf. *American Annals of the Deaf,* pp. 520–522.

Boothroyd, A. (1990). Impact of technology on the management of deafness. *Volta Review, 92*(4), 74–82.

Braverman, B. (1981, December). Television captioning strategies: A systematic research and development approach. *American Annals of the Deaf,* pp. 1031–1036.

Brawley, R. J., & Peterson, B. A. (1983). Interactive videodisc: An innovative instructional system. *American Annals of the Deaf, 128,* 685–700.

Brown, J. S., & Burton, R. R. (1978). Diagnostic models for procedural bugs in mathematical skills. *Cognitive Science, 2,* 155–192.

Colburn, M. J. (1982). *Computer-guided diagrams of learning disabilities: A prototype.* Master's thesis, University of Saskatchewan. (ERIC Document Reproduction Service No. ED 222 032)

Colburn, M. J., & McLeod, J. (1983). Computer-guided educational diagnosis: A prototype expert system. *Journal of Special Education Technology, 6,* 30–39.

Daynes, R. (1984). Who, what, where, why, and how much of videodisc technology. In R. Daynes & B. Butler (Eds.), *The Videodisc Book* (pp. 7–21). New York: John Wiley & Sons.

Eastmond, D. V. (1984). Math assessment videodisc. *Computing Teacher, 12*(3), 57–59.

Hayes-Roth, F., Waterman, D. A., & Lenat, D. B. (1983). *Building expert systems.* Reading, MA: Addison-Wesley.

Hofmeister, A. M. (1976). *Educating the mildly handicapped child.* Logan, UT: Utah State University, Center for Persons with Disabilities.

Hofmeister, A. M. (1984a). *Development of a microcomputer/videodisc aided math instructional management system for mildly handicapped children.* (Tech. Rep. No. G008101536). Logan, UT: Utah State University, Center for Persons with Disabilities.

Hofmeister, A. M. (1984b). *CLASS.LD* [Computer program]. Logan, UT: Utah State University, Center for Persons with Disabilities.

Hofmeister, A. M., Atkinson, C., & Hofmeister, J. (1975). *Programmed Time Telling.* Eugene, OR: E-B Press.

Hofmeister, A. M., & Friedman, S. (1984). Matching technology to content and learners: A case study. *Exceptional Children, 52*(23), 26–31.

Johnson, D. D., & Whitehead, R. (1989, July). Effect of maternal rubella on hearing and vision: A twenty year post-epidemic study. *American Annals of the Deaf,* pp. 232–241.

Katz, L. (1984, October). Deaf awareness: Let your fingers do the talking. *Video Computing,* pp. 5, 12.

Leutke-Stahlman, B. (1988, July). Documenting syntactically and semantically incomplete bimodal input to hearing-impaired subjects. *American Annals of the Deaf,* pp. 230–234.

Lowry, W., & Thorkildsen, R. (1990). *The effects of a videodisc-based direct instruction program in fractions on math achievement and self concept.* Paper presented at the American Educational Research Association, Boston, MA.

Luther, A. C. (1989). *Digital video in the PC environment.* New York: McGraw-Hill.

Nugent, G., & Stone, C. (1981). Think it through: An interactive videodisc for the hearing impaired. *Proceedings of the Johns Hopkins First National Search for Applications of Personal Computing to Aid the Handicapped* (pp. 49–51). Los Angeles, CA: IIEE Computer Society Press.

Pitsch, B., & Murphy, V. (1992). Using one computer for whole-class instruction. *The Computing Teacher, 19*(6), 19–21.

Prinz, P. M., & Nelson, K. E. (1984). *A child-computer-teacher interactive method for teaching reading to young deaf children* (Working Papers, Vols. 1 & 2). Washington, DC: International Symposium on Cognition, Education, and Deafness. (ERIC Document Reproduction Service No. ED 247–720)

Prinz, P. M., & Nelson, K. E. (1985, April). *Alpha interactive microcomputer system for teaching reading, writing, and communication skills to hearing impaired students.* Paper presented at the meeting of the National Conference on Microcomputers in the Education of the Hearing Impaired, Washington, DC.

Rule, S., Salzberg, C. L., & Schulze, K. (1989). The role of videodiscs in special education methods courses. *Journal of Special Education Technology, 10*(2), 80–85.

Stefik, M., Aikins, J., Balzer, R., Benoit, J., Birnbaum, L., Hayes-Roth, F., & Sacerdoti, E. (1983). The architecture of expert systems. In F. Hayes-Roth, D. A. Waterman, & D. B. Lenat (Eds.), *Building expert systems* (pp. 89–126). Reading, MA: Addison-Wesley.

Thorkildsen, R. (1982). *Interactive videodisc for special education technology* (Tech. Rep. No. G007904510). Logan, UT: Utah State University, Center for Persons with Disabilities.

Thorkildsen, R. (1984). *Interactive videodisc social skills program: Development and field testing of a microcomputer/videodisc based social skills curriculum for the severely emotionally disturbed child* (Tech. Rep. No. G00801537). Logan, UT: Utah

State University, Center for Persons with Disabilities.

Thorkildsen, R. (1985). Using an interactive videodisc program to teach social skills to handicapped children. *American Annals of the Deaf, 130*(5).

Thorkildsen, R. (1989). *Research on videodisc-based math instruction in mainstreamed classrooms.* Paper presented at the Association for Educational Communications Technology Conference, Dallas, TX.

Thorkildsen, R., & Findlay, P. (1991). *A Level I/Level III videodisc program on time telling: Production and field test results.* Paper presented at the American Educational Communications and Technology Conference, Orlando, FL.

Thorkildsen, R., Fodor-Davis, J., & Morgan, D. (1989). Evaluation of a videodisc training program. *Journal of Special Education Technology, 10*(2), 86–97.

Thorkildsen, R., & Friedman, S. G. (1986). Beginning reading with the interactive videodisc: A test of instructional design. *Learning Disabilities Quarterly, 9*(2), 111–117.

Thorkildsen R., & Reid, R. (1989). An investigation of the reinforcing effects of feedback in computer assisted instruction. *Journal of Special Education Technology, 9*(3), 125–135.

Thorn, B. S., & Thorn, F. (1989, March). Television and vision: Reading captions when vision is blurred. *American Annals of the Deaf,* pp. 35–38.

Walker, R., & Butler, L. (1984). Front-end systems analysis and media selection. In R. Daynes & B. Butler (Eds.), *The videodisc book* (pp. 27–33). New York: John Wiley & Sons.

Woodward, J., & Gerstern, J. (1992). Innovative technology for secondary students with learning disabilities. *Exceptional Children, 58* (5), 407–412.

Suggested Activities

Paper and Pencil

Find an article published in a recent journal issue that describes the use of interactive videodisc with exceptional individuals. What level system is used in the article? What are the videodisc system characteristics and exceptional individual attributes that interact? What could have been done to improve the system's instructional value?

Observation

Visit a special education or other setting that uses interactive videodisc technology. What hardware and software were used? Describe the procedures that were employed during the lesson. What was not done that could have been undertaken to improve the use of interactive videodisc? Interview the person in charge of the setting, and determine how the technology is used differently for individual and group activities.

Practicum

The National Kid Disc is typically available for rent. This videodisc is a Level I application and can be used interactively with the remote control unit. There is a section about sign language on the disc that provides the necessary audio and video sequences for an instructional unit. For a Level I application, supplementary materials will be required. Run National Kid Disc and design these supplementary materials to accompany the Level I application. Also, the sign language section on National Kid Disc provides excellent audio and video sequences to teach sign language for a Level III application. Level III applications require a microcomputer and an interface device to connect the microcomputer to a videodisc player. Information on developing Level III applications is available in the Level III applications manual (see "Resources" section below). Write a computer program to control a presentation of the sign language material.

Resources

Organizations

Technology and Media Division. This organization of professionals and other persons is interested in advancing technology concepts and applications with exceptional persons. Write to the Council for Exceptional Children, 1920 Association Drive, Reston, VA 22091.

KUON Videodisc Design/Production Group. This university-based unit is involved in videodisc design and production. Write to KUON-TV,

P.O. Box 83111, University of Nebraska, Lincoln, NE 68501.

Journals

Videodisc Monitor. This publication advances a number of issues related to videodisc technology. Write to Future Systems, P.O. Box 26, Falls Church, VA 22046.

Videodisc News. This publication publishes information on videodisc technology. Write to Videodisc Services, Box 6302, Arlington, VA 22205.

Books

Daynes, R., & Butler, B. (Eds.) (1984). *The videodisc book: A guide and directory.* New York: John Wiley & Sons.

Iuppa, N. (1984). *A practical guide to interactive video design.* White Plains, NY: Knowledge Industry Publications.

The Videodisc Compendium. A catalog of videodiscs for education and training—1,200 titles. Write to Emerging Technology Consultants, Distribution Center, P.O. Box 12444, St. Paul, MN 55112.

Categorical Applications

This section describes general and specific computer applications with individuals who have mild disabilities, speech and language disorders, severe and physical handicaps, and sensory impairments. It also describes general and specific computer applications with gifted/talented individuals.

Technology facilitates teaching/learning outcomes. *(Photograph courtesy of Apple Computers, Inc.)*

CHAPTER

Computers and Individuals with Mild Disabilities

Cynthia M. Okolo
University of Delaware ∎

School districts typically assign a disability label to students who receive special educational and related services. Although this practice facilitates the aggregation of state and national child count data, the differential labels assigned to students with mild disabilities have questionable validity. In fact, students with learning disabilities, mild mental retardation, and mild emotional disturbance or behavioral disorders are more alike than they are different. In this chapter, those students who receive these diagnoses will be referred to as "students with mild disabilities." The use of a noncategorical label for this population has been supported by empirical evidence regarding similarities in their characteristics and the instructional interventions they typically receive (e.g., Heller, Holtzman, & Messick, 1982; Lilly, 1977).

INDIVIDUALS WITH MILD DISABILITIES

Approximately 70% of the students who receive special education services have a mild disability (Office of Special Education Programs, 1990). Regardless of their primary label, students with mild disabilities are usually performing below grade level in core academic subjects such as reading, written expression, and mathematics (Deshler, Schumaker, Alley, Warner, & Clark, 1982; Hallahan & Kauffman, 1986) and must learn to compensate for cognitive deficits such as poor memory or short attention span (Hallahan, Kauffman, & Lloyd, 1985; Krupski, 1981). Furthermore, students with mild disabilities are often inefficient learners, and without explicit instruction from teachers or therapists they appear unaware of strategies, such as rehearsal or self-monitoring, that can offset their cognitive deficits (Baumeister & Brooks, 1981; Wallace & Kauffman, 1986). Also, without carefully sequenced and structured instructional practices, they experience substantial difficulty generalizing information (Belmont, Butterfield, & Ferretti, 1982; Kramer, Nagle, & Engle, 1980).

Students with mild disabilities often struggle to develop automaticity in basic-skill areas such as decoding and math facts. Lack of basic-skill mastery has a deleterious effect on their use of higher-order skills such as reading

111

comprehension and math problem solving (Goldman & Pellegrino, 1987; Torgesen, 1984). Furthermore, these exceptional individuals often lack the vocabulary and experiential knowledge necessary for success in content-area subjects such as science and social studies (Cognition and Technology Group, 1990). Over their school careers, poor reading skills, inefficient learning strategies, and decreased motivation to pursue academic tasks act to widen the gap between the background knowledge of students with mild disabilities and their nondisabled peers.

In addition to cognitive and academic deficits, students with mild disabilities also experience social and motivational difficulties that further interfere with their success at school. Research (e.g., Chapman, 1988; Pearl, 1982; Schunk, 1989) has indicated that these exceptional learners lack intrinsic motivation to pursue academic tasks, are easily frustrated, have low self-concept and self-efficacy, and do not believe they are responsible for their successes and failures. Not surprisingly, these exceptional students often lack appropriate social skills and consequently have difficulty forming and maintaining interpersonal relationships (Mercer & Mercer, 1989).

The above discussion focused on the difficulties and deficits of individuals with mild disabilities. However, these are not unalterable traits or insurmountable obstacles, and they should be viewed by teachers and therapists as challenges that can be at least partially overcome through a combination of effective instructional methods and compensatory tools. Indeed, intervention studies have provided considerable reason for optimism. Instructional techniques have been developed to help students automatize basic skills (e.g., Hasselbring, Goin, & Bransford, 1987) and acquire proficiency in higher-order skills (Graham & Harris, 1988; Palinscar & Brown, 1984). Effective procedures have been developed to help these exceptional students transfer their knowledge to new problems and settings and to self-regulate their learning (Cognition and Technology Group, 1990; Ellis, Lenz, & Sabornie, 1987). Also, researchers have demonstrated that students' motivation can be improved through interventions such as attribution re-

training (Försterling, 1985; Pearl, 1985) and goal setting (Schunk, 1985), and that social skills instruction and cooperative learning arrangements are effective for promoting more harmonious and enduring relationships between students with disabilities and their peers (Johnson & Johnson, 1986).

Computers and other electronic technologies are a powerful addition for professionals working with individuals with mild disabilities. Not only can they be used to deliver many of the effective practices described above but they also have the potential to transform the manner in which teachers teach. Computer software can provide basic-skill practice and facilitate complex tasks such as written expression and information management. Technological tools such as electronic organizers, spelling checkers, and thesauri can aid students with memory deficits, poor spelling skills, or weak vocabulary knowledge. Videodiscs and multimedia can provide professionals and students with feasible means for representing and manipulating realities that exist outside the class- or therapy room, and electronic networks can expand the types of authentic and meaningful learning activities in which students can engage. In many instances, technology-based learning activities improve students' motivation and self-efficacy (e.g., Lepper, 1985; Malouf, 1987–1988).

It is hoped that this introduction supports the position that computers and other electronic technologies offer many advantages for professionals trying to meet the needs of students with mild disabilities. Highlights of the ways in which technology can compensate for or help overcome students' deficits and difficulties are delineated in Table 6.1. Much of the remainder of this chapter is devoted to a more detailed discussion of these applications.

A BRIEF REVIEW OF THE LITERATURE

This section provides a review of the literature related to (a) how computers and other electronic technologies are being used with stu-

TABLE 6.1
Characteristics of individuals with mild disabilities and technology-based applications

Student Characteristic	Technologies and Applications
Deficits in basic academic subjects and skills	Drill-and-practice software, integrated learning systems, hypermedia
Need for repeated practice and review	Drill-and-practice software, integrated learning systems, teacher tool software, hypermedia
Memory deficits	Personal productivity tools
Short attention span	Gamelike software activities, simulations, instruction supported or delivered by videodiscs
Inefficient learning strategies	Problem-solving software, personal productivity tools
Lack of background knowledge	Content-area software, videodisc macrocontexts, hypermedia
Lack of higher-order skills	Writing tools, simulation and problem-solving software, instruction supported and delivered by videodiscs, content-area software, electronic networks, personal productivity tools
Motivational deficits	All technology-based applications

dents who are mildly disabled, (b) the impact of technology on students' academic achievement, and (c) the impact of technology on students' motivation. Research in these areas has burgeoned since the early 1980s, and the following review highlights key findings.

When considering research regarding the impact of technology on students' achievement and motivation, it is critical to keep in mind that "media are mere vehicles that deliver instruction but do not influence student achievement any more than the truck that delivers our groceries causes changes in our nutrition" (Clark, 1983, p. 445). It is not the computer or any other technological device, in and of itself, that produces learning and motivation, but rather it is specific features of technology-based instructional activities and the instructional context that supports them.

Surveys of Technology Use

Based on a national survey of over 1,000 schools, Becker (1990) reported that the number of professionals who use computers for instruction doubled between 1984 and 1985 and between 1988 and 1989. Students who are low achievers or who have mild disabilities are frequent participants in computer drill-and-practice activities (Becker & Sterling, 1987; Cosden, 1988; Mokros & Russell, 1986). Because these students often need repeated practice in order to develop basic-skill automaticity, drill-and-practice activities can serve an important function. However, the predominance of drill-and-practice activities has raised concerns that students with mild disabilities are missing out on opportunities to use technology in more productive and personally rewarding ways (Mokros & Russell, 1986).

Even in regular classrooms, however, technology use for personal productivity is relatively rare. Becker (1990) noted that word processing activities are on the increase, particularly at the secondary school level. However, applications such as spreadsheets, data bases, mathematical graphing programs, publishing programs, and outlining and prewriting programs were used by less than 15% of the schools in Becker's sample.

A recent national survey found that 96% of the public schools had a VCR and 15% had at least one modem, but newer and more expensive technologies remain in short supply. For example, only 4% of the schools surveyed had a CD-ROM drive, 3% had a laser disc player, and 1% used integrated learning systems ("High-Tech," 1990).

Technology and Student Achievement

Given the patterns described above, it is understandable that much of the existing research regarding the effectiveness of technology for students with mild disabilities has examined the impact of drill-and-practice software. In general, this body of research has shown that when computer-assisted instruction (CAI) incorporates principles of effective instruction and is appropriate for an individual's instructional needs, it can facilitate the mastery of basic skills including math computation (Okolo, in press a), spelling, decoding, word identification, and vocabulary (e.g., Hasselbring, 1984; Hasselbring et al., 1987; Jones, Torgesen, & Sexton, 1987; Majsterek & Wilson, 1989; Roth & Beck, 1987; Saracho, 1982; Swan, Guerrero, Mitrani, & Schoener, 1990).

Technology-based instruction also can enhance students' higher-order skills. Computer-assisted and interactive-videodisc instruction have improved students' achievement in areas as diverse as fractions, ratios, and percents; reading comprehension; mathematical and health problem solving; reasoning and study skills; social studies; and community living (Browning, White, Nave, & Barkin, 1986; Horton, Lovitt, Givens, & Nelson, 1989; Kelly, Carnine, Gersten, & Grossen, 1986; Woodward et al., 1986). It must be noted, however, that systems that incorporate sound instructional principles and that model explicit procedural strategies have proven the most effective (Woodward & Carnine, 1988). Poorly designed systems, regardless of the media through which they are presented, are unlikely to improve students with mild disabilities' achievement. The design and implementation of effective systems are described in Chapter 13.

As described above, word processing is a more frequent activity in today's class- and therapy rooms. Although students with mild disabilities and their nonexceptional peers may make more revisions when provided with word processing capabilities, these tend to be surface-level changes in spelling, punctuation, and text length (Cochran-Smith, 1991; Daiute, 1986; MacArthur, 1988). However, students' written-expression skills often improve when word processing is incorporated into a systematic program of written-expression instruction (Cochran-Smith, 1991). In studies where word processing has had a facilitative effect on students' written products, low achievers appear to make the greatest gains (Bangert-Drowns, 1989). Word processing can help students shift from a preoccupation with the mechanics of writing toward an interest in writing as a communicative act (Kahn, 1988). Numerous studies have found that students have positive attitudes toward writing with word processors, believe that their writing improves, are more relaxed about writing with word processors, and are proud of their finished compositions (Cochran-Smith, 1991).

Technology and Student Motivation

Students with mild disabilities have expressed positive attitudes toward computers in a number of studies (e.g., Gardner & Bates, in press; Okolo & Owen, 1991). Teachers have reported that students are eager to participate in computer activities and that the promise of time at the computer is an effective incentive for promoting improved instructional-related performance and behavior (Cosden, 1988; MacArthur et al., 1985; Okolo, Rieth, & Bahr, 1989). Observational studies have shown that students experience high levels of time on-task when they participate in computer-based activities (Cosden & Abernathy, 1990; MacArthur, Haynes, & Malouf, 1986; Rieth, Bahr, Okolo, Polsgrove, & Eckert, 1988) and that important motivational outcomes may be achieved through computer use. Metaanalyses of studies investigating the impact of CAI (e.g., Kulik, Bangert, & Williams, 1983; Kulik, Kulik, & Bangert-Drowns, 1985) have shown that students who use it tend to develop more positive attitudes toward course material and learning in general. Other motivational outcomes associated with instructional technology have included enhanced intrinsic motivation (Lepper & Malone, 1987; Malouf, 1987–1988; Rieber, 1990), more adaptive attributions for successes and failures (Okolo, in press b; Swan et al., 1990), and increased self-efficacy (Graham & Harris, 1989).

Limitations of Existing Research

Much of the research summarized above has taken place in laboratories or under controlled experimental conditions. Furthermore, many studies have been of short duration, spanning only a few weeks or months. Although existing research has provided important demonstrations of technology's potential, they are only the first step in ensuring that technology has a positive impact on teaching and learning as it occurs on a day-to-day basis. Teachers and therapists working with students with mild disabilities rarely enjoy the level of support that is built into most research and demonstration projects. Although technology has been touted as a time-saver, professionals have reported that it is extremely challenging and time-consuming to incorporate new technologies into the instructional setting (Wiske et al., 1988). Criticisms of the "narrow" way in which professionals use technology with exceptional students often ignore the limitations encountered by even the most highly motivated and well-intentioned users! Moreover, technology use is always embedded in a complex context of factors (Semmel & Lieber, 1986), and further research is needed to explicate those factors that support or hinder the effective use of technology in "typical" class- and therapy rooms.

GENERAL HARDWARE AND SOFTWARE CONSIDERATIONS

In a perfect world, teachers and therapists working with exceptional individuals would have instructional settings equipped with as many computers and other technologies as needed. In the real world, however, they must share access to limited technological resources. Although we tend to think that a one-computer one-student ratio would be ideal, many of the activities described below can be accomplished as effectively by pairs or small groups of students (Cox & Berger, 1985; Dalton, Hannafin, & Hooper, 1989). Available evidence has suggested that when a computer is the primary source of instructional information or practice, group size should be limited to two or three students per computer (Cox & Berger, 1985). To guarantee equal participation, professionals working with students with mild disabilities may need to enforce rules for equitable access by requiring students to take turns at the keyboard and by discouraging them from interfering with each other's turn (Bahr, 1990; Malouf, Wizer, Pilato, & Grogan, 1990).

When students work in dyads, it may be advantageous to pair a student with mild disabilities with a peer who can model or explain the target skill or behavior. Cooperative goal structures also are a viable way to increase student performance at the computer (Johnson, Johnson, & Stanne, 1986) and encourage task-related student interaction (Bahr, 1989). In order for group activities to be effective, these exceptional students may need guidance in providing explanations that will enable their peers to complete the task (Lieber & Semmel, 1987). They also may require direct teaching and subsequent teacher monitoring of pro-

Computers can be used by small groups of students. *(Photograph by David M. Aultz)*

social and cooperative behaviors (Malouf et al., 1990).

Because technology resources are limited, teachers and therapists also must prioritize the goals and purposes for which computers and other technologies are used. It should be clear from the research discussed above that there is no one best or most effective way to use them. However, research has indicated that if instructional technology is to have optimal impact, it must be used by professionals in a systematic manner as part of their ongoing instructional programs. In other words, instructional technology must be integrated with the curriculum (Macro Systems, 1989; Panyan & Hummel, 1988; Winkler, Shavelson, Stasz, Robyn, & Fiebel, 1985). Thus, special educators and other professionals should give first priority to technology activities that are consistent with their curricular goals and that can support their students' attainment of those goals.

The remainder of this section provides an overview of four broad categories of technology utilization pertinent to professionals working with students with mild disabilities. These general uses include instructional applications, computer-managed instruction, personal-productivity tools, and teacher tools. The types of general technology-based activities that exemplify each category, the ways in which these activities can help students and their teachers and therapists, and the guidelines to consider when implementing these activities are described.

Instructional Applications

The following six general instructional applications can be used with individuals with mild disabilities in class and therapy settings.

Basic Skill Instruction

As described above, drill-and-practice in basic skills has been a predominant use of technology in special education. Computer-based drill-and-practice programs have effectively assisted students in acquiring basic skill automaticity, and thus are consistent with curricular goals for many students. However, not all drill-and-practice programs are created equal. Software programs are more likely to be effective if they incorporate general principles of effective instruction. Factors to consider when choosing drill-and-practice software and the rationale for their importance are summarized in Table 6.2.

Drill-and-practice software also should incorporate domain-specific principles of instruction. For example, research by Hasselbring, Goin, and Bransford (1987) has demonstrated that students automatize math facts more effectively if professionals (a) first assess a student's present level of automaticity, (b) choose facts for practice that are closely related to automatized facts, (c) focus on a small set of facts at a time, (d) require students to reduce their retrieval times, and (e) provide frequent review of mastered facts. The DLM Math Fluency program (Hasselbring & Goin, 1989) embodies these principles, and this program has helped students automatize math facts in numerous field tests. However, these domain-specific principles are not utilized in most math drill-and-practice programs. Rather, programs typically present students with facts selected at random from a large set of fact families. Students' math facts practice is rarely systematic, sequential, or individualized, and therefore students experience less than optimal learning opportunities. In an attempt to capture students' interest, many software programs have incorporated video game features such as fantasy themes, fast-paced responding, auditory and visual embellishments, and variable levels of performance (e.g., Chaffin, Maxwell, & Thompson, 1982; Malone, 1981). Although the idea of embedding learning activities in video game formats has considerable intuitive appeal, research suggests that they be used judiciously. Video game features may detract from the time available for practice and learning (Okolo, 1991b) and may distract students' attention from the skill they are supposed to practice (Christensen & Gerber, 1986). Gamelike features may also be most appropriate for students who have low motivation for a particular activity (Malouf, 1987–1988; Okolo, 1991a; Okolo, Hinsey, & Yousefian, 1990).

Regardless of the type of program a teacher or therapist selects, drill-and-practice software

TABLE 6.2
Features of effective drill-and-practice software

What to Look for	What to Avoid	Rationale
Programs that provide high rates of responding relevant to the skill to be learned	Programs that take too much time to load and run or that contain too many activities unrelated to the skill to be learned	The more time students spend on task, the more they learn.
Programs in which graphics and animation support the skill or concept that is being practiced	Programs with graphics or animation that are unrelated to the program's instructional objective	While graphics and animation may facilitate student interest in an activity, they may also distract students, interfere with skill mastery, and reduce practice time.
Programs in which reinforcement is used sparingly and approximates the type of reinforcement schedule students encounter in the classroom	Programs that provide a reinforcing graphic or activity after every correct response	If students are reinforced too frequently for correct responses, they may no longer exhibit those responses when fewer or no reinforcers are offered. Furthermore, excessive time spent engaging in the reinforcing activities detracts from time to learn and interferes with the development of automaticity.
Programs in which reinforcement is clearly related to task completion or mastery	Programs in which the events that occur when students are incorrect (e.g., an explosion) are more reinforcing than the events that occur when the student is correct (e.g., a smiling face)	Some programs may actually encourage students to practice the incorrect response in order to view the event that they find more reinforcing.
Programs in which feedback helps students locate and correct their mistakes	Programs in which students are merely told if they are right or wrong or are told to "try again"	Without feedback that informs them of the correct answer after a reasonable number of attempts, students may become frustrated and make random guesses.
Programs that store information about student performance or progress that can be accessed by the teacher at a later time	Programs without record-keeping features	Students may encounter difficulties with the skills covered by a program that require teacher intervention. However, teachers often find it difficult to monitor students as they work at the computer. Access to records of student performance enables the teacher to determine if a program is benefiting a student and whether the student needs additional assistance.
Programs with options for controlling features such as speed of problem presentation, type of feedback, problem difficulty, and number of practice trials	Programs that must be used in the same way with every student	Options are cost-effective; they enable the same program to be used with a broad range of students. Furthermore, they permit a teacher to provide more appropriately individualized instruction.

should never be used with students who have not yet acquired a conceptual understanding of a skill. Students with mild disabilities should use drill-and-practice software to practice information they already know but are slow at retrieving. Otherwise, computer-based practice will have minimal effects on their automaticity and, in some cases, only encourage the rapidity with which they use strategies that interfere with automaticity, such as finger counting (Hasselbring, Goin, & Bransford, 1988). Drill-and-practice activities are more likely to be effective if students engage in short, spaced practice periods that intersperse to-be-learned material with frequent review of mastered information (Salisbury, 1990). Finally, drill-and-practice in basic skills should not be utilized as a prerequisite for engagement in more complex and meaningful activities. Rather, drill-and-practice activities may be more effective and motivating when both preceded and followed by meaningful skill applications (Hofmeister, 1983; Pea, 1987).

Problem Solving

Open most educational software catalogs and you will find numerous programs that are purported to develop students' problem-solving skills. These programs are typically of two types: simulation and activity-oriented problem-solving software. Simulation software programs portray complex events such as the solution of a crime, the ecology of a rain forest, or a pioneer's cross-country wagon train journey. Often students assume the role of a character, such as a detective, scientist, or pioneer, and work through a series of decisions and problems to reach a desired goal. Activity-oriented problem-solving programs address broad problem-solving skills such as visual spatialization or concept formation. These programs engage students in a sequence of increasingly different activities that necessitate the use of specific problem-solving abilities. Most problem-solving programs are open ended, entail much self-directed reading and decision-making, and include students' graphics, animation, and gamelike features. However, it is important for professionals to realize that students with mild disabilities may learn little

from problem-solving software without direct instruction and intervention. Problem-solving programs rarely teach or guide the student toward an understanding of correct or efficient problem-solution strategies (Wiebe & Martin, 1990). These exceptional students often fail to "discover" effective problem-solving strategies on their own. In fact, Duffield (1990) has reported that in some of the most commonly used problem-solving software programs, students can obtain more rapid and successful results if they use less rather than more sophisticated strategies! Effective use of problem-solving software must include considerable learner guidance and support through elaborated feedback, modeling of explicit problem-solving strategies, and guided practice (Woodward et al., 1986). Often this support must be provided by the teacher or therapist in conjunction with student use of the software program.

Word Processing

Computers can facilitate many aspects of the writing process that are consistent with current theories of effective written-expression instruction. Word processing lends itself well to a process-writing approach, which is characterized by the interactive stages of planning, writing, and revision. Because word processing functions such as delete, move, and copy relieve many of the logistical burdens of revising, word processing can make it easier for students with mild disabilities to interactively write and revise, as good writers are known to do.

Poor writers often view writing as a test-taking rather than communicative activity (Thomas, Englert, & Gregg, 1987). Word processing and desktop-publishing programs can encourage students to write for a wider audience that includes peers and parents, and the computer itself may stimulate more social interaction during writing activities. Because text on the computer screen can be read by anyone passing by, students may be more likely to read and comment on each other's writing as they wait to use a computer or move about the class- or therapy room (Bruce, Michaels, & Watson-Gegeo, 1985). Computer-generated copies of compositions can be easily shared and discussed by groups of students. Peer-editing activities can help focus students' attention on what is unclear or missing from their compositions, thus helping them to become more effective writers.

It is important to keep in mind that writing is a complex task that requires the integration of many skills. The use of a computer and word-processing software adds additional task demands. Without instruction and practice in keyboarding and word processing functions, students may focus on the mechanics of operating the word processor rather than on the content of their writing (Cochran-Smith, Kahn, & Paris, 1988; Daiute, 1986). Many professionals have recommended that students learn to type at least well enough so they do not have to hunt for each key on the keyboard (Morocco, 1987; Morocco, Dalton, & Tivnan, 1989). Keyboarding fluency can be developed through short practice sessions that focus on the sequential introduction of and practice with key locations and sequences (Neuman & Morocco, 1987). Professionals should beware of game software that encourages students to hit keys as rapidly as possible to fire missiles, shoot spaceships, and so on, because these programs may encourage students to sacrifice technique for speed. In order to be effective, students' keyboarding practice should be closely monitored by the teacher or therapist, who can reinforce the use of proper technique (Neuman & Morocco, 1987).

Students with mild disabilities may require a substantial amount of practice to develop keyboarding fluency (Okolo et al., 1990). Given that the average elementary school student receives only about 2 hours of keyboarding instruction (Sormunen, Adams, Berg, & Prigge, 1989), professionals may find it advisable to integrate keyboarding with a regularly scheduled subject such as language arts (Sormunen & Wickersham, 1991). In fact, keyboarding instruction may be more motivating and effective when taught as a skill that is useful for learning other subjects (Anderson-Inman, 1990). Some software programs, such as Type to Learn (Sunburst), emphasize keyboarding across the curriculum. Other criteria have been suggested (Knapp, 1984; McClean, 1987) that teachers and therapists may wish to consider when choosing keyboarding programs:

1. Sequential introduction of keys in small sets

2. Feedback about typing accuracy and speed, referenced to previous performance

3. Screen display of upper- and lowercase letters

4. Options for students to correct their errors during practice activities

5. Use of real rather than nonsense words in practice exercises

6. Options for teacher-created lessons

Despite the importance of keyboarding skills, students' lack of them should not preclude their use of word processing programs. This caveat is especially true of young children and learners with mild disabilities, whose developmental maturity or lack of fine-motor skills may limit keyboarding proficiency.

Students also will require introduction to and practice with word processing functions (e.g., delete, move) and word processing components (e.g., spelling checkers, thesauri). Although these features may seem self-evident to adults, students with mild disabilities may encounter considerable difficulties when using them. Spelling checkers are an illustrative example. Dalton, Winbury, and Morocco (1990) reported that typical spelling checkers identify only slightly more than half of students' errors and offer corrections for slightly less than half of these. When a spelling checker offers alternative spellings, students who are impulsive or who have weak word identification skills may have difficulty making the correct choice. Students will need backup strategies they can rely on when the spelling checker cannot offer an alternative. In addition, students who lack confidence in their abilities may find it difficult to "reject" the program's feedback that an idiosyncratic or slang word is misspelled. Finally, students who rely solely on a spelling checker may not correct errors, such as homonym substitutions, that the pro-

Individualized instruction can be accomplished with computers. *(Photograph by David M. Aultz)*

gram cannot identify (Dalton et al., 1990). As with keyboarding, students with mild disabilities will require direct instruction about and practice with word processing functions as well as tools and strategies for their effective use.

Telecommunications and Electronic Networks

The opportunity afforded by technology for extending learning beyond class- or therapy room walls has generated substantial enthusiasm in the educational community. Students with mild disabilities are corresponding with other students from around the world, collaborating with peers to develop solutions to important problems such as acid rain, and apprenticing themselves to experts in a domain of interest. Telecommunications activities require access to a phone line, computer, modem, and appropriate software. Local area networks (LANs) connect computers to each

other, often within the same building. If one computer in a LAN is connected to a phone line, all computers on the network can communicate with outside bulletin board systems, eliminating the need for a phone line in each class- or therapy room. Both types of networking opportunities are becoming more common in educational settings, and their hardware and software requirements are discussed in Chapters 1, 2, and 13.

SpecialNet (GTE Education Services) is an electronic network designed by and for special education professionals. GTE offers classroom accounts at a reduced rate and charges significantly less for messages sent after peak hours. The network operates a bulletin board entitled KidsTalk, which is monitored by the International Center for Telecommunications in the Classroom in Flint, Michigan. In addition to corresponding with other students in electronic peer-support projects, students with mild disabilities and their nonexceptional peers are communicating with their state senator regarding current events of concern and corresponding with senior citizens who serve as telefoster grandparents.

Electronic networks can facilitate social-interaction skills and the development of long-distance friendships. Ongoing correspondence with persons whom exceptional students do not know or will never meet can help them realize the importance of describing information and events in a clear and comprehensible manner. In addition, students who are otherwise reluctant writers may be highly motivated by the collaborative and communicative activities that networks offer (Newman, 1987). Thus electronic networks can facilitate the attainment of important instructional goals for students with mild disabilities.

As professionals gain more experience using electronic networks, they are finding some activities more effective than others. Collaborative projects that require students to engage in a joint activity, do not rely on the response of a particular person, enable professionals and students to work off-line and then transmit files locally, and are characterized by the interdependency found in cooperative-learning groups seem to have the best chances for success and are the least costly (Laboratory of Comparative Human Culture, 1989; Newman, 1987). The Computer Learning Foundation and the International Society for Technology in Education have published an excellent telecommunications guide and set of lesson plans for instructional activities that can be accomplished through electronic networks (Clark, Kurshan, & Yoder, 1989).

Videodiscs

Videodiscs are flexible instructional tools that can be used in a variety of subject areas (Woodward & Gersten, 1992). In fact, videodisc-based curricula are beginning to appear on state and local school district lists of approved "textbooks" (Allen, 1990). Levels of videodisc instruction and their respective hardware and software components are described in Chapter 5. Three instructional uses of videodiscs will be described below.

First, videodiscs can be used to support teacher-directed lectures or discussions by bringing a concept or event to life. For example, Windows on Science (Optical Data) contains the video sequence of a tornado as filmed by a Minneapolis helicopter news crew. This sequence more than justifies the adage that a picture is worth a thousand words; no amount of verbal or written description could compete with the power of this camera footage. Videodiscs have enabled teachers and therapists to simulate potentially dangerous situations, such as drug and alcohol abuse or the operation of electrical equipment, without risk to their students. Indeed, videodisc-supported instruction is purported to be more efficient than traditional teaching methods and to result in increased retention of information, increased motivation, and reduced behavior problems (Bosco, 1986). An increasing number of videodiscs come equipped with software programs that permit the user to customize the sequence of video information, to add captions, and to annotate video frames for future reference. These features increase the flexibility with which videodiscs can be used to accommodate the needs and characteristics of students with mild disabilities.

A second and related use of videodiscs is for the creation of macrocontexts, or instructional contexts that are sufficiently broad and rich to facilitate instruction in a variety of skills and content areas. Video representations of events and problems enable students to form rich mental models of problem situations (McNamara, Miller, & Bransford, in press). They can supply the background knowledge that students with mild disabilities often need to successfully construct meaning from text or to solve complex problems (Bransford et al., 1988; Van Hanegan et al., in press). When instruction is anchored in rich and realistic auditory and visual contexts that cut across a variety of different areas, students are more likely to transfer what they have learned (Bransford & Vye, 1989; Cognition and Technology Group, 1990).

Researchers at Vanderbilt University's Cognition and Technology Group are developing a series of 6 to 10 videodiscs designed to promote problem-solving skills. The series, Adventures of Jasper Woodbury, and its associated data bases utilize principles of anchored instruction. Students are introduced to the situations encountered by Jasper Woodbury and provided with a rich source of relevant video information. The video information is not discipline specific, but rather provides links to mathematics, science, and history to facilitate generalization of problem-solving skills across the curriculum.

Third, many videodisc programs are designed to deliver instruction and operated by the professional during whole-class instruction. An example is the Core Concepts series (Systems Impact), which provides instruction in mathematical topics such as fractions, decimals, and percentages. The teacher or therapist operates the videodisc with a hand-held remote-control device and is able to access individual video segments and remedial loops and exercise control over the pace of the program. As the videodisc presents instruction, the professional can circulate among students and assess their progress. When additional instruction is necessary, the teacher or therapist can easily access a video segment, freeze the frame, and annotate it with additional explanations or clarification (Kelly, Gersten, & Woodward, in press).

Videodiscs can also be controlled by an external computer, most often to deliver instruction to individuals or small groups of students. Commands or choices entered through the computer keyboard determine the video information presented to the viewer(s). The Science Quest videodisc series is an interactive science curriculum comprised of videodisc-based lessons and activities. Through a combination of computer hardware and software, students conduct experiments, listen to experts discuss a topic, and collect data to solve science-oriented problems (Litchfield, 1990). Systems such as this one afford highly individualized instruction and provide students with mild disabilities with opportunities to review and repeat activities. However, they presume that students will be able to make optimal use of the multiple learning opportunities they afford. This is not always the case for exceptional students, who may not realize that they do not understand a concept or need additional practice. As with any individualized system, professionals must teach students how to make optimal use of the system and must monitor students' performance and progress.

Hypertext, Multimedia, and Hypermedia

Hypertext permits the design of nonlinear instructional activities in which learners can follow multiple paths depending on their particular needs. This format gives students with mild disabilities active control of their own learning in ways not possible with traditional computer-based activities. Students can focus on instructional information of most importance or interest to them, set personal learning goals, and acquire information in highly individualized ways that may facilitate interconnections with prior knowledge (Schmalhofer & Kahn, 1988). Combinations of audio and visual effects, including input from VCRs or videodiscs, sound effects, and speech synthesizers, comprise a new and exciting form of instructional presentation: multimedia. When hypertext capabilities are added, the resultant application is termed hypermedia. Hypermedia and multimedia environments are purported to enhance quality of instruction and depth of student learning and to be highly motivating alternatives to traditional instructional activities.

Hypertext, multimedia, and hypermedia offer unprecedented opportunities for individualized instruction. In addition to providing multiple learning paths, they can contain a variety of different help functions and rich sources of background knowledge that can be accessed as needed. Higgins and Boone (1990) have developed and field-tested a hypertext basal reading series in which students can select pictures and animated graphics sequences that illustrate and expand the written text, obtain definitions, and learn strategies for word identification and reading comprehension. This program can enable students with mild disabilities to receive the individually tailored instruction they require within a regular or special class setting. As the costs of the technology continue to decrease, these systems will undoubtedly become more prevalent in special and regular classrooms.

Computer-managed Instruction

Individualization of instruction to address a particular student's strengths and needs is a hallmark of special education programs. Student achievement increases when teachers make data-based instructional decisions (Fuchs, Deno, & Mirkin, 1984). In addition, students' motivation and interest in their academic programs often improve when they have frequent and immediate access to information about their progress (Hunter & Dickey, 1990). However, the systematic collection and analysis of individualized information is time-consuming, labor-intensive, and hence infeasible for many professionals. Computers are excellent tools for collecting, recording, storing, and analyzing such data. Sophisticated software programs increase the ease with which teachers and therapists can accomplish the above activities and can enhance the types of data-based instructional decisions they make.

Integrated learning systems (ILSs) are a variant of computer-managed instruction (Mageau, 1992). These systems are being used with increasing frequency for students with mild disabilities and other low achievers. The typical system contains both instructional and management components. Instructional activities are drawn from a broad selection of reading, math, and language arts software that spans several grade levels. The management component collects information about student performance during instructional activities and assigns students to individual lessons based on these data (Sherry, 1990). Integrated learning systems are designed to run on networked computers in a school computer lab and typically cost from $60,000 to $180,000 for 20 to 30 stations.

Professionals should keep in mind that ILSs are only as good as the instruction they provide. Teachers and therapists deserve some guarantee that these systems incorporate the principles of effective instruction reviewed above. In some cases, these systems may be unable to make accurate decisions about and prescriptions for exceptional students (Hativa, 1988; Hativa & Lesgold, 1990). Systems may interpret students' keyboarding errors or misunderstanding of directions to be substantive errors, therefore making incorrect assessments about students' knowledge and, consequently, inappropriate instructional recommendations. ILSs offer a potentially powerful instructional and management environment; however, their use must be monitored to ensure that exceptional students are responding correctly and are receiving appropriate instructional prescriptions.

Personal Productivity Tools

In addition to its potential as an instructional delivery and management system, electronic technologies offer tools that can help students with mild disabilities increase their own efficiency and productivity as learners. Word processors, data bases, spreadsheets, and electronic networks are excellent examples of personal productivity tools. As described earlier, word processors reduce some of the mechanical burdens of writing and can facilitate the use of more sophisticated writing strategies. Data bases can help students analyze relationships, look for trends, test and refine hypotheses, organize and share information, keep lists up to date, and arrange information in more useful ways (Watson, 1988). Spreadsheets not only help students compute repetitive calculations with ease; they can enable

students to observe relationships among sets of information, explore numerical patterns, and gain insight into concepts such as variables and functions (Clements, 1989). Electronic networks provide students with access to on-line data bases and information sources that can be searched for the most up-to-date information on a topic of interest.

Perhaps one of the most exciting benefits of technology is its potential use as a cognitive tool. Technology-based programs such as word processors and spreadsheets not only facilitate the accomplishment of a task but also model effective ways of performing it. Salomon (1988) purported that personal productivity tools can be internalized by the learner and subsequently used as cognitive tools when they extend the learner's cognitive activities in new and important ways and if they operate in an explicit and understandable manner.

Outlining programs, which are designed to help writers interactively create and revise a written document, provide an illustrative example. By displaying the contents of an outline at different levels of detail, a student may obtain different perspectives on the document, analyze part-whole relations, and experiment with alternative organizational schemes (Pea, 1985). If students with mild disabilities come to see the value of outlining and understand how it works by virtue of using a computer program, they may subsequently apply an outlining strategy to other tasks that require them to organize information.

The notion of cognitive tools is a powerful one that has significant implications for the instruction of students with mild disabilities. Teachers and therapists should realize, however, that their students will not autonomously intuit the strategies embodied in these tools, internalize them, and generalize their use across varied tasks and settings (Perkins, 1985). Undoubtedly students will need explicit instructions to transform personal productivity tools into cognitive tools.

Teacher Tools

Computers and other technologies also offer professionals at least three options for improving their professional productivity. First, technology can help teachers and therapists organize and analyze classroom information more effectively and efficiently. Excessive paperwork is a frequent lament of professionals working with students with mild disabilities, and application programs such as data bases and spreadsheets can reduce record-keeping burdens. Data bases offer a convenient format that can keep track of student demographic information, classroom supplies, or instructional plans. Through search and report components of data base programs, teachers have an efficient tool for locating pertinent information or organizing information into relevant categories.

Spreadsheets or specially designed gradebooks can be used to keep track of student progress and grades. Cumulative scores, individual progress, and class statistics can be computed with a few keystrokes. Although electronic spreadsheets and gradebooks take somewhat longer to set up than paper and pencil records, they save time in the long run and offer students and professionals access to systematic and frequent progress reports.

Commercial software has been developed to assist with other common classroom tasks that entail the organization and analysis of classroom information. These include programs that analyze the readability of text materials; transform, analyze, and report standardized test data; and develop and manage student IEPs.

A second type of teacher tool is software that facilitates communication among professionals and between professionals, parents, and students. Word processing software can play a major role in easing the burdens associated with written correspondence. Options for editing and revising text permit users to create multiple copies of letters and other correspondence in which only a few lines of information change from copy to copy. For example, with access to a computer, printer, and word processing software, a teacher or therapist could feasibly write monthly letters to parents that contain general information about classroom activities (which would stay the same from letter to letter) and a few sentences about each student's performance (which

would be tailored to the individual). Desktop-publishing programs also enable professionals and students to create newsletters and other printed documents that describe school events and student activities. Commercial software programs that contain predesigned forms and templates, such as certificates of recognition, can be used to readily convey progress information and recognition to students and their parents.

Finally, technology can assist educators and therapists in developing instructional materials. Word processing programs enable the user to create a variety of instructional activities with considerable ease. Word processing can save a professional a year of valuable career time by obviating the need to re-type dittos (Adams, 1989). The multiple fonts and formatting styles available in most word processing programs allow teachers or therapists to enlarge print size for primary readers or for students with visual disabilities. Bold print and italics can be used to attract students' attention and highlight important information.

A variety of options exist for teachers and therapists to create their own technology-based instructional activities. Word processing programs can form the basis for computer-based instructional activities such as prewriting, peer review files, sentence-combining activities, and revising exercises (Messerer & Lerner, 1989). Shell programs typically provide a predetermined instructional format into which professionals can enter their own content. They often permit professionals to adjust options such as sound effects, type and frequency of feedback, and mastery criteria for an individual student. Authoring systems are more sophisticated and open-ended than shell programs. They are more time-consuming to use but also more flexible, and thus can accommodate diverse instructional goals. Many newer authoring systems support the development of hypertext and hypermedia applications.

SPECIFIC COMPUTER APPLICATIONS

This section presents examples of specific computer applications (e.g. instructional applications, computer-managed instruction, personal-productivity tools, and teacher tools) that can be used in meeting the needs of individuals with mild disabilities. Examples to illustrate the types and range of commercially available software-based programs in each of the above areas will be described. Where possible, programs that are available in both Apple and IBM versions are discussed. These examples are by no means exhaustive, as there are more than 10,000 educational software programs on the market (EPIE, 1988). Add to this figure the growing number of videodiscs and other technology-based applications, and you can appreciate that any attempt to adequately portray the diversity of specific technology applications within a limited number of textbook pages will fall short.

Instructional Applications

Technology can be used to meet instructional goals across a variety of skill areas and age ranges. Examples of software for early learning, basic academic skills, problem-solving, reading comprehension, written expression, and content-area subjects are described below.

Early Learning Programs

A variety of software programs have been designed to accomplish important early learning goals (Schwartz & Lewis, 1991–1992). Discovery-oriented programs are designed to permit students with mild disabilities to learn about the computer (e.g., keyboards and other input devices) and to explore cause-effect relationships. In Playroom (Brøderbund), students can explore a playroom scene by clicking a mouse on different areas of that room. Features of the playroom change with the student's choice and the program presents activities related to early numeracy and literacy skills. Muppets on Stage is a discovery-oriented software program designed to work with the Muppet Learning Keys Keyboard (Sunburst), an alternative keyboard designed especially for young children. This colorful keyboard has enlarged and special keys, plugs into a computer's joystick port, and can be used with many other early learning programs.

Word processing programs such as Dr. Peet's Talk/Writer (Hartley) have been designed with young children in mind. Drill-and-practice programs also are available to develop readiness and early academic skills, often in a game format. Laureate Learning Systems offers a variety of programs that can help students with mild disabilities develop language, vocabulary, and categorization skills. All Laureate programs utilize synthetic speech and provide a range of options for program operation that can be modified by the teacher.

The Reading Magic Library (Tom Snyder Productions) offers a unique approach to early literacy. Designed to be shared by children and their parents or teachers, the program presents part of a story and then stops and awaits instructions about how the story should proceed. The child and adult discuss what should happen next and the program branches to that choice.

In addition to individual software programs like those described above, companies have put together comprehensive early childhood curricula. For example, the Writing to Read program (IBM) is based on the premise that children can write what they say and read what they write. Students engage in five types of reading and writing activities at technology-rich learning centers. The Apple Learning Series: Early Language (Apple) is a package of hardware, peripherals, and separate software programs that include Muppets on Stage, Muppetville, Muppet Word Book, and Touch 'N Write (Sunburst); Sound Ideas: Consonants, Vowels, and Word Attack (Houghton Mifflin); ColorMe (Mindscape); Where Did My Toothbrush Go? (D. C. Heath); and Talking Text Writer (Scholastic).

Most early childhood experts recommend that technology-based activities capitalize on young children's curiosity and encourage interaction among students (Haugland & Shade, 1988). Teachers and therapists should be on the lookout for difficulties that young children will encounter when interacting with the computer. These include text that must be read, complex loading procedures, and unfamiliarity with location of keys. Davidson (1989) offered many helpful suggestions for introducing computers to developmentally young learners.

Basic Academic Skills

A dizzying array of software has been developed to assist students in their mastery of basic academic skills. The majority of these are in mathematics. The DLM Math Fluency program (DLM) is based on the principles of effective automaticity instruction described above (Hasselbring et al., 1987). Students are introduced to one to three math facts at a time, which they practice through straightforward drill activities. Mastered facts are reinforced with further practice in a game format. The program assesses students' initial level of fact knowledge and keyboarding speed, assigns appropriate practice and remedial activities, enables the professional to generate student worksheets, and collects extensive student-performance records.

Math Masters (DLM) is another CAI program designed to provide practice in basic math facts. Students can practice math facts through a drill or game format, and professionals or students can modify the problems to be practiced (e.g., speed and manner of response, amount of repetition, duration of activity, input device, and type of feedback). Teachers and therapists can generate student worksheets for additional practice and the program compiles comprehensive records on student performance.

The DLM Reading Fluency program (DLM) contains a series of titles that are designed to improve students' decoding and vocabulary skills. The Hint and Hunt series focuses on rapid decoding of short medial vowel words,

Computers develop reading, mathematics, and other abilities. (*Photograph by David M. Aultz*)

the Construct-A-Word series enables students to practice blending beginning and ending sounds to create words, and the Word Wise series contains vocabulary building activities. Each of these programs utilizes synthesized speech and is based on empirically derived principles of effective instruction in decoding (e.g., Roth & Beck, 1987; Torgesen, 1984) and vocabulary instruction (McKeown & Beck, 1988).

A number of programs have been developed to improve students' spelling skills. For example, Spell It Plus! (Davidson) and Magic Spells (Learning Company) contain a variety of spelling-related activities. Like many programs, some activities require students to spell a word after it has been flashed on the screen while other activities present words in a scrambled format. These spelling activities, however, have questionable correspondence to the typical ways in which students spell words from long-term memory and from dictation. Programs that utilize synthetic speech to present a word, such as the Talking Text Speller (Scholastic) and Speller Bee (First Byte), approximate more closely the types of spelling tasks students encounter in the class- or therapy room. However, not all students have access to computers with speech synthesizers.

Numerous other examples of drill-and-practice software are available in just about any educational software catalog. Professionals should keep in mind the principles of effective drill-and-practice software described above when considering the purchase of any of these practice programs.

Problem-solving Abilities

Many programs have been developed to improve students' mathematical problem-solving skills. The Math Shop Series (Scholastic) presents problems that merchants in a shopping mall might encounter. Sailing through Story Problems (DLM) is designed around a pirate theme and has 12 levels, beginning with practice in locating relevant information and concluding with multistep problems. Like most word-problem activities, these software programs require students to read a moderate amount of information in order to solve problems. Students with reading disabilities may require some additional teacher assistance.

A different approach to mathematical problem solving is illustrated in simulation programs such as Survival Math (Sunburst) and Oregon Trail (MECC), in which students solve math problems in the context of running a business or traveling across the country on a wagon train. What Do You Do with a Broken Calculator? (Sunburst) is another discovery-oriented program in which students must solve mathematical problems when calculator keys are disabled. Designed to help students think creatively about multiple solutions to a problem, this program contains a variety of options and levels.

Sunburst and Wings for Learning publish a wide variety of activity-oriented problem-solving software that addresses a range of age and skill levels. Titles include Teddy and Iggy (Sunburst), which targets primary-age children's memory and sequencing skills; The Factory (Wings for Learning), which targets intermediate age students' spatial visualization and concept formation skills; and High Wire Logic (Sunburst), in which older students use Boolean logic to classify a set of objects. Fortunately, publishers are beginning to develop guidelines to help professionals use these programs more effectively. For example, teachers and therapists can now purchase a curriculum guide, What's Your Strategy? (Wings for Learning), that contains lesson plans for problem-solving activities that utilize manipulatives and The Factory program.

The HOTS program (Thinking with Computers) is a computer-supplemented approach to developing thinking skills designed for low-achieving students in grades 4 through 7. The program uses Socratic teaching to stimulate the development of skills such as drawing inferences from context, generalizing information across contexts, and synthesizing information (Pogrow, 1990). The software associated with the program is selected for its motivational value and includes games, adventure stories, and simulations.

Reading Comprehension

Some computer programs emulate traditional reading comprehension activities in which students are asked to read a selection and answer questions. Kittens, Kids, and a Frog (Hartley) presents short selections at first- and second-grade reading levels and then questions students about main idea, details, sequence, events, and predictions. The program has an extensive editing utility that enables professionals or students to create their own questions and prompts. Designed for older students, Comprehension Connection (Milliken) provides on-line help to facilitate understanding of content-area text and includes instruction in identifying the main idea and defining vocabulary words. Reading Comprehension: The Main Idea (Morning Star) uses a direct instruction approach to provide sequential practice in identifying the main idea of pictures, sentences, paragraphs, and short stories. The program also includes a comprehensive management component.

Other software programs are available that attempt to emulate or facilitate strategies that are associated with effective reading comprehension including asking questions about text, making predictions about what will happen next, and monitoring the outcomes of those predictions. Tiger's Tales (Sunburst) is designed for beginning readers, and through a combination of text and graphics students make predictions about the outcomes of short simple narratives. Reading Realities (Teacher Support Software) is a high-interest, low-vocabulary software program that presents directed reading-thinking activities on topics of interest to adolescents (e.g., peer pressure and career preparation). The Semantic Mapper (Teacher Support Software) is a flexible program that helps students develop concept maps that depict a text's main ideas, details, and interrelations among them.

Multimedia applications can effectively model the interactive processes involved in text comprehension. Discis books (Discis Knowledge Systems) are available on CD-ROM for the Macintosh computer and include 10 popular titles. Book pages are displayed on the screen with the original text and illustrations. In addition, the text is enhanced by the multimedia additions of voice, music, and sound effects. The story is highlighted phrase by phrase as it is read by the computer, and students can click on any word or picture for additional information that will enhance or extend their understanding. Some titles in the series are available in Spanish, French, and Cantonese.

Written Expression

Word processors, desktop publishing programs, and hypermedia writing tools and writing assistance programs can be used to develop students with mild disabilities' written language abilities:

Word Processors, Desktop Publishers, and Hypermedia Writing Tools. Many different word processing programs are in use in today's class- and therapy rooms. Popular titles include Bank Street Writer (Scholastic), Magic Slate (Sunburst), and Appleworks (Claris). These programs include features such as dictionaries, spelling checkers, and thesauri. Networked versions often include electronic mail functions.

FrEdWriter is a freeware word processing program available for a nominal fee from CUE SoftSwap. It contains many essential word processing features and functions, including a utility to prepare files for telecommunications activities. Because the program is freeware, professionals can make each student an individual copy. A Spanish version of FrEdWriter is also available, as are a number of model lessons that utilize FrEdWriter.

Talking word processors are especially appropriate for students with mild disabilities. Programs such as Talking Text Writer (Scholastic) and KidTalk (First Byte) utilize synthesized speech, enabling students to hear what they have written and to have dictionary definitions and other help features read to them. Both programs permit the user (e.g., student, teacher, therapist) to enter phonetic spellings for words that are not deciphered correctly by speech synthesis rules.

In recent years, a number of programs have been developed to enhance students' motivation to write and extend their writing experiences. Introductory desktop publishing programs such as Children's Writing and Publishing Center (Learning Company), facilitate

Computer concepts learned at school can be used at home. *(Photograph by David M. Aultz)*

the production of student-generated correspondence that contains text and graphics. Hypermedia writing programs, such as Super Story Tree (Scholastic), allow students to create interactive-branching stories in which the reader makes choices about what happens next. The writer can integrate multimedia options such as graphics, sound, and music with text. CUE SoftSwap distributes a similar program, entitled HyperStories, for Macintosh computers.

When considering programs such as these, teachers and therapists should keep in mind that with their sophistication comes complexity. Students with mild disabilities will need time and instruction in order to master the many commands necessary for utilizing their graphics and editing capabilities. These programs are good vehicles for collaborative writing projects, and professionals may consider assigning individual roles to members of student teams in order to facilitate their use.

Writing Assisting Programs. As described earlier, mere access to a word processor will not improve students' written-expression skills. However, professionals can structure the use of word processing software and utilize related written-expression tools to assist their students at each step of the writing process. A number of commercial and freeware programs are designed to facilitate the first step of the writing process (i.e., planning). These include Bank Street Prewriter (Scholastic) and Prewrite (Mindscape). The Semantic

Mapper, described above, also is appropriate for helping students generate and organize ideas prior to writing.

Other programs are available that help students with mild disabilities develop more sophisticated composing strategies during the writing process. Word processing programs such as Bank Street Writer, Magic Slate II, and FrEdWriter contain enhancements that permit the teacher or therapist to enter "prompt boxes" that cannot be altered by the student. Within these boxes professionals can guide students' writing with prompts such as story starters, outlines, or procedural reminders.

The revision process also can be facilitated by computer software. Programs such as Writer's Helper (Conduit), Ghost Writer (MECC), and Grammatik Mac (Reference Software) analyze written text and flag errors in syntax, sentence structure, and word usage. Students then are able to go back into their composition to correct these errors. Some of these programs also assist in the revision process by reformatting students' text. For example, Quill (D. C. Heath) displays a composition on the screen one line at a time. Ghost Writer (MECC) displays each sentence by printing only the punctuation and conjunctions; all other text is replaced by dashes. By removing surrounding sentences or displaying only the basic structure of each sentence, the ease with which students can make sentence-level revisions is enhanced.

Before special educators and other professionals use these programs, they should be cognizant of their limitations. Planning programs will not help students who do not know how to generate ideas through brainstorming. Revision programs cannot respond interactively to a student's emerging composition as a teacher or therapist does. Error checkers will catch only the most basic writing errors and analyze students' writing in quantitative, not qualitative, fashion. Sentence-level revision activities ignore more important aspects of students' writing such as overall coherence and audience appeal. Furthermore, these programs will be of no use to students who have not been taught how to implement the suggested revisions.

Content-Area Subjects

Simulation programs, electronic networks, computer-based laboratories, and data bases can be used with and by students with mild disabilities in the following content-area subjects.

Simulation Programs. Social studies and science classes can be enhanced by the use of computer-based simulations. Simulations can portray real-life situations, ranging from immigration to laboratory experiments to drug and alcohol use, in which students could not otherwise participate. Simulations help students to view all sides of a problem and experience the consequences of decisions or actions. Access to a projection panel or large screen monitor enables simulations to become a central feature of whole-class instruction. Because simulations branch to different paths, depending on the prior sequence of events, the same simulation can yield many different outcomes.

Broderbund publishes the Carmen Sandiego series, in which students act as detectives and collect clues to locate Carmen and her gang of thieves. Students must use reference skills, geographical and historical knowledge, and deductive reasoning to make sense of information offered by the program. Carmen may be tracked throughout the United States, Europe, the world, or through time, depending on the program purchased. Also, Mindscape offers a variety of programs that can supplement the science and social studies curricula. For example, That's Life series contains two exploratory and two simulation programs designed to reinforce physiology, ecology, genetics, and zoology concepts. The Social Studies Explorer series contains simulations in American history and world geography. Wings for Learning produces an exploratory science series that includes Trip to the Rainforest and Trip to the Kelp Forest.

Tom Snyder Productions has developed simulations for the social studies classroom that are called "groupware." They are designed to be used with students in grades 5 through 12 in combination with print materials, groups discussion, role playing, and classroom de-bates. Titles include the Decisions series, National Inquirer, and Our Town Meeting.

Electronic Networks. Over 3,000 classes in the United States and foreign countries are enrolled in the National Geographic Kids Network elementary science curriculum (Julyan, 1990). Participating classes join a research team with students from schools grades 8 through 12 around the country. Teams collect and share data and correspond through a telecommunications network. Examples of units available through the network include Hello (an introductory unit), Acid Rain, Weather in Action, and Water Quality. Future units for which plans are under way are Trash, Health, and Energy. In all units, students are provided with a topic to investigate and then form questions, collect data, analyze results, and report their findings.

Microcomputer-based Laboratories. Microcomputer-based laboratories (MBLs) have been designed to improve the manner in which students learn science. MBLs are comprised of measuring tools—such as a thermometer, light meter, and seismoscope—attached to a computer. These tools are used to take continuous measurements of scientific phenomena such as temperature, light, harmonics, and wave motion. Data collected by these instruments are recorded and stored in a computer program, which facilitates easy access and display. MBLs entitled Speed and Motion, Earthquake Lab, and Body Lab are available from Brøderbund. Sunburst publishes MBLs on temperature and motion.

MBLs help eliminate the mechanical aspects of experimentation and thus free students to focus on the substantive content (Linn, 1986). However, MBLs were never intended to teach scientific topics. Rather, they must be used in conjunction with instruction about scientific principles, phenomena, and the scientific process of designing, conducting, and interpreting experiments (Lieberman & Linn, 1991).

Data Bases. Data bases are excellent tools for teaching students with mild disabilities facts and problem-solving strategies in content-

area subjects. A number of commercial data bases have been developed for science and social studies topics. Sunburst publishes data bases for the Bank Street School Filer that address topics such as local communities, whales, and astronomy. Mindscape has compiled data bases about rocks and minerals; elements, compounds, and mixtures; nutrition; the American presidency; the first United States Congress; and families of the world. CUE SoftSwap distributes data bases that include colonial America, the solar system, and United States and black history.

Computer-managed Instruction

Integrated learning systems were defined above. Because each of these packages contains so many different features, it is impossible to describe them fully here. The reader is referred to Smith and Sclafani (1989), who offered guidelines for selecting ILSs and described some of the most commonly used systems. A few individual software programs have been developed to assist teachers and therapists in collecting and analyzing student-performance data. The Progress Monitoring program (Performance Monitoring Systems) is a data-base management system for tracking student academic or behavioral performance over the school year. The user defines the behavior to be recorded and the manner in which it was measured, sets a goal for the student, and enters individual scores. The program can print line graphs and customized reports that summarize student progress.

The Monitoring Basic Skills Progress measurement series (PRO-ED) is comprised of three programs to monitor student progress in reading, spelling, and mathematics. The Basic Reading and Basic Spelling programs automatically administer curriculum-based measures to the student at a grade level designated by the teacher or therapist, score the student's performance, provide feedback, and save scores. Professionals have reported that the automatic data collection feature considerably reduces the amount of time required to monitor student performance (Fuchs & Fuchs, 1989). These programs also graph student performance, delineate skills that students have mastered (where appropriate), make instructional recommendations, and offer suggestions to facilitate student goal setting.

Personal Productivity Tools

Personal productivity tools are software or devices that can help a student perform tasks more efficiently and learn more effectively. These tools have the potential to make students with mild disabilities "smarter" by improving their access to information, modeling procedures and strategies, and compensating for cognitive limitations.

Many of the software programs described in the instructional applications section above could be used as personal productivity tools. Word processing and writing assistance programs can facilitate students' independent writing. Data base programs such as the Bank Street School Filer (Sunburst) and FrEdBase (CUE SoftSwap) have been developed with students in mind. Again, because FrEdWriter and FrEdBase are shareware, they are good choices for productivity tools because a copy can be made for each student. Of course, a student must be familiar and comfortable with a software program and able to use it autonomously before it can function as a productivity tool.

Hand-held electronic devices also make good candidates for personal productivity tools. Many of us would be lost without our electronic organizers, which store calendars, schedules, addresses, and reminders in one device. These devices can be a boon for students with mild disabilities who demonstrate poor memory or limited organizational skills. Homeworker (Davidson) is a software program designed to serve a similar function by helping students organize their time and study activities. However, it lacks the convenience of a device that can be carried in one's pocket.

Other hand-held devices can provide students with specialized information or knowledge necessary for success in academic and vocational subjects. For example, manufacturers produce special cards for electronic organizers that compute common mathematical and scientific equations and translate languages. Franklin produces a hand-held dictionary that provides close to 275,000 definitions for 83,000 words. It gives the pronunciation by speaking each word and provides the correct spelling for words that are entered phonetically. Although this version costs nearly $200, professionals or students can purchase a less sophisticated hand-held device for under $40 that verifies and corrects the spelling of over 80,000 words, identifies and defines commonly confused words, and contains educational games. Technological tools such as these can play an extremely important role in supporting the academic activities of students with mild disabilities across a variety of settings.

Teacher Tools

The following three teacher tools can be used by professionals to meet the needs of their students with mild disabilities:

1. *Organizing Information and Communicating with Others.* Gradebook programs fulfill a ubiquitous classroom function by facilitating the process of storing and computing student grades. Mindscape, MECC, and CUE SoftSwap among other companies publish programs that are relatively easy to use. As discussed earlier, data bases and spreadsheets can help teachers and therapist organize and make sense of grades and other teaching-learning related information. Integrated applications packages, such as AppleWorks (Claris) or Microsoft Works (Microsoft), offer word processing, spreadsheet, and data base components within one software package. Teachers and therapists can copy information from one component of the program to another. For example, professionals could use an integrated software package to organize information about instructional activities. First they would create a data base file that delineated the title of an activity, the curricular areas under which it could be classified, the goals that it could help accomplish, and the appropriate group size. They would also include a field in the data base that referenced a word processing file name. Then they would create files in the word processing component that contained lesson plans for each data base entry.

Other programs contribute to the ease with which professionals can communicate with others. For example, Certificates and More (Mindscape) can create a variety of class- or therapy room materials, from achievement awards to calendars to gameboards. The program comes with 10 templates for many common classroom forms and organizational devices. Or professionals can create their own materials by selecting borders, fonts, and clip art from the program's options. Labels, Letters, and Lists (MECC) permits the user to enter student records and then generate lists, name tags, customized letters, and commonly used forms for correspondence.

2. *Creating Instructional Materials.* Ways in which word processing software can facilitate the development of instructional materials were described above. Many commercial software and freeware programs have been developed specifically to generate worksheets and other print-based activities. Multiple Choices (Mindscape) can be used to develop nine different multiple choice activities including crossword puzzles, scrambled words, matching, true-false, and multiple choice. The program transfers content entered into one of the activities into any of the other eight activities without retyping. Programs such as this enable professionals to create a variety of activities that contain the same content and thus provide the repetition and review often needed by students with mild disabilities. MECC also publishes a variety of programs to assist teachers and therapists in developing print materials such as Computer-generated Mathematics Materials and Quickflash.

Professionals also have many options for modifying and developing computer-based instructional materials. With increasing frequency, commercial programs permit the user to modify characteristics of program operation and content. Davidson programs such as Word Attack, Math Blaster, and Spell It permit the user to modify some features of operation (e.g., sound effects) and allow teachers or therapists to enter their own content through an editing system. Math Masters (DLM) allows a broad range of control over the manner in which the program operates as well as the mathematical content that students will prac-

tice. Quickflash (MECC) is a shell program adaptable to many different types of instructional activities that entail multiple choice or paired-associate learning. Freeware programs that permit professionals to enter their own content include Player's Choice, Juegos Selectos (a Spanish version of Player's Choice), Language Arts, and Shell Games (CUE SoftSwap).

A range of authoring systems is also available for professionals who wish to develop their own software programs. In contrast to earlier versions, recent authoring systems are easier to use and enable teachers and therapists to incorporate multimedia into instructional activities. Examples of these systems include Guide (Owl), a menu-driven system for IBM and Macintosh computers; HyperCard (Claris), a hypertext authoring tool that comes free with Macintosh computers; and Linkway, IBM's version of HyperCard. HyperStudio (Roger Wagner Publishing) and Hypercard IIGS (Apple) are adaptations of HyperCard for the Apple II GS, and TutorTech (Techware) runs on all Apple II computers.

SUMMARY

The research reviewed in this chapter has demonstrated that computers and other technologies can improve the achievement and motivation of students with mild disabilities. However, there is no pat formula for how to best use technology. Rather, technology can be used in many different ways to provide, support, and supplement a diversity of educational activities. Four broad categories of technology-based activities were presented in this chapter: instructional applications, computer-managed instruction, personal productivity tools, and teacher tools. Guidelines, recommended activities, and commercial and freeware products related to each category were presented and discussed.

The large number of different technology-based applications examined in this chapter testifies to the power and flexibility of electronic technology and its potential for improving educational experiences for teachers, therapists, and students with mild disabilities.

Technological devices continue to become smaller without sacrificing their power or sophistication. Technology-based systems are becoming more user-friendly—witness our current obsession with graphical user interfaces (GUIs)—and with the decreasing cost of mass-storage devices, more information can be stored less expensively. These factors will help increase the future availability of technology in both home and school settings for a wider variety of instructional purposes.

Even as technology becomes more sophisticated and numbers of applications increase, two critical considerations reiterated throughout this chapter are unlikely to change. First, instructional technology, in and of itself, is not the key to improved educational outcomes for students with mild disabilities. Rather, it is the way in which professionals use technology that matters. Technology use should be consistent with curricular goals and compatible with students' instructional needs. Its use should be integrated into ongoing instructional programs and directed toward accomplishing achievement and motivational outcomes that are of importance to teachers and students.

Second, technology use must be accompanied by teacher-directed instruction, guidance, and monitoring. Rather than replacing the teacher or therapist, technology has underscored the supremacy of the professional's role in the instructional process. Very few technology-based activities can introduce students to new skills and concepts as effectively as a teacher or therapist can. To date, most instructional applications are best suited for practice, review, or extension of teacher-directed instruction. Students with mild disabilities must be taught the prerequisite skills and knowledge necessary to take advantage of the opportunities afforded by tools such as word processing, electronic networks, and data bases. Moreover, these exceptional students must be taught functions and features of various technology applications and strategies to use them optimally. Their understanding of technology-based tasks, their progress toward the acquisition and mastery of skills, and the products they produce must be overseen by a knowledgeable professional who can clarify misunderstandings, provide additional instruction as needed, and encourage students to use more sophisticated strategies. Finally, the teacher or therapist must play a key role in helping students generalize information and models learned through technology to the class- or therapy room and to the world outside the school walls.

REFERENCES

Adams, R. C. (1989). Computers in schools: What's the real use? *NEA Today, 7*(6), 26–31.

Allen, M. (1990, November 13). Texas approves a "textbook" on videodiscs. *Wall Street Journal,* p. 1.

Anderson-Inman, L. (1990). Keyboarding across the curriculum. *Computing Teacher, 17*(8), 36.

Bahr, C. (1989, April). *Effects of goal structures on mathematics achievement, verbal interactions, and attitudes among mildly handicapped junior high school students using computer-based drill-and-practice.* Paper presented at the annual meeting of the Council for Exceptional Children, San Francisco.

Bahr, C. (1990, January). *Strategies for using computers in dyads.* Paper presented at the annual meeting of the Technology and Media Division Special Education Technology Conference, Lexington, KY.

Bangert-Drowns, R. L. (1989, March). *Research on word processing and writing instruction.* Paper presented at the annual conference of the American Educational Research Association, San Francisco.

Baumeister, A. A., & Brooks, P. H. (1981). Cognitive deficits in mental retardation. In J. M. Kauffman & D. P. Hallahan (Eds.), *Handbook of special education* (pp. 87–107). Englewood Cliffs, NJ: Prentice-Hall.

Becker, H. J. (1990, April). *Computer use in United States schools: 1989. An initial report of U.S. participation in the I.E.A. Computers in Education Survey.* Paper presented at the 1990 meeting of the American Educational Research Association, Boston, MA.

Becker, H. J., & Sterling, C. W. (1987). Equity in school computer use: National data and neglected considerations. *Journal of Educational Computing Research, 3,* 289–311.

Belmont, J. M., Butterfield, E. C., & Ferretti, R. P. (1982). To secure transfer of training, instruct self-management skills. In D. K. Detterman &

R. J. Sternberg (Eds.), *How much can intelligence be increased?* (pp. 147–154). Norwood, NJ: Ablex.

Bosco, J. (1986). An analysis of evaluations of interactive video. *Educational Technology, 26*(5), 7–17.

Bransford, J. D., Hasselbring, T., Barron, B., Kulewicz, S., Littlefield, J., & Goin, L. (1988). Uses of macro-contexts to facilitate mathematical thinking. In R. Charles & E. A. Silver (Eds.), *The teaching and assessing of mathematical problem solving* (pp. 125–147). Hillsdale, NJ: Lawrence Erlbaum.

Bransford, J. D., & Vye, N. J. (1989). A perspective on cognitive research and its implications for instruction. In L. Resnick & L. Klopfer (Eds.), *Toward the thinking curriculum: Current cognitive research* (pp. 173–205). Alexandria, VA: ASCD.

Browning, P., White, W.A.T., Nave, G., & Barkin, P. Z. (1986). Interactive video in the classroom: A field study. *Education and Training in Mental Retardation, 21*, 85–92.

Bruce, B., Michaels, S., & Watson-Gegeo, K. (1985). How computers can change the writing process. *Language Arts, 62*, 143–149.

Chaffin, J. D., Maxwell, B., & Thompson, B. (1982). The ARC-ED curriculum: The application of video game formats to educational software. *Exceptional Children, 49*, 173–178.

Chapman, J. W. (1988). Cognitive-motivational characteristics and academic achievement of learning disabled children: A longitudinal study. *Journal of Educational Psychology, 80*, 357–365.

Christensen, C. A., & Gerber, M. M. (1986, March). *Effects of game format in computerized drill and practice on development of automaticity in single digit addition for learning disabled students* (Tech. Rep. No. 29). Santa Barbara: University of California, Project TEECH.

Clark, C., Kurshan, B., & Yoder, S. (1989). *Telecommunications in the classroom*. Brea, CA: Diversified Printing and Publishing.

Clark, R. E. (1983). Reconsidering research on learning from media. *Review of Educational Research, 53*, 445–459.

Clements, D. H. (1989). *Computers in elementary mathematics education*. Englewood Cliffs, NJ: Prentice-Hall.

Cochran-Smith, M. (1991). Word processing and writing in elementary classrooms: A critical review of related literature. *Review of Educational Research, 61*, 107–155.

Cochran-Smith, M., Kahn, J., & Paris, C. L. (1988). When word processors come into the classroom. In J. Hoot & S. Silvern (Eds.), *Writing with computers in the early grades* (pp. 43–74). New York: Teachers College.

Cognition and Technology Group at Vanderbilt. (1990). Anchored instruction and its relationship to situated cognition. *Educational Researcher, 19*(5), 2–10.

Cosden, M. A. (1988). Microcomputer instruction and perceptions of effectiveness of special and regular education elementary school teachers. *Journal of Special Education, 22*, 242–252.

Cosden, M. A., & Abernathy, T. V. (1990). Microcomputer use in schools: Teacher roles and instructional options. *Remedial and Special Education, 11*, 31–38.

Cox, D. A., & Berger, C. F. (1985). The importance of group size in the use of problem-solving skills on a microcomputer. *Journal of Educational Computing Research, 1*, 459–468.

Daiute, C. (1986). Physical and cognitive factors in revising: Insights from studies with computers. *Research in the Teaching of English, 20*, 141–159.

Dalton, B., Winbury, N. E., & Morocco, C. C. (1990). "If you could just push a button": Two fourth grade boys with learning disabilities learn to use a computer spelling checker. *Journal of Special Education Technology, 10*, 177–191.

Dalton, D. W., Hannafin, M. J., & Hooper, S. (1989). Effects of individual and cooperative computer-assisted instruction on student performance and attitudes. *Educational Technology Research and Development, 37*(2), 15–24.

Davidson, J. J. (1989). *Children and computers together in the early childhood classroom*. Albany, NY: Delmar.

Deshler, D. D., Schumaker, J. B., Alley, G. R., Warner, M. M., & Clark, F. L. (1982). Learning disabilities in adolescent and adult populations. *Focus on Exceptional Children, 15*(1), 1–12.

Duffield, J. A. (1990, April). *Problem solving software: What does it teach?* Paper presented at the annual meeting of the American Educational Research Association, Boston.

Ellis, E. S., Lenz, K., & Sabornie, E. J. (1987). Generalization and adaptation of learning strategies to natural environments: Part 2. Research into practice. *Remedial and Special Education, 8*(2), 6–23.

EPIE (1988). *The Educational Software Selector (TESS): The 1988 supplement*. Water Mill, NY: Author.

Försterling, F. (1985). Attributional retraining: A review. *Psychological Bulletin, 98*, 495–512.

Fuchs, L. S., Deno, S. L., & Mirkin, P. K. (1984). Effects of frequent curriculum-based measurement and evaluation on pedagogy, student achievement, and student awareness of learning. *American Educational Research Journal, 21*, 449–460.

Fuchs, L. S., & Fuchs, D. (1989). Enhancing curriculum-based measurement through computer applications: Review of research and practice. *School Psychology Review, 18,* 317–327.

Gardner, J. E., & Bates, P. (in press). Attitudes and attributions on use of microcomputers in school by students who are mentally handicapped. *Education and Training in Mental Retardation.*

Goldman, S. R., & Pellegrino, J. (1987). Information processing and educational microcomputer technology: Where do we go from here? *Journal of Learning Disabilities, 20,* 144–154.

Graham, S., & Harris, K. R. (1988). Instructional recommendations for teaching writing to exceptional students. *Exceptional Children, 54,* 506–512.

Graham, S., & Harris, K. R. (1989). Components analysis of cognitive strategy instruction: Effects on learning disabled students' compositions and self-efficacy. *Journal of Educational Psychology, 81,* 353–361.

Hallahan, D. P., & Kauffman, J. M. (1986). *Exceptional children* (3rd ed.). Englewood Cliffs, NJ: Prentice-Hall.

Hallahan, D. P., Kauffman, J. M., & Lloyd, J. W. (1985). *Introduction to learning disabilities* (2nd ed.). Englewood Cliffs, NJ: Prentice-Hall.

Hasselbring, T. S. (1984). Using a microcomputer for imitating student errors to improve spelling performance. *Computers, Reading, and Language Arts, 1*(4), 12–14.

Hasselbring, T. S., & Goin, L. I. (1989). *DLM Math Fluency Program* [Computer program]. Allen, TX: DLM.

Hasselbring, T. S., Goin, L. I., & Bransford, J. D. (1987). Developing automaticity. *Teaching Exceptional Children, 19*(3), 30–33.

Hasselbring, T. S., Goin, L. I., & Bransford, J. D. (1988). Developing math automaticity in learning handicapped children: The role of computerized drill and practice. *Focus on Exceptional Children, 20*(6), 1–7.

Hativa, N. (1988). Computer-based drill and practice in arithmetic: Widening the gap between high- and low-achieving students. *American Educational Research Journal, 25,* 366–397.

Hativa, N., & Lesgold, A. (1990, April). *Computerized management of practice—Can it adapt to the individual learner?* Paper presented at the annual meeting of the American Educational Research Association, Boston, MA.

Haugland, S. W., & Shade, D. D. (1988). Developmentally appropriate software for young children. *Young Children, 43*(4), 37–43.

Heller, K. A., Holtzman, W. H., & Messick, S. (Eds.) (1982). *Placing children in special education: A strategy for equity.* Washington, DC: National Academy Press.

Higgins, K., & Boone, R. (1990). Hypertext: A new vehicle for computer use in reading instruction. *Intervention in School and Clinic, 26*(1), 26–31.

High-tech have-nots. (1990, December 10). *Business Week,* p. 98.

Hofmeister, A. (1983). *Microcomputer applications in the classroom.* New York: Holt, Rinehart & Winston.

Horton, S., V., Lovitt, T. C., Givens, A., & Nelson, R. (1989). Teaching social studies to high school students with academic handicaps in a mainstream setting: Effects of a computerized study guide. *Journal of Learning Disabilities, 22,* 102–107.

Hunter, M. W., & Dickey, J. (1990, January). *A computer-based information system to support ongoing academic adjustment by at-risk secondary students: Initial design and field test.* Paper presented at the Technology and Media Division Conference on Special Education Technology, Lexington, KY.

Johnson, D. W., & Johnson, R. T. (1986). Mainstreaming and cooperative learning strategies. *Exceptional Children, 52,* 553–561.

Johnson, R. T., Johnson, D. W., & Stanne, M. B. (1986). Comparison of computer-assisted cooperative, competitive, and individualistic learning. *American Educational Research Journal, 23,* 382–392.

Jones, K. M., Torgesen, J. K., & Sexton, M. A. (1987). Using computer guided practice to increase decoding fluency in learning disabled children: A study using the Hint and Hunt I program. *Journal of Learning Disabilities, 20,* 122–128.

Julyan, C. L. (1990). Lunchroom garbage: Findings from student-scientists. *Hands On, 13*(1), 11–14.

Kahn, J. (1988). *Learning to write with a new tool: A study of emergent writers using word processing.* Unpublished doctoral dissertation, University of Pennsylvania, Philadelphia.

Kelly, B., Carnine, D. W., Gersten, R., & Grossen, B. (1986). The effectiveness of videodisc instruction in teaching fractions to learning handicapped and remedial high school students. *Journal of Special Education Technology, 8*(2), 5–17.

Kelly, B., Gersten, R., & Woodward, J. (in press). Research on teachers' implementation of an interactive videodisc curriculum. In T. Grady (Ed.), *Technology and curriculum.* Alexandria, VA: ASCD.

Knapp, L. R. (1984). Finding the best typing tutorials. *Classroom Computer Learning, 5*(4), 70–71.

Kramer, J. J., Nagle, R. J., & Engle, R. W. (1980). Recent advances in mnemonic strategy training with mentally retarded persons: Implications for educational practice. *American Journal of Mental Deficiency, 85,* 306–314.

Krupski, A. (1981). An interactional approach to the study of attention problems in children with learning handicaps. *Exceptional Education Quarterly, 2,* 1–11.

Kulik, J. A., Bangert, R. L., & Williams, G. W. (1983). Effects of computer-based teaching on secondary school students. *Journal of Educational Psychology, 75,* 19–26.

Kulik, J. A., Kulik, C. C., & Bangert-Drowns, R. L. (1985). Effectiveness of computer-based education in elementary schools. *Computers in Human Behavior, 1,* 59–74.

Laboratory of Comparative Human Culture. (1989). Kids and computers: A positive vision of the future. *Harvard Educational Review, 59,* 73–86.

Lepper, M. R., (1985). Microcomputers in education: Motivational and social issues. *American Psychologist, 40*(1), 1–18.

Lepper, M. R., & Malone, T. W. (1987). Intrinsic motivation and instructional effectiveness in computer-based education. In R. E. Snow & M. J. Farr (Eds.), *Aptitude, learning and instruction: Vol 3. Conative and affective process analysis* (pp. 255–286). Hillsdale, NJ: Lawrence Erlbaum.

Lieber, J., & Semmel, M. I. (1987). The relationship between group size and performance on a microcomputer problem-solving task for learning handicapped and nonhandicapped students. *Journal of Educational Computing Research, 3,* 171–187.

Lieberman, D. A., & Linn, M. C. (1991). Learning to learn revisited: Computers and the development of self-directed learning skills. *Journal of Research on Computing in Education, 23,* 373–395.

Lilly, M. S. (1977). A merger of categories: Are we finally ready? *Learning Disability Quarterly, 10*(2), 56–61.

Linn, M. C. (1986). Computer as lab partner. *Teaching Thinking and Problem Solving, 18*(3), 1–12.

Litchfield, B. C. (1990). Science Quest: A multimedia inquiry-based videodisc science curriculum. *Instructional Delivery Systems, 4*(3), 12–17.

MacArthur, C. A. (1988). The impact of computers on the writing process. *Exceptional Children, 54,* 536–542.

MacArthur, C. A., Haynes, J. A., & Malouf, D. B. (1986). Learning disabled students' engaged time and classroom integration: The impact of computer assisted instruction. *Journal of Educational Computing Research, 2,* 189–198.

MACRO Systems. (1989, November). *Evaluation of the integration of technology for instructing handicapped students (high school level)* (Final Report, Executive Summary). Silver Spring, MD: Author.

Mageau, T. (1992). Two teaching models that work. *Electronic Learning, 11*(4), 16–22.

Majsterek, D. J., & Wilson, R. (1989). Computer-assisted instruction for students with learning disabilities: Considerations for practitioners. *Learning Disabilities Focus, 5,* 18–27.

Malone, T. W. (1981). Toward a theory of intrinsically motivating instruction. *Cognitive Science, 4,* 333–369.

Malouf, D. B. (1987–1988). The effect of instructional computer games on continuing student motivation. *Journal of Special Education,* 27–38.

Malouf, D. B., Wizer, D. R., Pilato, V. H., & Grogan, M. M. (1990). Computer-assisted instruction with small groups of mildly handicapped students. *Journal of Special Education, 24,* 51–68.

McClean, G. (1987). Criteria for selecting computer software for keyboarding instruction. *Business Education Forum, 41*(5), 10–11.

McKeown, M. G., & Beck, I. L. (1988). Learning vocabulary: Different ways for different goals. *Remedial and Special Education, 9*(1), 42–46.

McNamara, T. P., Miller, D. L., & Bransford, J. D. (in press). Mental models and reading comprehension. In P. D. Pearson, R. Barr, M. Kamil, & P. Mosenthal (Eds.), *Handbook of reading research* (Vol. 2). New York: Longman.

Mercer, C. D., & Mercer, A. R. (1989). *Teaching students with learning problems* (3rd ed.). Columbus, OH: Merrill Publishing.

Messerer, J., & Lerner, J. W. (1989). Word processing for learning disabled students. *Learning Disabilities Focus, 5,* 13–17.

Mokros, J. R., & Russell, S. J. (1986). Learner-centered software: A survey of microcomputer use with special needs students. *Journal of Learning Disabilities, 19,* 185–190.

Morocco, C. C. (1987). *Teachers, children, and the magical writing machine: Instructional contexts for word processing with learning disabled children.* (Final Report, EDC Writing Project). Newton, MA: Education Development Center.

Morocco, C. C., Dalton, B., & Tivnan, T. (1989). *The impact of computer-supported writing instruction on the writing quality of learning disabled students.* (Final Report, EDC Writing Project). Newton, MA: Education Development Center.

Neuman, S. B., & Morocco, C. (1987). Two hands is hard for me: Keyboarding and learning disabled children. *Educational Technology, 27*(12), 36–38.

Newman, D. (1987). Local and long distance computer networking for science classrooms. *Educational Technology, 27*(7), 20–23.

Office of Special Education Programs. (1990). *Twelfth annual report to Congress on the implementation of the Education of the Handicapped Act.* Washington, DC: Author.

Okolo, C. M. (1991a). *The effects of CAI formats on students' mathematics performance and continuing motivation.* Manuscript submitted for publication.

Okolo, C. M. (1991b). Learning and behaviorally handicapped students' receptions of instructional and motivational features of computer-assisted instruction. *Journal of Research on Computing in Education, 24,* 171–188.

Okolo, C. M. (in press a). The effects of CAI format and initial attitude on the arithmetic facts proficiency and continuing motivation of students with learning disabilities. *Exceptionality.*

Okolo, C. M. (in press b). The effects of computer-based attribution retraining on the attributions, persistence, and mathematics computation of students with learning disabilities. *Journal of Learning Disabilities.*

Okolo, C. M., Hinsey, M., & Yousefian, B. (1990). Learning disabled students' acquisition of keyboarding skills and continuing motivation under drill-and-practice and game conditions. *Learning Disabilities Research, 5,* 100–109.

Okolo, C. M., & Owen, V. (1990). *The effects of gender and learning disability on students' computer experience and attitudes.* Manuscript submitted for publication.

Okolo, C. M., Rieth, H. J., & Bahr, C. (1989). Microcomputer implementation in secondary special education programs: A study of special educators', mildly handicapped adolescents', and administrators' perspectives. *Journal of Special Education, 23,* 107–117.

Palinscar, A. S., & Brown, A. L. (1984). Reciprocal teaching of comprehension-fostering and comprehension-monitoring activities. *Cognition and Instruction, 1,* 117–175.

Panyan, M., & Hummel, J. W. (1988). *Evaluation of the integration of technology for instructing handicapped children at the elementary school level.* Baltimore: Johns Hopkins University, Center for Technology in Human Disabilities.

Pea, R. D. (1985). Beyond amplification: Using the computer to reorganize mental functioning. *Educational Psychologist, 20,* 167–182.

Pea, R. D. (1987). Cognitive technologies for mathematics education. In A. H. Schoenfeld (Ed.), *Cognitive science and mathematics education* (pp. 89–122). Hillsdale, NJ: Lawrence Erlbaum Associates.

Pearl, R. (1982). LD children's attributions for success and failure: A replication with a labeled LD sample. *Learning Disability Quarterly, 5,* 173–176.

Pearl, R. (1985). Cognitive-behavioral interventions for increasing motivation. *Journal of Abnormal Child Psychology, 13,* 443–454.

Perkins, D. N. (1985). The fingertip effect: How information-processing technology changes thinking. *Educational Researcher, 14*(7), 11–17.

Pogrow, S. (1990). A Socratic approach to using computers with at-risk students. *Educational Leadership, 47*(5), 61–66.

Rieber, L. P. (1990, April). *Animated graphics, incidental learning, and continuing motivation.* Paper presented at the annual meeting of the American Educational Research Association, Boston, MA.

Rieth, H., Bahr, C., Okolo, C., Polsgrove, L., & Eckert, R. (1988). An analysis of the impact of microcomputers on the secondary special education classroom ecology. *Journal of Educational Computing Research, 4,* 425–442.

Roth, S. G., & Beck, I. L. (1987). Theoretical and instructional implications of the assessment of two microcomputer word recognition programs. *Reading Research Quarterly, 22,* 197–218.

Salisbury, D. F. (1990). Cognitive psychology and its implications for designing drill and practice programs for computers. *Journal of Computer-Based Education, 17,* 22–30.

Salomon, G. (1988). AI in reverse: Computer tools that turn cognitive. *Journal of Educational Computing Research, 4,* 123–139.

Saracho, O. N. (1982). The effects of a computer-assisted instruction program on basic skills achievement and attitudes toward instruction of Spanish-speaking migrant children. *American Educational Research Journal, 19,* 201–219.

Schmalhofer, F., & Kähn, O. (1988). *Acquiring computer skills by exploration versus demonstration* (Tech. Rep. No. 88.3). Montreal: McGill University, Laboratory of Applied Cognitive Science.

Schunk, D. H. (1985). Participation in goal setting: Effects on self-efficacy and skills of learning disabled children. *Journal of Special Education, 19,* 307–317.

Schunk, D. H. (1989). Self-efficacy and classroom learning. *Psychology in the Schools, 22,* 208–223.

Schwartz, I., & Lewis, M. (1991–1992). Selecting basic concept courseware for preschools and early elementary grades. *Computing Teacher, 19*(4), 15–17.

Semmel, M. I., & Lieber, J. A. (1986). Computer applications in instruction. *Focus on Exceptional Children, 18*(9), 1–12.

Sherry, M. (1990). Implementing an integrated instructional system: Critical issues. *Phi Delta Kappan, 72*(2), 118–120.

Smith, R. A., & Sclafani, S. (1989). Integrated teaching systems: Guidelines for evaluation. *Computing Teacher, 17*(3), 36–38.

Sormunen, C., Adams, M., Berg, D., & Prigge, L. (1989). *A national study of instructional practices and perceptions of elementary school teachers about typewriting/keyboarding.* Little Rock, AR: Delta Pi Epsilon.

Sormunen, C., & Wickersham, G. (1991). Language arts and keyboarding skills development: A viable approach for teaching elementary school students. *Journal of Research on Computing in Education, 23,* 463–469.

Swan, K., Guerrero, F., Mitrani, M., & Schoener, J. (1990). Honing in on the target: Who among the educationally disadvantaged benefits most from CBI? *Journal of Research on Computing in Education, 22,* 381–403.

Thomas, C. C., Englert, C. S., & Gregg, S. (1987). An analysis of errors and strategies in the expository writing of learning disabled students. *Remedial and Special Education, 8,* 21–30.

Torgesen, J. K. (1984). Instructional use of computers with elementary aged mildly handicapped children. *Special Services in the Schools, 1*(1), 37–48.

Van Hanegan, J., Barron, L., Young, M., Williams, S., Vye, N., & Bransford, J. D. (in press). The Jasper series: An experiment with new ways to enhance mathematical thinking. In D. Halpern (Ed.), *Concerning the development of thinking skills in science and mathematics.*

Wallace, G., & Kauffman, J. M. (1986). *Teaching children with learning problems.* Columbus, OH: Merrill.

Watson, J. (1988). *Teaching thinking skills with databases.* Eugene, OR: International Council for Computers in Education.

Wiebe, J. H., & Martin, N. J. (1990, April). *The impact of a computer-based adventure/action game on achievement and attitudes in geography.* Paper presented at the annual meeting of the American Educational Research Association, Boston, MA.

Winkler, J. D., Shavelson, R. J., Stasz, C., Robyn, A. E., & Fiebel, W. (1985). Pedagogically sound use of microcomputers in classroom instruction. *Journal of Educational computing research, 18,* 285–293.

Wiske, M. S., Zodhiates, P., Wilson, B., Gordon, M., Harvey, W., Krensky, L. L., Lord, B., Watt, M., & Williams, K. (1988, March). *How technology affects teaching* (Tech. Rep. No. TR87-10). Cambridge, MA: Harvard Graduate School of Education, Educational Technology Center.

Woodward, J., & Carnine, D. (1988). Antecedent knowledge and intelligent computer-assisted instruction. *Journal of Learning Disabilities, 21,* 131–139.

Woodward, J., Carnine, D., Gersten, R., Gleason, M., Johnson, G., & Collins, M. (1986). Applying instructional design principles to CAI for mildly handicapped students: Four recently conducted studies. *Journal of Special Education Technology, 8,* 13–26.

Woodward, J., & Gersten, R. (1992). Innovative technology for secondary students with learning disabilities. *Exceptional Children, 58*(5), 407–421.

Suggested Activities

Paper and Pencil

Make a list of five instructional goals that you consider most important for students with mild disabilities at a particular age level (i.e., preschool, primary, intermediate, high school, or postsecondary). Obtain reviews of software and videodiscs from journals, resource guides, or catalogs and list five technology-based products that could help you accomplish each instructional goal.

Observation

Visit a school that uses computers and other technologies. Observe how technology is being used in regular classrooms, computer labs, and special education classrooms. Note how students with mild disabilities use technology in each of these three settings. Do technology applications used by students with mild disabilities differ from those used by non-disabled students? Do students with mild disabilities use technology differently across settings? Interview teachers of the classes and labs you have visited about these differences.

Practicum

Develop a week- to month-long unit that utilizes technology as a central component of the instructional activities. Describe the unit's goals and objectives and the technology and nontechnological materials necessary to accomplish them. Consider any prerequisite skills that students will need to use these materials and activities that will help students transfer the skills they will learn. Decide how you will evaluate students' attainment of objectives.

As you teach your unit, keep records of student progress and student reactions to the technological applications you have chosen. Consider how the technology facilitated the accomplishment of your objectives and its impact on student learning and performance. Describe any unintended outcomes of the technology being used and consider ways in which the unit could be improved in the future.

Resources

Organizations

Apple Computer Office of Special Education and Rehabilitation. This office works with national education, rehabilitation, and advocacy organizations to identify technology needs of people with disabilities, develop programs that respond to those needs, and ensure the accessibility of Apple equipment. It also coordinates the National Special Education Alliance, a coalition of nonprofit resource centers across the country that provide services and demonstration sites related to technology use for individuals with disabilities. The Office of Special Education and Rehabilitation publishes a resource guide entitled *Apple Computer Resources in Special Education.* An on-line data base of resources available to people with disabilities, entitled Apple Solutions, is available via AppleLink, SpecialNet, or as a hypercard stack. Write to Apple Computer, 20525 Mariani Avenue, Cupertino, CA 95014.

Center for Special Education Technology. This center is a federally funded project designed to promote the appropriate use of computer, video, and audio technology in special educa-

tion. The center operates a bulletin board (Tech.line) on SpecialNet, publishes manuals and fact sheets about special education technology, and sponsors conferences and working groups. Write to the Center for Special Education Technology, 1920 Association Drive, Reston, VA 22091.

IBM National Support Center for Persons with Disabilities. This center was established to help educators and other service providers, employers, public officials, and individuals learn how technology can improve the quality of life for people with disabilities. The center responds to requests for information on ways in which computers can help individuals with disabilities and publishes resource guides. Write to the IBM National Support Center for Persons with Disabilities, P.O. Box 2150, Atlanta, GA 30055.

International Society for Technology in Education. This organization is comprised of professionals interested in educational technology. It publishes a practitioner-oriented journal, *The Computing Teacher;* a research journal, *Journal of Research on Computing in Education;* a newsletter; and a variety of special-interest group publications. It also produces a number of valuable print and software-based materials, offers inservice education courses, and produces a software preview guide. Write to the: International Society for Technology in Education, 1787 Agate Street, Eugene, OR 97403.

Technology and Media Division. A division of the Council for Exceptional Children (CEC), this is an organization of professionals interested in the effective use of technology for individuals with disabilities. It publishes a quarterly journal, *Journal of Special Education Technology,* and the *TAM Newsletter.* It also sponsors an annual conference. Write to TAM, c/o Council for Exceptional Children, 1920 Association Drive, Reston, VA 22091.

Software and Hardware

Apple Computer
2025 Mariani Avenue
Cupertino, CA 95014

Brøderbund
17 Paul Drive
San Rafael, CA 94913-2101

Claris
5201 Patrick Henry Drive
Box 58168
Santa Clara, CA

Conduit
University of Iowa
Oakdale Campus
Iowa City, IA 52242

CUE SoftSwap
P.O. Box 271704
Concord, CA 94527-1704

Davidson & Associates
3135 Kashiwa Street
Torrance, CA 90505

Discis Knowledge Systems
45 Shepard Avenue East
Toronto, Ontario, Canada

DLM
One DLM Park
Allen, TX 75002

D. C. Heath
125 Spring Street
Lexington, MA 02173

First Byte
3333 East Spring Street
Suite 302
Long Beach, CA 90806

GTE Education Services
8505 Freeport Parkway
Suite 600
Irving, TX 75063

Hartley Courseware
P.O. Box 419
Diamondale, MI 48221

Houghton Mifflin
P.O. Box 683
Hanover, NH 03755

IBM
P.O. Box 2150
Atlanta, GA 30055

Laureate Learning Systems
110 East Spring Street
Winooski, VT 05404

The Learning Company
6493 Kaiser Drive
Fremont, CA 94555

MECC
3490 Lexington Avenue North
St. Paul, MN 55126

Microsoft
One Microsoft Way
Redmond, WA 98052-6399

Milliken Publishing
1100 Research Blvd.
P.O. Box 21579
St. Louis, MO 63132-0579

Mindscape Software
Dept E
1345 Diversey Parkway
Chicago, IL 60614-1299

Morning Star Software
P.O. Box 5364
Madison, WI 53705

National Geographic Society
Educational Services
Department 5397
Washington, D.C. 20036

Optical Data
30 Technology Drive
Warren, NJ 07059

Owl International
14218 NE 21st Street
Bellevue, WA 98007

Performance Monitoring Systems
P.O. Box 148
Cambridge, MN 55008

PRO-ED
8700 Shoal Creek Blvd.
Austin, TX 78758-9965

Roger Wagner Publishing
1050 Pioneer Way
Suite P
El Cajon, CA 92020

Scholastic
2931 East McCarty Street
P.O. Box 7502
Jefferson City, MO 65102

Sunburst Communications
101 Casleton Street
Pleasantville, NY 10570-9905

Teacher Support Software
1035 N.W. 57th Street
Gainesville, FL 32605-4483

Tom Snyder Productions
Educational Software
123 Mt. Auburn Street
Cambridge, MA 02138

Thinking with Computers
P.O. Box 42620
Tucson, AZ 85733

Techware
P.O. Box 151085
Altamonte Springs, FL 32715

Wings for Learning
1600 Green Hills Road
P.O. Box 660002
Scotts Valley, CA 95067-0002

Computers and Individuals with Speech and Language Disorders

CHAPTER

Paula S. Cochran
Northeast Missouri State University
Glen L. Bull
University of Virginia

The availability of powerful, creative, effective computer applications for assisting persons with communication disorders was anxiously anticipated just a few years ago. Even though the advent of personal computers was exciting to some professionals from the start, it was acknowledged that early applications were often too primitive and too inflexible to be clinically useful. University faculty and members of professional organizations such as the American Speech-Language-Hearing Association (ASHA) met to discuss strategies for incorporating the latest technologies into communication disorders training programs (Bull et al., 1985). The lack of appropriate software in the early 1980s caused some experts to suggest that speech-language pathologists should learn computer programming for the purpose of writing their own software to meet the needs of individual clients (see, e.g., Ventkatagiri, 1987). Developers promised that more powerful, more affordable, more portable technology was coming soon.

Those promises became reality with the availability of specific computer hardware and software applications for persons with communication disorders. Once proponents of clinical applications of computers were armed with only anecdotal evidence and enthusiasm, but now the results of controlled efficacy studies are available. Although a short time ago most clinical applications of computers appeared to be electronic workbook versions of traditional therapy activities, now computer applications serve a variety of useful roles in therapy. Whereas once the appearance of a computer was remarkable, computers are now a routine part of the landscape in schools, hospitals, and clinics, and most ASHA members report that they use computers at work (Hyman, 1985) (see Figure 7.1). Just a few years ago only a few individuals with communication disorders had the opportunity to benefit from new clinical applications of computers; however, now many do so every day.

143

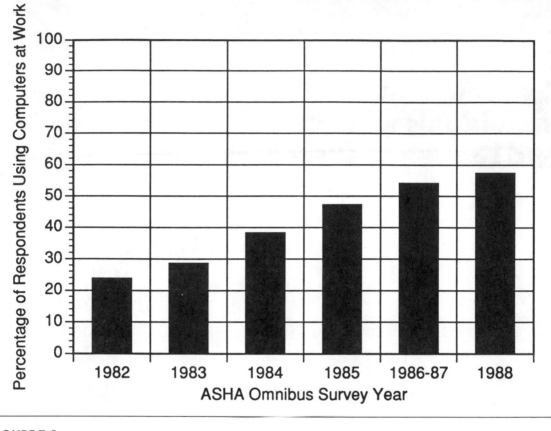

FIGURE 7.1

INDIVIDUALS WITH COMMUNICATION DISORDERS

A communication disorder generally refers to any impairment of an individual's ability to use oral language to communicate with other people. Thus communication disorders include problems with hearing, articulation (producing speech sounds), voice, fluency, or language. Language disorders, in contrast to speech disorders, may include difficulties comprehending, planning, or producing appropriate words and sentences according to a socially shared code. Speakers of a dialect are not considered to have a communication disorder unless their ability to communicate with other members of their dialect group is impaired. It is important to note that language disorders may go beyond difficulty with the form of language (sounds and structure) to include difficulties adapting language to fit the circumstances and using it effectively in various situations.

Projections based on U.S. population data suggest that in 1990 there were approximately 288,000 persons with speech impairments and 2,106,000 persons with hearing impairments in the United States (Fein, 1983). These numbers are expected to increase by the year 2050 to 399,000 and 3,651,000, respectively. Fein (1983) also noted that "between 1980 and 2050, the numbers of persons with speech and hearing impairments will increase at faster rates (53% and 102%, respectively) than the total U.S. population (36%) as a direct result of the aging of the U.S. population" (p. 47).

Some communication disorders result from known organic causes. For example, a cleft palate or cerebral palsy may cause an individual to have difficulty producing certain speech sounds. Often, however, no organic cause is apparent in the presence of a speech or language disorder. Mental retardation is one of the most common reasons that children fail to acquire language normally, but a variety of other reasons, ranging from hearing loss to emotional disturbance, may be responsible. Thus, some communication disorders involve delayed, arrested, or disordered acquisition of skills. Other communication disorders, such as adult aphasia, involve the sudden impairment or loss of communication ability. Such a condition may be temporary (as in the case of a vocal pathology that can be surgically treated) or permanent (as in the case of sudden hearing loss). In summary, persons with communication disorders may be any age and may be experiencing a temporary or permanent, sudden or gradual change in their ability to exchange information with other people through normal means. Intervention designed to assist persons with communication disorders, therefore, may have a very wide range of goals including remediation, compensation, or rehabilitation.

Professionals who provide direct intervention services for persons with speech and language disorders are called *speech-language pathologists. Audiologists* are professionals who specialize in the evaluation and rehabilitation of hearing impairments. In the United States, most states require a master's degree or equivalent in order to meet state licensure and/or teaching certification requirements in speech-language pathology or in audiology. Speech-language pathologists and audiologists provide services in a wide variety of work settings that include schools, hospitals, private and public clinics, rehabilitation centers, state residential institutions, nursing homes, and private practice offices. This chapter describes the ways computers are used by speech-language pathologists to assist persons with speech or language impairments. Computer applications for persons with sensory impairments such as hearing loss are covered in Chapter 9.

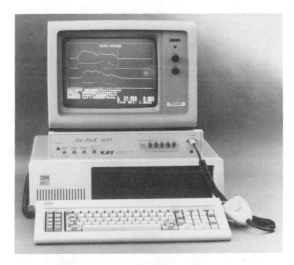

The computer can provide visual biofeedback about aspects of a person's speech or voice.
(Photograph courtesy of Kay Elemetrics Corporation)

GENERAL HARDWARE AND SOFTWARE CONSIDERATIONS

Administrative Applications

Speech-language pathologists use computers for both administrative and clinical purposes. Administrative purposes include report writing, individualized education plan (IEP) and individualized habilitation plan (IHP) generation, billing and record keeping, and electronic communication with other professionals. Such administrative activities are described in Chapters 12 and 13. The present chapter focuses instead on the clinical applications of computers, or applications that are used directly with persons who have speech or language disorders.

Clinical Applications

At this time in the development of computer applications in communication disorders, there are three main categories of clinical use of computers with and by persons who have speech or language disorders. The three categories of clinical applications are defined by their purposes (see Table 7.1). Each type of clinical application is discussed in the next section.

TABLE 7.1
Clinical applications of computers for persons with speech-language disorders

Clinical Purpose	Clinical Role
Remediation or rehabilitation	• Instructor • Context for therapy • Materials generator • Biofeedback device • Datakeeper • Expert system
Evaluation or diagnosis	• Hearing and hearing aid testing • Voice/speech analysis • Speech sample analysis • Language sample analysis
Augmentative/ alternative communication	• Dedicated device • Academic/vocational assistant • Electronic aid training device • Communication board designer

TABLE 7.2
Speech and language disorders and types of computer applications

Disorder	Types of Applications
Articulation	Phonologic analysis, intelligibility analysis, drill-and-practice, and games
Voice	Biofeedback programs and client information
Fluency	Biofeedback and relaxation programs
Syntactic	Language sample analysis, drill and practice, games, and tutorials
Semantic	Language sample analysis and cognitive rehabilitation
Pragmatic	Problem solving and simulations
Hearing Impairment	Visual feedback, sign language instruction with CAI, and telecommunication applications

Computer Roles in Remediation and Rehabilitation

It is possible to review many clinical applications of computers in communication disorders and label software/hardware packages according to categories well established by researchers in educational technology. Such traditional categories include tutorials, simulations, drill-and-practice, and others (see Table 7.2). These categories are of limited value when considering the clinical applications of computers for communication disorders. It is more instructive to consider the roles that a variety of computer applications may play in the remediation and rehabilitation of communication disorders. That is, speech-language pathologists have choices to make about how computers will or will not be integrated into a plan that addresses the needs of a specific student or client. How the computer is used implies important assumptions that go beyond whether the software itself is independently labeled as a tutorial versus a simulation. The roles computers play in intervention may depend more on the procedures of the clinician than on specific hardware and software features.

SPECIFIC COMPUTER APPLICATIONS

Computer as Instructor

The computer acting as an instructor during speech-language therapy is probably the role most beginning clinicians and most lay people imagine first. In this role, the computer is assumed to be deliberately "teaching" the user something, or at the very least providing a structured opportunity for the user to practice a predetermined skill. Generally, the pattern of interaction between the computer and the user goes something like this:

COMPUTER [*Presents information or stimulus question and waits for a response from the user*]: Which one is a vehicle?

PERSON WITH SPEECH-LANGUAGE DISORDER [*Responds by pressing a key or using an alternative access device such as a joystick*]: *Presses number 2 to match the picture of a car on the screen.*

COMPUTER [*Provides feedback about the correctness of the response*]: Yes, a car is a vehicle.

Thus a familiar stimulus-response-reinforcement pattern is used as the structure for two-way interaction between the computer and the user. Usually software designed to teach language in this manner keeps track of correct and incorrect responses and provides individual performance records upon request.

Although software designed to address language deficits in this way has been widely available for several years, there is little data-based research demonstrating its efficacy in improving communication skills (Nippold, Schwarz, & Lewis, 1992). For example, several studies have explored the use of language tutorials and drill-and-practice software by persons who have mental retardation. Researchers have used computers instead of humans to teach skills such as sight-word recognition (Conners, Caruso, & Detterman, 1986; Lally, 1981; Wright & Anderson, 1987) and picture recognition and categorization (Wilson & Fox, 1983). For the most part, success in such studies is measured by the percentage correct received during the computer activity rather than by changes in effective communication with another person.

Several data-based studies have considered the independent use of computers by adults who have acquired speech-language impairments (Katz, 1984, 1986; Mills, 1986a, 1986b). The computer has functioned successfully as an instructor when target behaviors involve improving written language skills (e.g., reading comprehension, spelling, sight-word recognition). For some adults, intervention plans include helping them gain an increased sense of control and responsibility for their own rehabilitation. In such cases, the independent use of computer applications

capable of serving in the role of instructor may be particularly effective.

In summary, computer applications designed to teach language concepts in the absence of a communicative context or a conversational partner are widely available. There is a lack of empirical evidence to support the isolated individual use of such computer applications by persons with speech or language disorders to improve their oral language skills. There is evidence to support the independent use of a computer when such use is intended to improve written language skills or overall independent learning habits.

The Computer as a Context for Therapy

Susie is a language-delayed 5-year-old who is working on correct use of present- and past-tense action verbs in therapy (e.g., *The boy was walking. He walked.*). Susie is pressing on the W key and watching the face on the computer wink at her. She and her clinician have just finished creating the funny face by picking the eyes, ears, nose, mouth, and hair from a collection of features that come as part of the computer program Facemaker (Spinnaker, 1984). Now they are causing parts of the face to move by pressing certain keys.

CLINICIAN [*Pressing S key*]: Look! I'm making him smile. He's smiling. He's smiling at you.

SUSIE: No, he's smiling at *you*. Let me do it. [*Presses S key*]

CLINICIAN [*Hiding her eyes*]: What's happening?

SUSIE: He's smiling! [*Presses W key*] He's winking too!

CLINICIAN [*Peeking*]: I saw him! He winked! He winked at me.

Computer programs such as Facemaker can function as a context for a speech or language therapy session. In this role, the computer provides an ongoing focus for communication between the clinician and the person with a speech or language disorder. The software employed during this kind of activity need not be designed to provide explicit programmed instruction. Rather, open-ended, flexible software that is guided by the input of the users is well suited to provide a context for a therapy session. Activities based on this kind of software are user-controlled and center on the goals and strategies initiated by the learner rather than the computer. Such software has been labeled "learner-centered" software (Mokros & Russell, 1986; Russell, Corwin, Mokros, & Kapisovsky, 1989). An even more flexible and extensible subset of learner-centered software has been labeled "learner-based tools" (Bull & Cochran, 1991). Many case studies and examples of specific learner-based software programs used in speech and language therapy have been described elsewhere (Bull, Cochran, & Snell, 1988; Cochran & Bull, 1991; Russell et al., 1989; Steiner & Larson, 1991).

As Susie's example illustrates, the instructional value of learner-based software often depends on the occurrence of a three-way interaction between the student, the computer, and the clinician or teacher. In this case, the clinician provides the appropriate emphasis on action verbs to meet Susie's individual needs. Susie has the opportunity to hear and use the target language in the context of real communication with another person. Because the clinician's input during the use of the computer provides practice with specific language targets, a very wide selection of educational software programs can be the basis for such language therapy activities.

There have been several experimental studies of the use of computer-based activities as a context for speech or language therapy with children (Harn, 1986; O'Connor & Schery, 1986; Ott-Rose, 1990; Prinz, 1991; Schetz, 1989; Shriberg, Kwiatkowski, & Snyder, 1989, 1990). Such studies do not assume that the computer is replacing the clinician but rather that the computer serves in the place of alternative materials or activities. Taken together, the results of these studies suggest that when a clinician and child use a computer together, a context for therapy exists that is at least as effective as that provided by more traditional materials.

In addition to concern about efficacy in achieving clinical goals, researchers share an interest in children's motivation and preferences regarding computer-based activities. Fazio and Rieth (1986) studied the free-play choices of preschoolers attending a nursery school program. They found that normally achieving preschoolers chose a computer activity 84% of the time and their peers with mental retardation chose to use a computer 70% of the time, despite the presence of a wide variety of alternative activities. Both groups of children showed a marked preference for software considered to be user-controlled rather than drill-and-practice in format (Fazio & Rieth, 1986). In addition, two studies have tallied the preferences of preschool children using closely matched computer-based and traditional table-top speech and language therapy activities (Ott-Rose, 1990; Shriberg et al., 1989). In both cases, most children (15 out of 18, Shriberg et al., 1989; 4 out of 5, Ott-Rose, 1990) expressed a preference for the computer-based version.

Using a Computer to Generate Materials

Speech-language pathologists typically use a number of visual materials to help convey the meaning of words and to serve as stimulus items for a person working on improving speech or language skills. Many of these materials are consumable rather than reusable. Stickers are taken home, worksheets are completed, and pictures are colored as reinforcement for good work. Computer programs that could be used to develop consumable as well as reusable therapy materials have proliferated, although many clinicians remain unaware of the possibilities.

User-friendly flexible software for quickly producing fancy text and graphics (e.g., signs, greeting cards, calendars, banners, certificates) is available for all major brands of microcomputers. Print Shop (Brøderbund), Print Shop Companion (Brøderbund), and Certificate Maker (Springboard) are among the programs of this type most widely available in public schools. Such software can also be used to create a context for therapy when the clinician and client use it together to accomplish a

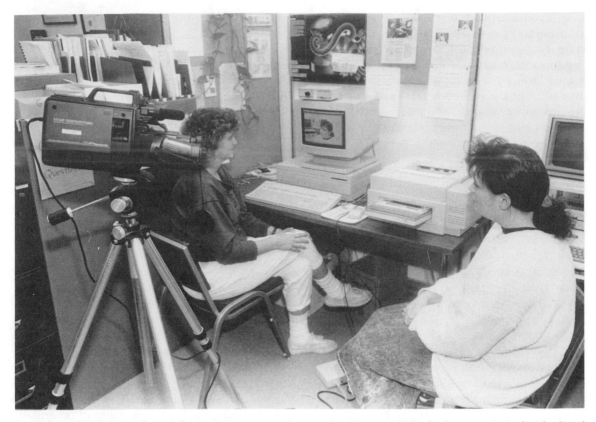

A graphics digitizer can be used to capture images that are familiar to a client for later use in individualized therapy materials. *(Photograph by Ray Jagger)*

shared goal (Cochran & Bull, 1991). Schrader (1990) has described hundreds of ideas for speech and language therapy activities that make use of graphics software as well as other utilities such as word processing, spreadsheet, and data base software.

Clip art libraries and affordable scanners have made it possible for clinicians to develop professional-looking therapy materials that are customized to match the needs of individual clients. For example, items from clip art collections can be used to develop games or worksheets that include pictures of exactly the vocabulary targets for a particular client. If a scanning device is available (see Chapters 2 and 3), images from a video camera or printed pictures can be transferred to the computer. The images captured through this process can be shrunk, expanded, rotated, or incorporated into other pictures. In this way, a clinician could build a library of images pertinent to particular clients and language objectives.

These images can be printed out to produce consumable materials or integrated into clinician-made computer activities.

Computer as a Biofeedback Device

A stutterer may bring the vocal folds together before airflow from the lungs is initiated. A businessperson making important presentations may bring the vocal folds together too abruptly and eventually develop contact ulcers. A person with a hearing impairment may use inappropriate pitch or excessive nasality while talking. Often individuals with speech or language disorders are not aware of all the characteristics of their own speech. It would be much easier to change inappropriate habits and behaviors if they were able to identify them. This is much the same difficulty encountered by a student trying to master the production of a foreign language.

Sometimes auditory feedback—the sound of a person's own speech—is not enough to help the person make changes. Other forms of feedback that may be needed are visual and tactile (touch). Attempts to develop instruments to analyze speech and assist with the treatment of speech and hearing disorders span a century or more. Alexander Graham Bell attempted to create a device to make speech "visible" for persons with impaired hearing. A half-century later, workers at Bell Laboratories devised a machine to translate speech into visible patterns (Potter, Kopp, & Green, 1947). Although only a few individuals were able to learn to read those visible-speech patterns, such efforts have been followed by nearly 50 years of ever-improving speech science instrumentation. As a result, instruments have been developed that can analyze certain aspects of a person's speech or voice and display those features visually. Such a visual display provides immediate information about a person's physical behavior, and is therefore labeled *biofeedback*. For example, it is possible to watch a tracing of the pitch or loudness of your voice as you say a word or a phrase such as "Every good boy does fine." The addition of computers to speech science instruments has increased their power and flexibility, and made them cost-effective for widespread clinical use.

There is a rich literature documenting the efficacy of computer-based speech and voice analysis in the evaluation and treatment of persons with speech and voice disorders (for a recent overview of microcomputer-based speech and voice biofeedback systems see Volin, 1991). For example, Rushakoff and Edwards (1982) described how a computer was used to significantly improve the attitude and speech performance of a 20-year-old college student receiving therapy for distorted sibilant (s-like) sounds. As therapy progressed for this client, she was shown how to use the computer for practice and feedback. She then scheduled herself to use the computer independently several times a week. Her reluctant attitude in therapy improved appreciably, and she was soon dismissed from the clinic.

There were several reasons why the young woman's attitude and skills improved (Rush-akoff & Edwards, 1982). In practice sessions with a speech-language pathologist, she had had a tendency to feel dragged along. Once she began using the computer independently, she assumed major responsibility for her own improvement. She also indicated that she felt good about being able to work on her speech in private, without another person there to observe her mistakes. Finally, she felt glad that she was able to control how long a session lasted and how many times a week she practiced. According to Rushakoff and Edwards (1982), the computer's ability to provide appropriate biofeedback and self-paced practice was the primary reason for the successful outcome for this client. This is not to say, however, that such tools challenge the need for skilled clinicians. Rather, they extend the reach of the clinician. As Volin (1991) recently wrote, "None of these machines knows how to choose a target; not one of them knows how to select an appropriate task" (p. 77). The biofeedback and speech analysis capabilities of computers have simplified some previously complex clinical tasks (such as estimating a person's habitual pitch) and added to the number of potentially effective strategies for helping people improve their communication ability.

Computer as a Datakeeper

Although using computers to record, summarize, and present clinical data seems like an obvious application, there is a lack of commercially available software designed primarily for this purpose. Most clinicians would agree that manual tracking of correct-incorrect responses is sometimes tedious or is difficult to accomplish without slowing down or interrupting ongoing communication with the client. While computer-based data collection does not entirely eliminate the difficulties, it may have advantages in some situations.

The Pacer/Tally software developed by Beukelman, Yorkston, and Tice (1988) is designed to assist clinicians with two tasks in particular: timing the presentation of stimulus items and tallying client responses. Clinicians can develop lists of written stimulus items that are presented one at a time by the "pacer"

An audiologist fine-tunes the settings of a hearing aid with the help of a computer. *(Photograph by Ray Jagger)*

component of the software, in accordance to the timing parameters chosen by the clinician. The "tally" component facilitates the accurate recording of correct-incorrect responses during any off-computer clinical activity.

Computer Managed Articulation Treatment (Fitch, 1984) is another example of software that primarily fills the role of data manager. Text on the screen guides the clinician through a set of drill-and-practice exercises for 10 of the most commonly misarticulated sounds. The clinician either provides a speech model by reading the stimulus item aloud and asking the client to imitate or just listens as the client reads the screen. The clinician judges responses as they occur and codes them by pressing a key on the computer. As criteria are met, the tasks presented by the computer increase in difficulty. Response data are stored on disk, and reports can be generated at a later time.

Videodiscs and Expert Systems

Videodisc technology is already being used in two ways in communication disorders intervention. Videodiscs are technically similar to the more familiar music compact discs (CDs) except that they can store both video and audio information. Videodiscs are played on special laser videodisc players that can be controlled by either a remote control or a computer (see Chapter 5 for more information about videodisc technology). Researchers have been developing and testing new interactive videodisc materials for use in aural rehabilita-

tion (Kopra, Kopra, Abrahamson, & Dunlop, 1987; Miller, Slike, Bailey, & Hobbis, 1987; Tye-Murray, Tyler, Bong, & Nares, 1988). It is likely that other specialized videodiscs will follow shortly.

Meanwhile, a second use of videodisc materials in speech and language therapy involves repurposing existing videodiscs. Videodiscs can provide ready access not only to large numbers of high-quality photographs but also to broadcast-quality action video. In a study of 30 nondisabled kindergartners, Flowers (1990) found that most children talked more and used more complex language in response to videodisc action segments than in response to traditional still pictures. Ott-Rose (1990) used action segments from the videodisc Paul McCartney's Rupert and the Frog Song (Pioneer Artists) to teach present progressive action verbs to five language-delayed preschoolers. Both researchers used a computer attached to a videodisc player to select and play certain segments of the videodisc during interaction with children. Software tools for facilitating the use of videodiscs in speech and language therapy have been developed (Bull & Cochran, 1990; Cochran & Bull, 1989; Cochran, Bull, & Allen, 1988). With open-ended tools, clinicians have the opportunity to develop speech and language activities based on the wide range of commercially available videodiscs including for example, *The Wizard of Oz, Star Wars, National Zoo Disc,* and Walt Disney's *Lady and the Tramp.*

The use of a computer as an *expert system* is another clinical application that will see greater development and use in the future. Expert systems are usually designed to make very complex tasks (such as medical diagnosis or seismograph interpretation) more explicit. By identifying the procedures and deductions of an acknowledged human expert, computer programmers may be able to develop computer-based expert systems for use by professionals who have less expertise. The computer running expert system software could guide the professional through a series of questions or reminders, making sure that all important factors are taken into consideration.

Possibly less elaborate but equally effective expert systems may be developed to assist persons with communication disorders (Bull et al., 1988). The computer might serve as an information retriever or reminder for persons whose ability to plan and carry out everyday tasks is limited. One such use of a computer with a head-injured patient has been reported (Kirsh & Levine, 1984). With increasingly portable computer technology becoming available, one can envision a computerized "coach" that would help a language impaired person complete routine interactions such as ordering lunch, making a phone call, or asking for change.

Computers and the Evaluation of Disorders

There are a number of computer applications that assist in the evaluation of persons with communication disorders. New technologies have resulted in new methods of hearing testing, hearing-aid fitting, and evaluating speech-reading abilities, among other advances (Sims, Kopra, Dunlop, & Kopra, 1985; Stach, 1989). See Chapter 9 for more information about computer applications for persons who have sensory impairments.

There are also many computer applications designed to assist with the evaluation and/or diagnosis of speech or language disorders. Some, involving biofeedback and the acoustic analysis of speech, have been described above. Many diagnostic applications involve the analysis of speech or language samples recorded during communication between the clinician (or other communication partner) and the person with a possible communication disorder. Speech-sample analysis software exists for every major brand of personal computer (Masterson & Pagan, 1989; Palin & Mordecai, 1982; Shriberg, 1986; Weiner, 1982). Not to be confused with programs that analyze the acoustic characteristics of speech directly, speech-sample analysis software uses information about speech as it was transcribed by a clinician using special encoding rules. Thus a misproduction of the word *got* by a child who substitutes /d/ for /g/ might be transcribed by the clinician as [dat]. Using this transcription and many other examples, the computer could tabulate errors and help identify error patterns that have implications for remediation.

Similarly, language-sample analysis software is also available for every major brand of microcomputer (Bennett & Alter, 1985; Long & Fey, 1988, 1989; Miller & Chapman, 1985, 1990; Mordecai, Palin, & Palmer, 1982). A clinician who analyzes a language sample without a computer may spend several hours transcribing the conversation from tapes and then analyzing what was said in terms of grammatical structures, vocabulary, and conversation (discourse) rules. Many clinicians dream of the day when technology will permit them to transfer samples directly from audiotape into a computer for grammatical analysis, thus bypassing the tedious transcription phase. While this is not yet possible, currently available computer applications can assist in making language sample analysis faster and more thorough. Long (1991) viewed this role of the computer assisting the clinician as follows:

> Microcomputers can simplify clinical transcription by providing efficient methods for recording and editing responses. They can process large quantities of client data, thereby relieving the clinician from many tasks that are both time-consuming and, because of their repetitiveness, mentally exhausting. Current software can also scan for subtle patterns within the data. Nevertheless, it is the clinician, not the microcomputer, who remains in charge of the assessment process; although technology can get the data to the clinician, only a clinician can derive information from that data. (p. 2)

Computers and Augmentative/ Alternative Communication

Countless individuals, for many different reasons, are not able to talk. For some people, handwriting provides an alternative to talking, but writing everything they want to say is usually excruciatingly slow. For some people with severe physical impairments, even handwriting or sign language is not an option. In some instances, a computer can be used as an alternative or augmentative communication

A 2-year-old child uses the Muppet Learning Keys keyboard. *(Photograph by Glen L. Bull)*

device. Most popular microcomputers can be modified for use as alternative/augmentative communication (AAC) devices through the addition of special software, special access devices, keyboard emulators, and/or speech synthesizers (Biklen, 1992; Brandenburg & Vanderheiden, 1987a, 1987b, 1987c; Vanderheiden, 1985). Modifying an existing computer in this way may result in a less expensive and more flexible device than one that is custom-built from specialized components.

Specialists in the planning and design of augmentative/alternative communication "systems" use this term carefully. They think of a person's AAC system as a combination of strategies, techniques, and special devices that facilitate 24-hour-a-day communication (Blackstone, 1987). All means of expression on the part of the person with impaired communication are valued and encouraged. This may include eye-contact, gestures, and vocalizations as well as messages encoded through a special device. Each component of a person's system should be designed to complement the rest. For example, since eye contact with other people is often a major avenue of communication for persons who cannot speak, a device that uses signaling methods other than visual focus may be preferred. In this way, one means of communication is not sacrificed for another unless absolutely necessary. It is important to note that extremely sophisticated computer-access devices are now available, so that a person with nearly any type of volitional motor control, no matter how subtle, can be given control over a computer.

Many factors must be taken into account in planning an AAC system for another person. Such factors include the person's most frequent communication partners, communication needs and opportunities, motoric control and range of motion, ability to comprehend graphic symbols and/or text, memory and planning ability, visual acuity, mobility, and personal preferences. In addition to the factors important for successful personal communication are academic or vocational considerations. Ideally, a recommended communication system should be compatible with the person's academic or vocational plans and activities.

Some augmentative/alternative communication equipment is termed "dedicated" because it can function only for the purpose of communication. An AAC system that includes a general-purpose computer, in contrast, may give the user access to many other functions, such as doing mathematical calculations, electronic mail, writing and storing large amounts of text, producing art work, or using the same software as other people in a classroom or office. Dedicated devices tend to be more portable than most computers, and the most sophisticated can be more expensive. Some devices (such as the TouchTalker by Prentke-Romich) can serve either as a dedicated device or can be attached to a personal computer for work or school. The advent of smaller, more reliable, more powerful laptop computers has greatly increased the possibilities in AAC system design.

Whether a major-brand personal computer becomes a long-term component of a person's AAC system or not, often a computer can be useful in the process of determining the best option. First, a computer can help a clinician determine a person's prognosis for effective communication utilizing an electronic aid. Many schools and clinics do not have a comprehensive selection of dedicated electronic communication aids available for evaluation situations. Using a computer, some special access devices, and a variety of communications software, clinicians can simulate many different electronic aids during an assessment. Second, a computer and communication software might be used to teach some of the skills that the potential user will need in order to make full use of a new AAC device once it is obtained. Such skills might include symbol recognition, conversational turn-taking, use of scanning arrays, or direct selection with an adaptive device such as a head pointer.

Yet another use of computers to assist persons who need AAC systems is to provide clinicians a faster, more efficient way to accomplish such tasks as generating pictures or symbols for a communication board and identifying appropriate vocabulary items. Several software programs for assisting in the design of communication boards are available, making it possible to plan and produce multiple versions in less time than creating one layout by hand. A recent addition to this collection is the Vocabulary Selection Toolbox (Beukelman, 1989). This program for the Macintosh helps a clinician identify and prioritize the optimal vocabulary for a person's AAC device depending upon the person's age, sex, education, and individual communication opportunities.

SUMMARY

Computers serve a wide variety of needs for persons who have speech or language impairments. For persons who cannot talk, a computer may provide an augmentative/alternative communication system. Computer applications also have an important role in the evaluation and treatment of persons who have impaired speech or language abilities. During speech-language therapy, a computer may function in the role of instructor, materials generator, datakeeper, biofeedback device, expert system or as a context for interaction between the clinician and client.

DEDICATION

This chapter is dedicated to the memory of Gary E. Rushakoff, our chapter coauthor in the first edition of this text, whose contributions to computer applications in communication disorders and patience *with clinicians just starting to use them should not be forgotten.*

REFERENCES

Bennett, C., & Alter, K. (1985). *Word class inventory (Apple II)* [Computer program]. Austin, TX: PRO-ED.

Beukelman, D. (1989, November). *The Building Bridges Project: A vocabulary selection toolbox.* Presented at the annual convention of the American Speech-Language-Hearing Association, St. Louis, MO.

Beukelman, D., Yorkston, K., & Tice, R. (1988). *Pacer/Tally* [Computer program]. Tucson, AZ: Communication Skill Builders.

Biklen, D. (1992). Typing to talk: Facilitated communication. *American Journal of Speech-Language Pathology, 1*(2), 15–17.

Blackstone, S. (Ed.) (1987). *Augmentative communication: An introduction.* Rockville, MD: American Speech-Language-Hearing Association.

Brandenburg, S. A., & Vanderheiden, G. C. (1987a). *Communication, control, and computer access for disabled and elderly individuals. ResourceBooks 1: Communication Aids.* Madison: University of Wisconsin, Trace Center. (ERIC Document Reproduction Service No. ED 283 305)

Brandenburg, S. A., & Vanderheiden, G. C. (1987b). *Communication, control, and computer access for disabled and elderly individuals. ResourceBooks 2: Switches and environmental controls.* Madison: University of Wisconsin, Trace Center. (ERIC Document Reproduction Service No. ED 283 306)

Brandenburg, S. A., & Vanderheiden, G. C. (1987c). *Communication, control, and computer access for disabled and elderly individuals. ResourceBooks 3: Software and hardware.* Madison: University of Wisconsin, Trace Center. (ERIC Document Reproduction Service No. ED 283 307)

Bull, G. L., & Cochran, P. S. (1990). *Videodisc activity toolkit version 1.0 (Macintosh)* [Computer program]. Kirksville, MO: Northeast Missouri State University, Department of Communication Disorders.

Bull, G. L., & Cochran, P. S. (1991). Learner-based tools. *Computing Teacher, 18*(7), 50–53.

Cochran, P. S., Bull, G. L., & Allen, B. (1988, November). *Creating a shared context: Using videodiscs in language therapy.* Paper presented at the annual convention of the American Speech-Language-Hearing Association, Boston, MA.

Bull, G., Cochran, P., Lang, J. K., Pierce, B. R., Seaton, W., Smaldino, J. J., Mahaffey, R. B., & Chial, M. (1985). Technology infusion: A resource guide. *Journal for Computer Users in Speech and Hearing, 1*(2), 96–116.

Bull, G. L., Cochran, P. S., & Snell, M. E. (1988). Beyond CAI: Computers, language, and persons with mental retardation. *Topics in Language Disorders, 8*(4), 55–76.

Cochran, P. S., & Bull, G. L. (1989, November). *The Building Bridges Project: Watch and talk clinical toolkit.* Presented at the annual convention of the American Speech-Language-Hearing Association, St. Louis, MO.

Cochran, P. S., & Bull, G. L. (1991). Integrating word processing into language intervention. *Topics in Language Disorders, 11*(2), 31–48.

Conners, F. A., Caruso, D. R., & Detterman, D. K. (1986). Computer-assisted instruction for the mentally retarded. *International Review of Research in Mental Retardation, 14,* 105–134.

Fazio, B. B., & Rieth, H. J. (1986). Characteristics of preschool handicapped children's microcomputer use during free-choice periods. *Journal of the Division for Early Childhood, 10*(3), 247–254.

Fein, D. J. (1983). Projections of speech and hearing impairments to 2050. *Asha, 25*(9), 47.

Fitch, J. (1984). *Computer managed articulation treatment.* Tucson, AZ: Communication Skill Builders.

Flowers, D. (1990). *A comparison of the use of three media to elicit oral language from kindergartners.* Doctoral dissertation, University of Virginia, Charlottesville, VA.

Harn, W. E. (1986). Facilitating acquisition of subject-verb utterances in children: Actions, animation, and pictures. *Journal for Computer Users in Speech and Hearing, 2*(2), 95–101.

Hyman, C. (1985). Computer usage in the speech-language-hearing profession. *Asha, 27*(10), 25.

Katz, R. C. (1984). Using microcomputers in the diagnosis and treatment of chronic aphasic adults. *Seminars in Speech and Language, 5,* 11–22.

Katz, R. C. (1986). *Aphasia treatment and microcomputers.* Austin, TX: PRO-ED.

Kirsh, N. L., & Levine, S. P. (1984, April). *A compensatory microcomputer intervention for patients with cognitive limitations.* Paper presented at the Conference on Models and Techniques in Cognitive Rehabilitation, Indianapolis, IN.

Kopra, L. L., Kopra, M. A., Abrahamson, J. E., & Dunlop, R. J. (1987). Lipreading drill and practice software for an auditory-visual laser videodisc system (ALVIS). *Journal for Computer Users in Speech and Hearing, 3*(1), 58–68.

Lally, M. (1981). Computer-assisted teaching of sight-word recognition for mentally retarded school children. *American Journal of Mental Deficiency, 85*(4), 383–388.

Long, S. (1991). Integrating microcomputer applications into speech and language assessment. *Topics in Language Disorders, 11*(2), 1–17.

Long, S., & Fey, M. (1988). *Computerized profiling version 6.1 (Apple II)* [Computer program]. Ithaca, NY: Ithaca College, Department of Speech Pathology & Audiology.

Long, S., & Fey, M. (1989). *Computerized profiling version 6.2 (Macintosh and MS-DOS)* [Computer program]. Ithaca, NY: Ithaca College, Department of Speech Pathology & Audiology.

Masterson, J., & Pagan, F. (1989). *Interactive system for phonological analysis (ISPA) (Macintosh)* [Computer program]. University: University of Mississippi.

Miller, G. D., Slike, S. B., Bailey, H. J., & Hobbis, D. H. (1987, November). *Interactive videodisc technology: Audiometric testing and sign language instruction.* Scientific exhibit presented at the annual convention of the American Speech-Language-Hearing Association, New Orleans, LA.

Miller, J. F., & Chapman, R. S. (1985). *Systematic analysis of language transcripts (SALT) version 2.1 (Apple II)* [Computer program]. Madison, WI: Language Analysis Laboratory, Waisman Center on Mental Retardation and Human Development.

Miller, J. F., & Chapman, R. S. (1990). *Systematic analysis of language transcripts (SALT) version 1.3 (MS-DOS)* [Computer program]. Madison, WI: Language Analysis Laboratory, Waisman Center on Mental Retardation and Human Development.

Mills, R. H. (1986a). Microcomputer applications in aphasia and head trauma. In J. Northern (Ed.), *A personal computer for speech, language, and hearing professionals* (pp. 85–99). Boston: Little, Brown & Co.

Mills, R. H. (1986b). Computerized management of aphasia. In R. Chapey (Ed.), *Language intervention strategies in adult aphasia* (pp. 333–344). Baltimore: William & Wilkins.

Mokros, J. R., & Russell, S. J. (1986). Learner-centered software: A survey of microcomputer use with special needs students. *Journal of Learning Disabilities, 19*(3), 185–190.

Mordecai, D. R., Palin, M. W., & Palmer, C. B. (1982). *Lingquest 1: Language sample analysis* [Computer program]. Columbus, OH: Charles E. Merrill.

Nippold, M. A., Schwarz, I. E., & Lewis, M. (1992). Analyzing the potential benefit of microcomputer use for teaching figurative language. *American Journal of Speech-Language Pathology, 1*(2), 36–43.

O'Connor, L., & Schery, T. K. (1986). A comparison of microcomputer-assisted and traditional language therapy for developing communication skills in nonoral toddlers. *Journal of Speech and Hearing Disorders, 51*(4), 356–361.

Ott-Rose, M. (1990). *A comparison of videodisc and traditional therapy materials to teach action verbs.* Master's thesis, Northeast Missouri State University, Kirksville, MO.

Palin, M. W., & Mordecai, D. R. (1982). *Linquest 2: Phonological analysis (MS-DOS)* [Computer program]. Columbus, OH: Charles E. Merrill.

Potter, R., Kopp, G., & Green, H. (1947). *Visible speech.* New York: Van Nostrand.

Prinz, P. M. (1992). Literacy and language development within microcomputer-videodisc-assisted interactive contexts. *Journal of Childhood Communication Disorders. 14*(1), 67–80.

Rushakoff, G. E., & Edwards, W. (1982, November). *The /s/ meter: A beginning for microcomputer assisted articulation therapy.* Paper presented at the annual convention of the American Speech-Language-Hearing Association, Toronto, Canada.

Russell, S. J., Corwin, R., Mokros, J. R., & Kapisovsky, P. M. (1989). *Beyond drill and practice: Expanding the computer mainstream.* Reston, VA: Council for Exceptional Children.

Schetz, K. F. (1989). Computer-aided language/concept enrichment in kindergarten. *Language, Speech, and Hearing Services in the Schools, 20,* 2–10.

Schrader, M. (1990). *Computer applications for language learning.* Tucson, AZ: Communication Skill Builders.

Shriberg, L. (1986). *Programs to examine phonetic and phonologic evaluation records (MS-DOS)* [Computer program]. Madison: University of Wisconsin, Software Development and Distribution Center.

Shriberg, L. D., Kwiatkowski, J., & Snyder, T. (1989). Tabletop versus microcomputer-assisted speech management: Stabilization phase. *Journal of Speech and Hearing Disorders, 54*(2), 233–248.

Shriberg, L. D., Kwiatkowski, J., & Snyder, T. (1990). Tabletop versus microcomputer-assisted speech management: Response evocation phase. *Journal of Speech and Hearing Disorders, 55*(4), 635–655.

Sims, D., Kopra, L., Dunlop, R., & Kopra, M. (1985). A survey of microcomputer applications in aural rehabilitation. *Journal of the Academy of Rehabilitative Audiology, 18,* 9–26.

Stach, B. A. (1989, November). *The Building Bridges Project: A microcomputer-based speech audiometer.* Presented at the annual convention of the American Speech-Language-Hearing Association, St. Louis, MO.

Steiner, S., & Larson, V. L. (1991). Integrating microcomputers into language intervention with children. *Topics in Language Disorders, 11*(2), 18–30.

Tye-Murray, N., Tyler, R. S., Bong, B., & Nares, T. (1988). Computerized laser videodisc programs for training speechreading and assertive communication behaviors. *Journal of the Academy of Rehabilitative Audiology, 21,* 143–152.

Vanderheiden, G. C. (1985). *Non-vocal communication resources book* (2nd ed.). Austin, TX: PRO-ED.

Ventkatagiri, H. S. (1987). Writing your own software: What are the options? *Asha, 29*(6), 27–29.

Volin, R. A. (1991). Microcomputer-based systems providing biofeedback of voice and speech production. *Topics in Language Disorders, 11*(2), 65–79.

Weiner, F. (1982). *Phonological analysis by computer (Apple II)* [Computer program]. State College, PA: Parrot Software.

Wilson, M. S., & Fox, B. J. (1983). Microcomputers: A clinical aid. In H. Winitz (Ed.), *Treating language disorders: For clinicians by clinicians* (pp. 248–255). Austin, TX: PRO-ED.

Wright, A., & Anderson, M. (1987). Does a computer system help to teach a sight vocabulary to children with severe learning difficulties? *British Journal of Educational Technology, 1,* 52–60.

Suggested Activities

Pencil and Paper

Locate a review of clinical software in *Asha* or the *Journal for Computer Users in Speech and Hearing.* Compare this review with reviews of educational software in Closing the Gap's newsletter or the EPIE index. What additional factors are considered when software will be used for clinical purposes?

Observation

Interview a speech-language pathologist in a local school system. Does that school system have computers to which the speech-language pathologist has easy access? Is there specialized software available as well?

Practicum

Find a computer that has a speech synthesizer. Run a program that makes use of synthesized speech. Without looking at the screen for clues, write down what the speech synthesizer says. Did you have difficulty understanding the speech? Do you think it would be easier to understand with practice?

Resources

Organizations

American Speech-Language-Hearing Association. This organization certifies speech-language-pathologists and audiologists, provides information to the public, and publishes several scholarly journals. Write to ASHA, 10801 Rockville Pike, Rockville, MD 20852.

Computer Users in Speech and Hearing (CUSH). This international organization has members interested in all aspects of computers and communication sciences and disorders. For more information about activities and membership write to CUSH Business Office, Attn: William Seaton, Ph.D., P.O. Box 2160, Hudson, OH 44236.

Journals

Asha Magazine. This monthly publication for members regularly publishes software reviews and new product announcements. Write to American Speech-Language-Hearing Association, 10801 Rockville Pike, Rockville, MD 20852.

Augmentative Communication News. Published 10 times a year, this newsletter is intended for anyone interested in current ideas, news, and research related to augmentative and alternative communication. For subscription information, write to ACN, One Surf Way, Suite 215, Monterey, CA 93940.

Journal for Computers Users in Speech and Hearing. This journal is published by a national nonprofit organization twice annually. It includes information on special topics and new products, clinical suggestions, peer-reviewed research reports, and detailed software reviews. For membership and subscription information write to Computer Users in Speech and Hearing Business Office, Attn: William Seaton, Ph.D., P.O. Box 2160, Hudson, OH 44236.

Self-instruction Modules

ASHA Project IMPACT (Apple or MS-DOS). This 2-year project resulted in the development of instructional modules (videotapes, disks, manuals) designed to provide self-paced instruction to professionals in communication disorders who wanted beginning-level instruction pertaining to computer applications. For more information, write to ASHA Publication Sales, 10801 Rockville Pike, Rockville, MD 20852.

Managing information in communication sciences and disorders with Appleworks software. By W. H. Seaton (1990). This "bookware" includes a book and several diskettes of exercises and templates, as well as a second on-disk resource manual that can be printed out. The instruction about AppleWorks is tailored to meet the needs of speech-language pathology and audiology professionals. For ordering information, contact Seaton & Sibs, 5929 Sunset, Hudson, OH 44236.

Technical Information

Communication, Control, and Computer Access for Disabled & Elderly Individuals: Resource Books 1, 2, and 3. Edited by Sara A. Brandenburg & Gregg C. Vanderheiden. These extensively illustrated manuals provide an overview of adaptive devices available for persons with special needs. Write to College-Hill Press/Little Brown, 34 Beacon Street, Boston, MA 02108.

IBM National Support Center for Persons with Disabilities. This office provides exceptional individuals with information and referrals pertaining to IBM equipment and special needs. Write to IBM National Support Center for Persons with Disabilities, P.O. Box 2150 (A06S1), Atlanta, GA 30055.

National Special Education Alliance. This network of centers provides information and referrals pertaining to Apple and Macintosh equipment and special needs. Write to Apple Computer, NSEA Foundation, 1307 Solano Avenue, Albany, CA 94706.

ABLENET. This hotline provides information about hardware and software for special needs. Call 1-800-322-0956.

Free Subscriptions

Assistive Device News. For a free subscription to this inhouse newsletter about augmentative communication and computer applications, write to Elizabethtown Hospital and Rehabilitation Center, Elizabethtown, PA 17022.

Classroom Computer Learning. This magazine focuses on computer applications in education. For a free subscription, write to Subscription Dept., 2451 E. River, Dayton, OH 45439-9907.

Electronic Communication

CompuServe Information Service. This electronic mail and bulletin board service is widely used and features some bulletin boards of special interest. For information and a start-up packet, write to CompuServe, P.O. Box 20212, Columbus, OH 43220, or call 1-800-848-8199.

PennPal Network. This is an electronic mail network for teachers, parents, and professionals as well as students who use adaptive devices. For more information, write to Pennsylvania Assistive Device Center, 150 S. Progress Avenue, Harrisburg, PA 17109.

SpecialNet. This national electronic mail and bulletin board network specializes in topics related to special needs, including current information about legislation, employment opportunities, professional conferences, and many professional organizations including the American Speech-Language-Hearing Association (through the ASHA Update Bulletin Board). For subscription rates and information write to SpecialNet, 2021 K Street NW, Suite 215, Washington, DC 2003, or call 1-202-835-7300.

IBM PC User Group Bulletin Board. This bulletin board is for general interests. At this time neither fees nor registration is required, but users pay for the telephone time. All baud rates are supported. With modem, call 1-404-835-6600 (computer link). Join Conference 20 for Special Needs.

Recommended Books

Beukelman, D., Yorkston, K., & Dowden, P. (1985). *Communication augmentation: A casebook of clinical management.* Austin, TX: PRO-ED.

Fitch, J. L. (1986). *Clinical applications of microcomputers in communication disorders.* Orlando, FL: Academic Press.

Russell, S. J., Corwin, R., Mokros, J. R., & Kapisovsky, P. M. (1989). *Beyond drill and practice: Expanding the computer mainstream.* Reston, VA: Council for Exceptional Children.

Hardware/Software

Facemaker
Spinnaker Software
215 West First Street
Cambridge, MA 02142

Print Shop
Brøderbund
P.O. Box 12947
San Rafael, CA 94913

Print Shop Companion
Brøderbund
P.O. Box 12947
San Rafael, CA 94913

TouchTalker
Prentke Romich
1022 Heyl Road
Wooster, OH 44691

Also see related references in Reference Section.

Computers and Individuals with Severe and Physical Disabilities

CHAPTER 8

Lou Esposito
Rehabilitation Engineer, Madison, Connecticut
Philippa H. Campbell
Temple University ■

Humans were designed to function unimpeded in their environment. However, individuals with severe mental and physical disabilities have difficulty functioning (e.g., moving, communicating) in most environments. The evolving computer hardware and software technology is one solution to the problem these exceptional persons are experiencing at home, in the schools, and in the community. However, computers can enhance opportunities for individuals with disabilities only when appropriate equipment and software have been selected and modified, as needed, for the individuals' specific requirements. The diverse uses of the computer are both attractive and mind boggling (Heim, 1992). Computers have been used with infants, children, and adults with severe mental and physical disabilities including applications to (a) access children to computers; (b) train computer usage; (c) acquire educational skills; (d) teach problem-solving skills; (e) communicate; and (f) interface with the environment for recreational, vocational, and daily living activities (see Behrmann, 1984; Bowe, 1984; Burns, 1984b; Gergen & Hagen, 1985; Hagen, 1984a).

INDIVIDUALS WITH SEVERE AND PHYSICAL DISABILITIES

This chapter will provide basic information on applications of computers with individuals with severe mental or physical impairments. This population varies along different dimensions, each of which must be considered when selecting or adapting equipment for specific functional uses.

Severe Mental Disabilities

While a single definition to define individuals with severe mental handicaps has not been universally accepted, this exceptional population is generally defined within the mental retardation category. According to Grossman

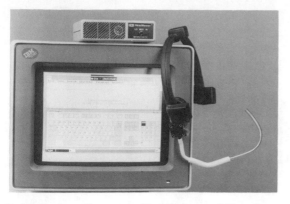

Individuals with severe disabilities and the physically challenged need special interface devices.
(Photograph courtesy of Prentke Romich Company)

(1973), "Mental retardation refers to significantly subaverage intellectual functioning existing concurrently with deficits in adaptive behavior and manifested during the development period" (p. 3). Within this definition, severely mentally handicapped persons are distinguished by their intellectual quotient (Stanford-Binet IQ scores between 35 and 20 or Wechsler IQ scores between 39 and 25). As Heward and Orlansky (1991) noted, however, the degree of functional impairment (e.g., nonverbal, nonambulatory) and educational needs (e.g., self-care instruction, language development) should also be used to classify individuals as severely mentally retarded. Some of the major characteristics manifested by these exceptional individuals include

- Aggression toward others . . . that can inflict bodily harm

- No attention to even the pronounced social stimuli

- Self mutilation . . . such as head banging, biting oneself

- Rumination . . . self-induced vomiting

- Self-stimulation . . . purposeless, repetitive behaviors

- Durable and intense temper tandrums

- Imitation . . . to mimic or repeat a behavior

- Extremely brittle medical existence . . . presence of life-threatening conditions (Gast & Berkler, 1981, p. 434)

Persons with severe mental disabilities need training in toileting, dressing, feeding, and other self-care areas. They also need experiences to develop or extend their language capabilities. Computer technology can be used to advance self-care and language skills.

Individuals with Physical Disabilities or the Physically Challenged

Individuals who are physically challenged have significant disabilities in posture and movement. These disabilities may be acquired through accident or disease, for example, paralysis (e.g., quadriplegia or paraplegia). Some individuals are born with movement disabilities that range from mild to severe. Individuals may be totally unable to move their arms, legs, or bodies but may be able to move their heads or eyes. Some individuals have upper extremity movement but movement may be limited or uncoordinated. Physical and occupational therapists can provide assistance necessary to understand physical abilities (and limitations), and rehabilitation engineers can design solutions that accommodate an individual's motor disability and allow for computer use.

Individuals with physical disabilities may also have additional associated handicaps, such as vision, hearing, or cognition problems. When a number of associated problems are present, these individuals are often labeled as severely handicapped or multiply handicapped. Severely handicapped implies that the individual also has a significant degree of mental retardation. Each of these associated problems needs to be taken into account to design effective programs for computer usage. Applications that have been successfully used with individuals with visual or auditory impairments can often be combined with those designed for individuals with physical disabilities to synthesize appropriate applications for individuals with multiple handicaps. Specialized training procedures, some of which are described in this chapter, will need to be implemented with individuals with severe handicaps.

TABLE 8.1
Movement characteristics of individuals with severe mental and physical disabilities and computer interface options

Movement Characteristics	Interface Options
Some control of upper extremities, no fine motor control	Deltoid aids, universal cuff, pointers or typing tools
Good head control	Head or mouth stick
No head control and no control of uppers	Voice input, puff, and sip switches
Control of eye gaze	Eye types
Control of specific muscle (facial or otherwise)	Muscle twitch switch, EMG switch, foot switch
Unilateral control (e.g., one arm, one hand)	Keytronic keyboard, setable control switches, keyboard macro software

Table 8.1 lists the movement characteristics of severely mentally handicapped and physically challenged persons and possible computer interface options. Additional behaviors (stated as instructional objectives) and uses for computers are delineated in Table 8.2.

A BRIEF REVIEW OF THE LITERATURE

There has been a steady increase in the literature on computer applications with and by individuals with severe and physical handicaps. Specific areas to be considered include access to computers, control switch interfaces, precomputer training, and assessment and training for control switch activation.

Access to Computers

Individuals with severe disabilities and the physically challenged will require greater attention to selection of hardware, the interface mechanism, and the method of stimulus presentation than will individuals with other types of special needs. Hardware decisions are made at several different points when using computers but need to be considered at this stage in order to match interface needs with hardware possibilities (e.g., Lahm, 1985). Some interface devices can be used only with specific types of hardware, or a school may only have certain types of hardware available for use with students (Johnson, 1992).

The possible types of hardware that might be used with a given individual should be generally identified before attempting to select an interface device for computer access. The ways in which the computer may be used will vary depending on (a) application selected (e.g., computer-assisted instruction, communication, environmental control multiple function); (b) age of the individual; (c) interfaces to the computer that are possible given an individual's degree of motor impairment; and (d) uses that are possible given a student's cognitive abilities. These uses can change during an individual's life and through various types of training. Operation of the computer access method (e.g., control switch interface device) and cognitive skills (e.g., cause and effect) can be taught to infants, young children, and individuals with cognitive impairment, thereby increasing the applications performed by computer.

Control Switch Interfaces

A wide variety of interface devices are available to overcome physical problems and en-

TABLE 8.2
Selected examples of computer usage and instructional objectives

Instructional Objective	Use of Computers
Signal for adult attention	Teach switch activation skills (to use to signal for attention)
Increase receptive language	Software (with voice synthesizer and switch activation), e.g., First Words (Laureate Learning Systems)
Perform independent recreation leisure skills	Computer games
Assess developmental milestone skill level	Software (such as Discover Your Baby, BTE Systems)
Teach motor coordination	University of Washington software and computer games (with use of switch)
Teach switch activation	Software (such as Ontario Crippled Children's Program) with switch interface
Teach academic skills	Computer-assisted-instruction software
Enhance academic abilities	Computer-assisted-instruction software
Teach problem-solving skills	LOGO, robotics, with switch or Koala pad
Allow for expressive "oral" communication	Communication software programs (with or without voice synthesis)
Allow for expressive written communication	Word processing software (with required adaptations, such as keyboard emulator, switch interface, etc.)
Perform business-oriented vocational skills	Business software (with required adaptations)
Teach environmental control	Software systems that allow for multiple function through direct access and/or voice input/output

able individuals to communicate with and through computer hardware. These include specialized computer keyboards (e.g., membrane or enlarged boards), keyboard emulators (e.g., Mod Keyboard System), voice activation, and numerous types of switch interfaces. Control switches of various types can give an individual access to a computer through many different types of movement. These switches can be purchased commercially from a variety of sources or can be fabricated from readily available plans (Campbell, McInerney, & Middleton, 1983; Wright & Nomura, 1985). Some examples of the types of control switch interfaces that can be operated using various movement patterns are listed in Table 8.3. The operation of these control switches varies in terms of both cognitive and motor difficulty. Typically, those switches that

operate using the least conventional forms of movement (e.g., eye or mouth) require the most sophisticated cognitive skills. Control switches activated by a reach and touch pattern can be operated by infants, young children, and other individuals who may lack complex cognitive skills.

Some uses of the computer require activation of only one switch closure. More complex systems of interaction with the computer, however, require operation of more than one switch closure. A person with disabilities may control direction of a scanner (e.g., using a directional joystick) or may operate one control switch to turn the machine on and additional closures to perform scanning and other functions.

Computers are often used as one component in a multiple function system or in com-

TABLE 8.3
Movement patterns and types of control switches

Types of Control Switches	Movement Patterns
Rocking lever	Normal or abnormal upper extremity patterns
Paddle switch	Head movement (through use of a mouthstick or headstick)
Tread switch	
Plate switch	
Wobble switch	Head, arm, or gross body movement; can be normal or abnormal
Leaf switch	Movement pattern used dependent on placement of switch
Flexit switch	
Air cushion pneumatic switch (pressure switch)	Head, arm, or leg movement dependent on switch placement
Touch switch	
Lever switch	Head movement
Joystick	Arm/hand movements
Wobble switch	

bination with other devices, such as motorized chairs, communication aids, or environmental control systems (Romich & Vignini, 1985). For example, a physically challenged individual may activate a switch using a backward head movement to turn on the computer and hitting the switch twice to activate a motorized chair or other devices. Once the computer has been turned on, other movements (e.g., head forward) produce switch closures to perform various computer functions (e.g., move cursor on the screen). A user must have understanding of a number of different cognitive skills (e.g., cause and effect, reading a menu) in order to use control interfaces for multiple function use.

Precomputer Training

Some individuals with severe or physical disabilities may require training before being able to use the computer for educational, recreational, communication, or other functional uses (Behrmann & Lahm, 1985; Bourland,

Jablonski, Allen, & White, 1984; Campbell, Bricker, & Esposito, 1980). Infants, children, youths, and adults with severe handicaps may be able to activate a control switch interface but may not demonstrate the basic cognitive skills (e.g., ability to understand cause and effect) necessary for computer access. The type of training necessary to teach required cognitive skills can be delivered via computer software. Several programs are in the process of development but others are currently available (Behrmann & Lahm, 1984; Brinker & Lewis, 1982a.)

One program, Stimulus-Response Management System, operates software packages developed for the Commodore Vic20 or 64 that uses either a datasette or a disk drive (Esposito, 1985). These software packages can be used for both assessment and training but have greater use in training young children or individuals with severe handicaps (Esposito & Campbell, 1985). Several levels of basic cognitive skills training are possible. The first level trains an individual to activate the switch interface device under the control of consequences to that activation. This training level is comparable to the primary circular reactions described by Piaget (1952). The second level trains performance of the switch activation dependent on antecedents to the activation. This level is comparable to discriminated activation or Piaget's secondary circular reactions and is a critical prerequisite for computer use. Both timed and trial-by-trial training options are possible, allowing for implementation of a training program to best fit individual needs.

Other types of available software develop similar cognitive prerequisites but begin training at the secondary circular reactions level (see Behrmann & Lahm, 1984; Brinker & Lewis, 1982b). These software programs operate on Apple computers and have been specifically developed for use with infants with physical handicaps but could be used with individuals with cognitive impairments. It should be noted, however, that research on this type of precomputer training has validated procedures at particular levels and with particular populations (Campbell & McInerney, 1983; Brinker & Lewis, 1982a; Rosenberg, 1984.) Unfortunately, few studies have been conducted over extended periods of time to empirically investigate the effects of providing precomputer training for computer use in communication and other types of functional skills. These training methods show promise for making computer use possible for anyone. Longitudinal studies that follow individuals from cognitive training through to functional use of computers will determine the long-range effects of precomputer training strategies such as these.

Assessment and Training for Control Switch Activation

Several methods have been suggested in the literature to determine the best type of interface to use for providing computer access. Most exceptional individuals will use some sort of control switch. Other existing types of interfaces such as microphones for voice entry can be used for access without the use of a control switch (Burns, 1984a). Possibilities are increasing as new access methods become available.

Physically challenged students can use computers for many purposes. *(Photograph courtesy of IBM Corporation)*

Systematic assessment procedures must be used to determine both the type and location of the control switch the exceptional individual can use (Campbell, 1985; Campbell & Mulhauser, 1984; Rosenberg, 1984). Three variables considered are (a) configuration of the switch (e.g., pad, joystick, head pointer, or pneumatic) and the movement pattern used to provide closure (e.g., hand, arm pressure, head); (b) location of the control switch or device (e.g., arm, hand, foot mounted); and (c) outcome produced by switch activation (e.g., cursor scans letters on the screen). Assessment procedures must hold two variables constant while testing for the third. For example, the same switch would be used in several different locations to test for the most ideal location, or a location would be held constant while trying several different configurations or types of control switch interfaces. Where possible, assessment procedures should involve physical therapists and rehabilitation engineers to ensure a comprehensive differential diagnosis of the individual's movement and cognitive capabilities and the selection of the most efficient switch and its location.

Two systems for assessment and motor skill training have been developed and are commercially available. The first of these operates without a computer, using the TA-2 training aid device developed by Prentke Romich (see Prentke Romich, 1985). The device operates a number of assessment and training programs using built-in software. Decisions about switch type, location, and output following activation are made on the basis of numerical performance data, including measures of rate per minute of switch activation and percentage of correct activations. The programs allow for testing over several sessions in order to obtain stable measures of each of these variables (Campbell, 1985).

A second system uses the software Microcomputer Applications Programme to provide standard output following switch activation. Several different types of tests can be run using this software program and a standard switch: one test evaluates ability to use a scanning system for either communication or computer usage; another evaluates ability to activate a switch following presentation of visual input on the computer screen; the third test provides information about ability to activate a switch to terminate a visual input following presentation on the screen. This assessment system is divided into two parts, testing and practice. Individuals can use the practice portions of the software before being tested. The test portions provide numerical data about performance specific to the tests being run. However, computer-operated assessment programs may not always be necessary. The best type of control switch access for an exceptional individual may be determined through clinical observation measures. Programs that produce reliable and accurate data concerning control switch activation, however, are a necessity for individuals with such severe movement dysfunction or incoordination that data concerning rate of activation are necessary to determine the most ideal interface. Such programs are also a necessity for individuals who, because of chronological age or impairment, require training in the cognitive skills necessary to operate a control switch.

Other issues related to computer access for the individual with severe mental handicap and the physically challenged include intrusiveness of the computer system or interface device and funding sources. Many persons with physical disabilities may choose not to use a perfectly reliable system because they believe the system is too complicated or cumbersome or because they cannot afford to buy it.

GENERAL HARDWARE AND SOFTWARE CONSIDERATIONS

A variety of types of computer hardware and peripherals have been used with individuals with severe mental handicaps or physical impairments. Apple computers are the most frequently used, possibly due to their availability in educational settings and the resultant large variety of developed software and peripherals (Vanderheiden, 1983, 1984). Hardware and software decisions must be made jointly to support the use that the computer will have for the individual (Lahm, 1985). Computer uses include basic skills assessment, computer-assisted instruction (to assess, remediate, and enhance skills), and performance of life functions (such as communication, mobility, environmental control, vocation, and recreation). Software is selected to meet one (or more) of the objectives designed for a given individual. Table 8.2 provides examples of uses of computers to support individual instructional objectives.

Since computer use supports performance of a desired objective, it is often wiser to make software decisions first, allowing the software to determine the hardware decision. As Russell (1983) noted and as stated in Chapter 3, not all software works on all computers. The objectives selected for the individual are of first importance. Both the software and, subsequently, the hardware must make the desired objective possible for the individual. More programs are available for the more popular computers (e.g., Apple and IBM and their compatibles) that have a wide and growing user base (Shanahan & Ryan, 1984) than for computers with a narrow or declining user base.

Selection of software should be based on a number of predetermined activities, including (a) specification of what the software must accomplish, (b) identification of existing software, (c) evaluation of software design (in relation to desired specifications), (d) preview of available software packages, (e) recommendations for potential use, and (f) postuse feedback. Software should enhance the objective selected for the client in a way that arouses interest, maintains attention, and provides interesting and humorous feedback (Kahn, 1985; Komoski, 1985).

Finding the appropriate software is made easier by using directories such as *The Educational Software Selector* (*TESS*), a software selector from EPIE Institute (see Chapter 4). This directory covers the entire software market and provides information on how software fits into the curriculum, what it is designed to do, who produces it, what it costs, and how to obtain it. A listing of contacts at schools currently using the software is provided and is particularly useful if the supplier does not have a policy that precludes previewing before purchase.

Several other resource lists of software are also available, including *The National Software Hardware Registry* (Vanderheiden, Bengston, Brady, & Wolstead, 1984) and the Special Education Software Center in Menlo Park, California (see Appendix E). *The National Software Hardware Registry* includes reviews of applications with persons with a variety of types of disabilities. The Software Center provides online information, accessible through computer and modem, as well as answers to information requests by telephone or mail. In addition, many states maintain software review centers, frequently located in either the states' departments of education or in universities. See Chapters 3 and 4 and Appendix E for additional information on software.

SPECIFIC COMPUTER APPLICATIONS

Many applications of computers with individuals with severe disabilities and the physically challenged allow users to perform single functions for specific reasons while others allow for performance of multiple objectives or functions (discussed in the next section). Most applications with infants and younger children will involve single functions of assessment and/or training of basic skills, computer-assisted instruction (CAI) or multimedia activities, and interfacing to perform

living skills such as communication or recreation. Older students and adults may also use any of these single functions (as well as others needed for environmental control or vocational pursuits) but are more likely to use multiple function systems combining communication, vocational, mobility, environmental control, and other functions. Multiple functions will be discussed in the Additional Computer Issues section.

Basic Skills Assessment and Training

Some of the applications that have been developed for assessment and training involve precomputer training of both cognitive and motor skills necessary for effective computer access. Other software programs are available to assess or develop other aspects of behavior or performance (Jorgenson, 1992).

A number of investigators have developed systems for using the computer to measure the overall developmental status of infants (BHT Group, 1984) or of preschool-age children (Lutz & Taylor, 1981). Both of these software packages, as well as others, allow professionals or parents to enter data about skills that children are able to perform. The computer selects a remedial program of activities designed to enhance performance in areas where children demonstrate weakness in relation to nonhandicapped children of similar chronological ages. Other assessment/training packages have been developed for use by teachers by both commercial and academic software producers (e.g., Barton, 1985). These approaches allow teachers and clinicians to develop a computerized individual education plan (IEP) for students by entering data about performance of basic skills.

Programs of these types can be used to assess skill levels of individuals with physical disabilities. However, any software program selected for this function must be evaluated on the basis of the theoretical approach used as well as in terms of the software operation itself. The cost of the program might also be considered. Normal models of milestone development are often inappropriate for remedial use with infants and children with physical disabilities (Campbell, 1985; Wilson, 1984) as are various curricular instructional approaches. These models do not become valid as a basis for programming simply because they have become computerized.

Computer-assisted Instruction

Computers can be used to assess instructional levels, remediate deficiencies in basic skills, or enhance instructional opportunities. Many programs have been developed for use with nondisabled children but can be easily used with children who are physically challenged through the addition of voice synthesizers, the Adaptive Firmware Card (Schwejda & Vanderheiden, 1982), or general purpose interface cards (Tinker, 1985). The primary obstacle for children with only physical disabilities is often the computer keyboard itself. Adaptations such as enlarged keyboards or touch-sensitive membrane panels allow a child with poor motor control to access standard software with direct input. Control switch interfaces, in combination with adaptations such as those mentioned above, allow bypass of the keyboard through scanning or other methods. Keyboard emulators bypass computer keyboards entirely by allowing an alternate character selection system, such as ASCII (see Appendix A), to be used for input to the computer. An augmentative communication aid is used to generate the ASCII signals that enter the computer as though they were keystrokes on the keyboard.

Programs that have been developed for use with preschool- or school-age students who are nonhandicapped are often appropriate for use with physically challenged persons (Lynd, 1983; Rushakoff & Lombardino, 1983). CAI software packages typically provide assessment, enhancement, or remedial practice around a specific area of instruction. Software that is selected for use should support the content of the educational program of a student, provide appropriate opportunities for assessment or practice, present material in interesting and motivating ways, and be appropriate for the individual's chronological age.

Some students with physical disabilities may also have cognitive impairment or dem-

onstrate delayed achievement. Age-appropriate CAI and multimedia programs may be difficult to locate or to use effectively to supplement regular instruction. Software programs that have been developed for normal learners may present too little opportunity for practice for students who may require more trials to acquire a particular concept or may present information at too fast a rate for learners with cognitive impairments. Initial assessment of the software program determines content and chronological age appropriateness. A computer programmer or rehabilitation engineer can often modify programs either to present more learning opportunities or to slow down rates.

Authoring systems offer additional opportunities for individualization in special educational and mainstream settings (Messinger, 1983). Several systems have been developed for use with both Apple and IBM (MS-DOS) computer systems as well as with other computers (see Hazen, 1985; Piszkin, 1985; Zuckerman, 1985). This approach allows professionals and therapists to design individual CAI software programs without having to learn to program the computer. See Chapters 3 and 6 for more information on authoring systems.

Interfaces to Perform Living Skills

Computer hardware, software, and peripherals enable individuals with severe disabilities or the physically challenged to perform living skills appropriate to their chronological age, such as operating appliances, controlling environmental devices (e.g., locking/unlocking doors, turning on lights), or performing bookkeeping skills (e.g., writing checks). Many adaptations have been made available, particularly for older children and adults and specifically for individuals who do not also have impaired cognitive functioning or additional sensory handicaps (Browning, Zembrosky-Barkin, Nave, & White, 1985; Enders, 1984; Gergen & Hagen, 1985; Nave, Browning, & Carter, 1983). Many living skills can be performed using single-function interfaces with a computer. As with other applications, pro-

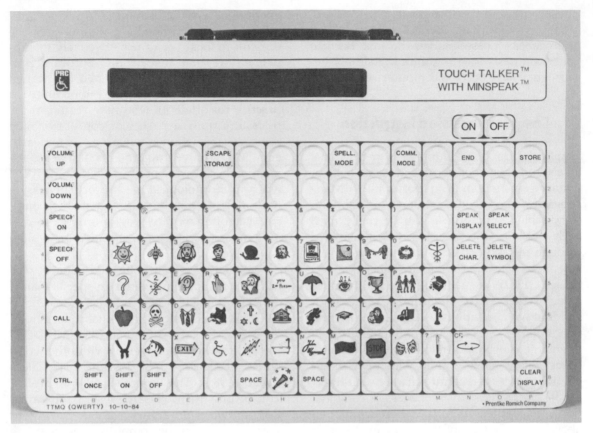

Augmentative communication devices permit exceptional individuals to express themselves.
(Photograph courtesy of Prentke Romich Company)

grams and peripherals are most readily available for the Apple, although many other types of computers have been used.

The first decision to be made when assessing a person with severe mental impairment or the physically challenged for use of the computer for some sort of living skill is to target an initial area of focus. The initial area will most likely be communication for infants and young children (and other individuals with severe impairment). Other areas of application may assume priority at specific chronological ages. For example, use of a computer to enable an individual to perform necessary vocational skills would be a high-priority target for an adult. Computer use for educational purposes (e.g., CAI or multimedia) would have greater priority for a school-age student.

The physical, sensory, and cognitive abilities of an individual must then be assessed in relation to performance of basic computer

skills. This information is obtained though use of computer access procedures described at the beginning of this chapter, in Chapter 4, and by referenced authors (Campbell, 1985; Lahm, 1985). Resultant decisions shape a focus for the type of software, hardware, and peripherals that will be used to interface an individual to the environment. These data also determine the extent to which precomputer training will be necessary for an individual as an initial step in accessing the environment. The final step is to select appropriate software, as discussed earlier and in Chapter 4, and to educate the individual to use both the software and hardware for functional uses. Some individuals may require little training in specific areas of living skills. However, some living skills areas, such as communication and vocational applications, will require additional training.

Numerous software programs and packages of hardware, software, and peripherals (e.g., Smartterm) are being experimentally and clinically used with physically challenged individuals. These packages become more sophisticated (more capable, complex, or useful) as hardware changes and as greater access is provided into mainframe and other types of larger computer systems. The following sections describe some single-function applications that have been used to help individuals perform various living skills. Keeping up to date on current applications can be a full-time job in the rapidly growing field of computer applications with populations with special needs. A review of current applications should be undertaken (and assistance sought from rehabilitation engineers and other individuals who are working with computers) before determining the exact application that will be used with a given individual.

Communication

A number of communication aids are available to assist individuals with physical disabilities to communicate expressively (Vanderheiden, 1985). Most existing aids address both oral and written expression, using one of two approaches. Some are independent of commercial computer equipment through self-contained software. Examples include the Touch Talker and the Minspeak system, marketed by Prentke Romich Company. Other aids operate using existing computer hardware. Many of the software programs that use commercial hardware have been developed for use by specific individuals with disabilities (Hagen, 1984b; Jung, 1980; Shirriff, 1980), while others have been developed for more general use (e.g., Traynor & Beukelman, 1984). Some systems allow only for expressive communication while others perform multiple functions of communication and computer access.

Many of the existing communication software packages operate through scanning systems or direct keyboard access that provide either visual or verbal output using voice synthesizers such as the Echo II or the Votrax Personal Speech System. Scanning systems can be quite difficult to operate for many physically challenged individuals (Heckathorne & Childress, 1983). A typical scanning system software package includes an alphabet or a number line. These symbols are scanned (at a controlled rate) for the user to activate a control switch interface to choose a letter or number. Number sequences, in turn, may signify a specific symbol. An individual with poor coordination or low rates of movement may require several minutes to generate a simple word.

The full use of commercial equipment as a comprehensive means for individuals with severe physical disabilities to communicate has not yet been realized (Vanderheiden, 1985). Required motor coordination and cognitive abilities for use of current equipment present one problem. An additional problem is that widely accessible computer hardware, such as Apple, IBM, or compatible systems, is fairly nonportable, restricting expressive communication to environments in which the computer is present. A few software systems have been developed for smaller portable computers, such as the Epson, in combination with voice synthesizers. Words + and Portable Voice II provide direct access to the keyboard to generate spoken or printed messages. While these systems are portable, they require good cognitive abilities and motor coordination to use.

Recreation

Computer software provides many opportunities for exceptional children and adults to enjoy individual and group recreational opportunities. Toys can be operated through a computer, although more often these are attached directly to a switch and operated through direct battery sources (Enders, 1984); young children with physical handicaps especially can benefit from playing with computerized toys (Burkhart, 1982; Hanline, Hanson, Veltman, & Spaeth, 1985). Software for games and activities of various types (see Chapter 3) has been created for the regular consumer market and can be used by physically challenged individuals. Many existing game programs are accessed through the joystick that can be purchased for most computers. Additional types of switch interfaces can also be used by plugging an interface into the game port of the computer while plugging the selected switch into the interface.

Games and other recreational activities using the computer should be carefully selected on the basis of the following factors: interests of the individual, chronological age of the individual, degree of motor coordination and speed, and type of access used. Ideally, the activities selected should be ones that are enjoyed by the person, are chronological age appropriate, and can be easily used with the selected access method and degree of motor control (Powers & Ball, 1983). Recreational activities should be used primarily for enjoyment, not to develop needed skills.

Vocational

The personal computer can be a vocational tool for a worker with a physical disability. To qualify as a tool, a device must be capable of producing a fairly predictable output across users and across user skill levels. Several factors have impeded the effective use of computers with workers (Nave, Browning, & Carter, 1983; Shworles, 1983). Among the most important are the following:

1. The mode of input, the media of output, the devices, and the software must be matched to both a client's abilities and the job to be done. Most rehabilitation counselors and teachers lack both computer literacy and knowledge of the function and operation of special aids.

2. Knowledge of access (to computer) technology is currently possessed by only a handful of people. Most of this technology is not evaluated. Furthermore, access methods change rapidly due to the changing computer field. Many aids are presently developed in vacuums. Local personnel with expertise, where they exist, simply cannot keep up with the technology.

Individuals with severe mental handicaps or the physically challenged must possess four skills in order to use computers effectively as a tool in the postschool environment. Ability to use special devices, interface with special technology, use regular office equipment, and demonstrate knowledge about the working environment are essential skills that can be developed through appropriate educational programming at the high school or postsecondary level. These skills will be necessary whether a student selects higher education, employment, or both following graduation (Esposito, 1985).

An emerging system designed to aid college students who have disabilities is the laptop portable computer in conjunction with a larger personal computer, kept in the dormitory. The smaller portable computer is used as a classroom notetaker that is interfaced later to the larger personal computer for additional work with the stored information (Evans & Sherill, 1983). An example of this system is the Epson lap-sized HX microcomputer using the TRINE software developed at the Trace Center (Vanderheiden, 1985). This software is an alternative word processing system that requires fewer keystrokes than usual word processors and uses an MS-DOS system.

The best approach for the student on a vocational track is a long-term one that starts in the early high school years (Tindall & Gugerty, 1984). The long-term approach allows for job awareness activities, identification of vocational goals, and extensive job searching. These objectives should be approached systematically and, ideally, overseen by a repre sentative from the state's department of vocational rehabilitation. The high school vocational program for a person physically challenged includes rehabilitation engineering, work exposure and training, vocational counseling, and overall case management. A simulation of selected job goals can be performed during the high school years to verify that the student will have job opportunities. This simulation should include job site analysis and modifications as well as the fabrication of adaptations to accomplish work at the job site.

Certain existing software systems open up areas of vocational pursuit that were traditionally only available to workers with upper-extremity dexterity. Computer-assisted drafting (CAD), computer-assisted manufacturing (CAM), MacPaint, and MacOffix, for example, all operate using a mouse to move the computer cursor. The traditional mouse (or digitizer) is moved by using gross upper-extremity movements. Many individuals with physical disabilities who are unable to use finger movements may be able to use the mouse. More recently, a control system has been developed that moves the cursor to the place on the screen where the user is looking (Personics, 2352 Main Street, Concord, MA 01742). A lightweight headset measuring subtle changes in both the angle and rotation of the head translates these movements into cursor commands, enabling an individual to operate mouse-oriented business software with only head movements.

Computer-based tools for an employee with disabilities can be a business necessity (e.g., word processing, bookkeeping, accounting, or payroll) or can be the center of a complete environmental control (e.g., voice input-output, telecommunication, or other multiple function system). The use of the computer must fit the needs of the job so that the equipment enhances employee performance or allows accomplishment of a job that would not be possible without the computer. At present, most physically challenged individuals employed with computers are performing single-function business applications using existing software packages developed for the business community and accessed through voice, control switch interfaces, or other methods. While these applications have enabled some clients to hold jobs, the multiple-function systems that are currently emerging offer greater opportunities for many individuals. The continued funding and implementation of special computer industry programs by IBM and other companies will advance computer vocational opportunities for physically handicapped persons.

ADDITIONAL COMPUTER ISSUES

Multiple-function systems are those that allow an individual to perform more than one function with the same type of equipment. For example, a switch control interface may allow an individual both to access and operate a communication aid and to activate a motor-

ized wheelchair. The incorporation of computers as the basis for multiple functions has significantly increased both the amount and types of control that the user can have over aspects of the physical environment.

Many systems that use computers utilize keyboard emulators of one sort or another. The MicroDEC II system (Heckathorne & Leibowitz, 1985) uses an Apple and two switch closures to combine computer operation, environmental control, and telephone use. The Lainey System transmits information through an external communication aid such as the Express III or Minspeak to integrate communication, environmental control, computer access, and mobility (Romich & Vignini, 1985). Both of these systems, as well as others, enable an individual to combine functions required for independence in vocational pursuits and home living, thereby increasing the opportunities for employment. A variety of device opportunities exist in the area of environmental control systems, although the company that manufactures the X-10 USA system has a virtual monopoly on power line carrier equipment. This basic technology can be accessed through a variety of means, including voice. The CASH III Computer Workstation for the handicapped voice-controls 32 individual appliances, lights, or other devices that plug into wall outlets in addition to seven pieces of office equipment, such as intercoms, dictation machines, or automatic doors. In addition, all the vocabularies required to voice-

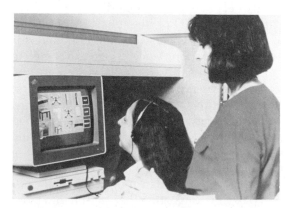

Computers help individuals with severe disabilities and the physically challenged to function in their environment. *(Photograph courtesy of IBM Corporation)*

operate major software programs, such as WordPerfect and Lotus 1-2-3 (see Chapter 3), are also included.

This system is representative of a new segment of multiple-function computer technology known as voice input/output system (VIOS) that is a separate and distinct area of computer science. Numerous manufacturers have announced computer-oriented voice input products and voice output equipment (Fox, 1991). This new computer market segment has not been caused by the machine communications needs of people with physical disabilities. Rather, the new voice systems are being developed for industry to assist individuals who need to input data without being at their computer keyboards. The net gain for people with physical disabilities will be falling prices for the technology and more individualized applications.

New Directions and Future Trends

The component nature of the new VIOS technology makes applications ideal for selection by rehabilitation engineers and others who need to solve vocational or educationally oriented problems for the physically challenged. Demands for VIOS are expected to increase as more cost-effective whole systems enter the market. But even now there is an ample range of VIOS technology for engineers to put to immediate use. Some simple forms of this technology already exist for many home and business microcomputers. The Texas Instruments (TI) speech command system is compatible with the TI professional computer and allows for some voice-activated commands for software operation. Voice Master is a complete hardware and software utility system for the Commodore, Apple, and Atari computers. The system includes speech synthesis, word recognition, and Voice Harp, a music-oriented software. Voice may be added to almost any program using Voice Master. The software also allows an increased level of understanding of the speech of an individual with cerebral palsy by translating that speech into more recognizable forms, enabling communication to be more easily understood.

Telecommunications, computer bulletin board systems, and electronic data access offer many opportunities for individuals with disabilities (see Chapters 1 and 6) and make interaction with people a practical reality. Computer networking, a principle component in office automation, can be an opportunity lifeline for an individual with disabilities. The technology is not new, but the value of telecomputing has not yet been realized. Connections can be formed from modem to modem, modem to bulletin board, and modem to large data banks (e.g., HEX, CompuServe, etc.).

The use of simple robots or turtles, particularly in connection with the computer language LOGO (see Appendix C; Fay, Okamoto, Brebner, & Winter, 1982; Gray, 1984; Hutinger, 1985), allows exceptional individuals to learn control over computer operation and programming by manipulation of the robot. Research in the robotics industry, however, has produced robots with sophisticated vision systems and with touch-sensitive grippers that can select and manipulate very small objects. This same robotics research will help people with disabilities be more self-sufficient in educational and vocational settings.

Computer simulation through videodisc, artificial intelligence, and other innovative technologies (see Chapter 4 and 6) is currently being developed and researched in the computer industry. While many of these developments remain experimental and costly for average use, the technologies offer the possibility of providing instruction for individuals with disabilities. Computers are changing the way we educate our children, conduct business, and do our jobs because they are effective, efficient, and rapidly becoming almost inexpensive. Most technology is designed for individuals other than those with physical disabilities, yet exploring new ways to use the evolving technology in applications with individuals with physical disabilities will continue to provide untold benefits.

SUMMARY

Three important factors must be considered when designing programming using computer technology: method of access to be used, chronological age of the individual, and educational or life-functioning area(s) to be enhanced. Individuals with physical disabilities and average intelligence are often able to use software designed for nonhandicapped people once computer access has been obtained.

This chapter provided information about literature on computer access, methods to determine the most ideal access device(s) and training, specific applications of computers for single-function uses in CAI and for life functioning, examples of existing devices and software packages designed to enhance the growth of individuals with physical disabilities, multiple-function systems, and examples of current technology and its possible future applications with consumers with disabilities.

Any information on technology growing as rapidly as computer systems is probably outdated as it is being written. However, technology is appropriate only when its application results in greater independence for the user. Computers (and the various types of technology associated with their use) can enhance the development of individuals with severe mental disabilities and the physically challenged. Newer and more sophisticated applications than those described in this chapter can be made when a teacher, parent, rehabilitation counselor, or other professional understands the area(s) of functioning to be enhanced. Consultation with a rehabilitation engineer (or other person who is knowledgeable and up-to-date in the computer field) can subsequently produce an effective and cost-efficient application of current technology.

REFERENCES

Barton, L. (1985). *An integrated microcomputer based program for the management of programs, data, IEP's and computer assisted language systems.* Poster presentation at the 12th Annual TASH Conference, Boston, MA.

Behrmann, M. M. (1984). A brighter future for early learning through high tech. *Pointer, 28*(2), 23–26.

Behrmann, M. M., & Lahm, L. (1984). *Proceedings of the national conference on the use of microcomputers in special education.* Reston, VA: Council for Exceptional Children.

Behrmann, M. M., & Lahm, L. (1985). Assess, teach, evaluate: A teaching hierarchy for computer based instruction. In M. Gergen & D. Hagen (Eds.), *Computer technology for the handicapped. Proceedings from the 1984 Closing the Gap Conference* (pp. 181–184). Henderson, MN: Closing the Gap.

BHT Group. (1984). *Discover your baby.* Mountain View, CA: Author.

Bourland, G., Jablonski, E. M., Allen, G. B., & White, J. (1984). On microcomputers, instruction, and the severely developmentally disabled. In M. M. Behrmann & L. Lahm (Eds.), *Proceedings of the national conference on the use of microcomputers in special education* (pp. 135–153). Reston, VA: Council for Exceptional Children.

Bowe, F. (1984). *Personal computers and special needs.* Henderson, MN: Closing the Gap.

Brinker, R. P., & Lewis, M. (1982a). Contingency intervention. In J. D. Anderson (Ed.), *Curricula for high-risk and handicapped infants* (pp. 37–41). Chapel Hill, NC: TADS.

Brinker, R. P., & Lewis, M. (1982b). Making the world work with microcomputers: A learning prosthesis for handicapped infants. *Exceptional Children, 49*(2), 163–170.

Browning, P., Zembrosky-Barkin, P., Nave, G., & White, W. (1985). *Computer technology for the handicapped in special education and rehabilitation: A resource guide* (Vol. 2). Eugene, OR: International Council for Computers in Education.

Burkhart, L. J. (1982). *Homemade battery powered toys and education devices for severely handicapped children.* Millville, PA: Author.

Burns, M. (1984a). Alternate interface devices for the physically handicapped. In M. M. Behrmann & L. Lahm (Eds.), *Proceedings of the national conference on the use of microcomputers in special education* (pp. 178–180). Reston, VA: Council for Exceptional Children.

Burns, M. (1984b). A justification for the use of computer-assisted instruction with the physically handicapped. In M. M. Behrmann & L. Lahm (Eds.), *Proceedings of the national conference on the use of microcomputers in special education* (pp. 171–177). Reston, VA: Council for Exceptional Children.

Campbell, P. H. (1985). *Training aid 2 application manual.* Shreve, OH: Prentke Romich.

Campbell, P. H., Bricker, W. A., & Esposito, L. (1980). Technology in the education of the severely handicapped. In B. Wilcox & R. York (Eds.), *Quality education for the severely handi-*

capped: The federal involvement. Washington, DC: Bureau of Education for the Handicapped.

Campbell, P. H., & McInerney, W. (1983). *The use of control interface devices with multihandicapped individuals with cognitive dysfunction.* In Proceedings of the Sixth Annual Conference on Rehab Engineering, San Diego, CA.

Campbell, P. H., McInerney, W. F., & Middleton, M. Q. (1983). *A manual of augmented sensory feedback devices for training severely handicapped students.* Akron, OH: Children's Hospital Medical Center of Akron.

Campbell, P. H., & Mulhauser, M. B. (1984). *Use of electronic switch interface devices in discrimination training with severely handicapped students.* Unpublished manuscript.

Enders, A. (Ed.). (1984). *Technology for independent living: Sourcebook.* Washington, D.C.: Rehabilitation Engineering Society of North America.

Esposito, L. (1985). *The stimulus-response management system.* Unpublished manuscript.

Esposito, L., & Campbell, P. H. (1985). *Use of computer programs to train switch activation skills with young children with handicaps.* Presentation at 8th Annual RESNA Conference, Memphis, TN.

Evans, R. O., & Sherrill, T. (1983). A computer program to assist persons with physical or visual impairments in notetaking. *Rehabilitation Literature, 44*(11–12), 331.

Fay, G., Okamoto, G., Brebner, J., & Winter, F. (1982). The electronic schoolhouse: New technology in education of the severely retarded. *Pointer, 26*(2), 10–12.

Fox, J. (1991). Voice: The next interface. *PC Today, 5*(11), 8–13.

Gast, D. L., & Berkler, M. (1981). Severe and profound handicaps. In A. E. Blackhurst & W. E. Berdine (Eds.), *An introduction to special education.* Boston, MA: Little, Brown.

Gergen, M., & Hagen, D. (1985). *Computer technology for the handicapped. Proceedings from the 1984 Closing the Gap conference.* Henderson, MN: Closing the Gap.

Gray, L. (1984). LOGO helps remove children's handicaps. *Educational Computer, 4*(1), 33–38.

Grossman, H. J. (Ed.). (1973). *Manual on terminology and classification in mental retardation.* Washington, DC: American Association on Mental Deficiency.

Hagen, D. (1984a). Jason says "yes." *Pointer, 28*(2), 40–43.

Hagen, D. (1984b). *Microcomputer resource book for special education.* Henderson, MN: Closing the Gap.

Hanline, M. F., Hanson, M. J., Veltman, M. A., & Spaeth, D. M. (1985). Electro-mechanical teaching toys for infants and toddlers with disabilities. *Teaching Exceptional Children, 18*(1), 20–29.

Hazen, P. (1985). *Microcomputer software for individually managed instruction.* Baltimore: Johns Hopkins University, Applied Physics Laboratory.

Heckathorne, C. W., & Childress, D. S. (1983). Applying anticipatory text selection in a writing aid for people with severe motor impairment. *IEEE Micro, 3*(3), 17–23.

Heckathorne, C. W., & Leibowitz, L. (1985). The MicroDEC II system: Integrated device control and computer access. In M. Gergen & D. Hagen (Eds.), *Computer technology for the handicapped* (pp. 81–87). Henderson, MN: Closing the Gap.

Heim, J. (1992). Remote communications software: The next best thing. *PC World, 10*(1), 155–164.

Heward, W. L., & Orlansky, M. D. (1991). *Exceptional children* (4th ed.). Columbus, OH: Merrill/Macmillan.

Hutinger, P. L. (1985). Activating children through technology: Notes on using microcomputers with very young children. In M. Gergen & D. Hagen (Eds.), *Computer technology for the handicapped* (pp. 168–174). Henderson, MN: Closing the Gap.

Johnson, L. B. (1992). Choices at your fingertips. *PC Today, 6*(1), 24–31.

Jorgenson, E. (1992). Missouri's basic education initiative supports job training. *T.H.E. Journal, 19*(8), 60–62.

Jung, P. (1980). New learning aids offer help for the handicapped. *Apple, 1*(1), 22–23.

Kahn, T. M. (1985). *The paradox of special education software: Everyone is special.* Presentation at the Special Education Software Conference, Alexandria, VA.

Komoski, K. (1985). *The formidable task of evaluating educational software.* Paper presented at the Special Education Software Conference, Alexandria, VA.

Lahm, E. A. (1985). HUMAN-SD: A validated tool for selecting computer systems for handicapped users. In M. Gergen & D. Hagen (Eds.), *Computer technology for the handicapped* (pp. 6–13). Henderson, MN: Closing the Gap.

Lutz, J. E., & Taylor, P. A. (1981). A computerized home-base curriculum for high-risk preschoolers. *AEDS Journal, 15*(1), 1–9.

Lynd, C. (1983). A consumer's guide to computer-assisted learning. *Exceptional Parent, 13*(4), 49–56.

Messinger, M. (1983). CP = computer proficient. *Exceptional Parent*, 13(4), 57–60.

Nave, G., Browning, P., & Carter, J. (1983). *Computer technology for the handicapped in special education and rehabilitation: A resource guide.* Eugene, OR: International Council for Computers in Education.

Piaget, J. (1952). *The origins of intelligence.* New York: Norton Books.

Piszkin, T. (1985). Courseware authoring for the computer neophyte. In M. Gergen & D. Hagen (Eds.), *Computer technology for the handicapped* (pp. 154–158). Henderson, MN: Closing the Gap.

Powers, J., & Ball, T. S. (1983). Video games to augment leisure programming in a state hospital for developmentally disabled clients. *Journal of Special Education Technology*, 6(1), 48–57.

Prentke-Romich. (1985). *The TA-2.* Prentke Romich Co., 8769 Township Road 513, Shreve, OH 44676.

Romich, B. A., & Vignini, C. (1985). Integrating communication, computer access, environmental control and mobility. In M. Gergen & D. Hagen (Eds.), *Computer technology for the handicapped* (pp. 71–77). Henderson, MN: Closing the Gap.

Rosenberg, S. A. (1984). *Development of a microprocessor based workstation for S/P multihandicapped students.* (Final report, U.S. Department of Education Grant No. G008300312). Omaha, NE.

Rushakoff, G. E., & Lombardino, L. J. (1983). Comprehensive microcomputer applications for severely physically handicapped children. *Teaching Exceptional Children*, 16(1), 18–22.

Russell, S. J. (1983). Had we but world enough and time: LOGO in special education. *Classroom Computer Learning*, 4(3), 34–39.

Schwejda, P., & Vanderheiden, G. (1982). *Adaptive firmware card for the Apple II.* Madison, WI: Trace Research and Development Center.

Shanahan, D., & Ryan, A. (1984). A tool for evaluating educational software. *Teaching Exceptional Children*, 16(4), 242–247.

Shein, F., Lee, K., & Pearson, B. (1983). *Ontario Crippled Children's Centre* (Appendices C1, C2, C3). Ontario Crippled Children's Centre, 350 Rumsey Road, Toronto, Canada M46 1R8.

Shirriff, B. (1980). The microcomputer as a communication device for non-vocal children with limited manual dexterity. *Proceedings of the Association for the Development of Computer-based Instructional Systems* (pp. 152–156). Bellingham, WA: Western Washington University.

Shworles, T. R. (1983). The person with disability and the benefits of the microcomputer revolution: To have or to have not. *Rehabilitation Literature*, 44(11–12), 322–330.

Tindall, L. W., & Gugerty, J. J. (1984). *Effective microcomputer assisted instruction for the vocational education of special needs students.* Madison: University of Wisconsin–Madison, Vocational Studies Center.

Tinker, R. (1985). *Technology compensatory activities: Severely physically-impaired persons.* Technical Education Research Centers, 8 Eliot Street, Cambridge, MA 02138.

Traynor, C. D., & Beukelman, D. R. (1984). Nonvocal communication augmentation using microcomputers. *Exceptional Education Quarterly*, 4(4), 90–103.

Vanderheiden, G. C. (1983). *The practical use of microcomputers in rehabilitation.* Madison, WI: Trace Research and Development Center.

Vanderheiden, G. C. (1984). *Comparison of Apple, Epson, IBM . . . microcomputers for application in rehabilitation systems for persons with physical handicaps* (Revision D). Madison, WI: Trace Research and Development Center.

Vanderheiden, G. C. (1985). *Non-vocal communication resource book* (2nd ed.). Austin, TX: PRO-ED.

Vanderheiden, G. C., Bengston, D., Brady, M., & Wolstead, L. M. (1984). *The national software hardware registry* (2nd ed.). Madison, WI: Trace Research and Development Center.

Wilson, J. (1984). Cerebral palsy. In S. Campbell (Ed.), *Pediatric neurologic physical therapy.* New York: Churchill Livingstone.

Wright, C., & Nomura, M. (1985). *From toys to computers: Access for the physically disabled child.* Christine Wright, P.O. Box 700242, San Jose, CA 95170.

Zuckerman, R. A. (1985). *Microcomputers software for individually managed instruction.* Kent, OH: Kent State University, Department of Special Education.

Suggested Activities

Paper and Pencil

Find an article that describes computer applications with the severely handicapped and one that addresses computer applications with the physically challenged. Compare and contrast (a) how these two exceptional populations are defined and (b) the computer applications used with these individuals.

Observation

Visit a center in the community for individuals with cerebral palsy. Interview the director or supervisor and outline the present computer applications and those planned for the future.

Practicum

Use a head stick to type on a computer keyboard, or try to operate a computer using an access device such as the Eyetyper or a control switch interface.

Resources

Organizations

National Easter Seal Society. This organization of parents, professionals, and concerned citizens engages in research, publishing, and educational activities in order to improve the education and life of exceptional persons. Write to National Easter Seal Society, 2023 West Ogden Avenue, Chicago, IL 60612.

United Cerebral Palsy Association. This organization of interested persons supports a number of activities to improve the lives of individuals with cerebral palsy. Write to United Cerebral Palsy Association, 66 East 34th Street, New York City, NY 10016.

Journals

Bulletin of Science & Technology for the Handicapped. This is a quarterly newsletter that reviews a variety of technologies that apply to individuals with a disability. Write to American Association for the Advancement of Science, 1776 Massachusetts Avenue, Washington, DC 20036.

Computer-Disability News. This is a quarterly newsletter that addresses a number of computer issues and publishes personal interviews. Write to the National Easter Seal Society, 2023 West Ogden Avenue, Chicago, IL 60612.

Books

Vanderheiden, G. C. (1985). *Non-vocal communication resource book* (2nd ed.). Austin, TX: PRO-ED.

Browning, P., Zembrosky-Barkin, P., Nave, G., & White, W. (1985). *Computer technology for the handicapped in special education and rehabilitation: A resource guide* (Vol. 2). Eugene, OR: International Council for Computers in Education.

Hardware/Software

Adaptive Firmware Card
Adaptive Peripheral
4529 Bagley Avenue North
Seattle, WA 98103

CASH III Computer Workstation
Cascade Graphics Development
1000 South Grand Avenue
Santa Anna, CA 92705

Computer Assisted Manufacturing (CAM)
Hitachi America
50 Prospect Avenue
Tarrytown, NY 10591

Echo II
Street Electronics
1140 Mark Avenue
Carpenteria, CA 93013

Epson HX
Epson America
2780 Lomita Blvd.
Torrance, CA 90505

Express III
Prentke-Romich
1022 Heyl Road
Wooster, OH 44691

Lainey System
Prentke Romich
1022 Heyl Road
Wooster, OH 44691

MacOffix
Emerging Technology
470 Walnut
Boulder, CO 80301

Microcomputer Applications Program
Ontario Crippled Children's Centre
350 Rumsey Road
Toronto, Ontario, Canada M4G 1R8

Micro DEC II
Digital Equipment
Two Iron Way, Box 1003
Marlboro, MA 01752

Minspeak
Prentke Romich
1022 Heyl Road
Wooster, OH 44691

Mod Keyboard System
Tash
70 Gibson Drive, Unit 1
Markham, Ontario, Canada L3E 2Z3

Portable Voice II
Words +
1125 Stewart Court
Sunnyvale, CA 94086

Smartterm
Hayes Microcomputer Products
5923 Peachtree Industrial Blvd.
Atlanta, GA 30092

Stimulus Response Management System
Family Child Learning Center
1909 Third Street
Cuyahoga Falls, OH 44221

TA-2
Prentke-Romich
1022 Heyl Road
Wooster, OH 44691

Touch Talker
Prentke-Romich
1022 Heyl Road
Wooster, OH 44691

TRINE
Trace Center
University of Wisconsin
Madison, WI 53706

Voice Harp
Covax
675D Conger Street
Eugene, OR 97402

Voice Master
Covax
675D Conger Street
Eugene, OR 97402

Votrax Personal Speech System
Votrax
500 Stevenson Highway
Troy, NY 48084

Words +
Words +
1125 Stewart Court
Sunnyvale, CA 94086

X-10 USA
X-10 USA
185A Legrand Avenue
Northvale, NJ 07647

CHAPTER

Computers and Individuals with Sensory Impairments

Ronald R. Kelly
National Technical Institute for the Deaf
Rochester Institute of Technology ■

All human beings have an incredible potential for learning. There is nothing more amazing than a child's developmental progress in acquiring a full complement of psychomotor, cognitive, and language skills. There is also nothing more discouraging to a parent or teacher than to see a child's potential development hindered by a sensory disability (Beggs, 1992). During the 20th century, parents and educators have searched for technological advances to improve the development of handicapped learners. Indeed, technology has offered hope to sensory-impaired individuals, although it has yet to fulfill expectations.

We currently seem to be experiencing the golden age of technology. Only 22 years since humans first walked on the moon, robot spacecraft from Earth now electronically and photographically survey the planets of this solar system on their way to the stars, and anything seems technologically possible. Yet these events may raise false expectations for educators and parents concerning the application of computer technology to education.

Almost daily, the news media inform us of the rapid advances in computer technology. Personal computers offer greater capabilities than the mainframe computers of the 1950s. New supercomputers from Cray Research perform between 600 million and 1.2 billion calculations per second, while current mainframe computers perform approximately 5 million calculations a second and some desktop computers perform up to 1,000 calculations per second. Computers talk to us and recognize voice commands. Computer applications have entered almost every facet of human endeavor in the Western world, influencing the way people work and live.

Unfortunately, how to apply computers to the education of individuals with sensory impairments in order to maximize instructional and learning benefits is not readily apparent (Cronin, 1992). The educational potential of the current technological revolution may not offer the same potential to people who cannot read or process information normally. The task facing professionals and parents of visually and/or hearing-impaired individuals is how to apply computer technology to meet learning needs complicated by sensory impairment. A successful match between learner and technology requires an understanding of the strengths and limitations of both sensory-impaired individuals and computer technology.

INDIVIDUALS WITH SENSORY IMPAIRMENTS

Both visually impaired and hearing-impaired people comprise highly heterogeneous groups, which complicates the educational process. A teacher of either the hearing impaired or visually impaired with a small pupil-teacher ratio (e.g., 7:1) is often faced with far more instructional complexity than a teacher with 25 students in a regular classroom, because a variety of human dimensions interact to create unique combinations of learning problems and information processing requirements. For both the visually impaired and the hearing impaired, the complicating variables that influence individual performances include (a) age at onset of sensory impairment; (b) severity or degree of impairment; (c) causal factor of the impairment; (d) multiplicity of handicaps; (e) timing of earliest developmental or educational inter-

Computerized portable braillers can be used in the home, school, and community.
(Photograph by Jimmy D. Lindsey)

ventions; (f) type of family support—home environment; (g) cognitive potential; and (h) chronological age (see Lowenfeld, 1981; Myklebust, 1964; Warren, 1977). When educators of the sensory impaired discuss the need for individualized instruction, their perspective is based on practical necessity.

Visual Impairment

The only common feature of the visually impaired is visual loss. Jan, Freeman, and Scott (1977) observed that there is no universally accepted definition of blindness—over 65 different definitions of visual impairment exist throughout the world. From an ophthalmological perspective,

> visual impairment or visual disability can be used to describe a visual limitation of 20/70 or worse. The "20/70" refers to the diagnosis made by using the Snellen chart; it means that the person could see no more at a distance of 20 feet than someone with adequate vision can see at a distance of 70 feet. Those persons whose visual acuity falls between 20/70 and 20/200 are considered **partially sighted** and therefore deserving of rehabilitative services. . . . The clients in a rehabilitation setting whose visual acuity falls between 20/200 and 20/500 are described as having **partial vision, low vision,** or **useful vision.** Clients with 20/500 or worse . . . are termed **totally blind or having no useful vision.** (Vander Kolk, 1981, p. 2)

An ophthalmological definition is not always adequate for educational or rehabilitative purposes. The visually impaired may vary in their abilities to use the existing sight they have (Lowenfeld, 1981). Vander Kolk (1981) observed that two persons with diagnosed 20/200 vision may function in different ways. One person may be able to move about independently, read regular printed materials, and function similarly to a normally sighted person. The other person, however, may have trouble reading regular print, will not be able to see at night, and may function as if totally blind. These two individuals may also vary considerably in their ability to use low-vision aids. Clearly there is a discrepancy between measured vision and how an individual translates it into functional vision. Functional use of impaired vision is in part due to the interaction of the personal variables that influence performance. As Lowenfeld (1981) noted, success for visually impaired persons "is basically dependent upon the strengths of each individual" (p. 229).

In terms of planning appropriate educational experiences for the visually impaired, individualization and independent learning activities are key components. Six major concerns that Chorniak (1977) suggested should be considered when planning learning experiences for the visually impaired are individual differences, physical encounter, stimulation, structure (wholeness and relationships), reinforcement, and independence. Lowenfeld (1981) cited similar educational principles: individualization, concreteness, unified instruction, additional stimulation, and self-activity. Technological advances in aids, tools, and equipment have made learning more efficient for totally blind and partially sighted students (Chorniak, 1977), but there is a continuing need to improve the instructional/learning efficiency of the educational environment. People with visual impairments need an extraordinary educational environment.

Computer applications for key educational needs of the visually impaired appear to be particularly relevant to individualization, structure, unified instruction, and independent learning activities. Computers also have the potential to improve the quality of life at home and work for visually impaired individuals.

Table 9.1 lists general computer applications with visually and hearing-impaired individuals. Specific concepts are addressed later in this chapter.

Hearing Impairment

Hearing impairment also introduces incredible complexity into the education and development of an individual. "The implications of an auditory impairment vary from person to person and from one circumstance to another. This makes it difficult to define rigorously

TABLE 9.1
Visually and hearing-impaired individuals and general computer applications

Exceptionality	General Computer Applications
Partially sighted	CAI, large print video display, large print printers, and speech synthesis
Blind	Speech synthesis, hard copy braille, refreshable (paperless) braille, text to braille, braille to text, text to tactile equivalent, and CAI
Hearing impaired	Language development, speech synthesis, telecommunications, and CAI
Deaf	Language development, speech synthesis, interactive video, Real-time Graphics, telecommunications, and CAI

what is meant by terms such as hearing loss, deaf, and hard of hearing" (Myklebust, 1964, p. 3). Furthermore, the usefulness of the various terms and definitions "depends on our purposes, and the important purposes for which these terms are useful are social, educational, and medical" (Davis, 1970, p. 84). In terms of hearing levels,

> we find a zone of uncertainty from 70 to 90 dB (ISO). . . . Within this zone some individuals are socially deaf, but more of them are merely very hard of hearing. . . . We propose to confine the term deafness to hearing-threshold levels for speech greater than 92 dB (ISO). A good reason for selecting this particular boundary is that the most authoritative medical rule . . . reads "if the average hearing threshold level at 500, 1000, and 2000 Hz is over 92 dB (ISO), the handicap for hearing everyday speech should be considered total." Our criterion thus has a medical sanction in a social and economic context. (Davis, 1970, p. 84)

A long-standing definition of hearing impairment was provided by the Committee on Nomenclature of the Conference of Executives of American Schools for the Deaf (1938). According to this definition, the deaf are "those in whom the sense of hearing is nonfunctional for the ordinary purpose of life." This committee classified the deaf into two groups: (a) congenitally deaf, or those who are born deaf; and (b) adventitiously deaf, or those who are born with normal hearing but in whom the sense of hearing becomes nonfunctional later through illness or accident. However, when planning educational interventions, Myklebust (1964) recommended that educators adopt a more useful definition for hearing impairments. According to Myklebust, the deaf are those persons whose hearing loss has precluded normal acquisition of language, while the hard of hearing are those individuals whose hearing loss is not great enough to prevent language acquisition. Silverman and Lane (1970, p. 386) included in their functional definition of deaf children those who have not developed the expressive and receptive skills of communication before the onset of deafness. This means they cannot talk or understand the speech of others as do children of the same age with normal hearing. Also included in this definition are those children who have acquired some of these skills of communication before the onset of deafness but whose incompetence in language still calls for special educational techniques.

The most obvious effect of a hearing impairment is the negative impact on the development of expressive and receptive communication skills and patterns of language. Unfortunately, these happen to be critical components of both human development and the educational system. A hearing impairment has extensive implications for learning, personal development, and social interaction. In fact, "the loss of hearing sensitivity in young children alters the character of their linguistic intake, which in turn interacts with their development and maturation and affects the acquisition of language (and speech) to the degree that many deaf children enter adolescence and adulthood without the ability to communicate effectively in English" (Bochner, 1982, p. 107). This situation, in turn, influences the educational experiences of the hearing impaired:

Since academic subjects have required English as a mode of instruction, the greater instructional emphasis has always been placed on teaching English. As a result, deaf children have had less exposure to the amount and quality of school subjects than have their English-speaking peers. . . . The fourth-grade achievement levels exhibited by the average deaf high school graduate could be considered a result of both English deficits and a lack of knowledge and information about the world. (Hofmeister & Drury, 1982, p. 359)

English/language skills, conceptual development, communication, and academic content are critical areas to consider in planning appropriate experiences for the hearing impaired. There are also implications for individualization and independent study. Computer applications appear to have potential for these areas of need.

Deaf-Blind Impairment

The combination of hearing and visual impairments creates even greater instructional complexity for parents and educators. The dual handicap of blindness and deafness is relatively rare. (It is estimated that there are fewer than 1,000 deaf-blind children below the age of 21 in the United States.) Multiple sensory impairments, particularly from birth or prior to language acquisition, require comprehensive and systematic educational interventions if even the slightest gains in development are to be made. Educational planning is complicated by the fact that functionally defining deaf-blindness is influenced by a variety of factors. Dinsmore (cited in Warren, 1977) suggested five possible categories:

1) those children who have had vision and hearing for several years, so that verbal and visual memory are available, 2) those who have been deaf from early in life but have had vision for some years, 3) those who have been blind from very early in life but have had auditory function for some years, 4) those who have been both visually and auditorily impaired from early in life, and 5) those who have variously combined partial losses. (p. 174)

Unfortunately, professional perspective influences the definition of deaf-blindness, and thus has the potential for affecting the educational planning and implementation. Warren (1977) maintained that

> those who are primarily interested in deafness tend to view such children as deaf with the additional handicap of visual loss, while those primarily interested in blindness tend to regard the hearing impairment as secondary . . . the child with the dual handicap may fail to receive a program that is geared optimally to his capabilities. (p. 174)

It is difficult to say whether computer applications offer the same potential for deaf-blind individuals as they do for either the visually impaired or the hearing impaired. The existing literature on educating the deaf-blind is sparse and has neither an experiential nor a historical-educational perspective to provide guidance. Rather than generalized applicability, computer applications to meet the needs of the deaf-blind may fall into the realm of individual case situations.

A BRIEF REVIEW OF THE LITERATURE

There are no easy technological solutions to meeting the educational needs of the sensory impaired. To date, computers have been used to address a variety of unique communication and instructional needs created primarily by sensory disabilities. This is not to suggest that these computer applications have satisfactorily resolved the educational needs of sensory-impaired learners; however, these applications are an important step forward and will provide the foundation for future development.

Kleiman (1984) has described six computer capabilities that meet some of the specific needs of the visually impaired:

1. *Computer speech synthesis*—the computer can state which line the cursor is on and speak the words on that line, which makes almost all of the computer's capabilities accessible to blind people.

2. *Large print displays*—the computer can display large, high-contrast print on the video screen or through the use of an appropriate printer.

3. *Tactile forms*—for people who cannot read any print regardless of size, various devices can convert printed letters to a tactile code of vibrating patterns or to braille.

4. *Braille word processing*—special braille printers can interface with computers to take advantage of the word processing capabilities.

5. *Computerized letter recognition*—speech synthesizers and text-to-speech programs can convert words stored in the computer to speech, large letter displays, braille, or to tactile signals.

6. *Conversion of print to speech*—the Kurzweil Reading Machine can convert print to speech by combining conversion capabilities.

Regarding the hearing impaired, it is not surprising that various computer applications address these learners' unique educational needs for English/language, mathematics, and communication skills. Watson's (1979) historical review of computer-assisted instruction (CAI) for the hearing impaired and others with handicaps appears to focus on English and mathematics skills. Two national symposia on the use of computers in the education of the hearing impaired (see Stepp & Reiners, 1982, 1983) also support the view that computer use focuses on communication and language skills pertinent to instruction and assessment. Specifically, the unique educational needs of the hearing impaired are reflected in computer applications in the areas of basic skills (e.g., reading comprehension, writing techniques, mathematics instruction), speech-reading instruction and practice, sign language instruction and practice, auditory listening skills, assessment of skill levels in the above areas, telephone communication, and computer management of the educational programming.

Pertinent to the needs of other exceptional populations and students with special needs, there are also excellent guides available that focus specifically on selecting computer technology for the elementary and secondary levels, vocational education, and higher education. These guides are excellent starting references for those who want to incorporate computer-based components into existing curricula.

GENERAL HARDWARE AND SOFTWARE CONSIDERATIONS

Computer hardware and software for sensory-impaired individuals should adequately serve the user's specific needs and a structured plan is required that shows how the computer will be integrated into the educational environment, implemented in the home, or utilized at work. Careful planning is the key to success ("Hearing Aids," 1992).

When selecting computer equipment for the visually impaired, the prime consideration is the interface capabilities with the assistive devices required for the individual (e.g., speech synthesizer, large print displays on the terminal or printer, tactile devices, and letter recognition for converting text to speech). The availability of appropriate software for the computer equipment under consideration should also be a principal criterion in hardware selection. Some software is compatible with a wide array of computers, while other software is not (see Chapter 3).

For the hearing impaired, interface and compatibility considerations are not as necessary for educational computer applications, since assistive devices are not often involved. Thus selecting equipment for the hearing impaired is similar to selecting equipment for a nonhandicapped user. Special considerations for computer applications with the hearing impaired would be necessary if the implementation required a sophisticated and complex systems design like interactive video (see Newell, Sims, & Clymer, 1984) or specific research and related training. In discussing

the use of computers for speech training and research, Nickerson, Stevens, Rollins, and Zue (1983) listed some desired features of a computer system:

1. flow mode display capability
2. freeze and capture capability, which, when coupled with flow mode capability, provides the important option of monitoring continuous speech and capturing the contents of the display (the last two seconds of speech) for careful inspection at any time
3. auditory capture and replay
4. data analysis capability to make measurements of duration, amplitude, and frequency directly from a display
5. flexibility . . . to experiment with different displays and display formats and to evolve an effective system though use (p. 319)

Some of the limitations of the computer system that Nickerson et al. (1983) identified in their speech-training research were:

1. lack of the ability to store and retrieve prerecorded samples of speech and speech-like stimuli for use in auditory testing and training
2. lack of a spectrographic display
3. lack of ability to provide language training
4. lack of a carefully designed user interface (p. 319)

These considerations may or may not be applicable to the general educational application of computers. However, they should give general and special education personnel, as well as individuals with sensory impairments, reasons to think about exactly what is necessary for their specific application and implementation efforts. The most common and embarrassing situation is to purchase a computer system and then find out it will not do what it is expected to do. To prevent this from occurring, one needs to initially determine the computer system's function, capacity, speed, flexibility, expendability, portability, reliability and service, cost, compatibility with both hardware and software, and user compatibility (Chial, 1984). Six other specific criteria to consider in selecting computer software are usability, performance and accuracy, affordability, installation, documentation, and support (Schwartz, 1984a). These various considerations are discussed in Chapters 3 and 4.

The evaluation criteria for selecting computer hardware and software are really dependent on the specific sensory-impaired person's needs. In educational settings, selection could begin with the needs generated by the integrative educational plan and proceed from there. The computer applications illustrated in this chapter should serve as a point of departure for planning computer applications. There is nothing wrong with replicating either a curriculum or computer-based instructional system developed by others. However, the nature of serving the sensory impaired educationally involves extensive individualization.

SPECIFIC COMPUTER APPLICATIONS

Visually Impaired

In the literature on computer applications for the visually impaired, the primary focus is on assistive devices (e.g., speech synthesizers) pertinent to the handicap. Discussions of curricular or course content issues related to computer applications with the visually impaired are almost nonexistent. However, one notable exception to this lack of literature is the report of the Carroll Center for the Blind's Project CABLE, which described two courses developed to help individuals with visual impairments understand and use computer access devices for vocational purposes. (For further information, write to the Carroll House for the Blind, 770 Centre Street, Newton, MA 02158.) Thus it appears that current educational thought concerning computer applications for the visually impaired is dominated by the need to provide assistive aids for the vision handicap. This contrasts with the literature on computer applications for the hearing impaired, which covers a broader range of issues related to

curricula, methodology, and communication impairment.

Several important yet practical developments in computer applications with the visually impaired involve the use of synthetic speech, word processing text-editing for braille output, and large print displays on the screen or in hard copy. These developments have been central to providing the visually impaired relatively inexpensive access to computers along with a multitude of programs. Currently, it is possible for the visually impaired to interact with a computer through combinations of five types of information: synthetic speech, large print, low-vision aids, hard-copy braille, and refreshable braille.

Speech Synthesis

Briefly, speech synthesizers range from less than two hundred dollars (e.g., Echo+ discussed earlier) to several thousand dollars (e.g., Professional Vert). Goodrich (1984) stated that

inexpensive voice synthesizers are characterized by low-quality (but intelligible) pronunciation, limited exception dictionaries (the number of words that are not pronounced according to the general rules of English), limited review capabilities, and relatively slow speaking rates. Some may even limit the user's ability to review the text that already has been spoken. . . . Expensive voice synthesizers are characterized by high-quality pronunciation, large exception dictionaries, relatively fast speaking rates, and overall good review capabilities. (p. 410)

From an educational perspective, synthetic speech capabilities (see also Chapter 7) offer enormous potential for computer applications. Their use means that the visually impaired will have access to a considerable portion of the commercially available software without extensive adaptation. However, speech synthesizers will not provide access to graphic information. Through speech synthesizers, visually impaired learners will be able to use the same software programs as sighted students (Hagen, 1984). Speech synthesizers will allow a major improvement in resource use for regular and special educators as well as the visually impaired. A primary instructional problem for professionals involved with the visually or hearing impaired has been the constant and continuous need to adapt existing materials to meet specific communication requirements of the learners. Even more important, with these assistive computer aids, it is possible for individuals with visual impairments to achieve almost complete independence in accessing the information electronically stored in the computer memory banks. Processing information independently and self-directed control in the learning process are critically important to the development and growth of all people.

Large Print

As for large print, it can be generated either through software on a typical computer or by the use of specially designed equipment. For example, the Large Print Display Processor can enlarge letters up to 16 times. A problem with large print computers is that they reduce the amount of material displayed at one time and make review tedious and difficult (Goodrich, 1984). In addition to displaying less text at one time, large print computers generally require more space, are more expensive, and do not produce graphics (Morrissette, 1984). In spite of the limitations, such devices are workable alternatives for providing access to computers for the visually impaired who need this type of enhancement. When sufficient for the individual, low-vision aids such as magnifiers are less expensive and generally do not require modification of the computer equipment, thus offering a wider range in the selection of computers and software. Low-vision aids for the computer are primarily the same as normally used—magnifying aids for reading print on paper or the video system.

Braille Applications

Refreshable braille—or paperless braille— allows immediate feedback of information for editing purposes, while hard-copy braille provides a permanent record. Refreshable braille is a changeable tactile system that uses a series of pins that are raised or lowered to form braille characters. Currently, the refreshable braille systems are more expensive than voice synthesizers and have limitations such as the single-line display of the VersaBraille. However, work is being pursued on full-page refreshable braille displays that would also offer the possibility of two-dimensional graphics. For more detailed information on computer aids for the visually impaired, refer to Morrissette (1984) for an evaluation of large-print computer features, and Goodrich (1984) for a general evaluation overview.

The OPTACON is one of the more widely used technologies for accessing print, including computer text (Ruconich, Ashcroft, & Young, 1984). The OPTACON system translates visual text into a raised, vibrating, tactile print that is not braille but a tactile counterpart of visible symbols. With appropriate camera lenses, the OPTACON can read either the paper printout or the electronic video display. The clear advantage of the OPTACON is its versatility for accessing print on either hard copy or a video display, while one of its limitations is the slow speed of 20–60 words per minute. Ruconich et al. (1984) provided an excellent review of the OPTACON and other technologies discussed in this chapter for making computers accessible to blind people.

Individuals with visual impairments will use computers for the same purposes as sighted persons. Goodrich (1984) reminded us that the primary application of computers is information processing. The management of information is the major advantage of computer applications for word processing, data bases, spreadsheets, and games. The key to successful computer use is the degree to which it enhances an individual's education, work, or leisure.

ULTRA

An excellent example of a computer aid that enhances both the education and work capabilities of students with visual impairments is provided by Morrison and Lunney (1984), who described the development of the Universal Laboratory Training and Research Aid (ULTRA). The ULTRA is a portable talking laboratory computer that can be used as an instructional laboratory aid, talking computer terminal, a professional tool, and a personal computer. Even more important, the ULTRA enables people with visual impairments to perform important instrumental measurements and laboratory experiments independently. The ULTRA was initially designed within the context of a chemistry laboratory but offers far broader applications and potential. As Morrison and Lunney noted:

> The usual approach to accommodating a visually impaired student in a chemistry laboratory is to employ a sighted aide who makes visual observations and performs manipulations that the visually impaired student cannot perform. This approach can be acceptable if the aide is well trained and competent. However, we believe that the needs of visually impaired science students can be served better by giving them adaptive apparatus that they can operate without assistance because the value of independence in the laboratory has been clearly demonstrated (Cochin & Herman, 1981; Ricker, 1980; Weems, 1977). Indeed, if a visually impaired student plans to do laboratory work as a scientist, technician, or engineer, he or she will have to operate apparatus independently, so why should the student not start early with the right tools? (p. 418)

The ULTRA is easily connected to a variety of measurement instruments and sensors commonly found in undergraduate science laboratories. ULTRA converts the data readings from various instruments to speech or some other auditory output. Thus, a person with visual impairments can independently perform measurements of physical and chemical quantities and perform pertinent calculations. Synthetic speech is the primary mode of auditory output for the ULTRA. The use of rising and falling pitches enable users to locate maxima and minima in data.

The impressive features of the ULTRA are its portability and flexibility. Its physical dimensions are approximately 20 by 13 by 8 inches. In addition to its primary laboratory functions, it serves as a talking calculator, talking computer terminal, and a personal computer. The system is an open-ended profes-

sional tool that can grow to accommodate the changing needs and skills of the user. Also, "the ULTRA represents a significant step toward the goal of giving individuals with visual impairments better access to careers that involve laboratory work [and] represents the first serious attempt to use [computer] synthetic speech . . . to give visually impaired people independent access to scientific instruments" (Morrison & Lunney, 1984, p. 425).

VersaBraille

Another important educational application of computer technology for the visually impaired is the VersaBraille, a paperless braille machine. It is a portable stand-alone machine that functions like a word processor. Braille is displayed on a field of 20 cells containing six holes each through which rounded pins project to form the braille characters. The editing capability for braille, similar to word processing, is a key advantage. Information is stored on audiocassette tape for ease of retrieval. Furthermore, through the use of adaptors the VersaBraille can be interfaced with either computers or printers.

Moore (1984) described the utility of the VersaBraille in educational environments. Students with visual impairments in the Pittsburgh area attending junior high, high school, and the University of Pittsburgh used VersaBrailles in their classes and at home for a wide variety of school activities (e.g., preparing for classes, taking notes in classes, preparing papers and other homework assignments, and editing them in preparation for submission to teachers) and for personal uses such as daily diaries, addresses, and telephone numbers.

> At the junior and senior high school level, students developed procedures for using VersaBrailles each day for taking notes in classes. For example, at the beginning of the week, a student opened a chapter for each subject and reserved enough pages in the chapter to write class notes for a week. As she finished the notes for each class each day, she entered her name on to the tape; the next day, with the word search function, she found her name within seconds and was prepared to continue with notes. Tests and worksheets were pre-

pared on tapes by each teacher; the student read the question and, using the insert function of the VersaBraille, put in her answer. After the test or worksheet was completed, the VersaBraille was connected to a printer—in many cases, a school printer which was used in the computer lab—and, again within seconds, the braille was translated and a print copy was ready for the classroom teacher. If the printer had the capacity to send and receive, the teacher put the test on a cassette tape in braille by typing it on the printer keyboard. One teacher found she could prepare students' work on a microcomputer typing on the keyboard, then she downloaded to that student's VersaBraille. Long assignments such as research papers or science reports were written by students on their VersaBrailles, corrected and edited until copies were perfect, and print copies were quickly prepared for classroom teachers on the printer; this saved an enormous amount of time for the student and for the special teacher. (p. 143)

Students at the university level used the VersaBrailles in additional ways. They used telephone modems to access data banks and review the same information and literature as the other college students. Using this approach, the VersaBraille enabled the student with visual impairments to write research papers, correct and revise them until they had final drafts to submit, and have the papers printed in clean copy for their instructors. Students studying computer science found that by using a telephone modem with the VersaBraille to communicate with the mainframe computer, they could produce as much work in similar timeframes as their classmates. This was something they had not been able to accomplish before. Thus the VersaBraille application improved the efficiency of university students in completing their assignments.

Training is recommended for both students and professionals who wish to use the VersaBraille in an educational environment. For further information and discussion of the educational applications for VersaBraille, refer to Moore (1984).

Tactile Graphics Display

The American Foundation for the Blind has developed a new Tactile Graphics Display under a grant from the National Science Foundation. As Maure (1984) reported, the Tactile Graphics Display

> can be configured in single-line, multi-line, or full-page displays (Library of Congress standards). Because of its symmetrical dot configuration, multiple alphanumeric fonts, conventional six-dot braille, computer braille and graphics can be generated. Black pins on a white background provide a sharp contrast which enables the partially sighted to use the display, as well as the blind. (p. 134)

The design of this device using electronic control results in a low-cost assistive aid. Maure (1984) also described the features and design considerations for the Tactile Graphics Display. The flexibility and relatively low cost offer considerable potential for educational applications.

Kurzweil Reading Machine

One of the more impressive applications of computer technology for the visually impaired is the Kurzweil Reading Machine from Kurzweil Computer Products. The Kurzweil Reading Machine orally reads in synthesized speech almost any book, magazine, letter, or other printed material in any type size or type style. Individuals with visual impairments using this computer device "can control the speed of the artificial speech, whether uppercase and lowercase letters should be differentiated vocally, and whether words should be read in toto or spelled out" (Bowe, 1984, p. 112). Furthermore, the Kurzweil Reading Machine can also send anything it reads directly into a computer with approximately 80% accuracy for automatic entry. The primary limitation to the Kurzweil Reading Machine is the high cost, approximately $21,000. Kurzweil's $24,000 VoiceWriter, capable of recognizing 10,000 words and printing them as quickly as they are spoken, will also be an invaluable computer for visually impaired and seeing persons (Henry, 1986).

Historically, the search for a device that blind persons can use to read books goes back to the 19th century when it was discovered "that electrical resistivity of selenium was in-

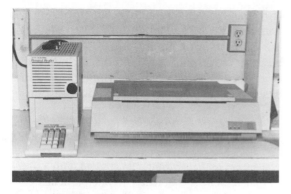

Kurzweil Reading Machine uses synthesized speech to orally read almost any book.
(Photograph by Jimmy D. Lindsey)

fluenced by light. Many technical applications followed that discovery, including at the turn of the century an apparatus for reading specially-prepared 'photophonic books'" (Cooper, Gaitenby, & Nye, 1984, p. 51). It took nearly 80 years to bring this dream to even partial reality, with the advent of the Kurzweil Reading Machine. Unfortunately, considerable work yet needs to be done in spite of the incredible advances in technology. For example, the intelligibility and comprehensibility of the speech now capable of being generated still needs improvement. Machine-produced sounds are still unnatural due to imprecise articulation and faulty intonation and syllabic tempo. In their comprehensive review of the evolution of reading machines pertinent to Haskins Laboratories' research, Cooper et al. (1984) made clear that "the problem of machine-to-man communication as encountered by the blind reader is still far from being completely solved" (p. 84).

Augmentative Writing Systems

In addition to the specific applications discussed here for the visually impaired, there are also more general and technical considerations pertinent to supporting their writing needs. Some of the considerations for implementing an augmentative writing system are keyboard support systems, switch systems, alternative interfaces, software, voice output, and enhanced print options. Shell (1989) provided an excellent overview of these areas, along with various implementation considerations.

Hearing Impaired

Specific computer applications for the hearing impaired are focused primarily on communication and educational problems generated by the sensory handicap. The literature on computer applications for individuals with hearing impairments is also focused on numerous examples pertinent to both communication skills and curricular/content issues, because a severe hearing impairment early in human development clearly influences the ability to process information from a language perspective. This language deficit also appears to influence the conceptual understanding required to function with higher-level mathematics.

Audiology and Speech

Complementary to the application of computers to curricular areas for the hearing impaired is the movement to use computers in providing and improving the clinical services of audiology and speech. Nickerson et al. (1983) demonstrated the viability of applying computers to speech training. Their system was built around a minicomputer that could measure pitch and nasalization and analyze the speech spectrum. Speech data were acquired not only from a voice microphone but also from a miniature accelerometer attached by two-way adhesive taped to the child's throat or nose. Attached to the throat, the accelerometer determined glottal waveforms, or the fundamental frequency of voiced speech sounds. Attached to the nose, the accelerometer provided measures of sound energy emitted through the nose to infer the degree of nasality. The primary emphasis in the project by Nickerson et al. was on the visual representations of various aspects of speech. In regard to the focus of training, most students showed improvements including (a) reduced incidence of nasalization in vowels, (b) shifting of average fundamental frequency into a more appropriate range, (c) reduced incidence of inadvertent changes in fundamental frequency in phrases and sentences, (d) reduced number of inadvertent pauses between words, and (e) improved spectrum of glottal output.

Unfortunately, overall speech intelligibility was not consistently increased with these improvements. The authors raised the possibility that their training was concentrated on aspects of speech that perhaps had less importance for speech intelligibility than some other areas. Regardless, the research by Nickerson et al. (1983) demonstrated that computer-generated displays can be effective in modifying speech in objective and measurable ways.

In terms of administrative potential, the data management capabilities of the computer make it a prime administrative tool for education, clinical services, and research pertinent to communication disorders (Schwartz, 1984b). In clinical tasks, computers have been used to assess patient data; store, retrieve, and report case history information and audiologic test results for adult clients; and to explain a client's hearing loss and present remedial actions via graphic display on the computer monitor (Lasky, 1984, p. 7). Chapters 7 and 12 provide a more detailed discussion of computer applications for administrative and clinical purposes in speech and language development.

Language

Evaluation of language development is another area of possible application for computers. Because of the time needed to administer tests to hearing-impaired students and to analyze their responses, many educators do not perform the analyses. "This may be due to knowledge insufficient for the task of analysis, or it may be due to the problem of isolating particular constructions. Very often, however, and independent of teacher expertise, the decision is made with respect to time" (Riley, 1983, p. 586). Computer-assisted evaluation (CAE) was conceived by a teacher at the California School for the Deaf in Fremont to support the language assessment needs of all teachers in the school. They have developed more than 30 evaluation sequences using the Blocks Authoring System. The kinds of language-related skills that can be assessed by the computer evaluation lessons are questions, negation, reading adverb clauses, reading other clauses, compounds and coordinates, alphabetization, on-the-job questions, information from the stub of a paycheck, filling out applications, and reading bills. Depending on the level of the students and the intended lesson, a combination of formats may be used, including dictation, scrambled picture description, spontaneous response, interview, and reading response.

> A dictation or scrambled format, for example, may be easier for a limited language student than a spontaneous format would be. The dictation mode presents the student with a series of sentences that focus on one particular construction . . . [while] the scrambled mode is flexible enough to use with a variety of language constructions . . . the spontaneous response, interview, and reading response formats are used with the higher level language constructions. (Riley, 1983, pp. 586–587)

There appear to be multiple advantages to computer-assisted evaluation. It fosters a more consistent and structured assessment process than the traditional classroom teacher evaluations, yet it flexibly meets the needs of classroom evaluation. It potentially offers the individual teacher more time to focus on the instructional process without detracting from the evaluation aspects. And it provides a practical structure in which teachers can work together in developing and implementing appropriate evaluation strategies. Chapters 7 and 12 describe a number of software programs on assessment that can be used to evaluate the speech and language abilities of hearing impaired individuals.

An interactive video system at the National Technical Institute for the Deaf, Rochester Institute of Technology in Rochester, New York (NTID/RIT) illustrates further computer applications pertinent to language and communication skills. Interactive video involves student-controlled self-instruction; the progress and direction of the interactive program are dependent on the responses of each individual student. The development of an interactive video system at NTID began in 1978 under the direction of Donald G. Sims and was named DAVID (dynamic audio video instructional device) (Sims, Scott, & Myers, 1982). DAVID consists of a videotape recorder, an Apple II or IIe microcomputer, and a video controller (Newell et al., 1984). DAVID can facilitate the speech and language drill-and-practice that consumes considerable classroom time. In most classrooms for the hearing impaired, drill-and-practice occurs in small groups or on a one-to-one basis. Interactive video presentations of drill-and-practice are as efficient as the student-teacher situation and much more exciting. A primary advantage of using DAVID "is that by relying on interactive video to teach the basics, the teacher is free to proceed with more complex instructional objectives" (Newell et al., 1984, p. 15). DAVID is used to provide speech-reading practice and sign language instruction, and to simulate job interviews for college students with hearing impairments at NTID/RIT. The speech-reading exercises have the students view a series of videotaped single sentences and then respond to the computer program by typing what was said. If the students access the help key, hints are provided. Correct responses are provided immediate confirmation and reinforcement. Sign language instruction consists of individual signs, signed sentences, and paragraph comprehension. Briefly, the college students with hearing impairments are asked to type the English translation on the computer in response to the computer-presented stimulus. "In addition to providing practice in signs, sentences, and paragraphs, each sign language lesson contains explanations of sign grammar principles with examples that students may view" (Newell et al., 1984, p. 17). The final example of DAVID simulates a job interview. It asks students to fill out an application form on the computer; then, based on the responses, a video interviewer asks pertinent questions. Depending on each student's response to questions, additional video sequences of the interviewer are selected for further question/response interaction. It is the position of those who developed DAVID that

> interactive video should be viewed as an instructional medium comparable to books, films, and overhead transparencies. As with any instructional medium, its use must be based on an analysis of the entire curriculum. The objectives of a lesson, the characteristics of those objectives, the planned learning activities, and the evaluation criteria should determine which medium is best for a specific

situation. Most receptive communication drills demand that the presentation of items be in real time with synchronous sound and motion, and that the student be expected to make an overt response to indicate an understanding of the material. (Newell et al., 1984, pp. 17–18)

RAM

A computer application related to English and language skills that can be used in various educational settings is the Reading and Microcomputer (RAM) Project implemented by the Texas School for the Deaf. This program addresses students with hearing impairments' reading comprehension problems through building their vocabulary skills. With RAM, students use computers to "approach vocabulary in a multitude of ways, including learning various possible meanings of a single word, completing analogies, analyzing context clues, and understanding words as they pertain to a specific situation" (Pollard & Shaw, 1982, p. 484). These computer-based independent vocabulary-building activities have resulted in reports from teachers in subject areas other than reading that students have increased their use of new words in both compositions and conversations. Ten reading teachers at the secondary level implemented the RAM Project using the Blocks Authoring System developed at the California School for the Deaf in Fremont. The use of this authoring system enabled the students to create their own Blocks lessons including graphics, color, large

Dr. Donald Sims, developer of DAVID, assists a student with the system. (*Photograph courtesy of the National Technical Institute for the Deaf/Rochester Institute of Technology*)

and small letters, and personalized feedback. The implementation procedures served approximately 200 students at the secondary level from 28 academic reading classes during any one week. Those involved in the RAM Project contend that the successful application of computers with students with hearing impairments requires an initial and continuing inservice training program, along with providing adequate preparation time for the teachers.

Reading

The research of Prinz, Nelson, and Stedt (1982) illustrated another application of computers to reading with students at the initial stage of schooling. Prinz et al. examined a computer-based method for teaching young deaf children to read prior to the primary grades. The children involved were between the ages of 2 and 6 and enrolled in the preschool program at the Pennsylvania School for the Deaf in Philadelphia. Phase 1 of the implementation took 10 weeks and involved individualizing the computer-based software for each child pertinent to the child's performance on the initial language evaluation and baseline reading inventory. The individually developed software resulted in an information set consisting of printed words and graphic representations of pictures to illustrate word meanings. Graphics of manual signs and finger-spelled words were also incorporated into the program. Thus teachers formulated individualized interactional programs for each child with the assistance of a computer programmer. The instructional sessions involved the children pressing keys with words, pictures, and words plus pictures on them. For example,

> on the key a child presses for "flower," besides the word there might also appear a small picture. Similarly, the computer display monitor would show both word and picture. . . . The particular words used initially were all drawn from the child's own central interests and instructional objectives; this was possible because the keys were readily changeable, because new words could be rapidly entered in the computer, and because permanent disk storage allows nearly instantaneous access to thousands of printed words and accompanying color graphics. (Prinz et al., 1982, p. 533)

Redundancy was a central part of the educational plan. Teachers also had the option of commenting on the child's message or asking the computer for more information. This might be done by asking the students if they wanted to see a different size or kind of dog or by telling them something additional about a dog—again with the appropriate display of print and graphics. As a result, this research project created an environment where the hearing-impaired preschool child could actually initiate and use printed information in an active and interactional way to exchange messages with other people. The findings of this research revealed that after 6 weeks of computer instruction, the children between 3 and 6 years of age showed improvement in word recognition and identification. Although the approach of this experimental research project offers considerable potential for the reading development of young deaf children, it also requires considerable expertise and time commitments from the teachers. Realistically, this degree of effort may be the minimum necessary to meet the complex communication needs of young deaf learners.

Mathematics

Mathematics instruction is also an area where educators of the hearing impaired have implemented computer-based learning experiences. Castle (1982) described the design, development, and implementation of a computer laboratory for mathematics at the California School for the Deaf in Riverside. In setting up this computer lab, the decision was made to use the Corvus Hard Disk Drive Network system to avoid separate disk drives for each computer terminal as well as the potential related problems associated with floppy disks when a large number of people handle them. The primary purpose of the computers has been to serve as a math tutorial lab for the high school mathematics department. "The high school math department classes take turns using the computer lab. Each class gets 40 minutes every seven school days. Therefore, the lab is a reward for the classroom, and it is rare when a student is not excited about working in the lab" (Castle, 1982, p. 497).

Math City software is the foundation of the math computer lab at the California School for the Deaf in Riverside. Math City consists of 783 lessons that range from simple counting to pre-algebra concepts. Each lesson can last from 10 seconds to 10 minutes, which reduces boredom or restlessness. Students can complete between 3 and 20 Math City lessons on the average during a 10 minute period. Flexibility is a part of the implementation approach: an authoring system enables teachers to develop tutorials and tests in any subject to be added to the sequence of lessons. Teachers and therapists can also prescribe a specific lesson or series of lessons for automatic repetition as related to the drill-and-tutorial plans. The language level of the Math City software ranges from second- to eighth-grade level. As with the other examples of computer applications in the classroom discussed in this chapter, the need for a continuing in-service training program for the participating teachers was stressed by Castle (1982).

LOGO

In addition to the specific instructional applications of computers to curricular subjects discussed so far, several educators have recognized the advantages of computer experiences that allow the students programming control (Grant & Semmes, 1983; Stone, 1983). The computer language known as LOGO enables children to write programs for the computer and control and operate it in much the same way as professional programmers. Grant and Semmes (1983) demonstrated the efficacy of LOGO with preschool age hearing-impaired children. The experimental project involved a set of preschool twins, one with a profound hearing impairment and the other with normal hearing. The project's objectives were to promote the development of spatial visualization, to provide time for problem solving and creative efforts, and to introduce a logical symbol system in addition to spoken language. The results of this project demonstrated that children at the preschool level could use LOGO commands and turtle graphics to have a successful learning experience. Furthermore, it was evident that

the introduction of the new language posed by the single keystroking program [written by Semmes] proved to be no problem whatever. . . . With one demonstration, both children grasped the concept that one keystroke could command an activity. As they progressed, they became more sophisticated in their "language usage," using terms such as **repeat, penup,** and **pendown** all with semi-abstract connotations. The parallel of LOGO to spoken language is striking. For example, the process of making a square is reminiscent of the linguistic principle of conjoining, which in this case is expanded to four elements. The finished square is composed of four equal commands, just as a compound sentence, subject, or predicate is composed of as many equal components as desired. (Grant & Semmes, 1983, p. 569)

Stone (1983) used LOGO with a group of 14 children with profound hearing loss who ranged from age 8 to age 14. The initial exposure for the students involved learning how to move a turtle (a small triangle) around the screen to draw various shapes. With only three commands—FD (forward), RTURN (right turn of 30 degrees), and LTURN (left turn of 30 degrees)—the students were able to create numerous shapes on the monitor screen.

For several children, an intriguing problem soon presented itself; namely, how to draw a circle. Two boys spent an entire week of their computer time working on this problem. Assistance was given by asking them to walk out a circle. This strategy proved very helpful and soon each of them had solved the problem and reached a very fundamental conclusion: Circles are no more than a series of short straight lines that turn a constant angle. These boys shared their discovery with others and soon circles were a part of every child's list of procedures. This experience highlights two very exciting benefits of the LOGO environment. Children create their own problems and then set out to solve them and are able to share their discoveries with others. The teaching strategy of having children walk out problems is a very powerful one that is used often. In addition, some large and small group time has been spent playing Computer. In these activities, one child playing the role of programmer gives directions to another child, who uses a piece of string to draw the lines he or she is commanded to draw. (Stone, 1983, p. 649)

Peter Jennings, ABC news anchor, speaks to a capacity audience of hearing-impaired college students and faculty using the Real-time Graphic Display at NTID/RIT.
(Photograph courtesy of the National Technical Institute for the Deaf/Rochester Institute of Technology)

Stone (1983) proposed that the real power of the computer using LOGO is its ability to be taught (programmed) by the hearing-impaired children. These hearing-impaired children, by gaining "control of the basic aspects of programming . . . are learning that the answer to a difficult problem lies in breaking it down into manageable parts and that the computer is a marvelous tool for facilitating this process" (p. 652). Appendix C describes and provides examples of LOGO and other programming languages that individuals with hearing impairments can use.

Real-time Graphic Display

Real-time Graphic Display of speech is another intriguing application of computers to the communication needs of the hearing impaired. Under the leadership of Ross Stuckless at the National Technical Institute for the Deaf, Rochester Institute of Technology, the Real-time Graphic Display has been in development since 1978 and was initially implemented in 1982 when the technology became available for practical classroom applications. "The system uses a court stenographer sitting in a class and entering speech sounds in phonetic shorthand into a minicomputer that regenerates English. The spoken English is then displayed (almost instantaneously) in the classroom on a television display. Hard copy of a lecture and student discussion can be printed out for student use immediately after class" (Stuckless, 1983, p. 619). Although still undergoing refinement, the Real-time Graphic Display of speech is a reality and is currently benefiting hearing-impaired college students in college courses at NTID/RIT.

ADDITIONAL COMPUTER ISSUES

A further area of interest is computer applications for the telephone to address the general communication needs of individuals with hearing impairments. In general, these exceptional people use some type of telecommunications device or a computer terminal to communicate via the telephone with either a visual display or hard copy. Computer-based telephone communication offers greater flexibility in terms of accessing telecommunications networks that provide electronic messages, bulletin boards, and real-time linking capabilities with both hearing and deaf friends, businesses, and services (Bowe, 1991; Middleton, 1983).

For example, deaf students in the San Diego city schools use a telecommunications network to send and receive private electronic messages and bulletin board announcements (Pflaum, 1982). However, computer networking can also be used for instructional purposes. Peyton (1988) described how an interactive network can be used to teach written English and help deaf learners to distinguish between conversational and written forms of language. Computer networks are also used for information exchanges on a more professional level. SpecialNet (see Chapter 1) is a computer-based instant communication network that provides current information for persons concerned with services and programs for handicapped individuals (Gibbs & Nash, 1983). In addition to data collection and information management, SpecialNet also provides electronic mail and bulletin board services. At the National Technical Institute for the Deaf, faculty and students use a local computer network for special interest conference purposes. There are from 10 to 15 professional topics listed on a continuing basis within this local conference computer network on which deaf people can comment. In this way, countless individuals can participate in exchanging views on topics of professional and personal interest on a continuing basis. Although electronic mail and bulletin board services offer considerable benefit to people with computer equipment, they do not permit telephone communication with people not owning similar equipment. Glaser (1982), however, described a device for deaf people's telephone communication that does not involve special equipment at the hearing party's location but uses the tones of a standard touch telephone to respond to the deaf person's equipment.

Countless other issues could be raised here in relation to computer applications for the sensory impaired. For example, Trachtenberg (1986) examined the role of the computer as a tutor, tutee, and a tool for deaf children. Also, the two components of computer-based education, computer-managed instruction (CMI) and computer-assisted instruction (CAI), have not been touched on. For an expanded discussion of CAI and the differences between CAI

and CMI, see Sims and Clymer (1986). There are also the issues of procedures and processes for developing software programs as well as the related issue of how teacher-developed software should be evaluated (Frillmann, 1982).

The development of artificial intelligence has focused on problem-solving and decision-making processes representative of human beings (Gevarter, 1983) and requires the sophistication of human language and a considerable store of knowledge. In contrast, robotics produces a robot conceptualized as a "reprogrammable, multifunctional manipulator designed to move material, parts, tools, or specialized devices through variable programmed motions for the performance of a variety of tasks" (Moore, Yin, & Lahm, 1985, p. 35). The Japanese expand this to include selected types of manipulators to be operated by humans. Moore et al. (1985) raised several pertinent questions. Can advances in artificial intelligence help special education students learn more effectively, and can robotics help handicapped people to be more self-sufficient in educational settings? Given the practical considerations of resources, time, and further refinement of these technologies, the answer is a cautious yes. In terms of immediate potential for widespread use, current implementation is probably not feasible other than on an experimental basis. However, it should be recognized that many of the computer program games do approximate some of the reasoning and learning concepts of artificial intelligence, at least in terms of intelligent responses to the learner making a series of possible decisions. However, one cannot really suggest that intelligence is present in these types of game programs (Hartnell, 1985). Deaf college students at NTID/RIT use computer-based games to improve their skills in language, reasoning, and decision making. For a more detailed analysis of the potential of artificial intelligence and robotics for future applications in special education, see Moore et al. (1985).

Some cautionary issues that teachers and therapists should consider pertinent to computers relate to philosophy, appropriate time for introducing students to computers, socialization implications, and potential threats to individual growth. Also, the issue of student experience with computers and its effect on their attitudes toward computer-based learning should be considered (Mackowiak, 1989). For a critical perspective on the computer in education, the edited text by Sloan (1985) provides excellent insights. Computers are not a panacea for the education of the handicapped, they are merely machines with the potential to be developed into marvelous educational tools. Computers can only be developed into first-class instructional tools by the people in education—not by outsiders and not by drivers of high-tech bandwagons. Individual educators are the key to computer applications for sensory-impaired people and other handicapped populations. Successful computer implementation can only be accomplished through thought, reflection, and quality planning.

SUMMARY

This chapter has described some of the educational problems faced by the sensory impaired. These problems are the focus for most computer applications for the sensory impaired. For the visually impaired, computer applications primarily involve assistive aids to overcome the vision handicap, including speech synthesizers, large print computer displays and printers, text-to-speech conversion, tactile devices, and braille interfaces. For the hearing impaired, computer applications focus on language and related conceptual problems, as well as speech/audiology clinical services. Individualization is necessary in all areas of application.

There are no clear directions for computer applications for the sensory impaired. This is probably as it should be, since educational use of computers is still in the early stages. The exciting challenge for professionals is that they have an opportunity to influence the development of computer hardware and software as important instructional tools for the sensory impaired.

REFERENCES

Beggs, W. D. A. (1992). Coping, adjustment, and mobility-related feelings of newly visually impaired young adults. *Journal of Visual Impairment & Blindness, 86*(3), 136–139.

Bochner, J. H. (1982). English in the deaf population. In D. G. Sims, G. G. Walter, & R. L. Whitehead (Eds.), *Deafness and communication* (pp. 107–123). Baltimore, MD: Williams & Wilkins.

Bowe, F. G. (1984). *Personal computers and special needs.* Berkeley, CA: Sybex.

Bowe, F. G. (1991). National survey on telephone services and products: The view of deaf and hard-of-hearing people. *American Annals of the Deaf, 136*(3), 278–283.

Castle, D. J. (1982). Mathematics software, a computer lab, and the hearing impaired. *American Annals of the Deaf, 127,* 495–504.

Chial, M. R. (1984). Evaluating microcomputer hardware. In A. H. Schwartz (Ed.), *The handbook of microcomputer applications in communication disorders* (pp. 79–123). Austin, TX: PRO-ED.

Chorniak, E. J. (1977). Education of visually impaired children. In J. E. Jan, R. D. Freeman, & E. P. Scott (Eds.), *Visual impairment in children and adolescents* (pp. 291–304). New York: Grune & Stratton.

Committee on Nomenclature, Conference of Executives, American Schools for the Deaf. (1938). *American Annals of the Deaf, 83,* 1.

Cooper, F. S., Gaitenby, J. H., & Nye, P. W. (1984). Evolution of reading machines for the blind: Haskins Laboratories' research as a case study. *Journal of Rehabilitation Research and Development, 21,* 51–87.

Cronin, P. J. (1992). A direct service program for mainstreamed students by a residential school. *Journal of Visual Impairment & Blindness, 86*(2), 101–104.

Davis, H. (1970). Abnormal hearing and deafness. In H. Davis & S. R. Silverman (Eds.), *Hearing and deafness* (3rd ed.) (pp. 83–139). New York: Holt, Rinehart and Winston.

Frillman, L. W. (1982). The development of your own programs for the microcomputer: A process approach. *American Annals of the Deaf, 127,* 625–631.

Gevarter, W. B. (1983). *An overview of artificial intelligence and robotics: Vol. 1.* Artificial intelligence: Part A. The core ingredients. Washington, DC: National Aeronautics and Space Administration.

Gibbs, L. K., & Nash, K. (1983). SpecialNet: Instant information/communication. *American Annals of the Deaf, 128,* 631–635.

Glaser, R. E. (1982). Telephone communication for the deaf. *American Annals of the Deaf, 127,* 550–555.

Goodrich, G. L. (1984). Applications of microcomputers by visually impaired persons. *Journal of Visual Impairment and Blindness, 78,* 408–414.

Grant, J., & Semmes, P. (1983). A rationale for LOGO for hearing-impaired preschoolers. *American Annals of the Deaf, 128,* 564–569.

Hagen, D. (1984). *Microcomputer resource book for special education.* Reston, VA: Reston Publishing Company.

Hartnell, T. (1985). *Exploring artificial intelligence on your Commodore 64.* New York: Bantam Books.

Hearing aids: New technologies. (1992). *Counterpoint, 12*(3), 16.

Henry, G. M. (1986, April 28). Can we talk? *Time,* p. 54.

Hofmeister, R., & Drury, A. M. (1982). English training for the primary and secondary level deaf student. In D. G. Sims, G. G. Walter, & R. L. Whitehead (Eds.), *Deafness and communication* (pp. 259–371). Baltimore, MD: Williams & Wilkins.

Jan, J. E., Freeman, R. D., & Scott, E. P. (1977). *Visual impairment in children and adolescents.* New York: Grune & Stratton.

Kleiman, G. M. (1984, September). Aids for the blind. *Compute,* pp. 122–124.

Lasky, E. Z. (1984). Introduction to microcomputers for specialists in communication disorders. In A. H. Schwartz (Ed.), *The handbook of microcomputer applications in communication disorders* (pp. 1–15). Austin, TX: PRO-ED.

Lowenfeld, B. (1981). *Berthold Lowenfeld on blindness and blind people: Selected papers.* New York: American Foundation for the Blind.

Mackowiak, K. (1989). Deaf college students and computers: The beneficial effect of experience on attitude. *Journal of Educational Technology Systems, 17*(3), 219–229.

Maure, D. R. (1984). Tactile graphics display. In J. E. Roehl (Ed.), *Computers for the disabled: Conference papers* (pp. 137–140). Menomonie: University of Wisconsin–Stout, Materials Development Center.

Middleton, T. (1983). DEAFNET—the word's getting around: Local implementation of telecommunications networks for deaf users. *American Annals of the Deaf, 128,* 613–618.

Moore, G. B., Yin, R. K., & Lahm, E. A. (1985). *Robotics, artificial intelligence, computer simulation: Future applications in special education.* Washington, DC: Cosmos.

Moore, M. W. (1984). VersaBraille applications in education. In J. E. Roehl (Ed.), *Computers for the disabled: Conference papers* (pp. 141–144). Menomonie: University of Wisconsin–Stout, Materials Development Center.

Morrison, R. C., & Lunney, D. (1984). The microcomputer as a laboratory aid for visually impaired science students. *Journal of Visual Impairment and Blindness, 78,* 418–425.

Morrissette, D. L. (1984). Large-print computers: An evaluation of their features. *Journal of Visual Impairment and Blindness, 78,* 428–434.

Myklebust, H. R. (1964). *The psychology of deafness* (2nd ed.). New York: Grune & Stratton.

Newell, W., Sims, D. G., & Clymer, E. W. (1984). Meet DAVID, our teacher's helper. *Perspectives, 2,* 15–18.

Nickerson, R. S., Stevens, K. N., Rollins, A. M., & Zue, V. W. (1983). Computers and speech aids. In I. Hocberg, H. Levitt, & M. Osberger (Eds.), *Speech of the hearing impaired* (pp. 313–324). Austin, TX: PRO-ED.

Peyton, J. K. (1988, Fall). Computer networking: Providing a context for deaf students to write collaboratively. *Teaching English to Deaf and Second-Language Students, 6*(2), 19–24.

Pflaum, M. E. (1982). The California connection: Interfacing the TDD and an Apple computer. *American Annals of the Deaf, 127,* 573–584.

Pollard, G., & Shaw, C. C. (1982). Microcomputer reading comprehension improvement program for the deaf. *American Annals of the Deaf, 127,* 483–486.

Prinz, P. M., Nelson, K. E., & Stedt, J. D. (1982). Early reading in young deaf children using microcomputer technology. *American Annals of the Deaf, 127,* 519–525.

Riley, D. C. (1983). Computer-assisted evaluation at the California School for the Deaf–Fremont. *American Annals of the Deaf, 128,* 585–594.

Ruconich, S. K., Ashcroft, S. C., & Young, M. F. (1984). Making microcomputers accessible to blind persons. *Exceptional Education Quarterly, 4,* 9–22.

Schwartz, A. H. (1984a). Evaluating microcomputer software. In A. H. Schwartz (Ed.), *The handbook of microcomputer applications in communication disorders* (pp. 126–146). Austin, TX: PRO-ED.

Schwartz, A. H. (Ed.). (1984b). *The handbook of microcomputer applications in communication disorders.* Austin, TX: PRO-ED.

Shell, D. F. (1989, Fall). Computer-based compensatory augmentative communications technology for physically disabled, visually impaired, and speech impaired students. *Journal of Special Education Technology, 10*(2), 29–43.

Silverman, S. R., & Lane, H. S. (1970). Deaf children. In H. Davis & S. R. Silverman (Eds.), *Hearing and deafness* (3rd ed.) (pp. 384–425). New York: Holt, Rinehart and Winston.

Sims, D. G. (1988, September). Video methods for speechreading instruction. In C. L. De Flippo & D. G. Sims (Eds.), New reflections on speechreading [Monograph]. *Volta Review, 90*(5), 273–288.

Sims, D. G., & Clymer, E. W. (1986). Computer assisted instruction for the hearing impaired. In J. L. Northern (Ed.), *Microcomputer applications in communication disorders.* Boston, MA: Little, Brown.

Sims, D. G., Scott, L., & Myers, T. (1982). Past, present and future: Computer assisted communication training at NTID. *Journal of the Academy of Rehabilitative Audiology, 15*, 103–115.

Sloan, D. (1985). *The computer in education: A critical perspective.* New York: Teachers College Press.

Stepp, R. E., & Reiners, E. (Eds.). (1982). Microcomputers in education of the hearing impaired: National conference. *American Annals of the Deaf, 127*, 463–717.

Stepp, R. E., & Reiners, E. (Eds.). (1983). Computer assisted research and instruction for the hearing impaired: National conference. *American Annals of the Deaf, 128*, 507–783.

Stone, P. S. (1983). LOGO: A powerful learning environment for hearing-impaired children. *American Annals of the Deaf, 128*, 648–652.

Stuckless, E. R. (1983). Real-time transliteration for speech into print for hearing-impaired students in regular classes. *American Annals of the Deaf, 128*, 619–624.

Trachtenberg, R. (1986). Computer applications in deaf education. In H. J. Murphy & J. A. Dunnigan (Eds.), *Computer technology and persons with disabilities: Proceedings of the conference.* Northridge, CA, October 17–19, 1985.

Vander Kolk, C. J. (1981). *Assessment and planning with the visually impaired.* Austin, TX: PRO-ED.

Warren, D. H. (1977). *Blindness and early childhood development.* New York: American Foundation for the Blind.

Watson, P. (1979). The utilization of the computer with the hearing impaired and the handicapped. *American Annals of the Deaf, 124*, 670–680.

Suggested Activities

Paper and Pencil

List three learning and instructional needs of the exceptional students you either are preparing to or currently teach. What computer applications described in this chapter could be used (or revised and used) with these pupils? Give a brief reason why you believe these applications would work.

Observation

Visit a school or a class for the visually impaired and the hearing impaired. How are computers being used in these instructional settings? What future plans do these settings have for computer instruction?

Practicum

Select a computer-based adventure game and play it enough to understand the procedural requirements and rules. Plan and conduct an instructional activity that teaches problem solving or decision making to language-deficient hearing-impaired learners.

Resources

Organizations

American Foundation for the Blind. This organization publishes numerous printed materials related to visual impairments, including the *Journal of Visual Impairment & Blindness.* Write to the American Foundation for the Blind, 15 West 16th Street, New York, NY 10011.

American Printing House for the Blind. This organization provides various materials (e.g., large print books, braille, etc.) to visually impaired individuals and special educators. Write to the American Printing House for the Blind, 1839 Frankfort Avenue, Louisville, KY 40206.

Alexander Graham Bell Association. This professional organization provides printed materials (e.g., *The Volta Review*) about hearing impairments to special educators, parents, and hearing impaired persons. Write to the Alexander Graham Bell Association, 3417 Volta Place N.W., Washington, DC 20007.

National Association of the Deaf. This organization serves as a clearinghouse for educational, communication, employment, and other information for hearing impaired individuals. Write to the National Association of the Deaf, 814 Thayer Avenue, Silver Springs, MD 20910.

SPEECH Enterprise. This nonprofit organization was founded by Sherry Lowry after her teenage son became blind. This organization focuses on Apple computer concepts as they relate to large print and speech. Write to SPEECH Enterprise, P.O. Box 7986, Houston, TX 77270.

Journals

Journal of Visual Impairment & Blindness. This journal is published 10 times a year and focuses on topics related to the education and rehabilitation of visually impaired individuals. Write to the American Foundation for the Blind, 15 West 16th Street, New York City, NY 10011.

Education of the Visually Handicapped. This quarterly journal publishes research and practical articles for teachers of the visually impaired. Write to Association for the Education of the Visually Handicapped, 206 N. Washington Street, Suite 320, Alexandria, VA 22314.

Volta Review. This journal is published nine times a year and focuses on topics related to educating hearing-impaired and deaf individuals. Write to the Alexander Graham Bell Association, 3417 Volta Place, Washington, DC 20007.

American Annals of the Deaf. This bimonthly journal also publishes articles that focus on educating hearing-impaired and deaf persons. Write to Convention of American Instructors of the Deaf and the Conference of Executives of American Schools for the Deaf, 814 Thayer Avenue, Silver Springs, MD 20910.

Books

Bowe, F. G. (1984). *Personal computers and special needs.* Berkeley, CA: Sybex.

Roehl, J. E. (Ed.). (1984). *Computers for the disabled: Conference papers.* Menomonie: University of Wisconsin–Stout, Materials Development Center.

Hardware/Software

Blocks Authoring System
Director
California State School for the Deaf
Fremont, CA 94538

Corvus Hard Disk Drive
Corvus Systems
2100 Corvus Drive
San Jose, CA 95124

DAVID
NTID/RIT
One Loom Memorial Drive
Rochester, NY 14623

Echo +
Street Electronics
1140 Mark Avenue
Carpenteria, CA 93013

Kurzweil Reading Machine
Kurzweil Computer Products
33 Cambridge Pkwy.
Cambridge, MA 02142

Large Print Display Process
Visualtek
1610 26th Street
Santa Monica, CA 90404

Math City
Mathware
1020 Manhattan Beach Blvd.
Manhattan Beach, CA 90266

OPTACON
Telesensory Systems
455 North Bernardo Avenue
Mountain View, CA 94043

Professional Vert
Telesensory Systems
455 North Bernardo Avenue
Mountain View, CA 94043

Real-time Graphic Display
NTID/RIT
One Loom Memorial Drive
Rochester, NY 14623

Tactile Graphics Display
American Foundation for the Blind
15 West 16th Street
New York City, NY 10011

ULTRA
Department of Chemistry
East Carolina University
Greenville, NC 27854

VersaBraille
Telesensory
455 North Bernardo Avenue
Mountain View, CA 94043

VoiceWriter
Kurzweil Computer Products
33 Cambridge Pkwy.
Cambridge, MA 02142

Computers and Gifted/ Talented Individuals

Evelyn J. Dale
California State University, Sacramento ■

In 1980, a pebble was dropped in the ocean of computer technology—Papert's book, *Mindstorms: Children, Computers, and Powerful Ideas*, was published. This book's particular concern is the new and revolutionary computer language LOGO. *Mindstorms'* ripples, however, go beyond this specific computer language to affect all aspects of computer education. The purpose of computer technology for students, Papert argued, is to empower them and, in so doing, develop independence, critical thinking, and problem-solving skills. This is possible because computers put the tools of the professional into the hands of the young, enabling their intellectual explorations to become increasingly mature and profound. This chapter explores ways in which computer technology can open the doors of intellectual and creative discovery for gifted and talented individuals. It is important that these exceptional individuals achieve their potential so that they can maximize their contributions to society (Shaklee, 1992).

GIFTED/TALENTED INDIVIDUALS

The Renzulli (1978) three-ring concept of giftedness will be used to define gifted/talented individuals (see Figure 10.1). This definition is based on past research that includes Terman's (1959) component of academic excellence, the United States Office of Education's component of multiple talent and criteria, and Witty's (1958) criterion of remarkable performance. Renzulli's concept is based on two assumptions: giftedness is not something an individual either has or does not have but a mode of behavior; and giftedness depends on three equally important components (i.e., above-average general ability, task commitment, and creativity).

The idea that giftedness is a mode of behavior is nothing short of revolutionary because it questions the organizational structure of programs that select students for a year or more. Renzulli suggests exchanging the traditional format for gifted education for his Re-

WHAT MAKES GIFTEDNESS

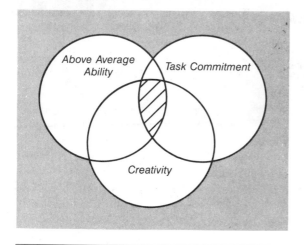

FIGURE 10.1 Renzulli's Three-Ring Concept. From *The Revolving Door Identification Model* by J. S. Renzulli, S. M. Reis, and L. H. Smith, 1981, Hartford, CT: Creative Learning Press. Copyright 1981 by Creative Learning Press. Reprinted by permission.

volving Door Identification Model (RDIM). With this plan, students with gifted potential are identified but remain in a mixed-ability class working on an enriched and challenging curriculum. When these students exhibit gifted behavior they are revolved into a special program designed to meet their new needs and interests. Renzulli's RDIM model can be modified to accommodate different gifted/talented programs already in place, but the main point is that students move into and out of the program according to their needs (Renzulli, Reis, & Smith, 1981).

Renzulli's second assumption is that giftedness is composed of three equally important clusters of human traits—above-average intellect, creativity, and task commitment—and that gifted behavior is not present without all three. This is important because it has generally been assumed that superior intelligence makes an individual gifted. The three-ring concept makes it clear that truly gifted behavior depends on all three traits.

Although above-average intelligence is essential to giftedness, research indicates that

the connection between high intelligence quotients or aptitude test scores and some gifted/talented behavior (e.g., creativity) is only distantly related. As Wallach (1976) pointed out, academic skills assessments are not accurate in predicting future achievements. What they do tell is "the results a person will obtain on other tests of the same kind" (p. 57). While intelligence is not the only factor in determining giftedness, it is necessary. How high that ability needs to be depends on the performance area itself (MacKinnon, 1968a).

Terman noted that the gifted people in his study who were most successful were those who worked diligently to accomplish their goals (1959). The work of Roe (1975) and MacKinnon (1968a) also underscored the importance of task commitment to gifted behavior. It is often easier to exercise the kind of task commitment required by special projects outside the traditional school environment. Unless programs for gifted/talented individuals are changed to meet this need, the discrepancy that exists between in-school and out-of-school achievements for many gifted persons will continue (MacKinnon, 1968b).

Creativity, the third ingredient of giftedness, is difficult to discuss because a positive correlation between creativity tests and actual creative products has not been established (Crockenburg, 1972). Furthermore, the validity of creativity tests has been questioned (e.g., Getzel & Csikszentmihayli, 1975; Nicholls, 1972) because these tests do not probe the test-taker's ability to identify and define the problem itself and may be measuring only one part of the total process. Wallach (1976) recommended other ways to assess creativity, such as judging samples of students' work and reading students' evaluations of their own creative accomplishments.

Renzulli's three-ring concept of giftedness works with many different types of gifted individuals; it not only helps to identify gifted artists, musicians, and scientists, it helps to identify those individuals with special needs. For example, learning-disabled gifted students are ignored in most educational settings (Senf, 1983). Baum (1984) has provided an excellent discussion related to how Renzulli's three-ring conception of giftedness and the

TABLE 10.1
Gifted/talented individuals and computer applications

Individual	Computer Applications
Academically gifted	Programming (e.g., BASIC, LOGO, Pascal)
	Computer-assisted instruction
	Word processing, data bases, spreadsheets, and graphics
	Telecommunications
Creative/talented	Computer-assisted design (CAD) and other art activities (e.g., using color graphics with the Amiga system)
	Music synthesis and Musical Instrument Digital Interface (MIDI)
	Analysis and cataloging of athletics, dance, acting, and other physical activities

Note. Many gifted and talented individuals are academically and creatively strong, and would therefore use computer applications from both areas.

RDIM model can be used to provide enrichment activities for the learning-disabled gifted student.

Possessing above-average ability, task commitment, and creativity means nothing until they are applied to such specific performance areas as cartooning, poetry, ornithology, or city planning. Such variety makes it seem impossible to provide for all gifted students. Fortunately, computer technology can help meet the diverse needs and interests of all gifted/talented persons. Table 10.1 delineates the major characteristics of this exceptional population and general computer applications that can be used to enhance these attributes. Again, when individuals with above-average but not necessarily superior intelligence apply creative thinking and commitment to particular projects, they are behaving in a gifted/talented manner.

A BRIEF REVIEW OF THE LITERATURE

Research into the general impact of computers in education is still investigative. This is particularly true in the gifted/talented literature because most gifted/talented programs are just beginning to incorporate computers into their curricula. What is currently published are articles that discuss existing programs and their curricula, computer activities for learning, and reviews of software programs. For a discussion of the impact of computers on the development of problem-solving skills among mathematically gifted and talented fifth- and sixth-grade students, see Hersberger and Wheatley (1989).

Kolstad and Lidtke (1983) have compared two Illinois computer projects for gifted/talented students. The purpose of both projects was to identify students' computer interests and use this knowledge to develop a computer curriculum. The first project began in 1972 in the elementary schools but was expanded in 1975 to include a more formal program for junior high school students. The other project started in the early 1980s and involved only junior high school students. Both programs used the University of Illinois' PLATO computing system to provide students with computer-assisted instruction (CAI) and programming experience. Both programs found students were least interested in CAI and most interested in computer games. They also found that time and supervision were essential to student progress.

Rotenberg (1985) has described two schools in Pennsylvania that use computers with gifted/talented students. In these programs the emphasis is on integrating the computer into the total learning process by using it as a resource tool. Instead of concentrating on CAI and programming, students use computers for word processing, data base management, communication, graphics, and speech devel-

Gifted/talented students can take their computers to and from class. *(Photograph courtesy of Apple Computers, Inc.)*

opment tools. The difference between the Illinois and Pennsylvania programs indicates a shift from the traditional CAI/programming approach to one that recognizes technology's ability to act as a powerful learning resource (Hamlett, 1984). According to the study "Computer Competence: The First National Assessment, National Assessment of Educational Progress Project" (Balajthy, 1988), little has changed in computer literacy programs. Instead of understanding how to use computer technology effectively, most students know only about the hardware.

Gifted computer science students, of course, need to pursue their interests as well. Options for advanced programming today include classes at secondary and postsecondary schools. A formal alternative for such young people is offered through the Center for the Advancement of Academically Talented Youth (CTY) at Johns Hopkins University. This program has a computer science strand that includes Computer Science I or Computer Science I for Girls; Programming Languages, Algorithms, and DataStructures; Automata Theory and Formal Languages; and Computer Science AP. CTY sponsors similar computer science programs at other sites across the country.

The California State University at Sacramento (CSUS) offers a program that is endorsed by Johns Hopkins' CTY but is based on a different approach. CSUS's Project Talent Search reflects the multiple needs and interests of the general gifted/talented population. For example, Talent Search's Computer Applications course focuses on the use of word processing, data base management, and spreadsheets for personal and academic enrichment. The course for introducing students to the field of computer science, Problem Solving with Computers, uses LOGO rather than BASIC and emphasizes the principles of logic and structured programming and is a prerequisite for the Pascal class that is designed for advanced programmers. Project Talent Search began investigating the effects of academic acceleration on students' social and academic achievement in 1985. Participating students were given a series of formal questionnaires over a 3-year period. The results of this study indicated that "bright, highly motivated early entrants to college can be quite successful in college and later in life" (Brody, Assouline, & Stanley, 1990, p. 138). The authors, however, pointed out that success is most likely when the verbal and mathematical SAT scores of the early entrants are the same or better than the means of the other entrants at the college (Brody et al., 1990).

Literature on computers and gifted/talented people is surprisingly limited. Books and articles in this field focus on the how-to aspect. Terry's (1984) book, *How to Use Computers with Gifted Students: Creative Microcomputing in a Differentiated Curriculum,* focuses on the practical aspects of developing and implementing an educational plan. Greenlaw and MacIntosh (1988) have published a brief but excellent discussion of a K–12 computer curriculum for gifted/talented students while Sisk (1987) has provided an analysis of technology's role in understanding intelligence. *Computer Connections for Gifted Children and Youth* is an excellent collection of articles written by such noted authorities as Papert and Dwyer, among others. This anthology covers topics such as how to get started, existing programs, and the personal and societal effects of the technology. Swassing's (1985) *Teaching Gifted Children and Adolescents* includes a chapter by Trifiletti on using computers to teach the gifted. *G/C/T* is a periodical that regularly publishes articles on computers for gifted/talented students. The November/December 1983 issue includes articles on family computing, the application of computers to gifted education, and how to develop a computer classroom. In the January/February 1985 issue,

articles discuss a curriculum guide for teaching computer literacy, using computers to solve math problems, and preschool computer games for learning. Niess (1990) has published a recent update on the professional's computer competencies for the 1990s. Emphasis is now on using computers as educational tools rather than abstractly knowing about them.

While the available literature on computers and gifted/talented individuals is limited, general public articles can be used effectively in gifted/talented programs. In fact, careful reading may identify some that were originally used in gifted/talented programs. For instance, Bollinger and Hopping's (1985) publication, "Reach for the Stars," discusses activities for developing an astronomy data base. While the article does not mention gifted/talented students, an associated biographical statement indicates that Bollinger teaches science to gifted students. Furthermore, software reviews published in journals and books rarely label packages as appropriate for gifted/talented persons. However, there are exceptions. The "Computer Center" in the November/December 1984 issue of *Curriculum Review* identified several software packages as especially appropriate for gifted/talented children; these packages are discussed later in this issue (Staff, 1984). Also, the Council for Exceptional Children's Software Search can provide teachers, parents, and gifted/talented individuals with a list of software recommended for gifted/talented persons.

GENERAL HARDWARE AND SOFTWARE CONSIDERATIONS

Many gifted/talented individuals have computers at home; many do not. To correct this imbalance, schools should provide all gifted/talented students, as well as their peers, with access to this technology. When computers are brought into the classroom, three basic areas need to be considered: educational setting, classroom management, and student learning. The overall purpose of computers in education is to integrate subject areas, extend learning, and contribute to the total learning process. Teachers of gifted/talented students must keep in mind that computer technology is still continuing to evolve for these exceptional students (e.g., using computers for voice and sculpturing purposes) and that numerous factors (e.g., gender) should be considered when implementing computer-based instruction (Middleton, Littlefield, & Lehrer, 1992).

Educational Setting

There is some debate about the best configuration for computers in the schools. Some say that the lab is best while others feel the computer belongs in the classroom. Proponents of the lab configuration have reality on their side. Many schools still have only a few computers to share among their staff, many of whom are uncertain about how to use the technology effectively. Pooling limited computer resources in a lab provides computer access for all students. The person in charge of the computer lab is likely to have some computer knowledge or is at least responsible for acquiring it. Finally, establishing a lab indicates administrative approval. After all, why would a lab exist if it were not meant to be used?

The computer lab is not always perfect. Lab supervisors are often teachers' aides who are chosen for their willingness to oversee a lab rather than qualified teachers with computer expertise. Since the lab is separated from the classroom, the computer may become its own subject (e.g., computer literacy) rather than a valuable tool to explore other fields. It is also easy for classroom teachers to lose contact with student learning and progress with a separate computer lab. Being out of touch with students is never desirable, but with gifted/talented students as with many handicapped learners it can be disastrous.

Placing the technology in the classroom is preferred to isolating it in the lab because it encourages the computer's integration into the curriculum and allows students to use the equipment as a professional might. The close proximity of the technology to the general

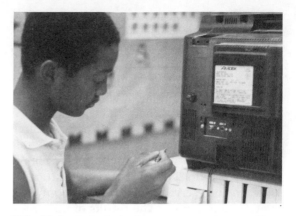

Gifted/talented students can support as well as benefit from their schools' computer programs. *(Photograph courtesy of Education and Technology Resources)*

learning environment enables students to use it the same way other learning materials are used—when needed rather than at an appointed time. In this context, computers can become powerful learning resources.

Unfortunately there are two major problems related to placing computers in classrooms—limited funds and expertise. Many schools consider themselves fortunate if they have enough computers for a lab; few schools have a computer for every classroom. Although the number of computers in schools is bound to increase, the problem of the lack of teacher expertise remains. As long as teachers are intimidated by the technology, little will be done with it in the classroom to improve education.

The solution to this dilemma is bound to the situation itself. If equipment and knowledge are limited, a separate computer lab is probably the appropriate solution. However, the long-range goal should be a computer lab in every classroom with teachers who know how to use the computer to enhance learning. Gifted/talented students need computers in the classroom so they can easily investigate a wide range of subjects, work on in-depth projects, and solve challenging problems. The ratio of computers to students, of course, depends upon the intent of the class itself. An elementary school classroom may need fewer computers than a secondary or college drafting class using computer-aided design.

Classroom Management

Teachers of gifted/talented programs have the same administrative teaching needs other educators have. There are a number of software packages (see Chapters 3 and 12) that they (and their students) find extremely helpful for such purposes. The three most useful applications are word processing, data bases, and spreadsheets. These programs can be used for writing and revising letters and reports, storing and retrieving important data, and generating and monitoring budgets. Data base managers help teachers and gifted/talented learners deal with voluminous information related to class projects or learning resources. For example, a data base of community mentors could be developed to store the people's names, addresses, phone numbers, areas of expertise, and the times they can consult with students.

Software packages that integrate these three applications (e.g., AppleWorks) make writing and keeping records especially easy. With them, information can be exchanged from one application to another. For instance, a mentor data base is used to identify experts in animal husbandry while the word processing program is used to write a personal letter to those who are selected requesting information and help. Such integrated software packages offer good value not only because they can be modified to meet special class needs but because students can use them for their own projects (see Computer Tools section in this chapter).

Unlike most classroom teachers, teachers in gifted/talented programs have to deal with students who are intellectually demanding in many different areas. These teachers are often faced with trying to meet these demands alone because they are the only teachers of gifted/ talented students in their school or district (Mills & Durden, 1992). Telecommunications can help. All that is needed to use the computer for communicating with the outside world is a modem, the software to run it, and a telephone line. Electronic bulletin boards (see Chapter 1) are already helping teachers exchange ideas and solve problems. Electronic mail, another useful function of telecommunications, is like regular mail except that the letter is transmitted electronically. Both these systems can put teachers and students in touch with others who have similar needs and interests.

Teachers and students involved with AT&T's Long Distance Learning Network (LDLN) have found the experience of working together across the miles intellectually invigorating and challenging. Information shared includes knowledge about software and hardware as well as ideas and developed curriculum (Lake, 1988). National Geographic's Kids Network uses telecommunications to bring together students from all parts of the world in the pursuit of scientific investigations and analysis.

Educational telecommunications networks also exist for teachers. California State University (CSU) provides telecommunications for teachers through CSUNet, which is part of InterNet, a nationwide telecommunications network. CSUNet links the 20 CSU campuses and is available for K–12 teachers through multiple public access ports. Teachers wishing to use the system log on through their local CSU campus and request an account number. Once the request is granted, teachers may use the system to access bulletin boards and data bases, participate in computer conferences, and send messages to other teachers via electronic mail. The data bases available include Software Clearing House, Video Clearing House, Video Disk Evaluations, and ERIC. CNN Newsroom On-Line provides teacher guides to the news that can be downloaded for use in the classroom. Students may participate in on-line curriculum projects such as the Kids to Kids Network. Teachers outside of California may access the system through a university that is an InterNet node and has public access ports. This network is exciting because it can connect educators across the nation. Information about CSUNET and other technology projects can be found in the *CTP Quarterly*, which is published by the California Technology Project and is sent to universities and educational technology units in state departments of education across the nation.

Student Learning

The purpose of computers in any educational program is to promote learning. With gifted/

talented individuals, learning needs to be independent and cover a wide range of subjects, which influences decisions regarding the kinds and numbers of computers as well as the software to be used.

The first thing to consider is how technology can serve the educational goals. Teachers should list their educational goals and then delineate the ways computers can be used in the gifted/talented program. They should include applications they know they need and those they may need at some future date. Also, they must find software that meets the needs they have identified. Software and hardware flexibility and expandability are important. For example, Publish It! provides a format for creating newsletters. The complexity and content of each newsletter depends upon the abilities, interests, and needs of those who use it. Hardware should be expandable to accommodate changes in technology and student projects. This is really true as computers become the controlling agent in a multimedia environment. For instance, the Apple II, II+, and IIe computers accommodate a wide range of needs simply because they have expansion slots to add peripheral interface cards. Purchasing equipment that can be enhanced as needs arise also helps to keep initial costs down. Later, when more funds are available, the system can be upgraded.

The question of how many computers are needed in a program for gifted/talented students is interesting. Much depends on the budget and the number of students. While it is possible for a well-organized teacher to manage with one computer in a class of 30, this would not provide for any in-depth investigations. However, it is not necessarily desirable to have one computer per student. What is really required is that everyone have access to the hardware and software when needed. Since individuals should use computers to solve a variety of problems that are not usually bound to the computer, it would not be necessary for everyone to use the computer at the same time. A possible exception to this might be a programming class, but even here students do not always need to work at the computer. In fact, a great deal of valuable thinking and planning takes place away from the computer.

Figure 10.2 illustrates how gifted/talented students might use a single microcomputer system to gather, sort, produce, and transmit information. While a program for gifted/talented individuals does not require a computer for every student, there should be a variety of computers available with which students can work and learn. For example, a classroom might have six expandable personal computers with one equipped with a modem for tapping larger information sources such as WilsonLine. This service is a collection of 14 data bases used worldwide by libraries, corporations, and government agencies. It provides access to such indexes as the *Applied Science and Technology Index, Biological and Agricultural Index, Book Review Digest, Education Index, Humanities Index, Readers' Guide to Periodical Literature,* and *Social Sciences Index*. Portable computers could be used for small, special purpose projects or collecting information outside the classroom. Information collected on these compact computers could then be downloaded to the microcomputer via a modem.

No program, particularly one with artistically talented students, should be without a printer with graphics and color capability. Dot matrix printers provide good-quality print and graphics at a reasonable cost. Laser printers are expensive for the average school budget but have a place in secondary and college courses, as do ink-jet printers. Inexpensive thermal printers such as the Scribe can provide color printing, but the supplies (thermal paper and special ribbons) are expensive. Furthermore, work printed on thermal paper deteriorates within a year or so. Letter-quality daisy wheel printers cannot produce graphics. Laser printers can produce letter-quality type and graphics.

Robotics is a new and challenging field for gifted/talented individuals. Keeping an up-to-date robot collection does not need to be expensive. For example, Robotic Workshop (Access Software) provides a fascinating introduction to the world of robotics. With this kit and additional Capsela parts, a wide variety of robots can be constructed and used to explore the physics of light and motion. LOGO can be used to control a variety of turtles such as the Turtle Tot (Campbell & Sears, 1989–1990).

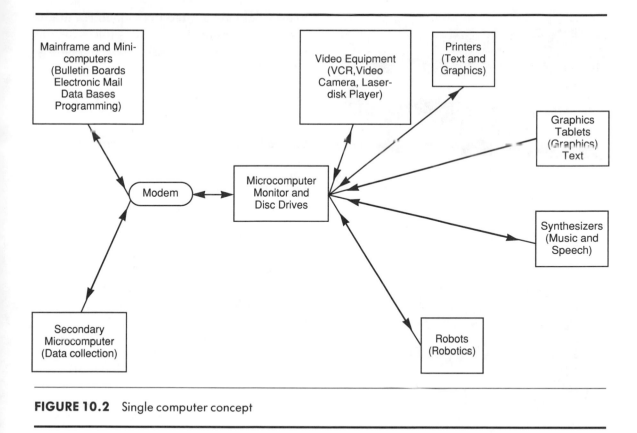

FIGURE 10.2   Single computer concept

Lego TC LOGO uses Lego building blocks and motors to construct robots that are then controlled by students' LOGO programs. These and other inexpensive robots provide an excellent introduction to this new branch of computer technology. The high cost required to establish a good robotics component will tend to preclude teachers of gifted/talented students from developing a highly sophisticated program. Advanced robotics investigations may be possible at local universities or colleges, however. For example, the University of California at Davis and California State University, Sacramento both permit qualified high school students to participate in their robotics programs.

SPECIFIC COMPUTER APPLICATIONS

The computer's versatility, ability to access information, and ability to provide learning tools make it especially appropriate for the gifted/talented user. Computers also stimulate the development of higher-level thinking skills essential for complex projects. Finally, the computer encourages creativity, enables information to be acquired at a remarkably rapid rate, and is compelling in its operation.

In his *Taxonomy of Educational Objectives*, Bloom (1956) describes six major categories of thinking: knowledge, comprehension, application, analysis, synthesis, and evaluation. Knowledge and comprehension, at the lower end of this scale, represent the most basic kinds of thinking. Synthesis and evaluation are the most advanced levels. According to Taylor (1983), learning for gifted/talented individuals should begin at the application level. Unfortunately, 90% to 95% of all learning at the elementary school level and 95% to 100% of all learning at the secondary level involves the two lowest levels, knowledge and comprehension. This is the case in many programs for gifted and talented students as well. What

A computer lab can be used to develop gifted/talented individuals' computer abilities.
(Photograph courtesy of IBM Corporation)

makes individuals gifted/talented is their behavior—giftedness depends upon above-average ability, task commitment, and creativity. Because computers provide such a variety of resources to tap these three areas, they are an increasingly important part of a gifted/talented person's educational process and life.

Software Criteria

While gifted/talented people form a unique and intellectually demanding group with special needs and interests, software is not usually specifically targeted for this population. As a result, it is important to outline basic criteria for evaluating software for gifted/talented individuals. This is not easy because there is such variation in their abilities and interests and the basic criteria may not apply

to every gifted/talented individual. For example, as part of a solar energy project for the California Science Fair in 1983, 6-year-old Jamie Lockwood built a computer to record each day's high and low temperatures and to calculate the day's average. This project required not only building a computer but reprogramming an electronically programmable read-only-memory (EPROM) chip. Jamie is an exceptionally gifted child whose level of development can be measured by the remark he made to his mother after his first visit to the physics lab at the University of California, Davis, "I thought I'd have to wait years before I could talk to someone who'd understand me." There can be no question that the criteria used to select software for Jamie Lockwood could be very different from the criteria used to select software for one of Jamie's gifted/talented peers.

Whether software is identified as appropriate for gifted/talented persons or not, the following criteria should be kept in mind:

1. *Flexible*—Does it support different areas of interest either in a specific field or in several fields?

2. *Modifiable*—Can the content or the order of operation of the software be changed? How much control does the user have?

3. *Expandable*—Can it be used to develop tools to explore one or more subjects?

4. *Responsive*—Does it offer different ways to alter the sequence of operation and speed?

While software packages for the gifted/talented should include the above points where possible, they should also support and encourage creative and intellectual development. Ability and interest dictate when a specific package is appropriate, not age. See Chapter 4 for an in-depth discussion of software evaluation procedures.

Computer Applications

Although the gifted and talented have special needs, their computer experiences do not always reflect this. In fact, they often take the same computer courses all students take. When special computer classes are developed for gifted/talented students, they usually focus on the computer science aspects of the technology. The computer becomes the subject—computer science. This is fine for a small portion of the gifted/talented population. While computer science as a subject should be left for those who have a strong interest in the theory and practice of computer applications, all gifted/talented people can benefit from the technology and should know how to use it for their own purposes. To do this, computers need to be integrated into the gifted students' total learning experiences.

The following discussion of applications for gifted/talented individuals is divided into three major categories: *computer-assisted instruction* involves how the computer can be used to teach specific concepts; *computer tools* focuses on software packages developed to explore different fields—these packages are either multi-purpose tools for examining many subjects or single-purpose tools for a specific field; and *computer science* examines the practice and theory behind computer technology. Gifted/talented people should know how to use software from the first two categories effectively and should be familiar with the programming component in the third category.

Computer-assisted Instruction

Computer-assisted instruction (CAI) explores different subjects (e.g., reading, geometry) and develops problem-solving and critical-thinking skills. CAI software covers drill-and-practice, tutorials, simulation packages, and, in certain instances, programming. When evaluating software for a specific subject area, it is important to consider, along with the four general criteria above, whether it challenges the intellect, stimulates critical thinking, and develops problem-solving skills.

Drill-and-Practice

Drill, practice, and tutorial packages (also see Chapter 3) traditionally offer users little control but help review old or introduce new information. Such applications should be mod-

ifiable in both content and learning sequence. These software packages offer gifted/talented students opportunities for independent, self-paced learning. Since a person may not be gifted or talented in all subjects, CAI can provide reinforcement in specific areas. MECC's Number Munchers presents math facts (multiples, primes, factors, equalities and inequalities) in drill-and-practice formats. Teacher options allow for a wide range of abilities and challenges.

Problem Solving

A variation of drill, practice, and tutorial software that develops problem-solving and critical-thinking skills is now appearing on the market. These programs present the user with a set of tools to solve and even create problems in a given environment; limited environments are usually employed to focus attention on specific thinking skills. For example, Factory (Sunburst) includes a square and three machines. These machines alter the square by adding holes, stripes, or turning the square. The player can use any combination of these machines to inductively or deductively build a factory or to create challenging problems for others to solve. The November/December 1984 *Curriculum Review* has an article that reviews seven problem-solving programs for gifted/talented individuals.

Simulation

CAI simulation software presents specific environments for the user to apply knowledge and test hypotheses. These environments are usually difficult or impossible to experience in the real world but are easy to experience with a computer. Flying a plane, traveling across the United States in the 19th century, or managing a nuclear reactor are all examples of such environments. They are especially useful for gifted/talented students because they provide a variety of opportunities for in-depth exploration. Tom Snyder Productions provides excellent problem-solving simulation for the classroom with only one computer. Simulations range from the *S.M.A.R.T. Choices* series in which students discuss ways to deal with issues such as drugs, sex, and responsible behavior in and out of school to the *Decisions, Decisions* series in which students participate in situations similar to those faced by Americans in the past. These software packages not only develop problem-solving strategies and critical-thinking skills but also promote cooperative learning as students work in teams to make decisions. Simulations also enhance hands-on experience. For example, a science student can first dissect a frog at the computer with Operation Frog by Scholastic and then perform the actual dissection in the laboratory. *Voyage of the Mimi* is an excellent multimedia simulation including videotapes, learning modules with disks, workbooks, and a teacher's guide. Although the entire set is expensive, it is engaging and well worth the expense, especially for a large school district.

Games

Computer games represent a special kind of CAI application whose educational value is often overlooked because the term *game* conjures up the image of players staring at a glowing screen as they blast space invaders out of the sky. In fact, computer games vary and can be divided into five basic categories: fantasy, adventure, strategy, simulation, and arcade (Levine, 1984).

Computer games for the gifted/talented need to be evaluated individually. Such games combine intellectual challenge with the compelling format of a game. Good computer games develop logical thinking, organization, and planning skills. They also stimulate off-computer activities. Players often create maps, game plans, conduct research, and discuss strategies with others in an effort to beat the computer. All this develops research, communication, and social skills. Unfortunately, today's computer games do not usually depend on in-depth knowledge of a specific field. When they do, the user develops specific knowledge and often continues investigating the subject after the game. Games have always been a source of intellectual challenge and pleasure for gifted/talented people. A computer simply provides a new format (Hamlett, 1984). Brøderbund's Carmen Sandiego software series (Where in the USA, Where in Europe, Where in the World, and Where in Time) promotes skills in researching, planning and organizing, and group cooperation in an effort to track down Carmen and her notorious gang.

Playing games is fun and often challenging, but creating your own game can be even better. With Think Quick (Learning Company), Lode Runner (Brøderbund), and the Strategic Simulations series (Electronic Arts), the user can not only play games but also make them. Pinball Construction Set (Electronic Arts) enables the user to first build a pinball game and then play it. Games can be saved on disks and shared with friends. Those interested in games that involve writing their own adventure stories may do so with Adventure Construction Set (Electronic Arts).

Computer Tools

Chapter 3 introduced the concept of application software and listed a number of word processing, data base, and spreadsheet programs that can be used with and by exceptional individuals. These application packages have a number of specific uses with gifted/talented individuals.

Word Processing

A word processor is an excellent tool for developing gifted/talented individuals' writing skills because it frees the user from the mechanics of writing and rewriting drafts, so that they can concentrate on prose content and its organization. This is especially important for gifted/talented youngsters whose ideas often outstrip their ability to write on paper. Magic Slate II (Sunburst) comes in three versions: 20-column, 40-column, and 80-column. The 20-column version features large letters and a picture menu with simplified commands. The 40-column version contains every feature in the 20-column version as well as more type styles and teacher/student planners for guided learning. In addition to these features, the 80-column version is a complete word processing package that can be used by adults as well as middle and high school students.

Microsoft Word (Microsoft) is a sophisticated word processing package, especially when used with a laser printer. In addition to the usual word processing capabilities, it has features such as (a) windows for referring to different documents at the same time and cutting and pasting between these documents; (b) a glossary for storing frequently used text; (c) traditional footnoting capabilities; (d) ability to use charts developed with Microsoft's Chart; and (e) telecommunications capabilities for receiving and transmitting text via a modem. See Chapter 3 for descriptions of other word processing programs that can be used with and by gifted/talented individuals.

Publish It and *Publish It 3* (TimeWorks) can also be used by gifted/talented individuals to develop their expository and creative writing abilities. They are designed to produce newsletters or newspapers and can mix graphics and text, use different styles of type, produce columned text, generate their own graphics (or import, scale, and resize graphics), and overlap text on graphics. *Publish It!*'s capacity to import *AppleWorks* and *Bank Street Writer* files is another useful feature.

Most word processing software comes with its own spelling checker. If it does not, see if there is an add-on spelling checker package such as TimeOut QuickSpell for your word processing software. Such a utility is well worth having, since students can fix typing and spelling errors quickly and easily. The ability to check a document immediately and have errors presented on the computer's screen is an invaluable tool. It not only helps students correct their work but also helps them learn how to spell. The student must decide whether the word identified by the computer is spelled incorrectly, and if so, they must determine how to spell it correctly. Learning is especially effective because feedback is immediate.

The major obstacle to successful word processing is keyboarding skills. There are, of course, software packages (see Appendix E) that develop keyboarding skills with the current QWERTY keyboard (Wetzel, 1985). However, there is another way to overcome this difficulty—change the keyboard. Today there is a microchip that converts the computer's difficult QWERTY keyboard to the Dvorak keyboard; Kaplan (1984) has an excellent description of the Dvorak panel. Gifted/talented

students who are interested in learning to use both types of keyboards could be taught how to do so.

Data Base Managers. As noted in Chapter 3, data base managers were originally developed to help businesses keep track of a wide variety of information. They are equally useful for other tasks involving collection, analysis, interpretation, organization, and retrieval of information. Gifted/talented students are often involved in such tasks. For this reason alone, they should know how to use this tool effectively. Working with data bases also helps to develop the higher-level thinking skills—analysis, synthesis, and evaluation. These skills are important not only because they cut across subject areas but because they also can be applied to off-computer as well as on-computer projects. Working with data bases develops computing and noncomputing knowledge and skills. It can also teach higher-order thinking skills (Watson & Strudler, 1989–90).

A data base can be used in astronomy to gather the following information for each star: name, light-years from Earth, magnitude (brightness), color and type, constellation, and seasons. After all information is entered, the Star Data Base can be used to find stars that are less than 10 light-years away, stars that are bigger than the Sun, the blue giants, the red dwarfs, the stars in the constellation Orion, those that are visible only in spring, or the yellow main-sequence stars that are less than 50 light-years away (Bollinger & Hopping, 1985). For an excellent explanation of how to use data bases with gifted first through fifth graders, see Brooks' (1990) article "Using Application Software with Gifted Students," in *Computing Teacher.* Data bases are useful tools for research in all fields and can be used for school, job, or personal projects.

Friendly Filer is an easy-to-use, fail-safe filing software system. It can search for seven items at a time with only parts of words. There are 10 fields per record and 24 characters per field. PFS: File is a flexible and sophisticated package. Although it is designed for adults, the average fifth grader can use it. Searches can be conducted for all or any combination of items in a file at one time; the fields per record and characters per field are unlimited. Files can be customized, and fields can be added and formats changed at any time. Chapters 3 and 12 have additional descriptions of data base programs gifted/talented individuals might use.

Electronic Spreadsheets. Electronic spreadsheets were also originally developed for business to keep track of financial matters that require recording and forecasting. Although electronic spreadsheets are designed to deal with money matters, they can be used by gifted/talented individuals to manipulate other kinds of data as well. For instance, a social studies project can use a spreadsheet to record and manipulate census data gathered from field research or government sources about cities across the United States. The completed spreadsheet can be used to produce a ranked listing of all the major cities in America according to their populations. This can easily be done for other attributes as well. Nonnumeric data can be evaluated by weighting it numerically. For example, categories for public transportation systems, levels of pollution, and numbers of parks and cultural centers can be ranked on a scale from 1 to 10. Cities can then be compared according to the value given each category. A final column totals each city's points and provides a final quality-of-life score for each city. This grand total is then used to rank the cities according to their total scores. Analysis of the results of such ranking is not only interesting in itself but can lead to a discussion of statistical ranking and a comparison of seemingly objective figures that may in fact produce biased results.

Electronic spreadsheets are easy to use. All that is needed is an understanding of basic arithmetic operations and grid layouts that use rows and columns. Dickinson (see Dickinson & Hopping, 1985) reported that his average fourth graders enjoy working with spreadsheets. Spreadsheets are also excellent for developing critical thinking skills since students can organize and analyze data and then hypothesize outcomes (Parker & Widmer, 1989). Microsoft's Multiplan is easy yet powerful enough for small businesses. This package includes capabilities such as the use of windows to view different spreadsheets and linking spreadsheets so changes made on one are automatically made on another.

Integrated Packages. It is possible to purchase a single software package that integrates a word processor, a data base manager, and an electronic spreadsheet among other functions (see Chapter 3). The advantage of such a package is that the commands are similar for each application. For example, AppleWorks uses many of the same key combinations in its word processing, data base, and spreadsheet sections. Since these applications are on one program disk, information from one application can be transferred to another without changing disks if the system has two disk drives. AppleWorks 3.0 versions for the Apple IIe and GS include many extra features such as a spell checker and multiline headers and footers. The GS version includes draw and paint tools, artwork import and incorporation features, color print options, and telecommunications capability. Beagle Brother's TimeOut series of add-ons make AppleWorks even more powerful. For example, TimeOut Graph builds a wide-range of graphs from AppleWorks' spreadsheet data and TimeOut's TextTools permits printing word processed files onto any type of premade form. Of course, since AppleWorks supplies all three applications in an integrated package, it is more expensive than a single application.

Special Tools. Word processors, data base managers, and electronic spreadsheets are general tools for exploring many different fields. There are also tools for conducting in-depth investigations in a specific field (e.g., art, music). Many of these specialized applications require additional hardware.

1. *Graphic art tools.* Graphics pads help gifted/talented individuals develop graphics for screen display or printing on paper. The Koala Pad by Koala Technologies (see Chapter 2) is an inexpensive and easy-to-use package that includes a touch tablet for drawing and the Koala Painter diskette. Dazzle Draw (Brøderbund) is a more sophisticated graphics package that uses

either a mouse, Apple Graphics Tablet, drawing pad (such as Koala Graphics Pad or Ergo Pad), or a joystick to create images. Dazzle Draw features include the ability to mix text with graphics, produce mirror images, use 16 colors and 30 multicolored patterns, and create more patterns. Different brushes and a spray can are also available. Dazzle Draw can produce an electronic slide show to display artwork and print in color as well as black and white. *Computers in the Artroom* by Greh (1990) is an excellent book about ways to use computers to develop students' artistic understanding and skills. The text includes a demonstration disk of student art work.

AutoCAD is a sophisticated graphics application for those interested in computer-aided drafting in architecture, industrial design, engineering, and archaeology. AutoCAD works with other specialized programs and computer-aided design (CAD) systems. This package handles graphics the way a word processor handles text. It can also develop graphic data bases and pass them to and from other specialized programs.

Digitizers transform anything shot with a video camera into a digital image that can then be seen on the computer screen, printed out, or saved on a disk. Such images can be enhanced with other software packages such as MacPaint or PageMaker.

Digitizing programs require their own hardware to photograph the image and communicate with the computer. Most are video digitizers requiring video cameras capable of accepting the digitizer's connectors. This setup permits the user to create original work. Optical scanners are different. Instead of a video camera, a device is used to digitize a two-dimensional image into the computer's memory where it can be captured, resized, cut, and pasted into a document or manipulated and colored with a paint program. Scanners range from tabletop to hand-held models. The size of the image that can be scanned is limited by the computer's memory and the scanner itself. High-resolution and double-high-resolution graphics are limited to a single

screen. In addition to the scanner itself, a cable and interface card that connect it to the computer and software to control it are required. LightingScan GS/LC (Thunderware) and *Quickie* (Vitesse) are two inexpensive hand-held scanners (Kohn, 1991). Marstek's Mars 105 Plus and Mars 800 models come with Digital Darkroom (Aldus/Silicon Beach) for high-end image enhancement. Optical character recognition is also possible with software such as Olduvai's Read It! OCR Personal (Holzberg, 1991).

2. *Music tools.* Computers are opening up the world of music to the novice and changing it for the accomplished musician. For most people, computer music has been limited to the constricted sounds of their home computer's speaker. All this is changing. Technological advances are improving computer speakers. For a good example, listen to the Macintosh. Quality sound, however, requires made-to-order hardware and easy-to-use software.

Today's music synthesizers provide professional quality music at reasonable costs such as MIDI (musical instrument digital interface), which is used on many music synthesizers and offers professional quality instruments at low cost. MIDI hardware can be used with Apple (see Cowart & Cummings, 1986), Commodore, IBM PC, and other computers. Non-MIDI sound hardware is also available. Leinecker (1990) has discussed music add-on cards and software for IBM PCs. With Ad Lib's synthesizer card and Visual Composer software or Creative Lab's Music Composer, a musician can begin to compose and listen to good-quality sound. More sophisticated sound can be produced with the Roland MT-32 sound module and Sound Globs.

Although hardware provides the equipment for generating sophisticated music with a computer, software runs the system. There are several music programs designed for wide ability ranges and therefore good for gifted/talented children. Mindscape's Bank Street MusicWriter applies the word processing concept to music. It can be used by beginning and experienced musicians to compose and practice music. Activision's Music Studio for the Commodore 64 is an inexpensive package that includes a special paint box for the novice and standard musical notation for trained musicians. This package permits the user to input lyrics as well use an electronic keyboard to input and play music. Professional Composer (Mark of the Unicorn) is a sophisticated piece of software for composing music with a Macintosh.

Multimedia Applications. As we move towards the 21st century, the computer has already become the controlling agent for multimedia explorations. In such a setting, the computer enables students to put together hypermedia productions that integrate music, voice, text, graphics, animation, and live-action video. Productions take many forms such as a multimedia video or an informational telepresentation (D'Ignazio, 1990).

A computer-based inquiry center involves additional equipment such as a laser videodisc player for instant access to slides and films, a VCR player for recording and playing tapes, a camcorder for on-location live-action videos, and a cassette player for recording sounds and dialogue (D'Ignazio, 1990). Software such as HyperStudio for the Apple IIGS, HyperCard for the Macintosh (Raker, 1989), or Linkway for the IBM (McMillan, 1990) is needed for the computer to control equipment such as the laser videodisc player and to produce interactive multimedia productions. The Visual Almanac is an interactive multimedia kit containing software on floppies and CD-ROM, a laser videodisc, and a book entitled *The Visual Almanac Companion*. Extra equipment, of course, is always useful. A video-overlay card permits visual images from the laser videodisc to be viewed on the computer's screen. A scanner or digital camera digitizes images so they can be incorporated into a computer program. Expanded RAM provides additional memory for large visual projects. Hard drives expand storage space for visual and textual data, and CD-ROM drives play audio and data disks.

The multimedia environment is especially appropriate for gifted/talented individuals because it is both open-ended and structured. Its openness resides in the almost limitlessness of the visual, audio, and textual resources. Its structure resides in the hardware and software that control it. Here at last is an environment in which creative, divergent thought can be used to produce unique solutions to intriguing problems—a place where process and product are joined.

Computer Science

Computer science covers the technical side of computing and can be divided into two basic levels: (a) controlling the computer through programming languages and an understanding of the computer's architecture, and (b) applying this knowledge to artificial intelligence.

Programming. Since it is often assumed that gifted/talented students ought to learn how to program, gifted/talented individuals across the nation are learning how to program computers at home, at school, or in special programs (e.g., Johns Hopkins' CTY). Whether the purpose is to develop problem-solving skills or to enter the computer science field, the computer languages that are most appropriate and the development of a suitable curriculum need to be considered.

All too often, the programming language selected is BASIC (see Appendixes C and F) because most computers come with it and those who know anything about programming know it. Programming languages should be selected on the basis of whether they support and develop students' interests, abilities, and needs. This is especially true for gifted/talented people who have such diverse abilities and interests. The primary value of programming is to develop independence, self-esteem, critical-thinking, problem-solving, and communication skills. Programming to develop computer science knowledge is important only for those who demonstrate an interest in the field.

All versions of LOGO can be used with and by gifted/talented individuals to develop thinking and communication skills as well as to obtain excellent preparation for the study of computer science. It supports individual learn-

Young gifted/talented students can quickly master basic computer concepts. *(Photograph by Jimmy D. Lindsey)*

problems or tasks are then presented to the computer and the results carefully observed. Free from social and psychological influences, the computer provides pure, limited intelligence with which AI researchers can test their scientific theories.

LOGO is an excellent computer language with which to begin exploring the field of artificial intelligence: it is an intriguing and fairly easy language to learn, and it is a procedural and list-processing language. LOGO is the front end of LISP, the major language used in artificial intelligence research. Thus LOGO provides a natural beginning and a comfortable bridge to this complex field.

ing styles and promotes problem-solving skills through its interactive and procedural structure. As an interactive language with clear error messages, LOGO helps programmers locate problems. Its modular or procedural structure also helps pinpoint errors because a program can be run in its entirety on a procedure-by-procedure or on a line-by-line basis. The ability to work from a general program to a specific line within that program effectively demonstrates the value of deductive thinking for solving problems. With LOGO, it is also easy to develop a program using the inductive method. (Dale, 1984).

Those who wish to study the field of computer science must also understand computer architecture and the theories and principles upon which computer technology is based. Learning assembly and machine languages and knowing how to use compilers and interpreters help achieve this goal.

Artificial Intelligence. The study of the field of artificial intelligence, or AI (see Chapter 5), can develop quite naturally from programming and is especially appropriate for gifted/talented individuals. The field of AI is the study of the nature of intelligence through the artificial or nonhuman means of a computer. Since the computer provides an environment in which all conditions can be controlled, a researcher can provide the machine with certain identifiable data and abilities. Specific

ADDITIONAL COMPUTER ISSUES

Computers do not exist in isolation. They have caused, are causing, and will cause major changes in societies around the world. Gifted/talented people need to be aware of the impact of computers for several reasons. First, many gifted/talented people are and will be decision makers. While they may not hold positions directly involved with computer use, their positions are likely to be affected by the technology. Second, as a group, gifted/talented individuals are inquisitive. They enjoy intellectually challenging puzzles. The computer presents a multitude of fascinating puzzles begging to be solved, and solving such puzzles brings a sense of control. It is a small step to extend this curiosity. For example, programming knowledge can be used to develop a simple program that methodically tries a series of symbols in an effort to find the secret password to a governmental agency or international bank. Lacking a firm understanding of the social, legal, and ethical issues of such behavior, many individuals see this as harmless behavior.

Computer crime, the most prominent computer issue today, can range from violation of copyright laws through copying protected software to embezzlement. Computer crime is especially tempting because it is often easy to do, difficult to detect, and, in the case of copying protected disks, practiced by so many. To combat illegal uses of the technology, it is important to discuss the social and personal implications of such actions thoroughly. Discussions should confront students with the difficult choices associated with many real-life situations. It is equally important to understand how the law affects the computer world. A chance to consider what the options are before encountering them in real life helps people make sensible and informed decisions. Regular and special educators can find a number of articles in the literature that provide a good introduction to computer crime and how to help students understand the practical, legal, and ethical issues involved.

Information control is closely associated with computer crime. In fact, it may be used as justification for the crime itself. The technology's capacity to access, manipulate, and retain vast quantities of information brings up the whole issue of who can have and use such information and whether it should be public or private. There is also a question of ownership. Should such information be sold to anyone with the money? What are appropriate and inappropriate uses of such information (Hannah & Matus, 1984)?

Investigating the legal, ethical, and social implications of computers with gifted and talented people involves thoughtful consideration of all aspects of a given issue. For example, members of a governing council on the fictitious planet Ecco examine the question of whether or not the use of computers in business and government should be restricted. Everyone considers the following questions. What hazards might a society face if business and government had unrestricted use of computers? What kinds of restrictions should be placed on business and government? What are future applications of computers and the potential benefits and losses to society (*Ethical Issues*, 1985)?

Since everyone is affected by computer technology in one way or another, it is important to consider what the effects might be and whether they are good, bad, or both. An awareness of the ways in which this technology is used to accomplish the ordinary (regulate a microwave oven's temperature) or extraordinary (navigate a satellite through outer space) develops a sense of its current capabilities and future potentials. Such knowledge is especially important for gifted/talented people because they are likely to make significant contributions in many fields, and understanding the world of computers will help make these contributions effective. It is also important to understand the technology's impact on careers. Which kinds of jobs are likely to be eliminated? Will the computer create new jobs? If so, in which fields? What about existing jobs? How will they be affected?

Computers are ubiquitous devices capable of entering any field and creating significant changes. For this reason alone, the exploration of their impact on society should not be considered in isolation nor should it be restricted to specific hands-on experiences. Rather, it should be discussed whenever relevant. Computers are becoming an indispensible part of society. It is essential that this be recognized and dealt with effectively (Weizenbaum, 1976).

SUMMARY

Computers present unique opportunities for expanding intellectual horizons in ways never before thought possible, and gifted/talented people are among those who are most likely to profit from the use of this technology. Identifying the best hardware and software for gifted/talented individuals is difficult because of the varied abilities and interests of this group of people. Schools need to consider how best to distribute their often meager computer resources. A lab outside the classroom should be seen as a temporary solution for gifted/talented students because they need the technology close at hand to pursue the many different kinds of special, in-depth projects in which they become involved. A multipurpose classroom lab with a qualified teacher is a better configuration. Classroom management is important too. Teachers in gifted/talented programs have administrative needs such as averaging grades and keeping track of attendance that the computer can effectively meet. Telecommunications hardware and software can also help these teachers meet the special needs of their students. For example, with a modem and the appropriate software, teachers and their students have access to sophisticated information resources at remote sites.

Gifted/talented individuals' learning is greatly enhanced by all aspects of computer technology. Computer-assisted instruction enables them to complete missed work, develop weak skills, accelerate learning, and explore problem-solving strategies. They can also use computers as application tools for general purposes (e.g., word processing) or focus on specific tasks (e.g., art or music). Gifted/talented persons can also learn programming languages (e.g., LOGO) to develop creativity, critical thinking skills, and problem-solving strategies and to investigate the field of computer science. Finally, gifted/talented people need to be aware of the current and future legal, ethical, and social implications of the technology.

REFERENCES

Baum, S. (1984). Meeting the needs of learning disabled gifted students. *Roeper Review, 7*(1), 16–19.

Bloom, B. (Ed.). (1956). *Taxonomy of educational objectives.* New York: Longmans, Green.

Bollinger, R., & Hopping, L. (1985). Reach for the stars. *Teaching and Computers, 2*(7), 12–19.

Balajthy, E. (1988). Results of the first National Computer Assessment. *Reading Teacher, 42,* 242–246.

Brody, L. E., Assouline, S. G., & Stanley, J. C. (1990). Five years of early entrants: Predicting successful achievement in college. *Gifted Child Quarterly, 34*(4), 138–142.

Brooks, S. (1990). Using application software with gifted students. *Computing Teacher, 18*(3), 41–43.

Campbell, S., & Sears, T. (1989–90). More robots in the classroom. *Computing Teacher, 16*(4), 9–11.

Cowart, R., & Cummings, S. (1986). A new musical revolution. *A+, 4*(2) 26–32.

Crockenburg, S. B. (1972). Creativity tests: A boon or boondoggle for education? *Review of Educational Research, 42,* 27–45.

Dale, E. (1984). LOGO builds thinking skills. In D. T. Bonnette (Ed.), *The 6th Annual National Educational Computing Conference* (pp. 224–226). Dayton, OH.

Dickinson, C., & Hopping, L. (1985). Teach dollars and sense with spreadsheets. *Teaching and Computers, 2*(6), 12–17.

D'Ignazio, F. (1990): Multimedia sandbox. *Computing Teacher, 17*(6), 16–19.

Ethical issues in computer use. (1985). Eugene, OR: International Council for Computers in Education.

Getzels, J. W., & Csikszentmihayli, M. (1975). From problem solving to problem finding. In I. A. Taylor & J. W. Getzels (Eds.), *Perspective in creativity* (pp. 741–775). Chicago, IL: Aldine.

Greenlaw, M. J., & McIntosh, M. E. (1988). *Educating the gifted: A sourcebook.* Chicago: American Library Association.

Greh, D. (1990). *Computers in the artroom.* Worcester, MA: Davis Publications.

Hamlett, C. (1984). Microcomputer activities for gifted elementary children: Alternatives to programming. *Teaching Exceptional Children, 16,* 153–157.

Hannah, L., & Matus, C. (1984). A question of ethics. *Computing Teacher, 12*(1), 11–14.

Hersberger, J., & Wheatley, G. (1989). Computers and gifted students: An effective mathematics program, *Gifted Child Quarterly, 33*(3), 106–109.

Holzberg, C. S. (1991). On the other hand: Five affordable Mac scanners. *InCider, 9*(1), 55–58.

Kaplan, G. M. (1984, January 24). Bye-Bye Qwerty. *PC Magazine,* pp. 338–343.

Kohn, J. (1991). Quickie vs. LightningScan. *InCider, 9*(1), 44–52.

Kolstad, R., & Lidke, D. (1983). Gifted and talented. In D. Harper & J. Stewart (Eds.), *RUN: Computer education* (pp. 222–226). Monterey, CA: Brooks/Cole.

Lake, D. (1988–1989). Telecommunications in the classroom. *Computing Teacher, 16*(4), 17–19.

Levine, N. S. (1984). A parents' guide to computer game selection. *Gifted Children Newsletter, 5*(11), 14.

MacKinnon, D. W. (1968a). Selecting students with creative potential. In P. Heist (Ed.), *The creative college student: An unmet challenge* (pp. 101–116). San Francisco: Jossey-Bass.

MacKinnon, D. W. (1968b). Educating for creativity: A modern myth? In P. Heist (Ed.), *The creative college student: An unmet challenge* (pp. 147–160). San Francisco: Jossey-Bass.

McMillan, G. (1990). Multimedia: An educator's link to the 90s. *Computing Teacher, 18*(3), 7–9.

Middleton, J. A., Littlefield, J., & Lehrer, R. (1992). Gifted students conceptions of academic fun: An examination of a critical construct for gifted students. *Gifted Child Quarterly, 36*(1), 38–44.

Mills, C. J., & Durden, W. G. (1992). Cooperative learning and ability grouping: An issue of choice. *Gifted Child Quarterly, 36*(1), 11–16.

Nicholls, J. C. (1972). Creativity in the person who will never produce anything original and useful: The concept of creativity as a normally distributed trait. *American Psychologist, 27,* 717–727.

Niess, M. (1990). Preparing computer using educators in a new decade. *Computing Teacher, 18*(3), 10–15.

Papert, S. (1980). *Mindstorms: Children, computers, and powerful ideas.* New York: Basic Books.

Parker, J., & Widmer, C. C. (1990). Using spreadsheets to encourage critical thinking. *Computing Teacher, 16*(6), 27–55.

Pollak, R. A., & Breault, G. (1985). On-line contemporary issues bring today's world to social studies classrooms. *Computing Teacher, 12*(8), 10–11.

Raker, E. J. (1989). Hypermedia: New technology tool for educators. *Computing Teacher, 17*(1), 18–19.

Renzulli, J. S. (1978). What makes giftedness? Reexamining a definition. *Phi Delta Kappan, 60*(3), 180–261.

Renzulli, J. S., Reis, S. M., & Smith, L. H. (1981). *The revolving door identification model.* Hartford, CT: Creative Learning Press.

Roe, A. (1975). Psychologist examines 64 eminent scientists. In W. B. Barbe & J. S. Renzulli (Eds.), *Psychology and education of the gifted* (pp. 119–126). New York: Irvington.

Rotenberg, L. (1985). Classroom happenings. *Teaching and Computers, 2*(6), 11.

Senf, G. M. (1983). The nature and identification of learning disabilities and their relationship to the gifted child. In L. H. Fox, L. Brody, & D. Tobin (Eds.), *Learning-disabled/gifted children: Identification and programming* (pp. 37–49). Austin, TX: PRO-ED.

Shaklee, B. D. (1992). Identification of young gifted children. *Journal for the Education of the Gifted, 15*(2), 134–144.

Sisk, D. (1987). *Creative teaching of the gifted.* New York: McGraw-Hill.

Staff. (1984, November/December). Cluster review: Software for problem solving. *Curriculum Review, 24*(2), 32–33.

Swassing, R. H. (1984). *Teaching gifted children and adolescents.* Columbus, OH: Charles E. Merrill.

Taylor, R. (1983). *Building a quality program for gifted students.* Paso Robles, CA: Bureau of Education and Research.

Terman, L. M. (1959). *Genetic studies of genius: The gifted group at mid-life.* Palo Alto, CA: Stanford University.

Terry, P. J. (1984). *How to use computers with gifted students: Creative microcomputing in a differentiated curriculum.* Manassas, VA: Reading Tutorium.

Wallach, M. A. (1976). Tests tell us little about talent. *American Scientist, 64*, 57–63.

Watson, J., & Strudler, N. (1989–1990). Teaching higher-order thinking skills with databases. *Computing Teacher, 16*(4), 47–50.

Weizenbaum, J. (1976). *Computer power and human reason: From judgment to calculation.* San Francisco: W. H. Freeman.

Wetzel, K. (1985). Keyboarding skills: Elementary my dear teacher? *Computing Teacher, 12*(9), 15–19.

Witty, P., (1958). Who are the gifted? In P. Witty (Ed.), *Education of the gifted.* National Society for the Study of Education Series, Vol. 57, Pt. 2. Chicago: University of Chicago Press.

Suggested Activities

Paper and Pencil

Identify and describe how three telecommunications sources can enrich the learning experiences of gifted and talented students. Use a word processor to write the paper.

Multimedia

Create a short multimedia production with gifted/talented students. Use the computer and at least one other medium such as a laser videodisc player. Discuss and list ways to improve and/or expand the project.

Observation

Visit a class for gifted/talented students. What computer technology applications do they use? What are the students' favorite and least favorite applications? Try to determine the applications discussed in this chapter that are not being used. Why are they not being used?

Practicum

Develop a computer data base of a favorite hobby (e.g., data on a book collection) or topic (e.g., names, companies, costs, compatibility of software for the gifted/talented). When finished, help someone else develop such a data base.

Resources

Organizations

Center for the Advancement of Academically Talented Youth, Johns Hopkins University.

Write to CTY, Johns Hopkins University, Charles and 34th Street, Baltimore, MD 21218.

Project Talent Search, California State University, Sacramento. Write to Talent Search, State Department of Education, 6000 J Street, Sacramento CA 95819.

Journals

CTP Quarterly. This journal is published three times a year. Articles are written by educators for educators and focus on the use of technology in the classroom. Write to *CTP Quarterly,* California Technology Project, P.O. Box 3842, Seal Beach, CA 90740-7842.

Gifted Child Today (G/C/T). This journal is published six times a year and focuses on a variety of issues related to gifted/talented individuals. Write to *G/C/T* Publishing Company, P.O. Box 6448, Mobile, AL 36660–0448.

Creative Child and Adult Quarterly. This journal is published four times a year and features lives and works of creative children and adults. Write to *Creative Child and Adult Quarterly,* National Association for Creative Children and Adults, 1340 State University, Muncie, IN 47306.

Books

Nazzaro, J. N. (Ed.). (1981). *Computer connections for gifted children and youth.* Reston, VA: Council for Exceptional Children.

Turkle, S. (1984). *The second self: The computer and the human spirit.* New York: Simon and Schuster.

Telecommunication Networks

CSUNet. CSUNet is a telecommunications network linking the California State University System, junior college campuses, state departments of education, and K–12 teachers among other individuals and agencies. Through CSUNet, users have access to InterNet, a global network system, and other networks such as NSFNet and NEARNet. The *InterNet Teachers' Guide* lists available facilities such as supercomputers, library catalogs, and *CNN Teachers' Guide.* Many states have network systems similar to CSUNet that are supported by state funds or their universities' financial resources. To use InterNet, call a local university or college or CSUNet (1-800-272-8743 [within California] or 1-800-985-9631 [outside California]).

Hardware/Software

Adventure Construction Set
Pinball Construction Set
Strategic Simulations Series
Electronic Arts
2755 Campus Drive
San Mateo, CA 94403

Apple II, II+, IIe
Apple Computer
20525 Mariani Avenue
Cupertino, CA 95014

Apple LOGO II
Apple Computer, Inc.
20525 Mariani Avenue
Cupertino, CA 95014

AppleWorks 3.0 and GS
Claris
5201 Patrick Henry Drive
Box 58168
Santa Clara, CA 95052

AutoCAD
Autodesk
2320 Marunship Way
Sausalito, CA 94965

Bank Street Music Writer
Mindscape
344 Dundee Road
Northbrook, IL 60062

Dazzle Draw
Brøderbund
17 Paul Drive
San Rafael, CA 94903

Decisions, Decisions/S.M.A.R.T. Choice
Tom Snyder Productions
90 Sherman Street
Cambridge, MA 02140-9923

Digital Darkroom/PageMaker
Aldus
411 First Avenue South
Seattle, WA 98104-2871

Friendly Filer
Grolier
Department 336
Sherman Turnpike
Danbury, CT 06816

IBM LOGO
IBM
P.O. Box 1328-W
Boca Raton, FL 33429

IBM PC
IBM
900 King Street
Rye Brook, NY 10573

Imagewriter
Apple Computer
20525 Mariani Avenue
Cupertino, CA 95014

Koala Painter
Koala Technologies
70 North 2nd Street
San Jose, CA 95113

Koala Pad/Koala Printer
Koala Technologies
70 North 2nd Street
San Jose, CA 95113

LightningScan
Thunderware
21 Orinda Way
Orinda, CA 94563

Lode Runner
Where in the U.S.A., Europe, World
or Time is Carmen Sandiego?
Brøderbund Software
P.O. Box 12947
San Rafael, CA 94913-2947

LOGOWriter
LOGO Computer Systems
555 West 57th Street,
Suite 1236
New York, NY 10019

MacPaint
Claris Corporation
5201 Patrick Henry Drive
Box 58168
Santa Clara, CA 95052

Magic Slate II
Sunburst Communications
101 Castleton Street
Pleasantville, NY 10570-4398
(800) 321-7511

Mars 105 Plus/Mars 128/Mars 800
Marstek
17795 Skypark Blvd. #F
Irvine, CA 92714

Microsoft Word
Microsoft
1 Microsoft Way
Redmond, WA 98052-6399

MT-32 Sound Module
Roland Corp
7200 Dominion Circle
Los Angeles, CA 90040

Multiplan
Microsoft
1 Microsoft Way
Redmond, WA 98052-6399

Music Composer
Creative Music Labs
Publisher/Distributor: Brown-Wagh
Publishing
16795 Lark Avenue
Suite 210
Los Gatos, CA 95030

Music Studio
Activision
2350 Bayshore Frontage Road
Mountain View, CA 94043

Number Munchers/Oregon Trail
MECC
3490 Lexington Avenue North
St. Paul, MN 55126

Operation Frog
Scholastic
P.O. Box 7503
2931 East McCarty
Jefferson City, MO 65102

Professional Composer
Mark of the Unicorn
222-T Third Street
Cambridge, MA 02142

Publish It!/Publish It! 3
Timeworks
444 Lake Cook Road
Deerfield, IL 60015

Quickie
Vitesse
13909 Amar Road
Suite 2
La Puente, CA 91746-1669

Read It!/OCR Personal 2.0
Olduvai
7520 Read Road
Suite A
South Miami, FL 33143

Robotic Workshop
Access Software
#A2561 So. 1560 West
Woods Cross, UT 84087

Sound Globs
Twelve Tone Systems
P.O. Box 226
Watertown, MA 02272

Tandy 1100 FD
Tandy/Radio Shack
1400 One Tandy Place
Fort Worth, TX 76102

Terrapin LOGO/LOGOPlus PC
Logo/Commodore LOGO
Terapin Software
400 Riverside Street
Portland, ME 04103

Think Quick!
Learning Company
6493 Kaiser Drive
Freemont, CA 94555

TI
Texas Instruments
Consumer Information
Houston, TX 77001

TimeOut Graph/TimeOut TextTools
Beagle Bros.
6215 Ferris Square
Suite 100
San Diego, CA 92121

Visual Almanac
Apple Multimedia Lab
Apple Computer
20525 Mariana Avenue
Cupertino, CA 95014

Visual Composer/Synthesizer Card
Ad Lib
50 Staniford St.
Suite 800
Boston, MA 02114

Voyage of the Mimi
Publisher: Holt, Rinehart and Winston
Distributer: Sunburst Communications
101 Castleton Street
Pleasantville, NY 10570-4398

Administrative and Instructional Applications

This section describes implementing the computer concept, administrative data management for special education, teaching applications, and evaluation models for technology applications.

Computer labs provide many exceptional individuals with technology-related experiences.
(Photograph by Jimmy D. Lindsey)

Implementing the Computer Concept

Jeffrey W. Hummel
Timonium, Maryland
Philip Archer
Nassau Board of Cooperative
Educational Services, New York ■

Microprocessor-based technology has the potential to assist in the management of special education information via information management systems (IMS), and more efficient information management can result in indirect benefits to the teaching-learning process. The applications of instructional computing (IC) and adaptive access/ augmentative communication (AAAC) can directly enhance education and services for exceptional individuals. After providing a brief history of the use of computers in special education, this chapter will review the decisions that need to be made in the process of planning to implement IC in special education. Specific attention will be given to membership on the planning committee, a plan to implement a pilot program of IC in special education, and a plan to revise and expand the pilot program. Information to aid the design of an IMS and a perspective on future applications is also provided. AAAC has been covered in other chapters. Specific reference to brands of hardware will be made only when such reference is required to make a point.

COMPUTERS AND SPECIAL EDUCATION

Prior to 1986

Cartwright and Hall (1974) reviewed the uses of mainframe computers in special education up through 1973 and reported that computers were used for direct instruction and assessment with students classified as emotionally disturbed, mentally retarded, hearing impaired, and visually impaired. They also reported that computers were used for teacher-training simulations and for data base management in the development and evaluation of programs. Other discussions (e.g., Magison, 1978; Overhue, 1977) have focused on the potential of computer-assisted instruction as a means of delivering individualized instruction. In the late 1970s and early 1980s, rationales (Goldenberg, 1979; Joiner, Vensel, Ross, & Silverstein, 1982; Taber, 1983) for the more extensive use of personal computers in special education were appearing more frequently. While there was an increased appreciation of applications beyond computer-assisted instruction (CAI), well-planned efforts to implement computers in special education were rare.

These increasingly prevalent rationales were based largely upon the potential of the microcomputer. In 1982 Joiner et al. provided an insightful discussion of the perceived benefits of the microcomputer compared to those of time-sharing mainframe systems. Their list of apparent benefits included (a) lower initial cost, (b) greater ease of installation and maintenance, (c) increased accessibility and local user control, (d) less disruption associated with downtime, and (e) no need for a cadre of experts. The increased interest in personal computers in the early 1980s culminated in the oversubscribed proceedings (Behrmann & Lahm, 1983) of the 1983 Council for Exceptional Children Hartford Conference.

The related factors of increased accessibility, particularly for teachers, and control over uses and specific software programs may have been central to the greater interest in microcomputers over mainframe-based systems. Educators could play with the microcomputer on their own time and had the option of seeking out software related to their own interests or the perceived needs of their students. Early active users brought the school's (probably underused) personal computers home or purchased their own. These teachers developed a sense of ownership and personal control over the computer as a tool to aid them with their responsibilities.

At the same time that a limited set of special education teachers explored the instructional applications of microcomputers and became disenchanted with the mainframe-based approach to CAI, mainframe systems were being used more for administrative applications, such as scheduling and attendance. There was a tendency to use microcomputers for instructional applications and mainframes for administrative applications. While it appears that computer applications were being developed on two different tracks, the factors that influenced implementation of computer applications in services and education for exceptional individuals have not been identified. Semmel Gerber, Semmel, Cosden, and Goldman (1984) have provided a conceptual

model for the analysis of factors that may influence the implementation of IC in special education programs. This model describes proximal and distal factors. Proximal factors are those that are close to the individual student, such as factors in the classroom. Distal factors are those that are relatively distant, such as school district policy. Federal and state legislative actions would be even more distal. Two studies (Hanley, 1983; Sheingold, Kane & Endreweit, 1983) and work by Semmel and his colleagues suggest that school district decision-making style may be an important factor for the implementation of IC.

Semmel and his colleagues found that although about half of the responding special education programs did *not* own any personal computers, in many of these programs the exceptional students had some access to microcomputers not provided by special education budgets. Based upon the low numbers of computers, they concluded that in 1984 the implementation of microcomputers was at a preliminary stage. In addition, there was generally a lack of budget lines and microcomputer-related organizational structures for hardware and software acquisition and for teacher training. One-third of the administrators reported that no training in microcomputers had been available in their districts in the year 1983–84.

Semmel and his colleagues also attempted to identify the educational personnel who were participating in decisions concerning the special education acquisition of microcomputers. In three-fourths of the responding 33 districts, the special education administrator participated. In about half, teachers and building administrators participated, as did a district computer committee. Only one of the districts reported that the special education program had a written policy on the acquisition of microcomputers. Districts also reported that similar personnel were involved in decisions regarding the allocation of microcomputers and in the purchase of software.

1986 to the Present

Special education administrators, teachers, and other personnel continue to grapple with

Students enjoy implementing the computer concept. *(Photograph by Jimmy D. Lindsey)*

the general technology concepts described above (e.g., functional local systems, hardware and software acquisition, accessibility, etc.), but in recent years they have also focused on a better understanding of how computer-related technology can be employed to deliver instruction and to improve exceptional individuals' quality of life in new, powerful, and effective ways. Because the previous chapters and the chapters to follow provide excellent reviews of extant literature from 1986 to the present, as well as the authors' professional experiences with special education technology integration during this time period, an in-depth summary of recent findings will not be given. However, a number of pertinent statements should be made about current computer and special education implementation events:

1. The number of special education programs using computers for IC, IMS, and AAAC

has increased significantly in the last few years. As was reported in Chapter 7, the number of teachers using computers has doubled between 1984–85 and 1988–89. Today very few school districts, if any, can be found that do not use technology with exceptional individuals for management or instructional purposes.

2. In addition to management applications, the predominant use of hardware and software is for instructional drill-and-practice. Special educators and other professionals are using state-of-the-art technology applications (e.g., laptop computers, interactive videodisc systems, AAAC, multimedia, etc.), but for the most part, this technology is not being used with or by the vast majority of individuals with disabilities, gifts, and talents.

3. Contemporary emphasis is moving toward integrating technology into all curriculum areas, homes, and communities. This is an exciting movement with respect to special education, because we are now trying to match the capabilities of technology with exceptional individuals' characteristics and curriculum demands. It is also exciting because exceptional individuals are using technology to control their lives at home or work (e.g., home control systems and employment-related adaptive devices), and communities are investing in technology (e.g., ramps, transportation vehicles with lifts, etc.) to promote access and usability.

4. Special educators and other professionals are using technology for personal productivity as well as instructional productivity. They are finding that their efficiency with management and teaching responsibilities increases as they use computer hardware and software (Beaver, 1992).

5. Although the research published since 1986 continues to be restricted and studies reported have methodological limitations, there is a developing body of literature empirically validating the benefits of using technology with and by exceptional individuals. As noted throughout this text, technology has been used in and out of the

instructional setting to develop or facilitate nonacademic abilities (e.g., sensory-perceptual, cognition, social-emotional, psychomotor, etc.) and academic knowledge abilities (e.g., reading, mathematics, written language, content areas, etc.). It has also been demonstrated to be effective for providing exceptional individuals with access to their environment and for promoting quality of life.

6. Recent concerns have also focused on developing appropriate models for integrating technology into instructional settings (D'Ignazio, 1992; Ray, 1992). This section ends with a discussion of these efforts.

Finally, Bialo and Sivin's (1990) research has also provided some guidance regarding the potential of computers in special education. They reviewed more than 60 published and unpublished sources for the period of 1986 to 1990 and noted that under the right circumstances, using technology to support learning can make positive differences. These circumstances are associated with effective instruction and include curriculum demands, the characteristics of the student population, the teacher's role, the student grouping patterns, the design of the software, and the access to technology. The right circumstances are related to what we know about effective instruction. When these circumstances are optimized, students are motivated, may develop more positive attitudes toward school, and do show important learning gains.

Technology Integration Models

There is an expanding set of concepts and ideas upon which successful computer implementation efforts can be built. The U.S. Department of Education's Office of Special Education Programs has funded three contracts with the objective of developing models for technology integration. Researchers at Johns Hopkins University, the Education Development Center/Technical Education Research Centers (EDC/TERC), and Macro Systems are developing these models.

With respect to the Johns Hopkins initiative, Phase I (1986–1989) involved three sets of researchers conducting research and reviewing the research of others with the goal of developing models for technology integration with associated strategies and support materials (Technology Integration Project, 1989). One outcome of Phase I was defining the goal of technology integration as making technology an integral aspect of instruction with emphasis on the role of the teacher's need for support and training. Teachers should be active decision makers who plan the use of technology and its linkage to nontechnology instruction. Interestingly, the findings of Casden and Abernathy's (1990) recent study also focused on special education technology integration and found that the teacher's role is prominent and suggested that clarification of this role will facilitate the implementation of technology.

Johns Hopkins' TIE model places a high priority on the correspondence of the curriculum of the school, of the curriculum needs of the learner, and of the curriculum content of the software (Hummell, Steeves, McPherson, & Panyan, 1990). Curriculum issues are basic to planning technology implementation, and planning must reflect an appreciation of the following three points. First, technology is a tool that can support the teaching of existing, formal curriculum objectives. Second, when technology and its use become the object of study for students, the formal curriculum should be changed to incorporate the intended learning objectives. Finally, this kind of curriculum incorporation, (i.e., the addition of some technology-related curriculum objectives) should be distinguished from linking the expanded use of technology with major curriculum revision. In Phase II (1989–1991) of the Johns Hopkins' initiative, the technology integration model, strategies, and support materials developed in Phase I are being field-tested.

The research efforts of the Merrimack Education Center (1990) and other agencies are providing technology integration models that also emphasize curriculum revisions. For example, EDC/TERC's "Make It Happen!" is the middle school version of the U.S. Department of Education's model on teachers developing new approaches to teaching. Like the

TIE model, the EDC/TERC model supports the importance of the teacher's role in the successful implementation of technology. However, the Merrimack Education Center's orientation and the EDC/TERC's "Make It Happen!" orientation, in comparison to Johns Hopkins' TIE model, highlight the linking of curriculum revision to technology and the emphasis on higher-order thinking skills. The "Make It Happen!" model also recommends school-wide change and describes requirements for teachers (e.g., a better understanding of students' needs, the benefits of technology, the curriculum, hardware and software, and assessment and instructional strategies). This model asserts that to be effective, teachers must be given the time to reflect and collaborate with their colleagues so that they can critically evaluate their practices and make appropriate adjustments in their instruction. In fact, both orientations emphasize the importance of ongoing school-based support and effective collaboration and communication structures.

The Macro System's high school version of the U.S. Department of Education's technology implementation models addresses the school district's development of a guiding philosophy and associated goals that reflect flexibility and sensitivity to local conditions. Good communication among involved parties who clearly understand the nature of their school's administrative organization structures is primary in the Macro System's orientation. These structures include (a) shared decision-making among teachers and administrators and effective communication management systems within buildings and across administrative levels; (b) collaborative decision-making between regular and special educators; and (c) improved collaboration between local education agencies and institutions of higher education for the development of preservice education.

While the information base for technology implementation is expanding, the challenge is still prodigious. Researchers at the Appalachia Educational Laboratory (1990) surveyed a broad set of teachers to identify the most serious impediments to the implementation of computers in the classroom. The impediments identified were (a) the limited number of computers for teacher and student use; (b) lack of planning to integrate computers into school and classroom activities; (c) lack of access to information about software resources and software reviews; (d) lack of access to quality software; (e) lack of access to software simulations, tutorials, and programs that address problem-solving and other higher-level thinking skills; and (f) lack of access to training in the operation and instructional uses of computers.

Two other problems hindering technology integration are the lack of access to dynamic technology developments and the capital investment that is required. In comparison to other arenas, education suffers from a cultural lag in access to technology. For example, the Apple IIe computer with its 8-bit processor is the dominant technology in the schools but this technology is deemed obsolete in other arenas. Also, the requisite capital investment for hardware and software and teacher training is substantial. Although school districts tend to have limited revenue sources, they must make some investment in the affordable technology of today (e.g., personal computers) while developing a vision of future technology developments (e.g., local area networks).

The rationale for networking computers is based upon shared resources and communication between computers. The network concept is simple (see Chapter 2) and can be local or remote. Local area networks, or LANs, typically involve a wire that connects all the computers in a room or a building. Remote networks connect computers at distant locations and might involve satellites. Several network reality questions must be considered for the early 1990s: Should school districts or a school building use networks at all? Can the existing computers be used in a LAN? How complicated is the required hard-wiring? Will the existing software run on a LAN and are network licenses available? Is there enough funding for establishing a LAN and providing teacher training on its use? Such questions about LANs must be addressed in local and regional contexts.

Finally, Gillman's (1989) analysis has provided insight into our failure to make appropriate use of much of the available technology in our schools. He attributed this failure to education's own slow response to change and to the specific structural deficiencies within the educational system. Given the social and competence requirements of today's changing world, Gillman concluded that this failure is untenable. He argued that we must develop policies and adopt structures for coping with change at all levels. He also argued that it is essential for professionals at all levels to plot a future course that accommodates change where risk is balanced by gain and where the pervasiveness of technology is acknowledged. Also, a recent report from the International Society for Technology in Education (1990), *Vision: TEST (Technology Enriched Schools of Tomorrow)*, offered recommendations that are compatible with Gillman's analysis but that made even more explicit demands on President Bush in particular and society in general. As a result of reviews of existing research, advice from over 150 educators, and visits to schools that use technology effectively, the International Society for Computers in Education generated the following recommendations: (a) President George Bush should establish a National Technology Trust Fund designed to ensure that no student is denied access to the use of computers; (b) every teacher's home and classroom should have a computer and every classroom should have a telephone and a modem; (c) a national educational computer-communications network should be established; (d) education should be restructured via the application of technology; and (e) technology must be integrated into the curriculum.

Many special education programs may still be in the early stages of computer use and can benefit from thoughtful planning for the implementation of IC. A number of key decisions must be made as districts consider the increased use of computers in their instructional programs. These decisions are discussed in the next section.

PERTINENT COMPUTER IMPLEMENTATION DECISIONS

The most important decision centers on the basic motivation for increasing the use of computers. The basic reason should be to enhance educational programs and not to keep up appearances or appease parents.

Public Law 94-142

A study conducted by Archer and Shaw (1986) provided direction regarding the implementation of IC in special education. This national survey of expert opinion regarding strategies for implementing personal computers will be referred to throughout this chapter. University, school district, and research and development experts on technology and special education were the respondents in this survey. A 5-point rating scale was used to determine perceived importance of implementation practices in areas of (a) administrative policy and budgetary consideration, (b) administrative management, (c) classroom management, (d) hardware and software, (e) instructional issues, (f) staff development, and (g) affiliations.

Eighty-seven percent of the responding experts indicated that the development of long-range and short-range goals was most important for effective computer implementation. Districtwide needs assessment was also a priority for 87% of the respondents. Any needs assessment of special education programs is likely to reveal that the requirements of Public Law 94-142 provide a rationale for using computers.

The requirements of Public Law 94-142 are to (a) prepare an individual education plan for all classified students; (b) provide individualized instruction; (c) monitor a given student's progress in relation to that plan; (d) maintain and deliver the various requisite reports to state education agency authorities; and (e) inform and involve parents in accordance with due process procedures. These can be viewed as sufficient rationale for special educators to explore the uses of computers. The various uses of computers are relevant to these requirements and to the more long-standing goals of special education. The exceptional student uses are IC and adaptive access/augmentative communication, or AAAC. The subdivisions of IC—computer-assisted instruction, computer-managed instruction,

A computer work center for teachers and exceptional students helps keep things organized.
(*Photograph by Philip Archer*)

computer-augmented learning, computer literacy, and tool applications (predominately word processing and data base management)—and AAAC are discussed in other chapters in this book. Information management systems, or IMSs, are discussed in this chapter under Designing an Information Management System. A more focused discussion of computer-assisted individual education plans, which is related to IMS, is provided in a different chapter in this book. Teaching students about IMS would come under tool applications, but the discussion of IMS in this chapter is focused on adults and IMS.

The First Implementation Steps

The basic steps in implementing the computer concept are to determine if there are any locally relevant mandated or restrictive policies regarding computer applications and conduct a needs assessment. Next, one must understand that the three basic computer applications (i.e., IC, AAAC, and IMS) are different in their purposes and how they affect and are affected by the five areas identified by Naron and Estes (1985). These areas include (a) the instructional program including curriculum and teacher competencies and instruc-

tional staffing; (b) administrative staffing; (c) communications in and out of school; (d) physical facilities; and (e) financial allocations. This chapter and most current efforts to implement computer applications for the handicapped are focused on IC and IMS. However, the requirements to implement AAAC may change in the near future. Already the integration of adaptive devices in educational programs has become an issue in due process hearings.

The first major decision is whether computers are needed. A second major decision, assuming that the first is yes, is to find out if any policy regarding the use of computers exists within the school, the school district, the state, or nationally. In the state of New York, all students must be computer literate under the Commissioner's Regulations in order to receive a high school diploma. Existing guidelines should be examined to determine what direction the program must take.

There are differences in general management philosophies and decision-making styles in different districts. However, efforts to implement IC are more likely to be successful if respected and interested teachers with leadership ability are engaged in the process. Efforts to implement IC will probably fail if administrators and teachers become adversaries instead of co-implementors. The computer implementation plan to be outlined in this chapter is relatively simple and straightforward. However, it requires the cooperation of all personnel in the school district. For example, it may be very difficult for teachers with full work loads to take on the responsibilities for planning IC implementation. An old notion of differential staffing may be useful here. Perhaps teachers who are very active in the planning process could be relieved of recess or study hall supervision or bus duty. At minimum they should be given some release time, and their contribution should be acknowledged.

Computer Program Coordinator

Given the importance of leadership, the careful selection of someone to monitor progress and ultimately coordinate the IC in the district is a priority. While different districts will approach this differently, it is imperative that the person selected to coordinate the implementation be knowledgeable in technology and instruction. It should be noted that 78% of the respondents in the Archer and Shaw study agreed that it was important to have a district-wide computer coordinator. This does not mean that this has to be a new position or that using computers educationally would be the person's only responsibility. The authors of this chapter have seen this responsibility successfully incorporated into a curriculum coordinator's role. What it does mean is that there must be an individual within the school district recognized by administrators, teachers, and staff as being responsible for the program. While it would certainly be a plus if the district coordinator were experienced in working with exceptional student populations, it is not necessary. Also, and as a general rule, the higher this person is placed within the hierarchy of the school district, the more positive the prognosis for having a program brought to fruition. However, it is far more important to have someone who is committed to the concept and willing to work at the upcoming tasks.

Teacher and Staff Involvement and Needs Assessment

The next major decision is to set up a planning committee. Many of the activities and decisions should be initiated as they become perceived as important within individual school districts. This is to say, in the same way students must be treated as individuals, school districts must design and schedule activities to meet their needs.

There will be different assets and problems with existing staffing patterns. There will be different demands from parents and different financial resources. With the establishment of a planning committee and the emergence of a leader or coordinator, a needs assessment should be initiated. Whether this is done under a formal structure involving surveys, interviews, and observations or in an informal setting, it is important to analyze needs. However, a formal needs assessment is likely to provide more useful direction. Eighty-seven percent of the respondents surveyed by Archer and Shaw felt that a needs assessment is a most important aspect in computer implementation.

The logical step following the needs assessment is to develop long- and short-range goals. These goals become the roadmap for the program. Most of Archer and Shaw's respondents (87%) agreed on the importance of this step. In addition, the adoption of these goals by the board of education or governing body of the school will also give strength to the planning efforts. While goals may be changed in future years, commitment to their basic intent should not waver.

Should mainframes or personal computers be used exclusively or in combination? While the push today is for personal computers, some superior instructional software may only be available through a minicomputer or mainframe. However, for most districts, microcomputers will be the logical and appropriate choice. Hardware and software issues must be addressed, library materials ordered, budgets established, interest groups kept abreast of progress, instructional strategies investigated, equity issues satisfied, professional in-service training implemented, class- and therapy room configuration explored, rules of conduct and safety developed, and insurance and maintenance options looked into, along with decisions concerning the proverbial kitchen sink. In other words, a large number of decisions need to be made.

One of the most important issues is deciding what decisions need to be made. While this may seem a little silly on the surface, it is really quite important. Many school districts implement a program by purchasing some computers and some software and putting them in a classroom. It should be understood that just buying equipment and materials is not implementing an IC program. Furthermore, district individuals responsible for implementing the computer concept should not be intimidated by the number and apparent complexities of decisions they need to make. They should keep in mind that they need not make every decision before they start, that they cannot know all of the significant factors, and that the results of incorrect decisions can provide insights into successful solutions.

THE PLANNING COMMITTEE

This section will discuss the major reasons for forming a planning committee, the membership of this committee, and the activities this committee should be undertaking. As would be expected, the first step is to decide if there can be a planning committee. If a school district has been using computers for a few years, it may be politically astute to call this committee the advisory committee or the computer policy advisory committee. Whatever its name, it is important to have a committee of individuals planning or monitoring the district's computer program.

Membership

The planning committee provides a forum for discussing the general and specific computer implementation issues. It increases the number of people involved in the decision-making process, strengthens the legitimacy of computers in the schools by showing that the school district is committed to the effective use of computers, provides a formal structure, implies continuity, and is expected to bring computers to the schools. If these were the only functions of the planning committee, it would be worthwhile to have it.

Committee membership is a central issue. It is advisable to keep the committee to a manageable number and to have representatives from the various groups that will be involved. It is recommended that the committee number between 5 and 10. If the school district has a coordinator of computers, that person should definitely be on the committee and should probably be its chairperson. Groups that should have representation are the administration, teachers, and staff. Other groups desirable to have represented on the planning committee include the district's committee on

the handicapped, the school board, parents, students, and a representative of the local community. A proposed planning committee membership list could include these members:

1. Three teachers (elementary, secondary, and special education)
2. One administrator (central office or school)
3. One staff member (central office or school)
4. One person from the committee on the handicapped
5. One student (nonexceptional or exceptional)
6. One parent
7. One school board member

TOTAL: Nine members

The above composition would provide both wide representation and a manageable size.

The planning committee has districtwide responsibilities and does not focus exclusively on the needs of exceptional students. A subcommittee to focus on the needs of exceptional students may eventually be needed.

Evaluate the effectiveness of other committees. Find a committee within the school district that is successful. Examine the membership and the strategies of this committee, and attempt to emulate them for the computer planning committee. While it may be the individuals on this other committee that have brought it success, it may also be the types of people involved, and this can be copied.

Committee Activities

After selecting a chairperson, carefully analyze the needs assessment. If the needs assessment appears to be leading in a direction contrary to the philosophy of the planning committee, decide how to direct implementation. For instance, if the teachers want to use computers simply for drill-and-practice, show other possible strategies. The needs assessment alone may not lead to an educationally sound plan. The planning committee needs to impose expertise on the results of the needs assessment. A study by Archer (1985) found no significant differences on a number of cognitive and affective variables between two strategies of computer use and a noncomputer instructional strategy with young handicapped children; data do not exist to support a single strategy of computer use.

Hardware and Software

Decisions on educational strategies are followed by decisions on software and then by hardware selection. While it is important that hardware selection not determine software or educational strategies, certain hardware considerations should be considered. The equipment must be durable, repairable, and standardized.

Funding

While the planning committee does not have the power to commit funding for this project, the committee does have the power and the responsibility to push for a commitment for funding. A long-term funding commitment is necessary if computers are to be integrated into the schools successfully. A 5-year plan detailing the money that will be needed for each year should be developed. All expenses should be included in this budget plan. Expenses involve more than simply the purchasing of equipment—money for teacher training should be included as well as for purchases of software, books, and magazines; travel to visit other programs; substitute teachers if the involved regular teachers will miss school days; additional personnel that may be required; equipment repairs; and planning team expenses. There will undoubtedly be other unanticipated expenses.

The proposed budgetary plan should be tied directly to a pilot project. Both the budgetary plan and the pilot project should be presented to the school administration and the board of education for approval. While a board of education probably cannot make a legal commitment for funding 5 years down the road, it can make a philosophical commitment that will make it more difficult for future boards of education to change the monetary commitment.

Staff Development

Probably no area is more important to the success of any new educational program than that of teacher training. This is particularly true of IC. Of the 68 separate items that the respondents were asked to rate in the Archer and Shaw study, only 2 were rated as being most important for effective computer implementation by 100% of the experts, and both of these involved staff development. The first item concerned the need for workshops or clinics for teachers, and the second was the need for budgetary allocations for these programs. Moreover, 96% of the respondents felt it was most important for the teacher workshops to take place within the local school district.

The schedule of in-service workshops needs to be coordinated with the implementation schedule. While an overview in-service course may be an effective beginning step for a large number of teachers, the specific computer content workshop will not be effective until the teachers have access to computers and begin to use them with their students. In most districts this will require an ongoing in-service program during the school year along with workshops geared to different levels of teacher expertise.

Pilot Project and Evaluation

The program needs to be evaluated if it is to have credibility. More important, evaluation should be used to improve the program while it is being implemented. This latter type of evaluation—formative evaluation—provides feedback from observation of student behavior, teacher reports, evaluation of hardware and software, and evaluation of physical settings and resources to enhance the ongoing development of the IC program. This information, or feedback, is given directly to the person responsible for the computer program. While this procedure need not be overly formalized, it should also not be haphazard. The objective is to improve programming, not judge district personnel.

A formative evaluation looks at the process of implementation; a summative evaluation is concerned with the end results. While both types of evaluation are valuable, 95% of the respondents to Archer and Shaw's questionnaire study viewed a formative evaluation as being most important for effective implementation, compared to 61% for a summative evaluation and 78% for a combination formative and summative evaluation. The planning committee should either be involved in or have total responsibility for a formative evaluation. Through this involvement, the committee can systematically gather information at all stages of the implementation process, analyze aspects of the program that are weak, and design strategies to strengthen the weak areas. It is imperative that the planning committee be aware of problems that certainly will occur during the IC implementation process.

IMPLEMENTING A PILOT PROGRAM

The major reason to have a pilot project is to develop a successful model that can be followed throughout the school district. A successful program will help instill confidence in other teachers that computers can be integrated into the program for exceptional students.

Pilot Project Considerations

A pilot program allows a district to look closely at a small number of IC variables and settings and immediately react to developing problems. It allows for dissemination of information to prepare the school and community for what is to come. Also, it gives the project its best chance for success. Using a pilot project to introduce exceptional individuals to computers has definite advantages.

A pilot project will implement computers as an instructional strategy slowly. Too often a new program is started throughout a school district. While this may work for the introduction of a new textbook, it will probably be disastrous for introducing computers. There are too many complexities involved to expect

success for all teachers. There are too many things for the planning committee to keep track of. Furthermore, if teachers become disenchanted, it can be disastrous for the program. Not only is it more difficult to get teachers to reattempt to use computers in instruction if they were unsuccessful in a previous attempt, but any such negative attitudes can be contagious.

Computers have the potential of individualizing instruction. Teachers need to know that computers are an instructional tool that should be integrated into the total educational program, that it is not likely that computers will replace teachers. The instructional use of computers should be designed by special educators, not computer specialists. Too often special educators lose control of their programs by allowing too much instructional decision making to be made by the computer specialist. Computer specialists have an important role to play, but this role should be in an advisory capacity, not the leadership role.

Five-Year Pilot Project

An outline of a 5-year strategy for implementing computers into instructional settings is depicted in Figure 11.1. By the end of 5 years, over 100 teachers would be using computers in instruction, any number of whom could be teachers of handicapped and gifted/talented populations. If the plan is extended for 2 more years, almost 1,000 teachers could be involved. The basic strategy is teachers helping other teachers.

Pilot Project Year 1

1. Establish planning committee.
2. Conduct needs assessment.
3. Develop long- and short-range goals.
4. Select four teachers for pilot project.

It is important to select good teachers who are respected by their peers. These teachers should want to be in the pilot program and have some knowledge of using computers in instruction. At least two of the teachers should

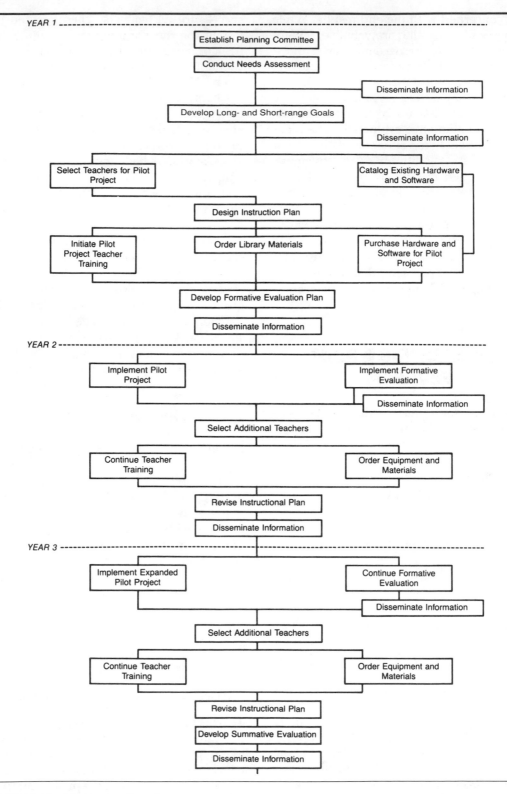

FIGURE 11.1 Pilot project flowchart

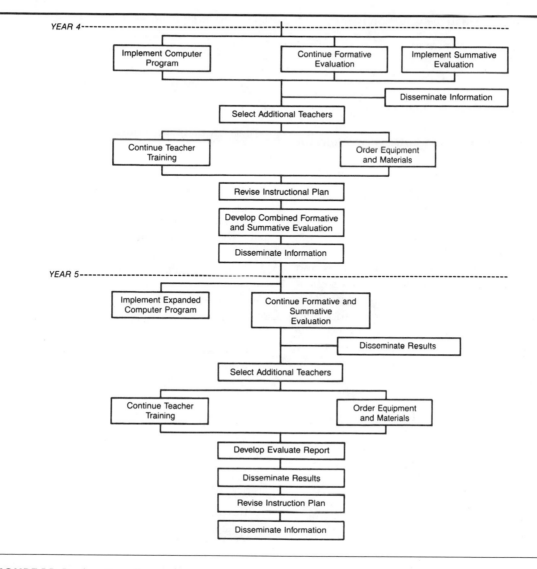

FIGURE 11.1 *(continued)*

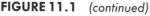

be special educators. Good teachers will be the core of the district's IC program.

5. Purchase hardware and software for four sites.

6. Develop and institute initial teacher training.

This initial training, directed at the four teachers selected, should be broad and include visits to other school districts using computers in instruction as well as more traditional formal courses. The teachers should be allowed to take the computers home for personal training.

7. Design instructional plan. The four teachers should be involved in this development.

8. Order library materials (books, magazines, etc.).

9. Catalog existing computer hardware and software. All new materials should be added to this inventory.

10. Develop formative evaluation plan.

11. Disseminate information.

All segments of the school community should be kept informed. In addition to a formal report to the superintendent and board of education, presentations should be made to interested groups and articles written for newsletters and local newspapers. It is especially important to keep teachers informed.

Pilot Project Year 2

1. Implement pilot project.

The pilot project will have four sites and four teachers. Set up the sites so that teachers are paired together and can act as teams. This will allow the teachers to interact and help each other. Schedule the same planning time for each team to facilitate communications.

2. Select new teachers for next year.

Pick eight teachers for involvement the following year. Use the same criteria as in Year 1. Set up teams that each have two new teachers and one of the original teachers in the pilot project.

3. Purchase hardware and software for next year's sites.

4. Continue in-service teacher training.

The training for this year should be on two levels: a more advanced level for the four original teachers and a beginning level for the eight new teachers. The four experienced teachers should be involved in the training of the new teachers. Part of the training for next year's teachers should include observations of the pilot project sites.

5. Implement formative evaluation.

Systematic evaluative information should be gathered, analyzed, and returned to both the planning committee and the teachers with the purpose of improving the program. Prob-

lems should be identified and strategies to resolve them implemented.

6. Order new library materials. This activity will be continued for all future years.

7. Revise instructional plan.

8. Disseminate information.

Pilot Project Year 3

1. Implement expanded pilot project.

This year there will be 12 sites in the district, the 4 original ones and the 8 new ones.

2. Select new teachers for next year.

Select 24 teachers for next year. Again, pair 2 new teachers with 1 experienced teacher.

3. Purchase hardware and software for next year's sites.

4. Continue teacher training.

A three-level in-service training system should be developed based on the experience and training of the teachers.

5. Continue formative evaluation.

6. Revise instructional plan.

7. Develop summative evaluation.

It is now time to plan to evaluate the results formally. This will be conducted the following year. Next year there will be 36 teachers involved, 12 of whom will be experienced.

8. Disseminate information.

Pilot Project Year 4

1. Implement expanded computer program.

This year there will be 36 sites with 12 experienced teachers and 24 new ones. It may now be time, depending on the size of the district, to stop referring to the sites as a pilot program and begin to call them something else (e.g., District IC Program).

2. Select new teachers for next year.

Select 72 new teachers for next year and place 2 with each experienced teacher.

3. Purchase hardware and software for next year's sites.

4. Continue teacher training.

A three-level sequence of training is probably sufficient. Much of the beginning-level training can be conducted by the more experienced teachers.

5. Continue formative evaluation.

6. Perform summative evaluation.

7. Revise instructional plan.

8. Develop combined formative and summative evaluation.

In the fifth year, a formal report should be developed combining the formative evaluations of the past 4 years and the summative evaluations of Years 4 and 5.

9. Disseminate information.

Pilot Project Year 5

1. Implement expanded computer program.

This year there will be 108 sites, 36 with experienced teachers and 72 with new teachers.

2. Select new teachers for next year.

Next year 144 teachers will be trained and teamed with experienced teachers.

3. Purchase hardware and software for next year's sites.

4. Continue teacher training.

5. Continue formative evaluation.

6. Perform summative evaluation.

7. Develop formative and summative evaluation report.

8. Revise instructional plan.

9. Disseminate results.

Revising and Expanding the Pilot Project

If the proposed 5-year schedule is followed, the pilot project is both revised and expanded automatically. However, there are three essential components for the success of this plan. First, teacher involvement is paramount. Experienced teachers must be willing to work with inexperienced ones. Trust must be developed between both groups, since cooperation is essential. The planning committee should work to achieve an atmosphere conducive to cooperative efforts. The second component is the feedback loop for revising the program. Many changes will be made throughout the implementation phase. It is necessary to have valid information if these changes are to be educationally sound. Third, information must be continually fed to the school community. As can be seen in this 5-year plan, funding requirements for hardware and software increase dramatically in Years 4 and 5 and in ensuing years. The best way to ensure the continuation of funding is to have knowledgeable people supporting the program. For this to happen, information needs to be disseminated.

One final word of advice is to have fun. Administrators, teachers, therapists, staff, and especially students should enjoy using computers. Granted not everyone will enjoy using computers, but most people will if given the appropriate background.

DESIGNING A SYSTEM

We are all familiar with the need to keep records, prepare reports, communicate with our co-workers and students' parents, and comply with any other related regulations. Computers and computer software can make the storage, manipulation, and transmission of this information simple. When designing an information management system (IMS),

Computer systems are being implemented in school classrooms, libraries, laboratories, and other environments. *(Photograph courtesy of Apple Computers, Inc.)*

one must appraise factors beyond the instructional program. Many professionals may not be as familiar with regional and state-level administrative arrangements as they are with instructional programs. They also may not have had the opportunity to learn about some regional or state information management systems that are already in place.

Information Management Systems

While the first factor to consider would be the current and anticipated use of information management in the school district, region, and state, a local education agency's (LEA) options may be constrained or otherwise influenced by information management systems in place or being planned by an agency (e.g., state department) outside the school district. State or regional IMS decisions may ultimately have to be used by the district. Thus it is very important to be aware of any current plans for IMS expansion or development in the state or region.

The results from a study conducted by Galloway (1984) support LEAs' taking a cautious approach to implementing an IMS system. In this 1984 survey to determine state education agencies' (SEA) initiatives to further implement technology in special education, Galloway noted that 12 states have already developed or use a statewide general IMS in special education. For these 12 states, the use and development of a general information system was a very high priority. In 10 states, a related high priority was the use of data exchange networks between LEAs and the SEA. Apparently several states are making IMS decisions that have an impact on LEA options. LEA personnel will want to monitor such SEA activities. Beyond existing SEA electronic communications activities, other factors that LEAs may want to take into consideration as they plan their IMS programs include size and population density of their state, region, and LEA, and the distance between buildings. When buildings are within a few miles of each other and there are unobstructed pathways for cables, such buildings can form local area networks. Wideband networks are required when such criteria cannot be met.

IMS Philosophy

Beyond information management decisions of SEAs, the local school district's philosophy of management may be very important. Becker (1983) stated that the preferred approach to its selection of an IMS would be to begin with the general philosophy of management. Process consultation, the study of organizational variables relevant to management, would provide a framework for exploring the LEA's operational philosophy of management. Exclusive, autocratic decision making and a prevalence of one-way communication offer a contrast to selective democratic decision making and a prevalence of two-way communication patterns. If professionals are selectively involved in decision making with administrators who listen to them, this should be reflected in the information management system. More specific questions to the management philosophy would be "Do teachers or only administrators decide on the objectives of the systems?" and "Will there be a two-way flow of information and teacher access to information analysis?" Naron and Estes (1985) have reported an interesting finding concerning school district management philosophy. They found that school district management philosophy may change and improve with the use of computers to support communication.

Becker (1983) has suggested that the general management philosophy should be viewed in the context of information management resources, including the hardware components, the manual and automated information processing procedures, additional budget or potential of additional budget, the system support functions, and the personnel who design, install, operate, and maintain the information management resources, as well as the user community. System support functions for the operation of the information

management resources include electrical power supply, environment control systems, security against damage and theft, and furniture and workspace.

IMS Accuracy

Accuracy of information is a basic consideration. Error-ridden systems are of no use. IMS errors are often wrongly termed "computer errors," as if only the computer were at fault. Becker (1983) used the term "information integrity," which encompasses all potential sources of error. In his framework, this term covers a broad number of sources of errors or problems including (a) accidental errors and omissions in the preparation of information for computer entry; (b) inadequate or faulty procedures used to manage the information either externally or in the computer; (c) the loss of information through hardware or software failure; (d) the complete loss of information management capability as a result of computer disaster; and (e) the unauthorized access and use of information management resources. To avoid the first two problems, the system must be matched to the needs of all the users, and the users must be well versed in the use of the system, particularly the data preparation and data entry requirements. Efforts to maximize information integrity involve much more than just hardware and software variables.

Information System Users and Information System Tasks

Existing teacher, staff, and administrative computer competencies and plans to enhance such competencies are obviously important information management resources. In a recent project on data base management in special education (see Hummel & Degnan, 1986), some administrators felt that only staff members had to learn about word processing and data base management. The administrators failed to recognize that to maximize benefits from the system, they had to understand what the system could do and how to use it. Staff personnel should not always have to translate administrators' requests into systems-appropriate input and translate systems output into messages administrators can understand. Administrators will benefit from working directly with the systems themselves.

The optimum situation would be for administrators, staff, and at least a subset of teachers and paraprofessionals to have some facility with the system. The fact that the manual collection, management, and entry of information is difficult results in district personnel thinking that using the IMS system is a clerical task. However, understanding the system's data management and data manipulation capabilities will enable administrators and teachers to be more effective users and thus reap greater benefits. At least some of the manual collection and management of information could be done by paraprofessionals. Also, entering data into the system may be best suited for staff members with excellent keyboard skills. However, there is no simple set of user decision rules. While some staff personnel may have relevant training and be able to operate systems better than administrators, other staff members may resist learning to use a simple word processing package. Some teachers may clamor for access while others will say, "That's not my job." Special education teachers, therapists, and supervisors or building principals are not likely to be interested in systems if all they do is enter data someone else wants. They are not likely to continue to be fully cooperative if all they do is respond to frequent requests to enter data that are not meaningful to them. Semmel, Cosden, Semmel, and Keleman (1984) have suggested that differentiated instructional staffing in association with differential computer expertise and responsibility may be the only way to approach this problem.

Opportunity 21 is the Sacramento City (CA) Unified School District's plan for preparing the children of Sacramento for the 21st century. As reported by Gillman (1989), if Opportunity 21 is to be successful, it must have an information management system—an integrated district information system—consisting of two components. The management component would provide management and operation sources to administrators, teachers, and other personnel. The instructional component would provide the link between the classroom and instructional-enhancing resources.

Nunn (1989) has developed an alternate management framework as a result of her systematic interviews with building principals. Nunn identified building principals as key players in technology implementation efforts and identified their information management needs that could be supported by technology (e.g., tasks related to communication, instruction, and management). This finding is consistent with the current increased priority that has been given to the leadership of principals and building-based management. Nunn's needs assessment resulted in the development of *The Principal's Assistant,* which gives the principal a central role in the process of using technology to support educational decision making. This guide was jointly sponsored by IBM and the Johns Hopkins Technology Project described earlier and provided answers to a series of questions to support principals in their use of technology to facilitate communications, instructional, and management tasks. These question were:

> With what tasks can the principal use the computer?
> What is the computer application solution?
> What are the benefits of that solution?
> What software features are available for that solution?
> What products are currently on the market?

The Principal's Assistant also described a technology tool framework, provided a catalog of MS-DOS tool programs for building administrators, and delineated pertinent computer management resources.

FUTURE

Future technological advances may be much less important than efforts to integrate technology into the lives of the handicapped. Predictions of the future of technology applications for the handicapped and gifted/talented individuals continue to include (a) Apple and IBM's redoubled commitment to meet the needs of the handicapped; (b) the Office of Special Education Programs' announcement of a universal interface (an interface device that crosses all the current operating systems) for the handicapped developed as a result of the success of the White House Commission; and (c) NASA's description of further technology transfer projects such as the Association for Retarded Citizens (ARC) bladder sensor project (Cavalier, 1985). An alternate set of events might result in professionals reacting like Luddites, sabotaging the technology and aggressively resisting its integration into public schools. Heinrich (1985) argues quite persuasively that the most important "educational technology" may take place outside of public schools with teachers losing their instructional decision-making options. However, if we act assertively on our understanding of robotics and adaptive peripherals as normalization devices, recognize that successful transitions to the world of work may require knowledge of utility applications such as word processing and data base management, and document technology-related effectiveness, the future may be very bright.

Because hardware advances are coming so rapidly, any predictions made now may be less useful than an assessment of the existing contexts. One might argue that special educators and therapists should not be overly concerned with predictions regarding the technology 5 years from now, and that they should understand the current realities of technology in education, understand the advanced state of technology integration in other sectors of society, and promote the successful development of technology applications and the continued integration of technology in curriculum areas. The more radical futurist may only alienate those minimally involved, convincing them that it is all passing them by.

The process of creation, storage, delivery, and editing of information is changing and will continue to change. The information society of Neisworth's *Megatrends* is here. The National Information Utilities Corporation and AT&T have joined forces to develop an education information utility. This utility, or a superior version, will be capable of rapid delivery of a comprehensive information service.

In the computer marketplace, inaccurate predictions concerning educational software have sent hardware and software producers to bankruptcy court, or at least out of the educational marketplace. The educational market is different from other markets. Schools simply do not have the capital to secure and turn over technology. While some schools struggle to remove discontinued hardware, upgrade to 16-bit processor microcomputers, or convert to all floppy disk drives, business and industry are exploring the limitations of linked megabyte hard drives and 32-bit processors. The cultural lag in technology is wider and deeper in education than in other sectors of our society.

Various authors (e.g., Brown, 1985; Head, 1985) writing about technology in the business world have indicated that even major corporations demonstrate a lack of appreciation of the potential and complexity of microprocessor-based technology. For example, Brown's analysis is particularly relevant to the above discussion of the design of IMSs. This researcher highlighted the three crucial IMS issues, including (a) the current lack of systematic methods of producing software in relation to business needs, (b) a rapid, explosive change in technology, and (c) the ever-increasing number of different information systems. Head stated that the preferred approach to the development of information management systems is a dynamic process in which the end user contributes over time to the formation of the system. She further argued that a static one-time assessment of end-point user needs generally does not work very well. End-point users require flexible opportunities for real computerized problem solving. This is not always so easy to provide. There needs to be proper balance among predictions of the technology of the year 2000, attention to systems matching needs, and end users' in-service education. Predictions such as those by Cook (1985) on the startling advances in disk storage are worthy of attention, but such predictions should not be a source of distraction to efforts to learn to use the current technology better. If special educators do not learn how to use their 8- and 16-bit machines effectively, they may never see any more advanced technology.

Beyond the recommendation to understand current technology better, we may continue to benefit from Moore, Yin, and Lahm's (1985) approach to understanding the future of technology applications in special education. They described the benefits of a "hybrid" approach to future developments of special education technology applications. In their "demand-pull" approach, the identified needs of the consumer are supposed to pull research and development efforts into the arena to help meet those needs. The Education Technology Center at Harvard (see Jackson, 1985) also advised movement toward demand-pull, with the recommendation that educators identify "targets of difficulty," or points in existing curriculum/instruction that may benefit from a contribution to technology. With a "technology push" orientation, an existing product or service must search for a consumer market, and commercialization and marketability are the goals. Currently marketing strategies are probably more related to software purchasing than to any other factor. With regard to special purpose software and adaptive devices, the needs of the handicapped and gifted/talented represent much too thin a market (if unsubsidized) for the demand-pull approach to work.

With the hybrid approach, special educators and therapists who are already at the interface of technology developments and the needs of the handicapped must search out development and application efforts outside education and human services. They must then develop special education counterpart scenarios that depict a special need/technology match. Feasibility ratings on the requisite technology transfer/adaptation must be made by groups or persons with some combination of expertise in special education and technology research and development. The next step requires a cost/benefit analysis on the economic and human benefits of completing the technology transfer/adaptation.

Moore et al. (1985) also focused on artificial intelligence, robotics, and computer simulation. Their panel reported that computer simulation would be the technology that would reach a large segment of the handicapped first, indicating that it might take as many as

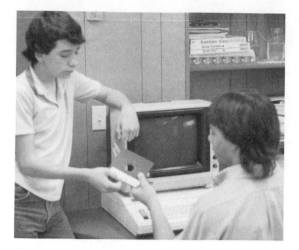

The needs of exceptional students must be considered during the implementation process.
(Photograph courtesy of Education and Technology Resources)

10 to 20 years for about 90% of the handicapped to benefit from this technology.

Also, Moore et al. reported that robotics has clear potential to help the physically challenged but would not result in significant gains for large numbers until the year 2000. There is interesting work being done by a multidisciplinary team at the Rehabilitation Research and Development Center of the Palo Alto VA Medical Center. They are conducting interactive evaluations with physically challenged clients using off-the-shelf hardware and customized software. They are exploring the general feasibility and the ultimate potential marketability of these systems. This project, although now focused on adults, will be examining the benefits for school-age populations.

Finally, Moore, Yin and Lahm (1985) described cost as the most significant barrier to the implementation of robotics and simulation. The opinions of the experts on their panel varied regarding the time necessary for artificial intelligence to benefit large numbers of exceptional persons. Not only was cost seen as a barrier, with some of the special education scenarios estimated to cost as much as $500,000, but training and technical difficulties were also viewed as very serious obstacles. To a large extent, the technologies of robotics and simulation are already being successfully integrated into other sectors of our society (such as manufacturing and military training). The implementation of robotics and simulation are more a matter of technology transfer and cost than a matter of basic development.

SUMMARY

This chapter provided a brief history of the use of computers in special education and reviewed decisions that must be made when implementing an instructional computing program. In the discussion of the implementation of an IC program specific attention was given to forming a planning committee, implementing a 5-year pilot project, and revising and expanding the pilot project. Information relative to the design and implementation of an information management system and the future of computer technology with exceptional individuals was also presented. In closing, and related to the issue of the future of computers in special education, let us not be so distracted by startling advances, or so overwhelmed by the complexities of the array of technologies, that we fail to use the more available and less complex technologies. It is clear that we need larger budgets for the purchase of hardware and software. It is also clear that we need better plans to use the limited access we have to technology effectively. Learning how to integrate technology successfully is just as important as securing it.

REFERENCES

Appalachia Educational Laboratory. (1989). *A model for assessing and meeting needs in instructional computing*. Washington, DC: AEDS/FAEDS Publications.

Archer, P. (1985, June). The impact of microcomputer instruction on handicapped children. *Proceedings of Invitational Research Symposium on Special Education Technology*. Washington, DC: Center for Special Education Technology, Council for Exceptional Children. (ERIC Document Reproduction Service No. EC 180 948)

Archer, P., & Shaw, S. (1986). INTERFACE: *Identification of effective implementation strategies for implementing microcomputer instruction into ongoing instructional services for the handicapped: Report*. (Contract No. G008430074). Washington, DC: U.S. Office of Special Education and Rehabilitation Services.

Beaver, J. F. (1992). Using computer power to improve your teaching. *Computing Teacher, 19*(5), 5–9.

Becker, H. B. (1983). *Information integrity: A structure for its definition and management*. New York: McGraw-Hill.

Behrmann, M. M., & Lahm, L. (Eds.). (1983). *Proceedings of the National Conference on the Use of Microcomputers in Special Education*. Reston, VA: Council for Exceptional Children.

Bialo, E., & Sivin, J. (1990). *Software Publishers Association report on the the effectiveness of microcomputers in schools*. Washington, DC: Software Publishers Association.

Brown, M. (1985). New technology but old methods. *Data processing, 27*(6), 16–18.

Cartwright, G. P., & Hall, K. (1974). A review of computer uses in special education. In L. Mann & D. Sabatino (Eds.), *The second review of special education*. Philadelphia, PA: JSE Press.

Casden, M. A., & Abernathy, T. V. (1990). Microcomputer use in the schools: Teacher roles and instructional options. *RASE, 11*(5), 31–38.

Cavalier, A. (1985, June). A bladder sensor for persons with urinary incontinence. *Proceedings of Invitational Research Symposium on Special Education Technology* (pp. 56–57). Washington, DC: Center for Special Education Technology, Council for Exceptional Children. (ERIC Document Reproduction Service No. EC 180 948)

Cook, D. (1985). Advances in disk storage technology. *Data processing, 27*(1), 29–32.

D'Ignazio, F. D. (1992). Technology vs. restructuring: Beware of the quick fix. *Computing Teacher, 19*(5), 54–55.

Galloway, J. R. (1984). *Plan Tech Conference: A Profile* (Report submitted for RFP 83–080, Office of Special Education and Rehabilitation Services). Washington, DC: National Association of State Directors of Special Education.

Gillman, T. V. (1989). *Change in public education: A technological perspective*. Eugene: University of Oregon. (ERIC Document Reproduction Service No. ED 302 940)

Goldenberg, E. P. (1979). *Special technology for special children: Computers to serve communication and autonomy in the education of handicapped children*. Austin, TX: PRO-ED.

Hanley, T. V. (1983). *Microcomputers in special education: Organizational issues* (Information Product

No. 1). Arlington, VA: SRA Technologies/ Cosmos.

Head, R. V. (1985). Information resource center: A new force in end user computing. *Journal of Systems Management, 36*(2), 24–29.

Heinich, R. (1985). Instructional technology and the structure of education. *ETCG, 33*(1), 9–15.

Hummel, J. W., & Degnan, S. (1986). *Options for information management and IEP development.* Manuscript submitted for publication.

Hummel, J. W., Steeves, K. J., McPherson, S., & Panyan, M. (1990). *Key aspects of The Johns Hopkins University Technology Integration Enhancement Model.* Manuscript submitted for publication.

International Society for Technology in Education. (1990). *Visions: TEST (Technology Enriched Schools of Tomorrow).* Eugene, OR: International Society for Technology in Education.

Jackson, G. (1985, June). Major technology based research issues. *Proceedings of Invitational Research Symposium on Special Education Technology* (pp. 38–40). Washington, DC: Center for Special Education Technology, Council for Exceptional Children. (ERIC Document Reproduction Service No. EC 180 948)

Joiner, L. M., Vensel, G., Ross, J. D., & Silverstein, B. (1982). *Microcomputers in education: Nontechnical guide to instructional and school management applications.* Holmes Beach, FL: Learning Publications.

Magison, E. (1978). Issue overview: Trends in computer assisted instruction. *Educational Technology, 18*(4), 5–8.

Merrimack Education Center. (1984). *Computer applications planning: A guide to planning and implementing a district-wide computer program.* Chelmsford, MA: Merrimack Education Center.

Moore, G. B., Yin, R. K., & Lahm, E. A. (1985). *Robotics, artificial intelligence, and computer simulation: Future applications in special education.* Washington, DC: Cosmos.

Naron, N. K., & Estes, N. (1985, April). *Technology in the schools: Trends and policies.* Paper presented at the annual meeting of the American Educational Research Association, Chicago, IL.

Nunn, J. (1989). *The principal's assistant.* Baltimore, MD: Center for Technology and Human Disabilities.

Overhue, D. (1977). Computer aided assessment and the development of basic skills. *Exceptional Children, 24*(1), 18–35.

Pogrow, S. (1985). The state of the art in educational administration software. *T.H.E. Journal, 13*(4), 78–81.

Ray, D. (1992). Educational technology leadership for the age of restructuring. *Computing Teacher, 19*(6), 8–14.

Semmel, M. I., Cosden, M. A., Semmel, D. S., & Keleman, E. (1984). Training special education personnel for effective use of microcomputer technology: Critical needs and directions. In R. E. Bennett & C. A. Maher (Eds.), *Microcomputers and exceptional children* (pp. 120–147). New York: Haworth Press.

Semmel, M. I., Gerber, M. M., Semmel, D. S., Cosden, M. A., & Goldman, S. R. (1985). *Special education administrator survey of microcomputer acquisition, allocation and access* (Tech. Rep. No. 7, Project TEECh). Santa Barbara: University of California, Santa Barbara.

Sheingold, K., Kane, J. H., & Endreweit, M. E. (1983). Microcomputer use in the schools: Developing a research agenda. *Harvard Educational Review, 53*, 412–432.

Taber, F. M. (1983). *Microcomputers in special education: Selection and decision making process.* Reston, VA: Council for Exceptional Children.

Technology Integration Project, (1989) *Final Report. Phase I.* Baltimore, MD: Center for Technology and Human Disabilities.

Suggested Activities

Paper and Pencil

Go to the library and find an article that describes how a local school district implemented its computer program. Did this system have a program coordinator? Why or why not? Who was this individual and why was this person selected? Did this district use a planning committee? Why or why not? If this district used the pilot project concept, how did their pilot project differ from the one described in this chapter? How did this district deal with the computer programs already in existence?

Observation

Determine if the local school district has a computer program planning or monitoring committee. If it does, ask to attend one of the meetings and volunteer to assist with the minutes.

Practicum

Visit the coordinator of special education in a local school district. Secure permission from this individual to take part in one of the computer evaluation processes taking place. Also determine what plans are being made to evaluate future computer applications and try to interview a special education teacher, staff member, exceptional student, and parent to determine their perceptions of future technology and evaluation procedures.

Resources

Organizations

National Association of State Directors of Special Education (NASDSE). This organization of special education administrators is involved in many special educational activities at the national and state levels, including the information service SpecialNet. Write to NASDSE, 1201 16th Street NW, Washington, DC 20036.

Journals

Exceptional Children. This journal is published nine times a year and focuses on leading issues in special education. Write to the Council for Exceptional Children, 1920 Association Drive, Reston, VA 22091.

Books

Goldenberg, E. P. (1979). *Special technology for special children: Computers to serve communication and autonomy in the education of handicapped children.* Austin, TX: PRO-ED.

Proceedings of Invitational Research Symposium on Special Education Technology. (1985). Washington, DC: Center for Special Education Technology, Council for Exceptional Children.

Administrative Data Management for Special Education

James E. Johnson, Ed.D.
Nazarene College, San Diego, California ■

Despite the availability and affordability of major advances in computer technology, many special education administrators, teachers, and therapists are still wondering if and how computer technology applies to their daily work load. This chapter will show professionals how computer technology can reduce the daily burden of paperwork, report writing, and data recording and retrieval required for exceptional students.

The main focus is on software and hardware considerations related to data management and data management systems. Despite this central focus on technology, the importance of the human element is not overlooked. Procedures, hardware, software, reports, and data management are all important in an advanced technological society (Remington, 1992). But the creative forces of human intervention are what make the machine and its product a worthy and valuable tool in the workplace. Simply put, computers are fast, accurate, and stupid. In comparison, people are relatively slow, often inaccurate, but decisively brilliant. Without the influence of the

human mind, the speed and accuracy of the computer are relatively useless. Coupled together, however, they produce an unlimited potential.

Basic information on data base management will be given and applications organized around four major content areas will be presented: (a) data collection and record keeping; (b) evaluation and diagnostic procedures; (c) individualized education programs (IEPs); and (d) central office and classroom applications.

CURRENT USE OF TECHNOLOGY FOR MANAGEMENT APPLICATIONS

The current development and use of computer technology in education closely parallel developments in business. Teachers, therapists, and administrators, like their private sector counterparts, need to access and retrieve information faster, more efficiently, and more reliably than ever before. Increased demands for greater accountability, projective planning techniques, interrelated budgeting and accounting procedures, and sophisticated communication and information processing strategies provide the obvious and most often indicated reasons for the sudden increase in the use of computers as administrative support tools. The increased use of computers in general and special education (as well as business) is closely linked to two key factors—user-friendly software with direct applications to personal or daily work tasks and the availability of computers for daily use.

Just a few short years ago the daily, personal use of computers for data management and other professional applications was considered by most too novel, too technical, and too expensive to be a potentially viable management resource. Today, computers are a must for those of us who store, retrieve, and organize information on a daily basis. As Kugell, the president of a leading software company, pointed out, "In the years immediately ahead, we'll see a more realistic view of personal computers as vital tools for office work" (Greensberg, 1986, p. 145).

Because mini- and microcomputers currently serve as effective tools for an increasing number of office functions, they will continue to be used for a larger and larger portion of the workday by an ever-increasing segment of office workers, teachers and therapists, and administrators. One specific reason for the increasing use of computers is the ability of beginning and moderate users to obtain easy-to-use (user-friendly) hardware and software for personal use and to use these systems to conduct more sophisticated applications in their daily work. As one noted business executive recently reported, "In the beginning, people were doing relatively trivial things with micros—a simple spreadsheet, some word-processing. But the quality of what users are doing has markedly improved over the last year. In many cases, users are doing very important things and saving big money" (Rubin, 1985, p. 35).

Although it has been 10 years since the advent of the personal computer, overall hardware development has focused primarily on increasing computer processing speed, expanding memory capacity, and developing larger disk storage capacity. As Bricklin, co-author of Visicalc and longtime PC-software visionary, aptly pointed out, "Since the introduction of the IBM PC a decade ago, the only important hardware innovations have been the laser printer and networks—and those really changed software" (Seymour, 1991, p. 89).

For many, computers brought the hope of "paperless offices." Realistically, the increased power of networked mini- and microcomputers allow PC workstations to handle many tasks previously performed by mainframes. The downsizing of the mainframe applications to the PC has created a new revolution of its own. As Sirkin (1991), a data processing consultant, reported:

> A product of the '70s, the PC has sparked a computing revolution of the '90s. . . . Although it does provide a much less expensive environment in which to develop and execute applications, there is another side to downsizing. . . . The migration to new technology requires a migration in responsibility. (p. 65)

Control issues regarding data collection and storage, confidentiality and security, and the increased need for audit/review procedures not only add new responsibilities but equally add the need for more education and training for all system users. "This means user department managers will require a better under-

Local education agencies can use mainframe computers to store and manipulate their records.
(Photograph courtesy of IBM Corporation)

standing of data processing, controls and security" (Sirkin, 1991, p. 65). Although Sirkin's comments were directed to data managers, they are also relevant for school office workers, teachers and therapists, and administrators working with data base systems.

The software explosion has been a significant factor in increasing the number of computer users. New computer users also affect the development of new software modifications and applications. Software initially designed for business and office applications is easily being modified to provide educational applications for teachers and administrators. As Kapor, chairman of Lotus Development Corporation, stated, "As a result of the tremendous progress in personal productivity tools, whole new groups of users are emerging—people with no previous computer experience, or with very specific vertical application needs, who have significant demands that will shape future software development" (Greensberg, 1986, p. 145). Special education professionals who are plunging ahead on the cutting edge are doing so with the advanced technology of faster computers, larger memory storage capabilities, and easier-to-use software for overall data management purposes.

The other factor adding to the increased use of computers in both business and education is availability of the computer for daily use. There is a wide range of differences on the part of educational agencies and businesses concerning their acceptance or willingness to provide computers for their employees. In 1985 extensive interviews were held with corporate managers at several Fortune 500 companies to assess the acceptance and impact of computers in corporate life (Rubin, 1985). Although dealing with companies in the private sector, the results are highly comparable to what might be expected if similar research were undertaken in the educational (public) sector. The results of the Fortune 500 research indicated that three prevailing attitudes exist about the use and importance of personal computers:

1. *Microcomputers in a mainframe world.* Severe restriction of the use of microcomputers by some companies that still regard microcom-

puters as a relatively minor part of computing systems dominated by mainframe and minicomputer terminals.

2. *Quiet revolution.* Requests for microcomputers are granted as they occur, and the companies are gradually coming to consider microcomputers at least as important as mainframes in their futures.

3. *Top-down commitments.* A few companies have made large, centralized commitments to microcomputers and are actively promoting the idea within the organization.

The development of a positive attitude toward using personal computers by any given school system (or corporation) depends largely on the ability of school managers to recognize the data management needs of the school system and appropriately rank the importance of funding requests for computers. Those school systems that begin to realize the information often needed and requested at the site level by an administrator, teacher, or therapist is most likely the same information stored and used by district-level supervisors and department managers have begun to place high priority on purchase requests for microcomputers by teachers and site administrators. As more personal computers are purchased and networking requests also increase, the next issue to appear relates to access to the school system's centralized data, usually stored and managed by a mainframe. The use of mainframes already within school systems, and their networking capabilities with independent or stand-alone microcomputer workstations, presents a very real problem for many school systems. Networking conversion expenses for mainframes becomes a costly factor, especially if mainframe terminals must be upgraded to serve as independent PC workstations or, as previously noted, the district decides to downsize the mainframe applications to PC applications. The advent of more powerful minicomputers (e.g., IBM System/36, IBM System/38, and Hewlett Packard 3000) with networking capabilities is modifying the mainframe concept. Because of the increased memory capabilities and more sophisticated networking capabilities of the minicomputers, it is often very difficult to determine whether a computer is indeed a mainframe or just a very powerful minicomputer. Recent minicomputer surveys have indicated that all of the major vendors have announced products that allow their machines to function as file servers for PC networks (Hindin, 1991). Cost factors, however, still favor the PC-based servers, but like the mainframe, minicomputers allow for multiprocessing and this feature for many large user systems would make the minicomputer worth the extra cost. In the future, other than possible memory differences, the functional differences may not vary for the newer versions of large host computers (mini or mainframe). However, the increased networking capabilities of newer minicomputers, with built-in networking software allowing easier use of personal computers both as terminals and as independent workstations, will make the minicomputer an attractive possibility for many school systems. With this in mind, the purchase of personal computers becomes more reasonable and does not become counterproductive to the overall data processing goals of the school system; personal computers are not in competition with a centralized host or mainframe concept.

School systems and educational leaders must continue to recognize the need and appropriateness of providing computers for teachers and administrators for daily use. They must be joined by others in providing technological assistance to teachers, therapists, and administrators to perform the daily paper-flow and information-processing tasks. Current trends clearly indicate this same continued level of effort on the part of many school systems to provide computers for teachers, therapists, and administrators. A significant factor supporting this effort is the direct assistance from major computer manufacturers: they are providing free hardware and software for special promotional events and are offering professionals financial discounts. Having hardware and software vendors actively seek the educational market has resulted in significant increases in the number of professionals using computers. This is criti-cal if applications for data management and for efficient and meaningful information storage and retrieval are to be available for all staff systemwide.

As software with greater capabilities evolves and continues to become more user-oriented, the need for regular and special professionals and administrators to use microcomputers becomes more apparent and cost-effective. By increasing the use of computers in a coordinated system for data management, there is an increase in efficiency and relief from the paperwork. The keys remain the same: good easy-to-use software, computers readily available to the system users, and capable trained people willing to use the system. The use of microcomputers by special education professionals and staff for data management becomes successful when the system is easy to access and available to a wide variety of people in different locations.

DATA BASE MANAGEMENT

Basic Definitions

The concepts and terms presented here will provide a foundation for understanding basic information and data base management procedures.

A *data base management system* is a program or integrated series of programs that allow a user to manage large quantities of information in a systematic and efficient manner. The information is often organized and managed through the use of technology, such as a computer, and is stored in the system as data. For example, a computerized data base management system for a school could sort and process personnel information (data) and student information (data) to produce class lists for each teacher in the school.

Data are simply usable pieces of information organized in some meaningful way. Data are stored, edited, and retrieved through the use of a data base software program (e.g., dBase IV, described later). For example, the name, address, and telephone number of a student are usable pieces of information and when organized in a data base are called data.

A *data base* is an organized collection of data for a specific purpose. The telephone directory is a very familiar data base. Classroom student lists, attendance records kept in a school office, and an inventory list of equipment in a classroom are also examples of data bases of organized information. One of the main purposes of a data base is the easy retrieval of specific information. To achieve this, information is organized within a data base using files. For example, a school data base might include organized information on professionals, students, and equipment located at a school. The information in the school data base could be separated and organized into several different files depending on how the information is to be used.

Files organize or group information within a data base related to a specific topic. Information is recorded or stored in a file by using a series of records. For example, using the school data base from the previous example, separate files could be made for each of the groups of data (i.e., one file for the teacher information, one file for the student information, and one file for the equipment information).

Records are a collection of data items treated as a unit. For example, the name, address, and telephone number are data items about one student and could make up one student record. The individual data items within a record are each identified separately and are called fields. For example, information collected in a student record might include name, address, home telephone, parent's name, address, home telephone, parent's name, and bus number. A teacher record might include name, teaching assignment, room, and years of experience. An equipment record might include type of equipment, cost, and location.

In summary, data base management systems manage data within a data base through the use of files, records, and fields. A user can easily sort and retrieve information, view data, add or delete data, and have information printed in a report for later use using data base management software. Information is quickly retrieved from a file by designating specific fields and by having the data base management system (program) analyze the information in each of these fields. For example, in a

data base file with student information, one report could be printed listing all the students alphabetically. A second report from the same student data base might list all of the students with special needs in reading, while a third report from the same data base might list the students who ride home from school on the bus.

Another direct application of a data base management system allows important data or information from more than one file to be retrieved and integrated into one single report. A staff member using a school data base program could create a report listing each teacher, the students assigned to each teacher, and the location of portable equipment for each period of the day. Using records from the teacher and student files, individual class lists and student schedules could easily be produced. Teachers and therapists could use the same data base and easily maintain records of student test scores, assignments completed, and future projects. Given adequate memory within the computer and software capable of handling more than one file at a time, data base management applications usually are only limited by the creativity of the user.

General Data Management Applications

Data base management systems enable administrators and teachers to store, analyze, and retrieve large quantities of data in a convenient and timely manner. Through the use of identified variables within the data base, information is easily sorted by specific characteristics which provide the capability of reviewing and organizing the same data in a variety of ways. The ability to design and present the data in different reporting formats is one of the central advantages to data base management systems. Independent data management programs, spreadsheets, and word processing programs offer the capability of general data management applications without the need for extensive technical training, and should be considered in any discussion of data base management applications.

Specialized computer hardware such as braille printers can be used in data collection and data base management. *(Photograph by Jimmy D. Lindsey)*

Independent or *nonindependent* data management programs such as dBase IV, Paradox, or Excel (see Chapter 3) are examples of data base management systems that use nonprogramming languages that are relatively easy to use and understand. With data base programming languages becoming more user-friendly, nonprogrammers (most special educators are nonprogrammers) enjoy the capability of sophisticated data management and detailed report writing without extensive training. One of the distinct advantages of independent data management programs is that they allow the user to utilize most general data management applications found in more technical and complicated data base management systems, but the user does not have to develop an entire program structure or system or learn how to program. Applications such as retrieving specific information about a student or maintaining confidential personnel information, staff lists, inventories of materials, directories of resources, accounting systems, mailing labels, and telephone and address lists are now easy to use. Through menus in the software programs or by use of the general program commands, these types of applications can be set up and implemented quickly and with minimal effort.

Data management applications are also possible through the use of electronic spreadsheets, even though spreadsheet programs were originally developed primarily for num-

bers manipulation for use with financial and budgetary forecasting. Although some spreadsheet programs have data management utilities integrated into them, spreadsheets are primarily used for computational purposes using single applications (e.g., teacher's yearly material money) requiring multiple calculations (e.g., using a formula in the spreadsheet to total all teachers' material money) or for generating alternate "what if" solutions (see Chapter 3). If the need is to count individual items in a report or the number of records in a data base or even to total a column of data in a report created from the data base, a data base management system typically would be more efficient for these types of applications, particularly if there is a need to sort the items (e.g., teacher money) by other characteristics (e.g., number of students in the class). Programs such as Lotus 1-2-3, Excel, Supercalc, and Quatro are examples of electronic spreadsheet programs. All of these spreadsheet programs have data base management capabilities integrated into the spreadsheet program.

Word processing as a computer application is primarily used for quick and efficient text editing purposes. Although some data management capabilities are included in many word processing programs, their speed and efficiency in that type of application rarely can match the capabilities of an independent data base management system. Many of the more frequently used word processing programs, such as Multimate and WordPerfect, do include integrated data management capabilities. Special education teachers, therapists, and administrators who require only minimal data processing, such as developing lists and inventories, and need a strong word processing program may find this application of data base management acceptable for their needs.

Compared to data base management with personal computers as just described, applications through the use of sophisticated computer programming languages such as FORTRAN or COBOL (see Appendix C) or through the use of minicomputer or mainframe languages offer wider application, greater power, and a higher level of user control over the computer in performing specific tasks for data base management. The primary reason for school systems to use this type of application would be their need to design a specific system that required multitasking and numerous applications across several departments (e.g., payroll, personnel, budget, etc.). It goes without saying that this type of system demands trained system programmers and system analysts to maintain and modify the software. Because personal computer data base management programs provide similar management capabilities and applications, most beginning and intermediate users would find the mainframe or minicomputer approach to data base management overwhelming and not worth the training required to learn these complicated systems.

Planning and Designing a Data Management System

General Planning and Designing Considerations

The planning considerations necessary for the development of successful data base management systems is most critical. Preplanning is essential to assure adequate system and program components to accomplish the desired tasks. Too often administrators and teachers wonder what they should buy at the beginning of the planning process. Ongoing planning is also necessary to ensure continued program operation (to minimize downtime), to maintain the existence of reliable and accurate information, and to obtain data for reports easily. Hornfischer (1985) highlighted six criteria to include in any formula to ensure successful computer planning:

1. The process must begin with organizational commitment (e.g., administrator and teacher support) and answer certain questions: (a) what is the goal of the user (e.g., retrieving staff information quickly, managing student information, making lists, tracking student progress)? and (b) where is the system going to be used and implemented (e.g., home, school, classroom, office, library)?

2. The second step is to determine the critical needs and to decide what to do first: (a) what is the user's present mode of data management? (b) what are the current resources for managing data? and (c) what are the priorities (e.g., purchase of equipment, software development, needs assessment and discussion with staff)?

3. The third step focuses on money. Questions that should be asked and answered at this level include (a) how much funding is available for use? (b) what are the sources of funding currently available? (c) how much should be spent in the initial acquisition and development of a system? and (d) how much should be spent for ongoing maintenance?

4. The fourth step addresses hardware and vendor selection: (a) what kinds of computer hardware and software are available that can do the required applications? and (b) what are the performance reports on the vendors being considered?

5. The fifth step considers vendor support: (a) what kind of follow-up support is provided? (b) is it part of the system package or additional? (c) is training provided or available? (d) is the vendor within the same city or region?

6. Hornfischer recommended that the process end with decisions related to flexible software concerns: (a) is a special program that must be written required? (b) can an existing preprogrammed software package be used? and (c) is it necessary to use a sophisticated program language or can an independent data management package be used?

The planning process begins with determining the overall needs and commitment of the organization and the expectations of prospective users of the data management system. Failure to determine the commitment and goals of the organization and to specifically define the critical needs of the users will most likely result in a data base management system that fails to meet the expectations or the demands of the users (see Figure 12.1).

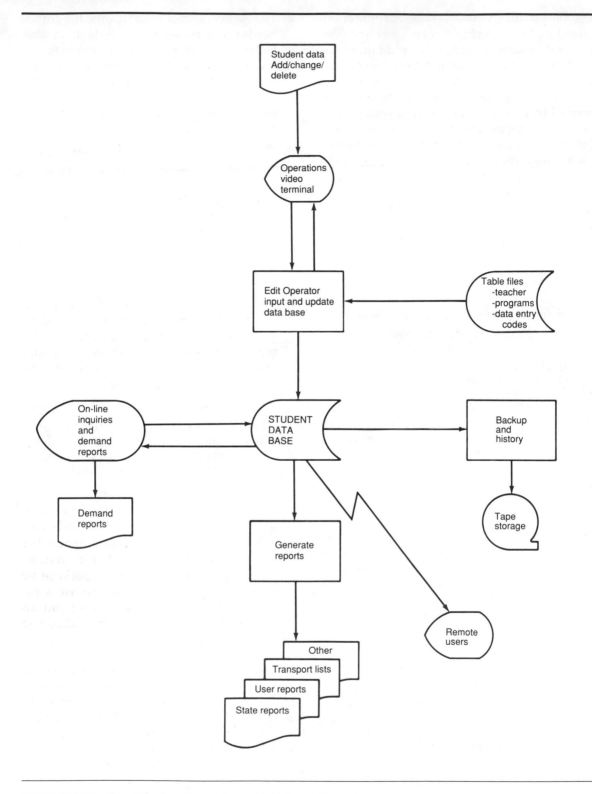

FIGURE 12.1 Special education management information system

Specific Planning and Design Considerations

In the development of data base management systems, careful thought and planning must be given to the basic system design and the components desired for the system. Reviewing general system and program components, determining specific system requirements, and determining which type of programmed management system will be most appropriate are all key decision areas for the system development process. Failing to address these system design factors in an initial planning and development phase usually results in a system unable to respond to the data processing needs desired. All users, particularly those just starting to use data management applications or those planning to develop or purchase a data base management system, should take time to review these basic components in system design. Several activities relating to these processes that might be helpful to administrators or teachers planning to develop or implement a data management system are listed in the Suggested Activities section at the end of the chapter.

The first issues for consideration in the system design process for data base management systems are the system and program requirements. Hardware and software requirements should be thoroughly reviewed and analyzed. The essential system requirements to consider include the following:

1. *Configuration.* Based on the location of system components, user access needs, data input and retrieval requirements, and types of numbers of components, a configuration design should be developed. This part of the design process begins to address issues such as how many pieces of equipment will be required, where they will be physically located, and how they will be connected to each other.

2. *Computer terminals and keyboards.* This component of the system design process addresses the issue of computer selection, including the selection of the types of terminals and keyboards that will support easy and efficient data base management.

3. *Computer screens (CRTs/video displays).* Based on user needs (e.g., need for color, graphics capability, and word processing), this component addresses the requirements for the selection of video display units.

4. *Memory.* Based on projected data needs (e.g., the number of files, records, and fields required and the amount of data to be stored or retrieved), memory requirements must be determined. Resident memory is almost as important in data management systems as permanent or storage memory (disk drives). Large resident memory capabilities greatly enhance the use of floppy disk storage systems, but for data management applications the use of a hard disk seems most advisable.

5. *Printers.* Besides the number and types of printers to be used (as discussed in issues regarding system configuration), speed, graphics capability, and print quality become key areas for decision making about this component.

6. *Multiuser interface.* The inability to exchange information across more than a single station becomes one of the greatest limitations of the microcomputer in the educational setting. Networking capabilities are becoming more and more dependable (see Chapter 2) and are within affordable price ranges for most school systems.

7. *Cables and hardware capabilities.* Transmission of data to peripherals (e.g., printers), or to other computers or storage devices, must be protected through the use of shielded cabling to ensure reliable data transfer.

8. *Training.* One of the critical system design components most often overlooked is training for new or inexperienced users. Consideration of any system component must include the review of training programs, materials, and time to be made available.

9. *Installation.* Installation costs, if any, must be a part of the system design process.

An office network can be established to manage data base systems. *(Photograph courtesy of Apple Computers, Inc.)*

10. *Maintenance.* A critical area most often underfunded and sometimes forgotten completely (until something does not work) is the ongoing maintenance of the equipment and programs.

11. *Support and consultation.* Good system design processes require support and consultation during all phases of the development and implementation process.

12. *Cost.* Administrators and teachers must avoid the temptation to save money by buying systems that do not meet the needs and specifications developed in the planning process.

Program requirements in the system design process must consider all applications and potential uses of the system by the user. Basic applications often considered in program requirement specifications include (a) word processing needs; (b) data processing needs; (c) spreadsheet needs; (d) mail list needs; (e) personnel information needs; (f) student information needs; (g) instructional program needs; (h) general office and management needs; (i) federal reporting requirements; (j) state reporting requirements; (k) local or district reporting requirements; (l) inventory needs; (m) access to communication and information networks (see Chapter 1); and (n) use of subscriber data base systems (e.g., CompuServe).

Types of Programmed Management Systems

In determining key system and program components in the planning/design process, the type of data management system to be used must be reviewed. In a system design process, consideration must be given to differences between independent data management programs and general application programs (Smith, 1985). One of the basic differences is the type of system used to manage files and store and retrieve data. Independent programs, such as dBase IV (Hsu, 1992), usually operate their filing systems on advanced con-

TABLE 12.1
Advantages and disadvantages of independent data management and general application programs

Independent Data Management Programs

Advantages
1. Based on advanced concepts used by mainframes and minicomputers
2. Able to customize data entry and report formats
3. Offer greater query capabilities for individual data elements or fields
4. Can use multiple files to share and pass data
5. Paradox and dBase IV are frequently used programs of this type

Disadvantages
1. Use a more technical language and command structure than menu-driven programs
2. Cost is often greater
3. Usually require more training to gain full use of all program capabilities
4. Often require large amounts of memory and a hard disk to operate effectively

General Application Programs

Advantages
1. Are easy to install and operate and usually provide a fully formatted data entry and update screen
2. Usually individual data records can be displayed and updated quickly
3. Separate program modules can often be purchased to provide alternate applications and report formats
4. They are relatively inexpensive and are available for use on all major brands of computers
5. Some commonly used programs in this category include DB Master and PFS Personal Filing System

Disadvantages
1. Cannot handle multiple files to share or pass data. Prevents ability to check data for accuracy except by total record
2. The ability to sequence program operations is limited
3. Report capabilities are often limited to single-line headings and listings with column totals
4. Many of the programs have limited or no arithmetic capability

cepts similar to those used on mainframes or minicomputers. These programs use a *relation data base system* that allows all data within a data base to *relate*, or be sorted, retrieved, and filed as independent pieces of information related to the file specification (e.g., fields). General application programs, however, usually use a *file manager system* that operates on a single data base or data file of information and uses preformatted file structures (e.g., PFS:File) to sort, retrieve, and file data.

File manager systems generally have menu-driven command structures, standard data entry formats, and standard reporting formats. Relational data base systems allow for the development of individualized file creation, data entry formats, and customized report formatting capabilities. The advantages and disadvantages of the two management systems are outlined in Table 12.1.

In evaluating and reviewing system and program requirements for a data base management system in the designing/planning phase, Smith (1985) gave six factors related to performance that should prove helpful in making a final selection for a data management program:

1. How easy will it be to operate?

2. Can it meet all the application needs designated in the system and program requirements?

3. Can information be sorted into various reporting sequences?

4. Can data be edited for coding or logical validity?

5. Is there flexibility of data field length of screen format?

6. Will it only work on one brand of computer?

File Structure Design

Another key area for consideration in the design/planning process is the development of the file structure and determination of the data elements (variables) to be included in the data base. Specific design considerations to be included for consideration in this phase involve the manner in which the data are entered, how files are created, and how information will be reported. Several key components to be considered in this phase include (a) file design (e.g., how fields are created and edited, how records are created and edited, and how files are accessed); (b) use and design of data entry formats (e.g., preformatted or the capability of creating customized data entry formats); (c) file handling procedures (e.g., save, delete, copy, revise, sort, merge, append, use of multiple files, etc.); (d) report design and specification (e.g., preformatted or the capability of creating customized report formats); (e) production of form letters and correspondence; and (f) documentation (e.g., does the system or program come with adequate documentation?).

General Guidelines for Software Evaluation

Although software evaluation is addressed in Chapter 4, there are a few general guidelines important to data management programs that

might be helpful to emphasize at this point as part of the design/planning process:

1. The software should be completely menu-driven but offer the experienced user the option of turning the menus off to increase speed of access.

2. The user should be able to discontinue the program in the middle of most major processing functions without losing data or leaving files open.

3. The program should provide a help option controlled by the user. The help option should be in a separate file that can be removed from the program disk and saved to another disk if more memory space is needed for data.

4. The management software should offer easy procedures for adding or deleting fields within the record and reloading data into newly restructured files (e.g., the school system has to add age as a new variable to its federal reports).

5. There should be verification of all destructive choices before proceeding. In some cases, a double destructive choice is helpful and should be included (i.e., restructuring the fields for certain records in the data base that will usually erase all the data currently entered in the file).

6. The program should offer the option of using the keyboard or mouse (where applicable).

7. The management program should monitor and evaluate input responses in such a way that the user is offered help without requesting it when making repeated mistakes.

8. The software should offer the option of running the program with or without sound or color (where applicable).

9. There should be a provision for discounted costs for multiple purchases of the program or a network environment.

Health and Safety Issues

An area not commonly covered in the design/planning process is health and safety issues.

Certain findings indicate unusual happenings for a large number of video display terminal users. According to Wallach and Ackerman (1982), there are certain conditions that increase the occurrence of symptoms that are more serious and long-lasting than minor eye strain and postural discomforts. They suggest that the following parameters have a direct physiological effect on users:

- CRT display within 2 feet of the operator
- Continuous use for 1 hour or more
- Regular daily usage
- Typical modern office environment
- Air pollutants and inadequate ventilation
- Higher positive charges on the face of the CRT
- Stress

Wallach and Ackerman also noted that some individuals are more sensitive to video display terminal exposure than others, and symptoms may occur for these people with 2 hours of continuous operation. Suggestions for reducing the hazards include (a) elevating the screen so the top of the screen is approximately level with the operator's eyes; (b) using a glare screen (under $30); (c) ensuring proper lighting and ventilation in areas surrounding the terminal; (d) having complete eye examinations for users at least once a year; (e) using proper furniture and chairs (no arms); and (f) having frequent breaks.

SPECIFIC APPLICATIONS FOR SPECIAL EDUCATION

Specific requirements and applications for special education management information systems and record keeping are evaluation and diagnosis and IEPs.

Evaluation and Diagnosis

Most of the current applications of the computer for evaluation purposes focus on stu-dent record keeping and test score computation, analysis, and reporting. A great number of software programs appearing on the market analyze data and generate lists of resources or instructional strategies for professionals. A few of these packages have the capacity to generate goals, objectives, and comparative and interpretive diagnostic statements. Almost all of the programs have at least one or more of the following capabilities: (a) diagnostic; (b) interpretation of test results; (c) information management of test results and data; (d) report writing; and (e) instructional strategies and student goals and objectives.

Several of the more commonly used assessment instruments offer these options. The Kaufman Test of Educational Achievement K-TEA), the Peabody Individual Achievement Test—Revised (PIAT-R), and the KeyMath—Revised all have computerized software programs for scoring and printing test results. They are called Assist for the K-TEA, Assist for the PIAT-R, and Assist for the KeyMath—Revised. The often-used Wechsler Intelligence Scale for Children—Revised also has its own software. Target is a complement management system that includes diagnostic support and also provides the user with these options. Also, WISC-R Compilation (*WISC-R,* 1983) provides diagnostic and interpretive statements for each subtest and lists short-term objectives related to the diagnosed weakness. Figures 12.2 presents a sample printout of the type of information that could be obtained from this type of program.

A good example of noncommercial software is Identification of School Behavior Problems (Kosberg & Kern, no date). This program received an honorable mention in the 1984 Software Competition sponsored by the Council for Exceptional Children.

In making a determination of what software, if any, should be purchased and used within a special education program for diagnostic/evaluation purposes, the decision should be based on the responses to three basic questions: (a) what information is needed? (b) how will the information be generated and saved? and (c) how will the information be retrieved or accessed? The answers to these questions depend on the system and program require-

---

Evaluation Report

Student: John Smith   Date: 11/10/92   Date Assessed:_____
1. Instrument: Wechsler Intelligence Scale for Children–Revised   Test Results:

(Test Results listed here for appropriate subtest)

2. Based on the test performance the following instructional program is recommended:

Annual Goal: (Goal is listed here from Goals/Objectives Data Base)

Short-Term Objectives: (Objectives listed here from Goals/Objectives Data Base)

FIGURE 12.2 WISC-R compilation sample printout

---

ments. For example, some data management systems permit information to be included in both a student's record and the system. Most IEP management systems include test score information, but it is entered into the system as data just as the student's name or address would be entered. As preprogrammed management systems become more sophisticated, this area should receive greater attention.

Future program capabilities may allow raw assessment results to be entered, and the system would then score the test, enter the scores into the student record, and generate a complete diagnostic assessment report based on predetermined assessment standards established by the special educator. This information would also allow for other system program components to generate prescriptive instructional guidelines without additional data input or user involvement. This is similar to how many of the current general application diagnostic programs operate.

If the system requirements are such that the diagnostic/evaluation data and reporting needs will be handled with independent programs (independent of the main student record system whether computerized or not), then the issues become more focused on the requirements needed for a diagnostic/prescriptive program. Although general software selection standards are applicable for all software purchases, there are several key questions to ask before buying a diagnostic/evaluation program (see Central Office and Classroom Con-

siderations section below for a list of general standards). The list of questions below provides some guidelines for the purchase or review of software for evaluation or diagnostic purposes:

1. Are the manufacturers of the program knowledgeable about assessment practices, classroom instruction, and timelines?

2. Does the program have good documentation, including easy-to-read manuals?

3. Are there skill books or written materials and other supplementary materials to accompany the program? If so, are they motivational? Can they be run on the computer also?

4. Is the program cross-referenced or adaptable to other curricula or programs?

5. Does the program generate objectives, and are they sequenced logically and progressively?

6. Does the program include all necessary variables for proper scoring and evaluation (e.g., chronological age, mental age)?

7. Are the questions and follow-up materials current? Does the manufacturer provide for update capabilities at reasonable cost?

8. If any of the programs include student use of the computer, will the sound generated

by the program disturb other students in the classroom?

9. Does the program really save time and effort?

10. Will the program generate printed reports of the data? Can the report format be changed to specific personalized needs?

11. Can the program be modified to reflect district assessment standards or criteria?

12. Has the program been tested and does it demonstrate reliability and validity?

Although the number of quality evaluation and assessment programs continues to increase, there is still tremendous potential for software development (Fisher, Blackaller, & Jackson, 1992). With the increased sophistication of voice-activated programs and graphics capabilities, it is not unreasonable to imagine diagnostic tests and assessment tools that could be standardized and administered through the computer for more effective assessment and diagnosis for children with limited speech or language, severe physical disabilities, or sensory impairments, or for students who are bilingual and in need of special education services. Coupled with increased capabilities for scoring and graphically displayed assessment results, the diagnostic and evaluation possibilities of the personal computer are exciting (Woodward, 1992).

Individual Education Programs

The basis for making a decision in a student's program is the IEP. Several factors inherent with IEPs and the IEP process make a standardized and uniform response regarding computerized IEP programs very difficult. Although the components and requirements for an IEP are clearly stated in Public Law 94-142, the information included on the IEP form varies from school system to school system. To add further difficulty to the standardization, data management system data entry forms are often different from the IEP form and may include different data elements or label fields with similar information but differ-

ent names. Three key issues to be considered regarding IEP programs for the personal computer are the following: (a) What is included on an IEP data entry form? (b) Who is going to provide the data management services? (c) What is the timeline?

What Is Included in the IEP?

Since there is little standardization or uniformity of IEP forms, there is little agreement on what should be included in computerized IEP programs. Some IEP programs provide only for student and program data (e.g., date of birth and program placement) used mostly for administrative purposes. Other software programs provide only for instructional data, such as goals and objectives or diagnostic and assessment information generated from computerized objective data banks. This information is used mostly by teachers and therapists at the classroom level. A few programs combine both student and program data with instructional data; however, significant differences occur in how much of the information is presented as part of the IEP. For example, some list goals and objectives based on test results recorded in the student record while others allow the teacher to select the objectives. In addition to differences in the type or amount of information included in the IEP, differences occur nationwide due to state legal requirements, mandated program requirements, and, most important, state reporting requirements. Learning Tools Special Education Management System is one of the few, if not the only, comprehensive data base management system that provides all three components in the computerized management of student information for the IEP. This system organizes and reports all needed student information for federal, state, and local reports; provides comprehensive case management for IEPs, parent notices, and other student reports; and maintains curriculum management of goals and objectives. Also, it is one of the few systems that allows the user to make the necessary modifications based on local district or school needs. Also, one of the appealing features of Learning Tools Special Education Management System is that the program is completely compatible with both Apple and DOS-based computers. Because of this feature and the design of the software, data are easily transferred among schools and district and state offices. Other programs, such as PennStar System or iepSystem, only generate IEP forms and provide computerized curriculum management of goals and objectives. A careful review of computerized IEP programs such as these reveals some common features that should be considered in the review or development of all computerized IEP programs and administrative packages:

1. The program allows for customized implementation based on local needs.

2. Program updates are provided at minimal cost or on an annual fee basis.

3. Documentation is easy to read and provides adequate detail including minimum hardware requirements.

4. Operation of the program is logical and easy to learn (within 3 or 4 hours of use/ training).

5. Training and support are included with purchase or at reasonable cost.

6. The program can be expanded with increased hardware capacity to include large student populations.

7. The program is menu-driven with well-defined prompt lines, clear input fields, and help feature.

8. Input errors are explained, specific, and understandable.

9. Data entry is streamlined and efficient.

10. Feedback is provided about processing status when program is running.

11. Formatting report options are menu-driven, or program allows for easy design.

12. Report options and formats provide reports to meet state and federal reporting requirements.

Who Is Going to Provide the Services?

Designating responsibility for implementing computerized IEP activities is just as impor-

tant as designating responsibility for implementing services listed on the IEP. Determining who will collect the data, what the format of the data will be, and who will enter the data into the student record system are major activities of computerized IEP program services needing clear and specific delineation of responsibility.

Instructions and documentation for data entry should be clear and a check system for errors implemented even if such a system is included in the program. These precautions should be developed to ensure that data errors can be traced to their origin. The purpose of detecting the origin of errors is not to focus attention on any person entering (or collecting) data incorrectly but to find the source of error so it can be corrected. Procedures to ensure confidentiality and limit access to appropriate personnel should also be included in the description and explanation of responsibilities.

What Is the Timeline?

One of the purposes of the IEP is to provide an efficient and organized way of summarizing all the necessary and required information for exceptional students to ensure timely and appropriate instructional programs. A manual for the IEP data management system that includes all the necessary and required steps, as well as instructions and responsibilities, ensures an organized computerized IEP system. Producing timely reports and information for IEP meetings, state and federal reports, and instructional planning for the classroom can occur only if there are procedures designated and scheduled to occur in the proper sequence.

CENTRAL OFFICE AND CLASSROOM CONSIDERATIONS

The importance of central office planning and support of computer use cannot be emphasized enough. The increase in the use of computers in special education can be attributed to the interest, support, and cooperation of special education supervisors, administrators, and teachers. Research (e.g., Hanley, Clark, & White, 1984) clearly demonstrates that there has been an increase in the use of computers in general education and that the increase in special education programs has been dramatic. It is estimated that at least one-half of the districts and one-third of the special education teachers in the United States use computers in some way.

The increased use of microcomputers in special education has focused on central office applications for student information management systems and classroom-level applications for computer-assisted instruction and computer-managed instruction. Computer-managed instruction has shown a steady increase in use and application mostly due to the increased capabilities of the software and hardware and the availability of microcomputers for teacher use.

Management Information Systems and Confidentiality

A major role of the central office is to combine individual computer use efforts into a cohesive system. For special education data management, the cohesive system is often called a management information system. Critical challenges for any central office in developing an effective management information system include (a) the accurate and orderly centralized recording of handicapped and gifted/talented students' data; (b) accounting for the movement of exceptional students within district programs and schools, regional county programs, or state programs; and (c) establishing an evaluation system based on collected data for district, state, and federal evaluation requirements. A centralized management information system must have clearly defined steps and procedures from the initial procedure of proper data collection to the final step of generating reports. In addition, there must be backup capabilities for the data base and capabilities for on-line inquiries and access by remote users. All of these and other necessary components of a typical special education management information system are diagrammed in Figure 12.1.

A key issue for special education management information systems is confidentiality. Procedures must be established to ensure that access to student files and records is limited to appropriate and authorized personnel. Protection of data stored within a computerized system can be accomplished by the use of normal security procedures such as building and office security and screening and monitoring of office workers or others visiting the office where records are maintained. Additional security precautions are disk- or file-locking programs or data encryption methods. Disk- or file-locking devices require the use of a password or key procedure in proper sequence to activate the disk or run a program. The other method, data encryption, scrambles the data when it is saved onto the disk and leaves it unreadable to unauthorized persons. Passwords or keys are also used to scramble and unscramble the data. Security procedures such as these are fairly inexpensive, ranging from $100 to $500.

Classroom Data Management Applications

Other than computer-assisted instruction, initial use of the computer in education focused on word processing. Although the introduction and use of computers for data base management is comparatively slow, many teachers and administrators have found this application not only a good learning tool to teach to students but also an excellent computer application procedure for their own use. However, finding suitable software for classroom instruction is not easy. Yet educational software companies are developing teaching programs with lessons already developed for the class- or therapy room for some of the data manager programs currently on the market. For example, Scholastic has developed four instructional packages to accompany PFS:File (a teacher's guide and three large data bases for students to explore, use, and modify). Units are also available for students to create and expand their own data bases.

Advanced data base management programs for special education classes include

Notebook computers can be used to generate and manage assessment data. *(Photograph by Jimmy D. Lindsey)*

Apple's AppleWorks (described in Chapter 3) and Scholastic's Bank Street Filer and PFS series including PFS:File and PFS:Report. Besides the typical applications for classroom instruction, such as developing a data base on the 50 states and doing comparisons of elevations, capitals, and populations, special educators and exceptional students are working creatively together to create information data bases on student progress, grades, and common interests among classmates. With the help of preprogrammed application templates, many of the software companies are rapidly developing entire libraries of application software designed for very specific purposes. The low cost of most of the applications make them very attractive. For example, PFS:School Record Keeper marketed by Scholastic consists of four ready-to-use forms that work with PFS:File and PFS:Report to produce 30 reports for such things as student record management and room event scheduling. 1-2-3 Report Writer from Lotus Development can easily print information from a 1-2-3 data base in a preformatted report format on a preprinted form.

As networking capabilities increase and communications software becomes less expensive, special education administrators, teachers, and therapists will begin linking data bases together and sharing information. In the same way, they will be able to transfer special education information more quickly and efficiently. Updating their students' current progress, goals and objectives or assessment results and having the capability for all team members to access the data almost immediately will increase the effectiveness of the IEP team and ensure better programming for handicapped and gifted/talented students. As advances continue with laptop and notebook computers, teachers, therapists, and administrators will be able to carry the information easily with them into IEP meetings or utilize data base information for daily planning or conferences with students and parents. Team members will be better and more quickly informed of need situations concerning students and be able to respond to those needs quickly. Depending on the sophistication of the data management system and the configuration, professionals may be able to access student files and enter data by the computer, thus avoiding the creation of paperwork that must be carried through school mail systems. Some school systems are also creating bulletin boards for their teachers and staff to expedite communication and reduce paperwork (e.g., notices and school events are posted). Requests for information or materials also can be posted, making limited resources more available for use.

SUMMARY

The availability of relatively low-cost sophisticated computer technology offers tremendous potential for increased efficiency for many special education administrative and instructional tasks. This chapter provided information on the development of the technological and human resources that support exceptional individuals in an educational setting and on the major administrative and data management issues and procedures to be considered in the development of data management systems. Key issues described included (a) system design, system and program requirements, and the advantages and disadvantages of independent data management programs and general application programs; (b) initial and ongoing planning efforts to ensure reliable data collection, accurate record keeping, and usable information for reporting purposes; (c) adopting current independent or stand-alone evaluation/diagnostic programs to ensure no duplication of efforts with existing data management systems and to ensure reliable and valid assessment results; (d) important concepts related to the effective use of computerized IEP programs; and (e) central office and classroom data management considerations.

Data management is an important part of the special education program. Special education administrators and teachers need to continue to provide better and more efficient ways to manage data for instructional programs, assessment, and administrative responsibilities in serving individuals with exceptional needs.

REFERENCES

Fisher, F., Blackaller, C. A., & Jackson, J. (1992). RESOURCES: Shareware: Case Studies in Special Education. *TAM Newsletter, 7*(1), 6.

Greensberg, K. (1986). The shape of things to come. *PC World, 4*(1). 143–151.

Hanley, T. V., Clark, L. S., & White, L. J. (1984, April). Microcomputers in special education: Findings and recommendations from case studies. Presentation at the 62nd Annual Conference of the Council for Exceptional Children, Washington, DC.

Hindin, E. (1991, April). The minicomputer tries a comeback. *Data Communications*, pp. 95–102.

Hornfischer, D. (1985). Today's computers—A formula for success. *T.H.E. Journal. 12*(8), 84–85.

Hsu, D. (1992). The basis of dBase IV. *PC Novice, 3*(3), 60–62.

Kosberg, B., & Kern, R. (no date). *Identification of school behavior problems.* Yonkers, NY: Andrus Children's Home.

Remington, M. (1992). Choosing your database. *PC Novice, 3*(4), 62–64.

Rubin, C. (1985). Blossoming productivity linked to micros. *InfoWorld, 7*(20). 30–37.

Seymour, J. (1991, July). Why software innovation is lagging. *PC Magazine, 10*, 89–90.

Sirkin, B. (1991, June). Few account for hidden costs of downsizing. *PC Week, 8*, 65.

Smith, G. (1985). *File manager systems and integrated systems—Advantages and disadvantages.* Sacramento, CA: Educational Research Consultants.

Wallach, C., & Ackerman, R. (1982, June). Health and safety and the microcomputer. Presented at 1982 Conference of Electrostatics Society of America.

WISC-R compilation. (1983). Novato, CA: Academic Therapy Publications.

Woodward, J. (1992). Computers spot students' math misconceptions. *Counterpoint, 12*(3), 15.

Suggested Activities

Paper and Pencil

Find several good books or magazine articles on data base management systems. Review the key components and procedures in designing data management systems. Pay particular attention to preplanning steps covering system and program design. Summarize your findings possibly in a checklist or step-by-step procedure manual. It might be helpful to list the system needs and the program needs of a system to be implemented in your school system.

Observation

Contact a local special education director or data process manager, and visit a district with a special education management information system currently in place. Use your checklist or procedure manual to evaluate and discuss the components of the system visited. Share any meaningful insights with the director or manager.

Practicum

Visit a local computer shop and ask to have demonstrated several data base management programs or systems. Ask the dealer or salesperson if you can try the program. Try to use more than one program. Especially try to use an independent data management program and a general application program. Compare and evaluate the differences.

Resources

Organizations

Council of Administrators of Special Education (*CASE*). This organization of special education administrators promotes effective practices for exceptional individuals, provides opportunities for the study of common problems, and promotes professional leadership. Write to CASE, Council for Exceptional Children, 1920 Association Drive, Reston, VA 22091.

Journals

Info World. This journal is an excellent weekly publication for all levels of users. Write to *InfoWorld*, P.O. Box 1018, Southeastern, PA 19398.

LANTIMES. This journal provides for an excellent source of information on local area networks and serves as a useful reference for network managers or network users. Write to *LANTIMES*, P.O. Box 652, Hightstown, NJ 08520.

PC Tech Journal. This monthly publication reviews new hardware, software, and peripherals within a more technical context. However, it is easy to read and provides information for users at all levels of ability. Write to Ziff-Davis Publishing, One Park Avenue, New York, NY 10016.

CASE Newsletter. This newsletter is published four times a year. Write to the Council of Administrators of Special Education, Council for Exceptional Children, 1920 Association Drive, Reston, VA 22091.

Books

Date, C. J. (1985). *An introduction to database systems* (3rd ed.). Reading, MA: Addison-Wesley.

Sage, D. D., & Burrello, L. C. (1986). *Policy and management in special education.* Englewood Cliffs, NJ: Prentice-Hall.

Hardware/Software

Assist for the K-TEA
American Guidance Service
P.O. Box 99
Circle Pines, MN 55014-1796

Assist for the PIAT-R
American Guidance Service
P.O. Box 99
Circle Pines, MN 55014-1796

Assist for the Keymath—Revised
American Guidance Service
P.O. Box 99
Circle Pines, MN 55014-1796

Bank Street Filer
Scholastic
2931 East McCarty
Box 7502
Jefferson City, MO 65102

dBase IV
Ashton-Tate
9929 West Jefferson Blvd.
Culver City, CA 90230

Excel
Microsoft
16011 NE 36th Way
Box 97017
Redmond, WA 98073-9717

Hewlett Packard 3000
Hewlett Packard
3000 Hanover Street
Palo Alto, CA 94304

Identification of School Behavior Problems
Andrus Children's Home
1156 North Broadway
Yonkers, NY 10701

iepSystem
IEP
Route 671
P.O. Box 546
Fork Union, VA 23005

Learning Tools Special Education
Management System
Learning Tools
248 River View Trail
Roswell, GA 30075

Lotus 1-2-3
Lotus Development
55 Cambridge Pkwy.
Cambridge, MA 02142

Multimate
Multimate
52 Oakland Avenue
East Hartford, CT 06108

Optionware
Optionware
Corporate Place 5 Barnard Lane
Bloomfield, CT 06002

Paradox
Borland International
4585 Scotts Valley Drive
Scotts Valley, CA 95066

PennStarr System
PennStarr Support Group
Box 213
Wisburg, PA 17837

PFS:School Record Keeper
Software Publishing
1901 Landings Drive
Mountain View, CA 94043

PFS:File
Software Publishing
1901 Landings Drive
Mountain View, CA 94043

Quattro Pro
Borland International
4585 Scotts Valley Drive
Scotts Valley, CA 95066

Target Management Systems
Teaching Pathways
P.O. Box 3152
Amarillo, TX 79120

WISC-R Compilation
Academic Therapy
20 Commercial Blvd.
Novato, CA 94947

WISC-R Computer Report
Southern Micro Systems
P.O. Box 2097
Burlington, NC 27216

WordPerfect
WordPerfect
288 West Center Street
Orem, Utah 84057

Teaching Applications with Exceptional Individuals

CHAPTER

J. Emmett Gardner
University of Oklahoma
Dave L. Edyburn
Vanderbilt University ■

When microcomputers were first intro-duced into schools, considerable effort was directed toward understanding how to program computers and developing computer literacy skills. Over time, experience and research regarding the effective use of microcomputers has shown that this initial emphasis was somewhat misfocused. Indeed, the following quote by Clark (1983) is often cited to focus attention on the influence that educational technology has had in teaching and learning:

> The best current evidence is that media are mere vehicles that deliver instruction but do not influence student achievement any more than the truck that delivers our groceries causes changes in our nutrition. (p. 445)

The work of two other writers in the mid 1980s provided additional insight regarding the perceived value of using computers in education. In *The Second Self,* Turkle (1984) described her research using extensive interviews and observations of computer users across the United States. Turkle suggested that our perceptions of computers are evocative and function much like a Rorschach inkblot test: an individual's beliefs regarding the effectiveness of computers reflect whatever the user chooses to project onto the computers. In a historical review of technological innovations in education since 1920, Cuban (1986) concluded that promises associated with the introduction of computers in classrooms will largely remain unfulfilled unless significant attention is placed on the instructional interactions within the classroom and the role technology will assume in these interactions.

As educators enter the 1990s, their attention is being refocused on teaching and learning and understanding how technology can be used to deliver instruction in new, powerful, and effective ways (Wepner, 1992). Special education and other researchers have noted similar trends, extensively documenting in the extant literature the ongoing interest in technology and its perceived value for educational and therapeutic purposes (Behrmann, 1984, 1988; Budoff & Hutten, 1982; Church & Bender, 1989; Ellis & Sabornie, 1986; Hassel-

TABLE 13.1
Computer applications facilitating special education teachers' personal productivity

Computer Application	Description	Related Strategies
Record keeping	Using the computer to maintain and manage information related to students and teaching responsibilities.	Using grade management software, electronic data bases and individualized education programs, and laptop computers to collect and analyze observational data.
Correspondence	Using the computer to facilitate personal communications between students, parents, and colleagues, and managing requests for information.	Using a word processor to create form letters or form documents. Creating a library file of frequently used phrases that can be copied and pasted into other documents.
Professional development	Using the computer to enhance the acquisition of information that supports one's teaching expertise.	Using telecommunications and CD-ROM to access information systems to obtain information for curriculum materials.

TABLE 13.2
Computer applications facilitating special education teachers' instructional productivity

Stage	Description	Related Topics and Strategies
Planning	Using microcomputers to assist in the outlining of instructional intervention and strategies.	Assessing student abilities and learning difficulties. Identifying software sources that enhance instructional objectives. Using computer lesson plans.
Preparing	Using microcomputers to facilitate the production of print and electronic instructional materials.	Utilities that create work sheets, certificates, flashcards, etc. Using authoring systems to create on-line lessons.
Managing	Ways to consider using microcomputers to conduct and manage instruction. Strategies that facilitate and manage student behavior and interests during computer-based learning activities.	Time management of classroom-based and lab-based computers. Monitoring students' computer performance. Effective feedback and praise relative to computer work.
Extending	Using existing technology and software creatively and effectively for additional instructional impact.	Review and maintenance of skills. Repurposing software. Remaining current with teaching/practice-oriented literature on technology. Using learner-centered software.

bring & Goin, 1989; Levin & Scherfenberg, 1987; Lindsey, 1986; Office of Technology Assessment, 1982). As a result of these and similar studies, professionals working with exceptional individuals have increased their awareness of and interest in technological applications. They are also working to ensure that technology is being used in ways that facilitate sound instructional practices with exceptional learners.

This chapter will review previously described computer concepts as well as introduce new general and specific computer teaching applications that can be used by professionals working with exceptional individuals in class- and therapy rooms. It is organized around two primary topics: personal productivity and instructional productivity. The term *personal productivity* is used to describe noninstructional tasks associated with record keeping, correspondence, and professional development responsibilities (see Table 13.1). The term *instructional productivity* is used to describe instructional methods related to planning, preparing, managing, and extending computer-affiliated instruction with special needs learners (see Table 13.2). In many cases, applications and strategies associated with one topic can be applied to contexts associated with other topics. More important, any strategy or application, when implemented with the clear purpose of improving educational opportunities for exceptional individuals, results in increased empowerment for the professional and facilitates the students' potential to learn.

THE USE OF TECHNOLOGY TO ENHANCE PERSONAL PRODUCTIVITY

The term *teacher empowerment* often refers to those activities that enable professionals to increase student achievement. One strategy for empowering teachers and therapists recommended in several recent educational technology policy statements focused on the merits of placing a computer on the teacher's desk

(International Society for Technology in Education, 1990; National Foundation for the Improvement of Education, 1989; Office of Technology Assessment, 1982). Putting aside the issue of whether a one-to-one ratio for teachers and computers will be achieved in this decade, the potential for using computers to enhance teacher productivity is clearly recognized and emphasized in these reports. Unfortunately, little insight into how technology can be used in specific applications to reduce the excessive demands of teaching is offered in these reports.

As already stated, the term *personal productivity* is used to describe a variety of computer-based activities that professionals perform when they are not directly involved with exceptional individuals. While these tasks may be noninstructional in nature, they are a necessary component of the teacher's or therapist's work. As Hannaford stated in Chapter 1 of this book, special education teachers often face an overwhelming number of noninstructional tasks and responsibilities. The utility of having a computer available to assist in personal productivity appears obvious. Projects and tasks can be done more efficiently, accurately, and faster by computers, especially those tasks that are repetitive or mundane. Indeed, the rationale for much of the interest in using technology to enhance personal productivity in special education is that professionals, by reducing the amount of time they spend on noninstructional tasks, will have additional time that can be reallocated for instructional productivity. Three types of tasks (record keeping, correspondence, and professional development) are examined below to illustrate how special educators and therapists can use technology to enhance personal productivity.

Record Keeping

Professionals working with exceptional individuals are required to maintain a variety of records that relate to academic histories, schedules, attendance data, and progress reports of attainment of specific goals and objectives (Charles, 1983). Other noninstructional events

Computers enhance the teaching/learning process.
(Photograph courtesy of Minnesota Educational Computing Corporation)

during the school year that place additional record-keeping demands on teachers and therapists include field trips, fund-raising events, enrichment reading, book orders, and so forth. Each of these tasks requires the management of considerable information as part of the overall class- or therapy room responsibilities. While all of these tasks are frequently performed without technology assistance, a number of general purpose productivity tools (e.g., word processors, data bases, and spreadsheets) can be used to increase the ease, efficiency, and accuracy of managing these records. Rosenberg, O'Shea, and O'Shea (1991) reported that when professionals use mechanisms (e.g., computers) to provide quick and easy access to student information, improved time management and reduced stress are key benefits. Other technology tools are also available that assist in specialized areas of record keeping such as managing grades, creating and managing individual education plans (IEPs), and collecting and analyzing behavioral data. The following sections will describe the use of these general and specialized tools and how they can be used to facilitate common record-keeping tasks.

General Record-keeping Tools

As stated in earlier chapters, a word processor is a versatile tool that can be used to create and store records when the information varies in format. AppleWorks (Claris), WordPerfect (WordPerfect), and Microsoft Word and Microsoft Works (Microsoft) are all common word processing programs that teachers and therapists can use to create files that contain their student schedules, assignment checklists, class lists, behavior contracts, or anecdotal observations. The value of these applications is twofold in that the information (a) is in a format readily accessible for reference and (b) is stored in a format that enables subsequent reuse and modification. For example, word processing files that contain students' class schedules can be easily opened on the computer, printed, and edited when changes in students' schedules occur. Something as simple as a class list typed into a word processing file can be copied and used to create a new list of group assignments for an enrichment activity or a list of travel partners and bus assignments for a field trip. Selections from a file of cumulative anecdotal observations written about a student could be utilized as part of a prereferral report.

A data base is quite useful for keeping track of similar information about students and class functions. As observed in Chapters 3 and 12, a data base is simply an electronic record-keeping system. Any information a professional writes onto a 3-by-5-inch index card, or records on an information sheet, has the potential to be stored and manipulated in an electronic data base. In the context of personal productivity, the issue is not so much what data bases are or can do but how they can be used to support the work of professionals. Thus the ease with which information can be retrieved and the ability to selectively reorganize existing fields of information to serve other functions and applications represent critical features of data bases. For example, most school offices maintain a student information card for all students with their addresses, parents' names, emergency contact information, and so on. Teachers and therapists may wish to construct and maintain a similar data base

First Name | Last Name
Address | Age | Grade
City | Birthdate
State | Zip
Home Phone No. | Student Lives with
Mother's Name | Mother's Work No.
Father's Name | Father's Work No.
Emergency Phone No.
Medical Concerns
Special Services

Counselor | School Psychologist

Period 1 | Teacher 1 | Room 1
Period 2 | Teacher 2 | Room 2
Period 3 | Teacher 3 | Room 3
Period 4 | Teacher 4 | Room 4
Period 5 | Teacher 5 | Room 5
Period 6 | Teacher 6 | Room 6
Period 7 | Teacher 7 | Room 7

Bus No. | Locker No. | Locker Combination | Next IEP Review
Other 1
Other 2
Other 3
Other 4

FIGURE 13.1 Sample Student Data Base Template

of student demographic information with data base programs like AppleWorks (Claris), Microsoft Works (Microsoft), or FileMaker (Claris). An example of the typical information that a teacher might store in a student data base is presented in Figure 13.1. This type of data base also contains information that can be used for a number of different purposes, such as creating personalized correspondence (e.g. using parents' names and addresses to print mailing labels or to personalize form letters), printing a variety of lists using different formats (e.g., each student's name and birthdate; each student's name, age, homeroom, guidance counselor, etc.), and retrieving student information at a moment's notice (e.g., What is Don's home address?).

A third general-purpose productivity tool for record keeping is an electronic spreadsheet. Spreadsheet programs such as AppleWorks (Claris), Lotus 1-2-3 (Lotus), and Wingz (Informix) are designed to store information in a column format and to perform mathematical calculations over a range of values. The use of a spreadsheet as a electronic gradebook is a common class- or therapy room application (discussed in additional detail in the next section) and permits the creation and storing of column-oriented information (e.g., a class list with various columns for daily scores or assignment checklists). For example, when a behavior management program is in effect, a spreadsheet can be created to serve as a template for entering daily performance scores and computing daily or weekly averages.

The value of acquiring a set of general record-keeping utility programs (e.g. data bases, spreadsheets, and word processors) is that once teachers and therapists learn how to use each program, they will recognize that they have the necessary tools to track almost any type of information in the format that is personally relevant. It is important to note, however, that while little time is saved in the initial development of record keeping files, considerable dividends are paid when the professional reuses this information without the need to retype some or all of the data. Thus the power and flexibility of general record-keeping tools make them an essential component of a software collection. Class- and therapy room data bases can be developed after professionals determine their unique information needs, and considerable time savings will result when this information is collected and stored in a convenient and flexible format.

Specialized Record-keeping Tools

Grade Management

Recording student grades is nearly a universal record-keeping task for professionals working with exceptional individuals. Electronic gradebook programs were designed to provide spreadsheet advantages in recording students' grades. While specially designed gradebook programs can be purchased, some professionals prefer to use a general spreadsheet program. Electronic spreadsheets can also be used to create templates that perform the function of grade management.

The chief advantages associated with electronic gradebook programs are (a) the ability to recalculate student grades as assignments are added or when students have the opportunity to make revisions for a change in credit; (b) the ability to compute statistics such as mean, median, mode, and standard deviation for sets of scores; (c) the ability to produce class rosters, profiles, and rankings; and (d) the ability to store teaching-learning comments and create progress notes for parents (Bluhm, 1987). However, due to the individualized nature of many assignments given

to exceptional individuals, the value of electronic gradebooks to special educators and therapists is questionable. Ultimately, the type of records that must be maintained on students will probably determine whether an electronic gradebook is a functional utility. The obvious drawback is the fact that a computer must be available to maintain the gradebook.

Electronic IEPs

The creation and management of IEPs significantly contribute to the workload of special education teachers and therapists. As a result, it is quite natural that the use of technology to facilitate IEP writing has been an ongoing interest to the field of special education. Computerized IEP systems differ from traditional data base programs in the sense that they are dedicated solely to IEP writing and evaluation processes, but they may offer some adaptability for local education agency information management needs. IEP systems are essentially prepackaged templates on which student data are entered in the creation of an IEP. The management benefits of computerized IEPs appear considerable. For example, in a study comparing computerized and noncomputerized IEPs, Ryan and Rucker (1986) sampled a combination of IEP-related variables that included the amount of time spent developing the IEP (e.g., time gathering data to prepare the IEP, and time spent writing the IEP), costs (e.g., participants' salaries, IEP printing costs, and the costs of computer hardware, software, and technical assistance), and the attitudes of participating teachers toward using computerized IEPs. They found significant difference in the areas of IEP writing time (on the average, 65 minutes for computerized IEPs versus 118 minutes for noncomputerized IEPs) and IEP preparation costs (approximately $67 to prepare computerized IEPs versus $84 for noncomputerized IEPs). Also, teachers who had the opportunity to use computerized IEP systems, compared to colleagues who used noncomputerized IEP procedures, also held more positive attitudes regarding the productivity value of these systems. Numerous other studies have addressed the pragmatics of using computerized IEPs

Computerized IEPs—Point and Counterpoint?

In an article entitled "Individualized Education Programs (IEPs) in Special Education—From Intent to Acquiescence," in the September 1990 issue of *Exceptional Children*, Steven W. Smith examines the norms and standards originally intended (circa 1975) for IEPs by Public Law 94-142 and contrasts them with the reality of present-day (circa 1990) IEP design and implementation factors. In his writing, Smith acknowledges that computerized IEPs help streamline the administrative areas of IEP production. However, Smith also argues—quite strongly—that the use of computerized IEPs appear to produce documents inferior to handwritten IEPs! You be the judge.

Numerous computer-managed instructional systems (CMI), or educational management systems that use computer software to manage the [individualized education program (IEP)], have been designed to relieve the burden of paperwork and cost created by the [Education for All Handicapped Children Act's (EAHCA)] mandate. . . .

Even though the issues of cost and time can be managed effectively by computer-assisted IEPs, as reported in the literature, the issue of a quality IEP is infrequently mentioned. . . . [The literature that focuses on finding effective computer-assisted systems to manage the IEP process and accompanying documentation] is important to analyze because its research focus has shifted from the original spirit and intent of the EAHCA [i.e., from IEP quality issues emphasizing factors such as multidisciplinary assessment, comprehensive educational planning, and parental involvement] to concerns about reducing the cost and time necessary to complete IEPs (minimal compliance) by computer assistance. The emphasis on being able to complete the IEP process and document in less time with less costs thereby fostering more favorable teacher attitudes toward the IEP is viable; however, the reason for the shift from developing quality IEPs to aiding the completion of the document remains conjecture.

Thus the [focus on finding effective computer-assisted systems to manage the IEP process] is one of the most curious stages of IEP research, not only because of the current acceptance of the IEP (despite its skeptical past), but because of the potential sentiment that a "quick fix" using technology can accomplish what other recommendations for improving IEPs have not. Perhaps the IEP's evolution toward a technocratic solution is special education's last effort to arrive at a state-of-the-art document. The IEP, as managed by computers, would now be generated by technicians, using formulas and following rules, rather than using the intended individualized or personalized problem solving to provide an appropriate education. Use of technology to formulate IEPs represents a response to the failure of special education practice to conceptually embrace the concept of what we know about IEPs versus what we do. Thus, efforts now are undertaken to ensure minimal compliance, the very nature of which the EAHCA was intended to preclude.

Sparse mention of quality [in the computerized IEP literature] leads to questions regarding IEPs generated by computers. Have the heal-all powers of technological assistance generated this phase of IEP research? . . . [Are] the obstacles to exemplary compliance [found in much of the IEP research literature] making quality IEPs a "non-issue"? Has exemplary compliance of the IEP become subordinate to the realities of time, effort, and money? Although answers to these questions are conjecture, one [computer managed instruction] effect on the IEP is clear—the IEP and its mission to provide individualized education within the spirit and intent of EAHCA has become a waning concern. Little if any suggestions are found [in the literature addressing using computer-assisted systems] for implementing IEPs toward the law's original intent of quality programming based on the values of an appropriate education. (Smith, 1990, pp. 10–11) and relevant features that should be included in them (Enell, 1984; Enell & Barrick, 1983; Honeyman, 1985; Hummel & Degnan, 1986; Jenkins, 1986, 1987; Kellogg, 1984; Lane, 1984; Lillie, 1983; Majsterek, Wilson, & Mandle-baum, 1990; White, 1984).

Although the obvious benefits of using computerized IEPs from the standpoint of efficient management of student information have been reported in the literature, Smith (1990) expressed grave concerns regarding whether the quality of computerized IEPs was any better than that of their paper and pencil predecessors. (See "Computerized IEPs" box.) Indeed, upon reviewing the literature on non-computerized and computerized IEPs, Smith pessimistically argued that computerized IEPs were less personal and focused IEP development processes toward meeting minimal compliance standards rather than facilitating the original norms and standards of the Education for All Handicapped Children Act (Public Law 94–142). The original standards included IEP quality issues emphasizing factors such as multidisciplinary assessment, comprehensive educational planning, and parental involvement.

Finally, IEPs do not have to be created using specifically designed commercial programs. They can be developed using a low-cost word processor. As is the case with other computer record-keeping strategies, the management and time benefits of using a word-processed IEP occur after the initial development of an IEP template.

Systematic Collection of Behavioral Data

One of the most recent breakthroughs of computer technology is the miniaturization of computer systems, which allows for easy transport of computers between educational settings. The new laptop computers, named after their ability to rest on the lap of the user, typically range in weight from 3 to 12 pounds and can possess desktop-computer capabilities. In addition to having a central processing unit, laptop computers contain built-in liquid crystal or plasma displays, floppy and/or hard disk systems for ample data storage, and built-in interfaces that allow for a variety of peripherals to be attached.

When laptop computers are combined with software that facilitates the systematic recording, graphing and analysis of observational data (e.g., procedures required when using applied behavioral analysis), professionals have at their fingertips hardware and software that can help them accurately collect a wealth of behavioral information regarding student performance. Laptop computers have been used to collect and analyze information regarding the frequency and duration of student behaviors as related to procedures that include event recording, time sampling, and duration and latency recording (Denny & Fox, 1989; Rieth, Haus, & Bahr, 1989; Repp, Karsh, Acker, Felce, & Harman, 1989).

The benefits of using portable computers to collect data include doing away with human error in the recording and summary calculations of sampled behavior and increasing the ability to collect information regarding continuous behavior and multiple categories of student behavior and information on more than one subject simultaneously (Rieth, Haus, & Bahr, 1989; Repp et al., 1989). However, potential impediments to using portable computers for observational data recording include (a) the absence of commercial observational data-collection software and thus the requirement of having to hire a programmer to customize and maintain software to fit the observational categories/data requirements of the teacher or researcher (Rieth, Haus, & Bahr, 1989), and (b) the degree of training required by observers to distinguish behaviors and operate the computer (Saudargas & Bunn, 1989).

Confidentiality of Information

One final point about computerized IEPs deserves to be made. Public Law 94-142 mandates that appropriate methods be employed to ensure confidentiality of records. Therefore it is important that professionals treat any form of computerized information containing confidential student information as they would a written document. Disks should be stored in a locked desk drawer or file cabinet, and information stored on a hard disk may need to be either encrypted or protected with a password system to control access. Also, computerized records directly associated with individual students must be considered part of their formal education record, and procedures must be established to facilitate parental inspection (Jacob & Brantley, 1986). Additional discussion regarding ethical and legal considerations for computer use in special education can be found in Jacob and Brantley (1986).

Correspondence

Correspondence represents the range of written communication that professionals have with parents, colleagues, and resource or professional organizations. Generally, these communications are informal or handwritten due to time constraints and the lack of clerical assistance. In contrast, the use of a word processor has considerable potential to improve the efficiency of communication between teachers, therapists, and parents or professionals and colleagues.

Several strategies can assist special education teachers and therapists in managing their written correspondence. Perhaps the most common strategy is simply using a word processor as a file cabinet to store and save copies of letters. Once written and stored, any document is available for reprinting as needed.

Certain correspondence can be classified as general, which means it can be reused with only minor changes (e.g., a request to parents for information requires changing only the inside address and salutation). Other types of documents are fairly standard but always require customization for individual students (e.g., a behavior contract for completing homework). In this case, by creating and storing on a computer disk a standard behavior contract that outlines the parameters involved in completing homework, the search and replace function of the word processor can be utilized to make changes that individualize the contract by adding the student's name, date of the contract, criteria and unique conditions, and so forth. Table 13.3 describes ways word processing features can be used to facilitate personal correspondence.

As a final word of advice and caution, the use of standardized form letters is increasingly common and often causes professionals to forget that the purpose of educational correspondence is to maintain parental communication and continuing collaboration. Therefore, it is important to keep all pertinent information in standard form letters updated and to ensure that correspondence properly reflects a personal tone.

TABLE 13.3
Word processing applications that facilitate personal correspondence

Application	Method
Creating a basic form letter	Create a form letter focusing on one topic that can be edited and revised to appear personalized. Basic features to be edited might include colleagues, students, or parents' names.
Editing a multipurpose form letter using cut and paste features	Edit a form letter that includes an introduction plus a series of related paragraphs by editing paragraphs that are relevant and cutting out the remainder.
Editing files using copy and paste features	Edit a word processing file that holds a variety of specific sentences and paragraphs by copying and pasting them into other word processing files based on correspondence needs.
Writing a letter using macro functions	Assign specific sentences and paragraphs to function keys. During word processing, insert these sentences or paragraphs by pressing a function key. Additional editing may follow. Some teachers write IEPs this way.

Professional Development

The topic of professional development opportunities for teachers and therapists has received increased attention in recent years due to nationwide school reform efforts. Two of the major goals of these efforts are to reduce the isolationism that professionals feel about being in their class- or therapy rooms all day and to increase the number of opportunities professionals have to interact with each other. A number of avenues exist through which technology increases the opportunities professionals have to share ideas with others, engage in provocative discussions, and gain access to data resources that provide information and assistance for improving instructional practices.

One type of professional development opportunity that is becoming commonplace is the use of teleconferencing to provide in-service training. *Distance learning* is a generic term used to describe a range of learning activities that take place when the professional and student are unable to be in the same physical location but can be interactively linked electronically from a central site through two-way television or computer and voice communications (Jordahl, 1991). In addition to greatly increasing access to information and services, distance learning is viewed as an important tool for providing high-quality presentations to remote locations (e.g., special educators in rural school districts) and to special interest groups gathering in central locations throughout the country or world. Readers interested in learning more about distance education are encouraged to contact the Arts and Sciences Teleconferencing Service at Oklahoma State University (Stillwater, OK) to obtain further information and a current programming schedule. Presently there is not a national center that charts the wealth of satellite teleconferencing available, but many professional publications do announce upcoming programs. *The Chronicle of Higher Education* is one source.

Another technology application that supports professional development involves the use of telecommunications. By adding a modem or fax modem (see Brown & Lusty, 1992) to the class- or therapy room computer and having access to a phone line, a professional has all

Technology enhancees personal productivity.
(Photograph by Jimmy D. Lindsey)

the necessary tools to use the computer to access a variety of electronic resources. Frequently these on-line resources are in the form of electronic information services that provide facilities for sending or receiving electronic mail, posting information requests, scanning software or text libraries, and accessing news services and electronic data bases, among other functions. For example, numerous on-line electronic networks, data bases, and bulletin boards specialize in providing technology-related information regarding special education and rehabilitation services and products (RESNA, 1990; Center for Special Education Technology, 1991a, 1991b; see "Directories of Electronic Information" box). SpecialNet (GTE), an electronic network devoted exclusively to special educators, provides a variety of bulletin boards focusing on information specific to disability areas (e.g., learning disabilities, mental retardation, deafness, etc.), technology-related topics (e.g., computers and hardware), classroom practices, and employment opportunities among other concerns. DIALOG (Dialog Information Services) hosts the Exceptional Child Education Resources data base of exceptional education literature. Table 13.4 provides some examples of information accessible through electronic information sources.

The use of telecommunication procedures increasingly provides teachers and therapists with access to information, resources, and the opportunity to collaborate with colleagues from around the country and across the world. Many networks and bulletin boards also pro-

TABLE 13.4
Examples of information accessible through electronic networks

Network	Board Name	Type of information
SpecialNet	BD.ED	Messages and topics related to behavior disorders
	LD	Messages and topics related to learning disabilities
	KIDS TALK	Messaging between students and teachers
	EDLINE	Daily news services profiling events in education
	EMPLOYMENT	Announcements about professional employment opportunities
COMPUSERVE		
	STUFORUM	Forum for students
	EDRESEARCH	Forum for discussing educational research
	DISABILITIES	Forum for discussing disability related topics
	AAE	Grolier's *Academic American Encyclopedia*
DIALOG		
	ERIC (File 1)	Bibliographic data base of educational literature
	Social Scisearch (File 7)	Bibliographic data base index of the social, behavioral, and related sciences
	Exceptional Child Education Resources (File 54)	Bibliographic data base of the exceptional education literature
	Magazine ASAP (File 647)	*Index to Current Periodicals*

Note. Contact information for each of these services is located in the Hardware/Software section at the end of this chapter.

vide electronic messaging and teleconferencing to facilitate communication and discussion between professionals. For example, the integration of electronic information into the curriculum involves using electronic mail to collaboratively plan with distant colleagues. By mutually creating instructional lessons and activities, teachers and students engage in cooperative planning and problem solving that provide a basis for real-life application of skills across the curriculum. A description of one such project is described in Kimmel, Kerr, and O'Shea (1987), and numerous current examples are provided on the KIDS TALK bulletin board on SpecialNet. Expanded information regarding telecommunications and spe-

cial education can be found in Gall (1988). The increased and varied use of telecommunications with and by exceptional individuals is also profiled in a special issue of the *Journal of Special Education Technology* (Gall, 1991).

In another context, electronic networks such as CompuServe, Prodigy, GEnie, and DELPHI provide professionals access to on-line general information sources such as *Grolier's Electronic Encyclopedia, Consumer Reports,* National Parenting Center publications, and the *Wall Street Journal.* Some networks offer electronic courses that provide college credit, and many networks offer libraries of public domain software that can be downloaded for use in the class- or therapy room.

Directories of Electronic Information Sources for Special Education in Print Form

The following directories provide addresses and descriptive information regarding a variety of resources for special education information in electronic form (e.g., information is accessible via telecommunications, CD-ROM, or floppy disks that can be copied onto hard disk systems). The directories are in print form.

Directory of On-line Networks, Databases and
   Bulletin Boards on Assistive Technology
The Association for the Advancement of
   Rehabilitation Technology (RESNA)
RESNA Technical Assistance Project
1101 Connecticut Ave., NW, Suite 700
Washington, DC 20036
Description: The directory is composed of three sections (electronic networks, on-line data bases, and bulletin boards) that exclusively identify electronic sources/systems of information on special education. Within each section, information is provided describing the system, its target audience, user hardware needs, how to access the system, and its cost. Sources' addresses and phone numbers are included in the information.

Directory of Software Data Sources
Directory of Assistive Technology Data Sources
Center for Special Education Technology
Council for Exceptional Children
1920 Association Drive
Reston, VA 22091
800-873-8255
Description: These directories do not exclusively focus on electronic sources of information. However, they provide a comprehensive listing describing features of software and hardware data sources with special education and regular education focus. For each data base, information is provided regarding how the data base is accessed, enabling the reader to ascertain whether electronic versions are available. Sources' addresses and phone numbers are included in the information.

One final note. The ERIC Clearinghouse on Handicapped and Gifted Children, located at the Council for Exceptional Children (same address as above), has written a document entitled Using Personal Computers to Acquire Special Education Information (1989). When writing, ask for ERIC Digest No. 429.

Recent advances in storage technology also provide alternative and more economical methods of accessing information without having to use telecommunications. Certain datasets of special education information can now be purchased and placed on personal computers that have sizable hard disk storage systems or compact disk read-only-memory (CD-ROM) players. For example, Apple Computer's SOLUTIONS (Apple Computer), Closing the Gap's CTG SOLUTIONS (Closing the Gap), and the University of Wisconsin–Madison's Trace Center for Adaptive Equipment's ABLEDATA (Newington Children's Hospital) data bases can be placed onto hard disk systems. The SOLUTIONS and ABLEDATA data bases are also available in CD-ROM form. CD-ROM systems, by virtue of their extended memory capabilities and use of laser disc technology, are able to include text, graphics, sound, and still and moving pictures (e.g., multimedia) in ways that are far superior to conventional floppy and hard disk systems (Schweback,

1992). Phillipo (1989) and Mendrinos (1990) have described a variety of CD-ROM-based information sources that are available, including Grolier's Electronic Encyclopedia (Grolier), Microsoft's Bookshelf (e.g., an electronic reference library that includes a dictionary, a thesaurus, a world almanac, facts and familiar quotations, etc.), and Whole Earth Catalog (Brøderbund).

THE USE OF TECHNOLOGY TO ENHANCE INSTRUCTIONAL PRODUCTIVITY

Various analogies have been used to describe the instructional use of computers in education. One often-cited metaphor is Taylor's (1980) analogy of the computer as a tutor (i.e., an object that teaches), tool (i.e., an object students use to learn with), and tutee (i.e., an object that students teach). But in Taylor's example, the emphasis is placed on functions of the computer rather than on the instruction managed by the professional. In describing computer-aided educational delivery systems, Bunderson and Inouye (1987) noted the teaching roles that teachers using computers must often assume. These roles include information processor (e.g., a lecturer, media user), coach and tutor (e.g., a deliver of feedback, an organizer and director of learning and practice), and lab instructor (e.g., an operator and monitor of computer equipment). The instructional roles that special education teachers and therapists occupy may be even more elaborate. Russell, Corwin, Mokros, and Kapisovsky (1989) described the teaching roles that special education teachers using computers should be prepared to occupy, and these roles include the teacher as an introducer (e.g., getting students started on new software), technical advisor (e.g., getting students through the mechanics of particular programs), arranger (e.g., building collaboration and cooperation skills between students), visitor (e.g., visiting students at the computer to check their work), silent partner (e.g., fostering student independence at the computer by refraining from action), booster (e.g., helping students when they are frustrated at the computer), mentor (e.g., requiring students to reflect and evaluate their computer performance), and learner (e.g., accepting the fact that students may learn things about or at the computer that the teacher or therapist does not yet know, which reverses the professional-student role). Clearly, more attention to the types of roles and the ways technology tools can be utilized by professionals working with exceptional individuals contributes to an increased understanding of the use of technology to enhance instructional productivity.

In contrast to the term *personal productivity,* which reflects the use of technology to enhance the productivity of noninstructional tasks, the term *instructional productivity* describes those tasks that teachers or therapists carry out that directly affect instruction. The use of technology for enhancing instructional productivity has generally received less atten-

tion than the area of personal productivity. In this section, specific tools and techniques to enhance the work of the professional in planning, preparing, managing, and extending instruction for exceptional individuals will be examined. The effective utilization of technology for instructional productivity has significant potential not only for improving teaching but also for facilitating learning.

Planning Instruction

Instructional planning is a daily task that special education teachers and therapists engage in as they assess, prepare, conduct, and evaluate lessons for their students. These professionals are well aware of the significant increase of time spent on these tasks due to their efforts to individualize instruction. The use of technology to assist in planning instruction can involve assessing students' abilities, identifying software to enhance instructional objectives, outlining instructional strategies, and developing computer lesson plans as a blueprint for conducting instruction. Each of these areas will be briefly examined in order to identify technology tools and strategies for improving instructional productivity.

Assessing Abilities

Assessment and diagnosis of exceptional individuals' abilities involve a number of tasks of considerable importance. Important functions of assessment include verifying that the student has a specific problem, obtaining specific and detailed information regarding the problem, and using the information to make decisions about the individual (Salvia & Ysseldyke, 1988). A variety of software programs have been designed to assist professionals in the diagnosis of learning difficulties. Often these programs will conduct an analysis of errors, provide feedback about areas of apparent difficulty, and suggest instructional interventions. For example, programs having one or more of these capabilities and used in the area of mathematical computation include Math Assistant I, II, (Scholastic), Math Fluency (DLM), and Monitoring Basic Skills Progress: Basic Math (PRO-ED). Similar programs that can be used in the area of reading include Reading Diagnostic I, II (Scholastic/ Microcomputer Workshops) and Monitoring Basic Skills Progress: Basic Reading (PRO-ED). In the area of spelling, Monitoring Basic Skills Progress: Basic Spelling (PRO-ED) can also be used.

When considering the purchase or use of these types of programs, professionals should investigate the cost, estimated time required for training, and determine whether the program is designed for student use or requires the teacher or therapist to enter selected performance data for analysis. Given time and practice using these programs, special educators and therapists will find these types of tools have significant potential for assisting in assessing student abilities.

Another development in the area of computer-assisted assessment tools is software programs that assist in the scoring and interpretation of standardized assessment instruments. An invaluable resource in this area is *The Psychware Sourcebook* (Klug, 1989), which provides a comprehensive listing of software programs for standardized assessment instruments and includes sample printouts that demonstrate the report capabilities of the programs. While professionals with considerable experience in administering a given standardized test may question the need for such programs, many users report that the scoring functions of a program assist in the timely preparation of diagnostic reports and reduce the likelihood of computational errors. In addition, programs that provide score interpretation and analysis feedback furnish a second opinion or nonbiased analysis that can be used to supplement clinical impressions of the performance indicators.

When a particular assessment instrument is regularly used, scoring, interpretation, and analysis software may hold some promise. However, teachers and therapists must be cautious in their use of the assessment information obtained via computer analysis. This software is subject to the same issues of reliability and validity associated with the use of standardized instruments in education. Computerized reports produce output based only on data and fail to contextualize other assessment information, such as the examinee's mood when the test data were being collected or other clinical observations (Sattler, 1990). Also, the accountability for using information from computer-assisted assessment tools rests on the shoulders of the individual who chooses to apply the information, not on the software that generates the information. Jacob and Brantley (1986) reported that courts are increasingly relying on the American Psychological Association's *Standards for Educational and Psychological Tests* (1985) as an authoritative source on the adequacy of computer assessment practices and on the National Association of School Psychologists' "Principles for Professional Ethics" (1985) to describe test users' accountability. The use of computers in psychoeducational assessment is best considered as experimental, and professionals who use computerized assessment and diagnosis tools must be specifically trained in the uses and limitations of computer-generated assessment information (Sattler, 1990).

Identifying Software That Enhances Instructional Objectives

Special educators and therapists working with exceptional individuals are confronted with no shortage of educational software to use with their computers. The challenge becomes one of identifying the most appropriate software to facilitate the learning of specific instructional objectives. This focus is referred to as the principle of *curriculum correspondence* (Edyburn, 1989) and represents the desire to align instructional software with instructional objectives. Curriculum correspondence stipulates that a direct connection must exist between what students do at the computer and the work they do at their desk. In other words, software must be matched to curriculum rather than curriculum matched to software. Application of the principle of curriculum correspondence requires that computer use be focused, intentional, controllable, and used to enhance mastery of specific instructional objectives associated with each student's IEP. The content areas and ability levels reflected in class- and therapy room materials must also correlate directly with the content and educational challenge attributed to the software being used. Thus, part of the professional's planning tasks requires that specific objectives that have the potential of being enhanced through the use of computers should be identified. One obvious method is to review exceptional individuals' IEPs, while another is to identify instructional objectives that appear to be consistently problematic or troublesome for particular students. These objectives, referred to as *targets of difficulty* (Pogrow, 1988), come to mind quickly for experienced teachers and therapists because their students seem to have difficulty with these objectives day in and day out. Because these objectives appear to be consistently hard for students to master and perhaps difficult to teach using traditional procedures, they make suitable targets for

professionals to consider when planning for the use of technology to enhance teaching and learning (Edyburn, 1989). Finally, once suitable objectives have been created, teachers and therapists should screen their local software sources for compatible programs or locate information about new programs to determine which ones are likely to provide the closest match to selected objectives. Edyburn (1990) has identified seven types of computer software resources (see "Locating Information about Software" box) that are helpful in providing teachers and therapists with software information.

It should be noted that when professionals adhere to the principles of curriculum correspondence and targets of difficulty, using software for general skill building (i.e., simply exposing students who need to develop remedial skills to a variety of math, language arts, and reading programs) can no longer be an acceptable sole rationale for using computers. Other factors must be considered.

Resources for Locating Information About Software

Looking for information about microcomputer software? The following information describes a multifaceted search process that identifies seven types of print-based information resources. Except where noted, all resources include software information for common microcomputers. Prices do not include shipping and handling.

1. Comprehensive Resources

The first type of resource to consider when looking for software is a comprehensive reference of educational software. These sources provide detailed information on programs in a variety of subject areas and grade levels.

The Educational Software Selector (TESS): The latest and the best of TESS (1991–1992 edition). Cost: $49.95. Available from: Educational Productions Information Exchange (EPIE), 103-3 West Montauk Hwy., Hampton Bay, NY 11946; (516) 728-9100.

This is the newest edition of *TESS* and contains detailed descriptions of over 3,000 recent and highly rated programs for all types of microcomputers and subject areas. Public and school libraries may also have other recent editions of this very useful reference (e.g., *The Educa-*

tional Software Selector (TESS), 1986–87, 3rd edition, and *The 1988 TESS Supplement*).

Software for the Schools 1987–88: A Comprehensive Directory of Educational Software Grades Pre-K through 12. Cost: $49.95. Available from: R. R. Bowker, P.O. Box 31, New Providence, NJ 07974; (800) 521-8110.

This book is similar in function to *TESS*. Indexes are available by computer and subject area. Programs are listed in alphabetical order and include information on price and publisher, each with a brief description. The hard cover makes it easier to handle than *TESS*, but this volume is becoming dated.

2. Focusing the Search to Find a Few Good Programs

One of the drawbacks of a comprehensive software reference is that it quickly becomes apparent how many choices one may have. It is also difficult to ascertain the qualitative differences between so many programs. Hence, several tools have been developed to focus your attention on a few good programs worthy of your attention.

Only the Best, 1992: The Annual Guide to Highest-Rated Educational Software, Pre-

school–Grade 12. Cost: $29.95. Available from: Educational News Service, P.O. Box 1789, Carmichael, CA 95609.

The editors compiled their software lists based on the results of published educational reviews of software. Programs that emerge from these national reviews with the highest possible score by three or more reviewers qualify as *Only the Best*. (A list of *Nearly the Best* is also included.) Recent editions may also be useful to consider purchasing: *Only the Best: The Cumulative Guide to the Highest-Rated Educational Software, 1985–1989, Preschool to Grade 12.* Cost: $49.95. *Only the Best: The Discriminating Software Guide for Preschool–Grade 12* (1990 edition). Cost: $26.95. Available from: R. R. Bowker, P.O. Box 31, New Providence, NJ 07974; (800) 521-8110.

1992 Survey of Early Childhood Software. Cost: $19.95. Available from: High/Scope Press, 600 N. River Street, Ypsilanti, MI 48198; (313) 485-2000.

Here is a tool that could be considered a blending of *TESS* and *Only the Best*, specifically for teachers of young children. Contains complete descriptions of 355 programs and evaluative information on software for Apple, IBM, Commodore, Macintosh, and Atari. Published annually. This resource is a "must" for early childhood teachers.

3. Software That Corresponds to the Curriculum

Effective use of computers implies that the software corresponds to the curriculum. By beginning with a specific objective, the software search is focused and the program ultimately selected will facilitate students' learning a particular objective.

Apple Access Curriculum Software Guides. Cost: $27.00 each.
  K–12 Science
  K–6 Mathematics
  6–12 Mathematics
  K–6 Reading, Writing, Language Arts
  6–12 Reading, Writing, Language Arts
  K–12 Social Studies

Apple Education Solution Guides. Cost: $24.00 each.
  English as a Second Language
  Foreign Language
  Business Education
Available through local Apple dealers.

These publications focus specifically on Apple software but are particularly valuable to subject-area teachers as well as special educators. Consider purchasing the appropriate guide when your district reviews each curricular area.

IBM Directory of Educational Objectives and Networkable Software for K through Eight in Language Arts, Reading and Math (June 1989). Cost: $14.95. Available through authorized IBM educational representatives.

This booklet provides scope and sequence charts that link curricular objectives in language arts, reading, and mathematics to commercial software programs made by IBM.

Macintosh Educational Software Guide 1990. Free. Available from: Apple Computer, Inc., 20525 Mariani Avenue, Cupertino, CA 95014; (408) 996-1010.

The first edition of a book that provides scope and sequence charts which link curricular objectives in computer science, early learning, language arts, mathematics, and social studies with commercial Macintosh educational software.

4. Special Needs Software

While the use of off-the-shelf software is desirable whenever possible, special software is often necessary for (a) teaching concepts not usually found in the mainstream curriculum (e.g., cause and effect, sign language); (b) taking advantage of adaptive equipment (e.g., switch, speech synthesizer); or (c) students' cognitive abilities. The following resources are useful in locating software designed specifically for special education.

Closing the Gap 1992 Resource Guide. Cost: $14.95. Available from: Closing the Gap, P.O. Box 68, Henderson, MN 56044; (612) 248-3294.

This is a comprehensive guide to the field of technology applications in special education. Published each February, this guide includes sections that address hardware, software, resources, and organizations. Annual subscription includes resource guide and five other issues for $21.00.

Apple Computer Resources in Special Education and Rehabilitation. Cost: $19.95. Available from: DLM, P.O. Box 4000, One DLM Park, Allen, TX 75002; (800) 527-4747.

An invaluable reference to Apple-related hardware adaptations, software, and information sources relating to the use of technology by individuals with disabilities using Apple computers.

Trace Resource Book: Assistive Technologies for Communication, Control and Computer Access, 1991 edition. Cost: $60.00. Available from: Trace Research and Development Center on Communication, Control, and Computer Access for Disabled Individuals, S-151 Waisman Center, University of Wisconsin-Madison, 1500 Highland Avenue, Madison, WI 53705; (608) 262-6966.

This comprehensive reference to adaptive hardware and special needs software provides extensive listings of products related to communication aids, switches and environmental controls, and hardware and software. A CD-ROM version of this reference is available as *HyperAbledata.*

The 1989–90 INNOTEK Software Resource Guide: A Guide for Selecting Software for Children with Special Needs. Cost: $20.00. Available from: National Lekotek Center, 2100 Ridge Avenue, Evanston, IL 60204; (708) 328-0001.

This resource guide contains information on 190 carefully selected programs that have been used in INNOTEK programs with children with special needs, ages 2–14 years. Includes important information on each program's compatibility with adaptive devices—an excellent resource.

5. Sources of Public Domain Software

Public domain software is a good value for the price. While there is no shortage of sources of public domain software, considerable time and energy may be required to review and select programs that have educational value. The following vendors have expressed interest in identifying and disseminating low-cost educational software.

A source of Apple Public Domain Software: CUE Softswap, P.O. Box 271704, Concord, CA 94527; (415) 685-7289

A source of IBM Public Domain Software: PC-SIG, Inc., 1030 E. Duane Avenue, Suite D, Sunnyvale, CA 94086; (800) 245-6717

A source of Macintosh Public Domain Software: EDUCORP, 531 Stevens Avenue, #B, Solana Beach, CA 92075; (800) 843-9497

6. Periodicals That Monitor New Software

One inherent problem with software reference tools is that they are unable to monitor new software developments because of the production time required. Thus, it is important to regularly review selected periodicals to stay informed about new products and resources. Some periodicals that special educators find useful include:

Apple II
  inCider
  Apple II GS Buyers Guide

IBM
  PC Computing
  PC Magazine

Macintosh
  Mac User
  MacWorld

General
  Classroom Computer Learning
  Teaching and Computers
  The Computing Teacher

7. Other Information Sources

Colleagues, professional journals, computer user groups, and local computer stores are examples of the vast number of other resources that can provide information on software. For example, IBM sponsors the National Support Center for Persons with Disabilities (800/IBM-2133) to locate special hardware and software. Professional conferences also provide a context in which to view software first-hand as well as learn from others about how well a program has worked. Finally, for those with access to telecommunications, AppleLink, CompuServe, and SpecialNet networks can connect you with other users, vendors, etc.

Note. The resources listed are adapted from "Locating Information about Software" by D. L. Edyburn, 1990, in *1990–91 Back-to-School Special Education Resource Guide* (pp. 14–15) by D. L. Edyburn, Technology and Media Division Newsletter, The Council for Exceptional Children. Adapted by permission.

Planning Events Related to Computer Instruction

Instruction represents the deliberate organization of external events to support learning processes (Gagne, 1985; Gagne, Briggs, & Wager, 1988). In the applied context of the class- and therapy room, professionals deliberately arrange external events of instruction to support the internal learning processes of students (Gagne, 1985). Considering that the arrangement of particular events and their direct relevance and the amount of information per event will vary with the circumstances of a particular lesson or lesson objectives, Gagne (1985) delineated the following processes of instruction to generally include within a lesson:

1. Gaining the learner's attention

2. Informing the learner of the objective

3. Stimulating recall of prior knowledge

4. Presenting the stimulus material

5. Providing learning guidance to the student

6. Eliciting student performance

7. Providing feedback to the student

8. Assessing student performance

9. Enhancing retention and transfer

When teachers and therapists consider each of Gagne's events and organize information, materials, and activities to fulfill the instructional purposes attributed to each event (see Gagne et al., 1988, pp. 177–197, for further discussion), instructional planning takes place. Typically, the most common form of instructional planning used is the lesson plan. Although Gagne's nine events of instruction echo a universal format for considering instructional delivery, Jones and Jones (1986) have incorporated other instructional elements into a practical lesson plan format usable by teachers and therapists. By adapting appropriate lesson design (Jones & Jones, 1986), applying pertinent principles of instructional events

(Gagne, 1985; Gagne et al., 1988), and incorporating teaching functions (Rosenshine & Stevens, 1986), an elaborated model of a lesson plan applicable to situations involving computer-based or computer-related instruction can be constructed (see Table 13.5).

In practice, the final choice of a computer-oriented lesson plan is up to the individual preferences of the user. Alternative versions of lesson plans applied to computer-based learning with exceptional individuals have been described by Male (1988), Male, Johnson, Johnson, and Anderson (1985), and Malouf, Jamison, Kercher, and Carlucci (1991a,b,c). It is important to note that the format of a computer-lesson plan is less critical, as compared to appreciating how the format will facilitate deliberate consideration and guidance of how computer instruction is going to take place. Table 13.6 provides an example of a completed computer-based lesson plan designed to emphasize the development of communication and thinking skills for students at grade levels 4 and up.

Finally, it should be observed that the steps used in planning computer instruction also represent a model for conducting instruction. When professionals actually perform Gagne's nine events, or the instructional events described in Table 13.6, deliberate instruction is taking place.

Preparing Instruction

An important component involved in preparing for instruction frequently is creating instructional materials. Special educators and therapists are well aware of the need to individualize instruction in order to meet the unique learning needs of their students. The use of technology tools to assist in creating instructional materials has clear implications for developing new and interesting instructional materials while simultaneously reducing the amount of time needed to complete such activities. This section calls attention to several software tools that facilitate the production of print and electronic instructional materials for exceptional individuals.

TABLE 13.5
Lesson design for computer applications with exceptional learners

Instructional Event	Function and Possible Applications
Anticipatory set	*Function:* To focus the students' attention and foster anticipation of the computer activity. To tie in previously learned information so that this information can be used to facilitate new learning. To develop the student's readiness for instruction. *Possible applications:* Verbally, through statements or questions, relate individual and/or group interests to foster anticipation of the computer activity. Briefly describe interesting and salient features of the computer program to be used. Ask the learner to review what has been learned during previous computer sessions. Call attention to already designed written information (such as tip sheets or cue cards) that can serve to aid or refresh students' memory. Review strategies that assist the student in accomplishing the computer tasks independently. Call attention to a bulletin board depicting the software program's theme(s) and objectives.
Informing the learner of the objective and its purpose	*Function:* To ensure that the learner is aware of the kind of computer achievement or performance (e.g., the conditions and criteria) that is expected, why the student will be doing it, and what information or behavior indicates to the teacher and student that learning has occurred. *Possible applications:* Verbally state the objectives of the computer activity (e.g., a short-term objective for one session, a long-term objective for an overall activity). Write the objectives down onto a checksheet and have the student take it to the computer. Post computer objectives on a bulletin board. Show the student a photograph or "screen dump" of how the computer screen appears when a particular objective is met. If an objective's conditions or criteria include a produced product (e.g., a story produced using a word processor, a computer-drawn picture), show the student an example of the finished product. (According to Gagne and colleagues [1988], communicating an objective "takes little time, and may at least serve the purpose of preventing the student from getting entirely off the track." It "also appears to be an act consistent with the frankness and honesty of a good teacher" [pp. 183–184]).
Instructional Input	*Function:* Through active instruction, (1) to facilitate students' perception of distinctive features of the computer, software, and supplemental materials that directly apply to the learning task and objective; (2) to provide a deliberately planned organization of the instructional information, teaching procedures, and materials necessary to complete the computer assignment; (3) to present instructional information and procedures about the computer activity broken into small concrete steps, concentrating on one factor at a time; and (4) to provide specific examples of or to demonstrate how computer-related information will be presented to the student and the student behaviors that represent correct performance. *Possible applications:* Task-analyze the computer activity. At each step, have specific feedback, events, and/or supplemental information prepared to present to the student. Prepare all materials to be discussed ahead of time. Maintain a library of sample printouts or screen pictures that help convey information to students.
Modeling	*Function:* To demonstrate the appropriate computer behavior. Modeling can be a subset of Instructional Input. Delivering instruction is a fluid and dynamic process. Modeling is based on Bandura's (1977) theory of observational learning. When modeling is used in an instructional context (such as using a particular software program

(continued)	or performing a computer-related activity), teachers should verbalize aloud the strategies and steps that are to be performed as they demonstrate them (Bell-Gredler, 1986).
	Possible applications: Physically demonstrate to the student how the software is to be used. During the demonstration, "think out loud," describing the strategies and actions that are related to using the computer, software, and support materials. Make sure the student observes an example that demonstrates the criteria for correct computer performance.
Monitoring to check for understanding	*Function:* To make sure that students understand the content, skills, and procedures required to successfully perform the computer activities by conducting frequent assessment of their computer performance. Checking for understanding is essentially a precondition of guided practice.
	Possible applications: During instructional input and modeling, pause to ask students whether they are following and understanding the information being presented regarding the computer activity. Ask students to verbally restate or physically perform key factors related to using the software.
Guided practice	*Function:* To monitor students' computer performance and provide feedback and guidance to facilitate the encoding of the information being learned. To ensure the accuracy of learning, especially during initial stages of the computer learning. To begin the process in which students actively use a computer program under direct teacher guidance.
	Possible applications: Generate a variety of questions, hints, and prompts for each factor outlined via task analysis under the Input section. In the presence of the student, model appropriate computer behavior and strategies, and then prompt the student through the same sequence. Emphasize the information that needs to be remembered, and the strategies to facilitate learning that are useful. After modeling appropriate computer behavior and strategies, remain with the student to provide feedback and then guide the student through the computer performance with gradually fading teacher assistance as the student assumes most, if not all, of the responsibility for directing the computer learning.
Summary	*Function:* To achieve closure by having students state, write about, or demonstrate on the computer what they have learned from the lesson (key factors, skills, and concepts covered in the Instructional Input section). To record the progress that has been made toward the computer learning objective(s). This can be done either by the teacher or the students.
	Possible applications: Review and discuss with the key factors/concepts addressed in the Instructional Input section.
Independent practice	*Function:* When students can perform particular computer tasks with little error and confusion, and are provided time to work on the computer with a minimum amount of teacher supervision, they acquire increased independence and responsibility in their learning activities.
	Possible applications: Reserve a block of time at the end of the lesson to allow for independent computer practice. Assign two or three problems or tasks, consistent with the lesson's objectives, that students must complete using the software independently. Depending upon the setting (classroom or computer lab), adapt Philip's (1983) scheduling strategies to allow students time for independent practice during unstructured school time.

TABLE 13.6
Sample computer lesson plan

Software: The Factory (Sunburst Communications)

Software Description: The Factory simulates an assembly line with machines for punching, rotating, and stripping (see Factory Help menu for descriptions). Students can build an assembly line and challenge others to duplicate their designs or can try to re-create designs presented by the software at different levels of difficulty.

Subject Areas: Language development, thinking and problem solving, sequencing, spatial orientation; mathematics/geometry

Grade Levels: 4 and up

I. Objectives
   A. Students will be able to design a sequence of actions and verbalize it step by step.
   B. Given a completed design, students will be able to create a sequence of actions which will produce the design.
   C. Students will be able to make hypotheses and communicate with team members about the outcomes when tested at the computer.

II. Materials Needed
   A. The Factory software
   B. Squares of blank paper (hard copy of "raw material") and pencils

III. Time required
   A. One hour
   B. Activity may be repeated.

IV. Procedures
   A. Procedures
     1. Assemble needed materials.
     2. Make sure you know how to work with The Factory software. Try out each of the options on the main menu (Build a Factory, Test a Machine, etc.). Try duplicating factories at easy, medium, and hard levels of difficulty.
   B. Anticipatory set
     1. Ask students if they have ever been to visit a factory where an assembly line was used. Ask if they have ever done a task in which each step was done by a different person (family cookie-making at Christmas, egg-decorating at Easter, etc.).
     2. Tell students that they will have a chance to design their own factory and to experiment with different types of machines.
   C. Input
     1. Show overhead of Factory Help menu and explain the different types of machines.
     2. Explain that rotation is counterclockwise. Review degrees of angles and the effect of different rotations on a piece of raw material.
     3. Allow students to test the machines (depending on number of computers—can be done with one and the whole class or with groups at the computers).
     4. Assign students to teams.
     5. Instructions to the teams: "Each person in the group should be an expert on one of the operations of a machine in The Factory. The group should come up with a design for a product which incorporates each person's machine twice. Once the group has agreed on a product, they should make sure each person in the group knows the sequence of steps to make the product, since the teacher may call on any member of the group to demonstrate the product that the group has chosen."

(continued)

      6. As you work today, concentrate on the following social skills:
- Taking turns and listening to each person's ideas
- Summarizing all of the steps until each person is successful

      7. Show students how to use the paper models of "raw material" to do off-line preparation for using the program. Using paper models is good practice for students (especially those who have difficulty visualizing rotations).

D. Guided practice
    1. Have teams meet and assign machines.
    2. Monitor groups as they try out the design process on paper.
    3. Monitor the use of target social skills within groups.
    4. As teams finish their designs, call on individual students at random within each team to describe the sequence of steps needed.
    5. Students move to computers to test out the factory.
    6. As each team finishes their product, collect their paper "raw material" and present it as a challenge to another team.

E. Closure
    1. Discuss with the groups the difficulty of the designs.
    2. Provide recognition for teams using certificates from Certificate Maker (Master Designers Awards; Master Craftsperson Awards, etc.).

F. Independent practice
    1. Assign a dollar value to each of the machines and ask students to calculate the cost of a particular design (e.g., $3.00 per punch; $2.00 per rotation; $1.00 per stripe).
    2. Given a particular factory design and a dollar amount to construct the design, challenge the teams to come up with less expensive ways to duplicate the product.

Note. From "Cooperative Learning and Computers: Maximizing Instructional Power with Minimal Equipment" by M. Male, 1991, *ConnSENSE Bulletin, 8*(1), pp. 12–13. Reprinted by permission.

Instructional Materials: Print

Professionals frequently prepare instructional materials that are in a print format. The value of a word processing program is clear when considering the variety of written assignments, work sheets, and study guides that teachers and therapists prepare. As discussed earlier, the search and replace functions allow the user to quickly and easily customize subsequent materials once the original file is prepared. A variety of specialized programs are available that provide the user with computerized tools for creating tests (e.g., All of the Above [Scholastic], All Star Drill [Tom Snyder], Classroom Toolbox [Sunburst]), work sheets (Worksheet Wizard [Scholastic/Edu-soft]), puzzles (e.g., Crossword Magic [Mindscape], Wordsearch [Hartley]), and other instructional activities (e.g., M-ss-ng L-nks and English Editor [Sunburst], Speed Reader II [Davidson], Timeliner [Tom Snyder]).

Another activity that professionals frequently engage in is creating instructional materials that serve to increase or maintain motivation to learn. Many teachers and therapists find it useful and enjoyable to utilize programs that allow them to prepare individual certificates of achievement, banners, signs, and posters (e.g., Create with Garfield [Scholastic], Print Shop [Brøderbund], Principal's Assistant [Mindscape]).

Instructional Materials: Electronic

One concern often mentioned by professionals is how difficult it is to find software that meets the unique needs of their students. The use of the computer to create electronic instructional materials represents an important trend that enables teachers and therapists to meet individual student needs with increasing ease and effectiveness. Software that allows modification of the instructional con-

Computer hardware and software promote instructional productivity. *(Photograph courtesy of IBM Corporation)*

tent of a program is frequently referred to as "modifiable software," "shell programs," or "mini-authoring programs." These types of programs provide an attractive alternative to computer programming because the general features and format of the program are already constructed, thereby allowing the user to simply enter (and save) the content of the lessons.

Professionals should be encouraged to develop a collection of modifiable software for several reasons. First, with only a few programs a teacher or therapist is able to provide computer-assisted instruction for all subjects in the curriculum. Second, modifiable software represents a tool that can be used to create instructional activities that are matched to the unique needs and abilities of individual students. Third, because teachers and therapists use modifiable software to construct individual lessons, their students are able to receive intensive practice on very discrete sets

of instructional topics that enable them to build mastery and fluency. Finally, modifiable software permits a high degree of curriculum correspondence between computer activities and other instructional activities within the class- or therapy room. Examples of modifiable software include QuickFlash! (MECC), New Game Show (Advanced Ideas), and Touch-Window LessonMaker (Edmark).

Multisensory approaches to learning are frequently used to overcome deficits in one or more of the senses. The capabilities of the computer to manipulate text, sound, and graphic images make it a powerful multisensory learning aid. Indeed, current developmental efforts suggest that multimedia applications will become increasingly available in the K–12 and college settings. A variety of programs is available to utilize multisensory instructional activities across the curriculum in the areas of writing (e.g., Talking Text Writer [Scholastic], Monsters and Make-Believe Plus

[Pelican]), spelling (e.g., Speller Bee [First Byte]), reading (e.g., Language Experience Recorder Plus [Teacher Support]), science (Science Toolkit Plus [Broderbund]), and social studies (e.g., Talking U.S.A. Map [Orange Cherry]. Multimedia tools (e.g., HyperScreen 2.0, [Scholastic], HyperCard [Apple], Linkway [IBM]) are also available.

Managing Instruction

The instructional models described in the section above on planning computer instruction also represent models for conducting instruction. The distinction between using the models for planning and practice is quite simple. As stated earlier, when a professional considers instructional events separately and organizes information, materials, and activities to fulfill the instructional purposes designated for each event, instructional planning takes place. When a teacher or therapist actively performs these instructional events, deliberate instruction takes place. Whereas planning computer-based instruction focuses on a broader model of instruction, the concept of managing computer-based instruction tends to focus on factors related to the incident-by-incident managerial issues and social interactions that take place between professionals and exceptional individuals once the instruction has begun. These factors include managing the presentation of computer-based information, managing students' access to computers, monitoring and mediating students' computer performance, and considering ways to evaluate students' computer performance when software programs provide insufficient record-keeping factors.

Managing the Presentation of Computer-based Information

The use of projection systems in conjunction with a computer enables a professional to effectively utilize a computer in the class- or therapy room as a tool for presenting information to students. The LCD panel connects to the computer and lies on top of an overhead projector to project the entire computer screen on the wall. This technology is quite effective in assisting with whole class instruction and in demonstrating how to operate a new software program. It can also be used in the writing classroom to illustrate both composition and revision strategies (Barbata, 1988; Moyer, 1988).

Certain products have been intentionally designed for whole class instruction. Tom Snyder Productions purposefully designs its software to be used in the one-computer class- or therapy room. With the aid of a projection system, the Tom Snyder software seeks to have the professional manage discussions while the computer displays and records the decisions of the class and presents new challenges to engage students in thinking and problem solving. Another way in which projection systems are used to facilitate computer activities is in conjunction with instructional applications of videodisc technology. Systems Impact has created a series of videodiscs in math and science that ingeniously incorporates effective individual instruction into whole group instruction by presenting instructional lessons and mastery checkpoints. Based on the performance of the class, the professional is directed to branch to the next chapter on the videodisc. The Learning Technology Center at Vanderbilt University has created Adventures of Jasper Woodbury, a videodisc-based series that seeks to improve students' problem-formulation and problem-posing skills through realistic and interesting real-life problem-solving adventures. In both cases, students' abilities to observe a much larger picture enhance and help focus their observational skills and attention toward using meaningful knowledge (Cognition and Technology Group, 1990).

Managing Students' Computer Access

According to Berliner (1988), "Time must be controlled after it is allocated or it is lost" (p. 13). Given the diversity of computer access conditions that can exist in a given school (e.g., one computer in each classroom or computers only in a lab), time-management strategies for accessing computers should be considered.

Philips (1983) described the following management strategies that can be used when only one computer is available:

1. *Total class instruction using simulation programs.* The computer is connected to a larger second monitor (21 inches or greater) or an LCD projection system so all students can view the output. Responses to the program are made by the class as a group, and the professional or a selected student enters information into the computer for the group. All students experience and participate in the instruction. Assessment of student learning is obtained through the use of follow-up commercial or teacher-made question sheets that students complete at their desks.

2. *Timed-use relay utilizing one program.* When there is a program that the teacher requires multiple students to access, the teacher or therapist begins by loading a program into the computer. Each student's time at the computer is scheduled for a specific interval which is kept by a timer set by the student. When the bell rings, a new student goes to the computer and resets the program and timer.

3. *Block-time format.* Each student in the class receives a weekly prescheduled allocation of computer time. The day and time of each student's access is posted next to the computer.

4. *Nonscheduled format.* Computer time before, during, and after school is blocked out. Sign-up sheets and procedural rules are maintained to manage and prevent scheduling problems that might arise.

5. *Judicious use of systematic procedures.* If the number and availability of computers vary (as additional computers are shared or acquired), the professional can employ variations in the format and procedures of strategies 1 through 4 to maximize efficiency and enforcement of access rules.

Whereas Philips' presented managing students' computer access from a pragmatic scheduling perspective, Dockterman (1990) conceived of management in the one-computer class- or therapy room from a perspective emphasizing teaching applications. According to Dockterman, managing microcomputer-based instruction should be considered in the context of one or more of the following uses of the computer:

1. *Smart chalkboard.* The use of the computer as a smart chalkboard seeks to capitalize on the ease with which computers can present information, draw and redraw illustrations, and animate movement. Through the use of a projection system connected to the computer, software and activities that were originally available to only one user are now projected for the whole class to use. For example, as a group, students edit word processing documents or participate in a problem-solving simulation like Where in the World is Carmen Sandiego? (Brøderbund).

2. *Discussion generator.* The use of the computer as a discussion generator involves using software that causes the students to engage in discussion and problem solving moderated by the professional. The role of the computer is simply to raise questions and issues and to present new challenges based on the choices made by the students. For example, a group of students could use Twistaplot Reading Adventures (Scholastic) or S.M.A.R.T. Choices (Tom Snyder).

3. *Group activator.* The use of the computer as a group activator is integrally tied to the use of cooperative learning in the classroom. As students work in groups, the computer is used as a tool to enable the group to carry out specific tasks that relate to their role in achieving a project goal. For example, in order to publish a class- or therapy room newsletter, students could work together using word processing, graphic, and desktop programs for composing text, illustrating concepts, and laying out pages.

4. *Discovery tool.* The use of the computer as a discovery tool enables students to engage in self-directed learning. This may involve instructional software that allows students

to explore new topics or telecommunications that enable students to conduct their own on-line searches. This use tends to be underutilized in many class- and therapy rooms today.

5. *Teacher secretary.* One important use of the computer, especially in the one-computer setting, is as a teacher's assistant or teacher secretary. Indeed, this chapter has already shown the value of this application.

Finally, in contrast to the class- or therapy-room-based computer setting, many schools believe it is cost-effective to group a large number of computers in a central classroom that functions as a computer lab. Typically, access to computer labs is divided between regular and special education classes, but unfortunately much of the software used with exceptional individuals has been designed for

nonhandicapped students (Hagen, 1984). In addition, lab software is typically shared by all students in a school, and there are no guarantees that software adjustments (e.g., rate and amount of information presented, level of difficulty, response criteria, type and amount of feedback and reinforcement, etc.) will remain unchanged. Imagine the routine involved in arriving at a lab, passing out programs to 15 students, and then having to readjust the instructional levels of 10 of those programs before the students can begin working. Therefore, when exceptional individuals access computers in lab settings, professionals should consider the following strategies:

1. Try to schedule access to the lab to coincide with the end of the planning period or at times when students are away at other activities. Have students report directly to the computer lab, and begin setting up pro-

---

Computer Cue Sheets:
Supplementing Software Documentation That's Too Elaborate or
at a Reading Level Too Difficult for Students to Understand

For exceptional students who may have difficulty reading software documentation or processing oral directions, or who tend to forget certain software programs' commands or tasks, creating supplemental tip or cue sheets that abridge, summarize, or supplement relevant information found in software documentation often provides exceptional students greater opportunity to work independently on challenging computer tasks. A computer cue sheet is analogous to a script or diagram of basic features and procedures found within a program. Cue sheets should be written at the lowest reading level and can contain one or more of the following types of information:

1. A summary of a program's main points, concepts, and objectives. This information can be provided either in print or by pictures of screens with commands or points.

2. Critical information regarding the content and design of the program based on functional categories (e.g., "Tips," "Commands," "Definitions," "Things to remember—that you have no

control over," or "Important things to remember—that only you can control").

3. A chronological flowchart that shows how the program works from beginning to end. Pictures of applicable computer screens may be reproduced.

4. Critical or frequently used key combinations (e.g., to get to the summary status screen from within the simulation, do the following: Press Escape, select option A, and press the S key for summary information).

5. Problem-solving strategies (e.g., "What to try, if . . . ," or "If you can't get beyond X, ask yourself these questions . . .")

As with any self-made instructional material, the form and format of a cue sheet is up to the teacher. Information presented should be concrete and uncluttered. Avoid mixing information categories within an individual sheet, and be attentive to the number of cues or tips per sheet.

grams for the period before students arrive.

2. Use a classroom aide or encourage a student, parent, or grandparent volunteer to arrive ahead of the class to assist with setup and remain as a computer counselor.

3. Get students started on their computer work as quickly as possible. Create computer assignment sheets for each student that provide them with clear instructions on the short-term computer objectives they are to accomplish during the lab session. Also, it is important to create specialized "cue" or "tip" sheets (see "Computer Cue Sheets" box). Maintain a computer progress notebook that has sections for each student and that can easily be carried to and from the lab.

4. Entrust the responsibility of adjusting and individualizing software features to the students. Whenever a new program is started, instruct the students on how to set custom features. For subsequent lab sessions, students' assignment sheets should also include what software features are to be set for that day's lab session. The professional monitors the students to ensure that the adjustments they make are accurate.

5. Use proximity control. Locate and be near those students who may need assistance when setting up programs. Grouping a row of students who need more frequent verbal prompting or physical assistance when getting started or during computer use will result in more efficient movement and availability than having to jump about the lab as different students wait to get started all across the room.

Cooperative Learning

The combination of cooperative learning and computer-based instruction represents an effective management strategy when computer resources are scarce and the quantity and quality of positive interactions between students are as significant an educational goal

as achieving instructional objectives at the computer. According to Male (1988), once the basic components of a computer-based cooperative learning environment have been established (see Table 13.7), professionals can use the following steps as a model for a cooperative learning lesson:

1. Assign students to heterogeneous teams and do team-building as necessary to establish trust and friendship.

2. Present the group goal (the "payoff" for working together).

3. Review the group skills to be emphasized (checking, praising, summarizing, etc.).

4. Make sure at least one student in each group can operate the software program.

5. Explain how each student's understanding or contribution to team effort will be evaluated.

6. Observe the group working both at the computer and at a table as they plan their strategies and complete their assignment at the computer. [The professional] keeps track of who should receive special recognition points for social skills during the "processing" discussion.

7. Review the group product.

8. Check for individual participation, understanding, and contribution.

9. Recognize outstanding group performance.

10. Lead the processing discussion. (pp. 128–239)

More extensive discussion regarding the application of computer-based cooperative-learning strategies with exceptional individuals can be found in Male (1988) and Male, Johnson, Johnson, and Anderson (1986).

TABLE 13.7
Essential components of cooperative computer learning

Component	Purpose/activities
1. Assign students to heterogeneous teams	Cooperative learning represents a conscious effort to create computer-learning teams that represent a mix of students who vary with respect to such characteristics as achievement and language/communication skills, gender, sex, cultural, problematic behaviors, and keyboarding skills. Groups can be assigned randomly or purposely structured to ensure heterogeneity.
2. Establish team identity	Building team spirit, trust, friendship, and a group identity provides an incentive for future teamwork and collaboration. Students in each group work on a variety of getting-acquainted activities that may or may not be computer related. Examples of activities include naming the group, naming the computer, and using a drawing program to design a team logo and banner.
3. Establish positive interdependence between team members	Members of the group must believe that group success is dependent on all members of the group being successful. Interdependence between team members can be facilitated by requiring one or more of the following: • *Goal interdependence:* "You're not finished until everyone in the group can explain how to teach the turtle to POLYGON [a basic LOGO command]." • *Task interdependence:* "Each of you will be an expert on a different aspect of the story—one on the setting, one on the characters, one on the plot. You must agree on how to put your story together." • *Resource interdependence:* "I will give only one work sheet to the group. You must record your group's prediction of what the turtle will do on the work sheet." • *Role interdependence:* "Each of you will have a job. One of you, for example, will be the Checker. The Checker's job is to make sure that everyone can explain how they came up with the answer. I will be giving your group credit for how well each of you does your job." • *Reward interdependence:* "If everyone on the team scores at least 80 points, then you can earn bonus points for your own grade."
4. Provide direct instruction of social skills	A principal rationale for using cooperative learning is to provide students a learning environment in which positive social skills are facilitated and reinforced. However, teachers should not assume that their students possess all of the prerequisite social skills needed for successful cooperation and collaboration. Thus students will likely need direct instruction in a variety of the social skills necessary for cooperative learning (e.g., praising, encouraging, listening, waiting for one's turn, explaining, clarifying, etc.). Direct instruction of social skills can include defining the skills, modeling the skills, discussing with students why the target skills are important, having students practice the skills through role playing or brainstorming, and monitoring to make sure that students continue to use the skills during the cooperative computer activities.
5. Establish individual accountability for each team member	Establishing individual accountability increases the likelihood that each individual will contribute to the group learning process. It provides the teacher with a way to evaluate individual student's contributions to the group as well as their personal mastery of learning objectives. At the beginning of cooperative learning activities, it is important that all students are made aware that they individually must demonstrate mastery to the teacher.
6. Provide students opportunities to discuss and process the social elements of their collaboration	Students will benefit from structured activities that provide them with the opportunity to discuss and process the social elements that took place within their group. Topics of discussion can include how the group helped each member learn, problems the group was able to solve, particular things the group or individuals did to help the problem solving process, and things the group thinks they need further assistance with.

Note. From "Cooperative learning and computers: Maximizing instructional power with minimal equipment" by M. Male, 1991, *ConnSENSE Bulletin, 8*(1), pp. 10–11. Adapted by permission.

Monitoring and Mediating Students' Computer Performance

Instruction is an active process. A teacher's or therapist's management responsibilities during computer instruction should be much like those of a "mentor," with the professional acting as a guide, counselor, and leader of instruction (White & Hubbard, 1988) and a coach and tutor (Bunderson & Inouye, 1987). At the same time, a second management responsibility is that of a "formative evaluator," with the teacher or therapist observing a student's performance during computer work and determining whether the student is making progress toward a given objective (and not in need of further assistance), or whether the student is having difficulty learning and in need of intervention and mediation.

One of the concerns expressed by Rieth, Bahr, Polsgrove, Okolo, and Eckert (1987) was that special education teachers were overly optimistic regarding computers' capabilities as independent tutors. Rieth et al. discovered that many teachers utilized a model that placed exceptional individuals at computers for the purpose of independent work only. Although the evidence was clear that the students were highly engaged in computer activity, teachers remained at their desks and did not interact with their students and software programs. Little monitoring and teacher mediation took place. Similar deficits in teacher-student interactions during computer work have also been cited by Cosden, Gerber, Semmel, Goldman, and Semmel (1987).

As with any instructional activity, computer learning should be built around an active process that is outcome based and includes the student, the computer, and the professional. Not only is it essential that student performance be monitored to ensure the quality of academic learning time, it is also essential that the teacher or therapist be prepared to guide computer learning when students encounter difficulty at the computer or when the software lacks sufficient content and design compatibility with specific learner characteristics or stated learning objectives. A major objective related to monitoring students' computer activity is the ability to acquire enough information in as short a period of time to determine whether a student is academically on-task or needs assistance. If intervention is needed, it should be direct and timely. Therefore, effective monitoring during computer activity can include one or more of the following strategies:

1. Be physically available and prepared to interact with students during computer work. Be up and about observing and formatively evaluating students' computer performance and providing assistance as needed.

2. Observe students' performance frequently to check their understanding. Concentrate on observing a student's computer work for a minute or two. For example, with drill-and-practice programs, wait for a summary screen and note the number attempted and number correct. If an unacceptable error rate is occurring and the program has a pause feature, invoke this function and intervene.

3. Be familiar with particular programs' auditory or visual feedback features that indicate correct or incorrect performance. Be on the lookout for sounds or familiar screen layouts that can serve as cues from across the room that a particular student deserves praise or needs assistance.

4. Be ready to interpret certain types of statements students make regarding their computer performance as cues that they need assistance. For example, if a student is overheard complaining, "Why can't I get out of the store?" or "This wasn't happening to me the last time I used this program!" closer monitoring and intervention may be needed. In addition, it goes without saying that professionals will need to know their software to discriminate these sorts of statements.

5. Collect on a consistent basis brief but descriptive anecdotal records or observational data about students' computer performance. As this information is accumulated, particular performance trends not previously spotted may emerge that accentu-

ate a student's need for supplemental instruction in computer-related skills.

One of the more pervasive aspects of monitoring computer instruction is the dialogue that takes place between the learner and professional when a student is in need of assistance that the software fails to provide. As in any instructional situation, factors associated with effective teacher-to-student communication during computer instruction (e.g., feedback and praise) are important variables to consider.

The ability to deliver immediate feedback is one of the features that increases the efficacy of using computers with exceptional individuals. In considering the elements of feedback as they pertain to the display of computer-based information, Flemming (1987) observed that feedback generally serves the function of rewarding or informing and that feedback principles assume that an agent mediating feedback (the computer or professional) is responsive and available. Generally, much of the educational software that presently exists functions adequately in providing immediate feedback and reward. However, the informative quality of the feedback leaves something to be desired. Therefore, when software provides only minimal feedback in situations where students require feedback that is more informative, teachers and therapists should be prepared to supplement the software with specific descriptive and corrective academic praise and feedback.

During the course of monitoring computer instruction, exceptional individuals should be questioned about their computer work, and teachers and therapists should be prepared to respond to questions or statements their students make about computer performance. When presenting corrective feedback regarding students' computer performance, it is recommended that professionals (a) keep directions simple and concrete, using explicit step-by-step statements; (b) emphasize and repeat main points, sometimes to the degree of being redundant; and (c) intersperse questions as a means of monitoring understanding (Rosenshine & Stevens, 1986).

Praise is one of the most obvious forms of feedback. Effective praise for computer work should not only reinforce the exceptional individual's behaviors but also descriptively focus on what is task-relevant about the computer performance. Praise should be given in moderation, and ideally should be specific rather than general (Rosenshine & Stevens, 1986). Certain aspects of Brophy's (1981) features of effective praise can be adapted and applied to computer activities:

1. Give praise contingent upon computer performance versus performance in general.

2. Praise specific components or criteria of computer performance versus general aspects of computer performance. It is better to call attention to a student's speed and accuracy when using a drill-and-practice program than to praise the student for making the "Hall of Fame" at the end.

3. Praise the student for effort and competence in performing computer-related tasks.

4. In praising students, focus attention on student factors such as their efforts and abilities rather than on features of the computer or software that enhanced their performance. For example, student-oriented praise would be: "Super, you are really writing more organized paragraphs since you've been using word processing. And your spelling has improved since you've begun editing your work! You're really making good use of the computer." Computer-oriented praise would be: "Wow, I can see how the word processor has helped your writing."

Evaluating Instruction

Managing instructional applications using computers should include both formative and summative evaluations. Frequently more formal assessment of student performance is a critical factor in successful student achievement. Unfortunately, many software pro-

Curricular goals, exceptional individuals' characteristics and teaching/learning principles should be considered when using multimedia applications. *(Photograph courtesy of Apple Computers, Inc.)*

grams have marginal record-keeping features. Because different software programs incorporate a range of record-keeping features, one or more of the following strategies may be appropriate as alternative ways to evaluate and maintain data regarding students' computer performance:

1. Create a classroom atmosphere that stresses the importance and routine nature of collecting specific information about students' computer performance. Make students aware that this information is used for purposes of teacher review, feedback, and problem solving, but at the same time stress that this information will not be used against them. As Papert (1980) suggested, inferior learning models stress a "got it"/"got it wrong" approach, rather than encouraging a "fix it" approach. According to Papert, computers are objects that students use to facilitate thinking. Exceptional individuals' computer performance should include evaluations for learning progress rather than mastery alone.

2. Use software programs that store performance information that is useful and adopt a routine that provides sufficient time to

access and interpret this information (Malouf et al., 1991c).

3. Record performance data from summary screens. If software programs do not have a permanent record-keeping function, design custom forms onto which student performance can be recorded.

4. Establish consistent procedures for the collection and recording of performance data. For example, when students arrive at summary screens, they must raise their hands and wait for the teacher or therapist to record their scores before being allowed to begin another trial.

5. Have students assume responsibility for recording their own performances. For example, when students check out programs to use, they each should take to the computer a personalized progress folder. Whenever they reach a particular stage in the program where performance information is displayed or accessible via a command, they should access this information and record it into customized forms that have been developed for such use. Periodically this information should be reviewed, transcribed onto a spreadsheet for graphing or charting, and placed in the student's folders for visual analysis and feedback.

6. Create and stick by a schedule of formally and informally collecting progress data. For example, always record student performance data after a set number of sessions or on the same day of the week. Set a schedule that requires each student to be observed at the computer for 5 minutes once a week, and write an anecdotal note immediately after the observation.

7. Design paper-and-pencil tests to measure students on skills and information learned at the computer. Design tests in ways that can probe for process errors and consider these tests a way to obtain information regarding the generalization of learning from the computer to another medium (Malouf et al., 1991c).

8. Elicit students' self-reports. When students appear to have problems, ask them to

describe what they find hard or why they are having difficulty. Students' self-reports can also be extremely important in clarifying whether or not they have mastered a particular skill or concept, especially when computer solutions can be achieved through trial and error. Another self-report method that can be used is the "think aloud" procedure to assess students' application of cognitive strategies or thinking skills. An example of a think-aloud application is to ask students to work at the computer and orally describe how they are thinking and problem-solving to complete the task.

Extending Instruction

The process of integrating technology into the curriculum to enable professionals to support professional and instructional productivity clearly involves a significant commitment of time, energy, and resources. It may also be useful to reflect on the fact that most computers in the class- and therapy rooms of this country have been in place less than 10 years. Much of the effort of the educational community during this time has been focused on selecting, acquiring, and implementing new application of technology. While all of these activities are necessary prerequisites to integrating technology into the curriculum, considerably less attention has been focused on the notion of extending instruction, or maximizing and maintaining the software's impact once it has been introduced into instruction and promoting continuing students interest in computer-based learning. This chapter closes its discussion by suggesting that renewed efforts should be placed on instructional practices that creatively and effectively utilize existing technology for additional instructional impact.

One common concern about instructional software is that it is consumable. That is, after students have used a program and mastered its content, the program must be returned to the shelf. The concept of "shelf time" suggests that a program is more valuable in the class- or therapy room when it is not sitting on the shelf. For example, tool or utility programs like word processors and graphic programs have flexibility and can be used on a daily basis resulting in less shelf time. Unfortunately, instructional software tends to have greater shelf time than tool programs because of its correlation with the curriculum (i.e., students master the content or become bored with the presentation before the content is mastered). The issue of shelf time suggests a number of strategies that should be considered in order to extend the effectiveness of instruction through technology.

One strategy that can be used to decrease the shelf time of a program is to schedule its reintroduction into the class- or therapy room for the purpose of reviewing the skills covered by the program or to check for the maintenance of skills. Reintroducing the software with a new purpose or learning objectives that are qualitatively different from the software's original objective is another strategy. There are a variety of ways software can be creatively reused as a context in which alternative learning activities occur. Examples of this strategy include cooperative learning (social skills), having students write journals or newsletter articles (written language skills), and having students give oral reports about their adventures in simulation programs (communication skills). Also, students could go through programs like Where in the USA is Carmen Sandiego? (Brøderbund) and use AppleWorks (Apple) to create a data base of cities. This activity would promote the development of perceptual, memory, organizational, and fine-motor skills among other abilities. Furthermore, using a lesson plan format like the one described earlier will certainly facilitate the planning and implementation processes associated with using software for alternatives purposes.

The effectiveness of extending instruction is also increased when professionals keep abreast of the instructional-oriented literature related to computer technology. Presently there are few forums that are specifically devoted to the discussion of creative applications of software or that encourage the exchange of educationally relevant ideas and promising practices for decreasing the shelf time of software. However, this type of information is available to teachers and therapists through newsletters published by several software publishers (e.g., Sunburst, Davidson, Tom Snyder) and through publications that accentuate the practice-oriented applications of technology in education (e.g., *Computer Teacher, Electronic Learning, Teaching and Computers, Technology Learning, Newsletter of the Technology & Media Division of CEC*). Three other information sources that can be used are networking with one's peers, attending conferences on technology and education, and joining or forming local computer users groups that focus on educational applications.

Finally, despite the constant constraint caused by limited resources for purchasing new software, limited availability of staff development opportunities, and limited technical assistance for integrating technology into the curriculum, the instructional application of technology with exceptional individuals can also be extended through professionals' recognition of the need to balance their instructional software collection with a variety of tool programs. After identifying a few basic tool programs, teachers and therapists can begin collecting and testing instructional strategies that effectively utilize these tools to enhance teaching and learning. These tool programs (e.g., word processors, data bases, telecommunications, and desktop publishing) will equip and enable their students to engage in "learning to learn" to pursue knowledge in any subject area. Once professionals and students have the opportunity to obtain a high degree of proficiency with these tools, a myriad of teaching-learning outcomes can be obtained. The value, power, and flexibility of tool programs are apparent from the limited shelf time these programs have. Russell et al. (1989) referred to this type of application as "learner-centered software," or software that places exceptional individuals in control of computer-learning activities and that encourage them "to think and use information to solve problems—or to create new problems to solve" (p. 4). In essence, any program can become learner-centered if the teacher or therapist uses the software to focus on the active development and exercise of mental skills and to improve learning strategies.

While a software collection of productivity tools for learning clearly empowers creative professionals, the use of technology to provide instruction is still a critical need. Software that utilizes sound instructional principles will always be welcomed in any class- or therapy room. More important, successful teaching applications of technology with exceptional individuals will remain a function of personal and instructional productivity (i.e., of how computers are used instructionally and not of how powerful the technology is or what the software is presupposed to teach).

SUMMARY

It was the purpose of this chapter to describe general and specific teaching strategies that can be used to implement personal and instructional productivity computer concepts in special educational and therapy settings. Personal productivity refers to using computers for nonprofessional tasks, and the noninstructional tasks described were record keeping, correspondence, and professional development. Instructional productivity refers to using computers for instructional purposes, and instructional procedures described included planning, preparing, managing, evaluating, and extending computer-affiliated instruction with exceptional individuals. Interestingly, applications and strategies associated with one topic can be applied to contexts associated with other topics. More important, any strategy or application, when implemented with the clear purpose of improving educational opportunities for exceptional individuals, results in increased empowerment for the professional and facilitates students' potential to learn.

REFERENCES

American Psychological Association. (1985). *Standards for educational and psychological tests*. Washington, DC: Author.

Barbata, D. (1988). Data projection panels: What are the choices? *Computing Teacher, 16*(1), 19–20.

Behrmann, M. M. (1984). *Handbook of microcomputers in special education.* Austin, TX: PRO-ED.

Behrmann, M. M. (1988). *Integrating computers into the curriculum.* Austin, TX: PRO-ED.

Bell-Gredler, M. E. (1986). *Learning and instruction: Theory into practice.* New York: Macmillan.

Berliner, D. C. (1988). The half-full glass: A review of research on teaching. In E. L. Meyen, G. A. Vergason, & R. J. Whelan (Eds.), *Effective instructional strategies for exceptional children* (pp. 7–31). Denver: Love.

Bluhm, H. P. (1987). *Administrative uses of computers in the schools.* Englewood Cliffs, NJ: Prentice-Hall.

Brophy, J. (1981). Teacher praise: A functional analysis. *Review of Educational Research, 51*, 5–32.

Brown, E., & Lusty, S. (1992). Buyers' guide: Fax-modems. *PC World, 10*(3), 190–198.

Budoff, M., & Hutten, L. R. (1982). Microcomputers in special education: Promises and pitfalls. *Exceptional Children, 49*(2), 123–128.

Bunderson, C. V., & Inouye, D. K. (1987). The evolution of computer-aided educational delivery systems. In R. M. Gagne (Ed.), *Instructional technology: Foundations* (pp. 283–318). Hillsdale, NJ: Lawrence Erlbaum.

Center for Special Education Technology. (1990a). *Directory of assistive technology data sources.* Reston, VA: Council for Exceptional Children.

Center for Special Education Technology. (1990b). *Directory of software data sources.* Reston, VA: Council for Exceptional Children.

Charles, C. M. (1983). *Elementary classroom management.* New York: Longman.

Church, G., & Bender, M. (1989). *Teaching with computers: A curriculum for special educators.* Austin, TX: PRO-ED.

Clark, R. E. (1983). Reconsidering research on learning from media. *Review of Educational Research, 53*(4), 445–459.

Clearinghouse on Handicapped and Gifted Children. (1989). *Using personal computers to acquire special education information.* Reston, VA: Clearinghouse on Handicapped and Gifted Children, Council for Exceptional Children. (ERIC Digest No. 429).

Cognition and Technology Group at Vanderbilt. (1990). Anchored instruction and its relationship to situated cognition. *Educational Researcher, 19*(5), 2–10.

Cosden, M. A., Gerber, M. M., Semmel, D. S., Goldman, S. R., & Semmel, M. I. (1987). Microcomputer use within microcomputer-educational environments. *Exceptional Children, 53*, 399–409.

Cuban, L. (1986). *Teachers and machines: The classroom use of technology since 1920.* New York: Teachers College.

Denny, D., & Fox, J. (1989). Collecting and analyzing continuous behavioral data with the TRS-80 model 100/102 portable laptop computer. *Journal of Special Education Technology, 4*(9), 183–189.

Dockterman, D. (1990). *Great teaching in the one computer classroom* (2nd ed.). Cambridge, MA: Tom Snyder Productions.

Edyburn, D. L. (1989). Using microcomputers in special education teacher training programs. *Capturing the Potential* [Missouri Technology Center for Special Education], *2*(2), 1–2.

Edyburn, D. L. (1990). Locating information about software [Special issue]. *1990–91 Back-to-School Special Education Resource Guide,* pp. 14–15. (Available from Technology and Media Division, Council for Exceptional Children).

Ellis E. S., & Sabornie, E. J. (1986). Effective instruction with microcomputers: Promises, practices, and preliminary findings. In G. A. Vergason, E. L. Meyen, & R. J. Whelan (Eds.), *Effective instructional strategies for exceptional children* (pp. 335–379). Denver: Love.

Enell, N. C. (1984). A cost comparison of preparing special education individualized education programs (IEP's) with and without computer assistance. (ERIC Document Reproduction Service No. ED 248 667).

Enell, N. C., & Barrick, S. W. (1983). An examination of the relative efficiency and usefulness of computer-assisted individualized education programs. (ERIC Document Reproduction Service No. ED 236 861).

Flemming, M. L. (1987). Displays and communication. In R. M. Gagne (Ed.), *Instruction technology: Foundations.* Hillsdale, NJ: Lawrence Erbaum.

Gagne, R. M. (1985). *The conditions of learning.* Chicago: Holt, Rinehart and Winston.

Gagne, R. M., Briggs, L., & Wager, W. (1988). *Principles of instructional design* (3rd ed.). New York: Holt, Rinehart and Winston.

Gall, R. S. (1988). Keys to the world: Microcomputer technology and telecommunications. In M. Behrmann (Ed.), *Integrating computers into the curriculum: A handbook for special educators* (pp. 231–258). Austin, TX: PRO-ED.

Gall, R. S. (Ed.). (1991). Telecommunications in special education [Special issue]. *Journal of Special Education Technology, 11*(2).

Hagen, D. (1984). *Microcomputer resource book for special education.* Reston, VA: Reston Publishing.

Hasselbring, T., & Goin, L. (1989). Use of computers. In G. Robinson, J. Patton, E. Polloway, & L. Sargent (Eds.), *Best practices in mild mental disabilities* (pp. 395–412). Reston, VA: Council for Exceptional Children, Division on Mental Retardation.

Honeyman, D. S. (1985). Data bases and special education IEP reports. *Electronic Learning, 4*(6), 24–26.

Hummel, J. W., & Degnan, S. C. (1986). Options for technology-assisted IEPs. *Journal of Learning Disabilities, 19,* 562–566.

International Society for Technology in Education. (1990). *Vision:* TEST (Technology Enriched Schools of Tomorrow). Eugene, OR: Author.

Jacob, S., & Brantley, J. C. (1986). Ethical and legal considerations for microcomputer use in special education. *Computers in the Schools, 3*(3/4), 185–194.

Jenkins, M. W. (1986). A new way of doing IEPs: Kill two birds with one stone. In M. Gergen (Ed.), *Computer technology for the handicapped: Applications '85* (pp. 286–288). Henderson, MN: Closing the Gap.

Jenkins, M. W. (1987). Effect of a computerized individual education program (IEP) writer on time savings and quality. *Journal of Special Education Technology, 8*(3), 55–66.

Jones, V. F., & Jones, L. S. (1986). *Comprehensive classroom management: Creating positive learning environments* (2nd ed.). Boston, MA: Allyn and Bacon.

Jordahl, G. (1991). Breaking down classroom walls: Distance learning comes of age. *Technology and Learning, 11*(5), 72–78.

Kellogg, R. C. (1984). Computerized individualized educational plans: One way. (ERIC Document Reproduction Services No. ED 250 838)

Kimmel, H., Kerr, E. B., & O'Shea, M. (1987). Computerized collaboration: Taking teachers out of isolation. *Computing Teacher, 15*(3), 36–38.

Klug, S. E. (1989). *The psychware sourcebook* (3rd ed.). Allen, TX: Developmental Learning Materials.

Lane, A. (Ed.). (1984). *Readings in microcomputers and individualized education programs.* Guilford, CT: Special Learning.

Levin, J., & Scherfenberg, L. (1987). *Breaking barriers: How children and adults with severe handicaps can access the world through simple technology.* Minneapolis, MN: AbleNet.

Lillie, D. L. (1983). Comparison of microcomputer-generated IEPs and teacher written IEPs: A pilot study. (ERIC Document Reproduction Services No. ED 232 386)

Lindsey, J. (Ed.). (1987). *Computers and exceptional individuals.* Columbus, OH: Merrill.

Majsterek, D. J., Wilson, R., & Mandlebaum, L. (1990). Computerized IEPs: Guidelines for product evaluation. *Journal of Special Education Technology, 10*(4), 207–219.

Male, M. (1988). *Special magic: Computers, classroom strategies and exceptional students.* Mountain View, CA: Mayfield.

Male, M. (1991). Cooperative learning and computers: Maximizing instructional power with minimal equipment. *ConnSENSE Bulletin, 8*(1), 1, 10–11.

Male, M., Johnson, D., Johnson, R., & Anderson, M. (1986). *Cooperative learning and computers: An activity guide for teachers.* Santa Cruz, CA: Educational Apple-cations.

Malouf, D. B., Jamison, P. J., Kercher, M. H., & Carlucci, C. M. (1991a). Computer software aids effective instruction. *Teaching Exceptional Children, 23*(2), 56–57.

Malouf, D. B., Jamison, P. J., Kercher, M. H., & Carlucci, C. M. (1991b). Integrating computer software into effective instruction, Part 1. *Teaching Exceptional Children, 23*(3), 54–56.

Malouf, D. B., Jamison, P. J., Kercher, M. H., & Carlucci, C. M. (1991c). Integrating computer software into effective instruction, Part 2. *Teaching Exceptional Children, 23*(4), 57–60.

Mendrinos, R. (1990). How CD-ROM has made two high school libraries vibrant information centers. *Electronic Learning, 9*(5), 30–31.

Moyer, J. (1988). Using a data projection panel for computer applications. *Computing Teacher, 16*(1), 17–18.

National Association of School Psychologists. (1985). Principles for professional ethics. In A. Thomas & J. Grimes (Eds.), *Best practices in school psychology.* Kent, OH: Author.

National Foundation for Improvement of Education. (1989). *Images of potential.* Washington, DC: National Education Association.

Office of Technology Assessment. (1982). *Technology and handicapped people.* Washington, DC: U.S. Government Printing Office.

Papert, S. (1980). *Mindstorms: Children, computers, and powerful ideas.* New York: Basic Books.

Phillipo, J. (1989). CD-ROM: A new research and study skills tool for the classroom. *Electronic Learning, 8*(8), 40–41.

Philips, W. R. (1983). How to manage effectively with twenty-five students and one computer. *Computing Teacher, 10*(7), 32.

Pogrow, S. (1988, May/June). How to use computers to truly enhance learning. *Electronic Learning,* pp. 6–7.

Repp, A. C., Karsh, K. G., Acker, R. V., Felce, D., & Harman, M. (1989). A computer-based system for collecting and analyzing observational data. *Journal of Special Education Technology, 4*(9), 207–217.

RESNA (Association for the Advancement of Rehabilitation Technology). (1990). *Directory of on-line networks, databases and bulletin boards on assistive technology* (2nd ed.). Washington, DC: Author.

Rieth, H., Bahr, C., Polsgrove, L., Okolo, C., & Eckert, R. (1987). The effects of microcomputers on the secondary special education classroom ecology. *Journal of Special Education Technology, 8*(4), 36–45.

Rieth, H., Haus, G. J., & Bahr, C. M. (1989). The use of portable microcomputers to collect student and teacher behavior data. *Journal of Special Education Technology, 4*(9), 190–199.

Rosenberg, M. S., O'Shea, L., & O'Shea, D. J. (1991). *Student teacher to master teacher: A handbook for preservice and beginning teachers of students with mild and moderate handicaps.* New York: Macmillan.

Rosenshine, B., & Stevens, R. (1986). Teaching functions. In M. C. Wittrock (Ed.), *Handbook of research on teaching* (pp. 376–391). New York: Macmillan.

Russell, S. J., Corwin, R., Mokros, J. R., & Kapisovsky, P. M. (1989). *Beyond drill and practice: Expanding the computer mainstream.* Reston, VA: Council for Exceptional Children.

Ryan, L. B., & Rucker, C. N. (1986). Computerized vs. noncomputerized individualized education programs: Teacher attitudes, time, and cost. *Journal of Special Education Technology, 8*(1), 5–12.

Salvia, J., & Ysseldyke, J. E. (1988). *Assessment in special and remedial education* (4th ed.). Boston: Houghton Mifflin.

Sattler, J. M. (1990). *Assessment of children* (3rd ed.). San Diego, CA: Jerome M. Sattler.

Saudargas, R. A., & Bunn, R. D. (1989). A handheld computer system for classroom observations. *Journal of Special Education Technology, 4*(9), 200–206.

Schweback, L. (1992). Get a taste of multimedia with NEC's CD gallery. *PC Today, 6*(2), 37–38.

Smith, S. W. (1990). Individualized education programs (IEPs) in special education—From intent to acquiescence. *Exceptional Children, 57*(1), 6–14.

Taylor, R. (Ed.). (1980). *The computer in the school: Tutor, tool, tutee.* New York: Teacher College Press.

Turkle, S. (1984). *The second self: Computers and the human spirit.* New York: Simon and Schuster.

Wepner, S. B. (1992). Technology links to literacy. *Reading Teacher, 45*(6), 464–467.

White, C. S., & Hubbard, G. (1988). *Computers and education.* New York: Macmillan.

White, G. T. (1984). Micros for the special education administrator. *Electronic Learning, 3*(5), 39–42.

Suggested Activities

Paper and Pencil

Review a number of IEPs and create computer objectives that correspond with the classroom curriculum.

Observation

Visit a classroom as well as a lab setting where exceptional learners are using computers. Observe how the teacher organizes instruction and interacts with the students during instruction.

Practicum

Arrange to spend a morning or afternoon in a special education classroom that is using computers. Acquire a software program that has never been used by the students. Plan, prepare, manage, and evaluate instruction based on a computer lesson plan.

Resources

Hardware/Software

Advanced Ideas
2902 San Pablo Avenue
Berkeley, CA 94702

Apple Computer
Office of Special Education and Rehabilitation
20525 Mariani Avenue
Cupertino, CA 95014

Brøderbund Software
17 Paul Drive
San Rafael, CA 94903

CompuServe Information Services
5000 Arlington Centre Blvd.
P.O. Box 20212
Columbus, OH 43220

Claris
5201 Patrick Henry Drive
Santa Clara, CA 95052

Closing the Gap
P.O. Box 68
Henderson, MN 56044

Davidson and Associates
3135 Kashiwa Street
Torrance, CA 90505

DELPHI
General Videotex
Three Blackstone Street
Cambridge, MA 02139

DIALOG Information Services
3460 Hillview Avenue
Palo Alto, CA 94304

DLM Teaching Resources
One DLM Park
Allen, TX 75002

Edmark
P.O. Box 3903
Bellevue, WA 98009

First Byte
2845 Temple Avenue
Long Beach, CA 90806

GEnie
General Electric Information Services
401 N. Washington Street
Rockville, MD 20850

Grolier Electronic Encyclopedia
Sherman Turnpike
Danbury, CT 06816

Hartley Courseware
P.O. Box 431
Dimondale, MI 48821

IBM
National Support Center for Persons with Disabilities
P.O. Box 2150
Atlanta, GA 30301-2150

Informix Software
16011 College Blvd.
Lenexa, KS 66219

MECC
3490 Lexington Ave. North
St. Paul, MN 55126

Mindscape
3444 Dundee Road
Northbrook, IL 60062

Microsoft
16011 NE 36th Way, Box 97017
Redmond, Washington 98073

Newington Children's Hospital
181 East Cedar Street
Newington, CT 06111

Orange Cherry Software
P.O. Box 390
Pound Ridge, NY 10576

Pelican Software
21000 Nordhoff Street
Chatsworth, CA 91311

PRO-ED
8700 Shoal Creek Blvd.
Austin, TX 78758

Prodigy Services
445 Hamilton Avenue
White Plains, NY 10601

Scholastic Software
730 Broadway, Dept. JS
New York, NY 10003

SpecialNet
GTE Information Services
2021 K Street, NW, Suite 215
Washington, DC 20006

Teacher Support Software
1035 N.W. 57th Street
Gainesville, FL 32605

Tom Snyder Productions
90 Sherman Street
Cambridge, MA 02140

Oklahoma State University
Arts and Sciences Teleconferencing Service
401 Life Sciences East
Stillwater, OK 74078

WordPerfect
1555 N. Technology Way
Orem, UT 84057

Evaluation Models for Technology Applications

CHAPTER

Earl H. Cheek, Jr.
Louisiana State University
Ronald R. Kelly
National Technical Institute for the Deaf,
Rochester Institute of Technology ■

Life's but a walking shadow, a poor player,
That struts and frets his hour upon the stage,
And then is heard no more; it is a tale
Told by an idiot, full of sound and fury,
Signifying nothing.

—Shakespeare, *Macbeth*

Just as Shakespeare's Macbeth (Kittredge, 1939) lamented the lack of meaning in life, we may lament the inadequate evaluation of computer technology applied to education. To what extent has computer technology in the schools contributed to the education of people, regardless of whether they are exceptional, normal, or gifted learners? Are computers reshaping the educational environment, or are computers merely expensive glitz and glitter, "full of sound and fury, signifying nothing"? If educators of exceptional individuals fail to respond to these questions as they implement computer technology in the classroom, there

will be no way to assess the true influence of computers on schooling.

Educators have a professional obligation to assess both the scope and effect of the instructional intervention. While encouraging creativity in developing innovative computer applications is desirable, it is only part of what needs to be done. For example, with any innovative instructional intervention, there is a clear risk in not being able to understand or explain what occurred as a result of the implementation. Unfortunately, the history of recent education is replete with examples of technological innovations that were implemented with great fanfare and ended up gathering dust in some closet. Lots of "sound and fury, signifying nothing"!

The theme of the special 25th year issue of *Educational Technology* examined the question "Computers in Education: Where Do We Go From Here?" The opening editorial observed that it was difficult to define what was meant by "here" in the present status of computers in education. Even though over a 5-year period, from 1980 to 1985, schools in the United States increased the number of computers in use from only a few thousand to over a million, such an increase in the placement of computers does not necessarily indicate any serious impact on the basic educational process for specific learners or groups of learners:

> Schools, by and large, have not purchased computers so that they might use the machines to teach students subject matter—other than computers! In other words, Computer Literacy is King. The schools are treating computers as a social artifact—something that children need to know about—just as they teach children how to use other machines useful in daily life. . . . So the "computer revolution" turns out to be much less revolutionary than one might suppose so far. It turns out to be little more than a form of vocational training. ("Computers in Education," 1985, p. 6)

This editorial emphasized that "if a computer is used solely to teach computer literacy, nothing changes in our schools—not as long as all other subject matter is taught traditionally" (p. 6). Fortunately, as evidenced by the numerous examples provided in this book, many of the educational programs serving exceptional learners are not focusing primarily on computer literacy.

As we turn to the task of identifying some appropriate evaluation models, it must be emphasized that data from evaluation research will not make decisions for people, nor are the findings infallible. Unfortunately, if precautions are not taken, people tend to convince themselves of the things they intensely advocate, even when there is no evidence to support their positions. It is very easy to delude oneself when attempting to sell others on something like high-technology education, especially when a strong professional and personal commitment is involved. The key is to take an educated commonsense approach to discerning nonsense from substance. Admonishing people to discern nonsense from substance is easy to do but more difficult to accomplish when it comes to examining computer technology applications in education.

COMPUTER EVALUATION CONCEPTS

Discerning Computer Nonsense from Substance

Before discussing options for evaluation, some simple ways to avoid confusion will be presented; otherwise, regardless of the evaluation paradigm implemented, it will be difficult to discern computer nonsense from substance. Even with the implementation of an extensive evaluation research effort, it is possible to set oneself up for failure. The reality of computer applications in education can be obscured in four ways:

1. Mirage-words

2. Romanticism

3. Modern witchcraft

4. Overstatement of facts and implications

As educators creatively pursue innovative instructional applications of computers for exceptional persons, they need to avoid the use of mirage-words. Mirage-words are defined as "the creation of a body of . . . terms and phrases that, utterly without justification, convey the impression that the speaker has just offered a solution to the problem at hand" (Greenfield, 1985). Mirage-words are inventive ways to avoid the reality of the task. Examples of mirage-words related to computer technology are *highly motivational* (for both students and teachers); *stimulating; easy implementation; high-technology learning; computer literacy* (exactly what does computer literacy mean pertinent to exceptional learners, or any learners for that matter?); *significant educational impact*; and *significant social benefits*. A recent newspaper article cited a research study conducted with low-income minority children. The research findings indicated that the children who used computers at home as well as at school "gained significant educational as well as social benefits. Their school attendance records improved, they had a better attitude toward learning, and they devel-

The personal computer was a major factor in the computer revolution. *(Photograph courtesy of Apple Computers, Inc.)*

oped strong feelings of self-esteem and accomplishment" ("Computers in the Home," 1985). The focus of concern here is how "significant" these educational and social benefits are. Are they significant only in a statistical sense? Are they significant in terms of a permanent influence on the child? Is the significance short-term or long-term? How do improved attendance, better attitude, and feeling of self-esteem relate to knowledge acquisition and other academic skills? Is this "significance" that crops up so much in educators' conversations real or merely "sound and fury?"

Be wary of the tendency to romanticize computer technology. In summarizing 34 papers presented at a symposium on computer applications for the hearing-impaired, Kelly (1982) observed many assertions reminiscent of the "age of romance." Romanticism, based on the feelings, expressions, and commitments of the people involved, emphasizes imagination, inspiration, and passion, rather than logic, restraint, and order (Kelly, 1982). Of the 34 papers presented at this computer symposium, 32 were qualitative, while only 2 were based on data. This indicated that the various claims about the contributions of microcomputers were not supported with evidence, especially for the numerous testimonies that computer use increased motivation and improved student performance, as well as the widely shared notion that we are entering a new and exciting era in education. This paucity of data in assessing the efficacy of computer-assisted instruction with deaf children has also been reported by Braden, Jeffery, and Shaw (1987). Perhaps true romantic assertions need to be tempered by the understanding that they emanate from the exuberance of people stimulated by participating in the implementation of a new educational tool. The process of integrating computer technology into the educational environment of exceptional persons has the possibility of being dominated by either romanticism or reason, or a combination. Regardless of which is allowed to dominate, the consequences will be the responsibility of the educators involved.

Educators involved in innovative instruction need to be careful not to get caught up in modern witchcraft. They must clearly avoid the sorcery of using statistics as camouflage, jargon to obfuscate, or methodology and objectivity to evade certain issues that are not easily quantifiable. This sorcery must be avoided both in the process of trying to convince themselves and when trying to persuade others. The reported results of all evaluation and research must be user-friendly so that any literate, thinking person can understand the implications. The goal of every evaluation or research effort should be to clarify and explain the circumstances of the events under examination. Persuasion using complex and confusing data is not effective. Confidence in the decision-making process is not fostered by statistical data shock accompanied by the reassurance of a contemporary statistical witch doctor who states, "Since you may not understand what these data mean, just rely on me to interpret the results and draw the implications." Educational administrators and teachers must not rely entirely on researchers, statisticians, or any other specialists to interpret the meaning and implications of a report. As much care should go into communicating the findings as went into the evaluation research design and implementation. For an interesting and broader discussion of sorcery in the social sciences, see Andreski (1972).

Educators cannot abrogate their responsibility to coordinate evaluation research with the development of instructional innovations.

Ideally, educators should plan from the beginning to document the influence of computers on exceptional students in order to discern nonsense from reason. Serious educators should not pass this responsibility on to specialists without remaining actively involved in the data collection, analysis, and interpretation. Anything less will result in modern witch doctors explaining the complex and the unknown. There is nothing wrong with using specialists in the evaluation component, as long as they are a tool and not a crutch. Educators should have not only appropriate data but a clear understanding of those data, so that correct conclusions and decisions may be made. As Kelly (1982) observed, it should always be remembered that "cum dato minimo, excretum bovis omnia vincit" (with little data, B.S. conquers all).

Always be conservative in making interpretations and projecting significance. Overstatement of facts and implications should be resisted. As Calvin Coolidge once said, "You don't have to explain something you never said." Recent news media releases suggest that some researchers and science reporters may feel pressured to overstate the significance and implications of their findings (Randolph, 1985). Media hype is occurring with increasing frequency in the most competitive fields (e.g., genetic engineering and artificial hearts) where there are prestige and commercial awards for the researchers who make major breakthroughs. For example, one New England university released the results of a preliminary study on Alzheimer's disease that involved only four patients. The resulting headlines in the news media made assertions such as "Researchers Describe Possible Alzheimer's Cure" and "Scientists Find First Breakthrough Against Alzheimer's" (Randolph, 1985). Only four patients, and yet someone in a university or the media gave the impression that such a study was a major breakthrough.

There is a parallel here with the application of computers with exceptional students. Computer technology involves intense competition for saturated markets, with the high stakes of financial rewards available to the companies that dominate major shares of those markets. In spite of the currently popular trend of more computers in the schools, and the widespread belief that computers are the wave of the future for education, such an outcome is not guaranteed. The current demand and enthusiasm for computers in education is due in part to a combination of mirage-words, romanticism, technological sorcery, and overstatement that has emanated from the exuberance of both educators and representatives of high-technology companies. If the age of reason is to prevail, a commonsense approach to evaluating the influence of computer applications on the schooling for disabled learners needs to be conducted. Otherwise, the computer age in education may be nothing more than expensive high-tech "sound and fury, signifying nothing" for exceptional persons.

Considerations for Selecting an Evaluation Model

The selection of an evaluation strategy to examine the implementation of computers with exceptional individuals should be determined primarily by (a) the purpose and scope of the computer application and (b) the nature of the question(s) to be answered.

In reflecting on the various kinds of computer applications in the schools, it appears that the potential purpose and scope of these efforts relate to one or more of the following categories:

1. To supplement traditional instructional activities

2. To replace, in part or whole, the curriculum delivery system

3. To expand involvement and quality of independent learning activities in specific skill or curriculum areas

4. To explore and develop innovative instructional strategies that are equal to or exceed the effects of the traditional instructional methods in use

5. To influence the attitudes and motivation of students

6. To examine student performance and achievement using computer-based delivery systems and traditional classroom activities

7. To compare the benefits and cost-effectiveness of traditional classroom activities and computer-based instruction

The specific purpose and scope of the computer applications for exceptional learners should provide direction as to what kind of evaluation model is necessary and, correspondingly, what types of questions it would be possible to address with that kind of model. In contrast to the popular misconception, not all evaluation efforts involve experimental research that examines the effects of manipulating an experimental treatment, nor data analysis requiring inferential statistics. A considerable amount of evaluation research consists of compiling and examining descriptive statistics. Descriptive statistics involve tabulating, depicting, and describing collections of data, in contrast to inferential statistics that characteristically involve attempts to infer the properties of a large collection of data from inspection of a sample of the collection (Glass & Stanley, 1970).

Before turning to a discussion of specific evaluation models, two related topics, unobtrusive measures and single-subject research, deserve comment. These issues are introduced here to emphasize both the need for developing a perspective different from the traditional research approaches and for introducing creativity into the evaluation planning. Too often professionals think that creativity is related only to the instructional process, while research and evaluation are associated with the dull tasks of documentation, busywork, and shuffling papers. In their classic text on unobtrusive measures and nonreactive research in the social sciences, Webb, Campbell, Schwartz, and Sechrest (1966) argued persuasively for multiple methods and novel procedures to overcome the weakness of depending on a single, fallible assessment approach:

Once a proposition has been confirmed by two or more independent measurement processes, the uncertainty of its interpretation is greatly reduced. The most persuasive evidence comes through a triangulation of measurement processes. If a proposition can survive the onslaught of a series of imperfect measures, with all their irrelevant error, confidence should be placed in it. Of course, this confidence is increased by minimizing error in each instrument and by a reasonable belief in the different and divergent effects of the sources of error. (p. 3)

In educational research, interviews, questionnaires, and testing appear to dominate the data collection procedures. Each of these methods has weaknesses in terms of both what they do not reveal and the reactive responses elicited from the subjects. People who know they are being observed or are a part of an experiment may respond accordingly and thus contaminate the results. Webb et al. (1966) described some examples of nonreactive and novel methods:

The floor tiles around the hatching-chick exhibit at Chicago's Museum of Science and Industry must be replaced every six weeks. Tiles in other parts of the museum need not be replaced for years. The selective erosion of tiles, indexed by the replacement rate, is a measure of the relative popularity of exhibits. (p. 2)

Library withdrawals were used to demonstrate the effect of the introduction of television into a community. Fiction titles dropped, nonfiction titles were unaffected. (p. 2)

To test advertising exposure—the "glue-seal record." Between each pair of pages in a magazine, a small glue spot was placed close to the binding and made inconspicuous enough so that it was difficult to detect visually or tactually. The glue was so composed that it would not readhere once the seal was broken. After the magazines had been read, exposure was determined by noting whether or not the seal was intact for each pair of pages, and a cumulative measure of advertising exposure was obtained by noting the total number of advertising breaks in the sample issue. (pp. 44–45)

The relative popularity of museum exhibits with glass fronts could be compared by examining the number of noseprints deposited on the glass each day (or on some sample of time, day, month, and so forth). The age of viewers can be estimated as well as the total number of prints on each exhibit. Age is determined by plotting a frequency distribution of the heights of the smudges from the floor, and relating these data to normative heights by age (minus, of course, the nose-to-top-of-head correction). (pp. 45–46)

Computer applications are often intended for enhancing reading skills and motivations and encouraging the students to pursue different areas of interest. Obviously, creative educators should be combining these kinds of information with the conventional types of research data in order to present a more complete picture on the effects of computer applications. Another way to assess the impact of computers on learners is to consider the increase on demand. At the National Technical Institute for the Deaf, Rochester Institute of Technology in Rochester, New York, the students' requests have resulted in expanded evening and weekend hours for the computer lab. Anecdotal evidence also exists that hearing-impaired college students with below-average language skills are individually and voluntarily increasing the time they spend studying English when their reading and writing assignments are done via computer gaming (E. Lichtenstein, 1985, personal communication). As a result, at the National Technical Institute for the Deaf/Rochester Institute of Technology (NTID/RIT) increased effort is being given to the development of faculty-designed computer games related to the reading materials assigned.

Single-subject research also offers considerable potential for evaluating the effects of computer applications with exceptional learners. This approach is more conducive to teacher-directed research and evaluation for several reasons. First, single-subject research more closely parallels the instructional perspective of individualized programming for exceptional students, while avoiding the problems associated with obtaining adequate numbers of subjects either within or between classrooms due to the requirements of group research designs. Second, it focuses on the

progress or development of individual students, rather than on group characteristics. "The individual is of paramount importance in the clinical science of human behavior change" (Hersen & Barlow, 1976, p. 1), and single-subject research designs reveal information on individuals as opposed to group data.

In its simplest form single-subject research uses the time series design proposed by Campbell and Stanley (1963) in their discussion of quasi-experimental methodologies. Briefly, this is a repeated measures approach in which the teacher examines an individual's performance of some skill or behavior over a series of repeated observations. The repeated performances of these observations in single-subject research are ideally suited to instructional development as Hersen and Barow (1976, p. 63) emphasize that single-subject designs are more oriented to technique building than to technique testing. The basic repeated measurers design can be illustrated as follows, where O represents the repeated observations and I represents the treatment or intervention:

$$O_1 \, O_2 \, O_3 \quad I_A \quad O_4 \, O_5 \, O_6$$

baseline   after-treatment
observations   observations

This repeated measures model can be used to examine a variety of behaviors and skills. In order to have a basis of comparison, a series of observations should be used to establish the baseline performance that will be compared to a later performance after the introduction of the treatment(s) or interventions. The baseline performance of an individual is assumed to be the current level of skill or behavior as determined by a series of pretreatment observations. A series of observations is necessary to provide a reliable assessment of the performance, because a single observation runs the risk of capturing an inconsistent performance or skill level of a student through poor timing when the student is distracted at a low or high functional period. In a time series model, it is also possible to administer a series or combination of instructional interventions: O, O, O, I_A O, O, O, I_B O, O, O. Furthermore, the inclusion of an additional student (or students) in this design is the equivalent of performing an independent replication of the single-subject research done with another student (Levin, Marascuilo, & Hubert, 1978). The more times the results of a single-subject research design are consistently replicated with other subjects, the more confidence one can have in the generalizability of the intervention or treatment strategies. Yet, if single-subject intervention data are only collected on one student, appropriate information is still provided for designing an individualized educational program.

With this repeated measures (observations) model, teachers have a powerful tool to develop instructional sequences on the computer and then to evaluate the effectiveness for one or more individuals. The key is to establish a baseline performance for each student for comparison purposes. For a broader discussion and more illustrations of applications for single-subject research design, refer to Hersen and Barlow (1976), Kratochwill (1978), or Tawney and Gast (1984).

In addition to collecting quantitative data through single-subject and/or repeated measures designs, one might want to balance these types of data with qualitative observations. By utilizing a combination of qualitative and quantitative approaches to assess the educational effects of computer utilization on individuals or groups of learners, it is possible to develop a broader understanding. In general, quantitative research focuses on a defined, singular dimension (i.e., test score, skill measurement, etc.), while qualitative research can focus on multiple dimensions by examining how various participants see and experience the educational treatment(s). However, the pitfall in implementing a combined qualitative and quantitative evaluation research study is that it requires expert research skills. For further information on qualitative research and the use of combined quantitative/qualitative approaches to evaluation, refer to Bogdan and Biklen (1982) and Cook and Reichardt (1979).

In turning to more specific evaluation models for program development, it should be remembered that there is a plethora of evaluation models, many of which will not be dis-

cussed here due to space considerations and limited application to the topic at hand. However, we need to develop an awareness of the diversity of available models that address evaluation from the perspective of systems analysis, behavioral objectives, decision making, freedom from goals, criticism, accreditation, adversary, and transaction. For a more detailed discussion of these evaluation models relative to their proponents, major audiences, methodologies, outcomes, and typical questions, refer to House (1978).

When an overall program evaluation is conducted, four distinct phases should be considered that are the constituent components of a comprehensive evaluation model (Posavac & Carey, 1980; Rossi, Freeman, & Wright, 1979). Each of these components or subparts represents an evaluation model and may be implemented as such. Almost all considerations for assessing computer applications with exceptional individuals should fall under one of the following four components of a comprehensive evaluation model:

1. Program planning

2. Monitoring program implementation

3. Assessing outcome

4. Analyzing cost-benefit and cost-effectiveness

The suggested purposes and scope of computer applications for exceptional persons listed at the beginning of this section relate primarily to the components of the evaluation model. It is on these components that this discussion will focus after a brief comment on some of the planning considerations of the first component.

Program Planning Considerations

Program planning consists of specifying the needs that a program should be addressing and identifying the operational strategies and services that will be implemented. Goals, objectives, and criteria for student success should be clarified. It is also a good idea to specify the parameters of program success. Program success should be defined in terms of

Professionals must carefully evaluate computer systems for exceptional individuals.
(Photograph by Jimmy D. Lindsey)

implementation phases and timelines. Ultimate program success, however, must always be seen in the light of the students' accomplishments.

Monitoring Program Implementation

The second evaluation model component is primarily a monitoring procedure to assess the extent to which goals and plans are being implemented. The kinds of questions addressed by this evaluation component are the following: (a) is an instructional program operating in conformity to the original design as planned? (b) how does the instructional program actually function? and (c) is the instructional program adequately serving the specified target population as planned? These three questions logically relate to the first three potential purposes and scope listed for computer applications pertinent to the instructional needs of exceptional persons:

1. To supplement traditional instructional activities

2. To replace, in part or whole, the curriculum delivery system

3. To expand involvement and quality of independent learning activities in specific skill or curriculum areas

Notice that none of these purposes or related evaluation questions require experi-

mental research or complex data analysis. The primary requisite is a monitoring process that focuses on the collection of data to describe the program and how it functions. For assessing computer applications in this context, it would be essentially a monitoring or audit process to describe the actual extent of the implementation: (a) a description of how the computer applications supplement the current instructional activities; (b) a descriptive analysis of where the computer applications replaced the current curriculum delivery system; or (c) a description of the expansion of independent learning activities per specific skill or curriculum area. These are merely descriptive responses to the questions at hand.

The evaluation focus of this monitoring process is on the extent of the program and who is participating in terms of students and instructional staff. Another critical aspect is assessing the participation of the intended student audience and the effectiveness of the delivery system. The methodology uses observation, interviewing of both students and teachers, and the compilation of descriptive information, in both narrative and numerical form. For a detailed discussion of monitoring the implementation and operation of programs, see Posavac and Carey (1980) and Rossi, Freeman, and Wright (1979).

A simple and effective approach to answering some of the questions in this type of evaluation approach is to develop a descriptive matrix to analyze the extent to which computer applications for disabled learners have supplemented, replaced, or expanded the instructional activities and skill development. Figure 14.1 provides an example of a descriptive matrix.

Depending on the completeness of the list of instructional activities and skill development for each curricular area, it should be possible to develop a descriptive analysis of the overall instructional impact of computers. This description could be presented in terms of percentages of computer applications, both for the overall instructional program as well as within each curricular area. If this type of descriptive analysis were updated on a periodic basis, it would be possible to chart the progress and changes developing in the vari-

	Instructional Activities			
Skill Development	"Traditional" Approach	Computer-based Activities		
		Supplemented	Replaced	Expanded
Language curriculum				
1.	—	—	—	—
2.				
3.				
4. etc.				
Mathematics curriculum				
1.	—	—	—	—
2.				
3.				
4. etc.				
Science curriculum				
1.	—	—	—	—
2.				
3.				
4. etc.				
Art curriculum				
1.	—	—	—	—
2.				
3.				
4. etc.				
Other curricula, etc.				

FIGURE 14.1 Example of a descriptive matrix to examine the extent of computer applications contributions to instructional activities and skill development

ous curricular areas for exceptional learners due to the continuing implementation of computer applications.

Assessing Outcome

The third evaluation model component involves considerations for assessing the results of the program. Essentially this is the research focus of program evaluation. The primary purpose is to answer whether the instructional intervention produced the intended outcome. This is the critical issue for the fourth,

fifth, and sixth potential purposes and scope listed for computer applications serving the instructional needs of exceptional individuals:

4. To explore and develop innovative instructional strategies that are equal to or exceed the effects of the traditional instructional methods in use

5. To influence the attitudes and motivation of students

6. To examine student performance and achievement using computer-based deliv-

ery systems and traditional classroom activities.

In order to examine and verify whether these instructional treatments or interventions are producing the intended effects, a research plan must be implemented. Such a plan requires clearly defined operational dependent measures for success or outcome, ones that will be assessed with a reliable and valid measurement instrument.

Most likely the purpose will be to examine casual effects pertinent to treatment and control groups. Therefore, the research plan should use a true experiment, if possible, in order to maintain better control of the potential alternative hypotheses that might confound the interpretation of the results. If a true randomized experimental design is not possible in which equivalent comparison groups are established through random assignment (e.g., a computer-intervention group and a control group), then a quasi-experimental research design may be utilized. A quasi-experimental design controls for the confounding variables through the use of a one-group time-series method (similar to the single-subject design discussed earlier), nonequivalent control group, or other appropriate research techniques. For a comprehensive discussion of experimental and quasi-experimental designs, refer to Campbell and Stanley (1963).

Under some circumstances, it may not be possible to conduct either a true experiment or quasi-experiment. However, it might be feasible to implement a less rigorous evaluation method as long as the limitations are understood. For example, due to either the topic and/or conditions, the only viable option might be to conduct a preexperimental single-group design such as a one-shot case study (a treatment followed by one set of observations), or a one-group pretest-posttest (two sets of observations). The major limitation to either of these nonexperimental designs is that neither controls for the potential confounding variables that would compete with the treatment or instructional intervention strategy as an explanation of the observed performances. This would, of course, restrict the interpretation of the results, ruling out any assessment of causality. The preexperimental route is certainly not recommended as the first choice and should only be used if there are no other possible alternatives. Other potential methods that are less rigorous include judgmental evaluations using participant ratings and expert opinions. The limitations of such approaches are rather obvious. For further insights into the preexperimental designs, see Campbell and Stanley (1963) or one of the evaluation texts on assessing outcome recommended at the end of this section.

Rarely will any single research methodology provide a perfect fit for a specific evaluation situation. In examining the range of alternative evaluation methodologies, it is possible to get discouraged on learning the inherent weaknesses and flaws within any one methodology. However, one does not have to select only one approach. "The issue is not choosing among individual methods. Rather it is the necessity for a multiple operationism, a collection of methods combined to avoid sharing the same weaknesses" (Webb et al., 1966, p. 1).

For further evaluation considerations pertinent to assessing outcome of a program intervention, refer to excellent discussions in either of the texts by Posavac and Carey (1980) or Rossi, Freeman, and Wright (1979). These texts provide clear explanations and descriptions of experimental, quasi-experimental, and less rigorous research designs.

Analyzing Cost-Benefit and Cost-Effectiveness

The fourth evaluation model component is one of the more complex and difficult to implement. In general, except for simple and clearly delineated projects, it is the one evaluation approach most often avoided. Two questions are addressed by this evaluation model: (a) what is the cost of the identified benefits? and (b) what is the cost in relation to comparative effectiveness of a similar program (or instructional approach)? These two questions pertain to the seventh of the potential purposes and scope listed for computer applications for disabled learners:

7. To compare the benefits and cost-effectiveness of traditional classroom activities and computer-based instruction

Cost analysis requires the acceptance of an economic perspective that educators have not historically focused on with any consistency. Cost-benefit analysis requires accurate estimates that specify both the tangible and intangible benefits of the instructional program. As difficult as that task may seem, cost-benefit analysis then requires the translation of the benefits into estimated or actual costs. If that is not possible, then it is necessary to find another means to relate the benefits in terms of some common denominator. The dimension of benefits is further complicated by the short-term and the often unknown long-term respects.

Cost-effective analysis is conceptually more straightforward, especially if it is integrated into the implementation plan. For example, if the plan focuses on replacing specific components of the traditional instructional approach with computer-based learning, then it is relatively easy to develop a comparative approach. However, if the purpose is to supplement the curriculum or innovate new instructional strategies that have no comparative component in the current traditional classroom approach, then cost-effective analysis becomes more difficult. The critical element is to have something to compare, so that judgments can be made concerning comparative efficacy and relative costs.

Both the simplicity and complexity of cost-analysis can be illustrated with an example concerning the purchase of a car. The clear comparative issue of a choice of two cars is transportation. Will both cars transport you from point A to point Z and what are the comparative costs of the cars? Direct costs such as gas price, mileage, oil consumption, and so forth can be calculated and compared relatively easy. But what about indirect costs like insurance, maintenance, depreciation, and other items not so easy to factor in? To complicate the analysis further, what if the original purchase prices of the two cars involved were $10,000 versus $29,000? At this juncture, the discussion would probably turn to benefits.

What are the comparative advantages of frugality versus those of comfort and luxury? Do certain benefits balance the scales or tip them in favor of either car in the cost-effectiveness comparison? If transportation were the only factor, then the outcome in cost-effectiveness would be won by the $10,000 car. But depending on precisely how benefits are factored into the analysis, the comparative outcome may not be so obvious.

Educators face similar complexities in cost-analyzing the benefits and comparative effectiveness of computer applications for exceptional persons. For detailed guidelines on how to conduct a cost-analysis, refer to Rossi, Freeman, and Wright (1979).

Who Needs Which Kind of Evaluation?

Such a simple question deserves a simple response. It all depends on perspective. A purist would adhere to a comprehensive perspective and require all four components to be evaluated. However, in the real world, such comprehensive luxury cannot always be afforded. What compromise is reasonable and yet still capable of providing adequate information? A basic rule should be to require the minimum data possible to make a decision or to respond to the most common inquiries.

For most education agencies, the most feasible evaluation perspective would probably focus on monitoring program implementation. A critical and persistent question most likely confronting regional agencies is, To what extent has computer technology influenced or changed the basic nature of education for exceptional students? To answer such a query, one would need to know the balance of percentage of computer applications that supplement, replace, or expand specific activities in relation to the overall curricular program. This is the kind of descriptive information that could be generated from monitoring program implementation.

Educational programs that provide direct instruction and clinical services to students would have to be attentive to all four dimensions of a comprehensive evaluation at one point or another. Depending on the specific purpose, they would periodically be monitoring program progress, assessing the outcomes of specific student development strategies and instructional interventions, or analyzing costs. While the administrative team of a direct service program might focus primarily on monitoring aspects and cost-analysis for benefit and effectiveness, the instructional staff and clinicians should focus on research and measurement to assess student outcome performance as a result of the computer applications.

In drawing this discussion to a close, it is clear that evaluation requires educated choices. There are no easy formulas for selection. The information presented here provides a foundation on which to build educated choices for assessing computer applications with disabled learners. With an intelligent and reasonable evaluation effort, it should be possible to discern whether all the "sound and fury" that have accompanied the entry of computers into the educational environment have indeed any "significant" implications for the education of exceptional persons.

CONCLUSION

Computers and Exceptional Individuals

A primary strength in using computers with exceptional individuals comes from the development of symbolic relationships between humans and computers. Humans provide the computer with detailed instructions needed to do work; the computer carries out the instructions quicker and more accurately than humans. The key lies in the human mind rather than in the computer. The mind provides instructions to the computer to assist exceptional individuals. Exceptional individuals are those within our society who, because of their mental, emotional, learning, social, physical, sensory, or communication abilities, require special consideration or assistance if they are to reach their potential in society.

Exceptional persons can be grouped as (a) mildly disabled—having mild disabilities in learning, perception, cognition, and socialization that require some specialized assistance; (b) speech and language disordered—unable to enter into meaningful exchanges of information; (c) severely and physically disabled—may be nonambulatory and many are unable to perform even the simplest tasks that require manual dexterity; (d) sensory impaired—suffering from the absence, loss, or reduction in functioning of vision or hearing; and (e) gifted and talented—possessing very high levels of ability in understanding, problem solving, and thinking or possessing high levels of creative ability and special prowess in one or more areas such as the arts.

Computers enable individuals in these categories to function more effectively in such areas as academic skills, personal adjustment, accelerated learning opportunities, communication, greater mobility, acquisition of spoken and written language, maintaining and directing attention, and independent living skills.

An analysis of current research reflects a note of cautious optimism about the use of computers with the exceptional person. There is very little in the way of empirical support for many of the statements that are made. Although most reports indicate that the use of computers with exceptional students has been successful, there is a tendency to weed out negative reports. There does continue to be an increase in the usage of computers with exceptional learners. Generally, the same results of research are noted with nonexceptional populations as are found with exceptional populations. The current educational uses of computers with exceptional learners can be grouped into use as compensatory tools, use in instructional management, and use in instructional delivery.

For many exceptional persons, the evolution of the computer signaled a potential change in the way certain aspects of their home life could be conducted. Currently computers are being used in home management, education, and as a compensatory tool.

Computers in our society will have an impact on exceptional persons—where and how they live, work, and go to school, and where and how they acquire information. This technology has great potential for improving the quality of life of exceptional persons, but there is nothing inherent in the technology which will make this automatic. The advent of new supercomputers, robotics, artificial intelligence, improved prostheses, new computer input devices, and information storage and retrieval will further impact the lives of exceptional individuals.

The Hardware and Software Domains

Hardware

The computer is a device that multiplies our capacity to perform certain types of tasks and enables individuals to engage in a variety of activities at a level of effectiveness previously thought unattainable. From the abacus invented by the Chinese about 4000 B.C. to the invention of the first computer in the early 19th century, and on to the breakthrough in computer design in 1946 when John von Neumann operationalized his concept of the stored program, this continuous evolution has led to the recent development of the microprocessor, or chip. These chips allow computer processing at speeds well over a million instructions per second and provide the means to use sophisticated input/output devices driven by complicated programs with large memory requirements.

A computer system is an interrelated set of components that work together as a unit. In its simplest form, a computer system consists of (a) an input device that enables the user to input data into the computer (e.g., keyboard); (b) a processing unit that includes a central processing unit (CPU); (c) a disk or tape system for storage of data; (d) the main memory; and (e) output devices such as a cathode ray tube (CRT) and various printing and/or plotting devices that produce hard copy of processed input.

The CPU, or microprocessor, is the device that controls the operation of the computer. It has the ability to receive data, decode it, and execute the instructions contained within data. Input/output (I/O) devices are the components of the computer system that allow one to command and control the processing data. Simply put, input devices provide the means for the CPU to read data for processing while output devices provide the end product. Devices used to enter data are keyboards, light pens, graphics tablets, optical character readers, the mouse, touch screens, and voice recognition devices. Output devices are CRTs, printers, plotters, and speech synthesizers.

One I/O device for storing and retrieving data is called a disk drive and is available for floppy diskettes or in the form of a hard disk. Another useful I/O device is the modem, which translates information into electrical waveforms that can be transmitted over telephone lines or broadcast over the air. Other interesting advances are the speech synthesizer and adaptive devices for the nonspeaking individual with a physical disability (e.g., text-to-speech synthesizers, specialized programmable keyboard emulators, and wireless systems that transmit computer information).

Computer networking consists of combining elements of two or three or more computer systems, enabling many groups to share information electronically. The three basic types of networks are the star network, ring network, and bus network. In selecting and purchasing computer equipment, consider the following: define the need, assess performance, provide maintenance, and provide feedback.

Software

Software consists of a set of instructions written in BASIC, Pascal, machine language, or some other code that a computer can understand and execute. It is soft because it is stored in RAM, the nonpermanent portion of a computer's memory. Instructions placed in the computer's memory may be deleted by simply turning the computer off, by loading another program into memory, or by using a computer command to clear memory.

One major class of software is systems software, which is designed to serve the function of the computer operator, the operating system. Operating systems consist of housekeeping programs provided by the manufacturer. Without an operating system, most computers are useless. They load and run programs, save programs, activate a printer, copy disks, rename programs, and perform many more functions. Operating systems are also a major factor in determining whether or not a given piece of software will run on a given computer.

The language computers understand is made up entirely of zeros and ones. In order to converse with a computer, specific types of programming languages must be used. Some of these languages are FORTRAN, BASIC, LOGO, Pascal, and PILOT.

Another major class of software is applications software, which is the largest segment of the software market and is designed for business, home, school organization, and management functions. These programs turn computers into smart typewriters, calculators, filing systems, and communication devices. Five categories of applications software are word processing, spreadsheet, filing or data base, graphics, and communications programs.

With the advent of the computer, schools can afford to set up laboratories dedicated to teaching programming, writing, or computer-assisted instruction. Publishers are developing educational software at a rapid rate, and many are talking of an educational revolution based on the computer. Categories of educational software are tutorials, simulations, demonstration/information, drill-and-practice, games, student utility programs, tests, and teacher utilities.

Software Evaluation and Development

Evaluation of software must be of primary concern to special educators and other professionals if selection and use of software is to be effective. Too often software is used as a reinforcer for completing assignments rather than teaching concepts and critical thinking skills. It is also frequently used without determining if appropriate information is presented in an educationally effective manner.

Since it is impossible for each special educator or therapist to evaluate all software prior to purchase, they must rely on external evaluators. When relying on these external evaluators, a number of issues should be considered: (a) what are the evaluator's credentials? (b) was the evaluation based on a team effort? (c) was the intended audience considered in the evaluation? (d) did the intended audience evaluate the program? and (e) how extensive was the evaluation?

In the event an external evaluation is unavailable, then an internal evaluation is critical. In developing an appropriate internal evaluation model, three areas to address are instructional information, educational adequacy, and technical adequacy and related technical information.

Frequently software necessary to meet the particular needs of the student, especially those from low-incidence populations (e.g., the deaf), are unavailable. At this juncture, teacher-developed software becomes essential. Special educators and other professionals can create the needed software by using authoring systems or more complex programming languages, or they can have someone else program the software. Regardless, professionals must possess knowledge of learning theory and principles, information on the content to be covered, and experience with the capabilities of the computer.

Issues of concern to special educators regarding software evaluation and development are (a) the lack of effective software evaluations; (b) illegal copying of software; (c) the lack of extensive field testing of software; (d) the need to adapt technology to the learner and the learner to the technology; (e) the need to develop a peripheral or adaptive input device that is common to all major computers; and (f) the need for compatibility of software with all hardware systems.

Interactive Videodisc and Exceptional Individuals

There is particularly great potential for the interactive videodiscs to help meet the special needs of exceptional individuals. Teachers and therapists continue to search for some educationally beneficial ways for students to spend their time in individual, small-group, or large-group settings. Traditional CAI and individualized self-administered assessment instruments require the student to have reading skills. This factor precludes a majority of the handicapped student population. Consequently, spoken instruction is necessary for student interaction. A videodisc player, with its rapid random access audition capabilities, makes interactive individualized spoken instruction possible.

A widely adopted classification system for instructional formats was proposed by the Nebraska Videodisc Design and Production Group in 1979. This classification system is based on the intelligence levels of different systems. The initial classification scheme include levels 1 through 3, but these levels have been augmented by a level 4. The different levels are as follows: (a) level 1—this system consists of a linear player with limited interactive functions designed primarily for home entertainment. Level 1 players include quick frame access, still frame, and fast visual scanning functions, two user-selectable audio channels, and chapter and picture stops; (b) level 2—the level 2 player adds the intelligence of an internal microprocessor to the above functions. However, it is difficult to record student responses on level 2 players; (c) level 3—systems at this level consist of a videodisc player linked to a computer, allowing other computer and videodisc-generated materials to be displayed on the screen; and (d) level 4—a level 4 system is distinguished from a level 3 system by the additional power of the microcomputer software.

A review of the literature reveals that levels 1 and 3 appear at present to have the most instructional value. Level 3 has received the most attention in industrial and military training settings. At this level, the individual learning station is a major instructional delivery system with resource available to support this type of instruction. Although there is a tendency by many to assume the superiority of the individualized learning station, research findings suggest that group-placed and other systems such as peer tutoring are just as effective. Therefore, the technologically based individual learning station must not be viewed as the ultimate delivery system for the public school.

The combination of a level 1 videodisc system and individual student workbooks results in a very flexible and comprehensive instructional system. In a typical level 1 system, the professional can move around the class- or therapy room more freely to check individual workbook activities, guide discussions, and control the videodisc player with the aid of a remote control panel. Additionally, videodisc applications can be organized into the areas of assessment and nonacademic and academic skills development. Videodisc applications are also being examined for personnel preparation purposes.

Categorical Applications

Individuals with Mild Disabilities

Individuals with mild disabilities are those with a learning problem or a behavior disorder. Labels commonly assigned to these individuals are learning disabled, mentally retarded, and behavior disordered. Instruction for these students should emphasize individualization with plans suited to each student's need for reinforcement and structure in learning, input and output channels, and unique learning rate. The computer can be a major element in the instructional plan if integrated properly to its greatest potential. That potential includes drill-and-practice, tutorials, problem solving, simulations, demonstrations, educational games, and application programs (e.g., word processing). Not only is the computer effective as an instructional tool, but it also enhances class- and therapy room organization and management.

A survey of the literature pertaining to mildly disabled students suggests that the use of computers will increase motivation, allow for more individualized instruction, and increase achievement and learning rate. Suggestions for instruction included stressing an instructional program that encompasses intellectual, personal, and social objectives and integrating technology into all subject areas. General and specific computer applications for individuals with mild disabilities can focus on developing nonacademic and academic abilities (e.g., perception, motivation, reading-word identification and comprehension, mathematics, content-area knowledge, etc.), using telecommunications and electronic networks, utilizing multimedia and interactive videodisc concepts, promoting computer-managed instruction, and promoting personal and instructional productivity.

Individuals with Speech and Language Disorders

Computers are also changing the ways an estimated 10 million individuals with communication disorders are treated. By the mid 1980s, computers were available in clinical setting ranging from hospitals to public schools. They are being used in many ways, including assessment, therapy, maintaining therapy data, report writing, and as augmentative communication aids for nonspeaking individuals. These uses are particularly effective in treating the various types of speech and language disorders: articulation disorders, voice disorders, fluency disorders, and language disorders. Computers are being used both for clinical treatment of patients and for administrative tasks. Clinical applications of the computer include its use as a diagnostic tool, use in augmentative communication, use as a tool for clinical analysis of voice, for the delivery of therapeutic services, and for the generation of therapy materials. A major administrative application of the computer is to document the services provided for an individual in order to make intervention decisions.

A review of the literature regarding speech and language disorders indicates that traditional categories of instructional software include drill-and-practice, tutorials, and simulations. Although there are literally thousands of educational software packages available to clinicians, relatively few of these packages have been evaluated in controlled tests to determine the amount of actual learning that takes place as a result of their use. In those relatively few tests, comparisons with alternative instructional methods are even rarer.

In selecting hardware for speech- and language-disordered individuals, there are several factors to consider: (a) a client's physical impairment may necessitate the addition of a sensor, or voice input to the computer; (b) those clients unable to read require the addition of either a speech synthesizer or a speech digitizer; (c) touch screens may be more useful in treating children than keyboards; and (d) in treating severely language delayed children, alternate keyboards are helpful.

Individuals with Severe Mental Disabilities and the Physically Challenged

When appropriate hardware and software have been selected to match disabilities, the computer is a solution to the problem of interface with the environment for many persons with severe disabilities and the physically challenged. Computers and related technologies have been used by and with there exceptional individuals to acquire educational skills, teach problem-solving skills; communicate; and interface with the environment for recreation, vocation, and daily living activities.

When selecting or adapting equipment for specific functional uses, a number of different dimensions must be considered. The most prominent dimension is the degree of physical impairment present. Some individuals may be totally unable to move their arms, legs, or body, but may be able to move the head or eyes. Others have upper extremity movement with movement patterns limited in number or performed with poor coordination or abnormally. A second dimension that must be considered is the number and type of associated handicaps that may be present. Many individuals with physical disabilities also have problems with vision, hearing, or cognition. Each of these factors will have to be considered in designing effective programs for computer use.

Computer accessibility is enhanced for the physically challenged through the use of control switch interfaces that enable them to communicate with and through the computer hardware. These include specialized computer keyboards, keyboard emulators, voice activation, and numerous types of switch interfaces. For some individuals, precomputer training may be necessary. This type of training can be

Adaptive devices such as page turners facilitate computer access and use.
(Photograph courtesy of ZYGO Industries, Inc.)

delivered through software currently available or in the process of development.

A variety of computer hardware and peripherals have been used with individuals with physical impairments. Hardware and software decisions must be made jointly to support the use the computer will have for the individual. There are many uses for computers including basic skills assessment and computer-assisted instruction (to assess, remediate, and enhance skills), and performance of life functions (such as communication, mobility, environmental control, vocation, and recreation). Software is selected to meet one or more of the objectives designed for a given individual.

Individuals with Sensory Impairments

Applying computers to the education of children, youths, and adults with sensory impairments is somewhat more difficult than one might realize at first, since the current technological revolution in computers may not have the same educational potential for people who cannot read or process information normally. Thus, the task facing professionals and

parents of individuals with visual or hearing impairments is how to apply computer technology appropriately to their educational experiences.

Individuals with visual and hearing impairments comprise highly heterogeneous groups; thus, the heterogeneity clearly complicates the educational process. Variables that further complicate the learning process for these exceptional persons are age at onset of sensory impairment; severity or degree of impairment; causal factor; physical origin of the impairment, multiplicity of handicaps; timing of earliest developmental or educational interventions; type of family support—home environment; cognitive potential; and chronological age.

The three categories of people with sensory impairments are visual impairment, hearing impairment, and deaf-blind impairment. Each of these impairments requires planning appropriate educational experiences with specific emphasis on individualization. Those individuals with visual impairments need physical encounter, stimulation, structure, reinforcement, and independence. People with hearing impairments must receive appropriate instruction in English language skills, conceptual development, communication, and academic content. Those individuals with deaf-blind impairments require comprehensive and systematic educational intervention.

A survey of the literature relating the application of computers with individuals with visual impairment suggests that the primary focus is on assistive devices pertinent to the handicaps. There is little discussion of curricular or course content issues in this area. The literature concerning computer application with the hearing impaired parallels that of the visually impaired with the emphasis on communication and educational problems generated by the sensory handicap. Also, technology should adequately serve the user's specific needs, a structured plan should be used to integrate technology into the educational environment, and the primary consideration should be the interface capabilities with the assistive device required for the individual and the availability of appropriate software for the computer equipment.

Individuals with Gifts and Talents

Over the years, education has struggled with the definition of giftedness. At the beginning of the 20th century, it was assumed that superior intelligence made gifted/talented people. As time passed, the narrowness of this definition was recognized. More recently, attempts to identify gifted/talented individuals have resulted in broader definitions of giftedness. In 1972, the United States Office of Education defined giftedness as superior performance in one or more of the following categories: (a) general intellectual ability; (b) specific academic aptitude; (c) creative or productive thinking; (d) leadership ability; (e) visual and performing arts aptitude; and (f) psychomotor ability. Other researchers (e.g., Renzulli) have broadened the gifted and talented definition.

A survey of the literature reveals that research examining the impact of computers on gifted/talented individuals is virtually nonexistent. One study that is available focused on programs in Illinois using the University of Illinois' PLATO computing system to provide students with CAI and programming experience. These studies found that students were least interested in CAI and most interested in computer games. Other studies have indicated an emphasis on integrating the computer into the total learning process by using it as a resource tool. Instead of concentrating on CAI and programming, students used computers for word processing, data base management, communication, graphics, and speech development tools.

Identifying the best hardware and software for gifted/talented individuals is difficult because of their varied abilities and interests. Schools need to consider how best to distribute their often meager computer resources. One of the more effective arrangements is to set up a school lab. These labs should be staffed by qualified professionals—teachers and therapists with accomplished classroom organization and management skills—and used state-of-the-art technology concepts (e.g., multimedia, telecommunications, etc.). Also, computer technology in the form of CAI enables gifted/talented students to complete missed work, develop needed skills, accelerate learning, and explore problem-solving strategies. Although learning to program is a primary function of computers and helps develop those various skills that gifted/talented students must acquire, the power and flexibility of computers will enable these individuals to develop skills needed in more diverse areas in the future.

Administrative and Teaching Applications

Implementing the Computer Concept

Microprocessor-based technology holds great promise. This electronic technology has the potential to assist in the management of special education information, and more efficient information management can result in indirect benefits to the teaching-learning process and has the potential to directly enhance education and services for exceptional individuals.

Through 1973, mainframe computers were used for direct instruction and assessment with exceptional individuals. They were also used for teacher training simulations and data base management in the development and evaluation of programs. In the late 1970s and early 1980s, rationales for using computers more extensively were developed, but actual implementation in special education was rare. Currently there is an acceleration of effort to use computers more extensively with disabled and gifted/talented individuals by integrating this technology into all curriculum areas. Although special education teachers and therapists are more involved in the process, the impetus behind this movement appears to be emanating primarily from administrators. Some special educators are concerned that so much emphasis on centralized planning may leave special education teachers with too little control.

Another current concern is that many special education programs do not own any computers. Thus many teachers and therapists may still be in the early stages of computer use and can benefit from thoughtful planning. In the process of planning to implement computers in special education and therapy settings, a number of important decisions must be addressed. First, the decision as to whether or not computers are really needed must be made. A second major decision, assuming computers do have a place, is to find out if any policies regarding the use of computers exist at the school district, state, or national level. If there are existing guidelines, they should be examined to determine the direction the program must take. Other major decisions that must be made are (a) appointing an individual to be responsible for monitoring the computer program; (b) setting up a planning committee; (c) conducting a computer needs assessment; (d) developing long- and short-term goals; (e) selecting the types of computers to be used; and (f) deciding what other decisions need to be made.

Technology makes learning fun for children, youths, and adults. *(Photograph by Robin T. Berard)*

Administrative Data Management for Special Education

The availability of sophisticated low-cost computer technology offers tremendous potential for increased efficiency for many administrative and instructional tasks faced daily by administrators, teachers, and therapists across our educational system. This is particularly true in record-keeping data base management for special education programs. Thus it is important to explore the use of computers for data management purposes and to provide generic and specific information on this aspect of computer use and technology for special education personnel.

In examining the topic of data collection and record keeping, the focus should be on system design, system and program requirements, and the advantages and disadvantages of file management systems and integrated systems. Planning efforts must be included in the initial designing phase and continued on an ongoing basis to ensure reliable data collection, accurate record keeping, and usable information for reporting purposes.

Computer assistance in the area of evaluation and diagnosis of exceptional individuals is becoming an increasingly more viable tool. The critical first step in successfully using this tool is to determine the pur-

pose for the evaluation and diagnostic process. Current independent or stand-alone evaluation/diagnostic software programs require careful analysis to ensure there is no duplication of effort with existing data management systems and to ensure that they provide reliable and valid assessment results.

The use of computer technology for special education becomes focused on individual education plans (IEPs) much like the programs and services for exceptional individuals focus on IEPs. Important concepts related to computerized IEP programs closely parallel key concepts in the IEP process itself. Issues such as what is included in the IEP, who is going to provide the services, and what the timeline is apply equally to both.

Central office and classroom considerations focus on health and safety issues for computer users, management information systems for special education, and confidentiality and general guidelines for software evaluation of data management systems.

Teaching Applications with Exceptional Individuals: Personal and Instructional Productivity

Cuban's (1986) review of technological innovations in education since 1920 concluded that promises associated with the introduction of computers in classrooms will be unfulfilled until significant attention is placed on the instructional interactions within instructional settings. As special educators and other professionals enter into the 1990s, their attention must be focused on teaching-learning outcomes and they must understand how technology can be used to assist them in achieving objectives using state-of-the-art hardware and software in more effective ways. It goes without saying that existing literature supports the position that professionals working with exceptional individuals have increased their awareness and interests with technological applications. To this end these professionals have and must continue to use computer applications for both personal productivity and instructional productivity.

The term *personal productivity* refers to using technology for noninstructional activities associated with record keeping, correspondence, and professional development. General record-keeping tools can be used to store and manipulate teaching-learning information. Word processing software assists the professional in creating files that contain their students' data (e.g., demographic and schedules), assignment or instructional sheets, behavioral contracts, and anecdotal notes among other pertinent information. This software can also support correspondence functions. Data base and spreadsheet programs can also enhance personal productivity related to storing, manipulating, and calculating teaching-learning data. Specialized record-keeping tools that also promote teachers and therapists' productivity are laptop computers (for systematic recording and analysis of observational data) and electronic grade books and IEP programs. Furthermore, professionals can employ technological concepts (e.g., telecommunications) and traditional activities (e.g., attending conferences) for professional development (i.e., increasing their hardware and software application knowledge base and collaborating with colleagues).

The terms *instructional productivity* is used to describe instructional methods related to planning, preparing, managing, and extending computer-affiliated instruction with exceptional individuals. Planning instruction involves implementing evaluation and diagnostic activities, identifying needed software, determining events related to computer instruction, and extending events to support learning processes. Preparing instruction entails designing summative and formative tests, creating printed instructional materials, and developing student-specific instructional software. Managing instruction involves supervising the presentation of computer-based information, managing access to the computer, monitoring student computer activities, and evaluating student performance.

Personal and instructional productivity applications and strategies associated with one topic can be applied to contexts associated with other topics. The most important teaching application objective, however, is that a strategy or application enhance the professional's productivity or efficiency and improve educational opportunities for exceptional individuals.

Evaluating Models for Technology

As professionals serving the educational needs of individuals with disabilities, gifts, and talents pursue quality innovations in computer applications, they have a professional obligation to assess both the scope and effect of the instructional intervention. Encouraging credibility in developing innovative computer applications is desirable, but it is only part of what needs to be done. Thus the final step in understanding or explaining what occurred as a result of implementation is evaluation. Almost all considerations for assessing computer applications by exceptional persons should fall under one of the four components of a comprehensive model: (a) program planning; (b) monitoring program implementation; (c) assessing outcomes; and (d) analyzing cost-benefit and cost-effectiveness.

REFERENCES

Andreski, S. (1972). *Social sciences as sorcery*. New York: St. Martin's Press.

Bogdan, R. C., & Biklen, S. K. (1982). *Qualitative research for educators: An introduction to theory and methods*. Boston: Allyn and Bacon.

Braden, J. P., & Shaw, S. R. (1987). Computer assisted instruction with deaf children: Panacea, placebo, or poison? *American Annuals of the Deaf, 132*(3), 189–193.

Campbell, D. T., & Stanley, J. C. (1963). *Experimental and quasi-experimental designs for research.* Chicago: Rand McNally.

Computers in education. Where do we go from here? (1985, January). *Educational Technology,* p. 6.

Computers in the home improve attitudes at school. (1985, May 3). *Times-Union Supplement,* Rochester, New York, p. 4.

Cook, T. D., & Reichardt, C. S. (1979). *Qualitative and quantitative methods in evaluation research.* Beverly Hills, CA: Sage.

Cuban, L. (1986). *Teachers and machines: The classroom use of technology since 1920.* New York: Teachers College Press.

Glass, G. V., & Stanley, J. C. (1970). *Statistical methods in education and psychology.* Englewood Cliffs, NJ: Prentice-Hall.

Greenfield, M. (1985, February 11). Mirage-words that we live by. *Newsweek,* p. 80.

Hersen, M., & Barlow, D. H. (1976). *Single-case experimental designs: Strategies for studying behavior change.* Oxford, England: Pergamon Press.

House, E. R. (1978). Assumptions underlying evaluation models. *Educational Researcher, 7*(3), 4–12.

Kelly, R. R. (1982). Microcomputers in education: Ages of romance, or age of reason? *American Annals of the Deaf, 127,* 693–697.

Kittredge, G. L. (Ed.). (1939). *Macbeth. The Kittredge Shakespeare.* Boston, MA: Ginn.

Kratochwill, T. R. (Ed.). (1978). *Single subject research: Strategies for evaluating change.* New York: Academic Press.

Levin J. R., Marascuilo, L. A., & Hubert, L. J. (1978). N = nonparametric randomization tests. In T. R. Kratochwill (Ed.), *Single subject research: Strategies for evaluating change* (pp. 167–196). New York: Academic Press.

Posavac, E. J., & Carey, R. G. (1980). *Program evaluation: Methods and case studies.* Englewood Cliffs, NJ: Prentice-Hall.

Randolph, E. (1985, April 28). Sources, media hype science news. *Democrat and Chronicle* [Rochester, NY], p. 7A.

Rossi, P. H., Freeman, H. E., & Wright, S. R. (1979). *Evaluation: A systematic approach.* Beverly Hills, CA: Sage.

Tawney, J., & Gast, D. (1984). Single subject research in special education. Columbus, OH: Charles E.Merrill.

Webb, E. J., Campbell, D. T., Schwarz, R. D., & Sechrest, L. (1966). *Unobtrusive measures: Nonreactive research in the social sciences.* Chicago: Rand McNally.

Editor's Note

The general purpose of the first edition of *Computers and Exceptional Individuals* was to present in a straightforward manner computer concepts for individuals with disabilities, gifts, and talents. Based on feedback from colleagues, students, and other consumers, I believe that the chapter and appendix authors and I met our objective in that this book's readability, literature reviews, discussions of generic and specific technologies, and descriptions of pertinent resources were rated practical, comprehensive, and state-of-the-art. There is another interesting event that somewhat provides evidence to support our feelings that *Computers and Exceptional Individuals* met its purpose. Cynthia Okolo (1990) conducted a study to investigate the effects of an introductory computer course on university students' attitudes toward the utilization of computers in instructional settings and their self-perceived confidence and competencies to use computers. The experimental group consisted of a class of nine undergraduate and graduate students; experimental group activities included readings, lectures, discussions,

and three lab projects. Pre- and posttest results indicated that the students in the experimental group had positive attitudes at both the beginning and ending of the course. These subjects' self-perceived confidence and competencies, however, were enhanced by the course. The required text in Okolo's study was *Computers and Exceptional Individuals*.

The second edition of *Computers and Exceptional Individuals* has the same general purpose as its predecessor, and the authors and I hope that you found it presents technology concepts in a straightforward manner. Besides limiting the use of jargon, we gave special attention to describing generic and specific hardware and software and to discussing how this technology can be used with and by exceptional individuals in the home, school, and community. In the 14 chapters and 7 appendixes, you have (or will) read that (a) hardware and software development is dynamic, and the number of special education programs and exceptional individuals using technology has increased significantly in the last few years; (b) computer-management procedures and instructional drill-and-practice continue to be the dominant applications, but other technologies are surfacing in and out of the class- or therapy room—laptop and notebook computers, interactive videodisc systems, adaptive devices, and multimedia; (c) professionals are using technology for personal productivity as well as instructional productivity; (d) exceptional persons are using technology to control their lives at home or work, and schools and communities are investing in hardware and software to foster these individuals' environmental access and functions; (e) research studies published after 1986 are restricted and have methodological limitations, but they continue to validate the advantages of using technology with and by exceptional individuals for instructional non-academic and academic purposes, to provide environmental access, and to promote quality of life; and (f) recent concerns have centered on designing effective models for integrating technology into instructional settings. This text again postulated that there is no single "best" or effective use of available technologies (i.e., technology in and of itself is not the key to teaching-learning outcomes). However, this edition, as compared to the first, repeatedly states the current philosophy for technology implementation: Special education professionals designing or integrating computer-managed or computer-assisted instruction must first identify their exceptional individuals' strengths and needs, delineate precise curriculum or quality-of-life goals, and be cognizant of effective pedagogical principles. Then they should match the capabilities of available hardware and software with user characteristics and educational objectives and employ empirically validated instructional procedures to achieve specific teaching-learning outcomes.

Professionals using computers must consider curricular goals, teaching/learning principles, user characteristics, and hardware and software attributes. *(Photograph by Ed Washington)*

There can be no doubt that, as Lonnie Hannaford, Carl Steinhoff, and Teresa Lyons noted in Chapters 1 and 2, computers and related technologies have become "almost invisible in our society" and what exists is "just a portent of what is to come." Wherever we go or whatever we do (e.g., stores, banks, restaurants, cultural and sporting events, etc.), technology directly or indirectly affects our activities. Also, the technology we thought was state-of-the-art last year (e.g., 5.25-inch diskettes and the Apple IIe) continues to be functional but has a more advanced replacement (e.g., 3.5-inch diskettes and Macintosh LC). Furthermore, as stated by Ronald Kelly in Chapter 9, almost daily we read in newspapers or periodicals about new computer developments or applications. Like you, in recent years I have read a myriad of these technology-related articles or heard media reports that presented the diverse advances or uses of technology. Four that specifically remain with me are (1) how computers are making teachers more innovative ("Survey Shows," 1990), (2) how interactive videodiscs are replacing textbooks ("Laser Videodiscs," 1990), (3) how technology will help the blind see (Stone, 1990), and (4) how we will "wear" computers to work and use these computers to connect with anyone or any computer in the world ("Computers to Wear," 1991). I know I will never forget the first article I read reporting IBM and Apple's agreement to develop joint technologies! I will also never forget a radio announcement that one of their projects would be the marketing of a hand-held computer with CD-ROM capabilities.

Finally, two years ago it excited me that my son's first-grade teacher was using computer-assisted instruction in reading for reinforcement purposes. Interestingly, these drill-and-practice activities were specifically related to curriculum objectives because the software came with the basal reading series. Today, however, nothing would please me more than for my son's third-grade teacher to use multimedia, telecommunications, and other applications that are congruent with curriculum goals and his abilities. Maybe my four-year-old daughter will experience this state-of-the-art philosophy and technology when she is in the third grade.

If you work with exceptional individuals or have an exceptionality yourself, do everything you can to learn about and use state-of-the-art technology. Hardware and software concepts described in this book are available and can be used today.

—Jimmy D. Lindsey
Southern University

REFERENCES

Computers to Wear Are in Work. (1991, September 6). *State-Times* [Baton Rouge, LA], p. 10-A. (By KRTN service)

Laser Videodiscs Replacing Textbooks. (1990, December 28). *Morning Advocate* [Baton Rouge, LA], p. 3-A. (By the Associated Press)

Okolo, C. M. (1990). Effects of an introductory computer course on special education students' attitude and evaluation of instructional software. *Journal of Special Education Technology, 10*(4), 233–240.

Stone, R. (1990, November 4). U.S. Researchers Bringing Light to Artificial Eye. *Sunday Advocate* [Baton Rouge, LA], p. 13-D. (First published in *The Washington Post*)

Survey Shows Teachers Innovative with Computers. (1990, September 4). *State-Times* [Baton Rouge, LA]. p. 16-A. (By the Associated Press)

Computer Terms

APPENDIX

Jimmy D. Lindsey
Southern University ■

Access time   The time needed to get data from main memory or from a storage device, e.g., diskette, tape, or a Winchester disk.

Acoustic coupler   A device used to transmit data over telephone lines by changing electrical signals into audio signals and vice versa.

Address   The number used to identify a specific location in a computer's memory.

Algorithm   A set of rules or procedures for solving a problem.

Alphanumeric   A term for alphabetic letters, numerical digits, and special characters (e.g., $, +, [ ]) that can be processed by computers.

APL   A terminal-oriented and symbolic programming language that was specifically developed for interactive problem solving.

Applesoft   A revised and extended version of the BASIC programming language developed for the Apple II family of computers.

Application   A particular task or program (e.g., manipulating student records) to which a computer solution can be applied.

Application program   A computer program designed to address unique user needs (e.g., a program that monitors school or testing data).

Application software   Computer programs developed to perform specific user applications.

Architecture   Often refers to the design or organization of the central processing unit (CPU).

Argument   The value (number or variable) contained in parentheses following a function and on which a function operates.

Arithmetic expression   A combination of arithmetic operators and numbers (e.g., 8 – 4 =) that directs a specific operation to be conducted.

Arithmetic/logic unit (ALU)   The area of the central processing unit where arithmetic and logical operations are performed.

Array   A programming procedure in which a series of related items (e.g., vectors, determinants, matrices) are arranged to perform a specific task.

Artificial intelligence   A new branch in computer science that uses computers to solve problems that require knowledge, intuition, or imagination.

ASCII   Acronym for American Standard Code for Information Interchange, which has assigned a binary number to each alpha and numeric character and several nonprinting characters to control communication devices and printers. For example, the ASCII code for the letter *a* is 01000001.

Assembler A program that takes a computer's nonmachine language and converts it into a form that the computer can use.

Assembly language A low-level symbolic language that permits a computer programmer or user to develop a program using mnemonics instead of numeric instructions.

Asynchronous A communication procedure whereby computer information and data are transmitted as soon as they are ready instead of at fixed intervals.

Background A programming procedure in which one or more noninteractive tasks are running on the computer while the user is using another interactive (foreground) task.

Background processing The automatic carrying out of a low-priority computer program when higher priority programs are not being executed by the computer.

Backup The copying of one or more disks, diskettes, tapes, or files on a storage medium to ensure safekeeping of the original.

BASIC Acronym for Beginners' All-purpose Symbolic Instruction Code, an interactive programming language developed at Dartmouth College for computers and beginning users.

Batch processing The automatic execution of a particular set of computer programs, usually without human direction or interaction during the execution.

Baud The modem unit of speed for data transmitting and receiving approximately equal to a single bit per second. Common baud rates are 300, 1,200, 2,400, etc.

Bidirectional The ability of a printer to print from right to left as well as from left to right or the ability to transfer data on a bus in either direction.

Binary The number system having two digits (e.g., 0 and 1) in which each symbol represents a decimal power of two. Also a system that has two functions or levels (e.g., off and on).

Bit The smallest unit of data (binary digit 0 and 1) recognized by a computer. For example, all letters, numerals, and symbols processed by a computer are digitized and expressed as a combination of bits or 0's and 1's.

Bit-map graphics The latest graphic technology that permits the control of individual pixels on a monitor to produce elements such as arcs, circles, sine waves, etc., of superior resolution that block-addressing technology cannot accurately display.

Board A circuit or plastic resin board containing electronic components such as chips and the circuits needed to connect them.

Boot The act of starting a computer by loading a program into its memory from an external storage medium such as a disk, diskette, or tape.

Branch A programming procedure to send a program execution to another line or statement other than the next one in sequence.

Branch instruction The instruction used to transfer control from one sequence of a program to another.

Buffer A temporary storage area used to hold data that is being passed between computers and other devices (e.g., printers) because the devices operate at different speeds or different times.

Bug A mistake in a computer program or a malfunction in a computer hardware component.

Bus A group of parallel electrical connections that carry signals or impulses between computer components or devices.

Byte The number of bits used to represent a character. For computers, a byte is usually eight bits.

Capacity The number of items of data (e.g., words, bytes, characters) that a storage device is capable of containing.

Card A storage medium in which data are represented by means of holes punched in vertical columns in a paper card.

Card reader An input device that can transfer data punched into cards to a computer's memory.

Cathode ray tube (CRT) A vacuum tube that generates and guides electrons onto a fluorescent screen to produce such images as characters or graphic displays on video display screens.

Central processing unit (CPU) Electronic components in a computer that control the transfer of data and information. CPUs also perform arithmetic and logic calculations.

Character A single printable letter (A–Z), numeral (0–9), or symbol ($, &, %) used to represent data. Nonvisible elements such as spaces, tabs, or carriage returns are also characters.

Character code A code (e.g., ASCII) that assigns numerical values to characters.

Character printer A printer that prints one character at a time like a typewriter.

Chip The piece of semiconducting material (usually silicon) on which an integrated circuit is fabricated. The word *chip* correctly refers to the piece of silicon itself, but it is often used to mean an integrated circuit and its package.

Circuit The system of semiconductors and related electrical elements through which electrical currents are directed or flow.

COBOL Acronym for COmmon Business Oriented Language, a high-level programming language that is well suited to business applications involving complex data records (e.g., school records and accounts) and large amounts of printed output.

Code A computer program that translates a source program written in a high-level language into a series of machine language instructions.

Cold start The process of starting a computer when the power is already on (or as if the power had just been turned on) by loading the operating system into memory and then loading and running a program.

Column A vertical arrangement of graphics points or character spaces on the screen.

Command A user instruction to the computer (e.g., word, mnemonic, or character) that is generally given through a keyboard and that causes a computer to perform a predefined function.

Compact disk—read-only memory (CD-ROM) A compact disk capable of storing 550 MB of information including text, audio, and graphics among other media.

Compatibility The ability of computers to work with other computers that are not necessarily similar in design or capabilities. Also, compatibility can refer to the ability of an instruction, program, or component to be used on more than one computer.

Computer A programmable electronic machine that can store, retrieve, and process data for educational, scientific, business, and other purposes.

Computer language *See* Programming language.

Computer network An interconnection of computer systems, terminals, and communications facilities.

Computer program A series of commands and instructions that guide the activities of a computer.

Computer science The field of knowledge that includes all aspects of computer design and use.

Computer security The protection of computer hardware, software, and data from unauthorized access or use.

Computer system The combination of hardware and software used as a unit to receive, manipulate, store, retrieve, and transmit data.

Computing The act of using electronic equipment for processing data.

Configuration The assortment of equipment (e.g., disks, tapes, printers, etc.) in a particular system.

Control The sequence or order in which statements of a program are carried out.

Core The older type of nonvolatile computer memory, made of ferrite rings, that represents binary data by switching the direction of polarity of magnetic cores.

CP/M Abbreviation for Control Program for Microprocessors, an operating system used by many computers.

Cursor A movable, blinking marker (usually a box or a line) on the terminal video screen that defines the next point of character entry or change.

Daisy wheel A print head shaped like a wheel with many spokes that forms full characters similar to those of a regular typewriter rather than characters formed of dots.

Data Facts, numbers, letters, and symbols used, created, processed, or stored in the computer.

Data base A large collection of organized data (e.g., information on individuals, test scores) that is required to perform a task.

Data base administrator (DBA) The individual responsible for the orderly development, operation, and security of a data base.

Data base management system (DBMS) A collection of related programs for loading, accessing, and controlling a data base.

Data communication The movement of coded data (e.g., sending and receiving) by means of electrically transmitted signals.

Data diskette A diskette that is used entirely or primarily to contain data files.

Data processing The application in which a computer works primarily with numerical data, as opposed to text.

Debugging Detection and elimination of all mistakes in a computer program or in the computing system itself.

Deferred execution The saving of a program line for execution at a later time as part of a complete program.

Device A piece of computer hardware that performs some specific functions such as an input device (e.g., keyboard to get data into CPU), output device (e.g., printer or monitor to take data out of the computer), or input/output device (e.g., terminal or disk drive to perform both inputting and outputting of data).

Diagnostic A program that examines the operation of a device, board, or other component for malfunctions and reports its findings.

Digit One of the symbols of a number system (0–9) that is used to designate a quantity.

Digital computer A computer that manipulates digital data and performs arithmetic and logic operations with these data.

Digital printer An output device that uses an automatically controlled pen to graph data.

Direct memory access (DMA) A method for transferring data to or from a computer's memory without CPU intervention.

Disk A rigid, flat circular plate of varying size and storage capacity with a magnetic coating for storing data.

Disk access time The time required to locate a specific track on a disk.

Disk/diskette drive A device (single or dual) used to read data from or write data onto one or more diskettes.

Diskette A flexible, flat, circular plate (usually $3^{1}/_{2}$, $5^{1}/_{4}$, or 8 inches in diameter) permanently housed in a paper or plastic envelope with magnetic coating that stores data and software.

Disk operating systems (DOS) An optional software system that enables a computer to control and communicate with one or more disk drives.

Display A display device or monitor that exhibits information visually.

Display screen A device such as a cathode ray tube that provides a visual representation of data.

Distributed data processing A computing approach in which an organization uses computers in more than one location, rather than one large computer in a single location.

Distributed processing system A set of interacting computer systems or data bases situated in different locations.

DOS *See* Disk operating system.

DOS shell A user-friendly software program designed to make working with DOS easier.

Dot-matrix printer A printer that forms characters from a two-dimension array of dots.

Double density Recording procedure for diskettes that permits them to store twice as much data as in normal or single-density recordings.

Downtime The period of time when a computer is not working.

Draft-quality printer A printer that produces high-speed readable characters that are less than typewriter quality. This printer is typically used to generate internal office documents.

Drive A peripheral device that holds a disk or diskette so the computer can read data from and write data on it.

Edit To change or modify text by replacing, moving, or inserting data or information in a document.

EDP Abbreviation for Electronic Data Processing.

Electronic file cabinet A storage unit that stores data much like a regular file cabinet. However, the electronic filing cabinet can store a great deal of information in a small area, access and change this information quickly, organize information more efficiently, and store information more securely.

Electronic mail A feature that allows short memos or messages to be sent to another computer.

Electronic spreadsheet   A type of software program that can perform in minutes complex financial tasks that would take hours to complete manually.

Emulator   A program that allows a computer to imitate a different system, thus enabling different systems to use the same data and programs to achieve the same results but sometimes at different performance rates.

Ergonomics   The science of human engineering that combines the study of human-body mechanics and physical limitations with industrial psychology.

Error message   The text displayed by the computer when an incorrect response is typed. The error message may also identify the problem and indicate what to do next.

Execute   To perform or carry out a specified action or sequence of actions such as those described by a program.

Expression   One or more formulas in a program describing a calculation or calculations to be performed.

Extended Industry Standard Architecture (EISA)   A computer bus system designed by several companies that extends the Industry Standard Architecture's (ISA) 8- and 16-bit bus to 32 bits.

Fanfold paper   A continuous sheet of paper whose pages are folded accordion-style and separated by perforations. This type of paper can be used to print lengthy documents without having to insert individual sheets of paper manually.

Fifth-generation Computer Development Project   A plan initiated by the Japanese to develop before 1990 a new generation of computers that will mimic human recognition systems. These computers will be designed to have the sense of sight, hearing, smell, and they will be able to sense temperature.

File   A collection of logically related records or data treated as a single item. A file is also the means by which data and information are stored on a disk or diskette.

Filename   The sequence of alphanumeric characters assigned by a user to identify or name a file that can be read by both the computer and the user.

Firmware   A program on a silicon chip that combines elements of both hardware and software.

First generation   The first commercially available computers, which were produced from 1951–1959 and were characterized by their use of vacuum tubes.

Flexible disk   *See* Diskette.

Floppy disk   *See* Diskette.

Flowchart   A form of algorithm that uses symbols and interconnecting lines to show the logic and sequence of specific program operations (program flowchart) or a system of processing to achieve objectives (system flowchart).

Font   A complete set of letters, numerals, and symbols of the same type style of a given typeface (e.g., typefaces such as Baskerville, Century, and Helvetica; fonts such as Baskerville Italic, Baskerville Bold, and Baskerville Bold Italic).

Foreground processing   Data or information processing that has top priority over background or lower-priority processing.

Format   (1) The form in which information is organized or presented. (2) To specify or control the format of information. (3) To prepare a blank disk to receive information by dividing its surface into tracks and sectors.

Form feed   The capability of a printer to advance fanfold paper automatically to the top of the next page or form when the printer has finished printing the previous form.

FORTRAN   Acronym for FORmula TRANslator. A widely used high-level programming language well suited to scientific problems and applications that can be expressed in terms of algebraic formulas.

Fourth-generation computer   A modern digital computer that uses large-scale integration (LSI) and very large-scale integration (VLSI) circuitry.

Function   A preprogrammed calculation that can be executed on request from any point in a program.

Function key   A key that causes a computer to perform a function (e.g., clearing the screen) or carry out a program.

General purpose computer system   A computer system that has been designed to deal with or solve a variety of problems.

Graphics   The use of lines and figures, as opposed to the use of printed characters, to display data or information.

Graphics digitizer An input device that converts graphic and pictorial data into binary inputs for use in a computer.

Graphic user interface (GUI) "Gooey" is the communication link (e.g., pull-down menus, pictures/icons) between the user and the operating system.

Hand-held computer A portable computer that can be programmed to perform a wide variety of applications.

Hang For a program or system to malfunction and perform no useful work.

Hard copy Output in permanent form on paper or paper tape as opposed to input in temporary form as data on a visual display or CRT.

Hard disk A disk such as the Winchester disk that is not flexible. It is more expensive than a diskette, but it has the ability to store much more data.

Hardware The physical equipment that makes up a computer system.

Hardwired This refers to a permanent, as opposed to a switched, physical connection between two points in an electrical circuit or between two devices linked by a communication line. For example, local computer connections are typically hardwired, but all connections through a modem are switched because they use telephone lines.

Head A component that reads, writes, or erases data on a storage medium such as a disk or diskette.

Help service Messages displayed on the video screen that provide information on how to use applications and other system services.

High-level language A programming language, such as BASIC, Pascal, or FORTRAN, that is relatively easy for humans to understand. Typically, a single statement in a high-level language corresponds to several instructions in machine language.

Hypercard An authoring software program that can be used to develop a multimedia program in a short time and permits the user to interactively look through the program (i.e., Hypercard stack or data base) for specific purposes.

Hypercard Stack A computer program or data base designed with Hypercard.

Immediate execution The execution of a program line as soon as it is typed to try out a statement to see how it works.

Impact printer A printer that forms characters on paper by striking an inked ribbon with a character-forming element.

Indefinite loop A section of a program that will repeat the same sequence of actions indefinitely.

Information processing All the operations performed by a computer.

Information retrieval The procedures used to recover specific stored information and data.

Information services Publicly accessible computer repositories for specific or general information and data (e.g., literature bibliographies, stock exchange data).

Input The act of entering data, or data entered into the computer.

Input/output device A device that is used to get data from the user into the central processing unit and to transfer data from the compiler's main storage to an auxiliary storage medium or to an output device.

Instruction A command that tells the computer which operation to perform next.

Integrated circuit A computer electrical circuit on a silicon chip.

Interactive Capable of carrying on a dialogue through a keyboard with the user as opposed to simply responding to commands.

Interface An electronic assembly that connects an external device (e.g., a printer) to a computer.

Interpreter A computer program that translates each source language statement into a sequence of machine instructions and then executes these machine instructions before translating the next source language statement.

Inverse video The display of text on the display screen in the form of dark dots on a light background instead of light dots on a dark background.

I/O Abbreviation for Input/Output. Pertaining to procedures for transferring information into and out of a computer.

Job A program or task for a computer to execute (e.g., saving a file).

Joystick A device for entering X-Y coordinates by moving a lever to change the position of a cursor on a graphic display screen.

K The symbol for the quantity 2^{10}, or 1,024. K is always in uppercase to distinguish it from lowercase k used for "kilo," which is 10^3, or 1,000.

Kbyte (KB) 1,024 bytes.

Keyboard The set of keys on a terminal that allows alphanumeric characters or symbols to be transmitted when keys are depressed. It inputs text and instructions to the computer.

Keystroke The act of pressing a single key or a combination of keys on the computer's keyboard.

Keyword A special word or sequence of characters that identifies a specific statement or command (e.g., SAVE, RUN).

Language A set of rules, representations, and conventions used to convey information.

Laptop computer A computer that runs on battery or alternating current and weighs between 6 and 15 pounds.

Large-scale integration (LSI) The combining of about 1,000 to 10,000 circuits on a single chip. LSI circuits include memory chips, microprocessors, calculator chips, and watch chips.

Laser printer High-resolution printer that produces hard copy by using laser technology to fuse the ink to the paper.

Letter-quality printer The printer used to produce final copies of documents in print comparable to that of a typewriter.

Light pen An electrical device resembling a pen that can be used to write or sketch on the screen of a cathode ray tube to provide input.

Line number A number identifying a program line in a program (e.g., 10 PRINT "HELLO").

Line printer A high-speed printer that prints an entire line of characters at a time.

Liquid crystal display (LCD) A type of screen for notebook and laptop computers that reflects existing light (reflective LCD) or has its own light (backlit LCD).

List processing The word processing application that permits many copies of a form document to be produced, with certain information changing from one copy to the next (e.g., the production of personalized form letters).

Load To transfer information from a peripheral storage medium (e.g., a disk) into main memory for use or execution.

Local Hardwired connection of a computer to another computer, terminal, or peripheral device such as in a local area network.

Loop A sequence of instructions in a program that can be executed repeatedly until certain specified conditions are satisfied.

Low-level language A programming language (e.g., assembly language) that is relatively close to the form that the computer's processor can execute directly.

Machine language The basic language of a computer.

Magnetic bubble storage A memory that uses locally magnetized areas that can move about in a magnetic material, such as a plate of orthoferrite. Because it is possible to control reading in and out of this magnetic material, a very high capacity memory can be built.

Magnetic disk A disk made of rigid material (hard disk) or heavy mylar (floppy disk) and used to hold magnetized material.

Magnetic tape or Magtape Magnetic tape used as mass storage media and packaged on reels. Since the data stored on magnetic tape can only be accessed serially, it is not practical for use with personal computers and is often used as a back up device on larger computer systems.

Mainframe A very expensive computer (e.g., IBM 4300) that is physically large and provides the capability to perform applications requiring large amounts of data.

Main memory The memory component of a computer system that can store information for later retrieval (e.g., random access memory and read-only memory).

Main storage The fastest general purpose memory of a computer.

Management information system An information system designed to supply organizational managers with the necessary information needed to plan, organize, staff, direct, and control the operations of the organization.

Mass storage A device like a disk or magtape that can store large amounts of data readily accessible to the central processing unit.

Mbyte (MB) 1,048,576 bytes, or 1,000 Kbytes.

Medium The physical substance upon which data is recorded (e.g., magnetic disks, magnetic tape, punched cards).

Memory   The main high-speed storage area in a computer where instructions for a program being run are temporarily kept, or a device where information and data can be stored and from which they can be retrieved.

Memory location   A unit of main memory that is identified by an address and can hold a single item of information of a fixed size.

Menu   A displayed list of options a computer user can select from by typing a letter or by positioning the cursor.

Menu-driven   A computer system that primarily uses menus for its user interface rather than a command language.

Micro channel architecture (MCA)   IBM's latest generation 16- and 32-bit bus designed for the PS/2 personal computer that permits more than one CPU in a computer.

Microcomputer   A computer based on large-scale integration that is physically very small and can fit on or under a desk.

Microcomputer system   A system that includes a microcomputer, peripherals, operating system, and applications programs.

Microprocessor   A single-chip central processing unit incorporating LSI technology.

Migration path   A series of alternatives outlined by a computer manufacturer that enables new computer equipment to be introduced into the present system. This permits users to increase their system's computing power by adding or trading in components rather than giving up all their current hardware and software.

Minicomputer   A type of computer (e.g., IBM System/36) whose physical size is usually smaller than a mainframe, but whose performance exceeds that of a microcomputer.

Mnemonic   A short easy-to-remember name or abbreviation that can be used for many functions, including commands in programming languages.

Mode   A state of a computer or system that determines its behavior (e.g., processing, waiting for command, etc.).

Modem   Acronym for MOdulator/DEModulator. A device that converts computer signals into high-frequency communications signals, and vice versa, and sends and receives these signals over telephone lines.

Monitor   A hardware television-like or CRT device that can be used as an output display screen. With respect to software, a monitor is a part of the operating system that allows the user to enter programs and data into memory and run programs.

MOS   Abbreviation for Metal-Oxide Semiconductor, which is the most common form of LSI technology.

Mouse   A device, attached to a computer by a cable, that can control the movement of a cursor by being rolled along a flat surface by hand.

Multikey sort   Using more than one parameter to qualify a record for inclusion in a specified group or to order a set of records.

Multimedia   Computer presentations incorporating two or more types of media including text, audio, graphics, animation, still or motion video, and voice.

Multiplexer   A device that permits more than one communication line to share one computer data channel.

Multiprocessing   The execution of two or more programs by a computer that contains more than one central processor.

Multiprogramming   A scheduling technique that permits two or more tasks to be in an executable state at any one time. When the computer has only one CPU, then more than one program can appear to be running at a time because the CPU is giving small slices of its time to each program.

Multitasking   The execution of several tasks "at the same time" without having to complete one before starting another. Although computers can perform only one task at a time, the speed at which a computer operates is so fast that it appears as though several tasks are being performed simultaneously.

Musical instrument digital interface (MIDI)   Standard for how musical instruments and computers communicate (e.g., keyboard synthesizers are input devices for MIDI-equipped computers).

Natural language   A language (also called problem-oriented language) that permits computer users to prepare programs in English or other spoken languages.

Nested loop   A loop contained within the body of another loop and executed repeatedly during each pass through the containing loop.

Network A group of computers connected to each other by communications lines to share information and resources.

Nonimpact printer A printer that produces a printed image without striking the paper.

Nonvolatile memory Memory that does not lose its contents when a processor's power supply is shut off or disrupted.

Normal The video display format that is made up of light dots on a dark background.

Notebook computer A computer the size of a notebook that runs on battery or alternating current and weighs 4 to 8 pounds.

Numerical analysis The branch of mathematics concerned with the study and development of effective procedures for computing answers to problems.

OCR Abbreviation for Optical Character Registration. Characters printed in a special type style that can be read by both machines and people.

Off-line A term describing persons, devices, or equipment not in direct communication with a computer's central processing unit.

On-line Directly under the control or in communication with the computer. For example, data are introduced immediately into the central processing unit.

Operating system A collection of computer programs that controls the overall operation of a computer and performs such tasks as assigning places in memory to programs and data, processing interrupts, scheduling jobs, and controlling the overall input/output of the system.

Option module An add-on printed-circuit module that allows expansion of a system.

Output device A unit (e.g., monitor, printer) used for taking information from a computer and presenting it in the appropriate form to the user.

Paddle A hand-held device connected to the computer that can move the display cursor left/right or up/down.

Parallel transmission Sending more than one bit at a time.

Parity A one-extra-bit code used to detect recording or transmission errors by making the total number of 1 bits in a unit of data—including the parity bit itself—odd or even.

Pascal A high-level programming language that has become very popular because it facilitates the use of good structured-programming techniques.

Peripheral A device (e.g., printer, modem) that is external to the CPU and main memory but connected to them by appropriate electrical connections.

Personal computer A small and inexpensive microcomputer that can be used in the home for household tasks, business, education, and entertainment, among other activities.

Pixels Shortened form of "picture elements." Definable locations on a display screen that are used to form images on the screen. Higher-resolution graphic displays can be produced by increasing the number of pixels.

Pocket computer A portable, battery-operated computer that can be programmed to perform a wide number of applications.

Port A physical area for the connection of a communications line. This line can be between the CPU and anything external to it (e.g., a modem, a printer, a second computer, or another communications line).

Power supply A transistor switch that converts AC power into DC power or steps down the power supplied to certain devices. A power supply also energizes components such as monitors, integrated circuits, and keyboards.

Print The act of transferring data from a computer's internal memory to a printing device.

Printer The printing device (e.g., dot matrix, letter quality) that produces a paper copy or hard copy output of a document.

Print head The element in a printer that forms a printed character.

Printout A general term that is used to refer to almost anything printed by a computer peripheral device.

Processing Generally, the arithmetic and logic operations performed on data in the course of executing a computer program.

Processor The functional part of the computer system (the CPU or central processing unit) that reads, interprets, and executes instructions.

Program The complete sequence of instructions and routines needed to solve a problem or to execute directions in a computer.

Program disk A disk containing the instructions of a program.

Program execution The process of putting a program in the computer, along with any other information required, and instructing the machine to execute or run the program.

Program library A collection of available computer programs and routines.

Program line The basic unit of a written program that consists of one or more statements separated by colons.

Program maintenance The process of keeping a program operation at an acceptable level, including correcting undetected bugs and making appropriate revisions or changes to meet new requirements.

Programmer The human author or writer of a program.

Programming language The words, symbols, mnemonics, and specific rules that permit an individual to construct a computer program.

Program testing Executing a program with test information to determine whether or not the program can be executed.

PROM Acronym for Programmed Read-Only Memory. A memory that is programmed by the user, not the manufacturer.

PS/2 Operating system developed by IBM and Microsoft to take full advantage of the capabilities of 80286 microprocessors and to do multitasking.

Punch card A cardboard card used in data processing operations in which tiny rectangular holes punched at specific locations denote numerical values and alphanumeric codes.

Query language A set of commands used to extract from a data base the data that meet specific criteria.

Radio-frequency modulator A device for converting video signals produced by computers to a form that can be used by a standard television set.

RAM Acronym for Random Access Memory. Memory that can both be read and written into (i.e., altered) during normal operation and is used in most computers to store the instructions for programs currently being run.

Read To get information from any input or file storage media.

Read-write memory Memory whose contents can be both read and written but that is erased and permanently lost unless saved when the computer's power is turned off.

Real time Refers to computer systems or programs that perform a computation during the actual time that a related physical process transpires so that the results of the computation can be recorded or used to guide the physical process.

Record A collection of related data items.

Remote Typically refers to peripheral devices (e.g., printers, video terminals) that are located at a site away from the CPU.

Reserved word A sequence of characters or word reserved by a programming language for some special use. For example, the words CALL, END, GOTO, and SAVE, among other words, are reserved words in Applesoft BASIC and cannot be used as variable names in a program.

Response time The time it takes the computer system to react to a given input (e.g., the interval between the pressing of the letter *a* and the visual displaying of an *a*).

Reverse video A feature on a display unit that produces the opposite combination of characters and background from that which is usually employed (e.g., black characters on a green screen if green characters on a black screen is normal).

ROM Acronym for Read-Only-Memory. Memory that is programmed on a solid-state storage chip at the time of a computer's manufacture and cannot be reprogrammed by the computer itself.

Rotational delay time The time required for the disk to attain the desired position at the read/write head.

Routine A part of a program that accomplishes some task subordinate to the overall task of the program.

Run The single and continuous execution of a program by a computer on a given set of data.

Screen The display surface of a video monitor or the pattern or information displayed on the screen.

Scrolling The changing of all or part of the content on a display screen by shifting information out one end (usually at the top) to provide room for new data appearing at the other end (usually at the bottom) which produces an effect similar to that of moving a scroll of paper past a fixed viewing window.

Self-test A procedure that permits a program or a peripheral device to check its own operation.

Semiconductor A material such as silicon with a conductivity between that of a metal and an insulator that can be used in the manufacture of solid-state devices (e.g., transistors, integrated circuits) that comprise computer logic hardware.

Semiconductor storage A memory device whose storage elements are formed as solid-state electronic components on an integrated circuit chip.

Serial access Refers to sequential devices (e.g., magnetic tape) that require data, information, or instruction retrieval only by passing through all locations between the ones that are currently being accessed and ones that are desired.

Serial transmission Sending one bit at a time. *See* Parallel transmission.

Simulation software A computer program (e.g., flight simulation) that has the instructions needed to represent the functioning of another system or event.

Single-density The normal or standard recording density for disks and diskettes. For example, 250,000 bytes can be stored on a single-density 8-inch disk.

Single thread A simple operating system (as opposed to a multitasking system) that carries out a specific task from beginning to end without interruption.

Soft copy Alphanumeric and/or graphical data presented in nonpermanent form (e.g., on a video screen).

Software The tasks (e.g., instructions in programs) that make computers perform particular functions.

Sort Rearranging the records in a file (e.g., alphabetically or numerically) so that the order is convenient to the user.

Special purpose computer system A computer system capable of solving only a few selected types of numerical or logical problems.

Stand-alone graphics system A graphics system that includes a microcomputer storage, terminal, and other input/output devices.

Startup disk A disk containing software recorded in the proper form that is loaded into the computer's memory to set the system into operation.

Storage capacity The number of items of data that a memory device is capable of containing.

Storage unit A place (e.g., disk, diskette, tape) where files and documents can be saved for later use.

String A programming procedure whereby an item of information consisting of a sequence of data or instructions is put together (e.g., A/B*66 = 26).

Subroutine A programming procedure whereby a part of a program is carried out on request from any point in the program and control is returned to the point of the request on completion of the procedure.

Supercomputer A very large and expensive computer system, characterized by fast processing speeds, that is capable of executing many million instructions per second.

Symbol An element of a computer language's character set (e.g., mark, number, or alphabet) that represents a numeral, operation, or relation.

System A combination of software and hardware that performs specific processing operations.

System board The main module (or motherboard) in a personal computer system box that contains the CPU, memory, and the interface circuitry for the keyboard, a printer port, and a communications port.

System unit The unit or structure that houses the system board, disk drives, power supply, and modules.

Tape A recording medium for data or computer programs. Tapes are available in permanent form (e.g., perforated paper tape) and are used as a mass storage medium because they store more data than disks. However, it takes much longer to write or recover data from tapes than from disks.

Task   A program in execution.

Terminal   An input/output device used to enter data into a computer and record the output either as hard copy (e.g., printers) or as soft copy (e.g., video terminals).

Terminal emulation   A communication whereby a terminal acts as a terminal of a different design so that it can be used on various systems.

Third generation   A series of computers that use integrated circuits and miniaturization as their main components.

Thumb wheels   Dials that provide input into a computer system.

Time-sharing   The providing of computer service to more than one user by working on each user's task part of the time.

Top-down program design   The process of breaking a large and complicated problem into a series of smaller and easier-to-solve problems.

Touch-sensitive panel   An input device that is made up of sets of horizontal and vertical wires mounted on a thin plastic sheet that is then combined into a grid separated by a third plastic sheet and mounted on a display screen.

Track   The portion of a moving storage medium (e.g., a disk or a tape) that is accessible to a given read/write head position.

Track ball   A device that can be used to move the cursor on a video display. It consists of a box-shaped mounting that holds a ball that moves at the speed and in the direction of the ball's motion.

Tractor feed   An attachment used to move paper through a printer. The roller that moves the paper has sprockets on each end that fit into the fanfold paper's matching pattern of holes.

Turnaround time   The time between the initiation of a computer job and its completion.

Turnkey system   A computer that is ready to be used without adding any hardware or software because it is complete as packaged for a particular application.

Universal Product Code   A machine-readable code based on parallel bars used for labeling products in a point-of-scale automation system (e.g., grocery items).

Upgrade   To reconfigure a personal computer as new features are developed or when existing features are enhanced.

User-defined key   A key that can remember and store a number of keystrokes needed to execute a particular operation. When the key is pressed, it carries out the keystrokes in the proper sequence, thus saving the user from having to press each key in the sequence.

User-friendly   A term that implies the computer system or software is easy to use.

User group   Individuals who use similar hardware and/or software and meet in person or via computers to share ideas.

Very large-scale integration   The accumulation of hundreds of thousands of electronic circuit elements (VLSI) on a single semiconductor chip.

Video disk   A disk (also called optical disk) that can store both text and pictures.

Video graphics array (VGA)   The display standard for 640 × 480 resolution color displays with a refresh rate of 60 hertz (i.e., the time needed to redraw a display screen) and 16 colors or 256 colors capability. A super VGA display has an 800 × 600 resolution.

Video terminal   A terminal that displays data on a CRT.

Virus   A harmless or harmful program within software or on a disk that is hidden and executes unwanted commands (e.g., changes date and time) at specific signals.

Volatile memory   Memory that loses its contents when power is removed unless battery backup is available.

Warm start   The restarting of the computer after the power is already on without reloading the operating system into main memory and often without losing the program or data already in main memory.

What you see is what you get (WYSIWYG)   The match between computer interface and printer that results in what is seen on the screen being produced in the hard copy.

Winchester disk   A hard disk capable of storing larger amounts of data than a diskette that is permanently sealed in a drive unit to prevent contaminants from affecting the read/write head.

Word processing system   A system that processes text by performing such functions as inserting, deleting, moving, replacing, and printing text, among other activities.

Word wrapping The automatic shifting of words from a line that is too long to the next line.

Wraparound The automatic continuation of text on a display screen or printer from the end of one line to the beginning of the next.

Write The process of transferring data and information from the computer to an output medium.

Write-enable notch The square cutout in one edge of a disk's jacket that permits information to be written on the disk. If there is no write-enable notch, or if it is covered with a write-protect tab, information can be read from the disk but not written onto it.

Write-once-read-many (WORM) Optical drive that permits the user to write permanently to a disk until it is full and then read the disk as many times as necessary.

Write-protect To protect data and information on a disk by covering the write-enable notch with a write-protect tab. Write-protect procedures also prevent new information from being written onto the disk.

Write-protect tab A small adhesive sticker used to write-protect a disk by covering the write-enable notch.

Computer Theories and Principles

APPENDIX

Robert E. Farrell
Texas Instruments, Inc.
Duane K. Troxel
University of Colorado–Denver ■

Counting is an ancient activity. The ability to measure, predict, and organize is fundamental to an ordered life—and counting is at the heart of these activities. Biology, astrology, astronomy, mathematics, physics—indeed, all the arts and sciences—have, throughout human social and technological evolution, relied on this ability to quantify—to count.

The current computer revolution is made possible by technologies principally developed over the past 300 years. It is difficult to credit a single individual with the invention of computers. As the development of photography was made possible by advances in optics, chemistry, and mechanics, computers too owe their existence to the contributions of numerous innovations incorporated and harmonized within the new technology.

The 12 years of progress from the Soviet Union's launching of Sputnik in 1957 to America's flag-planting ceremony on the moon can be largely credited to modern computers. It takes a computer that may work at rates approaching the speed of light to process the more than half-million instructions per second

used to maintain life support systems and navigate the void of space.

Humanity's progress from counting on fingers and toes to electronic computation stretches back uncounted millennia. Historically, developments leading to modern computers advanced with glacial sluggishness. Only the past 40 years have witnessed the head-spinning developments that characterize the frenetic pace of modern life.

THE MECHANICAL AGE

The Abacus

Over the centuries various devices were invented to perform increasingly more complex computations. Perhaps first among those fundamental innovations was the abacus. The abacus is a manual calculator that uses counting beads threaded on rods. Each rod holds a place equivalent to ones, tens, hundreds, etc., of the decimal system. Fifteen hundred years ago, merchants and government officials around the Mediterranean Sea adopted the abacus as their first business machine. Abacuses enabled skilled users to add and subtract quickly. In fact, some abacus users can calculate so rapidly that they are still employed in many countries today.

Logarithms

The next aid to calculation was designed by John Napier of Scotland, who found the drudgery of routine computation exceedingly tiresome. To simplify complex multiplications, Napier discovered logarithms. A logarithm is the exponent of a base number, indicating to what power that base must be raised to produce another given number. By laboriously compiling log tables, Napier gave the world a shortcut to complicated mathematical solutions. In the late 1620s, William Oughtred developed the slide rule, scored with logarithmic scales, enabling users to make rapid mathematical calculations without the use of tables. In 1617 Napier devised a nonlogarithmic aid to multiplication known as Napier's bones. These segmented bone rods enabled users to multiply large numbers by summing engraved numerals across horizontally adjacent segments.

Calculators

In 1642 the Pascaline eclipsed Napier's bones and Oughtred's slide rule. This boxed wheel-and-cog device, named for the brilliant French mathematician Blaise Pascal, was the world's first mechanical calculator. A series of meshed wheels computed numbers in much the same way a car's odometer compiles mileage. Each wheel from right to left represented a set of numbers in the decimal system. Values in each column increased from zero to a maximum of nine. An odometer reading of nine-tenths of a mile advances the next column by one when an additional tenth of a mile is added. This process of carrying ten to the next column is carried through the tens, hundreds, thousands, and ten thousands columns as the car

accumulates more and more miles. In much the same manner, the Pascaline performed multiplication by repeated additions.

Binary Arithmetic

In 1673 young Gottfried Leibniz extended the mathematical powers of mechanical calculators beyond the function of addition found in the Pascaline. His calculator completed mathematics' basic quartet of computation, adding the capabilities of mechanical subtraction multiplication, and division to the addition achieved by Pascal's device. Leibniz went on to devise calculus and binary arithmetic—the latter to play a significant role in the evolution of modern computers.

Punch Cards

After Leibniz, 130 years passed before another innovation fundamental to computing emerged. It came from the weaving industry where precision patterns, not calculations, were all-important. In 1804 Joseph Marie Jacquard, a French silk weaver, contrived a method to program weaving looms. Using an immense array of punched paper cards, Jacquard automated his looms to fabricate a host of intricate designs. Each card controlled a single pass of the shuttle. By substituting one batch of cards for another, he could change from one complex pattern to another. The ability to program a mechanical device to perform a complex series of operations would find its highest expression in the electronic computer.

The First Computer

Amazingly, a 19th century mathematician created a working computer—on paper. If technology had been sufficiently advanced to fabricate the components required for his invention, computers might have appeared in the 19th rather than the 20th century.

Difference Engine

Charles Babbage (1791–1871), an Englishman, is widely regarded as the father of computing.

Babbage, like Napier, Pascal, and Leibniz before him, originally set out to reduce the amount of routine drudgery computation demanded. First, he proposed the Difference Engine, a calculator that could reckon and print out lengthy mathematical tables. In 1823, after obtaining the support of the prestigious Royal Astronomical Society, the British government awarded Babbage 1,500 pounds sterling to build his calculator. After many troubled years and many thousands more pounds, the machine was still unfinished. The government withdrew its support and Babbage shelved his plans for the Difference Engine. He hadn't given up. He merely conceived of a machine vastly more powerful than the Difference Engine.

Analytical Engine

Charles Babbage's Analytical Engine, unlike its predecessor, the Difference Engine, was designed not only to solve mathematical problems but also to carry out a wide range of calculating tasks as instructed by its operator. It was to be a general nature machine, the first general purpose programmable computer. In fact, on paper the Analytical Engine was the first machine to embody the concept of memory. Theoretically, it would be capable of storing numbers 40 digits long. It even had a control part to orchestrate its own complex operations. It would employ punched cards to enter data and instructions.

Babbage's second brainchild was stillborn. The Analytical Engine simply could not be built. Parts could not be made for it. But his concept was workable. And his sometime collaborator on the project, the Countess of Lovelace, Augusta Ada Byron (the daughter of the poet Lord Byron), has become known as the first programmer. The Analytical Engine was designed to deal with algebraical patterns just as the Jacquard loom dealt with patterns of flowers and leaves.

Hollerith's Census Device

Just a decade before the close of the 19th century, Herman Hollerith invented an electro-mechanical tabulator to tally the 1890 United States census. His device processed punched cards at a rate unapproached by other methods. Like the cards in Jacquard's loom, the location of each punched hole represented coded information. Hollerith's cards coded age, sex, and race as well as other demographic information required for a census. So rapidly could Hollerith's machine tabulate that he completed the census in one-third the time used by earlier methods. Hollerith went into the business for himself. In 1924, that business took the name International Business Machines, or IBM. But electronic computers were still two decades away.

THE ELECTRONIC AGE

In the 1930s a number of inventors made contributions that would later be incorporated into the modern desktop marvels called personal computers. Germany's Konrad Zuse, unaware of Babbage's Analytical Engine, designed an electric programmable calculator that calculated according to a binary rather than decimal scheme. The simplicity of a 2-numeral system was much easier to represent in computer circuitry than the clumsy 10-numeral system. Furthermore, the binary approach permitted Zuse to incorporate a mathematical system of logic worked out by the self-taught British mathematician George Boole. The system of Boolean logic enables one to code propositions in mathematical terms symbolically. A proposition is either true or false. Such a system is ideally adaptable to the two-state condition of binary circuitry Zuse had adapted.

Binary Electronic Circuitry

Working independently of Zuse and each other, two American scientists also concluded that binary math using Boolean logic was a natural solution to the problem of devising a high-speed electronic calculator. Claude Shannon advanced his discovery in his master's thesis, published in 1937. In 1937 George

Stibitz of Bell Labs constructed an electronic circuit that could perform binary addition. By 1940 Stibitz had joined forces with a fellow Bell employee, Samuel Williams. Together they constructed a device capable of surpassing Leibniz's marvel. It could add, subtract, multiply, and divide using electronic relays.

Computers and World War II

Word War II hastened the advent of modern computing. Modern warfare requires high speed calculation. Calculating and adjusting the precise trajectory of artillery shells is a matter of life and death. Howard Aiken, a Harvard mathematician on duty with the U.S. Navy, was recruited to build such a machine. Using Babbage as his guide, he developed the Mark I, which used a decimal rather than a binary system. Finished, the gigantic computer was 51 feet wide, stood 8 feet tall, and contained 750,000 components. It could perform calculations in a day that formerly took months. Meanwhile, in Germany, Konrad Zuse had by 1941 already completed a programmable Z3 version of his calculator based on a binary system, thereby rendering Aiken's Mark I obsolete 2 years before it was completed.

The British were developing electronic calculators to fill another wartime need, intelligence. British Intelligence assembled a special team of the British's finest minds for the purpose of cracking German codes. Using vacuum tubes instead of electromechanical relays, the team built a new type of computer they named "Colossus." Colossus was a single-purpose computer dedicated to the vital task of decoding wireless transmissions of the German High Command. The success of Colossus and the team that built it has been chronicled in a number of recent World War II espionage books.

ENIAC, the Electronic Numerical Integrator and Calculator, like the Mark I, grew out of the need to aim artillery guns accurately. In 1943, John W. Mauchly and J. Presper Eckert of the University of Pennsylvania were awarded a $400,000 contract to build the gadget. The finished ENIAC was a marvel of complexity. Standing 18 feet tall and 80 feet long, it became the cliché still used to portray computers in popular cartoons. Though made more complex, and therefore slower, by the use of decimal rather binary mathematics, vacuum tube technology speeded up ENIAC tremendously. The more than 17,000 vacuum tubes propelled some 100,000 electronic components to compute at nearly the speed of light.

Reprogramming ENIAC was a nightmare. Thousands of wires had to be rerouted to perform special tasks. To overcome this limitation, Mauchly and Eckert designed EDVAC, the Electronic Discrete Variable Computer. EDVAC took a quantum leap beyond ENIAC. It employed mathematics and permitted programs to be stored electronically without rewiring. Professor John Von Neumann, a brilliant Hungarian-born mathematician, joined the EDVAC team and in 1945 published the first document on electronic digital computers to be widely circulated. Ironically, before EDVAC could be completed in 1951, a British scientist, Maurice Wilkes, who had heard Mauchly and Eckert lecture on their proposed computer, went home to Cambridge University in England and built his own. Two years before EDVAC was completed, Wilkes upstaged the pair by unveiling the EDSAC, the Electronic Delay Storage Automatic Calculator, to the world.

EDSAC was a multipurpose computer. To switch from one task to another, one had only to enter new instructions into the computer's memory. It is this stored-program concept that enables users of modern desktop computers to shift from balancing checkbooks to letter writing to vaporizing alien invaders on command.

Postwar Computers and Business

Postwar computers were put to work crunching commercial data instead of artillery trajectories. In 1950 England introduced the world's first business computer, LEO, which stands for Lyon's Electronic Office. Months later Mauchly and Eckert entered a competitor into the fray. UNIVAC, the Universal Automatic Computer, became perhaps the best-known commercial computer in the world at that time. UNIVAC was acquired by Remington Rand but was eventually eclipsed by IBM's series of computers.

It is during this postwar period that modern computers emerged. Each new generation of computers is characterized by the technology that manipulates and directs the data flowing through the system. The first generation of computers of (1951–1958) utilized vacuum tube technology. They were massive sedentary machines requiring air conditioned environments and a team of operators. Next came transistorized mainframes (1958–1964), somewhat smaller than tube-driven computers but still room-size. The third generation of computers was characterized by integrated circuitry (1964–1971). And the fourth and present generation of computers (1971–present) was made possible by integrated circuits, which shrank the mainframe behemoths down to desk size and liberated them from isolated rooms with special environments. Each development has led to successively more sophisticated computers. But regardless of the nature of the technology, counting is at the heart of everything computers do.

Mainframes and Minicomputers

In December 1954, IBM introduced the first mass-produced computer used primarily for business purposes, the IBM 360. It became the Model T of the computer industry, with over 1,500 installed at the time it was phased out in 1969. During this time, IBM also introduced the IBM 704, which performed floating point operations and arithmetic operations on numbers with fractional parts. Expressing numbers in floating point, also known as scientific notation, permitted numbers representing very small and very large quantities to be used conveniently. To help take advantage of this improved arithmetic ability, the programming language FORTRAN (See Appendix C) was developed as well as a special program known as a compiler to translate FORTRAN into the codes needed to operate the machine. This special program tool took $3^1/2$ years to write and had 25,000 lines of machine instructions.

In 1963 a small company near Boston, Digital Equipment Company, introduced the first computers designed to go where the computing needed to be done, the world's first minicomputers. These computers used transistors and could fit into a box on top of a desk. Thus began the trend that put computer power into the hands of individuals. Unlike massive mainframe computers, minicomputers required little in the way of special environments. They could be programmed by nonspecialists. The PDP-8 was one such computer. It costs $18,000 but was not as powerful as today's popular desktop microcomputers costing one-tenth that amount.

In 1964 IBM created a new wave of computers, the third generation, with its introduction of the IBM System/360. Programs were compatible across the 360 family. That is, any program one 360 could run could also be run by any other member of the 360 family. One could begin with a low-end 360 model and move upward without having to buy all new programs. The 360 family was innovative in another way. They were general purpose computers, not strictly dedicated to business or scientific applications but capable of performing a host of useful jobs. This series of computers also boasted an operating system that could determine priorities and schedule the work performed. No longer did a human operator have to decide which job was next in line.

Programming computers to schedule jobs made computers more productive. Each computer could perform many tasks almost concurrently in much the same way we might be baking a cake, making coffee, recording a TV program, and organizing a drawer. We get one thing going and move to the next, coming back only when the next step is ready to be taken. Modern computers are capable of shifting from one task to another in fractions of a second, enabling many users tied to the same computer via terminals to work on different projects at the same time. This is called time-sharing. Time-sharing reduces the cost of using expensive computer time by spreading the charges across many users.

The Microchip

In 1969, Intel, an integrated circuit manufacturer in Santa Clara (Silicon Valley), California, was contracted to build a set of chips for a calculator. The Intel engineers asked themselves, "Instead of following the usual method to create logic for the calculator, why not design a programmable chip instead of a single-purpose one? After all, the users would never know they were holding a computer in their hands instead of a calculator." Coupled with two other Intel products, a random access memory (RAM) chip (which allowed the processor chip to save results or programs) and a read-only memory (ROM) chip (engraved with permanent programs), the calculator was actually a primitive microcomputer. Surprisingly, large companies could not believe there was a market for personal computers. They argued that a general purpose computer would require peripheral devices to input data and retrieve it in a usuable form (see Chapter 2). Terminals, keyboards, monitors, printers, and card readers would increase costs to the point of putting such a device out of the reach of the general public. In addition to that, a relatively difficult body of knowledge would need to be mastered before users could put their machines to work. And just what, pondered mainframe moguls, would people want computers to do for them?

Personal Computers

A few farsighted individuals had faith that the age of home computing had arrived. The first available personal computers were constructed by do-it-yourself electronic hobbyists. In July 1974, *Radio Electronics* magazine featured plans for a do-it-yourself computer for the nominal charge of $250. Any electronics hobbyist could assemble a real digital computer from a half-dozen printed circuitry boards. Completed, the crude device was capable of very little. Each keystroke of information had to be laboriously loaded into the machine by throwing a set of eight switches, which in combination translated to one letter or number.

Six months after *Radio Electronics* introduced its computer plans, rival *Popular Electronics* magazine featured a $400 kit to build an Altair 8800 microcomputer. The kit had widespread appeal, greatly broadening the base of personal computing. Overnight companies sprang up to provide products for the tiny market of home computerists. Microsoft's introduction of a BASIC interpreter made it possible for novice computer buffs to program their own machines. But the mass market still needed an everyperson's computer. Working in a backyard garage in California, a young engineer and his visionary friend were soon to make computing history and millions of dollars.

Steve Wozniak and Steven Jobs created Apple Computer in 1975. Their first computer, Apple I, was little better than the *Radio Electronics'* kit. But the much-improved Apple II, introduced in 1977, was a more complete computer. It came with a keyboard for input. One needed only to attach it to a TV receiver to experience the magic of computing. Homemade programs could be saved on audiocassette tapes. The Apple II proved to be the Volkswagen of personal computers.

Although the microcomputer industry was growing by leaps and bounds, it took the entry of a major computer company into the burgeoning market to signal skeptics that microcomputers were not a passing fad but a genuine grassroots computer movement. In 1981 the IBM Corporation announced its first personal computer. Since that time, new as well as old computer companies have designed and marketed personal or desktop computers. Furthermore, the development of thousands of business, school, and home application programs has fueled the phenomenal popularity of desktop computers. Businesses ranging from mom-and-pop candy stores to Fortune 500 companies have adopted computers to change the way they do things. But how do microcomputers work?

RECENT COMPUTER DEVELOPMENTS

It is impossible in this section to describe all recent computer developments that have applications in businesses, schools, and society, but it is important that some of these technological advances be identified. With respect to central processing units (CPUs) and stand-alone computers, Intel Corporation has produced and marketed new generation microprocessors—the 80386 and 80486. The 80386 processor has an operating speed of 5 million instructions per second, while the 80486 is reported to be four times faster than the 386. Also, Sun and NeXT among other companies have developed fast, memory-intense machines called workstations, IBM has introduced its PS/2 series with microchannel architecture, and Tandy/Radio Shack and NEC have produced computers capable of multimedia application (e.g., Tandy CDR-1000, NEC CDR-83). Notebook and laptop portable computers are now extremely affordable and have varied users. These portable computers weigh 4 to 16 pounds, can operate for 2 or more hours on a rechargeable battery, have 80386 processors, 16 MB of random access memory (RAM), visual-graphics-array (VGA) displays, and 120-MB hard disk drives. Palm-size computers (e.g., Poqet PC) and pocket-size devices (e.g., Sharp Wizard) are also on the market, but the introduction of the notepad PC (e.g., NCR 3125 Notebook) and computers that recognize handwriting (e.g., Go's PenPoint) appear to be the technology that will increase computer portability.

With respect to input and output devices, IBM introduced a 3$\frac{1}{2}$-inch, 2.88-MB super-floppy drive, and a personal computer hard drive capable of storing 1,050 KB can be purchased. Compact disk—read-only memory (CD-ROM) and write-once-read-many (WORM)—drives are becoming standard peripherals. CD-ROM drives can access 152 KB per second; CD-ROM disks can hold approximately 600 MB, or 200,000 pages of text. Modem, facsimile, optical-character-reader, touch-screen, light-pen, and voice-recognition technologies are also advancing.

With respect to output devices, monitors are becoming larger and have greater resolution. The laser printer is becoming industry standard and top-of-the-line printers can produce 20-plus pages of hard copy per minute. Also, modem, facsimile, and speech-synthesis technologies are improving each year.

ANATOMY OF A MICROCOMPUTER

Chapter 2 provided a brief and concise overview of the inner workings of the computer. It is hoped that the mystique of how computers operate will lessen, and regular and special educators and exceptional individuals themselves will look on the computer for what it is—a very logical and efficient machine.

At the heart of modern computing is the central processing unit or CPU. This tiny chip, no bigger than a baby's fingernail, in the blink of an eye performs millions of complex operations one step at a time. It processes or manipulates data according to sets of instructions or programs.

A CPU executes all of its instructions using binary arithmetic. Binary arithmetic codes groups of zeros (0's) and ones (1's) to stand for numbers, letters, and symbols found on a standard typewriter keyboard. For example, the CPU in the Apple I computer could represent the capital letter C as 01000011, p as 01010000, and U as 01010101. A single 0 or 1 in the binary system is a bit. A bit is the smallest unit of information a computer can use. Each grouping of eight bits (0's and 1's) is a byte. A byte is equivalent to one keystroke. That is, whenever the user enters one keystroke into the computer it is ultimately understood by the computer as a series of eight bits. Computerists have playfully given the name "nibble" to half a byte.

The first Intel microchip (1971) could process 4-bit numbers. The second Intel chip (1974) doubled that to 8 bits. The Apple I and II series used an 8-bit chip called the 6502. Next came Motorola's 16-bit 68000 chip, which could multiply two 16-bit numbers in 3.2 millionths of a second. And most recently (1981), Hewlett-Packard created the 32-bit superchip that beats at the heart of the world's fastest computers.

A microcomputer works by the harmonious orchestration of many parts, each with its own specialized activity. The CPU is the brain. It computes. It contains arithmetic and logical units. Computers are idiot savants. Though capable of lightning logic, they must be told precisely everything they must do and the order in which it must be done. Instructions that computers must always remember are permanently etched into ROM chips. Thus, when you turn a computer's power on, it has enough native intelligence to get further instructions by going to an input device (e.g., disk drive) and to display that information on the monitor's screen. Those instructions contained on floppy disks are loaded one bit at a time into the computer's "brain cells," known as RAM chips. A fundamental set of instructions is the operating system (see Chapter 3) whose job it is to perform housekeeping and traffic chores. The operating system directs data flow and schedules all work. There is also a clock chip to synchronize the millions of quicksilver activities computers can perform.

WHERE WILL IT END?

Having recently passed its 10th birthday, the personal computer industry has moved beyond its explosive growth period. The current era is characterized by refinement and standardization. Proprietary operating systems are giving way to two or three basic standards. Speed, size, memory capacity, quality graphics, telecommunications, and computing power are the selling points competing for consumer dollars. Prices have fallen dramatically. Computing power costing millions of dollars less than 20 years ago is available for about a thousand dollars today. Computers are making their way into homes where they make possible such tasks as stock market trading, household management, letter writing and budgeting, music composition, electronic banking, and telecomputing via a computer keyboard.

Artificial Intelligence and robotics are the darlings of present-day microcomputerists. Whether machines will ever think and function like humans is the subject of much debate and research by governments, universities, and the private sector. But no matter how far people go toward making computers in their own image, the foundation of all that activity will no doubt continue to rest upon the ability to compute—to count.

Computer Languages

Stephen J. Puster
DeKalb County Public Works,
Atlanta, Georgia
Kerry L. Kirby
Eugene Graham
Shreve-Area Council of Government,
Shreveport, Louisiana ■

It has been said that computers are the smartest machines that humans have ever invented. Computers are not smart, as reported earlier in this text, but in fact they can only perform the functions that a computer operator instructs them to do. These instructions are transmitted to the "brain," or central processing unit (CPU), through software programs. These software programs are written in a language that can be recognized by the computer. This language actually transmits instructions to the CPU that turns switches on and off inside the computer. Contrary to popular opinion, one does not need to be a skilled scientist or mathematician to develop a computer program. Even elementary school children are writing computer programs. For the most part, and as would be expected, all programming languages available today were developed for the convenience of the user and not the computer. The two major types of programs that can be used with computers are based on low-level and high-level computer language, respectively.

LOW-LEVEL VERSUS HIGH-LEVEL LANGUAGES

A low-level language is a language that can be used to write programs or instructions that are directly and easily understood by a computer's CPU. Machine language is an example of a low-level language. Yet low-level languages are more difficult for programmers to learn and use because the commands and structures do not correspond to English vocabulary and structures. However, one advantage of a low-level program is that it is able to run faster in a computer than a program written in a high-level language; a high-level language program (e.g., RPG or Report Program Generator) must be translated to a low-level language so that a CPU can understand it.

High-level languages are easier to learn and understand because they more closely resemble the English language. A high-level language makes communications between

Stephen J. Puster wrote the appendix text and Kerry L. Kirby and Eugene Graham provided the program examples.

humans and computers easier because it permits programmers to identify information-handling routines in a language convenient for human use. But a high-level-language program must be translated into a low-level language before a computer's CPU can understand the instructions. This translation is done by an interpreter or a compiler. The distinction between the two translators is based on the time of the actual conversion to machine language. An interpreter translates a high-level language program into a low-level language when the program is actually running in the CPU. A compiler, on the other hand, translates the entire high-level-language program into machine code before execution of the program begins. Compiled programs do not have to be interpreted during each execution and therefore run very fast. The primary advantages of high-level-language computer programs are ease of operation, reduced programming time, reduced documentation costs, program language commonality, elimination of specialists, real-time processing, program consistency.

MACHINE LANGUAGE

Machine language is a low-level language that is readily recognized by computers and is based on the raw sequence of 1's and 0's. In machine language, each letter of the alphabet, every number, and various symbols are made up of a set of eight 1's and/or 0's in a preset sequence that in actuality represents the particular letters, numbers, or symbols. For instance, "10000011" in machine language could represent the capital letter A, while another sequence could represent the lower-case letter a. Since machine language is rather cumbersome to use in writing lengthy programs, most programs are written in another language and either compiled or converted into machine language. Yet the majority of programs still written in machine language are done so to take advantage of the processing speed afforded by bypassing the need for using a compiler or an interpreter, or to

include a routine that is not readily available in another language routine.

ASSEMBLY LANGUAGE

Assembly language is a low-level language that is one step away from machine language. Assembly is used where performance is important and there is no reason for modification by the user. Word processing is a good example of this concept, since this application in a software program takes a lot of computer resources. Assembly language keeps the computer resource use of a word processing program to a minimum. Unlike business application programs that require the user to modify the program itself to address particular business changes, word processing programs are such that programmers or users do not need to make changes in the program structure.

Assembly language is sometimes inserted into high-level-language programs to increase their performance. The following program is written in Assembly Language and prints a grid of 156 row by 198 columns of dots on the Apple Computer's high-resolution screen. The dots are stepped by 3 both horizontally and vertically:

```
DOTSCREEN listing

770 A9 00       LDA 00          load accumulator with zero
772 8D 00 03    STA 03 00       put zero in row count
775 A2 00       LDX 00          starting column is zero
777 8E 01 03    STX 03 01       save the starting column
780 A0 00       LDY 00          need a zero in the Y register
782 20 57 F4    JSR F4 57       plot the point
785 AE 01 03    LDX 03 01       get the column count
788 E8          INX             increment column
789 E8          INX                         count
790 E8          INX                              by 3
791 8E 01 03    STX 03 01       save new column count
794 AD 00 03    LDA 03 01       get row count
797 E0 C6       CPX C6          is column count 198?
799 D0 EB       BNE EB          if not 198 then finish row
801 AD 00 03    LDA 03 00       get row count
804 18          CLC             clear the carry flag
805 69 03       ADC 03          increment row count by 3
807 8D 00 03    STA 03 00       save new row count
810 C9 9C       CMP 9C          is row count 156?
812 D0 D9       BNE D9          if not 156 then start another row
814 60          RST             return to BASIC

45 BYTES TOTAL LENGTH
```

FORTRAN

FORTRAN (FORmula TRANslation) was developed by IBM in 1956 as a scientific programming language. It is used for a variety of mathematical applications, varying from simple addition to complex problems involving higher mathematics and complicated algorithms. FORTRAN was the first widely used high-level computer language and is the best defined and standardized high-level language available today. FORTRAN, the earliest of the non-machine-specific high-level languages to be used, is a procedure-oriented language, and is still the most widely used language for scientific and engineering applications. In FORTRAN a complex computation such as "V is equal to the square root of P squared plus $(R-1)$ squared" would be written in FORTRAN as V = SQRT(P*2+(R-1)*2). What follows is a program in FORTRAN for finding the area of a circle with a diameter of 4 using the Monte Carlo Technique:

```
$JOB CUR      PAGES=10
C$NOEXTEN
      APPROX=AREA(2.,1000,-2.,2.)
      WRITE(6,10)APPROX
      STOP
10 FORMAT(/////10X,'THE AREA OF THE CIRCLE  SQR(4-X**2)  IS ',F10.2)
      END

      FUNCTION AREA(HIGH,N,A,B)
      INTEGER HITS
      REAL INTVAL
      F(X)=SQRT(4-X*X)
      INTVAL=B-A
      HITS=0
      I=1
      WHILE(I .LE. N)DO
         Y=RAND(HIGH)
      X=RAND(INTVAL)+A
         IF(F(X) .GF. Y)HITS=HITS+1
         I=I+1
      ENDWHILE
      AREA=2.*(HIGH*INTVAL*(FLOAT(HITS)/N))
      RETURN
      END

      FUNCTION RAND(RMAX)
      DATA IRAND/137462873/,MULT/65539/,LARGE/2147483647/
      IRAND=IRAND*MULT
      IF(IRAND .LT. 0)IRAND=(IRAND+LARGE)+1
      RAND=RMAX*(IRAND-1)/(LARGE-1)
      RETURN
      END
```

COBOL

COBOL stands for COmmon Business Oriented Language and was developed in 1959 by a committee formed by the secretary of defense. The primary purpose of this committee was to provide a programming language that was compatible between machines made by different manufacturers. Until 1968 when a new "Standard COBOL" was introduced by the United States American National Standards Institute, several versions of COBOL had been written. In 1969 this new Standard COBOL underwent a name change to become the American National Standards Institute (ANSI) COBOL. While FORTRAN was developed for use in the scientific community, COBOL was the counterpart for the business community. COBOL is not a particularly easy language to learn to use, although it uses commands like "add pay-raise to old-salary giving new-pay."

There are four distinct divisions in a COBOL program. The Identification Division is a small set of statements serving to identify the program name, the author, the date written, and the company name. The Environment Division is two subsections—"configuration" and "input-output." The "configuration" program subsection describes the type of computer on which the program is designed to run while the "input-output" defines which input and output devices are being addressed. The Data Division also has two subsections—"file" and "working storage." The "file" subsection is concerned with each of the files and the data used in the program. The "working storage" subsection describes all pertinent information that is not contained in any of the input-output records. The heart of the COBOL program is contained in the Procedure Division, which defines the steps required to perform the functions of the program. These steps include the calculations, the data-handling instructions, and the logical decisions.

The following is an example of a program written in COBOL:

```
IDENTIFICATION DIVISION.
PROGRAM-ID.  REPORT1.

* * * * * * * * * * * * * * * * * * * * * * * * * * * * *
* THIS PROGRAM WILL PRINT A PAYROLL REPORT.  THE EMPLOYEE'S   *
* NUMBER, NAME, REGULAR PAY, AND OVERTIME PAY WILL BE TAKEN FROM  *
* A PAYROLL FILE. IN ADDITION TO THE ABOVE, A TOTAL PAY WILL BE   *
* CALCULATED AND ALSO PRINTED.                                *
* * * * * * * * * * * * * * * * * * * * * * * * * * * * *

ENVIRONMENT DIVISION.

CONFIGURATION SECTION.
 SOURCE-COMPUTER. IBM-370.
 OBJECT-COMPUTER. IBM-370.
 SPECIAL-NAMES. C01 IS TOP-OF-PAGE.

INPUT-OUTPUT SECTION.
 FILE-CONTROL.
     SELECT IN-REC ASSIGN TO UR-3504-S-SYSIN.
     SELECT PRINT  ASSIGN TO UR-3504-S-SYSPRINT.
DATA DIVISION.

 FILE SECTION.
 FD IN-REC
     LABEL RECORDS ARE OMITTED
     DATA RECORD IS PAYROLL-CARD.

 01 PAYROLL-CARD.
 03 FILLER            PIC X(8).
 03 EMP-NO            PIC 9(5).
 03 NAME              PIC X(20).
 03 FILLER            PIC X(28).
 03 REG-EARN          PIC 999V99.
 03 FILLER            PIC X.
 03 OVT-EARN          PIC 999V99.
 03 FILLER            PIC X(8).
 FD PRINT
     LABEL RECORDS ARE OMITTED
     DATA RECORD IS OUTLINE.
 01 OUTLINE           PIC X(133).
     WORKING-STORAGE SECTION.
1  77 EOF-MARK        PIC 9     VALUE 0.
2  01 LINE-KOUNTER    PIC 99    VALUE 0.
   01 HEADER-LINE.
      03 TOP-HEADER.
3        05 FILLER    PIC X(40) VALUE SPACES.
4        05 FILLER    PIC X(14) VALUE 'PAYROLL REPORT'.
      03 TITLE LINE.
5        05 FILLER    PIC X(8)  VALUE SPACES.
6        05 FILLER    PIC X(7)  VALUE 'EMP NO.'.
7        05 FILLER    PIC X(17) VALUE SPACES.
8        05 FILLER    PIC X(4)  VALUE 'NAME'.
9        05 FILLER    PIC X(18) VALUE SPACES.
10       05 FILLER    PIC X(7)  VALUE 'REGULAR'.
11       05 FILLER    PIC X(4)  VALUE SPACES.
12       05 FILLER    PIC X(8)  VALUE 'OVERTIME'.
13       05 FILLER    PIC X(7)  VALUE SPACES.
14       05 FILLER    PIC X(5)  VALUE 'TOTAL'.
   01 DETAIL-LINE.
15    03 FILLER       PIC X(9)  VALUE SPACES.
      03 EMP-NO-OUT    PIC 99999.
16    03 FILLER       PIC X(10) VALUE SPACES.
      03 NAME-OUT      PIC X(30).
      03 REG-EARN-OUT  PIC ZZZ.99.
17    03 FILLER       PIC X(6)  VALUE SPACES.
      03 OVT-EARN-OUT  PIC ZZZ.99.
18    03 FILLER       PIC X(6)  VALUE SPACES.
      03 TOTAL-EARNINGS PIC $$,$$$.99.
19 PROCEDURE DIVISION

     MAIN-LOGIC.
20     OPEN INPUT IN-REC,
            OUTPUT PRINT.
```

```
21      PERFORM HEADER-ROUTINE.
22      READ IN-REC AT END MOVE 1 TO EOF-MARK.
23      PERFORM SUB-LOGIC UNTIL EOF-MARK = 1.
24      MOVE SPACES TO OUTLINE.
25      WRITE OUTLINE AFTER TOP-OF-PAGE.
26      CLOSE IN-REC, PRINT.
27      STOP RUN.

     SUB-LOGIC.

28      MOVE EMP-NO TO EMP-NO-OUT.
29      MOVE NAME TO NAME-OUT.
30      MOVE REG-EARN TO REG-EARN-OUT.
31      MOVE OVT-EARN TO OVT-EARN-OUT.
32      ADD REG-EARN, OVT-EARN GIVING TOTAL-EARNINGS.
33      WRITE OUTLINE FROM DETAIL-LINE AFTER 1.
34      ADD 1 TO LINE-KOUNTER.
35      IF LINE-KOUNTER = 45
36         PERFORM HEADER-ROUTINE
        ELSE
           NEXT SENTENCE.
37      READ IN-REC AT END MOVE 1 TO EOF-MARK.


     HEADER-ROUTINE.
39      MOVE SPACES TO OUTLINE.
40      WRITE OUTLINE AFTER TOP-OF-PAGE.
41      WRITE OUTLINE FROM TOP-HEADER AFTER 2.
42      WRITE OUTLINE FROM TITLE-LINE AFTER 3.
43      MOVE SPACES TO OUTLINE.
44      WRITE OUTLINE AFTER 1.

***** THERE ARE NO STATEMENTS FLAGGED IN THIS COMPILE
```

RPG

Report Program Generator (RPG) is a very high-level language. In RPG, the programmer tells the computer *what* to do and the computer figures out *how* to do it. RPG II is the latest version of RPG. It is not a procedural language like COBOL or FORTRAN, but it is a problem-oriented language. Because of this difference, some programmers have difficulty in learning RPG II. However, once learned, it is an excellent language and can be easily used even on small business computers. RPG II is designed so that the programmer can feed certain information into one of five different specification sections that tell the computer what the programmer wants in return. From the information fed into the computer on the specification sheet, the computer generates its own program.

The five different specification sections, or sheets, used in an RPG language program are File Description, File Extension, Input,

Calculation, and Output. They describe the size of the records in each file and define the input/output device used for storing each file. The File Description defines the characteristics of the input and output files. The File Extension is not used as frequently as the other types of specification sheets. This specification sheet is usually used to define tables within the program. Input specifications define in detail what is in each of the input files that were described in the File Description. The Calculation specification describes the calculations to be made within the program. On some machines the programmer can perform square root calculations but on most machines is limited to addition, subtraction, multiplication, and division. Finally, the Output sheet specifies in detail how each file is to be treated on the final report.

The following RPG program reads the number of seats available for a flight and prints a seat register using three columns:

```
0001   01-020 FCARDIN IP F     80          READ05
0002   01-030 FOUTPUT O  F    132     OF    LPRINTER
0003   01-110 LOUTPUT 0060106012
0004 S 02-010 ICARDIN AA   01
0005   02-020 I                          1   30FLIGHTL1
0006   02-030 I                          4    8 PLANE
0007   02-040 I                          9  110SEATS
0008   03-000 C   L1           SETON                OF40
0009   03-000 C        ROW    SUB  ROW    ROW    30
0010   03-005 C        COL1   SUB  COL1   COL1   30
0011   03-010 C               SETOF             102030
0012 S 00-300 C               SETOF               1535
0013   03-000 C        SEATS  COMP 1              3515
0014   03-000 C    15         SETON              30
0015   03-000 C    15
0016   03-000 COR 35          GOTO SKIP
0017   03-020 C        SEATS  DIV  3      ROW    30
0018   03-030 C               MVR         ADJROW 10
0019   03-040 C        ADJROW COMP 0                10
0020   03-050 C   N10  ROW    ADD  1      ROW
0021   03-060 C        LOOP   TAG
0022   03-070 C        COL1   ADD  1      COL1
0023   03-100 C        COL1   ADD  ROW    COL2   30
0024   03-105 C    30         GOTO SKIP
0025   03-110 C        COL2   ADD  ROW    COL3   30
0026   03-120 C        COL3   COMP SEATS         30
0027   03-130 C        SKIP   TAG
0028   03-140 C               EXCPT
0029   03-145 C    L1         SETOF              L1
0030   03-150 C    40         SETOF              OF40
0031   03-160 C    OF         SETON              40
0032   03-165 C        COL1   COMP ROW             20
0033   03-170 C   N20         GOTO LOOP
0034   04-010 OOUTPUT H 201    OF
0035   04-030 O               UDATE Y     8
0036   04-040 O                       52 'P A S S E N G E R L 1'
0037   04-050 O                       56 ' S T'
0038   04-060 O                       86 'PAGE'
0039   04-070 O               PAGE    91
0040   04-080 O       H 1      OF
0041   04-100 O                          14 'FLIGHT  PLANE'
0042   04-110 O       H 2      OF
0043   04-130 O                          21 'NUMBER  TYPE SEAT'
0044   04-140 O                          35 'PASSENGER'
0045   04-150 O                          63 'SEAT     PASSENGER'
0046   04-160 O                          91 'SEAT     PASSENGER'
0047   04-170 O       EF 2     01
0048   04-180 O              L1  FLIGHTZ  4
0049   04-190 O              L1  PLANE   14
0050   04-195 O              OF  FLIGHTZ  4
0051   04-197 O              OF  PLANE   14
0052   04-200 O              N15N35 COL1 Z 21
0053 S 04-000 O              15          21 '1'
0054   04-210 O              N15N35 COL2 Z 49
0055   04-230 O              N30N35 COL3 Z 77
0056   04-240 O              35          42 '***ERROR - NUMBER OF SE'
0057   04-250 O              35          66 'ATS FOUND WAS ZERO OR NE'
0058   04-260 O              35          76 'GATIVE ***'
     END OF SOURCE
```

BASIC

BASIC is the acronym for Beginner's All-purpose Symbolic Instruction Code: BASIC does not mean simple, although the instructions in this language are given to the computer in English-like commands. Of the computer languages described in this appendix, BASIC language is the closest to English in its use of vocabulary and sentence structures. Because of this similarity to English, BASIC is the most common high-level language in use today.

A BASIC program is a list of numbered lines of instructions that the computer carries out in numerical sequence. BASIC is an interpreted language and therefore tends to operate slowly. BASIC is now used in most popular microcomputers, and the wide use of BASIC among different manufacturers' machines has caused the rise of "dialects" within the BASIC language. Many machines use a variation of "Microsoft" or "MS-DOS" BASIC. Microsoft is the BASIC dialect used by IBM microcomputers, and those machines using one of these variations are commonly referred to as "IBM-compatible." There are other dialects such as "Atari BASIC" and "Apple-Soft BASIC," as well as others that are manufacturer's machine-specific. The primary commands among these various dialects are identical. For the most part, it is the addresses and formatting of procedures that make up the main differences within these BASIC dialects.

The following is an example of a program written in BASIC. This program gives the monthly payments on a loan when the interest rate and the length of the loan period are known:

```
0    REM : REGULAR PAYMENT ON A LOAN
4    HOME
5    HTAB 6
7    HTAB 6
10   INVERSE : PRINT ``REGULAR PAYMENT ON A LOAN''
15   NORMAL
16   PRINT : PRINT
20   INPUT ``   HOW MUCH DO YOU WANT TO BORROW?                $'';P
25   PRINT
30   INPUT ``   HOW MANY YEARS DO YOU WANT TO PAY IT BACK? '';Y
35   PRINT
40   INPUT ``   WHAT IS THE ANNUAL INTEREST RATE CHARGED?   '';I
45   REM : CALCULATION BY FORMULA
50   R = ((I/100) * P/12) / (1 - 1 / ((I/100) / 12+1) - (12 * Y))
55   D = INT (R * 100+.5) / 100: PRINT
56   REM : PRINTS RESULTS ON SCREEN
60   PRINT ``   WITH 12 PAYMENTS PER YEAR...''
65   PRINT ``   YOUR REGULAR PAYMENT WILL BE  $'';D
70   PRINT : PRINT : PRINT : PRINT
75   INPUT ``   DO YOU WANT A PRINTOUT?      '';A$
80   IF A$ = ``YES'' THEN GOSUB 150
81   IF A$ = ``Y'' THEN GOSUB 150
85   IF A$ = ``NO'' THEN 90
86   IF A$ = ``N'' THEN 90
90   PRINT : PRINT :INPUT ``   DO YOU WANT TO DO THIS AGAIN?    '';Z$
95   IF Z$ = ``YES'' THEN 105
96   IF Z$ = ``Y'' THEN 105
100  IF Z$ = ``NO'' THEN 110
101  IF Z$ = ``N'' THEN 110
105  HOME : GOTO 5 1
10   HOME : PRINT : PRINT :PRINT `` THIS PROGRAM IS ENDED!!! '': END
120  REM : SUBROUTINE 150 PRINTS RESULTS ON PAPER
130  REM : PRINTER INTERFACE CARD MUST BE IN SLOT #1
150  PRINT CHR$(4);``PR#1''
151  PRINT : PRINT : PRINT : PRINT : PRINT : PRINT
155  PRINT ``          BORROWING   $'';P
160  PRINT
165  PRINT ``          FOR '';Y;`` YEARS''
166  PRINT
170  PRINT ``          AT '';I;`` PER CENT INTEREST''
175  PRINT
180  PRINT ``          YOUR REGULAR PAYMENT WILL BE    -----    $'';D
181  REM : RETURNS DISPLAY TO SCREEN
185  PRINT CHR$(4);``PR#3''
190  GOTO 90
```

LOGO

LOGO is a beginning computer language designed for young people in 1967 by Seymour Papert and a group from Massachusetts Institute of Technology. It is a high-level interpreted language that allows the programmer to use simple commands to draw on the screen. Although LOGO was pilot-tested on elementary school children in 1967, it was almost a decade before the microcomputer arrived on the scene and the general public learned about the wonders of LOGO.

It can be said computer languages are taught for computer literacy, for self-perpetua-

tion of computer technology, and to teach children to think. The name LOGO is derived from the Greek *logo*, meaning "word" or "thought." It is not surprising, then, to learn LOGO was created to teach creative thinking—or more correctly, to teach children how to learn.

To enhance the LOGO learning process, the programmer is asked to direct a turtle. Children have a natural affinity for playing with animals and the turtle is seen as a friend. In LOGO, this little friend can be envisioned as dragging a pen, and the pen draws a line each time the turtle is directed by a command to move. This is an easy concept for children to grasp and want to make happen on the screen.

The primary result of LOGO programming is graphic images, which further enhances its use in the educational field. Because of this predominance of simple graphics, many programmers consider LOGO to be a "toy" language that is not suitable for adults and should not be given serious consideration. This is far from the truth. The basic data components in LOGO are numbers, words, and lists, just like those of the "more powerful" languages. It also has the ability to be recursive; that is, it can call upon elements from within the program to command other elements within the same program. Other functions common among LOGO and other languages are the ability to do arithmetic expressions, contain variables, assign values, perform input/output operations, make simple selections like if-then-else and test and contain loops within a program.

Two simple programs that may demonstrate the power and simplicity of LOGO follow.

The first is a routine to draw a square on the screen.

```
FORWARD 15
RIGHT 90
FORWARD 15
RIGHT 90
FORWARD 15
RIGHT 90
FORWARD 15
END
```

The second program is a more complex application and results in a gradebook.

```
TO ROSTER  :CLASS
  PRINT FIRST FIRST  :CLASS
  IF NOT BUTFIRST  :CLASS = [ ] THEN ROSTER BUTFIRST CLASS
END

TO GET  :I  :A
  IF :I = 1 THEN OUTPUT FIRST :A
  OUTPUT GET ( :I - 1 ) BUTFIRST :A
END

TO GETNAME :NAME :CLASS
  ; Return the record of :NAME
  IF :CLASS = [ ] THEN PRINT [NOT FOUND] OUTPUT [ ] STOP
  IF :NAME = FIRST FIRST :CLASS THEN OUTPUT FIRST :CLASS
  OUTPUT GETNAME :NAME BUTFIRST :CLASS
END

TO GETSCORES :NAME :CLASS
  IF :CLASS = [ ] THEN PRINT [NOT FOUND] OUTPUT [ ] STOP
  IF :NAME = FIRST FIRST :CLASS THEN OUTPUT FIRST
     BUTFIRST FIRST :CLASS
  OUTPUT GETSCORES :NAME BUTFIRST :CLASS
END

TO GETTEST :I :RECORD
  ; Retrieve the Ith test score from :RECORD
  IF :I = 1 THEN OUTPUT FIRST :RECORD
  IF BUTFIRST :RECORD = [ ] PRINT [THERE AREN'T THAT MANY
     TESTS] OUTPUT [ ] STOP
  OUTPUT GETTEST ( :I - 1 ) BUTFIRST :RECORD
END
TO CLASSBOOK :CLASS
  PRINT FIRST :CLASS

  IF NOT BUTFIRST :CLASS = [ ] THEN
     CLASSBOOK BUTFIRST :CLASS
END
```

The ease of LOGO and its widespread use in the classroom have encouraged LOGO's growth and led most manufacturers to develop a version of LOGO for their computers. With the exception of the IBM and IBM compatibles which use a common operating system, different versions of LOGO are required for LOGO computers made by different companies. Apple LOGO will not run on a Radio Shack/Tandy computer and vice versa; and neither will work on a Texas Instrument computer. This is common to most computer languages.

PASCAL

Pascal was published by Niklaus Wirth in 1971. Pascal is extremely popular and is probably, after BASIC, the high-level language most used on microcomputers. One of the principle reasons for the design of Pascal was to create a programming language that could be used to teach a careful, disciplined approach to programming and problem solving. Another

intended purpose of Pascal was to provide a language that would be reliable, efficient, able to handle complex data structures. One outstanding feature that has helped Pascal gain popularity is its ability to enable programmers to find coding errors quickly.

The following program written in Pascal can find the distance between two integer points on the same line:

```
PROGRAM DISTANCE(INPUT,OUTPUT):
VAR
  POINTX, POINTY, DISTANCE : INTEGER;

BEGIN
  WRITE ('Enter two whole number points on a line ... ');
  READLN(POINTX,POINTY);
  IF (POINTX < 0) XOR (POINTY < 0)
    THEN
      DISTANCE := ABS(POINTX) + ABS(POINTY)
    ELSE
      IF (POINTX < 0) AND (POINTY < 0)
        THEN BEGIN
          POINTX := ABS(POINTX);
          DISTANCE := POINTX + POINTY;
          DISTANCE := ABS(DISTANCE)
        END
      ELSE
        IF (POINTX > 0) AND (POINTY > 0)
          THEN
            DISTANCE := ABS(POINTX-POINTY);
WRITELN('The distance between the points is ',DISTANCE :6)
END.
```

C

C is a relatively new language in the programming world. It has the ability to deal directly with the codes in machine language and at the same time can address the complex problems that are handled by high-level languages. Because of this unique ability, C is characterized as a medium-level language.

Programs written in C are not machine-specific and are not dialectic, so they can be moved from machine to machine with a great deal of ease. C is not interactive in its use as BASIC is; however, it is a highly extensible language that allows programmers to develop their own functions with minimum of difficulty. The following is an example of a C program that converts kilometers to miles:

```
/ Convert Kilometers to miles
    for k = 0 to 50              */
main ()
(
    int   start, end, kilo;
    float factor;
```

```
start  =  0;
end    =  50;
factor =  1.609;
for (kilo = start; kilo <= end; ++kilo)
  printf( ``%3d %6.2fn'', kilo, kilo*factor);
)
```

PL/I

PL/I was developed by IBM to be used as a synthesis of the best features of COBOL and FORTRAN. It was designed to combine the strengths of FORTRAN with the strengths of COBOL so that one language could be used for both business and technical applications. The version available for microcomputers (PL/M) was intended as a major general-purpose language, but it is rather complicated to use and therefore has not caught on even though PL/I is one of the most versatile of existing programming languages.

There are three reasons why PL/I makes writing programs very convenient. First, the programmer can write programs describing complicated computations in terms that are simple to understand. Second, the programmer can specify execution procedures in familiar terms. Third, PL/I is capable of operating with a minimum amount of specific information.

ADA

ADA is one of the newest languages available for microcomputers. Like COBOL, ADA was developed by the Department of Defense. It was modeled after PASCAL and has been described as one of the most powerful programming languages available. Its power may be its drawback as well, since many programmers consider ADA too big for one programmer to handle. In the microcomputer field, only subsets of the complete ADA language are feasible to use.

FORTH

FORTH is a computer program language that can be utilized to make languages. In FORTH many commands are redefined or deleted, which makes it almost impossible to use without changing it. Because of its flexibility, FORTH is very fast and very extensible.

Even though FORTH is criticized as being difficult to learn, impossible to read, and sometimes even bizarre, it still attracts users. Those who take the time to learn FORTH seldom use any other language to program.

The following program, written in FORTH, prints 20 rows of 40 periods with each period separated by a space:

```
Line 1:   : NEWLINE  13 10 EMIT EMIT  ;
                        - The colon tells FORTH that what follows
                          should be compiled and that the word
                          will be named NEWLINE. The 13 and 10
                          are ASCII codes for a carriage return
                          and a linefeed respectively and are
                          pushed onto the stack and printed by
                          the two EMITs. This causes the cursor
                          to return to the leftmost position and
                          advance one line. The semicolon tells
                          FORTH that the end of the word has been
                          reached.
Line 1:   : GRID        - Starts the definition of the word GRID,
                          which is the name of the program.
Line 2:   NEWLINE       - Executes the word NEWLINE, which
                          advances one line.
Line 3:   20 1 DO       - This line sets up the loop that will
                          cause 20 rows of dots to be printed.
Line 4:   40 1 DO       - This line sets up the loop that will
                          cause the 40 dots across the screen.
Line 5:   46 32         - A period (ASCII 46) and a space
                          (ASCII 32) are pushed onto the stack.
Line 6:   EMIT EMIT     - Since the 46 (period) is on top of the
                          stack, it will be printed first and the
                          space next.
Line 7:   LOOP          - Terminates the column loop.
Line 8:   NEWLINE       - Same as line 2.
Line 9:   LOOP ;        - Terminates the row loop and ends the
                          word GRID.
The following is the actual format for this FORTH program...

( FORTH program to print a 20 X 40 grid of dots )

: NEWLINE 13 10  EMIT EMIT  ;

: GRID
     NEWLINE
     20 1 DO
               40 1 DO
                       46 32
                       EMIT EMIT
               LOOP
               NEWLINE
      LOOP ;
```

PILOT

PILOT is the acronym for Programmed Inquiry, Learning, Or Teaching. SuperPilot is the latest version of this language. PILOT is a highly specialized language that was developed to allow teachers to write their own instructional and tutorial programs. PILOT programs most often involve asking students questions, analyzing the answers, playing music, and showing pictures. PILOT is very easy to learn, and it is an attractive language for teachers who want to purchase prewritten programs as well as write their own programs.

FOR ADDITIONAL INFORMATION

Finally, if you would like more information on computer languages, check out the computer section in the local library. Another way to acquire the knowledge is to engage in in-depth reading and practice experiences. Also, Appendix F in this work lists books that focus on BASIC and different computer systems. Excellent texts on computer languages that could be read include the following:

Baron, N. S. (1986). *Computer languages: A guide for the perplexed.* New York: Doubleday.

Bentley, J. L. (1982). *Writing efficient programs.* Englewood Cliffs, NJ: Prentice-Hall.

Christie L., & Curry, J. W. (1983). *The ABC's of microcomputers: A computer literacy primer.* Englewood Cliffs, NJ: Prentice-Hall.

Covey, H. D., & McAlister, N. H. (1980). *Computer consciousness: Surviving the automated 80's.* Reading, MA: Addison-Wesley.

Curran, S., & Curnow, R. (1983). *Overcoming computer illiteracy—A friendly introduction to computers.* New York: Penguin.

Hollerbach, L. (1982). *A 60-minute guide to microcomputers: A quick course in personal business computing.* Englewood Cliffs, NJ: Prentice-Hall.

Peavy, W. E. (1983). *Microcomputer software selection guide.* Wellesley, MA: OED Information Sciences.

Ruan, P., & Hayman, J. (1984). *LOGO activities for the computer.* New York: Simon and Schuster.

Ruhl, J. (1989). *The programmer's survival guide.* Englewood Cliffs, NJ: Yourdon Press.

Spencer, D. D. (1981). *Data processing: An introduction (2nd ed.).* Columbus, OH: Charles E. Merrill.

Spencer, D. D. (1985). *Principles of information processing.* Columbus, OH: Charles E. Merrill.

Taylor, C. F., Jr. (1988). *Master handbook of microcomputer languages* (2nd ed.). Blue Ridge Summit, PA: Tab Books.

Teacher Competencies

Henry F. Thibodeaux III
Lafayette, Louisiana ■

The development of competencies for computer-using professionals for preservice and in-service purposes has been an ongoing concern of regular and special educators. Typically, these competencies are generated by educational technologists working alone or in collaboration with colleagues using inductive or deductive reasoning or task-analytic procedures. Competencies derived are then evaluated and rated, and those competencies pertinent to educational practices are adopted, categorized, and included in lists. As hardware, software, and technology-related instructional knowledge evolve, competencies are revised or eliminated.

The regular education technology-competency movement has been spearheaded by the seminal research of numerous technologists including David Moursand (1981), Seymour Papert (1980), and Robert Taylor (1980) among others (e.g., Jacobs, 1985; Niess, 1990; Tashner, 1984). This movement has also been supported by the activities of professional organizations (e.g., International Council for Computers in Education) and the publications of specific journals (e.g., *Computing Teacher, Electronic Learning,* and *T.H.E. Journal*).

For the most part, the framework used to delineate competencies for computer-using regular educators is grade-level based (e.g., elementary, middle, or secondary). With respect to computer competency concerns, Niess has reported (1990) two recent major changes. First, it is the opinion of present-day regular education technology authorities that keyboarding skills should be taught as early as possible and that elementary teachers do not need to know how to program. Second, Niess noted:

> Probably the most significant change has been in the verbs that were used in the competencies. Verb phrases changed from "should have knowledge" (in 1983) to "should use" (in 1989). . . . No longer is simply having knowledge acceptable. The teacher must use that knowledge in the classroom. (p. 11)

Finally, one of the most widely used lists of competencies for computer-using regular educators was developed by a project jointly funded by the Northwest Council for Computer Education and Oregon State University (see Niess, 1990).

The special education computer competency initiative has been fostered by the research of regular education technologists and the explicit and implicit research and writings of various special educators (e.g., Behrmann, 1984, 1988; Budoff & Hutten, 1982; Budoff, Thorman, & Gras, 1984; Hagen, 1984; Hofmeister, 1982; Lindsey, 1987, in press; Roston & Sewell, 1984; Taber, 1981a, 1981b; among others). Also, competencies for computer-using special educators have evolved because of the efforts of national, state, and professional organizations (e.g., Closing the Gap, Council for Exceptional Children's Technology and Media Division, U.S. Office of Special Education Programs) and the publication of special education journals (e.g., *Journal of Special Education Technology*). However, it has been the work of A. Edward Blackhurst and his associates (e.g., Kinney & Blackhurst, 1987) that has resulted in the delineation of specific technology competencies that professionals working with exceptional individuals should have. Blackhurst's continued activities are resulting in updated competencies for computer-using special educators.

For the most part, the schema being used to categorize competencies for special educators focuses on general expertise (e.g., hardware and software knowledge and abilities), type of exceptionality (e.g., sensory, learning, physical disabilities, etc.), age level (children, youths, and adults), and instructional practices (e.g., assessment and teaching). Competencies for special educators, like those for regular educators, are being derived using professional knowledge and task-analysis and are being modified as technology and special education practices evolve.

What follows is a listing of general competencies special educators may need to effectively utilize computer hardware and software concepts with exceptional individuals. These competencies were derived by integrating the competencies reported by Niess (1990), suggested by Kinney and Blackhurst (1987), and discussed or alluded to by the authors in this book. An age-level format, infant to postsecondary, is used to categorize generic competencies. Again, rapid developments in technology and our increased understanding of the benefits of using this technology with and by exceptional individuals will result in the revision or elimination of these competencies. Also, and as stated by Kinney and Blackhurst (1987), "care should be taken in interpreting lists of competencies that have been developed" (p. 111). They also asserted that only those competencies that are valid for the context in which the user will need them should be considered.

Ages 0 to 5: Infant, Toddler, and Early Childhood

- Have infant, toddler, and early childhood special education certification and related competencies

- Possess state and local education agencies' computer literacy competencies

- Be knowledgeable of infant, toddler, and early childhood special education computing topics and familiar with related educational materials

- Show understanding of everyday functions of hardware and software and be able to engage in general troubleshooting activities (e.g., running diagnostic programs)

- Be able to arrange the physical setting to maximize technology use

- Be able to execute basic computer operations such as using operating systems, loading and running programs (e.g., floppy, hard disk, CD-ROM), installing programs on hard disks, formatting disks, copying files, loading printers and replacing ribbons, etc.

- Have the ability to maintain and care for hardware and software

- Utilize varied sources to secure pertinent information on hardware and software

- Use hardware and software for professional development

- Exhibit knowledge of the present and future impact of computers on society (e.g., home, school, and community)

- Identify and address equality issues such as equal access for males and females, minorities, and all exceptional users

- Assist parents, colleagues, and students alike in seeing the benefits of using computer technology

- Help parents and colleagues identify, evaluate, select, and develop computer-related activities to meet teaching-learning objectives (e.g., multimedia, authoring systems, etc.)

- Support the development of appropriate technology-related concepts by state and local education agencies (e.g., in-services)

- Integrate hardware and software into the curriculum, not curriculum to the computer, and consider the user's characteristics

- Determine, utilize, and teach the use of adaptive and augmentative communication-related technologies with appropriate exceptional individuals

- Comply with copyright laws and address ethical computer issues

- Use technology for personal and instructional productivity (see Chapter 13)

- Utilize various procedures to teach exceptional individuals the appropriate use of input devices (e.g., keyboarding, voice recognition, switches, etc.) and output devices (e.g., monitor, printer, speech synthesizer, etc.), robotics, etc.

Ages 6 to 11: Elementary School

- Have elementary special education certification and related competencies

- Possess state and local education agencies' computer literacy competencies

- Show understanding of everyday functions of hardware and software and be able to engage in general troubleshooting activities (e.g., running diagnostic programs)

- Be able to arrange the physical setting to maximize technology use

- Be able to execute basic computer operations such as using operating systems, loading and running programs (e.g., floppy, hard disk, CD-ROM), installing programs on hard disks, formatting disks, copying files, loading printers and replacing ribbons, etc.

- Have the ability to maintain and care for hardware and software

- Be knowledgeable of elementary special education computing topics and be familiar with related educational materials

- Utilize varied sources to secure pertinent information on hardware and software

- Use hardware and software for professional development

- Exhibit knowledge of the present and future impact of computers on society (e.g., home, school, and community)

- Identify and address equality issues such as equal access for males and females, minorities, and all exceptional individuals

- Assist parents, colleagues, and students alike in seeing the benefits of using computer technology (e.g., problem-solving tasks)

- Help parents and colleagues identify, evaluate, select, and develop computer-related activities to meet teaching-learning objectives (e.g., multimedia, authoring systems, telecommunications, etc.)

- Support the development of appropriate technology-related concepts (e.g., in-services) by state and local education agencies

- Integrate hardware and software into the curriculum, not curriculum to the computer, and consider the user's characteristics

- Determine, utilize, and teach the use of adaptive and augmentative communication-related technologies with appropriate exceptional individuals

- Comply with copyright laws and address ethical computer issues

- Use technology for personal and instructional productivity (see Chapter 13)

- Utilize various procedures to teach exceptional individuals the appropriate use of input devices (e.g., disk drives, keyboarding, voice recognition, switches, etc.) and output devices (e.g., monitor, printer, speech synthesizer, etc), applications software (e.g., word processing), authoring systems, multimedia, desktop publishing, telecommunications techniques, robotics, etc.

- Write understandable and structured simple elementary-level programs in at least one language (e.g., LOGO)

Ages 11 to 14: Middle School

- Have middle school special education certification and related competencies

- Possess state and local education agencies' computer literacy competencies

- Show understanding of everyday functions of hardware and software and be able to engage in general troubleshooting activities (e.g., running diagnostic programs)

- Be able to arrange the physical setting to maximize technology use

- Be able to execute basic computer operations such as using operating systems, loading and running programs (e.g., floppy, hard disk, CD-ROM), installing programs on hard disks, formatting disks, copying files, loading printers and replacing ribbons, etc.

- Have the ability to maintain and care for hardware and software

- Be knowledgeable of middle school special education computing topics and be familiar with related educational materials

- Utilize varied sources to secure pertinent information on hardware and software

- Use hardware and software for professional development

- Utilize basic technology terminology

- Exhibit knowledge of the present and future impact of computers on society (e.g., home, school, and community)

- Identify and address equality issues such as equal access for males and females, minorities, and all exceptional individuals

- Assist parents, colleagues, and exceptional individuals alike in seeing the benefits of using computer technology (e.g., problem-solving tasks)

- Help parents, colleagues, and exceptional individuals identify, evaluate, select, and develop computer-related activities to meet teaching-learning objectives (e.g., multimedia, authoring systems, telecommunications, etc.)

- Support the development of appropriate technology-related concepts (e.g., in-services) by state and local education agencies

- Integrate hardware and software into the curriculum, not curriculum to the computer, and consider the user's characteristics

- Determine, utilize, and teach the use of adaptive and augmentative communication-related technologies with appropriate exceptional individuals

- Comply with copyright laws and address ethical computer issues

- Use technology for personal and instructional productivity (see Chapter 13)

- Utilize various procedures to teach exceptional individuals the appropriate use of input devices (e.g., disk drives, keyboarding, voice recognition, switches, etc.) and output devices (e.g., monitor, printer, speech synthesizer, etc.), applications software (e.g., word processing), authoring systems, multimedia, desktop publishing, telecommunications techniques, robotics, etc.

- Design computer teaching-learning activities to promote the development of moral, psychological, and sociological concepts

- Write understandable and structured middle-grade-level programs in at least one language (e.g., LOGO or BASIC)

Ages 15 to Adult: Secondary and Postsecondary Levels

- Have secondary or postsecondary school special education certification and related competencies

- Possess state and local education agencies' computer literacy competencies

- Show understanding of everyday functions of hardware and software and be able to engage in general troubleshooting activities (e.g., running diagnostic programs)

- Be able to arrange the physical setting to maximize technology use

- Be able to execute basic computer operations such as using operating systems, loading and running programs (e.g., floppy, hard disk, CD-ROM), installing programs on hard disks, formatting disks, copying files, loading printers and replacing ribbons, etc.

- Have the ability to maintain and care for hardware and software

- Be knowledgeable of secondary or postsecondary special education computing topics and familiar with related education materials

- Utilize varied sources to secure pertinent information on hardware and software

- Use hardware and software for professional development

- Utilize basic technology terminology

- Exhibit knowledge of the present and future impact of computers on society (e.g., home, school, and community)

- Identify and address equality issues such as equal access for males and females, minorities, and all exceptional users

- Assist colleagues and exceptional individuals alike in seeing the benefits of using computer technology (e.g., problem-solving tasks)

- Help colleagues and exceptional individuals identify, evaluate, select, and develop computer-related activities to meet teaching-learning objectives (e.g., multimedia, authoring systems, telecommunications, etc.)

- Support the development of appropriate state and local education agencies technology-related concepts (e.g., in-services)

- Integrate hardware and software into the curriculum, not curriculum to the computer, and consider the exceptional individual's characteristics

- Determine, utilize, and teach the use of adaptive and augmentative communication-related technologies with appropriate exceptional individuals

- Comply with copyright laws and address ethical computer issues

- Use technology for personal and instructional productivity (see Chapter 13)

- Utilize various procedures to teach exceptional individuals the appropriate use of input devices (e.g., keyboarding, voice recognition, switches, etc.) and output devices (e.g., monitor, printer, etc.), applications software (e.g., word processing), authoring systems, multimedia, desktop publishing, telecommunications techniques, etc.

- Design computer teaching-learning activities to promote the development of moral, psychological, and sociological concepts

- Use hardware and software to develop exceptional individuals' career awareness and vocational abilities and competitiveness

- Write understandable and structured secondary or postsecondary elementary-level programs in at least one language (e.g., BASIC or Pascal)

REFERENCES

Behrmann, M. M. (1984). *Handbook of microcomputers in special education.* Austin, TX: PRO-ED.

Behrmann, M. M. (1988). *Integrating computers into the curriculum.* Austin, TX: PRO-ED.

Budoff, M., & Hutten, L. R. (1982). Microcomputers in special education: Promises and pitfalls. *Exceptional Children, 49*(2), 123–128.

Budoff, M., Thorman, J., & Gras, A. (1984). *Microcomputers in special education.* Cambridge, MA: Brookline Books.

Hagen, D. (1984). *Microcomputer resource book for special education.* Reston, VA: Reston Publishing.

Hofmeister, A. M. (1982). Microcomputers in perspective. *Exceptional Children, 49,* 115–121.

Jacobs, J. E. (1985, August/September). Let's prepare computer educators—not computer science educators. *Computing Teacher, 13,* 17–18.

Kinney, T. G., & Blackhurst, A. E. (1987). Technology competencies for teachers of young children with severe handicaps. *Topics in Early Childhood Education, 7*(3), 105–115.

Lindsey, J. (Ed.). (1987). *Computers and exceptional individuals* (2nd ed.). Columbus, OH: Merrill Publishing.

Moursand, D. (1981). *Introduction to computers in education for elementary and middle school teachers.* Eugene: University of Oregon, International Council for Computers in Education.

Niess, M. L. (1990). Preparing computer using educators in a new decade. *Computing Teacher, 18*(3), 10–15.

Papert, S. (1980). *Mindstorms: Children, computers, and powerful ideas.* New York: Basic Books.

Roston, A., & Sewell, D. (1984). *Microtechnology in special education.* Baltimore, MD: Johns Hopkins University Press.

Taber, F. M. (1981a). *Microcomputers in special education: Selection and decision-making process.* Reston, VA: Council for Exceptional Children.

Taber, F. M. (1981b). The microcomputer: Its application to special education. *Focus on Exceptional Children, 14*(2), 1–16.

Tashner, J. H. (Ed.). 1984). *Improving instruction with microcomputers: Readings and resources for elementary and secondary schools.* Phoenix, AZ: Orynx Press.

Taylor, R. (Ed.). (1980). *The computer in the school: Tutor, tool and tutee.* New York: Teachers College Press.

APPENDIX

Software for Exceptional Individuals

Henry E. Teller, Jr.
Southern University and A & M College
David A. Stewart
Michigan State University
Ruth F. Kirsopp
Louisiana School for the Deaf

Microcomputers are a part of many teachers' repertoires of instructional aids. Their introduction into the classroom over the two past decades has revealed that many aspects of student learning and teacher behavior can benefit from the use of microcomputers. Programs for exceptional (and nonexceptional) students do not deny the value of microcomputer-based learning experiences. Consequently, the diversity of classroom applications of the microcomputer has led to the development of commercially available instructional software that covers all subject areas. For the astute teacher, classroom management files, individualized educational plans, and other utility programs can be handled on the microcomputer.

The rapid proliferation of new instructional software does raise the question of which ones will best suit the needs of a particular child. Software may be designed around the requirements of a certain exceptionality; however, like textbooks, the personal characteristics of the students and the instructional techniques of the teacher dictate its proper application. Several agencies have been estab-

lished to help teachers make an appropriate software choice. For example, the Special Education Software Center (Building B, Room S312, 333 Ravenwood Avenue, Menlo Park, CA 94025) offers a 24-hour information service with access to the center's software data base. The center can be reached by mail, toll-free phone, Teletype Device for the Deaf, or computer, and services are offered free of charge. Universities are also providing up-to-date information on instructional software. The Center for Advanced Technology in Education (College of Education, University of Oregon, Eugene) has compiled a data base retrieval system used to search for software reviews. In addition to agencies, journals are good resources for software information—the *Journal of Learning Disabilities* has a section entitled "Computers in the School" and the *Volta Review* carries a "Volta Software Review" section. How well one uses available resources will likely determine the effectiveness of one's computer-based instructional materials.

Following is a brief description of a number of instructional and/or utility software programs that can assist teachers of exceptional students or exceptional individuals themselves. The list is by no means complete, but examples of a variety software are presented. It is hoped, however, that the reader will gain insight into the diversity of available programs and be inspired to explore the field further. Most of these products are provided in both the IBM PC and Apple II formats.

EARLY CHILDHOOD

Title: Facemaker Golden Edition   *Publisher:* Spinnaker Software Corporation, 215 First Street, Cambridge, MA 02142   *Level:* Preschool and elementary

This program is a high-interest way to teach young children some of the basics of computer operation. The user builds different faces and then animates them. When pressing the keys to animate a face, the user is actually doing an elementary form of programming. The user learns about menus, cursors, the return key, the space bar, simple programs, and graphics. A memory game can also be played. The user presses the appropriate keys to reproduce winks, ear wiggles, or a smile or frown on the face.

Title: Match-Up   *Publisher:* Hayden Software Company, 600 Suffolk Street, Lowell, MA 01854   *Level:* Preschool to lower elementary

No reading is required to operate this program. Children learn to match objects within a group and to pick out objects that do not belong in a group. These activities are designed to give readiness practice in the areas of mathematics, reasoning, and language. All activities begin with pairing identical objects. Once the child's matching skills are established, the program presents more challenging analogies of similar versus dissimilar.

Title: Getting Ready to Read   *Publisher:* Society for Visual Education, Department VS, 1345 Diversey Parkway, Chicago, IL 60614-1299 *Level:* Prekindergarten to grade 2

A 7-disk presentation of critical skills. This highly interactive program combines audiocassettes, microcomputer software, and 24 skill sheets to teach readiness skills. The teacher controls the level of difficulty as the prereader develops visual and auditory skills separately, then integrates them to practice skills in reading readiness from learning letters to decoding.

SPEECH AND LANGUAGE

Title: Visible Speech Aid   *Publisher:* Software Research Corporation, Discovery Park—University of Victoria, Box 1700, Victoria, British Columbia   *Level:* Preschool through adult

Designed to be used by teachers of hearing-impaired children and speech therapists in providing oral articulation training to severely and profoundly hearing-impaired children. Graphic displays of pitch, rhythm, and amplitude provide immediate visual feedback to reinforce the student's speech patterns. Positive aspects of the program include storage space for speech patterns and a wide range of speech characteristics. The visible speech component comes with a speed control option but, like all features of this program, the user requires highly specialized skills to ensure that the learner is aware of correct and incorrect graphic representations.

READING

Title: Steps to Comprehension   *Publisher:* Educational Publishing Concepts, P.O. Box 715, St. Charles, IL 60174   *Level:* Grades 1–8

Designed for use with elementary students, this reading program includes 90 original cloze and traditional stories about careers, values, and the environment on 11 reading levels. Each story of 200–275 words contains a title page, text with color illustrations, and both literal and interpretive comprehension questions. Students read at their own pace, either advancing to the next "page" by pressing the space bar or returning to the previous one by pressing the back arrow key. Students receive immediate feedback for their answers. If an incorrect response is selected, the correct answer is supplied followed by a return to the related portion of the text along with an explanation of why the given answer is appropriate. When students demonstrate mastery of a reading passage by correctly answering a predetermined percentage of the comprehension questions, the cartoon-style color pictures become animated.

Title: Improving Comprehension Skills   *Publisher:* Society for Visual Education, Department VS, 1345 Diversey Parkway, Chicago, IL 60614-1299   *Level:* Grades 2–3; Grades 4–5—remedial

This 3-disk program is designed with remedial readers in mind. It features 60 high-interest stories that are written at the second- to third-grade level. Teachers or students may also enter their own stories and questions to match interests and reading levels. Incorrect answers make a reading screen reappear for hints. Correct answers are rewarded with positive reinforcements. Record keeping for individual and class performance is built into the program.

Title: Readable Stories   *Publisher:* Laureate Learning Systems, 110 East Spring Street, Winooski, VT 05404   *Level:* Grades 1–4

This program offers three linguistic levels and reader control of the pace. After each story the student is given multiple-choice questions concerning comprehension. The linguistic levels depend on sentence length, word order, and the use of clauses and idioms. This program is recommended for children with learning disabilities, and it is also effective with children with impaired hearing. A student performance printout is available for the teacher.

LANGUAGE ARTS

Title: Compu-Spell   *Publisher:* Edu-ware Services, P.O. Box 2222, Agoura, CA 91301   *Level:* Elementary

Uses memorization and positive reinforcement to teach spelling. Spelling words are presented individually or in sentences. Each time the student presses the space bar, one of the spelling words disappears and the student must type the correct spelling of that word. The program advances only when the word has been correctly spelled. This feature encourages students to attend carefully to the word before attempting to spell. The program allows teachers to insert their own spelling words, thereby constructing individualized spelling exercises.

Title: Wizard of Words   *Publisher:* Computer Advances Ideas, 2550 Ninth Street, Suite 104, Berkeley, CA 94709   *Level:* Grades 2–8

Contains a multilevel list of 38,000 words that is used in spelling games. The five different spelling games are enhanced with graphics and sound. The program is straightforward and easy to use and includes an authoring system that allows for the creation of personal word lists for use in the spelling games.

Title: Special Needs, Volume 2   *Publisher:* Minnesota Educational Computing Corporation, 3490 Lexington Avenue North, St. Paul, MN 55126   *Level:* Elementary—physically challenged

The spelling program is designed for easy use by physically challenged students. By using a touch pad, any key on the keyboard, or a game control unit, the student can select an answer when it is enclosed in the box outline. Multiple-choice answers are given, and the program automatically moves the box from one answer to another until an answer is selected. The teacher can change the spelling word lists and sentences.

Title: First Categories   *Publisher:* Laureate Learning Systems, One Mill Street, Burlington, VT 05401   *Level:* Preschool through adult

Develops categorization abilities in the following areas: body parts, foods, utensils, and vehicles. A flexible program suitable for a wide range of language-handicapped persons, including preschoolers with mental disabilities, school-age learning-disabled pupils, and fluent aphasic adults. A one-switch option enables pupils with severe motor impairments to operate the program. A built-in authoring system would have expanded the capabilities of this program to other areas.

Title: Discovery Writer *Publisher:* Scholastic, 50 West 44 Street, New York, NY 10036 *Level:* Kindergarten through grade 2

The program is based on the whole language approach and makes extensive use of combining text and graphics. A synthesized voice makes the story come to life. Children can write their own stories and publish them in a variety of sizes. Theme packs are available for each grade level that covers the curriculum areas.

Title: Super Story Tree *Publisher:* Scholastic, 50 West 44 Street, New York, NY 10036 *Level:* Grades 4–8

The program is a story-writing tool for students. Each page is plotted by the student, who has three different avenues to follow. The "continue" link moves the student to the next page. The "choice" link gives a maximum of eight alternative path choices. The "chance" links direct the reader to one of two different page choices. The program offers a wide variety of uses and is compatible with Scholastic Graphics and Sound Booster Packs, Superprint, and Print Shop. Exceptional students can use a mouse or the space bar to operate this program.

Title: Writer Rabbit: Early Writing and Thinking Skills *Publisher:* The Learning Company, 6493 Kaiser Drive, Fremont, CA 94550 *Level:* Grades 2–4

Writer Rabbit includes a variety of games designed to help students identify parts of a sentence, create sentences, and learn grammar concepts. The program also includes "Silly Story Party," which is the creative writing section of the program. A school version is offered that includes the disk, backup disk, teacher's guide with lesson plans, and reproducible masters.

MATHEMATICS

Title: Management System *Publisher:* Computer Courseware, Quest Systems, P.O. Box 12515, Alexandria, LA 71315 *Level:* Elementary

Designed for use with elementary-level students, this package includes two components: instructional materials and software. The instructional materials include a management book that outlines a diagnostic-prescriptive approach to teaching/learning basic math skills and organizes the other materials; diagnostic tests that measure the student's computational skills with whole numbers; work sheets and activity cards that provide self-checking practice in addition, subtraction, multiplication, and division; games; post-tests; and a teacher's manual that explains in detail how to set up the program and includes management tips and lesson plan forms. The software component contains attention-getting motivational activities with immediate feedback, a computer prescription that automatically tracks each student according to the student's needs, diagnostic tests, results of the last lesson each student has completed, test results with suggested lessons for remediation, and a record-keeping disk and profile of each student as well as the whole class for lesson planning.

Title: Academic Skills Builders in Math *Publisher:* Developmental Learning Materials, One DLM Park, P.O. Box 4000, Allen, TX 75002 *Level:* Grades 1–12

A drill program designed to provide remedial work for students with learning difficulties. The program is ideally suited for slow workers and those with limited mobility, as a small number of keys, the space bar, or a joystick/paddle can be used to respond to prompts.

Title: Milliken Math Sequences *Publisher:* Milliken, 1100 Research Blvd., St. Louis, MO 63132 *Level:* Grades 1–8

Twelve disks break down the basic mathematic skills for students in grades 1 through 8. Best used for drills and documentation of students' grasp of mathematic skills. For the younger students, the positive graphic reinforcements are ideal; however, they become time-consuming and irritating for older students. Students are allowed two mistakes before they are exposed to a full-screen flashing X that may have a negative effect on students' confidence.

Title: Meteor Multiplication   *Publisher:* Developmental Learning Materials, One DLM Park, P.O. Box 4000, Allen, TX 75002   *Level:* Elementary and secondary

A high-interest game in which meteors advance on the user's star station. The user may fire at the meteors only after correctly answering a multiplication problem. The game may be played at varying levels of difficulty. Responses are tabulated.

Title: Money and Time Adventures of the Lollipop Dragon   *Publisher:* Society for Visual Education, Department VS, 1345 Diversey Parkway, Chicago, IL 60614-1299   *Level:* Kindergarten through grade 2; Grades 4–5—remedial

The software offers three games per disk with two to three levels of difficulty. The program is easy to follow using a menu-driven operation. The format for Money Adventures is practicing counting, summing coin and bill values, and counting change. The format for Time Adventures is practicing setting the hour and minutes of a clock using a digital or manual-hands clock. Filmstrips and skill sheets are offered as an optional package for reinforcement and review.

OTHER CONTENT SUBJECTS

Title: Special Needs, Volume 2   *Publisher:* Minnesota Educational Computing Corporation, 3490 Lexington Avenue North, St. Paul, MN 55126   *Level:* Grades 2–6—physically disabled

This disk has five programs that are adapted for physically challenged students. The five programs are Arithmetic Practice, Change, Odell Woods, Odell Lake, and Wrong Note. Arithmetic Practice includes drills in addition, subtraction, multiplication, and division. Selection of difficulty level and speed is offered. Change is a drill involving making change from a purchase. Odell Woods is a simulation of the animal chain that requires thinking skills. Odell Lake is also a simulation of the food chain but uses different fish. Wrong Note is a drill using pitch sounds and matching them with the correct written form. All of these programs have been adapted to multiple-choice rotating answers that can be chosen by a single key, game stick, or touch pad.

Title: Comparative Buying Series   *Publisher:* MCE, 157 S. Kalamazoo Mall, Suite 250, Kalamazoo, MI 49007   *Level:* Grades 6 through adult

Demonstrates the real dollar value of the pupil's shopping power in four programs: Buying Wisely, Becoming an Informed Shopper, Understanding Sales Buying, and Cash versus Credit Buying. All programs are designed specially for persons with mental retardation or learning disabilities. The graphic displays add reinforcement and keep attention. The program spans the reading levels of grades 2 through 7 and comes with a guide specifying teaching strategies, objectives, and evaluation procedures. Teacher assistance may be necessary for the instructions.

Title: Mickey's Space Adventure   *Publisher:* Sierra On-Line–Disney Software, P.O. Box 485, Coarsegold, CA 93614   *Level:* Elementary

Map skills, planetary science, and creative problem solving are taught through an adventure game. Mickey Mouse and Pluto are helped by the user to find a downed spaceship on a far-off planet. All search for the lost memory crystal that is necessary to save the planet's inhabitants.

Title: Game of the States   *Publisher:* Milton Bradley Company, 443 Shaker Road, East Longmeadow, MA 02102   *Level:* Elementary and secondary

This game is designed to teach the user the facts about the United States of America through a game format. Five games are offered: Name the State, Name the Capital, Abbreviation, Name the Neighbors, and Major Cities. Each of the five games may be played at two levels of difficulty. Level 1 has a multiple-choice format. Level 2 requires the user to type the correct answer.

Title: Survival Math   *Publisher:* Sunburst Corporation, P.O. Box 40, 39 Washington Avenue, Pleasantville, NY 10570   *Level:* Upper elementary and secondary

Four simulations that apply arithmetic skills to real-life situations are included in this program. The simulations are Smart Shopper Marathon, in which the user tries to make the best buys using discount and unit pricing; Hot Dog Stand, in which the user runs a food concession stand at football games to raise money; Travel Agent Contest, in which a trip has to be planned for 7 days within a given budget; and Foreman's Assistant, in which the user must construct a room while keeping within the given budget and time.

Title: Scientific Method   *Publisher:* Micro Power and Light Company, P.O. Box 441, 56 Park Drive, Owatonna, MN 55060   *Level:* Upper elementary and secondary

The user is led through the scientific method in a simulated experiment. The skills of observation, stating a hypothesis, measurement, and verification are taught through the experiment.

TYPING

Title: LetterMan   *Publisher:* Behavioral Engineering, 230 Mt. Hermon Road, Suite 207, Scotts Valley, CA 95066   *Level:* Upper elementary and secondary

A high motivation game that uses the Pac-Man concept to teach typing and to increase typing speed. The speed of the game is set by the player prior to starting and uses words per minute as its unit of measurement. An option is available that allows users to specify their own lists of vocabulary, keying in on specific content areas such as science, social studies, history, business, and others. As there is a lack of content in the typing tasks—all words are given individually and not in sentences—the users do not gain practice in typing common phrases.

Title: Mavis Beacon Teaches Typing   *Publisher:* Electronic Arts, 450 Fashion Island Boulevard, San Mateo, CA 94404   *Level:* All grades

This program focuses on word/letter combinations and progress charts. Animated graphics and sound accompany the lesson. The program contains a data base so large that the same lesson never appears twice. It also contains employment agency tests and passages from literature.

UTILITY

Title: Kindercomp   *Publisher:* Spinnaker Software Corporation, 215 First Street, Cambridge, MA 02142   *Level:* Elementary

An introduction to using the keyboard and graphics of computers. In addition, the publisher claims that the program develops pattern recognition, number sequencing, and skills necessary for matching upper- and lowercase letters, and that it is useful for reinforcing reading readiness skills. A good introductory package that perhaps is lacking only in its control of guiding learning objectives. That is, it reinforces guesswork instead of encouraging careful attention to instructions.

Title: PC Voice   *Publisher:* ARTS Computer Products, 145 Tremont Street, Suite 407, Boston, MA 02111   *Level:* Elementary through adult

The PC Voice program enables the user to hear what is displayed on the IBM personal computer screen. The screen image is verbalized, thus easing eyestrain. Punctuation marks are spoken, and the pauses are inserted to reduce confusion. Output can be heard even though it is not readily seen by the user. A good program for visually impaired persons.

CAREER AWARENESS—VOCATIONAL EDUCATION

Title: Analyzing an Ad   *Publisher:* MCE, 157 S. Kalamazoo, MI 49007   *Level:* Preschool through grade 12

This program describes how advertisements are created and coaches the user on how to avoid exploitation. Buying decisions are examined. The user can create ads through simulation and make hard copy.

Title: Compu-Job   *Publisher:* Computer Aids, 20417 Nordhoff Street, Department M5, Chatsworth, CA 91311   *Level:* Secondary

This career guidance program provides information about jobs and strategies for locating, obtaining, and maintaining employment. Among the skills the student acquires are developing a resume, completing application forms, and using classified ads and the telephone to find a job. The student learns what to expect as an employee, how to develop good relationships with supervisors and other employees, and how to plan a budget and keep a checking account balanced.

Title: Daily Living Skills, I & II   *Publisher:* Encyclopedia Britannica Educational Corporation, 425 N. Michigan Avenue, Chicago, IL 60611   *Level:* Secondary through adult

The first program is divided into two parts—Part 1: Prescription Medicine and Product Labels and Part 2: Classified Ads and Telephone Directories. Survival reading is emphasized. Prescription Medicine gives a description of the parts of a prescription label and tells how to use medicine correctly. Product Labels calls attention to information one may want to obtain from the labels of various goods. Classified Ads and Telephone Directories offers directions on how to obtain information listed in classified ads and telephone directories. The second program is also divided into two parts—Part 1: Banking and Credit and Part 2: Job Applications and Paychecks. Survival reading is emphasized. The maintenance of checking and savings accounts, obtaining loans, dealing with job applications, and examining paychecks are presented in depth.

Title: Home Safe Home   *Publisher:* MCE, 157 S. Kalamazoo Mall, Kalamazoo, MI 49007   *Level:* Upper elementary and secondary

Major household hazards are highlighted, with an emphasis on prevention of accidents. Color graphics are used extensively, and sound and music are linked to the concepts presented. The program highlights the hazards of household fire, electrical shock, falls, and poisons. Branching gives the user an option of three reading levels (second, third, or fifth grade). May be very useful training for disabled persons living in group homes or halfway houses.

SCHOOL AND CLASS MANAGEMENT

Title: Report Card   *Publisher:* Computer Aids, 20417 Nordhoff Street, Dept. M5, Chatsworth, CA 91311   *Level:* Teacher

This classroom management program allows the teacher to keep accurate records on up to 50 activities for a maximum of 12 classes containing 40 students each. If there are incomplete assignments, the program allows a "no grade" mark to be used that can be replaced when the assignment is completed. Records can be listed in a variety of ways, including student's first or last name, grades received on individual assignments, or average grade. Although each assignment is given a numerical value, this program can print out reports including class and individual averages and letter grades, class activities and their results, and a class roster.

Title: School Information Management System   *Publisher:* Powell Systems, 3839 Bee Caves Road, Suite 104, Austin, TX 78746   *Level:* Teachers, school administrators, university personnel, and education agencies

A time-saving program designed to store and retrieve information on student and teacher records; inventories; comparability data; health records; tracking teacher in-service workshop requirements; materials cataloging; and school, districtwide, or internal personnel surveys.

Title: IEP Manager   *Publisher:* Rocky Mountain Educational Systems, 1390 Kalmia Avenue, Boulder, CO 80302   *Level:* Professionals designing IEPs for students with an academic level below the seventh grade

This program generates a complete IEP that satisfies the requirements of Public Law 94–142. It begins with an assessment summary program on intellectual functioning and data from up to 15 instructional areas. From this an assessment report recommends a starting grade level for objectives based on diagnosed deficiency in the student's education. The user then chooses from 1 of 15 instructional areas and the appropriate grade level. The IEP printout includes student information, professionals involved with IEP write-ups, annual goals, short-term objectives, and an evaluation chart. Although the objectives do not cover all the individual's needs, the program permits editing, revisions, or deletion according to user's interests.

Title: Parent Reporting   *Publisher:* Computer Aids, 20417 Nordhoff Street, Dept. M5, Chatsworth, CA 91311   *Level:* Teacher

Using this management tool, the teacher can personalize messages sent home to parents. Standard phrases describing classroom activities and/or individual participation are input so as to eliminate the need to retype repeated descriptions. As many as eight subject areas along with grades for each can be incorporated into the note to parents. This time-saving device permits the teacher to keep in constant contact with parents with regard to each student's weekly or daily progress. It is also an excellent tool for the teacher to use to keep parents in touch with the child's progress as related to the IEP.

INTEGRATED SOFTWARE AND WORD PROCESSING

Title: AppleWorks   *Publisher:* Claris, 5201 Patrick Henry Drive, Santa Clara, CA 95052. *Level:* Students and adults

An integrated software package with a simplified menu system that facilitates movement between levels. AppleWorks consists of a word processor, spreadsheet, and file pro-

gram. The desktop feature permits simultaneous retrieval of data from several different files. Thus letters and reports can be composed and printed using the file program and the word processor together. The spreadsheet may be used to record grades and compute averages of students in the class as well as a number of other types of data and formulas. Information in the file program may be stored and retrieved in a variety of ways. Apple-Works may be used to organize and maintain student records or as a teaching-learning tool in the classroom, particularly in the areas of writing and problem solving.

Title: Bank Street Writer III   *Publisher:* Computer Aids, 20417 Nordhoff Street, Dept. M5, Chadsworth, CA 91311   *Level:* Grades 2–12

This word-processing program facilitates the composition, editing, and revision of reports, themes, letters, original stories, and other written materials. Lessons on how to use the word processor, a fully integrated spelling checker, and an on-line thesaurus are featured. This program is not copy-protected.

CONCLUSION

This list represents a fraction of the available software programs. Given the current status of technology and awareness of the advantages of microcomputers, we are witnessing a boom in the number of software programs for exceptional children and their teachers. More important, however, the pragmatic application of all programs will rely upon the dedication and knowledge of the teacher. Teachers who wish to keep abreast of latest developments should refer to the latest editions of several comprehensive educational software catalogues, software publishers' catalogues, and reviews of educational software that appear monthly in the educational computing magazines and professional educational journals.

Sample BASIC Programs

Rick Hazey
Baton Rouge, Louisiana ■

This appendix contains sample programs in BASIC that illustrate ways a microcomputer and BASIC programming can be used to assist in teaching as well as averaging grades, making measurement conversions, and using mailing lists. All of the programs were written on an Apple IIe, but they will run on most personal computers (e.g., IBM PC, Radio Shack, and Commodore) with few or no changes. Specific comments have been included in the programs so that they may be easily modified. Users who have problems or incompatibilities arise when trying to execute these programs should consult the BASIC manual for their computer. A list of books at the end of this appendix provide specific information on different computer systems and programming in BASIC for business, educational, or leisure purposes.

INTRODUCTORY BASIC PROGRAMS

Program Title: Salutations

Salutations demonstrates the underlying structure of all programs. Information is input, then modified or used to make a decision, and then output. Complex as well as simple programs follow this structure, and it can be used as a model for your future programs.

```
10 REM*****************************
11 REM*                          *
12 REM* PURPOSE: A SIMPLE PROGRAM *
13 REM* THAT DEMONSTRATES THE     *
14 REM* BASIC FLOW OF A PROGRAM.  *
15 REM*                          *
16 REM*****************************
17 REM
100 HOME:INPUT``WHAT IS YOUR NAME:   '';NAME$
110 ? ``HELLO '';NAME$;
120 INPUT `` ARE YOU FEELING WELL TODAY (Y/N)  '';WELL$
130 IF WELL$=``Y'' THEN ? ``GOOD, I'M GLAD TO  HEAR IT!'':END
140 ? ``THAT'S TOO BAD. I HOPE YOU FEEL BETTER SOON!''
150 END
```

Program Title: What is Your Age

What is Your Age permits the individual to input data about birthdate and compute age for any year.

```
10 REM ************************************
15 REM *                                  *
20 REM * THIS PROGRAM WILL COMPUTE THE  YEAR *
25 REM * IN WHICH YOU WILL BE A GIVEN AGE. *
30 REM * YOU ENTER YOUR BIRTH YEAR AND THE *
35 REM * AGE TO BE COMPUTED.              *
40 REM *                                  *
45 REM ************************************
47 REM
48 REM  MAIN PROGRAM
49 REM
100 INPUT``ENTER THE YEAR YOU WERE BORN: '';BIRTHYEAR
110 INPUT``ENTER THE AGE TO BE COMPUTED: '';AGE
120 YEAR=BIRTHYEAR+AGE
130 PRINT``YOU WILL BE'';AGE;`` IN THE YEAR '';YEAR
140 PRINT:INPUT``WOULD YOU LIKE TO TRY AGAIN ? (Y/N)'';A$
150 IF A$=``Y'' THEN GOTO 100
160 END
```

GAME PROGRAMS

Program Title: Guess It

Guess It has the individual try to guess a number between 1 and 100 and prints whether the guess is too high or too low. Guesses are entered until the number is found and the total number of guesses is found and the total number of guesses is displayed.

```
10 REM ************************************
15 REM *                                  *
20 REM * THIS PROGRAM WILL ASK YOU TO GUESS *
25 REM * A NUMBER BETWEEN 1 AND 100. YOU  ARE *
30 REM * TOLD WHETHER YOUR GUESS IS TOO  HIGH *
35 REM * OR TOO LOW.                      *
40 REM *                                  *
45 REM ************************************
46 REM
47 REM PRINT INSTRUCTIONS AND SET NUMBER OF TRIES
48 REM    TO ZERO.
49 REM
50 PRINT``I WILL CHOOSE A NUMBER BETWEEN 1 AND 100.''
60 PRINT``YOU TRY TO GUESS THE NUMBER AND I WILL TELL''
70 PRINT``YOU IF YOU ARE TOO HIGH OR TOO LOW.''
80 PRINT``PRESS ANY KEY TO CONTINUE.''
90 GET A$
97 REM
98 REM MAIN PROGRAM
```

UTILITY PROGRAMS

Program Title: Grader

Grader simplifies the grading process by computing average grades. Similar programs can be written to calculate grading curves.

```
5 REM ******************************
6 REM *                            *
7 REM * PURPOSE: THIS PROGRAM WILL  *
8 REM *   AVERAGE GRADES AFTER THE  *
9 REM *   NUMBER OF GRADES AND EACH *
10 REM*    GRADE HAVE BEEN INPUT.   *
11 REM *                            *
12 REM******************************
17 REM
18 REM MAIN PROGRAM LOOP
19 REM
20 GOSUB 100
30 GOSUB 200
40 GOSUB 300
50 IF DOAGAIN$=``Y'' THEN GOTO 20
60 END
97 REM
98 REM PURPOSE: GETS THE NUMBER OF GRADES TO BE AVERAGED
99 REM
100 HOME
110 INPUT``PLEASE ENTER THE NUMBER OF GRADES YOU WOULD LIKE TO
       AVERAGE '' ;NUMGDS
120 ?:?``PLEASE ENTER EACH GRADE:'':?
130 RETURN
197 REM
198 REM PURPOSE: GETS EACH GRADE AND ADDS IT TO A RUNNING SUBTOTAL
199 REM
200 TEMP=0
210 FOR INDEX=1 TO NUMGDS
220 ?``GRADE '';INDEX;
230 INPUT GD
240 TEMP=GD+TEMP
250 NEXT INDEX
260 RETURN
297 REM
298 REM PURPOSE: COMPUTES AND DISPLAYS THE AVERAGE
299 REM
300 AVERAGE=TEMP/NUMGDS
310 HOME
320 ?``THE AVERAGE GRADE IS '';AVERAGE
330 ?:INPUT``WOULD YOU LIKE TO DO ANOTHER? (Y/N)'';DOAGAIN$
340 RETURN
350 END
```

READING PROGRAMS

Program Title: Short and Long "a"

Short and Long "a" provides practice in identifying words with long or short *a*'s. This program can be easily modified to give practice in the other vowel sounds.

```
10 REM *****************************************
15 REM *                                       *
20 REM *THIS PROGRAM WILL ALLOW THE CORRECT    *
25 REM *LONG OR SHORT VOWEL TO BE CHOSEN  FROM *
30 REM *IN A WORD. THE WORDS TO BE USED ARE    *
35 REM *ENTERED STARTING AT LINE 1000.         *
40 REM *                                       *
45 REM *****************************************
46 REM
47 REM PRINT INSTRUCTIONS AND SET NUMBER OF RIGHT
48 REM   AND WRONG ANSWERS TO ZERO.
49 REM
50 NW=0
60 NR=0
65 VOWEL$=``A''
70 PRINT``TYPE LONG OR SHORT FOR THE VOWEL '' ;VOWEL$
80 PRINT``THAT APPEARS IN EACH WORD''
85 PRINT:PRINT``PRESS ANY KEY TO CONTINUE.''
90 GET A$
97 REM
98 REM MAIN PROGRAM
99 REM
100 READ WORD$
105 IF WORD$=``END'' THEN GOTO 250
110 READ CORRECT$
120 PRINT ``IS THE VOWEL '';VOWEL$;`` LONG OR SHORT IN THE WORD ''
    ;WORD$;`` ? '';
130 INPUT ANSWER$
140 IF ANSWER$<>CORRECT$ THEN GOTO 200
150 NR=NR+1
160 PRINT``THAT'S CORRECT! PRESS ANY KEY TO CONTINUE.''
170 GET A$
180 GOTO 100
197 REM
198 REM PRINT MESSAGE FOR INCORRECT ANSWER AND RETURN
199 REM
200 NW=NW+1
210 PRINT``THAT'S INCORRECT. THE ANSWER IS '';CORRECT$
220 PRINT``PRESS ANY KEY TO CONTINUE.''
230 GET A$
240 GOTO 100
247 REM
248 REM EXIT PROGRAM HERE
249 REM
250 PRINT:PRINT``THAT'S ALL THE WORDS I KNOW RIGHT NOW.''
260 PRINT``YOU GOT '';NR;`` CORRECT AND '';NW; `` INCORRECT.''
270 END
997 REM
998 REM ENTER WORDS AND LONG OR SHORT HERE
999 REM
1000 DATA ``FIRST WORD'',LONG
1001 DATA ``SECOND WORD'',SHORT
1002 DATA ``THIRD WORD'',SHORT
1003 DATA ``END''
```

Program Title: Reading Comprehension

Reading Comprehension provides practice in reading and comprehending specific written materials by presenting the individual with a screen of text to be read followed by a series of questions. The program is designed to be easily modified. Each line of text is entered as DATA line starting at line number 5000. Questions and answers are entered similarly starting at line 6000. Using the program as a skeleton, many reading and comprehension sessions can be created without having to write a program each time.

```
10 REM *****************************************
20 REM *                                       *
30 REM * THIS PROGRAM ALLOWS TEXT TO BE        *
40 REM * ENTERED IN LINES AFTER 5000 AND       *
45 REM * QUESTIONS AND ANSWERS TO BE           *
50 REM * ENTERED AFTER LINE 6000.              *
60 REM * THE NUMBER OF CORRECT ANSWERS         *
70 REM * GIVEN IS DISPLAYED AT THE END.        *
80 REM *                                       *
90 REM *****************************************
97 REM
98 REM PRINT TEXT TO BE READ
99 REM
100 HOME
105 RT=0
110 READ A$
120 IF A$=``END'' THEN GOTO 200
130 PRINT A$
140 GOTO 110
150 PRINT:PRINT ``PRESS ANY KEY WHEN YOU ARE FINISHED READING''
    :GET A$
197 REM
198 REM PRINT QUESTIONS AND GET ANSWERS
199 REM
200 HOME
210 READ QUES$:READ ANS$
220 IF QUES$=``END'' THEN GOTO 300
230 PRINT QUES$;`` '';
240 INPUT A$
250 IF A$=ANS$ THEN PRINT ``THAT'S CORRECT!'' :FOR N=1 TO
    500:NEXT:RT=RT+1: GOTO 200
260 PRINT ``THAT'S INCORRECT. THE RIGHT ANSWER IS: '';ANS$
270 FOR N=1 TO 500:NEXT:GOTO 200
297 REM
298 REM PRINT SCORE
299 REM
300 HOME
310 PRINT ``THAT IS ALL OF THE QUESTIONS''
320 PRINT ``YOU GOT '';RT;`` CORRECT''
330 END
4997 REM
4998 REM LINES OF TEXT GO HERE
4999 REM
5000 DATA ``FOUR-SCORE AND .....''
5001 DATA ``
5002 DATA ``
5997 REM
5998 REM QUESTIONS AND ANSWERS GO HERE
5999 REM
6000 DATA ``QUESTION'',``ANSWER''
6001 DATA ``
6002 DATA ``
```

MATHEMATICS PROGRAMS

Program Title: Math Drill

Math Drill assists in teaching simple arithmetic skills by drilling random problems and reporting the number of correct answers at the end of the session. The random function used in Math Drill is unique to the Apple IIe computer, so users with other types of computers, will have to consult their BASIC manual to make the needed changes to use Math Drill.

```
10 REM *******************************
11 REM *                             *
12 REM * PURPOSE: TO GENERATE RANDOM  *
13 REM *  SINGLE DIGIT ARITHMETIC     *
14 REM *  PROBLEMS FOR DRILL.         *
15 REM *                             *
16 REM *******************************
17 REM
18 REM MAIN PROGRAM LOOP
19 REM
20 HOME:GOSUB 500
30 FOR INDEX=1 TO 10
40 HOME:GOSUB 200
50 GOSUB 600
60 NEXT INDEX
70 GOSUB 700
80 IF DOAGAIN$=``Y'' THEN GOTO 20
90 END
197 REM
198 REM GETS TWO RANDOM VALUES TO USE FOR THE PROBLEM
199 REM
200 X=INT(RND(1)*9+1):Y=INT(RND(1)*9+1)
210 Z=INT(RND(1)*2+1)
220 ON Z GOSUB 300,400
230 ?:?``WHAT IS THE RESULT OF '';X;`` '' ;A$;`` '';Y;`` '';
240 INPUT ANSWER
250 RETURN
297 REM
298 REM GETS THE CORRECT RESULTS FOR AN ADDITION
299 REM
300 A$=``+'':RESULT=X+Y
310 RETURN
397 REM
398 REM GETS THE CORRECT RESULTS FOR A SUBTRACTION
399 REM
400 A$=``-'':RESULT=X-Y
410 RETURN
497 REM
498 REM INTRODUCTION TO PROGRAM
499 REM
500 ?``THIS PROGRAM DRILLS SINGLE DIGIT ADDITION AND SUBTRACTION
    AND RETURNS THE RESULTS AFTER 10 PROBLEMS.''
510 ?:?``PRESS ANY KEY TO BEGIN. '';
520 GET A$
530 RETURN
597 REM
598 REM CHECKS CORRECT ANSWER AGAINST THE INPUT ANSWER
599 REM
600 IF ANSWER()RESULT THEN GOTO 650
610 ?:?``THAT'S RIGHT!''
620 FOR N=1 TO 500:NEXT N
630 RIGHT= RIGHT+1
640 RETURN
```

```
650 ?:?``THAT WASN'T THE ANSWER I WAS LOOKING FOR. PLEASE
    TRY AGAIN.''
660 FOR N=1 TO 500:NEXT N
670 RETURN
697 REM
698 REM FINAL RESULTS
699 REM
700 ?:? ``YOU GOT '';RIGHT;`` PROBLEMS CORRECT!''
710 ?:INPUT ``WOULD YOU LIKE TO TRY AGAIN (Y/N)'';DOAGAIN$
720 RETURN
```

Program Title: Temperature Converter

Temperature Converter allows the easy conversion of degrees in Celsius to degrees Farenheit and back again. During the process of writing programs such as Temperature Converter, the concept of making conversions is taught.

```
10 REM ***************************************
20 REM *                                     *
30 REM * THE PURPOSE OF THIS PROGRAM IS TO   *
40 REM * CONVERT DEGREES FROM CELSIUS TO     *
50 REM * FARENHEIT OR VICE-VERSA.            *
60 REM *                                     *
70 REM ***************************************
80 REM
98 REM MAIN PROGRAM
99 REM
100 HOME
110 PRINT ``THIS PROGRAM WILL CONVERT DEGREES CELSIUS''
120 PRINT ``TO DEGREES FARENHEIT AND VICE-VERSA ''
130 PRINT:PRINT ``PRESS ANY KEY TO CONTINUE'' :GET A$
200 HOME
210 INPUT ``DO YOU WANT TO CONVERT FROM CELSIUS OR FROM FARENHEIT
    (C/F)'';CON$
220 IF CON$=``C'' THEN GOTO 500
230 IF CON$=``F'' THEN GOTO 600
240 GOTO 200
497 REM
498 REM ROUTINE TO CONVERT CELSIUS TO FARENHEIT
499 REM
500 HOME
510 INPUT ``ENTER THE DEGREES CELSIUS YOU WANT TO CONVERT ''
    ;CELDEG
520 FARDEG=(CELDEG*1.8)+32
530 PRINT
540 PRINT CELDEG;`` DEGREES CELSIUS EQUALS '';FARDEG;`` DEGREES
    FARENHEIT''
550 PRINT
560 INPUT ``WOULD YOU LIKE TO DO ANOTHER CONVERSION (Y/N) '';A$
570 IF A$=``Y'' THEN GOTO 500
580 GOTO 100
597 REM
598 REM ROUTINE TO CONVERT FARENHEIT TO CELSIUS
599 REM
600 HOME
610 INPUT ``ENTER THE DEGREES FARENHEIT YOU WANT TO CONVERT'';
    FARDEG
620 CELDEG=(FARDEG-32)/1.8
630 PRINT
640 PRINT FARDEG;`` DEGREES FARENHEIT EQUALS '';CELDEG;
    `` DEGREES CELSIUS ''
650  PRINT
660 INPUT ``WOULD YOU LIKE TO DO ANOTHER CONVERSION (Y/N) '';A$
670 IF A$=``Y'' THEN GOTO 600
680 GOTO 100
```

Program Title: Distance Converter

Distance Converter converts miles to kilometers and back again and teaches the same skills as the Temperature Converter program.

```
10 REM ***********************************
20 REM *                                 *
30 REM * THE PURPOSE OF THIS PROGRAM IS TO *
40 REM * CONVERT DISTANCE FROM MILES TO   *
50 REM * KILOMETERS OR VICE-VERSA.        *
60 REM *                                 *
70 REM ***********************************
80 REM
98 REM MAIN PROGRAM
99 REM
100 HOME
110 PRINT ``THIS PROGRAM WILL CONVERT MILES''
120 PRINT ``TO KILOMETERS AND VICE-VERSA ''
130 PRINT:PRINT ``PRESS ANY KEY TO CONTINUE'' :GET A$
200 HOME
210 INPUT ``DO YOU WANT TO CONVERT FROM MILES OR FROM KILOMETERS
    (M/K)'';CON$
220 IF CON$=``M'' THEN GOTO 500
230 IF CON$=``K'' THEN GOTO 600
240 GOTO 200
497 REM
498 REM ROUTINE TO CONVERT MILES TO KILOMETERS
499 REM
500 HOME
510 INPUT ``ENTER THE MILES YOU WANT TO CONVERT '';MILES
520 KILO=MILES/0.6
530 PRINT
540 PRINT MILES;`` MILES EQUALS '';KILO; `` KILOMETERS''
550 PRINT
560 INPUT ``WOULD YOU LIKE TO DO ANOTHER CONVERSION (Y/N) '';A$
570 IF A$=``Y'' THEN GOTO 500
580 GOTO 100
597 REM
598 REM ROUTINE TO CONVERT KILOMETERS TO MILES
599 REM
600 HOME
610 INPUT ``ENTER THE KILOMETERS YOU WANT TO CONVERT'';KILO
620 MILES=KILO*0.6
630 PRINT
640 PRINT KILO;`` KILOMETERS EQUALS ''; MILES;`` MILES''
650 PRINT
660 INPUT ``WOULD YOU LIKE TO DO ANOTHER CONVERSION (Y/N) '';A$
670 IF A$=``Y'' THEN GOTO 600
680 GOTO 100
```

```
10 REM **************************************
15 REM *                                    *
20 REM * THIS PROGRAM WILL ALLOW THE CORRECT *
25 REM * SPELLING OF A WORD TO BE CHOSEN  FROM *
30 REM * A LIST OF WORDS. THE WORDS TO BE  USED *
35 REM * ARE ENTERED STARTING AT LINE 1000.   *
40 REM *                                    *
45 REM **************************************
46 REM
47 REM PRINT INSTRUCTIONS AND SET NUMBER OF RIGHT
48 REM    AND WRONG ANSWERS TO ZERO.
49 REM
50 NW=0
60 NR=0
70 PRINT``CHOOSE THE CORRECT SPELLING FROM THE LIST''
80 PRINT``OF WORDS THAT FOLLOW.''
85 PRINT:PRINT``PRESS ANY KEY TO CONTINUE.''
90 GET A$
97 REM
98 REM PRINT LIST OF WORDS AND WAIT FOR INPUT
99 REM
100 FOR N=1 TO 3
110 READ WORD$
120 IF WORD$=``END'' THEN GOTO 300
130 PRINT:PRINT WORD$
140 NEXT N
150 READ CORRECT$
160 PRINT:INPUT``WHICH WORD IS SPELLED RIGHT? '';ANSWER$
167 REM
168 REM CHECK FOR CORRECT ANSWER
169 REM
170 IF ANSWER$()CORRECT$ THEN GOTO 250
180 NR=NR+1
190 PRINT``THAT'S CORRECT! PRESS ANY KEY TO CONTINUE.''
200 GET A$
210 GOTO 100
247 REM
248 REM PRINT MESSAGE FOR INCORRECT ANSWER AND RETURN
249 REM
250 NW=NW+1
260 PRINT``THAT'S INCORRECT. THE ANSWER IS '';CORRECT$
270 PRINT``PRESS ANY KEY TO CONTINUE.''
280 GET A$
290 GOTO 100
297 REM
298 REM EXIT PROGRAM HERE
299 REM
300 PRINT:PRINT``THAT'S ALL THE WORDS I KNOW RIGHT NOW.''
310 PRINT``YOU GOT '';NR;`` CORRECT AND ''; NW;`` INCORRECT.''
320 END
997 REM
998 REM ENTER WORDS AND CORRECT ANSWERS HERE
999 REM
1000 DATA ``A. FIRST WORD'',``B. SECOND WORD'',
     ``C. THIRD WORD'',``C''
1001 DATA ``
1002 DATA ''
1003 DATA ``END''
```

SPELLING PROGRAM

Program Title:
The Correct Spelling and Meaning

Correct Spelling and Meaning allows particular spelling words to be identified from a list of correctly and incorrectly spelled words. The words also have to be matched to sentences to show correct usage.

ADULT-RELATED PROGRAMS

Program Title:
Regular Payment on a Loan

Appendix C has the BASIC program Regular Payment on a Loan. This is an excellent program to use to determine what your monthly payments will be on a loan when you know the principal to be borrowed, the interest rate, and the time to be used to repay the loan.

Program Title: Address Book

Address Book permits the user to keep track of a list of names, addresses, cities, states, zips, and phone numbers of relatives and friends. All of the information is entered in DATA lines starting at line 5000, and the end of the list is marked by the word END.

```
10 REM ******************************
11 REM *                            *
12 REM * ADDRESS BOOK ALLOWS A NAME, *
13 REM * ADDRESS, ETC., TO BE FOUND  *
14 REM * FROM A LIST OF UP TO 100    *
15 REM * NAMES, ADDRESSES,           *
16 REM * CITIES, STATES, ZIPS, AND   *
17 REM * PHONE NUMBERS.              *
18 REM *                            *
20 REM ******************************
21 REM
50 DIM FIELD$(6)
60 DIM INFO$(100,6)
80 PRINT``THIS PROGRAM ALLOWS YOU TO ENTER NAMES AND ADDRESSES''
90 PRINT``AND FIND THEM QUICKLY.''
97 REM
98 REM MAIN PROGRAM
99 REM
100 GOSUB 2000
110 GOSUB 2500
120 PRINT
130 PRINT``1) NAME''
140 PRINT``2) ADDRESS''
150 PRINT``3) CITY''
160 PRINT``4) STATE''
170  PRINT``5) ZIP''
180 PRINT``6) PHONE NUMBER''
190 INPUT``ENTER FIELD TO FIND: '';FIND
200 IF FIND>6 OR FIND<1 THEN GOTO 190
210 INPUT``ENTER '';FIELD$(FIND);`` TO FIND: '';FIND$
220 FOUND=0
230 FOR INDEX=1 TO LASTENTRY
240 TEST$=INFO$(INDEX,FIND)
250 IF TEST$=FIND$ THEN GOSUB 1500
260 NEXT INDEX
270 PRINT:PRINT FOUND;`` '';FIELD$; `` '';``FOUND.''
280 PRINT``PRESS ANY KEY TO CONTINUE. ''
290 GET A$
300 GOTO 120
1497 REM
1498 REM PRINT EACH ITEM AS IT IS FOUND
1499 REM
1500 FOUND=FOUND+1
1510 FOR N=1 TO 6
1520 PRINT INFO$(INDEX,N);`` '';
1530 NEXT N
1540 PRINT
1550 RETURN
1997 REM
1998 REM INITIALIZE FIELD NAMES ARRAY
1999 REM
2000 FOR N=1 TO 6
2010 READ FIELD$(N)
2020 NEXT N
2030 DATA ``NAMES'',``ADDRESSES'',``CITIES'',``STATES'',``ZIP'',
     ``PHONE NUMBERS''
2040 RETURN
2497 REM
2498 REM INITIALIZE DATA ARRAY
2499 REM
2500 FOR N=1 TO 100
2510 FOR M=1 TO 6
2520 READ TEST$
2530 IF TEST$=``END'' THEN LASTENTRY=N:RETURN
2540 INFO$(N,M)=TEST$
2550 NEXT M
2560 NEXT N
4997 REM
4998 REM ENTER ACTUAL DATA HERE
2999 REM
5000 DATA ``JOE SMITH'',``12345 MAIN'',``ANYCITY'',
     ``ANYSTATE'', ``12345'', ``343-4444''
5001 DATA ``JOHN JONES'',``222 ANYSTREET'',``ANYCITY'',
     ``ANYSTATE'', ``54321'',``778-6785''
5002 DATA ``END''
```

BOOKS ON BASIC

Finally, there are a number of excellent books that can be purchased to learn to program in BASIC using particular computer systems as well as to secure BASIC programs already written for these systems. Among these books are the following:

Coan, James S., & Coan, Louisa. (1985). *Basic Microsoft BASIC for the Macintosh*. Hasbrouck Heights, NJ: Hayden.

Ellis, Mark, Ellis, Robert, & Goldstein, Larry J. (1985). *Atari 400, 600XL, 800, 800XL, and 1200XL*. Bowie, MD: Brady Communications.

Lien, David A. (1985). *Learning Apple II BASIC*. San Diego: CompuSoft Publishing.

Regena, C. (1983). *Guide to the TI 99/4A*. Greensboro, NC: Computer! Publications.

Schneider, David I. (1985). *Handbook of BASIC for the IBM PC*. Bowie, MD: Brady Communications.

West, Raeto. (1985). *Programming the Commodore 64: The definitive guide*. Greensboro, NC: Compute! Publications.

APPENDIX

The SECTOR Courseware Evaluation Form

Robert C. Reid
Kim E. Allard
Alan M. Hofmeister
Utah State University ■

INTRODUCTION

This document has been prepared to assist computer users in evaluating instructional software using the SECTOR Courseware Evaluation Form. (The five pages of the form are shown at the end of this explanation.)

GENERAL PRODUCT DESCRIPTION AND SUMMARY

The first page of the evaluation form is reserved for general information including the program name, publisher, and price of the program. A grid has been established which includes (1) content, (2) instructional design, (3) record keeping/management, and (4) ease of use as general areas of concern. *At the completion of the evaluation*, these areas may be rated on a five-point scale from superior to poor. Package contents and hardware requirements are also documented on the front page

of the evaluation form. Package contents include materials such as teacher's manual or guide, supplemental classroom activities, flash cards, black line masters and backup diskettes.

Hardware requirements should include a description of the hardware necessary to operate the program. This should include what types of microcomputer the program is used with, the number of disk drives which may be necessary to operate the program, and any extra peripheral devices that are needed. Peripherals include memory expansion boards, 80-column boards, cassette tape drives, speech synthesizers, etc. Some programs do not require specific hardware but may recommend the optional use of paddles, joysticks, printers, or additional disk drives.

CONTENT

Space has been provided under each section to make comments on that aspect of the program. Criteria for each section has been out-

The material in this appendix is reprinted with the permission of Systems Impact, Inc., 2084 North 1200 East, Logan, Utah 84321.

lined in a checklist, and each is rated on a four-point scale of excellent, satisfactory, unsatisfactory, or not applicable. Criteria are:

1. *Objectives are fully and clearly defined.* Specific instructional objectives should be provided. These objectives should indicate to the potential user the skills the pupils should demonstrate on successful completion of the program.

2. *Target audience is clearly defined.* As with other instructional materials, a target audience or population should be defined by the publisher. Generally, the target audience will be defined by grade level or special population (e.g., mildly mentally retarded) or by the prerequisite skills the pupil needs to participate successfully.

3. *Outside activities are appropriate and effective.* While some computer assisted instruction (CAI) materials do not provide outside activities, the ones that are provided should be appropriate and geared to the skills being worked on within the instructional program. Omission of activities or reference to activities that would help integrate the program into the classroom curriculum should be considered.

4. *Prerequisite CAI skills are clearly defined.* CAI materials often require skills not required by other instructional materials. These generally include typing and hardware operation skills. These skills should be identified in the documentation accompanying the instructional program.

5. *Content is presented clearly and logically.* This is generally applicable in tutorial programs where a concept is being presented and built upon by the program. The appropriate sequencing of curriculum units will need to be considered.

6. *Content is transferable and generalizable.* Skills learned on the computer should be transferable to other environments. For example, a student may do well on math facts on the computer, but cannot answer the same questions on a worksheet. Skills which can only be used or applied on the computer may be of questionable value.

7. *Content is consistent with objectives.* Content of the instructional program should match the objectives defined for it. This is best done by examining the behavior that the program expects from the pupil.

8. *Vocabulary level is appropriate for subject level and learner level.* This criterion is particularly important in evaluating CAI materials because of the amount of reading usually required to use the programs. Appropriate vocabulary levels should not be restricted to the academic content, but should include the directions for use of the program as well as feedback on student progress. As the case with some basal texts, the vocabulary level for some CAI programs may be above that appropriate for the defined audience.

INSTRUCTIONAL DESIGN

Instructional design refers to the way in which the formation is presented to the student. Criteria for instructional design are as follows:

1. *Learner controls rate and sequence of instruction.* The learner should generally be in charge of the rate and sequence of instruction. Students should be interacting with screens of text and graphics and cueing the program to continue after they are complete. Many programs accomplish this by having the student press the RETURN key when they are ready to continue. In many drill and practice programs, however, the student response rate is set by the teacher. In such cases, learner control may not be applicable.

2. *Program can be used independently.* While some programs are designed to be used with a teacher present, most CAI materials are designed to be used independently by the student. Options should be available for the student to receive help from the teacher if necessary.

3. *Learner interacts only with appropriate segments.* A program can be a powerful teaching tool by branching the student to appropriate instructional segments based on responses. Remedial segments or new concepts should be presented based on the progress the student is making. This is particularly important with tutorial programs where new concepts are being presented and students are being tested on those concepts. The student should not waste valuable time relearning concepts they have already mastered, but rather should use computer time productively to work on new skills.

4. *Program utilizes a variety of display and response modes.* There are a variety of ways in which the student can respond in a computer program. The most traditional is typing in answers at the keyboard. When responding via the keyboard, the program usually incorporates several response modes, including answering open questions, multiple choice, or true and false. Because of the difficulty involved with anticipating a variety of student responses, many programs will opt for a straight multiple choice or true and false response mode. While this simplifies the programming process, it may also reduce the effectiveness of the program. Response models should be based on the learner's needs, not an ease of computer programming.

5. *Program minimizes necessary typing.* While some programs are designed to improve typing or spelling skills, typing errors or misspellings may be of secondary importance in other programs. Misspellings should be dealt with by the program and handled appropriately when encountered. Students should not be penalized for poor typing when engaging in a lesson which does not have improvement of typing skills as an objective.

6. *Program handles a wide range of student responses appropriately:* When presented with a question like, "Who was the first president?", a student may answer in a variety of ways. "Washington, George Washington, President Washington and President George Washington" could all be correct answers to this question. The computer program should take into account a wide range of both correct and incorrect responses and provide appropriate feedback to the student. If appropriate, the program should have some method of handling unusual responses that may be correct. This may be done by branching to a multiple choice question to clarify the response.

7. *New material is presented in context and is related to previous material.* This criterion applies mainly to tutorial programs where concepts are being developed. Computer programs are not always as randomly accessible as textbooks. In a book, students can easily flip back a few pages to review a point they may have missed or misunderstood. Because microcomputer programs are not so easily manipulated, new material must be carefully presented in context and related to what the student has already learned.

8. *Summaries and reviews are provided, important concepts are restated.* Because of the way in which programs, especially tutorial programs are structured, each section should be reviewed, and important concepts restated and reviewed at appropriate times during the program.

9. *Programs can be adjusted by user for local needs.* CAI programs should be easily incorporated into the classroom formula. The classroom curriculum should not have to be adjusted to complement the CAI program. Programs should be adjustable by changing variables such as length of time the program is used by each student each day. In the case of drill and practice programs, the rate at which the drill is presented is a variable that should be changeable. In some cases, such as spelling programs, it may be desirable to allow the teacher to determine what content should be presented.

10. *Appropriate use of graphics/color/sound.* Graphics, color and sound are used often in CAI programs. Sound can be very distracting to other students when used in a classroom situation. Many programs provide an option for the teacher to turn the sound off when desired. Graphics and color are sometimes used as integral parts of the instruction. More often, however, they are used as feedback. Graphics should enhance the instruction and motivational aspects of the program and not detract from the instructional process.

11. *Feedback is useful and appropriate.* Feedback in CAI varies from simple written "right" or "wrong" to fireworks going off, and happy or sad faces. Generally, feedback should let students know whether they are right or wrong and allow them to continue on to the next activity. Feedback may contain the correct answers or contain hints for the correct answers. Feedback should not be confusing to the student nor detract from the instructional message. Unnecessary extra feedback for correct answers is often boring and slows the progress of the student.

12. *Instruction is active rather than passive.* Many instructional programs, particularly those tutorials that are attempting to teach a concept, require the student to read excessively from the display screen. The student should interact with the program wherever appropriate by responding to questions which aid understanding and application of the content. The microcomputer does not serve the student or teacher well when used as an expensive page turner.

14. *Program has consistent display rate.* Presenting information on the screen at a consistent rate results in students paying more attention to the material presented and devoting less time to distraction. Continual variations in computer presentation response handling time distracts students.

15. *Displays are clear, understandable, and effective.* Given the size limitation of most display screens, often too much material is included on one screen. Graphics should be clear and easily recognizable. Some programs do not have the appropriate levels of contrast for the quality of television monitors most commonly found in classrooms.

RECORD KEEPING AND MANAGEMENT

The computer gives the teacher a great deal of potential for storing and interpreting student data. Criteria to be considered include:

1. *Program keeps accurate records of student response.* Programs should keep accurate records of how the student is doing. Besides maintaining whether an answer is right or wrong, the program may also keep track of the length of the instructional session.

2. *Program keeps ongoing student records.* Comprehensive programs that students work on a daily basis should maintain student information from session to session. This places the burden of tracking daily progress on the computer not on the teacher or student.

3. *Program includes diagnostic/evaluative testing.* Comprehensive programs, that is programs which cover a variety of skills and levels, often have some method, usually a diagnostic test to appropriately place the student in the curriculum. Evaluative testing determines if the student has met the objectives of the program.

4. *Program generates further assignments.* Many newer programs can generate assignment sheets or additional practice based on student progress.

5. *Program graphically depicts student progress.* Programs can graphically depict either the progress of individual students or the entire class.

6. *Program provides statistical information on student progress.* Programs can calculate per-

centages, including error rates and correct responses.

7. *Program allows printout and screen display of student records.* Data collected on students should be easily accessible to the teacher both on the screen and in hard copy if a printer is available.

EASE OF USE

The acceptability of any computer program is dependent on its practicality in the classroom. The ease of use criteria listed below apply to both the student and the teacher:

1. *Support materials provided are comprehensive and effective.* Support materials, i.e., teacher's manuals, worksheets, flashcards, etc., should enhance the use of the CAI program. Instruction on how to most effectively use the program should be clearly presented.

2. *Program is reliable in normal use.* Programs should obviously not fail while in use. In addition, programs, should be foolproofed so that unexpected keyboard activity will not "crash" the program.

3. *"HELP" procedures are available.* Many programs allow the user to push a key such as the "?" to obtain help in working with the program.

4. *Program can be exited by student or automatically when appropriate.* When appropriate, students should be able to end their work session without teacher assistance and without destroying any progress data that

may have been collected. Some programs allow the students to decide at regular intervals whether to continue with or end their session.

PROGRAM STRENGTHS AND WEAKNESSES

This section of the coursework evaluation form allows the reviewer to describe the strengths and weaknesses of the program in relation to specific application.

VALIDATION

CAI programs should have been field tested with the populations they were developed for. Field test data should be documented by the developers. Of particular interest will be the potential level of objectivity of the researchers. CAI has, unfortunately, a rather long history of obtaining results that could not be achieved by later independent researchers. By using a small group of high performing children for a short time, under novelty conditions, it is possible to make even the worst product look good. Some of our best students are "best students" because they learn in spite of poor instruction.

The credibility of field test data is considerably enhanced if it is known that the testers were not associated with the development of the product and that it was used with large numbers of representative students for long periods of time under normal classroom conditions.

SECTOR COURSEWARE EVALUATION FORM

PROGRAM
NAME: _____

_____

PUBLISHER: _____

PRICE: _____

	SUPERIOR	VERY GOOD	GOOD	FAIR	POOR
CONTENT					
INSTRUCTIONAL DESIGN					
RECORD KEEPING/ MANAGEMENT					
EASE OF USE					

I. PACKAGE CONTENTS

II. HARDWARE REQUIREMENTS

The S.E.C.T.O.R. project is a state-funded special education computer technology resource located at the Exceptional Child Center, Utah State University, Logan, Utah.

COURSEWARE EVALUATION FORM ②

Content

_____
_____
_____
_____
_____
_____
_____
_____
_____
_____
_____
_____

	EXCELLENT	SATISFACTORY	UNSATISFACTORY	NOT APPLICABLE
Objectives are fully and clearly defined.				
Target audience is clearly defined.				
Outside activities are appropriate and effective.				
Prerequisite skills are clearly defined.				
Content is presented clearly and logically.				
Content is transferable and generalizable.				
Content is consistent with objectives.				
Vocabulary level is appropriate for subject area and learner level.				

COURSEWARE EVALUATION FORM 3
Instructional Design

_____

_____

_____

_____

_____

_____

_____

_____

_____

_____

	EXCELLENT	SATISFACTORY	UNSATISFACTORY	NOT APPLICABLE
Learner controls rate and sequence of instruction.				
Program can be used independently.				
Learner interacts only with appropriate segments.				
Program utilizes a variety of display and response modes.				
Program minimizes necessary typing.				
Program handles a wide range of student responses appropriately.				
New material is presented in context and is related to previous material.				
Summaries and reviews are provided, important concepts are restated.				
Program can be adjusted by user for local needs.				
Appropriate use of graphics/color/sound.				
Feedback is useful and appropriate.				
Instruction is active rather than passive.				
Learner expectancies are established.				
Program has consistent display rate.				
Displays are clear, understandable and effective.				

COURSEWARE EVALUATION FORM 4

Record Keeping & Management

	EXCELLENT	SATISFACTORY	UNSATISFACTORY	NOT APPLICABLE
Program keeps accurate records of student response.				
Program keeps ongoing student records.				
Program includes diagnostic/evaluative testing.				
Program generates further assignments.				
Program graphically depicts student progress.				
Program provides statistical information on student progress.				
Program allows printout and screen display of student records.				

Ease of Use

	EXCELLENT	SATISFACTORY	UNSATISFACTORY	NOT APPLICABLE
Support materials provided are comprehensive and effective.				
Program is reliable in normal use.				
"HELP" procedures are available.				
Program can be exited by student or automatically when appropriate.				

COURSEWARE EVALUATION FORM 5
Program Strengths and Weaknesses _____

_____
_____
_____
_____
_____
_____

Validation

PROGRAM TESTED   From_____To_____

_____In house   _____Independent

_____Controlled   _____Uncontrolled

POPULATION(S) TESTED _____
_____

ASSESSMENT INSTRUMENT(S)_____
_____

EVALUATION SITE(S)_____
_____

RESULTS _____
_____

CONTACT PERSON _____
ADDITIONAL INFORMATION _____
_____
_____
_____

EVALUATED BY_____
DATE_____

Author Index

Abernathy, T. V., 114, 134, 230, 247
Abrahamson, J. E., 151, 155
Acker, R. V., 280, 308
Ackerman, R., 263, 269
Adams, M., 114, 138
Adams, R. C., 124, 133
Aikins, J., 105
Alessi, S. M., 54, 60
Allen, B., 151, 154
Allen, G. B., 163, 173
Allen, M., 121, 133
Alley, G. B., 111, 134
Alter, K., 152, 154
Anderson, M., 147, 156, 290, 307
Anderson-Inman, L., 119, 133
Archer, P., 7, 24, 232, 234, 236, 237, 247
Ashcroft, S. C., 186, 197
Assouline, S. G., 204, 219
Axelrod, S., 9, 21

Baby, J., 57, 60
Bahr, C. M., 9, 10, 21, 24, 114, 115, 133, 137, 280, 308
Bailey, H. J., 151, 155
Balajthy, E., 204, 219
Ball, T. S., 170, 175
Balzer, R., 105
Bangert, L., 89, 104
Bangert, R. L., 114, 136
Bangert-Drowns, R. L., 114, 133, 136
Barbata, D., 296, 306
Barbus, S., 9, 23
Barkin, P. Z., 114, 134
Barlow, D. H., 316, 317, 331

Baron, N. S., 367
Barrick, S. W., 280, 306
Barron, B., 134, 138
Barton, L., 166, 173
Bates, P., 114, 135
Battenberg, J. K., 9, 21
Bauder, D. K., 54, 61
Baum, S., 202, 219
Baumeister, A. A., 111, 133
Beaver, J. F., 229, 247
Beck, I. L., 114, 126, 136, 137
Becker, H. B., 113, 133, 243, 247
Becker, H. J., 7, 9, 22
Beggs, W. D. A., 179, 196
Behrmann, M. M., 7, 22, 142, 159, 163, 164, 173, 228, 247, 273, 306, 370, 373, 374
Bell-Gredler, M. E., 306
Belmont, J. M., 111, 133
Bender, M., 7, 22, 273, 306
Bengston, D., 166, 175
Bennett, C., 152, 154
Benoit, J., 105
Bentley, J. L., 367
Berg, D., 119, 138
Berger, C. F., 115, 134
Berkler, M., 160, 174
Berliner, D. C., 296, 306
Beukelman, D. R., 150, 154, 169, 175
Beykirch, H. L., 102, 104
Bialo, E., 230, 247
Bialozor, R. C., 5, 22
Biklen, D., 153, 154
Bilken, S. D., 318, 330

Subject Index

The editor expresses his sincere thanks to the following individuals for their assistance in developing the author and subject indexes: Rodney W. Woods, Patricia S. Douglas, Betty R. Weinhoff, Lorraine G. Palmer, Tiger Thibodeaux, Robin D. Thibodeaux, Mary I. Cormier, Rosemary Reese, Irene Burnett, Sandra Cofield, Gail M. Nichols, Orlando J. Palmer, Theodore L. Carter, Tracy L. Ringo, Monica R. Plant, Jennifer L. Wilson, and Renee Gayle.